KENT

TOLLESBURY

R. Blackwater

HEYBRIDGE

BRADWELL

Osea I.

MALDON

BURNHAM

R. Crouch

PAGLESHAM

NORTH FAMBRIDGE

R. Roach

Hawengore

SOUTHEND

LEIGH

BENFLEET

Canvey I.

Hole Haven

TILBURY

GRAYS

ERITH

GREENHITHE

GRAVESEND

PORT VICTORIA

CHATHAM

R. Medway

GILLINGHAM

QUEENBOROUGH

SHEERNESS

Isle of Sheppey

Harty Ferry

The Swale

FAVERSHAM

WHITSTABLE

MARGATE

RAMSGATE

SANDWICH

DEAL

DOVER

The Downs

South Foreland

North Foreland

Goo

Margate Sand

Kentish Flats

QUEENS CHANNEL

PRINCES CHANNEL

SOUTH CHANNEL

OAZE DEEP

THE WARP

Nore Sand

WEST SWIN

Maplin Sand

Foulness Sand

EAST SWIN

BARROW DEEP

BLACK DEEP

Long Sand

Buxey Sand

Spitway

THE GUNFLEET

Ray Sand Ch.

Nautical Miles

0   10   20

Based on Reynolds' New Chart of 1903 published by Edward Stanford, London

CW01429617

Cruising Hints

Books (Editions) by Francis B. Cooke

Cruising Hints (1904, 1904, 1907, 1928, 1935, 1948)
Seamanship for Small Yachts (1906)
Yacht Racing for Amateurs (1911)
The Corinthian Yachtsman's Handbook (1913)
In Tidal Waters (1919)
London to Lowestoft (1919)
Seamanship for Yachtsmen (1923, 1948)
Coastwise Cruising (1929)
Single-handed Cruising (1931)
Cruising Chats (1932)
Week-end Yachting (1933, 1948)
Small Yacht Cruising (1937)
Pocket Cruisers (1938)
Hints, Tips and Gadgets (1939)
The Single-handed Yachtsman (1946)
Practical Yachting Hints (1946)
Yachting with Economy (1960)
Yachting Yarns (1944)
Sailing (Foyles' Handbook) (1949, 1951)

~ CRUISING HINTS ~

by

FRANCIS B. COOKE

Seventh Edition
Illustrated by

PHILIP H. BROOKS   NORMAN S. CARR   ARCHIE WHITE   KATHLEEN COOKE

with a Foreword by
CHARLES STOCK

LODESTAR BOOKS

Lodestar Books

71 Boveney Road

London SE23 3NL

United Kingdom

www.lodestarbooks.com

First published by Edward Arnold & Co., London

First edition 1904

Second edition 1904

Third edition 1907

Fourth edition 1928

Fifth edition 1935

Sixth edition 1948

This seventh edition published by Lodestar Books 2011

A catalogue record for this book
is available from the British Library

ISBN   978-1-907206-01-6

Set in Miller Text and Adobe Jenson Pro

Printed in the UK by MPG Biddles, King's Lynn

TO

MY SON AND FORMER SHIPMATE

RONALD L. COOKE

IN MEMORY OF MANY HAPPY DAYS SPENT TOGETHER
"FOOLING AMONG BOATS."

For will anyone dare to tell me that business is more entertaining than fooling among boats? He must never have seen a boat, or never seen an office, who says so, and for certain the one is a great deal better for health. — R. L. STEVENSON.

(From the Sixth Edition of *Cruising Hints,* 1948)

About this Book

Francis B. Cooke was born in 1872 and lived to the age of 102. His first published writing was at age eleven, a review of Robert Louis Stevenson's novel *Treasure Island* in 1883, for which the *Manchester Guardian* paid him five shillings, a small fortune to a small boy. He went on to produce some thirty volumes and countless magazine articles on the subject of yacht cruising. Generations of cruising sailors have been encouraged and influenced by his experience, down-to-earth approach and accessible writing style, but he has been 'out of print' in conventional book form for many years. I hope this volume restores him to currency, and grants him a new and deserved lease on life with readers old and young alike.

I have set out to embrace and organise everything Francis Cooke had to say in his books about yacht cruising which retains a relevance to the present day; to know his view on any practical aspect I hope that this book will suffice, and so eliminate the need to search his many earlier titles and editions – which can still be recommended as charming books in their own right. To provide a window onto the cruising world of Cooke's heyday of around a century ago, I have retained his writings on Thames Estuary 'headquarters', and a number of his early cruising yarns which provide interludes between the main parts of the book. Francis Cooke included in his books the designers' drawings for many interesting craft, along with his own comments upon them. He remains a frequent point of reference for those interested in British yacht design of his period; often one reads or hears of some design that "Cooke wrote about it in ... which book was it now?" All such designs, and his commentaries, are here. All but a hundred or so words in this book are Cooke's, my contribution being only enough prepositions and the like to 'hold it all together', and some chapter headings.

The techniques and technology of traditional yacht cruising have changed pleasingly little in the past century and more – one of the great attractions of the pursuit, for most of us – so I have not encumbered an already long book with references to its many forebears. In some passages the approximate date of writing may readily be inferred; for the remainder, we are fortunate that it is of no consequence. Francis Cooke's own views changed little during his writing career; the reader may notice one or two instances where they did. But with so broad and detailed a subject, he helps us by making us think about each of his topics at all, whether or not we may regard his view as the right one. I myself am on my fourth, and surely ultimate, yawl (Plate 11, top) and three of those have had canoe sterns, so I beg to differ from his views on both of those design attributes. I should mention some areas in which modern developments make obsolete the advice given: Synthetic rope and sailcloth eliminate concerns regarding rot and sail stretching; and those in quest of a sea-anchor should be sure to study the modern Series Drogue. Importantly, *all* local pilotage, buoyage and regulatory information in these pages is out of date and emphatically *not* to be relied upon. It is included for historical interest only. Readers who are neither British nor of a certain age will be at a disadvantage with some of Cooke's vocabulary. The Glossary is intended to address this, in addition to defining all but the simplest nautical terms and phrases.

In composing this book I have acquired every edition of every cruising title by Francis Cooke except three volumes, for the loan of which I am grateful to David Measures and John Cookson in Lancashire, and Graeme Forrest in New Zealand.

I am delighted to be able to thank Francis Cooke's granddaughter Valerie Palmer, and through her the Cooke family, for their support of this project, particularly his three surviving daughters, all now in their nineties. Their elder sister, Kathleen – known as Kay – drew many of the knot illustrations in her youth. Francis B. Cooke remains in copyright until 2044, and the family are directing the book's royalties to a charity close to their hearts, Arthritis Research U.K.

Those line drawings bearing florid lettering, and others in their style, are by Norman S. Carr (1877-?), a prolific illustrator and occasional yachting writer of the early 20th Century. Those most recent, depicting details of *Iolanthe*, and others of that style, are by the well-known East Coast artist, writer and yachtsman Archie White (1899-1957) whose art works and books are well worth seeking out. The remainder, including the navigation marks and maps from *Coastwise Cruising*, are by Philip H. Brooks, about whom, unfortunately, I can discover nothing.

An avowed fan of Francis Cooke is Charles Stock, who at 83 has just 'swallowed the anchor' after a lifetime sailing every inch of the Thames Estuary and its tributaries in his tiny gaff-rigged yacht *Shoal Waters*, described in his delightful book *Sailing Just For Fun*. His achievement has been a model of 'Yachting with Economy', and I much appreciate his agreeing to write the Foreword.

The most comprehensive of Francis Cooke's books went under the name *Cruising Hints*, in six editions from 1904 to 1948, and so it seems fitting if a little presumptuous to adopt it again here. I would be grateful to be informed, for the benefit of any future edition, of any errors or serious omissions.

Finally, Francis B. Cooke's writing is not without its humour, intentional or otherwise; I particularly like the unclassifiable final sentence of Chapter 37.

Richard Wynne
Editor & Publisher
May 2011

CONTENTS

PART I – THE BOAT

PART II – HEADQUARTERS

PART III – CRUISING DESIGNS

PART IV – EQUIPMENT

PART V – DOMESTIC ECONOMY

PART VI – MAINTENANCE

PART VII – SEAMANSHIP

APPENDICES

List of Design Drawings

List of Plates

Foreword

Throughout the nineteenth century the pastime of yachting began to move away from large vessels with paid hands to smaller ones owned by keen amateurs, some of whom even sailed singlehanded. They soon gave way to the urge to put pen to paper. Fiennes Speed was an early one, describing his difficulty in finding anyone on the lower Thames who had ever sailed to Burnham, and his trip there in his twenty foot, five foot three inch beam *Viper*. Macgregor's account of his trip to Paris in the *Rob Roy*, behind a string of six lighters, towed by a tug working its way along a chain on the river bed makes good reading. Frank Cowper produced the first pilots for the growing numbers of venturesome voyagers, but Francis Cooke seems to have been the first to realise the need for a readable, easy to understand, *how to* book, sorting out those details relevant to small boats in tomes such as the superb Admiralty Manuals. Seamanship is a traditional art and craft; a delight to practise in all its aspects from a sailmaker's whipping to catching a fair tide at just the right time. This book explains them all.

Once I became interested in sailing, I soon got hold of Francis Cooke's *In Tidal Waters* and was hooked. Working at the Admiralty gave me access to the three Westminster libraries and I read everything of his that they had. When it was published I bought *Pocket Cruisers*. After I left the Marines in early 1949 the shortage of craft and soaring prices meant my hard-earned savings only ran to a sixteen foot half-decker, but she took me from Maldon to the Wash and Poole Harbour, sleeping in army blankets under a tent of barrage balloon canvas. Looking back over sixty years and seventy-five thousand nautical miles, topped by the award of the Royal Cruising Club's annual Cruising Medal, I feel that my success was in no small part due to studying Cooke's *Cruising Hints*, which first appeared in 1904 and ran to six editions. This book summarises them all, together with some delightful yarns to whet the appetite for life afloat. Throughout the construction of *Shoal Waters* and her subsequent miles between Whitby, Dunkirk and the Solent, I kept a copy handy.

I recommend this book to all owners of cruising craft. Even those with modern plastic craft and all the modern goodies will find many useful tips for those days when the engine or the power winch fails to start, and the electrics die. All will find it a good read, and it will make them realise how right King Henry the Eighth was to give his subjects the right to sail all tidal waters, as he considered that practicing the art of navigation was an asset to the realm. It still is!

Chas. Stock
ex *Shoal Waters*

Preface

To the Sixth Edition of *Cruising Hints*, 1948

One of the charms of yachting is that it has no finality. New types of vessel and innovations in rig and equipment are frequently introduced and serve to keep one's interest alive. One is, indeed, always learning something new. When the first edition of *Cruising Hints* appeared more than forty years ago, it was a slim little volume of less than 150 pages, but as with the effluxion of time my experience and knowledge of yachts and yachting has increased, each succeeding edition has swollen in size. This sixth edition, by the way, is really the seventh, for that intended to be the fourth was subsequently called *The Corinthian Yachtsman's Handbook*, as I had included a section on racing and thought that Cruising Hints was not an appropriate title.

I have endeavoured in this new volume to tell the potential owner how to select, buy, equip, maintain and sail a small yacht, with suggestions as to where to keep her. That is a very big field to cover in one book and I don't suppose I have altogether succeeded in my purpose, but I hope what I have written will prove of service to beginners and others who, although not quite novices, have not yet had much experience of sailing.

The book was written at a time when we were changing over from war to peace conditions, and as prices are not yet stabilized, nor likely to be for some years, I have only ventured with caution into the realm of figures, and in the chapter on catering have assumed that rationing restrictions are only temporary. But if I have not told the reader the cost of the various items of equipment, I have indicated where they can be obtained and he can easily ascertain the price from the suppliers. For the benefit of the novice I have added a comprehensive glossary of nautical terms.

I have to thank the designers of the yachts whose lines appear at the end of the book for lending me the drawings for reproduction. Nearly all of the illustrations in the text were drawn by Mr. Archie White but a few retained from the last edition were the work of the late Mr. P. H. Brooks.

F. B. C.

Introduction

Few, if any, outdoor pastimes yield such a splendid return for one's money as that of cruising in a small yacht, and it is very certain that none is more beneficial to health. To those engaged in business, whose days for the most part are passed in the smoke-laden atmosphere of a city, yachting supplies that complete change of environment and conditions of life which constitute the ideal holiday. It would, indeed, be difficult to imagine a greater contrast. Instead of inhaling the poisonous fumes from countless motors, the yachtsman breathes the pure air of heaven straight off the sea, and in escaping from the nerve-racking turmoil of modern life to his little ship he finds that "peace which passeth all understanding." Moreover, in these days, when many thousands of people are killed or maimed every year on the roads, the sea is about the only place where one can feel reasonably safe.

Cruising on the sea is akin to touring on land, but, unlike the motorist, who has to seek accommodation each night and subsequently pay a heavy hotel bill, the yachtsman carries his home with him like a snail He has no tax to pay and his vessel is propelled by the wind which costs nothing. A small yacht costs no more to buy than a car, often a good deal less, and her depreciation is negligible, for if well built and properly cared for she will last a lifetime.

There is a fascination in cruising from port to port in one's own ship that can only be appreciated by those who have enjoyed its pleasures. How delightful to awake in some quiet anchorage far from the madding crowd and plunge overboard for a swim. Then, after breakfast, to make sail and start on a passage to some port, perhaps fifty miles distant, navigating one's own vessel. Throughout the livelong day there is not a dull moment, for the coastal scenery affords an ever-changing panorama, while little problems of seamanship and navigation are constantly arising to titillate and keep alive one's interest. Handling the gear provides sufficient exercise to keep one fit without making a labour of pleasure and one is able to visit many picturesque little waterside villages that are inaccessible by other means.

There are, of course, occasional days when the elements are in angry mood, and one has to fight one's way yard by yard against the forces of nature. But when at last the passage perilous has been won and the little yacht lies at rest in some delectable haven, the past discomfort is speedily forgotten and one thinks only of the successful issue of the struggle against wind and sea. It is such episodes that make one love one's craft and come to regard her almost as a thing of life. How snug and homely the cabin seems after a 'dusting' at sea! And with what zest one cooks and eats one's evening meal! Then as regards the actual sailing; if there is any pleasure greater than that of steering a smart yacht to windward in a fresh breeze, I have never experienced it, and yachting is a pastime that never palls. If the sea once claims you it will probably hold you for life, as custom cannot stale its infinite variety. There is always something fresh to be learnt, even by the most experienced, for the conditions that obtain from day to day are never quite alike. Yes, the sea is a glorious playground, but to make the most of it you must sail the boat yourself.

The old idea that yachting is an extravagant sport that can only be enjoyed by the wealthy has at last been exploded and many people now recognize that it is no more costly than most other outdoor pastimes. The expense indeed is so elastic that you can make it almost anything you like in reason. It is merely a matter of cutting your coat to suit the cloth. If you employ a paid hand and do nothing yourself, your sailing will cost you a pretty penny, but if you are content to do the work yourself the expense will be comparatively small.

Of the thousands of yachts in commission every season, the majority are owned by those whose sailing is confined to the weekends with, perhaps, a short holiday cruise in the course of the summer. To such yachtsmen professional assistance should be unnecessary, as there is no work that cannot be done efficiently and with pleasure by the owner and his friends. The employment of a paid hand in a yacht that is used only at the week-ends is economically unsound, as during the other five days there is little, or nothing, for the man to do. Even if you were fortunate enough to secure the services of a decent man, you would be likely to find him something of a nuisance. He would occupy the fo'c'sle, thus depriving you of valuable stowage space, and his presence would be a restriction on your conversation. Even when you went ashore your freedom of action might be hampered by the man, for, having told him to come and pick you up at a certain time, you would feel bound to keep the appointment, although you might subsequently have changed your mind and want to do something else.

But the inexperienced owner is not likely to obtain the services of a decent man, for in these days the really efficient paid hand is something of a *rara avis*. Formerly the fishing fleet was the nursery of yacht hands, but since the advent of the internal combustion engine, fishing craft are no longer propelled by sails. That source of supply therefore does not now exist and such good men as are available are pretty sure to be snapped up by the owners of racing craft and large cruising yachts.

In these circumstances it is possible, even probable, that the novice might fall into the hands of some waterside scrounger who would exploit him to the utmost. Should he get into the clutches of one of these 'sharks,' he will not be able to call his soul his own. A hand of that kind will rook an inexperienced owner right and left, obtaining a secret commission on almost everything he buys for the boat; and in that connection it may be remarked that the owner will be surprised at the quantity of new gear his man thinks it necessary to buy. Moreover, the man will probably claim the condemned gear as his perquisite. A fisherman once remarked to me: "We like to get hold of yacht rope; the skippers sell it cheap and it is better than anything we can afford."

The reader may pertinently ask: "How about the Corrupt Practices Act, or whatever it is called?" Well, I am afraid that that Act is not always so strictly observed as it should be. A man I knew, who owned a 30-ton cutter, once went to a certain yacht chandler to buy a new binnacle and compass for his vessel. He was wearing a reefer jacket and, having a beard, looked more like a professional seaman than a yachtsman. When he had made his purchase, the salesman handed him back a sovereign with the remark, "That's for you, Captain."

Then there is another point. A paid hand such as I have described will put every impediment in the way when his employer wants to go for a cruise, for he strongly objects to being taken away from his home waters at the week-end. He likes to go ashore on Saturday evening and forgather with others of the same kidney in the bar of his favourite pub. There he will pick his owner to pieces over a pint, or several pints. I once overheard a man of that sort remark to another:

"Yes, my Gov'nor's a proper little gent. 'E stands me a pint every time we comes ashore, and when 'e goes 'ome 'e leaves enough grub on board to last me most of the week. And as for sailin', why, we 'ardly ever goes outside the river."

It would appear therefore that if you buy your man unlimited beer, provide him with food, and are content to pass most of your time tied up to a mooring, you can be "a proper little gent," but otherwise I fear your character, as revealed to the habitués of the Anchor and Sail, will compare unfavourably with that of Adolf Hitler.

The reader must not run away with the idea that I condemn paid hands as a class, for I do nothing of the sort. There is no finer body of men in the country and I have the greatest admiration for those of the best type. They are courteous, hard-working, decent men, who take an interest in their ship; but there are black sheep in every fold and it is the novice who is likely to be landed with the 'wrong-uns.'

Now, if you sail the boat yourself and do all the work and cooking, your sport will cost you little and you will enjoy perfect freedom of action. Looking after yourself and cooking your own meals is no hardship; indeed, it is half the fun. You may say in answer to that, "That's all very well, but I can't cook." My friend, you will jolly soon learn how to cook when you have to do it. I once knew a man who thought he could not cook, and at first, when he went sailing, he subsisted on boiled eggs, which he had at every meal. His next stage in the Culinary art took the form of curry. Someone introduced him to Halford's curries, telling him that all he had to do was to boil the tin for a time before opening it. My friend used to count up the number of meals he would want while away and buy a similar number of tins of curry. He seemed a hopeless case, but happening to go on board his craft a few months later, I was greeted by a most appetizing smell of cooking. He had installed an oven stove and, opening the door with pride, displayed a chicken, sizzling merrily with a rasher of fat bacon tied over its breast in the most professional style. He had solved his problem by buying a little sixpenny cookery book. With the aid of such a book, anyone of average intelligence can cook simple dishes, which are all one needs when cruising.

Of course, if your sailing is mainly confined to the week-ends and you do not employ a paid hand, you will have to pay someone to keep an eye on your craft during your absence and see that she takes no harm. At almost every port there are watermen who undertake such jobs for a small fee. As the charges for such services rule higher at some ports than at others, I cannot give actual figures, but if you are a member of the Cruising Association, of which I shall write in a later chapter, you will be able to get your yacht looked after by the Association's official boatmen at fixed tariff rates. Anyhow, charges are usually quite moderate and for a few shillings a week a waterman will take care of a small yacht, put drinking water on board each week, pump her out and air sails when necessary, and look after the dinghy. The man, if required, will also undertake such work as scrubbing, re-painting and varnishing, fitting new gear and in fact fitting out generally, but of course the owner must pay extra for that.

In this book it will be my endeavour to tell the novice how to buy, equip, maintain and sail a small yacht; in fact, everything that he needs to know; and as I have owned and sailed such craft for more than half a century, he can rest assured that what I have to say is based on practical experience.

A Yarn

&

Euryanthe

As a warning, I will start by telling you about my own first experience of buying yachts. It is a story against myself, but if you take it to heart it may save you from making a fool of yourself as I did.

It happened at the beginning of the 'nineties, when I was a youngster not long from school, and was such a bitter experience that I remember it as clearly as if it had occurred but yesterday. I had had a sailing dinghy on the Upper Thames for some months and, finding sailing up and down Teddington Reach rather boring, I joined a syndicate which owned an old twenty-ton smack at Hole Haven. There were twelve of us in the syndicate, and I soon discovered that being one of such a crowd was anything but satisfactory.

Not only was it extremely uncomfortable but we were constantly in trouble, and after a few months I longed for a real yacht of my own. I therefore began to look about for a little cruiser. My quest took me one day to the Canal Basin at Gravesend, and there I happened upon *Euryanthe*. She was a pretty little cutter of about four tons, with a straight stem and long counter, probably built in the late 'seventies. Like most yachts of her time, she was rather narrow-gutted and drew nearly six feet of water, but in my ignorance such details did not strike me as important. She had just been fitted out and looked very smart, with her shining black topsides, set off by a gold line, and freshly varnished spars. And there was a board on her intimating that she was for sale.

Finding the man who had charge of her, I got him to take me on board. She had the cosiest cabin imaginable, with good headroom, and the usual settees, which formed seats by day and beds by night. The cushions were covered with blue velvet corduroy and there was a strip of blue carpet on the floor. There was a mahogany folding table between the bunks, and on the bulkhead a gimballed lamp fitted with a red silk shade with bead fringe. Natty little curtains of red silk hung over the portholes in the raised coach roof, on which was fitted a small skylight.

In the fo'c'sle was a large oil stove with an oven, and on opening a cupboard I found that it was full of crockery, including a soup tureen, of all things! Well, that cabin settled the matter so far as I was concerned, and learning that the owner was on the Stock Exchange, I took the next train up to town and called him out of the 'house.'

On hearing what I had come about, he took me to his office, and in a quarter of an hour I had bought *Euryanthe* for thirty pounds. It must be remembered that in those days a pound was a real golden sovereign, that would buy about three times as much as the flimsy bit of paper which is its modern substitute. Even so, the price seemed extraordinarily low, and I congratulated myself on having found such a 'snip.' All the same, that thirty pounds represented the savings of a good many years.

I arranged to take over *Euryanthe* on the following Saturday, when I proposed to sail her down to Hole Haven, where I had decided to keep her. You will readily imagine the eagerness with which I awaited the day that was to see me in command of my first yacht and how slowly the intervening time passed. But at last Saturday arrived, and accompanied by a friend who knew even less about sailing than myself, I proceeded to Gravesend. When we got on board, I discovered that we had come away without any butter, so I sent my companion into the town to buy some, while I made preparations for getting under way.

"If you are going out this tide, sir, you must hurry up," shouted the dockmaster, and looking round I saw that it was high water and several barges and smacks were passing through the gates. What was I to do? Looking down the road, I could see my friend Bill in the distance engaged in dalliance with a red-haired girl over a garden gate. I shouted and waved, but could not attract his attention. "Well," I thought, "he will jolly well have to get on board as best he can; I can't wait any longer."

Working in desperate haste and assailed by shouts from the dock-master and sundry loafers, I at last moved from my berth, and with the mainsail but half hoisted and the jib set upside down, made for the exit. After a slight collision with a smack, which cost me a bowsprit shroud, I was ignominiously shoved out into the tideway by a man with a long quant. As soon as *Euryanthe* was clear of the gates, I hove a line to the man, who moored her to the dockhead. For half a crown he temporarily repaired the broken bowsprit shroud and helped me to set the sails properly. By that time my friend had joined me on board, and we started on our trip down the river.

With a nice westerly breeze and the first of a spring ebb, we made a quick passage to the Haven, where we brought up near the Hard, giving her a generous scope of cable. Judging by the way in which she had overhauled several barges and smacks, *Euryanthe* was evidently no sluggard, and delighted me with her sailing qualities. But when Bill, on entering the cabin, announced that there was water on the floor, I was not so pleased. But, as I pointed out to him, we did not know when she had last been pumped and the water might have been accumulating for weeks and it had rained hard the previous night. So we pumped her out and hoped for the best.

After a meal, we went ashore to spend the evening at the Lobster Smack, where we met some of the crew of the smack in which I had previously sailed. In those days the Lobster Smack Inn, or 'Becky's' as it was usually called, was a favourite haunt of those who sailed in the Thames Estuary, and that Saturday night the cosy bar-parlour was crowded. Bill and I had not intended to stay late, but found the company so congenial that it was closing-time ere we left to return on board. It was a dark night, and at first we could not find *Euryanthe*, and it was perhaps a quarter of an hour before we located her. To our dismay, we found her aground and lying over at a most alarming angle. She had nearly dried out and there was only just enough water round her for the dinghy to get alongside. Whether we had not anchored quite in the channel, or whether she had blown out of it and taken the ground, I don't know ; but even to our inexperienced eyes it was obvious that she would not lift on the flood without assistance, and the tide was already coming in. It was evident that we must do something about it and do it pretty quickly.

There could be no doubt that the coaming would be submerged long before she began to lift to the tide, and it seemed to me that our only hope of refloating her was to cover up the lower side of the cockpit in some way. Searching the lockers, I found a tin of rusty wire nails and a hammer. Taking up two of the cabin floorboards, we nailed them across the lower side of the cockpit, backed by a spare sail. That was not so easy as it sounds, for at the fore-end of the cockpit there was nothing to which the boards could be fastened. However, I got over that difficulty by nailing a locker-lid to the bulkhead and resting the ends of the boards on that, keeping them in place with a rope stretched tightly from coaming to coaming. It was certainly something of a lash-up, but was the best we could improvise. As the lamp could not be used, owing to the heavy list of the yacht, we lit a candle in the cabin and with considerable misgiving awaited the rising of the tide.

Gradually the water rose until first the rail and then the side-deck were submerged. As it began to creep up the coaming my anxiety increased, for I had but little confidence in the temporary hatch we had contrived. It was a flimsy contraption, and I felt pretty sure it would leak. And it did, the water flowing through the cracks between the boards in a steady stream.

Soon we were standing in water above our ankles and bailing vigorously, one with a bucket and the other with that soup tureen. Hampered by lack of room and awkward stance, we got in each other's way, and the water slowly but surely gained on us. We could see it gradually mounting the boards, and soon the position began to look hopeless. We had, indeed, almost decided to abandon the ship and take to the dinghy, when she suddenly began to lift, and in ten minutes the coaming was clear and we were able to remove the boards. A little later she rose upright and all danger was over.

In the cabin the water was half-way up the bunk risers, but we were now able to use the pump. With one at the pump and the other bailing with the bucket, we soon had the yacht free from water, and when she floated, towed her into the channel and anchored her again. Everything was wet, but we were too exhausted to trouble about trifles like that. We just flopped down on the bunks as we were and in a few minutes were asleep.

Fortunately the next day was bright and sunny and we were able to dry things up. While we were having breakfast, two fellows from the smack came on board to look at *Euryanthe*. The floorboards had not yet been properly replaced, and one of our visitors began to prod about with his knife. "Gosh!" he exclaimed, "this boat is as rotten as sin." Then I knew why the late owner had sold her for thirty pounds. Further investigation showed that she had been attacked by dry rot and most of her timbers and planking were as soft as a sleepy pear. Moreover, she was obviously making a lot of water.

Having pumped her dry once more, we shifted our berth to one higher up the creek and then got all of the cushions and blankets out on deck to dry in the sun.

The following Saturday, when I went down to Hole Haven, all that could be seen of *Euryanthe* was her masthead sticking out of the water. I sought the man in whose care I had left her and indignantly asked: "Why didn't you pump her? I told you she was making water." Although it was more than fifty years ago, I still remember the man's reply:

"Why 'av'nt I pumped 'er out? Well, if you think as 'ow I'm a-goin' to sit up all night pumping the bloomin' Thames through that old basket for three bob a week, I ain't." With which impertinent, or perhaps pertinent, remark he left me.

Euryanthe was subsequently raised and berthed in a rill on the saltings, and I spent several week-ends putting tingles over the worst leaks. By such means I made her what I called reasonably tight. I don't mean to suggest that she leaked no more, for she did; but she only needed pumping once a day to keep the water from invading the cabin floor.

Now that *Euryanthe* was more or less seaworthy again, I decided to take a few days' holiday and go for a little cruise. Accompanied by two friends, who had never been yachting before, I sailed from Hole Haven one after-noon bound for Brightlingsea. It was fine and sunny, but the wind was very light, and darkness overtook us when we were near the Maplin Lighthouse. As I did not fancy going through the Spitway in the dark, I anchored on the edge of the Maplin Sands. Although quite calm, the continuous procession of steamers passing through the Swin scared me stiff, and I spent a miserable night dozing fitfully in the cockpit, while my passengers slept and snored in the cabin. I awoke them at six o'clock, and after breakfast we got under way and resumed our journey.

There was a nice south-easterly breeze and we made excellent progress for, despite her frailties, *Euryanthe* certainly sailed well. The Spitway was safely negotiated and then, with the flood tide to help us, we made a, quick trip into the Colne. It was grand sailing and we thoroughly enjoyed ourselves, but when our destination was in sight, disaster overtook us. As we were approaching the entrance to Brightlingsea Creek, we hit a floating boom end-on and it knocked a large hole in the rotten bow planking. Water poured into the ship and it was a toss-up whether we could get into the creek before she foundered.

Hauling the dinghy alongside in case we should have to abandon the yacht, we started to bail for all we were worth, but she was practically waterlogged as we entered the creek. Fearing that she might sink at any moment, I ordered my companions into the dinghy and told them to be ready to cast off should it be necessary. I had visited Brightlingsea before in the smack and knew there was a steep-to shingle point on the south side; known as Stone Point, if I remember rightly. That, I thought, would be an ideal spot on which to beach her, if I could only reach it; so I held on, with the yacht settling lower and lower.

She sank literally under my feet as she reached the Point, the deck being awash as she took the ground. It was just after high water, and with the tide ebbing rapidly, my companions were soon able to return on board and help me bail her out. This took some time, for even a four-ton yacht can hold the deuce of a lot of water, but in about an hour I was able to commence repair operations. Fortunately I had sufficient materials left over from my previous tingling activities and had become something of an expert at putting on patches.

The hole was rather larger than the palm of my hand and just below the waterline. Cutting a piece of sheet lead, about nine inches square, I put a tingle over the hole with a liberal backing of tar and brown paper. The planking was so rotten that some of the nails I pushed home with my thumb. I am afraid the job would have shocked a Lloyd's surveyor, but it was the best I could do, and I hoped that the tar would help the tingle to stick on. Noticing water running out from several other leaks, I took the opportunity to cover them with tingles, and by the time I had finished the yacht's bottom looked something like a patchwork quilt. But after we had refloated her that night, she was far tighter than at any time since I had bought her.

Of course, everything on board was sodden. We managed to get the blankets fairly dry in the wind and sun, but the bunk cushions were a much more difficult proposition, and for the next two nights we slept on the bare boards. When at last the cabin was once more habitable, we sailed for Burnham.

I still have pleasant recollections of that trip. It was one of those days of which the yachtsman dreams but so seldom experiences; brilliant sunshine, a fine sailing breeze, and the air like champagne. It was the last day of our short holiday, and making an early start, we reached our destination soon after ten o'clock. We devoted the rest of the morning to cooking a couple of ducks, and at 1.30 p.m. sat down to a dinner of which I still retain a pleasant memory.

That was the last sail I was destined to have in *Euryanthe*, for during the following week she was run down in the night and sunk by some unknown vessel. Her cable having been broken by the impact, she had been driven over the mud, where the wreck lay exposed at half-tide. She was almost cut in halves and beyond repair. I salved the spars, sails and gear, and sold what was left to a man in need of a little firewood. As she was uninsured, the thirty pounds I had paid for her had gone down the drain, as the saying goes, to say nothing of a good deal more which I had spent in trying to make her seaworthy. I had *Euryanthe* for just six weeks, during which she sank three times and caused me much worry and unhappiness ❧

Part I: THE BOAT

CHAPTER 1: *Tabloid Cruisers*

I think most of you will agree that sailing about in an aimless sort of way in your home waters is apt to become a trifle boring after a time. Yet many of you who own open or half-decked sailing boats do nothing else. I expect that you regard your craft as mere day boats and the idea that you might do a little modest cruising in them has never occurred to you. But, if you pick your weather, there is really no reason why you should not cruise in almost any sort of boat. That intrepid sailor, Mr. Uffa Fox, some years ago sailed from Cowes to Havre and back in a 14ft. racing dinghy, and he did not trouble to pick his weather either, for the conditions were pretty rotten when he started. Indeed, I believe he and his two companions were kept busy with the bailer for some hours.

I should not, however, advise any inexperienced yachtsman to emulate Mr. Fox, for it seems to me that an element of risk enters into such a venture that it is not altogether prudent to incur. But, given fine summer weather, there is no reason why the owner of a small half-decked or open boat should not make short passages from port to port and I am sure that he would derive infinitely more pleasure from such trips than from pottering about in the neighbourhood of his moorings.

When I was a lad, I sometimes went cruising with my brother in a little boat named *Norah Creina*, and I still have pleasant recollections of the topping times we had in her. She was what is known as a canoe-yawl, although actually rigged as a sloop, and measured 18ft. in length by 5ft. 6in. in beam. My brother usually kept her at Teddington, but during the summer used to sail her round to the Crouch and then spend his holidays cruising between Burnham and Ipswich. We slept under a tent on cork mattresses spread on the floor, and being of the bulb-fin type the boat was admirably adapted to the purpose and reasonably comfortable in fine weather. Occasionally, however, there was too much wind at night to enable us to keep the tent up and we then had to get what shelter we could under the well-cover. When such conditions obtained it was anything but comfortable, but when one is young, experiences of that sort are soon forgotten. *Norah Creina* was very fast and handy but damnably wet when going to windward in a short sea. To get over that trouble my brother had made a well-cover of waterproof canvas, stiffened with hardwood battens. In rough weather we could with this cover up the whole of the well, leaving only sufficient space at the aft end for our bodies. We were thus able to keep our gear fairly dry and contrived to live on board for two or three weeks at a time with reasonable comfort.

As proof of my contention that, given the will, you can go cruising in almost anything, I would mention that on one occasion I and another lad, in the early 'nineties, went for a ten days' cruise in a 20-ft. open boat which we chartered from the proprietor of the inn at Fambridge for five bob. That does not seem much to pay for the hire of a yacht, does it? But if you had seen the boat you would probably have thought it adequate. I have had some old 'tore-outs' in my time, but I think that boat was the most disreputable in which I ever sailed. She was held together mainly by tar of which she had evidently received many generous coats; her gear was of the rottenest and her sails a tragedy. But in that unpromising packet we cruised to Pin Mill and back, exploring most of the rivers and creeks en route. As we were both 'broke to the wide' our living was of the order that is known as plain and the total cost of the trip was fifteen shillings a head. It is true that bread and cheese bulked largely in the menu of every meal, but there was plenty of it and that after all is the great thing when one is young.

Although nearly forty years have elapsed, three incidents of that cruise are still fresh in my memory. The first occurred in Brightlingsea Creek when getting under way, the cable coming home with no anchor on the end of it. The chain must have carried away when we attempted to break out the anchor and the impression left on my mind was akin to that of sitting down on a chair that is not there. Curiously enough there had been quite a fresh breeze during the night and the boat must have thrown considerable strain on her ground tackle. Yet, when we recovered the anchor, which we did with the aid of a borrowed dinghy and grapnel, we found on it the shackle and a broken link, which had practically rusted through.

The second incident was experienced whilst en route from Pin Mill to Brightlingsea. When off the Naze the breeze piped up strong from the eastward and meeting the ebb knocked up a nasty sea. We should have had a pair of reefs in the mainsail, but the peak halyard having jammed, we could not lower the sail. With the boat rolling almost to her gunwale, we funked going aloft and so decided to hang on to the whole sail and hope for the best. I have never forgotten the way in which that old hooker ran up the Wallet. For a moment she would hesitate, poised on the top of a wave, and then rush forward on the scend of the sea, doing her damnedest to broach-to. As she stormed along she sucked up a wave astern which every now and then toppled over into the boat, thus keeping us busy with the bailer. It was anxious work, but somehow or other we contrived to reach our destination in safety. When we hauled our wind to beat up Brightlingsea Creek, the peak of the mainsail immediately dropped down of its own accord, the halyard having chafed through.

The third incident also occurred at Brightlingsea, and although neither fraught with peril nor excitement was the most annoying of them all. We got roped in to play in a cricket match, the home side being two men short. We batted first and were all out for 18 runs. I personally did not trouble the scorer as the local Larwood knocked out my middle stump with his very first ball. Our opponents then batted for the rest of the day, knocking up over 400 runs for the loss of only eight wickets. I was put to field in 'the country' and was kept on the run most of the day. Now, a heat-wave was in progress and the temperature something like 94 degrees in the shade. I was *not* in the shade, and to make matters worse the outfield was of the roughest description and not altogether guiltless of 'foreign matter.' When I ran to save a boundary there was always an element of uncertainty about it. If I was lucky I picked up the ball, but if the fates frowned on me I picked up a half-dry cow pat. Such is life! But what annoyed me more than anything was the uncalled-for hilarity of the crowd, who seemed vastly entertained by my activities. It was not until I returned on board in the evening that I ascertained the cause of their amusement. I had been wearing a pair of white duck trousers, the nearest approach to cricket kit that I could raise, and when I took them off I discovered that the seat was marred by a bright red patch. A tin of some alkaline preparation for removing paint had been upset on the thwart of the boat and in the morning I had evidently inadvertently sat on what was the equivalent of wet paint of much the same colour as that with which the G.P.O. adorn their pillar boxes. You may ask, what has all this to do with cruising? To which pertinent question I can only reply, nothing at all. But I mention the incident as a terrible warning to those who go cruising to stick to the business in hand and not be deluded into taking part in side shows.

The worst feature of cruising in an open or half-decked boat is that you can't keep your gear dry in wet weather, or even in fine weather if you get much spray on board.

Some years ago, with those old *Norah Creina* days still in my memory, I gave some thought to the tent question and designed one, based on the Cape cart hood, which at that time was largely used on motor-cars. The bearers were fitted with slides that travelled on rods on the outside of the well coamings. To erect it, you merely had to raise the tent and haul it aft, where it was secured to the main horse by a lanyard. The after end was closed by canvas curtains, which could be tied back when not wanted. When not in use, the tent folded round the fore-coaming, where it served to keep water out of the boat on rough days and the curtain, falling down to the floor, sheltered the bedding, etc., stowed under the fore-deck.

This Cape cart hood tent, however, was only practicable in a boat with parallel coamings and which also had sufficient space between the mast and the fore-coaming for the stowage of the tent. Boats with such characteristics are rather rare nowadays, most half-decked sailing craft having curved coamings to match the contour of the boat. The tent I had devised no doubt could have been modified by having the runner rods fitted to the deck, but it would have looked very unsightly and suggestive of a chicken-house. Then it occurred to me that what I had already devised as a cockpit tent for my small cruising yacht could be modi-

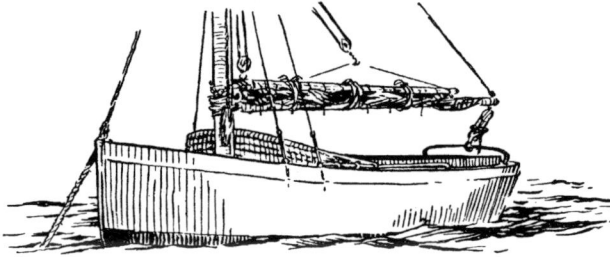

Cape cart hood tent

fied to serve as a tent for a half-decked boat. It is extremely simple and could be made to fit coamings of any shape.

For the sake of appearance and to reduce windage the tent, I think, should fit the coamings, and the top should be curved to allow rain to run off. The bearers, four or five in number, should therefore be curved, something like an enlarged coat-hanger. They can be made of hard wood or cane, the length of each being determined by the measurement from coaming to coaming at each position, the bearers being equidistantly spaced. Each spreader should have a hole bored through it in the middle, large enough to take a short length of hambro-line. The line should have a knot in one end, to prevent its being drawn through the bearer, and be long enough to pass round the furled sail and then tied. When erected the tent will fit the coamings and provide sitting headroom all over the well with an inch or two to spare. As the ends of the well will probably be rounded, the first and last bearers should be situated about a foot inside the coamings.

Careful measurements must be taken for the canvas cover, for as it will vary in width from station to station, a separate measurement must be taken at each station. As the furled sail must be pushed up the mast, the gooseneck should have a butterfly nut. The after end of the boom will, of course, rest in a crutch, as the boom must be horizontal before the tent is erected. The height of the boom from the floor can be determined by trial and error.

There must be an eyelet in the cover at each bearer station and, when erecting the tent, each bearer is fitted at its proper place by passing the hambro-line lanyard through the eyelet. The fore end is closed by being laced round the mast and the after end by canvas curtains, which can be folded back for ventilation purposes.

To erect the tent, the fore end should first be laced round the mast. Then, hauling the tent aft as you go, you pass each lanyard in turn round the furled sail until finally you secure the end of the tent to the boom-crutch with a lanyard kept on the tent for the purpose. The sides are fastened to brass screw-eyes on the outside of the coaming.

When erected, you will have a snug little cabin, with sitting headroom all over the well. Being made to the same shape as the well coamings and with a rounded top, it should look quite neat. Such a tent is quite simple, and when you have got everything organized, I don't think it will take very long to erect or take down.

Whatever form of tent you use it will be prudent to keep on board a water-proof ground-sheet, as when you bring up for the night the floor will often be wet with rain or spray. During the day the ground-sheet will be useful for protecting your blankets, etc. For a mattress I would suggest one of those Lilo things on which film-stars and other 'lovelies' lie on the beach sun-bathing (apparently with a camera man in attendance). They are waterproof and easily inflated, but care should be taken that there is nothing on the floor likely to cause a puncture.

To camp out under a tent when the interior of your boat and most of your gear are dripping wet is a miserable and depressing business, and the success or failure of your cruise is largely dependent upon the weather you experience. In the case of a half-decked boat, however, this difficulty can be overcome by the addition of a lifting cabin-top, which can easily be fitted to most boats of that

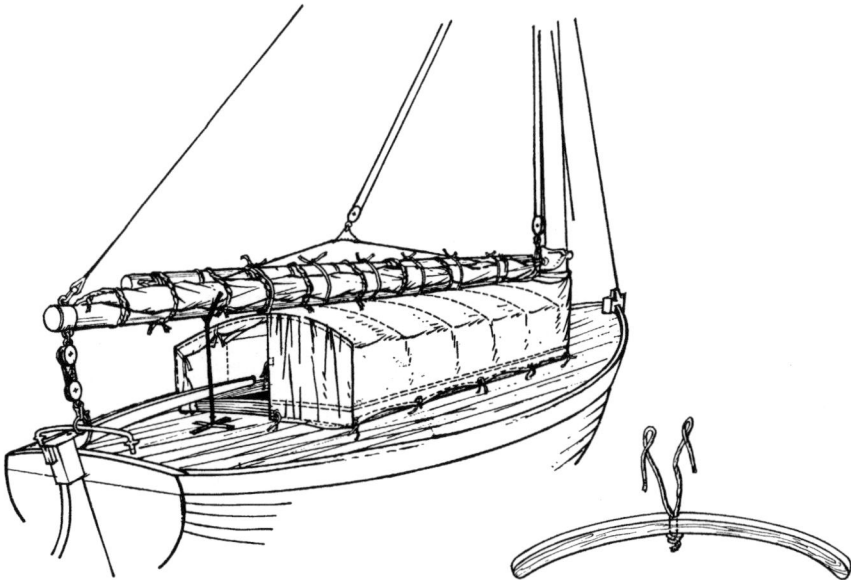

Another form of tent

type without much expense. The best lifting cabin-top that I have ever seen is that designed by the late Mr. G. Umfreville Laws. It has been fitted to many small craft and has, I believe, given general satisfaction. The advantages claimed for this cabin-top are: (1) Lightness. (2) Can be raised or lowered in a few seconds. (3) The supports act automatically. (4) It is adjustable to any strength or direction of wind. (5) Is adaptable to any size of yacht. Mr. Laws' description of the appliance reads as follows:

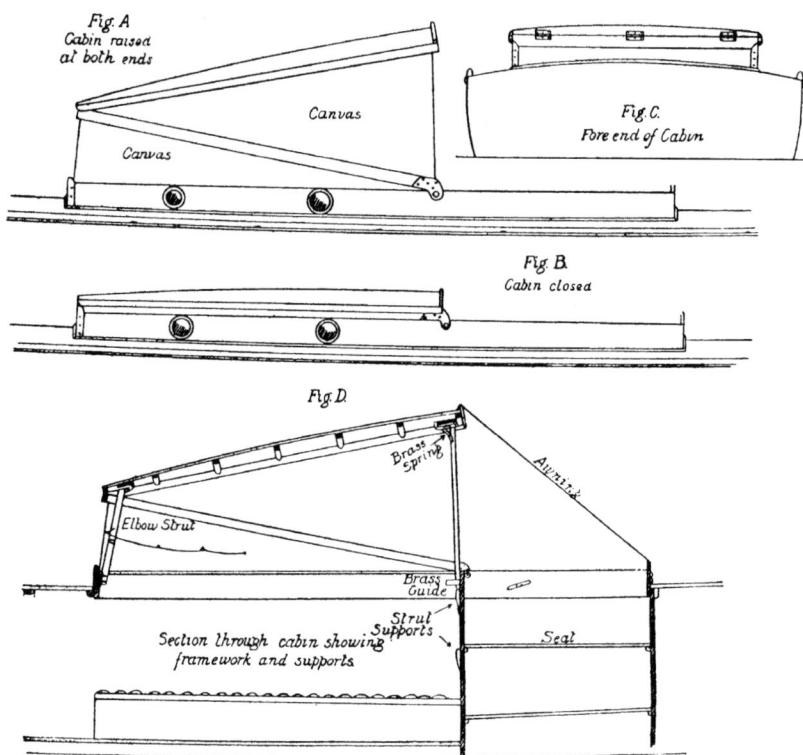

Laws' lifting cabin top

It will be seen from the drawings that the cabin-top lifts in two sections, both forward and aft. The coamings are in two parts, the upper part being strongly hinged at the fore end of the cabin-top, and at the aft end of the lower part. Figs. A, B and C show the hinges. Fig. B shows the cabin-top lowered and Fig. A shows it raised. The lower coamings are bound at the forward corners with brass angles, which project about 2 inches above to receive the upper coamings when lowered, and so prevent any lateral play. The cabin sides consist of light duck painted with Berthon flexible paint, and in them may be inserted, if desired, windows made of celluloid.

Although the arrangement looks fragile and flimsy when raised, it is in reality very firm, and will easily bear the weight of a man on top, raised or lowered.

The supports adjust themselves automatically, the forward ones being on the elbow-joint principle, and the after ones having fixed behind them, near the hinges, a strip of hard spring brass, which forces them against the bulkhead, so that they cannot fail to engage on the rests fixed thereon. All hinges must be very strong.

Fig. D shows the struts and rests. In order to prevent the canvas at the fore end bulging out when in the act of lowering, several small brass rings are sewn on to the sides and fore end and through these a small cord is rove and attached to the elbow struts, which, as they close, tauten the cords and thereby pull the slack of the canvas inwards clear of the coamings. The aft end of the raised cabin may be closed by means of a light awning stretched from the cabin to the after end of the coaming and buttoned or hooked round the sides. Should the wind be very heavy, half only of the cabin may be raised; and if the yacht is riding to the tide with the wind aft, causing her to sheer about, the aft end may be lowered and the forward end only kept up, and vice versa.

Before the fore end of the cabin can be raised, it is, of course, necessary to unship the boom from its gooseneck, or the spider-band. If the boat is fitted with roller reefing gear – which is generally the case now with up-to-date craft – this is easily done, as the boom can be unshipped from the gear by a simple pull aft. When the aft end only of the cabin is raised, the boom need not be unshipped, which is a further advantage of this method.

I have known quite a number of little boats fitted with the Laws cabin-top and their owners did a lot of cruising in them. Mr. Norman Carr, for instance, crossed the North Sea to Holland and cruised in the Dutch canals in *Dimsie III*, a pretty little craft designed by Mr. Laws and measuring only 17ft. on the waterline by 5ft. 3in. beam. Although Mr. Carr was well over 6 feet in height, he contrived to live very comfortably aboard *Dimsie III*.

CHAPTER 2: *A Perfect Love of a Boat*

I, like many other sailing men, have long searched in vain for the ideal small single-hander, but I think I have at last found her, or rather her lines, in a back number of the *Yachting Monthly*. She is a perfect love of a boat, and when my ship comes home, I shall be tempted to have her built. That is, of course, if I still remain in the same frame of mind; but yachtsmen's fancies as regards boats are as changeable as the seasons, and what seems desirable to-day may be the reverse to-morrow. The design I am in love with for the moment comes from the board of that enthusiastic yachtsman, Dr. T. Harrison Butler, and was published

H-B Singlehander sail plan, gaff main

in the *Yachting Monthly* of November, 1915. I am indebted to Dr. Butler for permission to reproduce the lines, which should make an exceedingly pretty and comfortable little cruiser. The boat has a very nice sheer and a bow that reminds me of the excellent small cruisers designed by Mr. J. Pain Clark. The underwater lines suggest weatherliness, and with a good length of keel she should be very steady on her helm. Her principal dimensions are: Length over all, 18 feet 6 inches; L.W.L., 16 feet; beam, 6 feet; and draught, 3 feet. Her displacement is 1.8 tons, and with an iron keel of .71 ton she should be stiff under her sloop rig of 200 square feet in area. Of course, the boat is very small, but it is astonishing what a lot of fun one can have even in a 'tabloid' cruiser. She strikes me as being just the thing for knocking about in the estuaries and creeks of the East Coast at week-ends, whilst a trip up to Lowestoft would be quite within her capabilities in any ordinary summer weather. Dr. Butler has given the boat a very snug sail plan, but in that I think he is right, for it is a mistake to over-canvas a boat intended for single-handed work. As far as can be judged from the sail plan the foresail is fitted with the Wykeham-Martin furling gear, one of the best shipmates I ever sailed with. I have used the gear on the headsails of several of my boats, and it has never yet 'sold me a pup.' To be able to set or furl a headsail practically instantaneously is a great boon to the single-hander, and no man who sails alone should be without the gear.

H-B Singlehander sail plan, gunter main

Dr. Butler has designed the boat with a Laws lifting cabin-top, an extremely clever device for increasing the headroom of small boats. As I know from personal experience, it is a gadget that works as well in practice as it looks on paper. Dr. Butler does not state what the headroom would be in his cabin, but as far as I can judge from the drawings it would be something like 5 feet with the cabin-top raised, which is ample for comfort. A special feature of this little cruiser is that the side seats in the cabin have a double top, so that the upper parts can be hinged over to meet, thus forming a flat floor on a level with that of the cockpit. The idea is that one or two mattresses could be spread on the floor for sleeping purposes. I do not, however, quite see the advantage of this scheme, as mattresses are awkward things to stow away in the daytime, and I should prefer to fit fo'castle cots like I had in my little *Snipe*. I always found them most comfortable and convenient, and they can be folded back to the sides of the yacht during the day with all the blankets and bedding inside. Dr. Butler suggests making a small well aft on one side of the rudder, covered by a hatchway, to accommodate an outboard motor, and this strikes me as a particularly happy idea. An Evinrude would drive a little ship like this at quite a respectable speed, and it possesses the advantages of being fool-proof and comparatively cheap to buy.

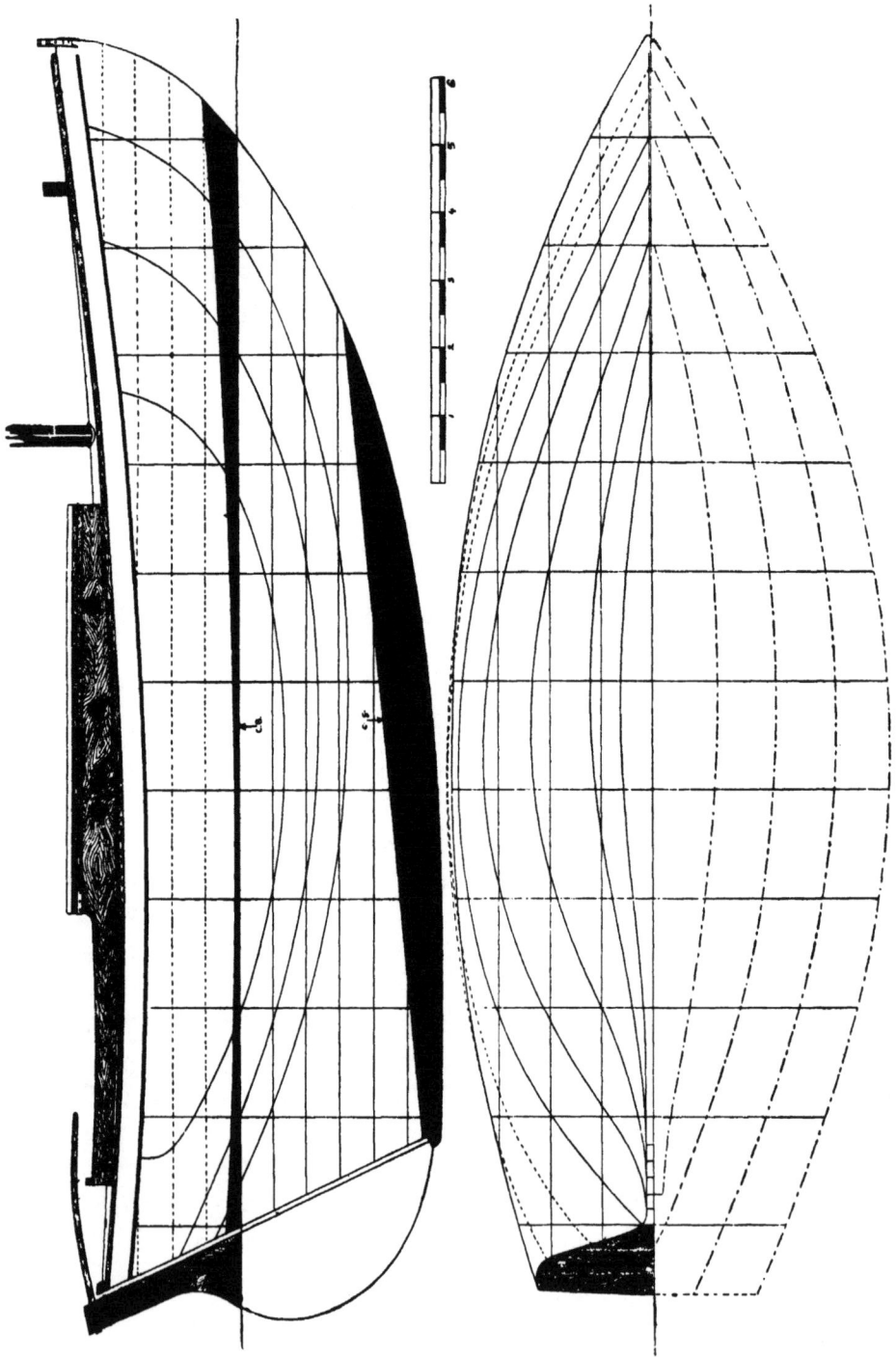

Drawing 1: Singlehander by T. Harrison Butler — Lines

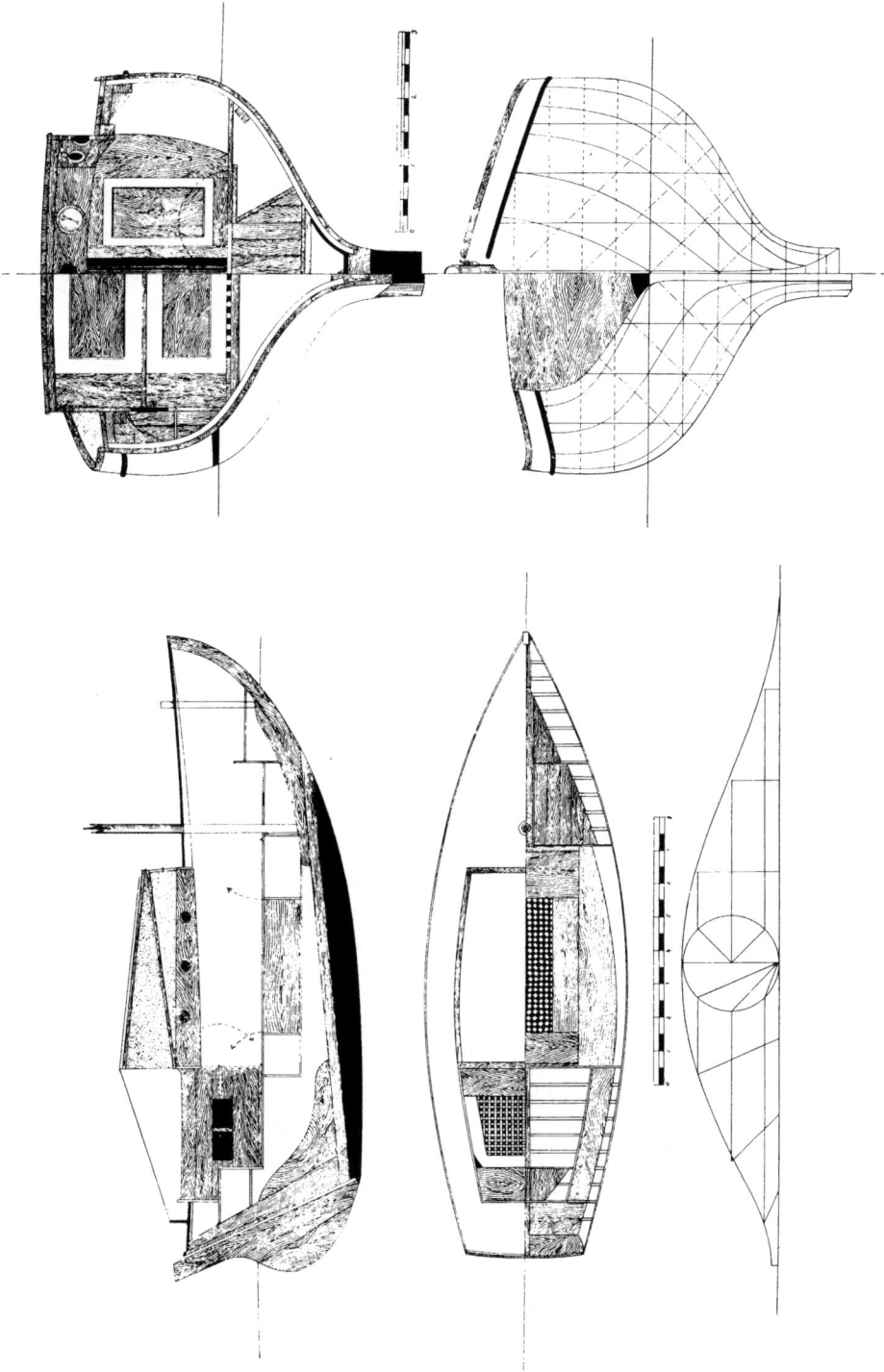

Drawing 2: Singlehander by T. Harrison Butler — Construction and Accommodation

CHAPTER 3: *Yachting with Economy*

I approach the subject of this chapter with more than a little diffidence, as at the time I write the war [WW-I]has not long been over and things are still in a state of flux. No one can at the moment forecast with any degree of accuracy what things will cost in the years to come, although it may be taken for granted that prices will rule higher than in pre-war days. Not only are materials in short supply but the cost of labour has increased considerably and such conditions are likely to obtain for a long time yet.

Even when matters are more stabilized it is doubtful if we shall ever again see a return to pre-war prices, for the cost of yachting has always been on the up-grade. When the famous racing yacht Britannia was built in 1893 she cost approximately £8,000, while the price of a similar vessel to-day would probably be at least four times as much; but it must be remembered that the purchasing power of the £ sterling is less than half of what it was.

Although it is obvious that our sport is going to cost us more, the outlook is not so black as mere figures would suggest, for if prices have advanced so has the income of the average man. I do not think therefore that the cost of yachting is likely to prove prohibitive. Some owners may have to rest content with smaller boats than they had contemplated and the poor man will have to do most of the work himself; but there is no particular hardship in that. But the point we now have to consider is what it will cost to keep a small yacht in the future.

To venture into the realm of figures under existing conditions would be both foolish and misleading, but it may be some guide to a potential owner if I tell him what it cost to maintain a small yacht before the war. Hazarding a guess, I should estimate the post-war advance at something like 80 per cent, and although that is only my own opinion, if he adds that percentage to the figures I shall give, I don't think he will be far wrong.

Well then, I will give you the information for what it is worth, but it must be remembered that the cost of upkeep depends a good deal on the size of the yacht and the amount of work you are prepared to do yourself. Even in these expensive days it will not cost very much to keep up a little boat of 3 or 4 tons, if you sail her and do most of the work yourself, but the larger the yacht, the more she will cost to maintain. To renew the running gear of a 3-tonner costs comparatively little, but that of a 7-tonner would be a considerable item, for she would need stouter rope and very much more of it, and rope is sold by weight. And the same thing will apply to everything connected with her.

I think the best I can do is to tell you what it has cost me to maintain yachts of different sizes before the war, then, by adding say 60 per cent to the figures you will have a pretty good idea as to what the cost would be to-day. It would be of little service if I went back too far, as prices have advanced so much in my time. To quote one example. When I was a youngster I had a new mast put into a 7-tonner for 28s., and 30 years later the same firm charged me nearly £10 for a mast for a 5-tonner. I will therefore confine myself to yachts I owned during the years immediately preceding the World War. They were craft of 7, 5 and 2½ tons respectively; all kept at the same place and under similar conditions.

In the case of a week-end yacht the principal item of expenditure is the employment of a waterman to take charge of the boat in the owner's absence. As I pointed out in the last chapter, this varies in different localities, but in such waters as the Thames Estuary and East Coast, it was, before the war, roughly about a shilling a week per ton. It has always been my practice to pay the same rate all the year round, as, during the winter, when the boat is laid up, the man stores my gear without charge and keeps an eye on the boat. Whether that custom obtains in other districts I cannot say, as mine is a rather exceptional case. The same man has looked after my yachts for almost fifty years, and in that I have been fortunate, for he devotes as much care and attention to the vessels in his charge as if they were his own property.

The following statements of expenditure represent the cost during an average year and being based on actual figures are beyond dispute:

7-ton Auxiliary Yawl

	£	s	d
Caretaker – 52 weeks at 7s. per week	18	4	0
Fitting out	7	15	0
New rope and bosun's stores	3	14	3
Sails (new balloon foresail)	2	0	0
Scrubbing and recoating with anti-fouling compo	2	17	6
Insurance	3	12	0
Petrol, paraffin and lubricating oil for engine	1	15	7
Stepping mast with crane	0	3	0
Lifting mast with crane at end of season	0	3	0
Rent of winter berth	0	10	0
Mooring fee paid to Fishery	0	10	0
Water rate	0	5	0
Paint	0	14	6
Coal for cabin stove	0	4	6
Sundries	0	3	6
£	42	11	10

5-ton Cutter (no engine)

	£	s	d
Caretaker – 52 weeks at 7s. per week	13	0	0
Fitting out	7	10	0
New sails	4	5	1
New rope etc	1	6	7
Scrubbing and recoating with anti-fouling compo	1	15	0
Insurance	1	4	3
Cabin furniture	0	14	9
Stepping and lifting mast	0	6	0
Lifting mooring	0	7	6
Mooring fee to Fishery	0	10	0
Winter berth	0	10	0
Water rate	0	5	0
Repairs to rudder	2	16	9
	£ 34	10	11

2½-ton Sloop (no engine)

	£	s	d
Caretaker – 52 weeks at 2/6 per week	6	10	0
Fitting out	5	10	0
Repainting during season – yacht and dinghy	2	6	4
Insurance	1	8	9
Scrubbing etc	0	10	0
New rope etc	0	6	10
New riding scope for mooring	1	8	2
Winter cover	2	4	4
Lifting mast	0	3	0
Lifting mooring	0	7	6
Rent of winter berth	0	10	0
Mooring fee to Fishery	0	10	0
Water rate	0	5	0
Bucket	0	2	6
	£ 22	2	5

The reader may be surprised that the cost of fitting out the 5-tonner was almost as much as that of the 7-tonner. The explanation is that the latter was a Falmouth Quay Punt and her spars, deck and coamings were painted. There was thus very little bright-work to be scraped. Insurance may also seem low, but I carry a quarter of the risk myself and insure with the East Coast Mutual, a club which, having no profits to earn, is able to base its premiums on bed-rock cost.

It will be seen from these statements that the cost of maintaining a 7-ton week-end yacht before the war was, in round figures, £42; a 5-tonner, £34; and a 2½-tonner, £22. Now, if they were owned in partnership the expense could be divided between the partners and the cost to each would be comparatively small. A 7-tonner will accommodate three people, a 5-tonner two and a 2½-tonner two. The annual expense of upkeep for each individual would be £14 in the 7-tonner; £17 in the 5-tonner and £11 in the 2½-tonner, which, it must be admitted, is not much to pay for sailing every week-end during the season, with, say, a three weeks' holiday cruise in the course of the summer.

In practice it pans out even better than that, for the yachtsman, by spending his holiday afloat, will save a considerable sum, which can be set off against the vessel's upkeep. When cruising one has little expense beyond the cost of food, and when you buy it in the raw and cook it yourself, food costs comparatively little. In my experience, one can live on board for twenty-five shillings a week, and allowing five shillings for incidental expenses, a holiday afloat should not cost more than, say, thirty shillings a week per head. Now, what would you spend if you went to a popular seaside resort for your holiday and put up at a hotel or boarding house? Even before the war I don't think you could have secured accommodation for less than three guineas a week, and on top of that you would have to pay for amusements, which would swell the expense to at least £4 a week. On a three weeks holiday you would therefore have saved something like £7 10s. 0d. if you went cruising, and if you set that off against the upkeep of the yacht, the expense of owning a small craft, instead of being the extravagance that some people seem to think, is really extraordinarily economical.

For week-end trips the cost of food before the war worked out at about four shillings a head. Your meals on board must of necessity be of the order known as 'plain' and to do it at the figures I have mentioned you must eschew fancy dishes and expensive drinks. But you will have plenty of good wholesome food, and if your drinks are confined to tea and coffee, it won't hurt you.

CHAPTER 4: *Partnerships and Syndicates*

Choosing a sailing partner is almost as chancy a business as choosing a wife. A man may be a delightful companion ashore but it is only after you have been cooped up with him in a small yacht for a time that you really know much about him. He may be a slap-dash, casual sort of fellow whose untidy habits will annoy you to distraction. Such an one will never stow things away in their proper places, or belay ropes on their right cleats, and the result will soon be chaotic. No one who takes a pride in his ship could put up with such a state of affairs for long and the partnership would probably soon be dissolved. On the other hand if you are associated with the right sort of chap, the pleasure of your cruising will be enhanced, labour reduced and the expense halved. Two old friends of mine sailed together for nearly fifty years, the partnership only being ended by the recent death of one of them. I can recall other sailing partnerships that endured for half a lifetime.

Partnerships are usually entered upon either for the sake of companionship or from motives of economy. Man, being by nature a gregarious animal, loves to herd with his fellows, and the idea of sailing alone is abhorrent to many people, although it has much to recommend it. When single-handed you are perfectly free to do just what you like. If you don't feel inclined to sail, you can remain on your mooring, and when you get under way you are at liberty to lay your course in any direction you may fancy. You can have your meals when it suits you and, having so much more room in the cabin, you enjoy greater comfort. And as for feeling lonely – well, there simply is not time to feel lonely, as there is always something to do in a yacht. It is only idle people who feel lonely.

Now, if you have a partner you are bound to study him, and unless both are prepared to adopt a give-and-take policy, the partnership will not long endure. Personally, I find it infinitely more interesting to sail alone and, although I have done so for many years, I have never felt at all lonely. Any spare time I have on my hands I devote to reading and writing, and incidentally have written several books and hundreds of articles on board. I have thus been able to combine business with pleasure and the one pays for the other, leaving a considerable margin to keep the wolf from the door. Before entering into partnership you will be wise to make sure that your potential partner's disposition is compatible with your own. Go for a cruise with him and if at the end you like him as much as you did at the start, there is every prospect of the partnership proving a success. It is only by trying each other out in that manner that you can be sure that you will get on well together. It is important that you should agree at the outset who is to be skipper, because you can't have two skippers in a boat without a risk of confusion that might lead to an accident. If one partner has had considerably more experience than the other, he should be skipper, otherwise you might take it in turns. I do not suggest that one should boss the other, but the initiative should fall to the one who is for the time being in authority.

In the last chapter I referred to a 'working partnership,' by which I meant an arrangement whereby one sails regularly in the yacht, paying a share of the cost of upkeep and catering expense. That may suit an owner better than a full partnership, as he retains full control of the yacht, while being relieved of some of the expense. It is equally satisfactory to the working partner, who gets his sailing at comparatively small cost and, if a novice, obtains a certain amount of practical experience. The working partner's contribution should be confined to ordinary expenses and not include costly items such as new sails, which may be expected to last for a good many years. I would advise the beginner, however, to have at least a season 'on his own' before entering into any partnership, as he will learn much more if he has to think out everything for himself.

At week-ends the financial side of the question presents no difficulty. Each partner makes a note of what he has spent for food, etc. and the matter is adjusted at the end of the trip. But when away for some time, as during a holiday cruise, that rough-and-ready way would not prove satisfactory, as each of the party would probably buy things from time to time and might forget to make a note of his expenditure. I can recommend the following plan in the case of partnerships and syndicates. Before starting on the cruise, let each one of the party contribute, say, £2, which should be put into a common purse, or a small canvas bag. Then everything bought should be paid for out of the 'ship money.' Take the money with you when you go ashore, and pay for everything you buy, even drinks, with it, except perhaps tobacco and cigarettes. I make that exception as one of the party may be a non-smoker, or smoke less than his companions. If the 'kitty' runs dry before the end of the cruise, there should be another whip round to replenish it. Any balance left at the end of the trip can be equally divided. This is, I think, a perfectly fair and convenient arrangement, as everyone pays alike and it eliminates such questions as, "Whose turn is it to pay for drinks?"

Syndicates are not very common nowadays, but they have their attraction for the impecunious, who otherwise might not be able to sail at all. Youngsters fresh from school seldom have enough money to buy a boat, or even to take a partnership in one. By clubbing together, sailing may become a feasible proposition. I joined a syndicate in my young days and it may be of interest to those possessed of much enthusiasm and little money if I tell them about it.

Several of us hailed from the same public school and were old friends. Persuading others to join us, we were able to form a syndicate numbering twelve members, each pooling the sum of £5. We thus had £60 with which to buy a boat, but realizing the importance of keeping a few pounds in hand for emergencies, we hoped to get a vessel of some sort for £50, or even less. We were all youngsters with the exception of one, who had reached the comparatively mature age of thirty-three, and as he was a more or less experienced yachtsman, we appointed him skipper.

To accommodate a round dozen, it was obvious that a craft of some size would be necessary and it seemed likely that such a vessel, at any price we could afford to pay, would take some finding. But we were lucky in our quest and happened on a suitable boat at Faversham. After a good deal of haggling in the bar-parlour of the Shipwright's Arms, during which numerous pots of beer were consumed, we became owners of the *Two Sisters* for the sum of £35. That could hardly be deemed an extravagant price to pay for a vessel of rather more than 20 tons, complete with all necessary gear, and a 16-foot boat in excellent condition.

The *Two Sisters* had been superannuated from work on the Whitstable oyster beds, and although more than eighty years old, was still more or less seaworthy.

It is true that she leaked more than was desirable, but that defect was, if not actually cured, at least mitigated to some extent by the application of tingles without and Portland cement inside. Her sails were of the stoutest flax canvas dressed with oil and ochre, and as many of the blocks were 'blind' and her running gear of tarred hemp, which became stiff and untractable in cold weather, she was uncommonly heavy to work. To set the mainsail, we had to lead the halyard falls to the windlass, an old-fashioned barrel affair that extended right across the fore-deck. To get the sail down, it was usually necessary for two of us to sit on the gaff and ride it down. She was as slow as a hearse in anything short of half a gale of wind, but all the same we thought her a wonderful craft and scornfully referred to yachts that passed us as 'racing machines.'

When we bought the *Two Sisters* her only sleeping accommodation consisted of two berths in the fo'c'sle, and the skipper claimed one by virtue of his office. For the other we drew lots and the unsuccessful ten had to camp out as best they could in the hold. Now this hold had carried oysters for many many years, and although we had scrubbed it out with a zeal that would have put Lewis Carroll's seven maids to shame, it still smelt strongly of what the Fleet Street reporter might term 'the succulent bivalve.' The hold, moreover, was always damp and often draughty, as the boards which formed the hatch covering did not meet by inches. It will readily be understood, therefore, that our sleeping quarters were, in the winter, of the order known as Spartan. On one occasion some of the party attempted to alleviate the discomfort by slinging hammocks across the hold, whilst their comrades, wrapped in blankets, courted sweet Morpheus on the floor beneath. For the first few hours all was well, but then trouble arose from an unexpected cause. Not only were the hammocks new but also the lanyards by which they were suspended and, assisted by the motion of the boat, the new rope gradually stretched. In the early hours of the morning, the backsides of the lordly ones who occupied them were bumping on the faces of the sleepers below, and in a short time the whole crowd was engaged in an unseemly fight in the dark.

As the result of that little episode it was decided that the hold must be converted into a proper cabin and with that object in view we sailed the *Two Sisters* round to Brightlingsea. There we were fortunate enough to happen upon the late Mr. Robert Aldous, who took a most sympathetic interest in the matter when we explained what we wanted done and how little money we had in hand to pay for the job. "You don't want to waste money on that old thing," he said, "you can do most of it yourselves." His men carried out the structural alterations, such as cutting away the deck, extending the hatch coamings and putting on a cabin-top, but all the internal work we did ourselves. We had not much experience of carpentering, but Mr. Aldous showed us how to set about it, supplied the necessary materials and lent us such tools as we lacked. I believe the old gentleman thoroughly enjoyed himself. He would often come aboard in the afternoon for a mug of tea and, sitting on an old box, would laugh at us and 'pull our legs.' When, after much pressing, he rendered his account, the amount was so small that it could hardly have covered the cost of the materials and labour. He was a fine old chap and I am glad to place on record his kind and generous treatment to a lot of youngsters whose only recommendation was their keenness.

When the alterations were completed we had a fine big saloon that would easily accommodate the lot of us. Wide bunks on either side provided beds for the majority and the rest slept on the floor. In the centre was a large table, firmly stepped, at which we sat on benches clamped to the floor. Across the forward end was installed a large stove with an oven which we had picked up cheap. We had taken the opportunity while she was ashore thoroughly to clean her out and give her a coat of paint. The saloon had been lined with match-boarding, which was painted white, and mounted on the cabin-top were a skylight and companion of teak, which Mr. Aldous had sold us for £2. They were coated with mould when we bought them, but they scraped up like new, as he said they would. Such was the ship in which we spent our week-ends, winter and summer, and also our summer holiday, during which we cruised between Lowestoft and the Wight.

And now a few words about our methods. At first everyone did much as he liked and, as most of us jibbed at domestic chores, confusion was apt to reign. I remember one occasion when the skipper said "Who is going to cook breakfast?" Meeting with no response, he continued, "As no one seems very eager, I will see about it myself," with which remark he retired to the fo'c'sle. The rest of us were delighted at having at last made the skipper do a job of work, for he was one of those men who only like work when someone else does it. And so we sat about on deck, patiently awaiting a summons to breakfast. But what a long time he was! It was nearly an hour before he reappeared on deck, filling his pipe. "If you chaps want any breakfast, you had better see about it," he said. On going below, we found no signs of preparation for a meal, but on going through into the fo'c'sle, we found a dirty frying-pan and there could be no doubt that he had merely cooked and eaten his own breakfast. Judging by the eggshells and bacon rind he had left on a plate, the skipper had 'done himself proud.'

We had learnt our lesson, and rules were drawn up and adopted and there was no further trouble. We took it in turns to attend to the catering and cooking each week-end, two of the syndicate being responsible for buying the food and two for cooking it. As washing-up was regarded as a particularly poisonous job, a different squad undertook the work after each meal, and boredom was thus to a large extent alleviated. The catering party were limited to three shillings a head for each week-end trip and they were expected to provide, *inter alia*, a large joint of some sort. This usually took the form of a big piece of boiling beef, which we cooked on board and had hot on the Saturday night, with the usual trimmings of dumplings, carrots and onions. The joint was served cold for lunch the next day, and also for supper on Sunday for those who remained on board. For breakfast we had either sausages or eggs and bacon.

The only alcoholic drink allowed was beer, of which we usually carried a two-gallon jar. It must be remembered that in the days of which I write things were much cheaper than they are to-day. We sometimes bought as many as two dozen eggs for a shilling, the best sausages were only eightpence a pound, and the price of most other things in proportion.

We stationed the *Two Sisters* at Hole Haven, and the weekend ticket to Benfleet, the nearest station, was only half a crown. Our catering and travelling expenses were thus only five shillings and sixpence a week-end, for which insignificant sum we had the time of our lives. During our absence the caretaker of one of the gunpowder hulks looked after the boat, charging half a crown a week for his services, and as we did all our own work in the way of repairs and renovations to gear, the cost of upkeep was trivial. As far as I remember about a shilling a head per week covered that item.

If I have dwelt at some length on this 'yachting in the rough,' it is because I am anxious to show that it is possible for even the most impecunious to go in for sailing. Of course, it would be quite impossible in these times to run a boat as cheaply as we did the *Two Sisters*, as everything costs so much more, but I don't see any reason why it should not be done at, say, double the price. Even in these expensive days food does not cost a great deal, if you buy and cook it yourself. The purchase of a suitable boat should present no great difficulty as now that most fishermen have gone over to motors, there must be lots of old smacks to be picked up cheaply.

Because I have told you of the humble manner in which I went sailing in my young days, please don't think that I recommend the novice to start in what the East Coast longshoremen call a 'little old tore-out.' If you can afford it, by all means get a good little yacht to begin with, or, if money be no object, even have one built to suit your ideas. The point I wish to emphasize is that any old crock, even a converted ship's boat, is better than no boat at all, and there is this to be said about it; you will probably learn far more seamanship in an old hooker than in a yacht of modern type, as the former takes much more handling. Moreover, by studying her defects you will get an idea of the sort of craft to buy 'when your ship comes home,' as the saying goes.

And now, having cleared the decks of preliminaries, so to speak, we can pass on to the selection and purchase of a suitable craft.

CHAPTER 5: *Selecting a Yacht*

In the selection of a yacht one has a wide choice, for there are many different types. Some are beamy and others narrow-gutted; some draw a lot of water and others are of light draught; some are keel boats and others have a centreplate or lee-boards; some have a straight stem, while others have an overhanging bow; some have flush decks and others a coach-roof. Then there are transom, counter and canoe sterns and many different kinds of rig. In fact, unless built to a standard design, every yacht has her own individual characteristics.

Those who cruise in small craft to-day are fortunate, for they have infinitely better vessels than yachtsmen of the last generation. Not only is the modern cruiser of a more efficient type, but she is better equipped and rigged. She is, moreover, safer, as the gear can be almost entirely handled from the deck. It is seldom, indeed, that one has to go aloft nowadays.

Things were very different when I began yachting. The small yacht of those days was a miniature edition of her larger sister and rigged in a similar manner. She carried a long fidded topmast and a long reefing bowsprit, spars that made for heavy and sometimes dangerous work. To carry a bare topmast on end was considered unseamanlike, and when the topsail was taken in, the topmast had to be lowered, which entailed a deal of work. First, the topmast shrouds and stay had to be slackened and then the topmast lifted a few inches by hauling on the heel-rope so that the fid could be withdrawn. A hand had to go aloft to do that, unless the spar was fitted with a tumbler fid. This was a permanent fitting, weighted at one end and having a line at the other. The tumbler fid was an ingenious contrivance in theory but did not always work in practice. When out of action it was supposed to house automatically in the heel of the spar, whilst a pull on the line brought it into operation. In practice, however, it did not always pan out according to plan, for if the weighted end of the fid happened to be on the side that the yacht was heeling it would not house properly and someone had to go aloft to make it 'do its stuff.'

After the fid had been removed, the topmast was lowered and the heel lashed to the mast. Then the shrouds and stay had to be shortened and set up again. For shortening purposes, the topmast shrouds were in two parts, connected by shackles or sister-hooks, and when the spar was housed the lower portions of the shrouds were removed. This, of course, took time and was not so easy as it sounds when the weather was rough. When the topmast was sent up again, the process was reversed.

In light weather we carried a large club-headed topsail, which was a beast to set, or hand, as the yard had a way of getting foul of everything it possibly could. In stronger breezes we used a jib-headed topsail, which, although less trouble to set than the club-headed one, also entailed a good deal of work, as the luff, in either case, had to be laced to the topmast. Someone therefore had to go aloft to lace or unlace the sail when the topsail was set or lowered. Getting the topsail down in a squall was no picnic for the masthead man, as he had to stand on the cap of the mainmast, while the vessel rolled or pitched heavily beneath him.

In those days even a small yacht had four or five jibs, and when the mainsail was reefed the jib had to be changed for a smaller one to restore the balance. And when a small jib was set the bowsprit had to be reefed. That was nearly as much trouble as housing the topmast, as bowsprit shrouds, bobstay and topmast stay had first to be slackened, so that the fid could be withdrawn. Then, the bowsprit having been pulled in the required distance, the fid was re-shipped in another hole. Finally, the bowsprit shrouds, which were fitted with tackles, the bobstay and topmast stay had to be set up again.

Shifting jibs in heavy weather was often the devil of a business, for the wildly plunging fore-deck afforded precarious foothold. It was a case of one hand for yourself and the other for the ship, and you were pretty sure to get wet through in the process. But it was a job that had to be done, for, apart from balancing the sail plan, a big jib could not be carried with safety in bad weather as the bowsprit was nearly as long as the boat, and the sail usually cut low on the foot. If a sea were shipped in the jib, the bowsprit was likely to be broken off short at the stemhead, an accident by no means uncommon.

Sailing such yachts in heavy weather was a strenuous business, but afforded fine training in seamanship and was thrilling sport. Few, however, regretted the passing of the old-time yacht, as she was succeeded by vessels infinitely more comfortable and easy to handle. It was not only the rig that was unsatisfactory but also the hull, which possessed features that are now considered definitely bad. The old yacht usually had a straight stem, deep forefoot and flat low counter, which slammed abominably when the vessel was at anchor in rough water. She was also inclined to be 'hard-headed,' and even a small yacht of the type often needed two men at her helm when reaching in a strong breeze. Her one redeeming feature was that she would lie-to in bad weather until the cows came home, as the saying goes.

Some of the yachts I sailed in those days were narrow-gutted, deep-heeled craft, relics of the plank-on-edge era. They were wonderful ships to windward, but as wet as a half-tide rock. Instead of lifting to the seas they went slap through everything and sailing them to windward in a strong breeze was something like riding on the back of a porpoise. One, in particular, was a yawl measuring 60 feet over all by 10 feet beam, with a draught of 9 feet 2 inches and carrying a huge spread of sail. I remember vividly my first trip in that vessel, from Rochester to Burnham in the depth of winter. We had just taken her over from her last owner and, unable to find the reef-tackle, had to beat down Swin in a strong easterly breeze and driving snow under the whole mainsail. The yacht was buried almost to her skylights in the harder squalls, and having high bulwarks with inadequate scuppers, the decks were full of water.

We were soon soaked through and I have never been so cold in my life before or since. It was dark when we rounded the Whitaker gas buoy and then had to run up the Whitaker Channel in the pitch-black night with nothing to guide us but the lead and compass, for the West Buxey buoy was not lit in those days. By working on and off the edge of the sands and sounding all the way, we got safely into the Crouch, but it was a hair-raising experience that will ever remain in my memory.

Of late years, designers have devoted considerable attention to the small cruiser and have succeeded in evolving a type of yacht that is almost ideal for the purpose. With comparatively small displacement, she can be driven by much less sail, and a moderate forward overhang tends to make her dry at sea. In place of the flat slamming counter of her predecessor, she has either a well-tucked-up counter of V-section, a canoe or transom stern. Which is the best of the three is largely a matter of opinion, as each possesses its advantages. The small cruiser of to-day is a good deal faster, particularly to windward, than the old-time craft, more weatherly, handier and a better sea boat, and she can be sailed by a much smaller crew.

Long topmasts and bowsprits are things of the past and now rarely seen. When a topsail is carried at all it is set with a yard on a pole mast and bowsprits have become shorter and shorter. In fact, many such craft nowadays have no bowsprit at all, a single headsail being set on the stemhead. The introduction of the Bermudian rig has simplified matters still further, for the mainboom is short and the sail set with a single halyard. With all of the sail plan inboard, the vessel can be worked from the deck and it is never necessary to go aloft unless something carries away. When that happens, a man is hoisted aloft in a bosun's chair to put things right.

Nowadays, too, no cruising craft is considered adequately equipped unless she has an auxiliary engine to propel her when the wind fails or when she cannot be sailed with advantage. The engine is also most useful when going into or coming out of a harbour, or to extricate the vessel from 'tight' places. Indeed, so much does the modern yachtsman rely upon his engine to get him out of difficulties, that at one time it seemed likely that handling vessels under sail would become a lost art, but the introduction of ocean racing – a comparatively new form of sport in this country – has fortunately prevented that, and we are now breeding a race of fine amateur seamen, who race over wide tracts of open sea, taking the weather as it comes.

It is an old saying that what the racing man uses to-day the cruising man will use to-morrow, and there can be no doubt that the latter has derived considerable benefit from racing. He, for instance, owes the overhanging bow to racing, for it was originally evolved to cheat the measurement rule. From the same source he has also derived such things as hollow masts and spars, wire rigging and gear, lead ballast, the Bermudian rig, rigging screws and other items of equipment. A few yachts are still designed with a straight stem, but in ever-decreasing numbers, and it seems likely that that form of bow will in course of time disappear altogether.

When buying a boat many things have to be considered. In the first place it is essential that you should have an idea as to the sort of sailing for which you intend to use her. Do you want her just for pottering about in the estuary of a tidal river, with perhaps an occasional short trip round the coast to a neighbouring port, or does your fancy lie in the direction of extended cruising over wide tracts of open sea? Then again, will your sailing be confined to the week-ends, or do you contemplate living on board all the summer?

Those are some of the questions to which you will have to find answers before you can come to any conclusion as to the size and type of craft best suited to your requirements. And there may be others which you cannot altogether ignore. If, for instance, you are a family man and wish to take your wife and children with you on your cruises, you will require a good deal more accommodation. Well then, let us first go into this question of tonnage.

The tonnage of the yacht you buy must be governed by the sort of cruising for which you want her. It is sheer waste of money to buy a 10-tonner when a 5-tonner will do the work equally well. If you have only the week-ends at your disposal, it is obvious that you will not be able to go very far afield and a craft of 4 or 5 tons will probably be large enough for the sort of cruising for which you have time. As a matter of fact it is possible to do quite a lot of cruising in craft even smaller than that. In the little *Snipe*, 2½ tons, which I owned about fifty years ago, I did far more cruising than in the 7-ton *Seabird* which superseded her, and although she was only 18 feet long by 6 feet beam, I managed to live on board in reasonable comfort. Of course I was only a boy and when we are young all our geese are swans. Still, for week-end purposes, with perhaps a holiday cruise of two or three weeks' duration in the course of the summer, a craft of 4 or 5 tons should be large enough for most people. She would cost comparatively little to maintain and very little work would be needed to keep her clean and tidy.

It must be remembered that the cost of upkeep mounts rapidly as the tonnage is increased. Rope, for instance, is sold by weight, and the larger the yacht, the more she will require, and it will have to be much larger in size and consequently heavier than that for a little yacht. And the same thing applies to everything else in connection with her. Then, too, the larger boat will cost much more to buy in the first place.

Expense, however, is not the only consideration; you must also take into account the work that will be necessary to keep the yacht in a state of efficiency and cleanliness. If you buy a craft of, say, 8 or 10 tons, much of your time will be sacrificed to the domestic department and your sailing unduly curtailed. And the same remark applies to keeping her gear in order.

Of course, if you are going to make the vessel your home and live on board all the summer, you must of necessity have a larger ship. You could not be really comfortable unless you had standing headroom in the cabin and ample locker accommodation. If you are going to be away from home for months on end, you will have to carry with you a considerable wardrobe and far more stores of all kinds than would be required for weekend trips, and I doubt whether a craft of less than 7 tons would fill the bill. If your wife and children are to accompany you, sleeping accommodation is another factor that must be taken into account.

Another important point is the depth of water at the place you propose to make your headquarters. If circumstances compel you to station the yacht at a place that dries out at low tide, it is desirable that she should be of a type that will take the ground without listing to any great extent. A keel boat, drawing 4 or 5 feet of water, would be a hopeless proposition under such conditions. Living on board would be intolerable when she was aground and such a boat would be liable to strain if she had to take the ground every tide. Moreover, your sailing would be much curtailed as you would only be able to leave, or return to, your moorings for perhaps a couple of hours on either side of high water. Such conditions call for a craft of very light draught that will take the ground without much list. That suggests either a centreplate boat or a barge yacht, so let us first consider those types.

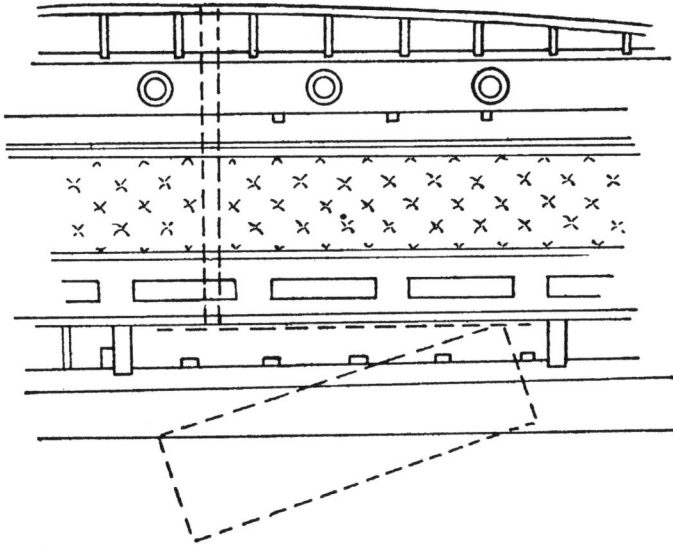

Centreplate below cabin floor

The centreplate, no doubt, is a handy contrivance for giving a vessel the necessary lateral resistance to enable her to sail to windward, but its case is horribly in the way and quite spoils the accommodation below decks. It prevents your stretching your legs, and I personally object to putting on my trousers in the cockpit on a wet day. But if you have to sail from a place where there is little water and the boats dry out at low tide, it is perhaps the most satisfactory solution to a rather difficult problem. With a natural draught of not much more than a foot, and a flat floor, such a yacht will take the ground almost upright and will be able to leave, or return to, her mooring for perhaps six or eight hours each tide. All the same I dislike a centreplate, for, apart from spoiling the cabin, it is often a cause of trouble. The plate is usually raised or lowered by means of a lanyard, which more often than not is of flexible wire rope. Nothing could be more unsuitable, as, being constantly wet and dry, it soon rusts. Since it is out of sight, the owner seldom has any knowledge as to its condition, until one day it breaks. Then he is betwixt the devil and the deep sea, as the plate hangs below the yacht by a single bolt, rendering the vessel unmanageable. To get the plate back into its case is the deuce of a job. If he is very lucky he may be able to coax it back by means of a rope passed under the keel forward and then hauled aft, but it is very seldom the plan succeeds, and it is possible that the plate may be bent in the process. In most cases it is only by hauling the yacht out on a slipway, or enlisting the services of a diver, that the plate can be housed, and either method involves considerable expense. If chain were used for the lanyard such mishaps would seldom occur.

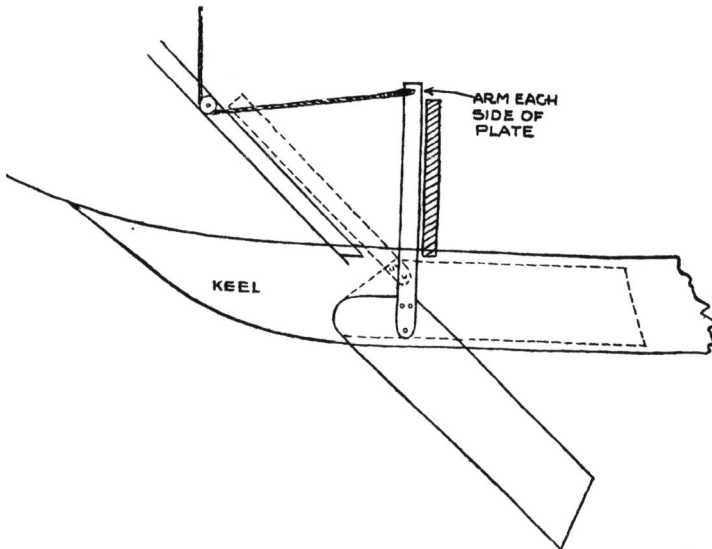

L-shaped centreplate

I have been referring to the common form of triangular or rectangular plate, but there are others far more satisfactory. The L-shaped plate, for instance, houses for the most part in the vessel's keel and as the case has only to accommodate the arm, it is much smaller and does not encroach so much on the cabin space. The lifting tackle, moreover, is of rope, and since it is visible an eye can be kept on its condition. Even if it broke, the plate would not fall out of the case. Then there is a form of plate that is housed entirely below the cabin floor and raised by a lanyard led through a tube to the deck or cabin-top. The tube, far from being in the way, makes a useful handfast to hold on to when moving about below in rough weather. But both of these plates entail more draught than would be desirable when there is scarcity of water and the boat has to take the ground every tide. Drawing perhaps 2 feet 6 inches or 3 feet, the yacht, when aground, would heel over quite a lot and be uncomfortable to live in, so must be considered unsuitable for the particular conditions of which I am writing.

Among other faults the ordinary kind of plate possesses may be mentioned the liability of the case to work and leak when the yacht is sailed hard to windward. Under such conditions great lateral stress is placed on it and the fastenings are often inadequate. A minor objection is that water is apt to squirt up through the lanyard hole and make the cabin wet. That can be obviated by stuffing a rag in the hole before getting under way, but one is apt to forget it until the mischief has been done. In order to get sufficient headroom in the cabin, the floorboards of a centreplate craft, such as I have described, must be placed almost on the keelson and there is thus little room left for bilge water, which is apt to invade the cabin when the yacht is in stays, and that makes things unpleasantly wet. The only way in which this can be prevented is to sponge the bilge quite dry before getting under way and that is an intolerable nuisance. It usually means lifting the floorboards, as all of the water cannot be removed with the pump, some of it being trapped between the timbers. It may not be much, but even a little will wet the cabin floor. The same thing applies, of course, to any flat-floored craft with no reverse curves in her sections.

The barge yacht would appear to be ideal for such conditions, as she draws but a few inches of water and sits upright when aground, but the little barge yacht is a poor sort of craft. In the hands of a novice she would be definitely unsafe. An ordinary yacht, with most of her ballast in the form of a lead or iron keel, can be hove down with impunity, because the more she heels the greater becomes the righting power of her keel. Provided that the water does not invade the cockpit, she can be hove down almost on to her beam-ends, and will right again as soon as the pressure on her sails has been eased. But the barge does not possess those qualities. She has enormous initial stability, but when heeled to a certain angle, that stability vanishes in a moment and over she goes, her capsize being assisted by the windage on her flat bottom. As most small barges have a very moderate sail area, they seldom heel to that extent, but it might happen in a heavy squall. This is no mere theory, for years ago a barge actually capsized in that manner in the course of the annual Thames barge match and so far as I remember one of her crew was drowned.

Many yachtsmen are prejudiced against barge yachts on account of their unsightly appearance. It is true that few have much to recommend them in that respect, but mere appearance is of no consequence. If your ship serves you faithfully and well, you will get an affection for her that will blind you to her aesthetic shortcomings. But if the barge does look something like an old orange-box, she has a great deal of room in her, for owing to her straight sides and flat floor, every inch of space can be utilized. This type of yacht, however, has one serious disadvantage. Before her bottom can be scrubbed, she must be placed on a 'gridiron' or blocks.

The small barge yacht was first introduced by the late Mr. E. B. Tredwen in the early 'nineties, and has attained considerable popularity in shallow districts, such as Southend and Leigh-on-Sea. Necessary lateral resistance is provided by lee-boards, although a few have been built with a centreplate. I have never sailed one myself, but have often watched the behaviour of such craft and have not been impressed by their behaviour in rough weather, at any rate those of 6 tons and under. They wallowed in the trough of the sea and every wave seemed to hurl them farther to leeward. I once saw one take charge in a squall and drive on to the sands and dry out. Opinions as to their seagoing qualities seem rather divided. Mr. Tredwen assured me that they were excellent sea boats, and he certainly did a good deal of cruising in his 12-ton *Pearl*, in which he visited many ports at home and abroad. I myself have seen Mr. H. G. Lynn's 14-ton barge *Heron* sailing well on a rough day, and these larger barges seem quite a different proposition, probably owing to their weight.

But if opinions differ on the subject of barge yachts, there can be no doubt as to the efficiency of the semi-sharpie chine yacht, with a bottom shaped like a broad V. Years ago I often watched Mr. Howard Messer's 8-ton *Skate*, a vessel of that type, sailing in the Blackwater, and was much impressed by her performance. She was not only fast but extraordinarily handy, and in crossing the North Sea on several occasions proved herself a good sea boat. I believe the first boat of semi-sharpie type was Thomas Fleming Day's 5-ton *Sea Bird*, which crossed the Atlantic some forty years ago. A yacht of the *Skate* type is, in my opinion, far superior to any barge yacht that has yet been built, and she certainly goes to windward in the most extraordinary manner in the short seas encountered in the neighbourhood of the Thames Estuary. As an instance of her speed to windward, I would quote a race sailed from West Mersea to Harwich under the burgee of the Blackwater Sailing Club in 1909, when *Skate* finished only nine minutes behind *Cherub*, a smart fast-cruiser designed by Payne. The yachts had a beat over the greater part of the course in a hard wind and heavy sea, and *Cherub* was a ton larger than *Skate*, and cost just about five times as much to build. *Skate* is an excellent sea-boat, and has made several trips across the North Sea, to say nothing of many long passages round the coast. She is extremely handy, and I have seen her beat up a very narrow creek against the tide under a foresail, and also under her mainsail alone.

Where a craft of this nature scores over the ordinary barge yacht is in the ease with which she can be scrubbed. When one side of her bottom has been scrubbed, she can be lifted over on to the other chine and the job completed on the same tide. *Skate* was fitted with a centreplate and carried a certain amount of ballast inside. When a centreplate yacht has to take the ground frequently it is not uncommon for stones and mud to work up into the case and jam the plate. That usually also happens when the boat is laid up in a mud berth. Mr. Messer eliminated this trouble in a rather ingenious way. He designed the case much

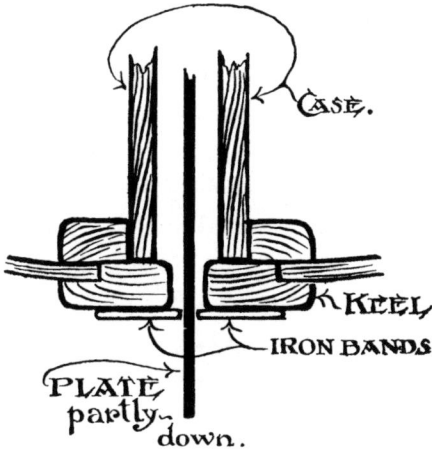

Skate's centreplate case

wider than usual, reducing the slot at the bottom to the normal width by means of iron bands, as shown in the illustration. Any stones or mud that managed to get into the case were soon washed aft and fell through a space left at the after end of the slot for the purpose.

Hitherto I have had in mind the Southend district, where the bottom is of sand, with a coating of mud, but if your craft is to be stationed in shallow waters where the bottom is of soft mud, your choice of a craft will be much wider, as a shoal-draught keel boat will be quite a practicable proposition. The keel of such a yacht would cut into the mud when she took the ground and she would not list excessively.

In my young days we used to reckon that no boat of 4 or 5 tons could be expected to sail decently to windward unless she had at least 4 feet 6 inches draught, but a good deal has been learnt about boats since then. I believe it was Linton Hope who made the discovery in the 'nineties that it is not so much the area of the keel or centreplate that makes for weatherliness as the length of the cutting edge. It was found that a dinghy fitted with a narrow dagger-plate was almost as weatherly as one with the ordinary triangular plate of much greater area.

The modern type of yacht, with forward overhang and practically no deadwood, has a very long cutting edge, and equal or superior weatherliness can be obtained with considerably less draught. The 11-ton sloop *Escapade*, designed and owned by Mr. Walter Stewart, for instance, sails extraordinarily well to windward on a draught of only 3 feet 9 inches. She originally had a centreplate, but Mr. Stewart found that she sailed so well to windward without it, that he removed it altogether. The 9-ton cutter *Windfall* also sails extremely well to windward on a draught of 3 feet 6 inches as did the 5-ton cutter *Forsitan*, which I owned some years ago, on a draught of only 3 feet 3 inches.

I am inclined to think that it is not the length of the cutting edge alone that does the trick, for the stability of the boat probably has something to do with it. Stability is obtained either by beam or ballast. If the vessel is a narrow one, she must have considerable draught if her keel is to afford an efficient righting lever. If she is beamy she has great initial stability and needs less ballast.

Now, most shoal-draught yachts are of the beamy type and I think it is largely due to their beam that they have sufficient lateral resistance to hold them to the wind. *Escapade*, with a waterline measurement of 30 feet, has 10 feet beam; *Nightfall*, whose waterline measurement is 27 feet, has 9 feet beam, and *Forsi-*

tan, with a waterline measurement or 21ft, has 7 feet 10 inches beam. As yachts of this type heel very little in ordinary weather, owing to their great initial stability, practically all their draught is brought into effective use to hold them to the wind. The narrow vessel, on the other hand, has but little initial stability and even in a moderate breeze heels to a considerable angle when on a wind. Her draught when sailing is thus a good deal less than when she is lying upright at anchor. A beamy shallow craft like *Forsitan*, with a nominal draught of 3 feet 3 inches, heels so little when sailing to windward in a moderate breeze that her effective draught is probably 3 feet or very little less; but a narrow yacht of the same size, with a draught of 4 feet 6 inches, deriving her stability from her keel, would in similar circumstances heel to such an extent that her effective draught would be reduced to about 3 feet 6 inches. It will be seen, therefore, that the draught on paper is not the same as the draught when sailing. And what is more, the keel of the shallow beamy boat, which sails almost upright, is far more effective, as it offers more lateral resistance than that of the deep vessel, sailing 'on her ear.' This, I think, explains why a shallow-draught yacht of good design is able to sail creditably to windward.

The advantages of shallow draught in waters such as those of the Thames Estuary and East Coast rivers cannot be denied. It enables the yacht to make use of the many swatchways and short cuts through the sands that there abound, and seek a snug berth at night in creeks inaccessible to her deep-draught sister. If she has the misfortune to run aground on the ebb tide and dry out, she will not list to any great extent, while the deep-draught vessel would lie over at such an angle as to render her cabin uninhabitable for the time being.

It may pertinently be asked why, if the shoal-draught cruiser has all these advantages, does anyone own a craft drawing more water than absolutely necessary? Surely there must be a snag somewhere. Well, I think there is, and having had considerable experience of both types, I will tell you some of the disadvantages of light draught, as I see them.

Although the shallow-draught yacht may sail decently to windward in smooth water, she has not as a rule sufficient weight to drive her through a rough sea, while in order to obtain adequate headroom in the cabin she usually has a good deal of freeboard and often an unduly high cabin-top. Both of these traits are apt to militate against her sea-going qualities in rough weather, and under such conditions the deep-draught vessel has a definite advantage. The average light-draught yacht is also apt to be inordinately lively in a seaway and the violent motion is extremely tiring. To get a meal under way is usually impracticable in heavy weather, and if you are not what is termed a 'good sailor' you are likely to 'lay all before you,' as Kipling would say. In bad weather every sea seems to hurl the boat bodily to leeward and your progress to windward is apt to be slow. Yachts of that sort, too, are often rather wild on the helm and difficult to sail single-handed. If you lash the helm to go forward, the transference of your weight from aft to the bow upsets her trim and she will probably come up into the wind before you have completed your job. I don't suggest that all small light-draught yachts are like that, but many are.

The rolling propensity of the shoal-draught yacht is, in my opinion, one of her worst traits, for it renders her most uncomfortable at anchor when a fresh wind blows against the tide. Under such conditions she is partially wind-rode and, lying athwart the tide, rolls her heart out. Cooking under such conditions is very difficult and living on board extremely uncomfortable.

Now a yacht like my old *Fancy*, a Falmouth Quay Punt of 7 tons, which I owned some years ago, was always comfortable at anchor. Drawing approximately 6 feet, she had such a grip on the water that she was nearly always tide-rode and the motion seldom more than a slight pitching. And of course a big-bodied vessel like *Fancy* is more comfortable than one of light displacement in every way, as she has full standing headroom in the cabin. When under way in rough weather the seas do not stop her much and conditions must be bad indeed to prevent one cooking a meal. But I found her heavy draught a great inconvenience in the waters I sailed. When I wanted to sail round to the Blackwater from the Crouch, I sometimes had to jill about for an hour or more before there was sufficient water for her through the Raysand Channel.

It will be seen, when this question of light or heavy draught is considered, that there is a good deal to be said on both sides. Indeed, what you gain on the swings you seem to lose on the roundabouts, and I think in the long run the most satisfactory sort of craft is neither the one nor the other but a compromise. A yacht of moderate draught will give you some of the benefits and mitigate some of the evils of both types, but, as I have pointed out, you must be guided in your choice to a large extent by the conditions obtaining in the district where you propose to establish your headquarters.

The canoe form of stern has become very popular for small cruising yachts of late years, but there is nothing novel about it, for it is as old as the hills. For centuries it has been used for life-boats, whaling boats and various other kinds of small vessel, as long experience has proved it the best and safest when running before a following sea. It is in fact a form of streamlining, and as everything in nature that is intended to travel through air or water is streamlined, a sharp stern would appear to be the proper ending for a boat. In that connection it may be remarked that the designer of vessels has always played the sedulous ape to nature and every boat is modelled more or less upon the shape of a fish. If you took a mackerel and cut it in halves lengthwise, the lower half would bear a strong resemblance to the hull of a modern yacht, and if yachts travelled entirely under water, they would in all probability be modelled upon a whole fish. Even in our sails we owe a debt to nature for the modern Bermudian mainsail is based upon the wing of a bird. The designer, however, cannot follow nature too closely, for whilst fishes and birds operate only in their natural element, the sailing yacht is dependent upon two elements, namely, wind and water. Moreover, she needs a crew to sail her and living accommodation has to be provided for that crew. Fishes and birds are free from such encumbrances, although it is recorded that Jonah once made a single-handed cruise in the belly of a whale. Although in general principles based upon the shape of a fish, the yacht must be something of a compromise.

Although the canoe stern is undoubtedly a very fine one from the point of view of seaworthiness, it has certain disadvantages, of which the most important is the restriction of deck-room aft, where it is badly wanted. In the case of a cutter, whose boomend extends beyond the stern, the lack of adequate deck-room renders reefing the mainsail very difficult, but nowadays the tendency is towards shorter booms, and this disadvantage of the canoe stern is not so apparent as it was a few years ago. It is not, however, only on deck that space is limited with this form of stern, for it entails a considerable reduction of locker space aft, and it is there that the spare sails are kept in most small cruisers. If the sail locker is not sufficiently large to accommodate all the sails, room must be found for them in the fo'c'sle, where they are apt to be a nuisance.

The transom stern is also commonly employed, but I think it probably owes its popularity to economy, as it is cheaper to build than a counter or overhanging canoe stern. The chief objection to it, in my opinion, is that a rudder hung on the transom nearly always makes a noise when the yacht is brought up and the tide against the wind. This is due to wear of the rudder irons, for if there is the slightest play there will be noise. It is probably not very much really, but a yacht is like a sounding board, and when one is in the cabin the slightest noise is magnified sufficiently to cause annoyance. But when the rudder is slung outside the yacht in this way, one usually has a fine roomy sail locker, and the absence of a rudder trunk, often a source of trouble, is a blessing.

Personally, I prefer a counter stern, provided that it is well tucked-up and not too flat. It not only enhances the appearance of the yacht but affords a reserve of buoyancy aft which adds to the vessel's seaworthiness in bad weather. Overhanging bows and sterns, of course, increase the sailing length of a vessel and sailing length is one of the chief factors that make for speed.

CHAPTER 6: *Conversions*

Having settled upon the most suitable draught for your local waters, you can now consider the question of type. Small cabin yachts in decent condition are always rather difficult to come by, and at the time I write are as scarce as strawberries in December. It is extremely improbable therefore that you will be able to buy just what you want, but will have to rest content with what you can get.

In selecting a yacht for cruising purposes, the average yachtsman is content to sacrifice something in the way of speed to comfort below decks, and I am rather inclined to think that he is right. One spends a great deal of time in the cabin in the course of a season, and it is therefore essential that one's quarters be fairly snug and roomy. To some men, however, speed is almost a necessity, for, having business engagements to fulfil, they have to catch certain trains. Business must, of course, be placed before pleasure, and if the catching of trains is a matter of moment everything must be sacrificed to speed. It is essential for a yachtsman in such a position to have a craft that can be relied upon to beat over a foul tide in a comparatively light breeze, so that he may make sure of getting back to his moorings in good time to catch his train, and if the vessel satisfies his requirements in that respect he must be prepared to make sacrifices in other directions.

The racing yacht: The only boat likely to fulfil the requirements of such an owner in the matter of speed is a vessel of light displacement and modern design, but modern fast-cruisers cost a deal of money to buy, and are beyond the reach of the yachtsman of limited means. He will, however, be able to find what he wants in the ranks of the outclassed racing yachts, of which there are usually plenty in the market at very reasonable prices. Many of these boats, particularly if built under scantling restrictions, are as sound as when launched, but owing to a change in the measurement rule they have lost their *raison d'etre*. The adoption of the International Rules by the Y.R.A. a few years ago placed a large number of vessels out of court, and some of the smaller ones, such as the 24-footers, can now be bought for a mere song. These boats have a liberal supply of sails and gear, but as a rule have no cabin accommodation; but a coach-roof can be fitted, if the owner's ideas be not unduly extravagant, at comparatively trifling cost. The cabin will be but small, for the racing vessels built under the last rule were, like the sailor's pudding, all ends, but with the addition of a coach-roof of moderate height there will be comfortable sitting headroom over the sofas. The accommodation will serve very well for week-end sailing and for two or three weeks' cruising in summer weather, when one can pass the greater part of the day in the well, using the cabin for little more than sleeping purposes. Such a boat, in comparison with the average cruiser, is very fast, and, if her sail plan be cut down a little, is quite easy to sail single-handed.

She will, moreover, be quite man enough for any cruising that the owner is likely to have time for, and he will be able to make sure of getting back to his moorings in anything but a calm. Mr. S.C. Houghton, who owns the 24-footer *Tulip*, contrives to do quite a lot of cruising in her, making trips across Channel and for a considerable distance round the coast, and he is no mere fine-weather sailor, for he keeps his little craft in commission for the greater part of the year. It is evident, therefore, that an ex-24-footer makes a small cruiser that is not to be despised by a busy man with little leisure at his disposal.

There are usually several ex-24-footers in the market, and the price ranges from £25 to £50, according to condition. A few of them have been already fitted with cabins, and if such a one be in the market, and in good condition, it would pay a prospective purchaser to go to a rather higher price for her, as it would probably be cheaper in the long-run. The addition of a coach-roof, however, need not be an expensive matter if the owner is modest in his ideas. If the owner be a handy man in the carpentering line he will be able to do a good deal in the way of fitting lockers, etc., himself, and for about £20 he should be able to convert the boat into quite a nice little cruiser and supply her with such fitments as are absolutely essential. The cabin of a converted 24-footer will afford fairly comfortable accommodation for two persons, and if they owned the boat in partnership she would be a very cheap craft to buy and inexpensive to maintain, as a waterman would look after her in the owners' absence for half a crown a week. They would get some excellent weekend cruising in her, and on occasions could race in a handicap class. In light breezes she would be far faster than any ordinary cruiser of like tonnage, and under a snug trysail would go through a deal of bad weather if handled efficiently.

My brother bought and converted a 24-footer in the early years of the present century, and as I often sailed in her I had opportunities of studying her shortcomings. So far as I remember, my brother bought her for £60, but by the time the conversion was completed she had cost him well over £200, and in those days £200 was a considerable pot of money. She was a narrow-gutted craft with very long overhangs. The extremities of the boat were of little use for anything but stowing sails and suitcases. Although she was only two years old when my brother bought her, it was found that the steel floors had been badly corroded by contact with the metal keel bolts and had to be renewed.

Although her sail area had been considerably reduced, she was very fast in comparison with the average cruiser of anything like her size, but very wet in rough water, and heeled to such an angle when on a wind that it was quite impossible to get any sort of meal under way other than a 'thumb-piece.'

I think it was her speed that tempted my brother to buy and convert *Spillikin*. As it was essential that he should return to town on Sunday night, as he had to be at his office early on Monday morning, he wanted a craft that would turn over the tide in a light breeze. Of course, nowadays an ordinary cruiser with an auxiliary engine would serve the purpose better.

Another type of fast boat that can sometimes be picked up at a reasonable figure is the craft with a bulb-fin. As she is cheaper to construct in the first place than a "built-down" vessel, it naturally follows that her second-hand price is also lower, but nevertheless she will probably cost a good deal more than an ex-24-footer. The bulb-fin is probably the fastest and most weatherly type extant, but there are one or two little traits she has that I personally do not care about. Such boats usually have very flat floors, and, with the cabin floor placed low down on the keelson, the bilge water is apt to swish about over the floor boards and make the cabin wet. The short fin, also, makes the boat rather wild on her helm when she is before the wind, and they are unhandy craft to heave to. But one cannot have everything, and if speed is of importance to the owner he will get it in a bulb-fin yacht.

Yachts built under the International rating rule are much better suited to conversion than the old linear raters, as their overhangs are shorter and they have much more displacement and freeboard. Quite a number of outclassed 6-metre yachts have been thus converted and make nice week-end cruisers. Although perhaps a trifle narrow, they have so much displacement that quite a comfortable cabin, with adequate headroom, can be put in. Built to Lloyd's construction rules, such a boat should last for many years if properly cared for, and can sometimes be picked up very cheaply. One, I know, was bought for £135, already converted, before the war, and her owner must have almost paid for her by the prizes she has won in handicap racing.

A 6-metre boat is a craft of some 5 tons by Thames Measurement competition, and thanks to her generous freeboard she can be converted into quite a comfortable little cruiser for two people. She will be far faster than the average cruiser of her size and, as the rule does not encourage excessive sail area, she need not be cut down to any great extent. A description of the converted 6-metre *Rowan III*, which appeared in *The Yachtsman* of March 14th, 1936, gave a very good idea of what can be done with such a vessel. This boat, originally known as *Valdai*, was built from Mylne's design in 1930 and formerly raced in the Clyde class. Her principal measurements are as follows: Length overall, 35.3 feet; waterline, 22 feet; beam, 6.75 feet; draught, 5 feet; and sail area 420 square feet. Under a not unsightly cabin-top there was 5 feet 3 inches headroom and somehow or other – the Lord only knows how – two pipe-cots were fitted in the fo'c'sle. She was thus able to sleep four, although the owner admits that the comfortable capacity of the yacht is three persons. How two people managed to sleep in the fo'c'sle beats me, because the headroom could not have been more than about 3 feet, and she is a narrow boat. But they were boys, and youngsters regard as a lark what older people consider acute discomfort. Stowed in the fo'c'sle, too, were the spare sails and oilskins, and in compartments between the cabin and fo'c'sle were kept the sanitary bucket and clothes, an auxiliary motor was installed beneath the cockpit floor, and room also found for a cooking galley and wireless set.

This conversion of *Rowan III*, I think, serves to show that a fast handy little cruiser can be made out of an outclassed 6-metre boat. I do not suggest that such boats make ideal cruisers, for I don't think they do. They sail too much on the side, a feature that makes cooking under way difficult, and in my opinion good and regular meals are essential to enjoyable cruising. If you are well fed you can view bad weather with comparative equanimity, but if you are wet, cold and hungry, you may feel inclined to give up cruising and take to fretwork. Still, for week-end sailing a converted 6-metre boat seems quite a sound proposition, as for a reasonable price you will get a splendidly built craft that will last for many years if you keep her up decently. She will moreover be a good deal faster than the average cruiser and if you have a fancy for racing occasionally, she is likely to win a good many prizes in a handicap class.

Even smaller racing craft than a 6-metre have been successfully converted into miniature cruisers. The old Royal Corinthian Yacht Club Seabird class boat is a case in point. An old friend of mine and his son cruised in one of these boats for many years, sleeping at night under a tent spread over the boom. I often re-

RCYC Seabird after conversion

marked that she would make quite a nice little week-end cruiser, if fitted with a cabin, and during the summer of 1936 I happened upon one of these boats that actually had been converted. And what is more, there were three men cruising in her. Shortly afterwards, this little boat competed in the long-distance race of the West Mersea Yacht Club, which is sailed for the most part at night over a 70-miles course in the North Sea. As by the conditions of the race the competitors had to tow dinghies, she had little chance of figuring among the prize-winners, but it was no mean feat for such a little ship to complete the course. I am told that a similar boat crossed the North Sea and cruised in Belgian and Dutch waters, so it is evident that cruising in them is quite a practicable proposition.

Nola, another converted Seabird, owned by Mr. A. V. Bellamy, is stationed at Fambridge and I know her well. With a lofty Bermudian rig she is a pretty little boat and a good deal faster and more weatherly than most small cabin yachts. Of course, in a craft of this sort one cannot expect much headroom in the cabin. In one I inspected it was only 3 feet 7 inches, but I believe *Nola* has 2 inches more, which is sufficient to enable one to sit on a low bunk. The cockpit, too, is rather small. That of *Nola* is 3 feet 6 inches long – cramped quarters for two people, particularly when going about, as of course the tiller encroaches on the space. If one did not wish to go to the expense of having a cabin fitted, a Cape-cart tent, as described earlier, would be an excellent substitute and give one more room when under way.

The life-boat: Speaking of sharp-sterned yachts recalls to mind another type of craft that floats upon the face of the waters as a monument to misguided enthusiasm and waste of money. I refer to the converted ship's life-boat, of which examples may be seen at almost any port round the coast. Ever since the late Mr. E. F. Knight wrote his delightful book, *The Falcon on the Baltic*, in which he described a cruise in a converted life-boat, yachtsmen in ever-increasing numbers have attempted the impossible feat of making silk purses out of sows' ears, and it is a significant fact that the results of their labours are almost invariably for sale at what might be termed a nominal price. I cannot claim to have converted a ship's boat myself, for that is a form of lunacy from which I have hitherto been spared. I have done many, many foolish things in my time, but never that. Yet I can lay claim to a wider experience of this particular type of craft than most people, as in the days of my youth I owned three, which previous owners had converted, and sailed in quite a number of others. In the hope of saving budding yachtsmen from spending a lot of money on an enterprise that can only result in bitter disappointment, I will tell you of my experience with converted ships' boats.

In theory the conversion of a ship's boat is not without its attraction. The very name 'life-boat' is suggestive of seaworthiness, and they are usually roomy craft that give promise of good accommodation when decked. But perhaps the chief charm is the extremely low price at which they can be bought. I believe it is the practice of shipping companies to renew their boats after a certain number of years, and, being seldom used, they are often in quite good condition when superannuated. They can often be picked up for a few pounds, and the inexperienced buyer is apt to jump to the conclusion that by expending a few pounds more he will be able to convert the boat into a fine, roomy yacht. I would advise anyone obsessed with that idea to sit down quietly with a sheet of paper and a pencil and draw up an inventory of everything necessary for the complete equipment of a cruising yacht of 6 or 7 tons Thames Measurement. When he has done that, let him take a yacht chandler's catalogue and fill in the prices against the various items. I venture to prophesy that long ere the job is finished he will throw the paper on the fire and his idea to the winds.

It must be remembered that the condemned ship's boat when acquired will be a mere shell and every item of her equipment will have to be bought at the current market price. Such things as cabin cushions, bedding, cooking stoves and utensils, crockery, riding and navigation lamps, compass and binnacle, cabin lamp, and numerous other items of domestic use would cost a pretty penny in these days, and then there are such things as mast, spars, sails, standing rigging, running gear, blocks, anchors and chains to be considered. Why, a suit of sails alone would cost the best part of £50 for a craft of that size! Then ballast would have to be provided. An iron keel is an expensive item nowadays, and even if scrap iron be used for stiffening, the price will be anything but negligible. Then there would be the shipwright's bill for converting the hull.

Although they carry small sails for use when the wind is fair, ships' boats are designed mainly for propulsion by oars. They are consequently not built to take the heavy lateral stresses to which sailing yachts are subjected. To give her the necessary lateral resistance to enable her to sail to windward, such a boat, when converted, must have either a keel or centreplate, and as the keel is usually too narrow to permit of a slot being cut in it without seriously weakening the boat, the former is in most cases adopted. A ship's boat's keel is seldom much more than 4 inches thick, and she has neither keelson nor floors. A thin keel like this is often weakened to a dangerous extent when bored for the keel bolts, if not actually split during the operation. Although it is customary to put in a few oak floors to take the strain of the keel, the whole structure is far too light to withstand lateral stresses for which the boat was never designed. A ship's boat almost invariably leaks when going to windward in a strong wind and rough water, and her leaking propensities soon become chronic. If all of the ballast be placed outside in the form of a heavy iron keel the trouble is accentuated, so it is usual to stow most of the stiffening inside. This means raising the floor to such an extent that the topsides have to be built up and a high coach-roof superimposed on the deck to secure the necessary headroom in the cabin. The result is a high-sided unsightly vessel, which has so much windage as to mar her sailing qualities.

What the structural alterations would cost in these days of high wages and expensive materials, I do not care to estimate, but I feel pretty sure that by the time the vessel was ready for sea her owner would have spent more than a decent second-hand yacht in good condition would have cost him. And what has he to show for his outlay? An extremely unsightly boat that would soon leak like a basket and which would not sail for toffee, as we used to say in our schooldays. And what is more, when he came to sell her he would be lucky if he recovered much more than a tenth part of what she had cost him.

The first converted life-boat that I owned I bought for £10. One could hardly expect to get a 6-ton yacht for less, but all the same I am inclined to think that I had the worst of the bargain. I did not buy her from any love of the type, but it suited my purpose at the time. A 5-ton cutter that I owned had been sunk by a barge, and all I managed to salve from the wreck consisted of the spars, sails and gear. I therefore purchased this converted life-boat with the idea of putting my gear in her, as her own was only fit for the scrap-heap. In this old hooker I had many adventures, and incidentally about the most uncomfortable time one could very well imagine. I also learnt many things, as, for instance: Item 1 – That it was desirable to reverse the helm for sternway when going about in rough water. Item 2 – That when she missed stays beating up a river it was wise to wear her at once and not make a second attempt to stay. Item 3 – That it was expedient to lead the simple life and turn in early, as attempting to sit up with only 3 feet headroom gave one a stiff neck. Item 4 – That if I did not pump her dry before turning in I should be awakened at 3 a.m., or thereabouts, by finding myself lying in water. Item 5 – That on wet nights it was prudent to put on my oilskins over my pyjamas before turning in; and Item 6 – That when the rudder became unshipped from the silly little pintles on which it was hung, it was no use going overboard to try and ship it. One way and another, I think my owner-ship of *Tiercel* could be truthfully described as a liberal education, and it is very certain I learnt in her more practical seamanship than in any of the other craft I have owned.

My second converted ship's boat was, like the servant girl's baby, a very lit-tle one, being only 16 feet long. She had belonged to a brig that was wrecked on the Gunfleet, and had been converted by a working man, who sold her to me for £10. She had a tiny cabin in which I could just sit upright on a bunk about 3 inches from the floor, and the after part of the boat was quite open. The previous owner's carpentering was of the order that is usually termed 'rough,' her keel being merely a plank bolted on in its natural state, without even being shaped at the ends. But the little boat sailed astonishingly well for what she was, and during the first year of my ownership I sailed her more than 1,200 miles at week-ends and during a short holiday cruise. Two of her original thwarts were left in, the mast stepping through one, whilst the other helped to support the cabin bulkhead. This latter thwart was horribly in the way, and I resolved to have it removed, and being very pleased with the sailing of the little boat, I de-cided to have sundry other alterations effected. During the winter I took her to Paglesham, and had waterways and coamings fitted aft, a deeper keel bolted on, new spars and sails, the decks covered with canvas, and the old paint burnt off. When enamelled black with a gold line she looked quite smart, particularly as I had given her more ballast, and thus reduced her somewhat excessive freeboard. But I soon found that I had quite spoilt her. Her enlarged sail plan made her hard-headed, and the extra ballast rendered her wet and sluggish in a seaway. But, worst of all, she soon began to leak badly, and so I cut my loss and sold her, the £20 she fetched barely covering the cost of the alterations.

For my third converted ship's boat I paid a comparatively high price, namely, £55, but she was an exceptional craft. When she was half built the order had been cancelled, and a yachtsman buying her as she lay on the stocks had her completed as a yacht. The experiment must have cost him a pretty penny, as she was beautifully fitted throughout, and, what is more, she sailed very well. She had an iron fin keel giving her a draught of about 5 feet, and when I bought her she was sloop-rigged with a boom measuring 26 feet, and a large single head-sail. Thus rigged I found her a bit of a handful when I was alone, and being at that time rather keen on single-handed cruising, I reduced her sail area and converted her to cutter rig. She had a most comfortable cabin with about 5 feet headroom.

Although she was only three years old when I bought her, I soon found that she leaked more than a little, and so I had her garboards doubled. After that she remained fairly tight until I got caught in some dirty weather one night whilst making a single-handed passage from Burnham to Lowestoft. The heavy head sea was evidently too much for her, and when I arrived at my destination the following day I was disgusted to find that she had 6 inches of water over the cabin floor and a sprung mast. For a week she leaked like an old basket, and then suddenly 'took up,' and made less water than at any time since coming into my possession. This extraordinary behaviour was beyond explanation, and as I had lost all confidence in the boat I soon afterwards disposed of her.

In addition to these vessels that I owned, I have sailed in others, and without exception they leaked abominably. I find it difficult to understand how a man can be so foolish as to spend a considerable sum of money upon a conversion which, if it does not break his pocket, will certainly break his heart. For far less money than such a conversion would cost to-day, a real yacht in decent condition could be bought. If poverty compels you to have a ship's life-boat or nothing at all, look out for one that some other ass has already converted and which does not need pumping out more than once a day, for the operation of pumping, when practised at frequent intervals, is a back-breaking, soul-destroying business. And when sailing her you must work your tides if you want to get anywhere. A converted ship's boat will run and reach like a hare in a strong breeze, but, as I have already remarked, she will not go to windward for nuts. To stay her is an achievement and to make a passage to a neighbouring port an adventure. In such a craft it is not prudent to start away on the top of the tide with a fresh fair wind if you have any idea of returning to your mooring the same day, for beating to windward over a foul tide is outside the range of practical politics.

I once wanted to get one of my converted ship's boats from Hole Haven to Burnham in the winter, but easterly winds prevailed every week-end and al-though I tried week after week for three months, I never succeeded in saving my tide round the Whitaker Beacon. At last, when the Easter holiday came round I determined to plug away until I did get there and eventually arrived at Burn-ham, four days out from Hole Haven, in a state of semi-starvation, having been lost in a dense fog en route. Still, it would be churlish to condemn converted life-boats altogether, for in the three old 'tore-outs' that I owned as a boy I had a lot of fun and learnt a lot of seamanship.

The fishing smack: The conversion of a smack is a much sounder proposition than that of a ship's boat, for whilst the one was built for sailing purposes the other was not. It is, however, from the financial point of view a very dangerous undertaking on which to embark, as one's ideas are apt to run away with one. If you can make up your mind to have only such work carried out as is absolutely necessary to make her habitable, well and good, but if you try to turn her into a smart yacht you are doomed to disappointment. A vessel originally designed and built as a smack will never look anything else, for you can no more change her appearance than can a leopard change its spots. If you can pick up a suitable smack in reasonably good condition at a low figure, her conversion may be worth while, but only if you are prepared to carry out the work of conversion on the most economical lines, as we did in the case of the *Two Sisters*. But the trouble is that one's ideas are apt to expand as the work proceeds and one goes from one folly to another

A considerable portion of the internal accommodation of a smack is sacrificed to her hold, or fish-well, and ere a cabin can be constructed this must be removed. In some smacks the fish-well is designed to keep the fish alive as long as possible. It is divided off by means of water-tight bulkheads, the bottom of the vessel, between the bulkheads, being perforated so that the water may flow freely through the well. Now, when the bulkheads are removed each of those innumerable holes has to be plugged. This of course makes for expense, and the smack selected for conversion should therefore be one that has no fish-well.

If the vessel be of some 15 or 20 tons measurement, it is probable the owner will require two cabins, and before they can be built the craft must be completely gutted. It may then be found that, owing to the large quantity of inside ballast needed to give her the necessary stability, it is impossible to obtain sufficient headroom in the new cabins. The obvious remedy is a lead keel, and, to enable her to withstand the extra strain, additional floors will be called for. Then it may be discovered that the constant friction of the trawl heads has worn the decks so thin that they must be renewed, and for the sake of appearance you may be tempted to put in teak covering boards. Then, of course, you will feel bound to use teak for the cabin-top, skylight, companion and coamings to match the covering boards. The old-fashioned barrel windlass, with its wooden handspike, may be quite efficient in operation, but it will look odd against your yachty deck fittings and you will replace it with a costly capstan and let the expense go hang. Then nothing will content you but a new outfit of spars, blocks, sails and gear. The trouble is that these refinements are usually decided upon gradually as the work proceeds and you are apt to lose all count of them. Then, when at long last the bill comes in, you get the shock of your life.

Hitherto I have only considered the matter from the point of view of the conversion of a comparatively sound hull, but in many cases, when fishermen sell their smacks, they are anything but sound and the way is paved for further expense. When the shipwright has gutted the vessel, he may find that what is left is so rotten that the new work cannot be fastened securely, and it sometimes happens that so much has to be removed that very little of the original boat remains. It will be gathered, therefore, that the conversion of an old smack is, to put it mildly, something of a speculation.

It may be thought that my remarks on this subject are a trifle exaggerated, but as a matter of fact they are based upon instances that have come under my personal observation. I remember years ago a man buying an old smack of about 15 tons with a view to conversion, and as she was rather small for his requirements, he decided to have her enlarged at the same time. When the shipwrights engaged on the job had removed all the rotten wood, nothing of the original hull remained but the keelson and a few frames. Upon these fragments was built a yawl of nearly 50 tons, and if the cost to the owner was anything like what it was locally said to be, he could have bought for the money a modern yacht of similar tonnage in the pink of condition. When completed, this vessel was unsightly to look upon, alarmingly tender and as slow as a hearse. That was certainly an extreme case, but I know of others in which the cost of conversion amounted to more than ten times the purchase price of the smack operated upon. Quite recently I went for a sail in a converted 10-ton smack owned by a friend, and he told me that he had bought her in the West of England for £25. The shipwright's bill for the work of conversion amounted to £300, and a few years later new covering boards had to be put in at a cost of £70. So the vessel cost him approximately £400, although nothing was done that was not necessary and nothing ornate in the way of fittings supplied. My friend certainly has a fine useful ship, in which he and his wife have done a lot of cruising, but I doubt if he will see his money back, should he want to sell her.

The Falmouth Quay Punt: This is a type of vessel particularly well adapted for conversion into a yacht. Before the advent of the internal combustion engine, the quay punts used to sail far out into the Atlantic to meet incoming ships, and as the first to arrive got the job of acting as tender to the ship while she was in port, speed was of the first importance. These boats therefore sail very well and are fine sea boats, but draw too much water for the Thames Estuary and East Coast. They are usually of about 7 tons T.M. and draw approximately 6 feet. With full standing headroom in the cabin and about 5 feet in the fo'c'sle, they are very comfortable to live in. Such a craft would make an admirable ocean cruiser. The little 4-ton *Joan*, in which Mr. W. E. Sinclair made so many blue-water voyages, was a small Falmouth Quay Punt, and she carried him safely through many a gale until dismasted and lost while on a passage across the Atlantic.

CHAPTER 7: *The Canoe Yacht*

Another type of small craft that calls for consideration is that known as the "canoe yacht." Such vessels have become rather popular of late years, but with the frequent modifications that have been effected in the type, most of the old characteristics have been improved out of existence. The canoe yacht has, of course, been evolved from the old-fashioned sailing canoe, and the early craft of the type were nothing more than enlarged canoes fitted with cabins. They had long straight keels, straight stems, and life-boat sterns, with the rudder hung on the stern-post. They were seen at their best when running before a strong wind and heavy sea, the long keel keeping them from yawing about, and the sharp stern gently dividing the pursuing waves. But that, so far as I can see, was the only special feature that the early canoe yacht had to recommend her. The modern canoe yacht is a canoe in little more than name, for the only claim that she has to the title is derived from a stern that is sharp on the deck-line. As the stern is usually drawn out into a considerable overhang, it is to all intents and purposes a counter. For the rest, the boat may be of any form the designer happens to fancy, and some of them are craft of the bulb-fin type, and the majority have the now fashionable overhanging bow. Now, what advantage do these so-called 'canoe yachts' possess over small yachts of the ordinary type? For the life of me I cannot see any at all, but, on the other hand, they have several traits that strike me as distinctly detrimental. In the first place, such a yacht lacks deck room aft, where it is particularly useful, to say nothing of the sacrifice of a certain amount of valuable locker space. Then, again, it renders more difficult the operation of reefing the mainsail, as one's foothold is precarious and the end of the boom farther outboard than it is in the case of a yacht with the orthodox counter. This was brought home to me in a rather unpleasant manner many years ago when I owned a 7-tonner named *Seabird*. She was at that time a sloop and her boom, which was 26 feet long, extended far outside the boat.

One day, when single-handed, I had to pull down a reef in a rough sea in the Wallet and in order to reach some of the reef-points I was standing on the rudder-head. Suddenly I missed my footing and in a moment was overboard. Fortunately I clung to the boom and was able to haul myself along the spar and scramble on board again. Falling overboard is not at any time a pleasant experience and when one is alone it might easily be attended by fatal results.

In a yacht with a canoe stern the lead of the mainsheet is apt to be a little difficult, as one cannot have the usual quarter blocks, and if the lower block is secured to an eye-bolt in the deck, it gets in the way of the tiller. In *Snipe* the lower block travelled on a horse, fixed about 2 feet inboard from the stern-post.

This got over the mainsheet difficulty, but the horse did not allow the tiller much scope. Fortunately she was a handy boat and did not require much helm to put her about, but it made her rather slow in stays. In *Seabird*, the mainsheet block was attached to a sort of miniature horse bolted on to the sternpost. This proved quite satisfactory as the horse, being so close to the rudder-head, did not in any way impede the movement of the tiller and a stop at either end prevented the block from falling down too low.

I would not for a moment seek to imply that the canoe yacht is of necessity a bad type of craft, for I know of many that are most desirable little ships. The 6-tonner *Lora*, built in 1911 for Mr. J. Pain Clark, from the owner's design, is, for instance, as nice a little cruiser as one could wish for, but nevertheless I think she would have been improved had she been designed with a moderate counter like that of Mr. Pain Clark's previous boat, *Lona III*. But most of the yachtsmen who build these canoe yachts have graduated from the ranks of canoe sailors, and they do not seem to be able to break away entirely from their old traditions.

CHAPTER 8: *The Rig*

There is probably no subject in connection with yachting so controversial as that of rig, as most yachtsmen have their own views as to which is the best. When yachtsmen meet, this question of rig is pretty certain to be discussed sooner or later, and the introduction of the Bermudian form of mainsail has tended to add fuel to the fire. The views of sailing men on such matters have always differed, and it is to be hoped that they always will, for such divergencies of opinion help to keep one's interest alive. It would be a dull world if we all thought alike.

As the rig of a yacht must be largely a matter of the owner's personal preference, I have no wish to dictate on the subject. My remarks must be regarded merely as my own views, which I may say are based upon an experience of cruising in small craft extending over many years and in many boats. As I am only writing here of small cruising yachts of, say, 10 tons and under, the field is narrowed, for such rigs as the schooner would be quite out of place in a little ship of this size.

The rigs most commonly used in small cruising yachts are the cutter, sloop, yawl and ketch, and each of those may have either a gaff or Bermudian mainsail. It will, therefore, be as well before going any further first to consider the merits or otherwise of the two forms of sail.

THE FORM OF SAIL

The gaff mainsail is a sail of considerable antiquity, having been used not only in yachts but in such vessels as fishing smacks, pilot boats and small coasters for hundreds of years, whilst the Bermudian has only attained popularity since the first Great War. It would be a mistake, however, to think that the Bermudian sail was a new discovery, for it was known in the days of Samuel Pepys. There is in the Pepysian Library at Cambridge a manuscript written by a man named Fortree who, anxious to interest Pepys in a new rig, criticized one in current use, obviously of the Bermudian type, which is described as follows:

Of the Bermoodes saile

The Bermoodes saile is much the same with ye shoulder of Mutton saile, but hath no boom at all and riseth with a higher peeke being a perfect triangle but being so large at bottom and no boom to extend it, before a wind it cannot stand larger than the deck of the vessel but hangs in a great bagg and also by a wind it will bunt very much, which will cause a great deal of back saile: which will much hinder the way of the vessel; nor is it so yare to tack, for that the sheet must be always handed from side to side.

I have seen, too, a number of drawings by the famous marine artist, E. W. Cooke, executed in the early part of the last century, of yachts with sails of this type, and I remember a little cruiser named *Induna*, designed by the late Linton Hope in the 'nineties, that had Bermudian sails. The sail, of course, has long been used in Bermuda, from whence it derives its name, but the modern Bermudian sail, as we know it to-day, is a modification of these earlier ones, being far more lofty and much narrower on the foot.

The Bermudian sail in its present form was introduced for racing purposes a few years before the outbreak of the first Great War, and as it was found to be about 10 per cent faster to windward than the gaff sail, it soon came into universal use for racing. For a time cruising men fought shy of it, looking askance at the very long mast that was necessary to set it. In other ways, however, the Bermudian sail was attractive, for it needed but a single halyard and the weight and gear of a gaff was saved. The Bermudian sail thus began to make its appearance in cruising vessels and is now as popular, perhaps even more so, than the gaff mainsail. In its early stages, however, the sail had many undesirable features. As the tall mast required a rather complicated system of staying, two and sometimes more cross-trees being employed, the luff of the sail could not be attached to the mast by the usual hoops. It was therefore attached by means of slides travelling upon a brass trackway, screwed to the after side of the mast. The early form of trackway proved very inefficient, for if it got bent or dented, the slides would stick and prevent the sail from being hoisted or lowered, as the case might be. Very often, too, the sail could only be set or lowered when the yacht was lying head to wind. Various expedients were tried for overcoming this difficulty, that most commonly used in cruising craft being a wire jackstay from the masthead set up taut to the deck. The head of the sail was hanked to this

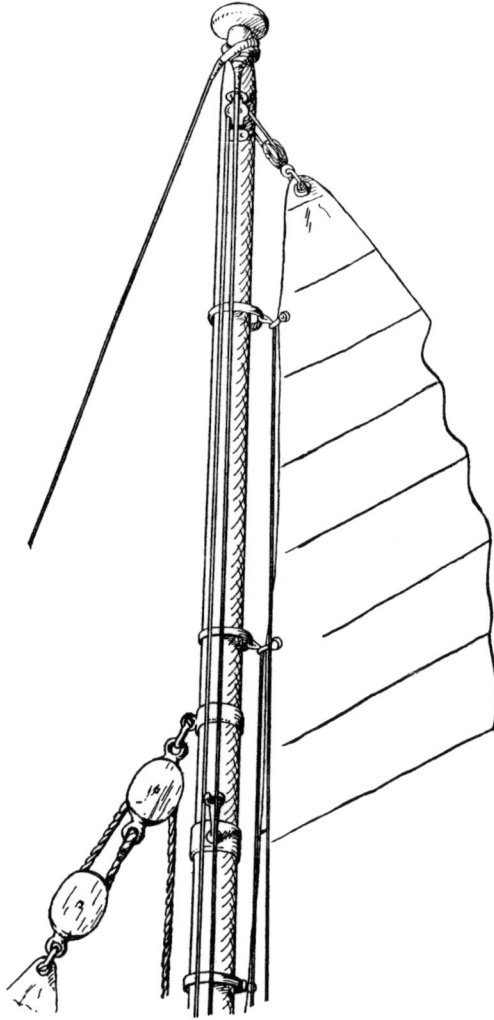

Bermudian sail set using hoops and guys, above crosstrees

jackstay and the lower part, below the cross-trees, was attached to the mast by hoops, in a similar manner to a gaff mainsail, the jackstay being led inside the hoops. Another method was the use of a couple of hoops above the cross-tree. To each of these hoops was attached a light rope guy, of which the end was passed through a hank on the luff of the sail before setting it. When not in use the two hoops rest on the jib halyard bolt, and when the sail is set they are taken up with it and a pull on the guys has the effect of pinning in the head of the sail to the mast and distributing the strain over the pole. The illustration shows the idea, but of course the upper of the two hoops should be much nearer the head of the sail, when the latter is set, than shown in the drawing. Neither of these methods, although still sometimes employed, is as effective as a trackway and slides, which have now been so improved as seldom to give trouble.

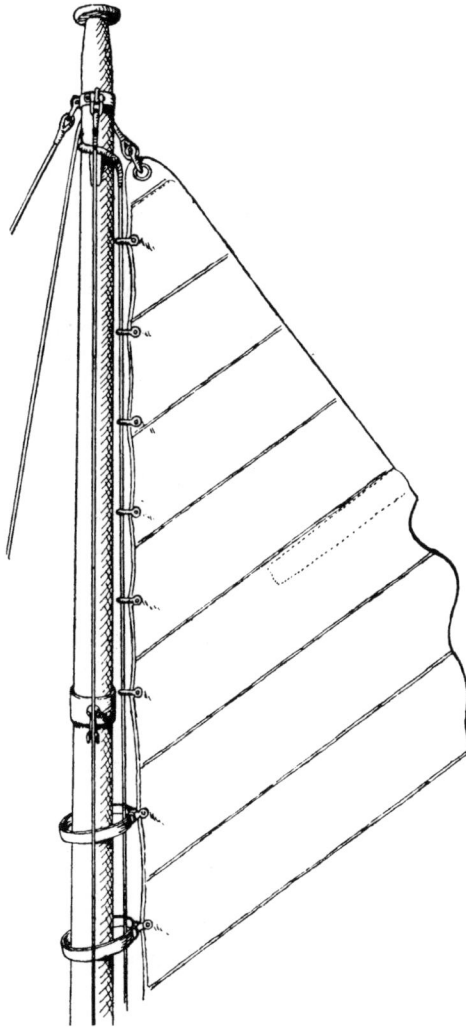

Bermudian sail set using a jackstay to deck, above crosstrees

But the gaff mainsail dies hard and having stood the test of centuries is never likely to disappear altogether, as many of the advocates of the Bermudian seem to think. It has endured for hundreds of years and will probably continue to do so long after the Bermudian has again been consigned to oblivion. I am inclined to think that the gaff sail will come into its own again in the future, but probably in a modified form.

Since the introduction of the aeroplane important discoveries have been made in the science of aerodynamics, but the lessons thus learnt have been almost entirely applied to the Bermudian sail. The possibilities of development in the gaff sail have not yet been explored in the light of modern science, and I should not be surprised if some day it were discovered that such a sail can be produced that will be equal, or even superior, to the Bermudian. After all, the

Bermudian excels only on one point of sailing, namely to windward, and I think it is generally admitted that the gaff sail is actually the more efficient when running and reaching. But what may happen in the future is hardly germane to the question under discussion, and I had better confine my remarks to the Bermudian and gaff sails as we know them to-day.

Let us first consider the advantages claimed for the Bermudian mainsail. These, I think, are as follows : (1) That it is faster and more weatherly when sailing to windward. (2) That it entails less weight and windage aloft, owing to the absence of a gaff and its attendant blocks. (3) That it requires but one halyard to set it instead of two.

That it is more effective to windward than a gaff sail cannot be denied, as experience has shown that it is about ten per cent faster on that point of sailing. It is probably a trifle less efficient on a reach and definitely slower when running. In racing, where windward work counts more than anything, the Bermudian must reign supreme, but I think the average cruising yacht does more of her work with a fair wind than a foul, as the owner who contemplates making a passage often does not start if he finds that the conditions will give him a beat to windward for the greater part of the passage. He waits for more favourable conditions or alters his programme and goes some-where else. If, however, the bulk of his sailing is in the river, the weatherliness of his yacht assumes greater importance, as frequent foul winds cannot be avoided.

The saving of the weight and windage of a gaff is a definite advantage, but not perhaps so great as might be thought, as the rig entails the use of a much taller mast. The benefit arising from the use of a single halyard is I think more imaginary than real, for the average Bermudian sail seems to take a good deal longer to set than a gaff mainsail. If the best results are to be obtained, the sail must be cut with a rounded leach and battens are necessary to make it stand. When setting or lowering the sail the battens have a way of getting foul of everything they possibly can, and even in the absence of battens the headboard often fouls the rigging. Jamming slides are not so common as they were, as the early flimsy trackways have given place to better and more substantial tracks. Even so, a Bermudian sail is not always easily hoisted or lowered unless the yacht is head to wind.

Now for some of the disadvantages of the Bermudian sail as I see them. In the first place it entails the use of a very tall mast, which is difficult to stay effectively and is moreover comparatively costly to make. Unless the mast is kept perfectly straight the set of the sails is impaired, and that usually means extra stays, which must be set up taut as fiddle-strings. That, it seems to me, must throw an undue strain on the hull generally and a thrusting strain on the mast-step in particular, which may cause leaks to develop.

When running before the wind, the boom can only be eased off to about an angle of 45 degrees with the centre-line of the vessel. If allowed to go further, the head of the sail will foul the cross-trees. The sail consequently loses a good deal of its effectiveness on that point of sailing. Then, in most Bermudian-rigged boats the runners have to be tended when beating, as unless the weather one is set up the luff of the jib cannot be kept taut, whilst the lee runner must be slackened to prevent the mainsail being girt across it. The centre of effort of a Bermudian sail has a tendency to move forward as it is reefed and some boats even carry lee helm when close-reefed. The outboard end of the boom, too, is inclined to drop as the sail is reefed, and I have seen several small Bermudian-rigged boats whose mainsails when close-reefed dropped to such an extent that the crew had to crouch in the cockpit to allow the boom to clear their heads when in stays. If the sail is reefed with tackle and pendant, that defect can be corrected by adjustment of the reef cringles to allow for it, but in most cases roller reefing gear is employed. This tendency of the boom-end to drop is probably accounted for partly by the shape of the sail and partly by the luff-rope over-riding as the boom is turned. With a view to correcting it, the boom is sometimes tapered and in other cases splines are fitted, but it seems to me that such expedients must in course of time stretch the sail out of shape. Taking it all round, I think one pays rather dearly for that extra ten per cent, of speed to windward.

Now let us consider the gaff mainsail. If your gear is in proper working order, the sail can always be set or lowered without trouble, either on or off the wind. If

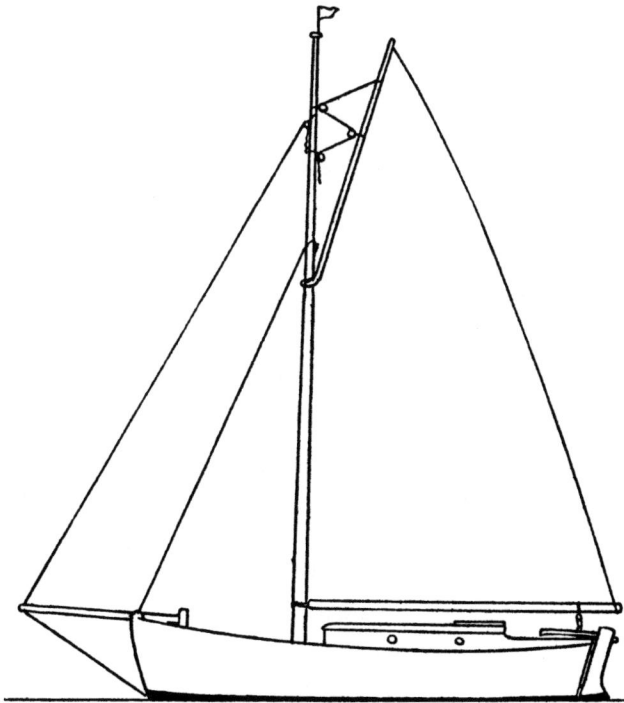

High-peaked gaff mainsail

Gaff and Bermudian sloops

caught in a bad squall, sail can be temporarily reduced in a moment by lowering the peak, and when sailing through a crowded anchorage, the tack can be triced up, giving one a clear view ahead. When sailing with a fair wind, the boom can be squared well off, thus enabling you to trim the sail to best advantage, and when beating, the runners can be kept set up, thus keeping the luff of the jib taut. Finally, in light winds a topsail can be set. Many gaff mainsails, however, are cut too flat on the head, with the result that the peak is inclined to sag to leeward and mar the weatherliness of the yacht. In my opinion, the sail should have a rather short gaff and a high peak. With such a sail the gaff will not sag unduly and the boat will hold a much better wind, although it of course entails the use of a rather longer masthead.

The gunter sail is not often used in cruising yachts nowadays. It is set on a short mast and has a very long gaff, or yard. When set it is much the shape of a Bermudian, but the doubling of the yard and mast makes for weight and windage that is saved in the Bermudian. When reefed, however, the yard comes down with the sail and the weight and windage of the tophamper is reduced, instead of there being a length of naked mast aloft, as is the case with the Bermudian. It is a very weatherly sail, but the long yard is awkward to handle and for that reason the gunter is not popular for cruising purposes.

Other single-masted rigs used in small yachts are the lugger and the una, but neither in my opinion is very suitable for cruising purposes. That prince of single-handed sailors, the late Mr. R. T. McMullen, certainly favoured the lug-sail, but he was the only yachtsman of note that I can recall who used the rig. A lug strikes me as a rather unhandy sail that requires a deal of setting and I think most yachtsmen will agree that the gaff mainsail or Bermudian is a better proposition. The sail that Mr. McMullen used was a working lug without a boom, the tack being made fast abaft the mast. I never could understand why he, with all his vast experience, should have favoured this particular sail for single-handed work, as it must be a perfect brute to reef.

That reefing such a sail was a very long and tedious job will be gathered from the following description of the operation which he gave in his book *Down Channel*:

When a reef has to be taken down, or sail temporarily shortened for a squall, I hook the reef-tackle into the fourth cringle of the after leach, lower away main halyards sufficiently, take in the slack of the upper tack-tackle until it is nearly two blocks, peak the yard again by 'setting up' halyards, and then bowse the sheet aft with the reef-tackle. When this is done, half the sail remains properly set, and the boat is under command during the process of reefing, or until the squall has expended its violence. If a reef is to be taken, the lower tack-tackle and main-sheet have to be transferred to the cringles above and the sister-hooks moused, the two hoops on the mast shifted a cringle higher, the tack and sheet rolled up and secured with short pieces of small manila rope having an eye spliced in the end, eighteen reef points tied, fall of main-sheet belayed – leaving plenty of slack, so as not to interfere with hoisting the sail, reef-tackle cast off, and upper tack-tackle overhauled. Then hoist away mainsail, taking

Gaff and Bermudian ketches

Gaff and Bermudian yawls

care to keep your head out of the way of the upper mainsheet-block when the sail flaps in the wind, peak with upper tack-tackle until the sail is girt from the tack to the peak, bowse down lower tack, throw her up into the wind and get the sheet aft. If the sail is not then as flat as it might be, I put a strap on the fall of the main halyards (which lead aft to the waist through a block at the foot of the mast), hook in a luff-tackle, shake up in the wind and bowse away until no more can be got, belay the slack of the main halyards and remove the strap and tackle.

That sort of thing may be all very well at sea, but it would not do for most of us who often have to reef in narrow waters. The lugsail is certainly very effective on a reach, but I doubt whether it is as close-winded as a gaff mainsail or a Bermudian when close-hauled. Running before the wind, the sail, in the absence of a boom, is very ineffective; so much so, indeed, that Mr. McMullen, in *Procyon*, carried a spar 21 feet long with which to boom out the sail when he had a fair wind.

The dipping lug is possibly the most powerful sail extant and is much favoured by fishermen in the West of England; but for the purposes of the average cruising yachtsman it strikes me as unsuitable. The yard is carried to leeward of the mast and the tack made fast near the stemhead. Every time the vessel is stayed, or gybed, the sail has to be lowered and passed over to the other side of the mast. The fishermen in the West of England, sailing the open waters of the Atlantic, are in the habit of making such long boards that this does not much inconvenience them, but to the yachtsman who frequently has to beat up comparatively narrow channels, the rig would be impracticable.

Of two-masted rigs the yawl and the ketch are the most popular for small cruising yachts, although owners who go in for blue-water cruising sometimes adopt the schooner rig. In this they are probably following the lead of America, where the rig has been in favour for many years. In the famous American ocean race from New London to Bermuda, a considerable proportion of the competing craft are usually rigged as schooners, many being from the design of Mr. John Alden, who has a world-wide reputation for vessels of this rig.

Amongst other advantages claimed for the ketch rig, it is contended that it lightens labour and frequently obviates the necessity for reefing, as the mizzen can be stowed in lieu of reducing the mainsail; or, if that should not prove sufficient reduction, the mainsail can be furled and the yacht sailed under mizzen and headsails. This theory is perfectly correct as regards large craft, but let us criticise it from the small-boat sailor's point of view. The little ketch may jog along to windward, after a fashion; but, should the water be rough, she will probably hold a very poor wind, sag away to leeward a good deal, and develop an obstinate tendency in stays. I venture to think that, under like conditions, a sister boat rigged as a cutter or sloop would, with a reefed mainsail, beat the double-sticked craft out of sight in a very short time, for she would not only point higher and handle better, but would also travel through the water considerably faster. Amongst other objections to the ketch rig for small vessels, the gear is practically doubled, and the mizzen-mast is apt to spoil the accommodation below decks. There are occasions when the mizzen might be a source of convenience, such as picking

Gunter sloop and lug yawl

up moorings or berthing alongside a quay; but, for all ordinary purposes, I am convinced that the cutter or sloop rig will be found more satisfactory

And now I approach the consideration of the yawl with some diffidence. In my books and elsewhere I have for many years heartily damned the rig for small craft, and if I now say anything in its favour I shall lay myself open to a charge of inconsistency. But in the past I have confined my remarks to the gaff yawl, about which I have not changed my views in the slightest degree. But of late years the Bermudian yawl has made its appearance and that is a very different proposition. The yawl that was my particular aversion had a footling little mizzen, about the size of a large pocket handkerchief, which was of no practical use and only made for complication of gear. I think it owed its origin to the big racing yachts of the late 'nineties, which sported the rig. But in such vessels the mizzen was used solely for rulecheating purposes, a generous allowance off their rating being granted to yawls. For a time it was the fashion to step a tiny mizzen almost on the taffrail, so that the rig allowance could be claimed. Cruising yachtsmen, probably thinking that there must be some particular virtue in the mizzen, adopted a similar rig, and little yawls with tiny mizzens attained some degree of popularity about that time and are not uncommon to-day.

A great deal of nonsense was formerly written in text-books and elsewhere about these small yawls. It was claimed that the mainsail need seldom be reefed, as the mizzen could be stowed instead; or should that not be a sufficient reduction, the mainsail could be furled and the yacht sailed under the mizzen and a head-sail. I have often wondered whether the writers had ever had any practical experience of sailing a small yawl to windward in rough weather under mizzen and headsails.

In my young days I owned two of these miniature yawls and, being more of an optimist than I am now, sometimes tried the experiment. I found that every sea hurled the vessel farther to leeward, while staying was outside the range of practical politics. Even in smooth water, staying was on the knees of the gods. I have seen small yawls get into a horrid mess through missing stays under such canvas, and any owner who plays monkey tricks of that sort in a crowded anchorage ought to be put in a home, for he is a menace to the safety of other craft. Of course, a boat of racer type, or even a smart modern cruiser, would stay under mizzen and headsails in smooth water with a good breeze, but she would probably do the same under headsails alone. The idea of sailing under mizzen and headsails is wrong in theory and bad in practice, for when sail is shortened the aim should be to concentrate the area amidships as far as possible.

The modern Bermudian yawl, however, is a very different craft, for she carries a mizzen of serviceable size and the back-draught from the Bermudian mainsail is thrown clear of it. If the jib is fitted with the Wykeham-Martin furling gear, sail can be reduced very rapidly without leaving the cockpit, as the jib can be rolled up and the mizzen lowered. One is then left with a neat sloop rig without the balance of the boat being affected. The Bermudian yawl, too, is nearly as weatherly as a cutter.

I have been told that I am prejudiced against the yawl rig, but I don't think I am. I have owned three of them and any remarks I have made on the subject were based on practical experience. They were gaff yawls and I found the same defects in all of them. The last was the 7-ton Falmouth Quay Punt *Fancy*, which I had a few years ago. Determined to give the rig a thorough try out, I had a new mizzen made, as the sail in the boat when I bought her did not set very well. The new mizzen was quite a sizable sail, with an area of, I should say, about 80 square feet, a very different proposition to the footling little mizzens in my previous yawls. I will try and give an unbiased opinion of the gaff yawl, stating the pros and cons as I see them. We will take the advantages first. The short boom certainly facilitates reefing the mainsail, for as the boom is all inboard, reefing the sail is a simple matter in comparison with that of a cutter or sloop. If the mizzen is a jib-headed sail and the jib fitted with furling gear, sail can be quickly reduced without leaving the helm, as the jib can be rolled up and the mizzen either lowered or the boom topped up to the mast. When running, the mizzen can be goose-winged (i.e. carried on the opposite side to the mainsail). That will ease the weather helm if the boat is inclined to be hard-headed and slightly increase her speed, as in that position the mizzen does not blanket the mainsail. It, however, tends to deflect the wind, and if you are in the habit of steering, when running, by the feel of the wind on the back of your neck, as I am, it is rather disconcerting until you get used to it.

Another advantage of the mizzen is that it can be used as a riding sail if you have to ride to a sea-anchor, but as the coastwise sailor seldom, if ever, has sufficient offing to ride to a sea-anchor, that advantage is imaginary rather than real. Moreover, there are precious few modern yachts that will ride to a sea-anchor by the bow.

Finally, the mizzen-mast makes a capital flag-staff for flying an ensign when under way. Well, those are all the advantages possessed by the yawl that I can think of, and now let us look at the disadvantages. She is slow to windward in comparison with a cutter or sloop, as she does not hold such a good wind. In order to secure adequate sail area, it is the custom to cut a yawl's mainsail with considerable hoist and very long on the head. The gaff, indeed, is usually as long as the boom, and has a tendency to sag to leeward when the yacht is on the wind. This might possibly be mitigated by the use of vangs, such as are used on the sprit of a Thames barge, although I have never seen a yawl's mainsail thus fitted. They have, however, been tried with success in schooners and I see no reason why they should not be equally effective in a yawl.

As the 'dirty wind' from the mainsail is apt to impinge on the lee side of the mizzen, the latter has to be so harshly sheeted to make it stand on a wind that it loses most of its driving power. When thus sheeted it is of little value beyond maintaining the balance of the sails. Being right outside the boat, the mizzen is an awkward sail to stow and coat and most owners, rather than take the trouble, merely top up the boom and stow the sail on the mast. The mizzen consequently soon gets dirty and mars the appearance of the yacht. The mizzen also checks the yacht's head from paying off, and if one has to bear away quickly, the mizzen sheet must be slackened, before she will do so. That takes an appreciable amount of time, which sometimes can ill be spared, as one also has to tend the mainsheet. The mizzen, moreover, makes for extra weight and windage aloft and entails a lot of extra gear, which, of course, adds to the expense.

In *Fancy* I soon gave up using the mizzen when beating to windward, as it was such an intolerable nuisance. The mizzen-mast was stepped almost on the transom and off-set so as not to interfere with the tiller. That meant that every time she went about, the mizzen sheet had to be readjusted and as she seemed to sail just as well without the mizzen, it was not worth the bother. The mizzen, therefore, was seldom used, except for reaching and running.

CHAPTER 9: *Size for the Single-hander*

It is astonishing how the ideas of yachtsmen vary with regard to the size of craft most suitable for single-handed work, the tonnage of the boat selected often being in inverse ratio to the size of the man. Thus we find little spare men sailing yachts big enough to accommodate a fair-sized family, whilst big stout men confine their well-developed carcases in little slips of vessels that look more suited to the Round Pond at Kensington than to the open sea. In selecting a boat for single-handed sailing the yachtsman should exercise a little discrimination in his choice, keeping in view the sort of cruising he intends to practise. If it is his intention merely to jog round the coast from port to port, a comparatively small yacht will be quite big enough for the job, and it is absurd to go in for a craft larger than necessary. If, on the other hand, he proposes to make long trips across open water, it is desirable that his yacht should be of sufficient size to keep the sea in any weather likely to be encountered.

So far as I know, the largest craft ever sailed single-handed by an amateur yachtsman was the yawl *Lady Harvey*. In that vessel Mr. Frank Cowper cruised for some years, circumnavigating the British Isles and exploring en route practically every river and creek round the coast. I remember the old *Lady Harvey* well, and she was certainly a lump of a boat for one man to handle for months on end. Built at Dover so long ago as 1867, she measured 29 tons T.M., her principal dimensions, as given in Lloyd's Register, being: Length between perpendiculars, 44 feet; beam, 13.4 feet; and depth, 7 feet. Her draft, I believe, was about 6 feet, and she was rigged as a yawl. Mr. Cowper, when he owned *Lady Harvey*, was collecting data for his well-known series of cruising guides, *Sailing Tours*, and his trip was therefore more or less a voyage of exploration.

Although snugly rigged, *Lady Harvey* must have been a handful at times for a light man of something under ten stone, but Mr. Cowper seems to have completed his cruise without experiencing any serious difficulty. Another yacht owned subsequently by Mr. Cowper was not much smaller than *Lady Harvey* and even older. I refer to the 24-ton yawl *Zayda*, which was built in 1859. Her length between perpendiculars was 45 feet 9 inches, and her beam 11 feet 3 inches. Speaking from memory, I should say that her sail area was rather larger than that of *Lady Harvey*, and her owner must have experienced some little difficulty in setting her mainsail. The anchor work in both of these yachts was very heavy for a single man, particularly one of the physique of Mr. Cowper, who, also, if he will forgive my saying so, was no longer in the first flush of youth. It is difficult to imagine what can have induced him to go in for single-handers of such size, as craft of half the tonnage would have served his purpose equally well and have been infinitely easier to handle. To my mind the best boat 'Jack-all-alone' ever owned was *Undine* (now known as *Singora*) which he designed and built himself. Even she was on the large side for single-handed work, measuring 18 tons T.M., but she was ketch-rigged and of a more modern and handy type than *Lady Harvey* and *Zayda*. Having once cruised in such a craft as Undine, it strikes me as amazing that Mr. Cowper should ever have bought a yacht like *Zayda*, which must, I think, be included in the category of what the yacht hand is pleased to term 'old tore-outs.'

In considering the question of the most suitable size of yacht, it must be remembered that it is not merely the labour of handling the vessel that has to be taken into account. There is also the matter of keeping her clean and in a state of general efficiency to be reckoned with. A yacht of the tonnage of *Lady Harvey* or *Zayda* as a rule carries two paid hands, or a man and boy at least, who will have the assistance of the owner and his friends in sailing her. Now, when the owner dispenses with the assistance of a professional crew and has no amateurs to help him, how is he going to sail the boat and also keep her in a smart and efficient state? It simply can't be done, and it seems to me that if a man elects to sail a craft of that size single-handed he must either neglect her or else spend most of his time in cleaning work. To pass most of the day under way and yet keep a yacht of some 30 tons in decent condition, is, I contend, beyond the powers of one man, and that is probably why neither *Lady Harvey* nor *Zayda* was particularly smart in appearance. But Mr. Cowper, I should say, does not care a tinker's D about mere appearance. Having a fancy for big boats, he gratified his desires in that respect and let what is somewhat vulgarly termed the 'spit and polish' side of the question go hang. Personally, if I had the same ideas as regards size, I should be inclined to take a leaf out of the book of the fishermen and paint the spars, blocks, and decks and dress the sails.

One can get a good idea as to the amount of work there is to be done in a 20-tonner from the pages of *Down Channel*, which, by the way, is one of the most fascinating and instructive yachting books ever published. The author, the late Mr. R. T. McMullen, narrates his experience of sailing alone in his yawl *Orion*, which he brought home to the Thames from Cherbourg. He was away cruising with his usual crew of two paid hands and the men complained bitterly of the hard work. Their behaviour became so mutinous that Mr. McMullen had to discharge them at Cherbourg. Then, to demonstrate that their complaints were not justified, he determined to sail the yacht home alone and carry out all the work that the men would have had to do in the ordinary course of their duties. Mr. McMullen gives in his book a detailed account of the work, which is most interesting, but far too long to quote here. As an instance, however, of the amount of labour involved, it may be mentioned that it took him eleven hours to get the yacht under way and clear of the harbour. A portion of the time was spent in attending to the domestic economy of the yacht and in preparing his meals. "If asked to give a strict account of my time," he writes, "it would not be possible, but one or two suggestions will go far to make it clear. Many things require to be held; you have to go and fix them, return to your own work, and then back to release them again. There is plenty of that in handling the mainsail. All ropes, after temporary use, were coiled down in their places." It must be said that *Orion* was equipped with far heavier canvas and gear than it is customary to use in yachts nowadays, and Mr. McMullen was a little man of not much more than nine stone in weight. An experience of this nature once in a lifetime may be all very well, but nobody could make a practice of doing such work, and if a man habitually sails a craft of from 20 to 30 tons single-handed it is, I think, pretty obvious that something must be neglected. This particular trip from Cherbourg to the Thames was undertaken more from necessity than choice, but Mr. McMullen was a very keen single-handed sailor and made notable cruises. The boats he had specially built for single-handed work ranged in size from *Leo*, 2¾ tons, to *Procyon*, 7 tons, and I doubt whether he would have advocated anything much larger than the latter for the purpose.

A large craft not only entails undue labour but also makes for unnecessary expense, both of which it is desirable to avoid. If it is the intention to use the boat merely for week-end trips and pottering round the coast, a craft of 4 or 5 tons should be of ample size for the purpose and would afford sufficient comfort below decks to satisfy the owner's wants, provided that she had adequate headroom. To be compelled to sit huddled up in the cabin, even for a week-end, is intolerable, and for that reason no boat with much less than 4 feet 6 inches headroom should be thought of. In choosing a yacht the factor of physical strength must not be overlooked, as a craft that a strong man can handle with comfort may speedily tire out anyone of slighter build. It is not, however, so much the size of the boat that must be considered in this respect as the area of the sails and weight of the ground tackle. There are those who will tell you that these factors are not of much importance, as lack of strength on the part of the owner can be compensated for by the use of more powerful purchases on halyards and sheets and the employment of an adequate windlass for the cable. But with that view I do not see eye to eye. The more mechanical power employed the longer it takes to do the job, and in single-handed work speed is often of the first importance. When getting the vessel under way, for instance, one cannot be at both ends of the yacht at once, and in preparing to leave a crowded anchorage, with a strong tide running, delay may spell disaster. It must be remembered that it is necessary to sight the anchor before the boat can be got under perfect control, and in practice this means that as soon as the anchor has been broken out of the ground the chain must be cast off the drum of the windlass and hauled in hand over hand. There simply isn't time to use mechanical power for the purpose. One's presence is urgently needed at the tiller and mainsheet, and if one got the chain in slowly with the aid of a windlass, the yacht would probably be athwart some other craft long ere the anchor was sighted. An anchor weighing some 40 lbs. on the end of a $\frac{3}{8}$-inch chain is quite heavy enough for a man of average physique to 'fist' up, and if one has to use much heavier ground tackle than that it will mean bringing up on the outskirts of the anchorage, probably a long way from a landing causeway.

The question of sail area must be viewed in a rather different light than it would be in the case of a yacht manned by a strong crew. In the latter instance the area can be considered as a whole, but the single-hander must look to the size of the individual sails. The main point he has to decide is the area of the largest sail he can handle efficiently and without undue strain. Although light winds for the most part obtain during the summer months, it would not be wise to base one's calculations solely on such weather, as a strong wind might prove overpowering. The single-hander has but himself to depend upon and if caught in a breeze is obliged to 'stick it out.' It is all very well in theory to talk glibly about heaving to and going below for a rest, but the yachtsman who confines his sailing to trips round the coast seldom has sufficient offing to do so with safety. He therefore has no alternative but to plug on until he makes a port or finds shelter under a weather shore. In considering the question of sail area he should for this reason keep in hand a certain reserve of strength.

The mainsail, being the most important, will naturally claim first attention, and rightly so, as the area of the other sails is largely dependent upon its size. In dealing with this question I cannot do better, perhaps, than give my own experience in the 7-tonner *Seabird* that I formerly used for single-handed work. When I bought her she was rigged as a sloop with a mainboom 27 feet in length and a foresail of, so far as I remember, something like 180 square feet. I suppose I can describe myself as a man of average physique, being rather more than twelve stone in weight, and I must confess that *Seabird* under her sloop rig made me very tired indeed in strong winds. To make matters worse she was a sharp-sterned boat and the boom-end 6 feet outboard. I sailed her in that trim for some time, but an experience I had one day when caught in a breeze convinced me that a little curtailment of the sail area was desirable. I got caught out in the Wallet in some dirty weather that necessitated reefing, and soon found that what was difficult in the river was next door to impossible in a seaway. There was a 'certain liveliness' about *Seabird* in rough water that rendered it far from easy to maintain one's foothold on deck. Indeed, she kicked up her heels like a colt in a paddock, and it was perhaps somewhat imprudent to stand on the rudder-head whilst vainly endeavouring to tie the last few reef-points. Anyhow, I suddenly found myself hanging on to the boom-end with my feet alternately dangling in space and diving under water, what time the boat did her best to shake me off. Neither by training nor inclination am I a gymnast, and I shall never forget the horrible scramble I had to get back on board. From that moment the sloop rig was doomed so far as *Seabird* was concerned, and I sailed her straight back to Burnham for alteration. The modification made in her rig was quite simple. I had 6 feet lopped off her boom and the mainsail cut down to fit, whilst the big single headsail gave place to foresail and jib. The alteration was a complete success, for although something was sacrificed in the way of speed, the enhanced comfort and ease in handling were ample compensation. The reduced boom measured 21 feet, the end being plumb with the sternpost, and I am inclined to think that that is about the limit in length that the average yachtsman will care to handle alone in a breeze.

If the yacht is of a size to require more sail to drive her a two-masted rig may perhaps be desirable. But I make the suggestion with all reserve, having a prejudice against such rigs for quite small craft. Far better, in my opinion, would it be to content oneself with a rather smaller yacht than to patronise the doubtful virtues of, say, the yawl rig with its complication of gear. The yawl rig, to my mind, is quite out of place in any vessel of less than 20 tons measurement. One can, however, imagine circumstances that would almost compel a man to have a boat a good deal larger than he would require for his own personal accommodation. There is, for instance, the married man who does not care to leave his wife and children at home whilst he goes cruising. For such a yachtsman the first consideration must be internal accommodation, as he has to provide sleeping berths for his passengers, and it is quite likely that the craft may be of 12 or 15 tons, requiring a sail area of 1,000 or 1,200 square feet. It would be beyond his strength to handle alone such a spread of canvas in a cutter rig, and so he must split it up into 'penny numbers,' so to speak. In such a case the yawl or ketch rig becomes almost a necessity, but I have more to say on that point when I discuss the question of rigs. Although it is possible to split up the sail area into sails of a workable size, the anchor difficulty in a large boat still remains, and anyone who sails single-handed a yacht that requires an anchor and chain of such weight as to call for the employment of a windlass, should never take up a berth in a crowded anchorage unless he has a mooring to ride to.

To buy a yacht larger than is necessary for the work for which it is proposed to use her savours somewhat of extravagance, and if it is the single-handed yachtsman's intention to confine his cruising for the most part to week-end sailing round the coast, the main point to consider is that of personal comfort. For that sort of work a little craft of 2 or 3 tons will do as well as one of 5 or 6 tons, provided that she is of good design and has sufficient displacement to afford the necessary headroom in the cabin. I do not suggest that such a vessel is fit to make a coastwise passage in a summer gale, but when such conditions of weather obtain the yachtsman will be well advised to stay in port, even if his boat be as large as 6 tons. There are those whose conversation would lead you to suppose that they enjoy nothing better than a bad 'dusting' in a small yacht, but it will usually be found that they are novices who have had no practical experience of really heavy weather. Most yachtsmen sooner or later get caught out in a blow and have to 'face the music,' but I have yet to meet the man who deliberately courts bad weather.

It is astonishing what a lot of pleasure can be derived from the smallest of cruisers, and what a deal of ground can be covered in them in the course of a summer, but it is essential that the boat should be of suitable type and design. Of the score of boats that I have owned my favourite was the 2-ton canoe yacht *Snipe*, and I still regret the day when I was tempted by a fat price to part with her. I picked her up when she was four years old for a mere song from a man who had acquired a big yacht. I cruised in *Snipe* for three years with the utmost pleasure and satisfaction, and then a friend, who had fallen in love with her, offered me almost twice as much as I had paid for the boat, and I parted with her. Built by Pengelly and Gore at Teignmouth in 1895, *Snipe*'s principal dimensions were: Length, 18 feet; beam, 6 feet; and draught, 3 feet 6 inches. With 13 cwts. of iron on her keel and a like quantity in the form of pigs inside, she was as stiff as the proverbial church under a sloop rig of moderate area, whilst, thanks to her generous freeboard, she had ample headroom in the cabin to sit upright on a bunk of moderate height. *Snipe*'s cabin accommodation was remarkable for a boat of her size, and two persons could live on board quite comfortably for weeks on end. On either side of the cabin was a folding cot, which let down over the sofa for sleeping purposes, and when folded back to the side of the boat during the day contained all the bedding and blankets, which were protected from damp by a sheet of Willesden canvas. At the fore end of the cabin was a small table, and on the floor a Turkey rug. The fo'castle was divided from the cabin by dark blue curtains, held back by broad red ribbons, whilst a red silk shade subdued the light from a gimballed lamp fixed to the mast. It was the snuggest and homeliest little cabin imaginable, and I have often had less comfortable quarters in a 5-tonner. *Snipe* was of true canoe form – that is to say, without overhang either fore or aft – and she was a little man in heavy weather. The boat was inclined to be wet in rough water, but what small craft that travels is not under such conditions? It was, however, only the foredeck that the water invaded, and it ran off harmlessly along the waterways.

Beating to windward in rough water, she sloshed through it in the most convincing style and never failed to come about when the helm was put down. Since I sold her nearly twenty years ago *Snipe* has only changed hands once, which would suggest that her later owners have found her as satisfactory as I did. Although now twenty-four years old, the boat is, I believe, still quite sound and tight, and the last time I saw her she looked as smart as ever. But she has been fortunate in her owners, and has always been well kept up. Messrs. Pengelly and Gore would appear to have been particularly happy in their small cruisers, as another of their creations, *Lady Frances*, is an equally good little ship. She is a trifle larger than *Snipe* and has a transom stern, whilst her beam is greater in proportion to her length. Her cabin is positively palatial for a 3-tonner, and she has quite a useful turn of speed.

In single-handed sailing one has to combine the roles of helmsman and crew, consequently when the yacht is put about one must look after the helm and also work the headsail sheets. This is quite easy to do, but it is essential that one has sufficient time in which to do it. For this reason the modern yacht with a short keel and her deadwoods cut away is not always the best type of single-hander, as she is far too quick in stays. What one wants is a craft that comes round slowly, but surely, so that the tiller may be lashed down and the headsail sheets tended comfortably whilst the yacht is coming round. To secure this quality a certain length of keel is necessary and the forefoot must not be unduly cut away. The long keel, moreover, makes for steadiness on the helm, and such a boat will often sail herself with tiller lashed for quite a long time. In the book he published on his voyage round the world Captain Slocum stated that the *Spray* would sail herself for days together, and with steady trade winds there seems no reason to doubt the statement. In our home waters the wind is seldom perfectly steady, and a yacht with her tiller lashed will generally call for a certain amount of supervision, but in my old *Seabird* I frequently cooked and ate my dinner whilst she reached along with the tiller lashed. It is also desirable that the yacht should be easy to get about on, or, in other words, should have sufficient beam to prevent her heeling to a great angle. A boat that sails much on her side is most uncomfortable for single-handed sailing, as she is difficult to get about in, both on deck and down below. As reefing is heavy work when undertaken single-handed, the boat should be stiffer than would be considered necessary in the case of a craft carrying a full complement of hands. Qualities such as I have referred to do not make for speed, but safety and comfort are, I think, of greater importance than fast passages, and the cruising man, as a rule, is not obsessed with a lust for speed.

CHAPTER 10: *Buying a Yacht*

Having carefully considered such matters as type, tonnage, draught, rig and accommodation, you will probably have formed a pretty good idea as to the sort of yacht you want, and the time has now come to go in quest of her. If you have had no previous experience you may be at a loss how to set about it. Well, the quickest way, I think, would be to insert an advertisement in one of the yachting journals, stating briefly your requirements. You might back this up by applying to a few of the brokers whose advertisements appear in such journals. In the course of a few days you will probably receive a number of replies, and then will come the task of separating the sheep from the goats.

You may be surprised to find that some of the yachts offered to you do not correspond with your advertised requirements. It may seem to you stupid that you should be sent particulars of craft larger, or of a different rig, to what you want, but there is method in the broker's apparent madness. He knows very well that the yachtsman's fancies are as changeable as the weather and that you may see particularly desirable features in one of the craft he offers you that may cause you to change your mind. But, don't be tempted to buy an unsuitable boat because she has, say, an exceptionally roomy cabin, or a very comprehensive inventory. Of course, you cannot expect to get exactly what you want unless you have a yacht specially designed and built for you, but you can hope to secure a vessel that will roughly satisfy your requirements in such matters as size, rig and type.

The particulars furnished should comprise such details as age, tonnage, dimensions, designer, builder, materials of which she is constructed, headroom, draught, age of sails and gear, ballast, cabin plan and inventory. Too much reliance, however, should not be placed on statements as to the yacht's condition, until it has been confirmed by survey, for they are as a rule merely based upon the owner's opinion. With these particulars before you, assisted by a photograph of the yacht, you should be able to form an idea as to whether she is likely to suit you. Out of perhaps a score of boats offered, you may find two or three that seem to fill the bill. If they are lying at ports within reasonable distance, you should apply for orders to view them and take an early opportunity of doing so. If you fancy a boat from the description supplied, do not delay in going to look at her, as small yachts in decent condition sell like hot cakes and if you wait for a few days you will probably find that the vessel has been snapped up by someone else.

Don't be too optimistic, for yachts offered for sale are not always what they seem. I have, in my time, made many, many long and expensive journeys to inspect yachts which appeared most desirable on paper, only to find that they were little better than old junk. One naturally expects the vendor to make the best of a boat, but some draw on their imagination to the extent of scandalous misrepresentation of facts. Unfortunately, one has no redress and in the course of your quest you may thus be induced to waste both time and money.

To illustrate what I mean, I will tell you of an experience I had some years ago. When in search of a small yacht I saw an advertisement of a 4-ton cutter which seemed very attractive, but she was lying at a place difficult of access from where I lived. To go and inspect her would involve a long cross-country journey, necessitating several changes, and as the trains did not fit in at all well, it would take a whole day, and a long one at that. Before deciding to make the journey, I wrote to the advertiser for further particulars, putting to him a number of questions as to the yacht's draught, headroom, age, equipment, etc. In reply I received a eulogistic description of the craft, from which I gathered that she was in excellent condition and had recently been fitted out at considerable expense. Her draught, I was told, was 4 feet 6 inches, and the headroom in the cabin 5 feet. She was said to have a full cruising equipment, including cushions, blankets, cooking stove and utensils, crockery, riding light and a small engine (make not specified). He assured me that both yacht and gear were perfectly sound and as he was shortly going abroad he was offering her at the low price of £90. Finally, he urged me to lose no time in going to inspect her as several others were after her.

Well, that all seemed so satisfactory that the next morning I got up at an unearthly hour and started on the long and tedious journey. I reached my destination in the middle of the day and found the yacht legged on the hard. Far from being the desirable little ship I had been led to expect, she was little better than old junk, long overdue for the scrap-heap. I could see at a glance that her draught was nearer 3 feet than 4 feet 6 inches, and her appearance suggested that nothing had been done in the way of fitting out beyond putting the gear on board. Her bowsprit was badly sprung and the bobstay consisted of a length of rusty iron rod, roughly bent at the ends to form hooks, to which was attached a piece of wire rope, also very rusty. The standing rigging was in a deplorable state and most of the running gear rotten. Some of the blocks, I noticed, were those little iron things sold for hauling up a wireless aerial, which cost about ninepence apiece. The uncoated mainsail was old and dirty, and the hull looked as if it had not been painted for years.

Climbing on board, I found that most of the space in the cockpit was occupied by the 'small engine,' which had rusted up solid and had evidently been out of action for years. The tiller, obviously a makeshift, was positively ludicrous, being a bit of bar iron no more than a foot long. In the cabin I found that the headroom was just 3 feet 11 inches under a rather high coach-roof, in which there was a large hole, over which a bit of linoleum had been roughly tacked. The bunk cushions were wet and had large holes in them, which exuded mouldy flock stuffing. Lying on one of the bunks were two filthy old army blankets, and on the floor stood a cheap hurricane lamp. Whether it was intended to serve as riding light or cabin lamp, I don't know, but it could not have been used for both purposes and would have been equally inefficient for either. There were no lockers in the cabin, other than those under the bunks, but there was a cupboard in the fo'c'sle in which there were a few Woolworth enamelled plates and mugs in poor condition. The cooking utensils consisted of a rusty tin kettle and frying-pan in similar condition. In fact, the only thing on board in a decent state was a Primus stove.

As a matter of curiosity I tested her timbers and planking in one or two places with my knife, and found them as ripe as a sleepy pear. In reply to my question as to her age, the owner had replied that he did not know exactly when she had been built but thought it was probably before the war. He did not say which war, but I suspect it was the Crimean. To inspect this old 'tore-out' I had wasted a whole day, to say nothing of an expensive railway journey.

That was certainly a very bad case of misrepresentation, but on many occasions I have been induced to waste time and money on inspecting unsuitable craft by what can only be described as deliberate lying. Such mendacity upon the part of sellers is not only reprehensible but foolish, for the veriest 'mug' can use a two-foot rule. Many yachtsmen, no doubt, have had similar experiences and unfortunately the victim has no redress.

On another occasion the owner of a boat I went to inspect had told me that the headroom in the cabin was nearly 5 feet. When I accompanied him on board to look at her, I found it impossible to sit upright on a very low bunk. Turning to him, I said, "You told me the headroom was nearly five feet."

"Well," he replied, "it's not much less."

Whipping out my rule, I measured and found that it was just 3 feet 4 inches.

"I thought it was more than that," was all he had to say when I pointed out the discrepancy. I am afraid I said quite a lot.

Of course, if one buys through the medium of a broker, one is not likely to be victimized in that manner, for yacht-brokers do not as a rule handle old junk. In my experience, however, most small yachts are bought and sold without the intervention of an agent.

Now here is another point. If one buys through a broker, one is usually supplied with an inventory of gear and equipment, and can tick off the various items and make sure of getting what one pays for. But, as I have said, in most cases small yachts are sold direct and an inventory is seldom available. One is merely told that everything goes with the boat except personal effects. To the inexperienced buyer that may sound quite satisfactory, but the term 'personal effects' is extremely elastic and often leads to unseemly squabbles.

What exactly is meant by 'personal effects'? A leading insurance company defines the term as "articles which would not appear in the yacht's inventory if the vessel were put up for sale," but I don't think that quite meets the case, as the views of owners as to what should be sold with a yacht are by no means uniform.

One, for instance, may regard blankets as part of the yacht's equipment and be content to part with them, while another might wish to keep them for use in the next vessel he buys. My own view is that personal effects should comprise such articles as are not essential to the sailing of the yacht. They would thus include such items as clothing, oilskins, sea-boots, books, charts, navigating instruments, binoculars, club burgees and cameras.

But even if no inventory is supplied, it is quite easy for a buyer to protect himself. If the seller says that everything goes with the boat except personal effects, he should be asked to name what he wishes to retain. The buyer should then make a list of the items and get him to sign it. By following that course the risk of any subsequent dispute will be entirely eliminated. In my time I have bought and sold more than a score of small yachts and have never had any disagreement.

I think, however, that it is more satisfactory to both parties when there is an inventory of equipment and it does not take long to compile if one does it on board. The seller, of course, is at liberty to omit anything he wishes to keep, but if he retains too much it may prejudice the sale of the yacht.

I would advise you not to place too much reliance on what the seller tells you about the yacht's sailing qualities, for, in my experience, every yacht offered for sale is a good sea boat, fast and weatherly. And do not take his word that she is sound. If the vendor gives a written undertaking to that effect, it is another matter, for you could sue him in the event of her proving otherwise. But he is not likely to do anything of the sort. Even the professional surveyor usually covers himself by some such qualification as 'so far as it was possible to ascertain.'

The novice, when buying his first yacht, cannot be expected to form a reliable opinion as to her condition, but he should be capable of judging whether she is the sort of boat that he wants and whether the cabin accommodation is all that he requires. If you take a fancy to a yacht and think she will serve your purpose, there will be no harm in making an offer for her subject to survey. You will have to pay the cost of the survey, but it will be money well spent. If the report is satisfactory, the knowledge that she is quite sound will give you confidence when you are cruising.

The importance of having a yacht surveyed cannot be over-stressed, for the condition of a yacht cannot be determined by her appearance. Paint and varnish, when applied to boats, often cover a multitude of sins. The first yacht I bought when a boy looked as smart a little ship as one could desire, and when I bought her for £35 I thought I had got a real bargain. But she had been attacked by dry rot and was really in a deplorable condition. I only had her for six weeks, during which she sank three times and ended her career by being run down in the night and so badly damaged as to be what is known to underwriters as a 'constructive total loss.' Having removed her spars, sails and gear, I sold what was left for ten bob to a man in need of firewood. As she was not insured, I lost the savings of years, but I gained some very valuable experience.

Now, when I speak of survey, I mean examination by a professional surveyor. It is no use taking a yachting friend to inspect the boat. He may be a fine sailor but not know so much about the construction of yachts as he thinks he does. Moreover, it is probable that the seller will be present when your friend examines the vessel, and the latter will feel rather diffident about carrying his inspection too far. He will probably merely try with his knife such parts of the vessel that are easily accessible, but that is not enough. The professional surveyor, on the other hand, knows just where to look and if necessary will have a portion of the lining removed so that he can test the condition of the wood behind it. He will not care a hoot about the owner's feelings; he has been employed to do a job and he will do it thoroughly, for his reputation is at stake. He will scrape off the paint in places and take specimens of the wood by boring with a gimlet, have a keel bolt knocked out to ascertain the condition of the fastenings, test the mast and spars to make sure that they are not sprung, or rotten, and make a thorough inspection of the sails, rigging and running gear.

Do not on any account ask a local fisherman or waterman to look at a yacht for you. Such men, although they spend their lives afloat, seldom have much knowledge of the construction of yachts, and even if the man be honest, his opinion will not be of much value. And there is always a possibility that he may be interested in the sale, in which case you may be badly had. Above all, beware of the local longshoreman who has for sale 'a nice little bo't; just the thing for a young gent like you.'

Most naval architects will survey a small yacht for a moderate fee and out-of-pocket expenses, but should you experience difficulty in finding one in your district, you can apply to Lloyd's Register of Shipping, who will send one of their own surveyors to examine the yacht. You must arrange with the seller to have the boat berthed on a hard, or hauled out on a slipway, for the purpose, as a vessel cannot be properly surveyed afloat, or in a mud berth. Many writers of yachting text-books give their readers instructions for testing for soundness by prodding the planking and timbers with a knife. I do not propose to follow their example, as I am convinced that the average novice might prod until he was black in the face without being much wiser, as the most vulnerable parts of a vessel are usually the most inaccessible, particularly when the cabin is lined. When you receive the surveyor's report you may find he recommends that certain parts of the yacht or gear should be renewed. If the craft is otherwise suitable, she should not be condemned on that account, as the recommended repairs may be comparatively trivial. Get an estimate from a shipwright for the work, and then, by adding the amount to the price asked for the yacht, you will be able to make up your mind whether it is worth your while to buy her. It is possible that if you point out the defects to the seller, he may make some abatement in the price.

It must not be concluded from what I have written on this subject that yachtsmen as a class are an unscrupulous lot when disposing of their boats, for they are not. In most cases the novice will get a fair deal, but there are black sheep in every fold and I am anxious to save the beginner from being 'picked up,' as I was when I bought my first craft. If he has the yacht professionally surveyed before completing the deal, he cannot go far wrong. It may cost him three or four pounds, but he must remember that if he buys a rotten or ill-found boat he may run a grave risk of losing his money and possibly his life as well.

When a yacht has lead ballast the seller does not, as a rule, omit to draw attention to the fact, which he is quite entitled to do, as lead is a commodity that commands a high price in a ready market. But where you are apt to be misled is in the quantity, particularly if it happens to be on the vessel's keel. In my experience, most estimates of the quantity of lead on a yacht's keel are exaggerated, or shall we say optimistic? If, therefore, you see it stated in the particulars of a yacht you contemplate buying that she has 3 tons lead on her keel, don't at once begin to compute by mental arithmetic what it is worth. In all probability there is nothing like 3 tons there, and even if there is, its cash value to you will be nothing, as you are not in the least likely to sell it separately. If you are wise you will regard the lead merely as ballast and ignore its cash value altogether. Of course, if you are a mathematical genius and measure up the lead keel very carefully, you could arrive at something like its correct weight, provided that the keel was all lead, but even then you could not accurately estimate its market value. I once discussed this question with a leading metal merchant and he told me that his firm had given up buying yacht lead on account of its impurity. Yacht lead, he said, seems to have an abnormal amount of dross, and sometimes foreign matter such as iron, cement and even bricks have been found imbedded in it.

In view of these facts I would strongly advise you not to be persuaded into paying more for a yacht than you can afford, with the idea of selling the lead keel and substituting a cheaper iron one. You must remember that before you can sell the lead, the keel must be removed and cut up into pigs of suitable size. This will cost a considerable sum for labour, and when you come to sell it you will have to accept less than the market price on account of the small quantity you have for disposal. Moreover, if you remove the lead keel and substitute an iron one, the latter will have to be specially cast and by the time it has been fitted it will probably have cost you nearly as much as you obtained for your lead. And it is more than likely that you will have quite spoilt the sailing qualities of the yacht.

Should the yacht you contemplate buying be lying at a port far distant from your home waters, you will have to consider the cost of getting her round the coast. You should make your offer for delivery at your headquarters and then the cost of the trip will fall to the vendor. If, however, you have to take delivery at the port where she is lying, you must reckon the expense of the trip as part of the purchase price and it will be necessary to get an estimate for the job. Probably the cheapest and most expeditious method will be to have her brought round on the deck of a steamer, if there is a line of cargo boats running between the two ports. If not, you must either sail her round yourself or pay men to do it for you. Should you adopt the latter course, make a contract for a fixed sum for the job and do not agree to pay the men so much a day whilst they are on the journey, for if you do, the passage is likely to be a very long one. I remember an instance in which an East Coast yachtsman bought a small craft at a Welsh port and engaged a couple of watermen to sail her round at so much per day. The season was half over ere she arrived at her destination and the cost of the boat had been increased by nearly 50 per cent. If the men know that they will only receive a certain agreed sum, they will not waste more time than they can help, as they will be only too anxious to get back home and resume their ordinary work.

There is one more word of warning that I must give before leaving this subject, and that is, don't be prevailed upon to pay the men you hire in advance. Many years ago I engaged a fisherman, who owned an old smack, to take some gear for me from Burnham to Hole Haven. I foolishly consented to pay him in advance as he said that he had to buy things for the trip. I saw nothing more of the man or my gear for three weeks, and I had almost given him up as lost, when he quietly sailed into the Haven. It appeared that, feeling thirsty en route, he had stepped ashore at Foulness for a drop of beer. He apparently found it so good that he stayed there until his money gave out. The ultimate result was that I had to give him a few shillings more to take him home again.

We have now come to the final stage of the deal, when the agreed purchase price is paid over to the vendor and delivery taken of the yacht. If she is a registered vessel certain formalities must be complied with. But perhaps it will be as well to mention that when I speak of a 'registered vessel' I mean one that has been registered at the Custom House. Many yachtsmen seem to think that a 'registered' yacht is one whose name appears in Lloyd's Register of Yachts, but that is not the case. That book is merely a work of reference, compiled from particulars furnished by the owners of the yachts, whilst the Custom House Register is the official register of ownership. A vessel's Certificate of Registry is a kind of title deed and consequently a document of value. As, in the eyes of the law, the person whose name appears in the Custom House Register is the owner of the vessel, you must take care to obtain from the seller the Certificate of Registry and a Bill of Sale, executed on the proper form provided by the Custom House. These documents will enable you to get the yacht registered in your name and you will be safe in paying over the agreed purchase price against their delivery. You may ask "How am I to know whether she is a registered vessel or not?" Well, look at her main beam and if you see carved on it a number and her tonnage, you will know that she has been registered and should demand the papers to which you are entitled. Having obtained the Certificate of Registry and Bill of Sale, you must send them to the Registrar of Shipping at the Custom House at her port of registry, together with the prescribed fee, which, if my memory be not at fault, is two shillings and elevenpence. These documents must be accompanied by a

Declaration of Ownership, executed by you on the proper form and signed in the presence of a magistrate or a commissioner for oaths. In due course you will receive from the Registrar a notification that the change of ownership has been made in the register. At the same time he will return to you the Bill of Sale and the Certificate of Registry, with the change of ownership duly endorsed on it.

You may ask what advantages, if any, are derived from registration if it is optional in the case of small craft under 15 tons. Well, if you visit a foreign port the possession of proper papers will save you a good deal of trouble, as they establish the identity of the yacht and you as the owner. Then it will enable you to obtain an Admiralty Warrant to fly the blue, or other special ensign, if you belong to a club possessing the Admiralty Warrant. But the mere fact of being a member of a club holding the Admiralty Warrant is not in itself sufficient to entitle you to fly the special ensign. You must also obtain, through the secretary of the club, an individual warrant for your own craft, which is only granted to the owner of a registered yacht, who is a British subject and sole owner, or whose partners are also members of the club.

Then again, the owner of a registered yacht can in the event of a collision claim to have his liability limited to £8 a ton, or £15 a ton if there is loss of life. I always think there is an element of doubt about this, however, as it can only be claimed when the accident occurs without the owner's fault or privity. I do not see how the owner of a small yacht who is in charge, or at any rate on board, can very well fail to be privy to any accident that may occur. But the principal advantage of registration is that you are legally recognized as the owner. The only disadvantage of registration, apart from the trouble involved, is that if your boat is over 5 tons register you are liable for light dues. Even that cannot really be regarded as a disadvantage as most of us cheerfully pay these dues. We make use of the lightships, buoys, etc., round the coast and it is only fair and just that we should contribute towards their upkeep.

As the owner has to pay dock and harbour dues on his registered tonnage, it is usually his aim to get his vessel's tonnage registered as low as possible and if he knows the ropes, he can often secure considerable reductions. He may, for instance, get his cabin certified as a 'chart room' and the fo'c'sle as 'quarters for so many seamen.' I remember the case of a steam yacht of 89 tons Thames Measurement, whose registered tonnage was certified as only 11 tons. On the other hand, I know a cutter of 12 tons T.M. whose registered tonnage is a fraction over 12 tons. I think there must be a good deal of luck about it and the registered tonnage must depend very largely upon the mood of the surveyor and the persuasive powers of the owner.

In buying and selling vessels hard cash is the only legal tender, and the vendor would be quite within his rights if he declined to accept your cheque. This may make matters a little difficult if you are buying a boat at a distant port and it is not convenient for you to pay over the money personally. You will readily appreciate that the vendor will not feel disposed to part with documents that constitute his title-deeds against the cheque of a stranger, who may not have sufficient funds at his bank to meet it. You, on the other hand, will be equally unwilling to pay over hard cash in the absence of the papers. At a first glance this would suggest a deadlock, but, as a matter of fact, the difficulty is easily overcome. All you have to do is to remit the money to some responsible third party, say a bank, in the vendor's district, with instructions to pay over the amount to him against production of the yacht's Certificate of Registry and a properly executed Bill of Sale. The bank will, of course, charge a small commission for attending to the business.

Before leaving this subject, I must mention that in the event of a yacht being sold abroad, or to a foreigner who has not taken out naturalization papers, it is the duty of the vendor at once to notify the Registrar that the vessel has been sold out of the country and to send in the Certificate of Registry for cancellation. Should he fail to do this he renders himself liable to a heavy penalty.

If the yacht has been bought through the intermediary of a broker, he will attend to the transfer of the papers and the delivery of the vessel to the buyer without charge, as he will receive his commission from the seller. I believe the recognized brokerage for selling a yacht is 5 per cent, but understand that some brokers of an optimistic turn of mind sometimes ask as much as 10 per cent in the case of a small yacht of comparatively little value.

I am sometimes asked by potential owners whether I know any firm who would advance money to enable them to build or buy a yacht. I know of several such firms but am not going to recommend any of them, as I regard the system as rotten in principle and unsound financially. In the first place it is expensive, for no firm is likely to advance money for such a purpose unless it can make a reasonable profit out of it. The interest on the loan consequently adds considerably to the price of the yacht. But my chief objection to the system is that it encourages people to buy what they cannot afford and tempts them to accept financial obligations that they may not be able to meet. Most of those who have written to me on the subject are youngsters, who are apt to view such matters through rose-tinted glasses. To be able to get possession of a small yacht on payment of a comparatively small sum is no doubt attractive, and when we are young we are inclined to turn a Nelsonian eye upon the future. But if you have not sufficient money to buy a boat outright, it is unlikely that you have the means to keep her up when you have got her, even if you are able to pay the instalments regularly.

No, I am convinced that it is a bad principle, and if you adopt it, you will be living in advance of your income. Nobody can forecast the future; something unexpected may happen to prevent your paying the instalments, and in such a case you will lose your boat and incidentally a considerable sum of money, as no firm would advance more than threequarters of the value of the yacht. Besides, it is beastly to have an incubus of debt hanging over your head. I know that the mere thought that I was sailing a boat for which I had not paid would completely spoil my pleasure. But youngsters are apt to think 'sufficient for the day is the evil thereof' and don't look farther than the end of their noses.

As I write I have before me the prospectus of one of these firms – they call themselves bankers, but I call them moneylenders – and their terms I expect are much the same as those of others. They advance money either for building a new yacht or for the purchase of an old one, up to three-quarters of the value. That is their limit, but I rather fancy that when you came to borrow you would find that in your particular case the most that they would be prepared to advance would be two-thirds or less. The rates they charge, as stated in the prospectus, vary from 6 per cent to 9½ per cent per annum, according to the circumstances of each particular case, and you can bet your boots that in your case the rate will be on or near the 9½ per cent mark.

The yacht, whether a new or an old one, must be registered at the Custom House as a British vessel, the borrower having to pay the charges for measurement and registration, and that will cost him several pounds. Then he has to obtain from the Registrar of Shipping a certified copy of the entry in the Register. If she is a new yacht he must produce a certificate from the builder of her cost, or, if she is still under construction, furnish the lenders with the builder's estimate. If the borrower is buying an old yacht, he must have her surveyed and lodge with the lenders the surveyor's report and estimate of value, which will cost him a good deal to obtain. Then, whether the boat is a new or an old one, he must supply the lenders with a comprehensive policy, to the full value, issued by an approved insurance company. Finally, he must execute a mortgage deed in favour of the lenders. Apart from all these vexatious formalities, the expense of obtaining the Certificate of Registry, survey report and insurance policy will be heavy, and on top of that he will have to pay perhaps 9½ per cent per annum interest on the loan and at the same time arrange to pay it off in instalments.

It seems to me that a yacht bought on those lines is going to be a pretty expensive one and my advice to anyone contemplating borrowing money in that way is to have nothing to do with it. To pay up to 9½ per cent interest at a time when the joint-stock banks will only allow ½ per cent for money placed on deposit is so financially unsound that I cannot believe anyone of mature years and experience would consider such a proposition for a moment. It is the youngsters who are likely to be caught, and I hope my remarks will serve to open their eyes to the folly of buying what they cannot afford.

CHAPTER 11: *Building a Yacht*

When you bought your first yacht you no doubt thought that you would keep her for years, but it is extremely unlikely that you will do anything of the sort. As you gain experience, so will your ideas develop, and after a season or two you will begin to hanker after something larger, or more up-to-date. You have now reached the stage when you will be tempted to build the yacht of your dreams, and if your financial circumstances permit, there is no reason why you should not follow your inclination. You will get no end of pleasure out of planning your new ship and watching her grow under the builders' hands.

There is an old saying current among yachtsmen that 'fools build yachts for wise men to buy,' and in a financial sense at least there is an element of truth in it. I think I pointed out in a previous chapter that the depreciation of a second-hand yacht, that has been well kept up, is almost negligible, but in the case of a new yacht that does not apply. Depreciation, indeed, may be said to begin even before she leaves the ways, for she has been designed to suit the owner's own ideas, which are not necessarily the ideas of other yachtsmen. If you decide to build, therefore, you must resign yourself to some loss of capital when you come to dispose of her in the future.

If you have no knowledge of the science of yacht designing, you will probably concentrate on the vessel's internal accommodation and begin to plan the lay-out of the cabin. This you will find a fascinating occupation for the winter evenings, and as you sketch out the internal arrangement of your ship, ideas will crowd in on you, with the result that you may try to get into a 5-tonner the accommodation of a 10-tonner. On paper it will all look very attractive, but if you succeed in persuading the naval architect you employ to incorporate all your ideas in the design, it is likely that you will ultimately have a craft of such heavy displacement in proportion to her waterline length, that she will require a large area of sail to drive her, and even then be very slow.

A cruising yacht must always be something of a compromise. If you want great speed you must sacrifice comfort to get it, or if your desires lie in the direction of a fine roomy cabin, you must be content with less speed. You will be well advised to be guided by the expert knowledge of your designer, who knows far more about the matter than you. Sketch out your cabin plan by all means and submit it to the designer for his consideration. Should he think that what you suggest is not practicable, abide by his opinion and allow him to make such modifications as he deems necessary. If you insist upon all your ideas being incorporated in the design, he will no doubt follow your instructions, but do not blame him if the result is disappointing.

Two friends of mine once had a 7-tonner built and insisted upon the designer carrying out their ideas, which he did under protest. One of them was a married man who wished to take his wife away cruising, and so she also had a finger in the pie. Between them they planned a cabin which might reasonably have been described as 'a home from home,' as the boarding-house advertisements say. As there was obviously insufficient room below decks for a ladies' cabin, the cabin-top was extended several feet forward of the mast and the fo'c'sle turned into a state room for the lady. Considering 6 feet of headroom essential, they insisted upon the designer providing it, which he could only do by means of a coach-roof nearly 2 feet high. The accommodation scheme included such items as a pantry, cooking galley, lavatory, hanging cupboard for the lady's costumes, and a little dressing-table complete with mirror and the usual oddments that ladies consider necessary to their toilet. Round this 'home from home' the wretched draughtsman had to design a boat. The result was a hideous high-sided craft that was about the slowest thing out of Burnham. Needless to say they did not keep her long, and having cut a considerable loss, bought a boat that would sail, even if she lacked some of the home comforts they desired.

If you decide to build, therefore, do not attempt the impossible feat of putting a quart into a pint pot. Select a designer in whom you have confidence, tell him your ideas and leave it to him to incorporate as many of them as are practicable. Of course, there will be no harm in giving him your views as to type and rig, and you should also indicate the sort of sailing for which you want the boat.

If the yacht is to be a little boat of 4 or 5 tons, you will be wise to have her built with a cabin-top, as a flush deck is not a practicable proposition in any craft of less than 7 tons Thames Measurement. I have seen yachts of only 5 tons with flush decks, but I cannot say that they appealed to me very much. Such craft are certainly pleasing to the eye, but I cannot imagine that they are comfortable to live in.

In considering this question you must remember that your cabin will be a small apartment, measuring perhaps 8 feet by 7 feet, in which two or possibly three people will have to live, and it is obvious that you will want all the air and light that you can get. By means of a cabin-top you will be able to secure additional headroom, which is vital to comfort, and as the coamings will be fitted with port lights that can be opened at will, you obtain both light and fresh air. If, on the other hand, you have a flush deck, your only means of ventilation will be a small skylight, opening but a few inches, which must be kept closed when it rains, or if you are beating to windward in a rough sea. These tiny skylights, moreover, usually leak, even when closed, and to my mind are generally unsatisfactory. With a cabin-top you can always open some of the ventilating scuttles when it rains and thus keep the cabin reasonably aired. In yachts of 7 tons and upwards flush decks are quite a different proposition, as you can have the skylight mounted on a narrow cabin-trunk, with ventilating ports in the sides. The idea of a flush deck, of course, is to give you more deck room, but in a little boat of 4 or 5 tons I think the advantage is imaginary rather than real, as one can walk on a cabin-top just as well as on a deck and it is a quicker and safer way of going forward.

For a good many years past I have advocated in my books and articles the over-all type of cabin-top, or raised deck, but for a long time designers of small yachts would not entertain the idea. They contended that it was ugly and made for increased windage. I am glad to see, however, that at last some of them are coming round to my way of thinking and small craft with a raised deck, or over-all cabin-top, have of late made their appearance in ever-increasing numbers. Their diffidence in accepting this form of cabin-top has much surprised me, as its advantages are so obvious. The ordinary coach-roof is a source of weakness in a yacht, as from the main beam to the after end of the cockpit there is not a single through beam, the side-decks and coach-roof being supported by a few short beams between the shelf and carlines. I have long thought this a rather flimsy arrangement, and that it is so will be gathered from the fact that it is often found necessary to use tie-bolts or angle-irons to hold the structure together.

The object of a cabin-top is to increase the headroom in the cabin, but a coach-roof fails to provide the extra headroom where it is most needed, namely, over the bunks. In most small yachts of 5 tons or under, there is not sufficient headroom under the side-decks to enable one to sit under them, and unless one can do that and lean back against the side of the boat there can be no real comfort. As a rule in such craft, one has to sit on the edge of the bunk with the coaming cutting into the back of one's neck, and after a time that becomes little short of torture. Apart from that, all the space under the side-decks is wasted. Of course, an over-all cabin-top eliminates the side-decks, but what of that? They are of little practical use, for even when not cluttered up with spare spars and sweeps, they are too narrow to walk on with safety. Indeed, in my experience, they are seldom used for that purpose. When going forward, one walks over the cabin-top, as it is more convenient and safer. But walking on the cabin-top, if it is of the coach-roof variety, usually leads to trouble sooner or later.

I dare say you have noticed that when anyone walks on a cabin-top it gives slightly under his weight. When it does that what happens? Well, as the cabin-top is cambered to allow water to run off, the effect of its giving is slightly to force out the coamings, and the continual working loosens the caulking between the coaming and deck and causes leaks. Now, in the case of an over-all cabin-top, or raised deck, the sides of the vessel are carried up to take the place of coamings and the top is a firm structure, built upon through beams. It can be walked on with impunity and adds enormously to the strength of the boat. It increases the room in the cabin to a surprising extent and, even in a little cruiser of 2 or 3 tons, one can sit back comfortably against the side of the boat. It will also facilitate the fitting of such items of furniture as a galley and hanging clothes cupboard.

I had a lot of correspondence on this subject with the late Mr. Harrison But-ler. At first he was averse to the idea but was at last converted, and several of his last designs incorporated an over-all cabin-top, which he called a turret deck. But I never succeeded in converting him to the raised deck, which he thought unsightly. But if well designed it is not at all unsightly, and I know several small yachts with a raised deck which are extremely pleasing to the eye. But the raised sides must be of a different colour from the topsides, so that the natural sheer line of the yacht is clearly indicated. If of varnished teak, or mahogany, the raised deck will enhance the appearance of the yacht, but if painted the same colour as the topsides, she will have a 'boxy,' clumsy look.

The difference between an over-all cabin-top and a raised deck is that the former has a fore coaming, while in the latter the fore-deck is carried into the cabin-top, thus forming what is in effect a flush deck from the bow to the after bulkhead. The raised deck, in my opinion, is much neater and increases the headroom in the fo'c'sle. Some time ago I went on board the 3-ton *Sirius*, which has a very shapely raised deck, and was amazed at her cabin accommodation. Not only was the cabin roomy and comfortable, but there was sufficient space in the fo'c'sle for a pipe-cot. One advantage a cabin-top has over a flush deck is that you can have a large cabin door giving access to a roomy comfortable cock-pit. You are thus able to walk straight into the cabin instead of climbing down a companion hatchway. On wet days you can leave the cabin door open, except when the wind is against the tide, and thus get plenty of light and ventilation.

And now I should like to say a few words on the subject of cockpits. Flush decks are usually accompanied by a shallow cockpit, often of the self-draining order, and they are extremely uncomfortable. As one sits practically on the level of the deck, with nothing round one but a coaming a few inches high, there is nothing to lean against, and if you sit to leeward when steering you feel as if you are about to tumble overboard backwards. And you get no protection at all from the wind. It is the custom, too, with such cockpits for the headsail sheets to be belayed outside on deck, and in such a position it is impossible to exert much power on the sheets when getting them in. I am sure that these shallow self-draining cockpits are a mistake in small yachts. More often than not they let in more water than they let out, and I have known several craft in which the owners made a practice of stopping the outlet pipe with a cork when under way. Even when the pipe is fitted with a nonreturn valve, this trouble is sometimes experienced, as the valve does not always function as it should. The self-draining cockpit is supposed to be a safety device, but is it? Personally, I think it a source of danger, as it is possible for the helmsman to be washed overboard. That ac-tually happened some years ago to the helmsman of the little *Ahto II* when off Ushant in heavy weather, and had it not been for the fine seamanship of the owner, young Ahto Walter, he would have been drowned. A similar accident was only prevented at a later date by the helmsman being secured with a life-line.

As far as I can see, the only real advantage derived from a self-draining cockpit in a small yacht is that it keeps the rain out of the boat when at anchor in wet weather.

There can be no doubt that a deep roomy cockpit is a great comfort when cruising, as one can sit on a seat about the height of an ordinary chair from the floor and have a comfortable back to lean against. If affords adequate protection from wind and water and you can sit to leeward when steering without feeling that you are about to tumble overboard. You have plenty of room to work, and if the headsail sheets are led through holes in the coaming, they are just the right height to enable you to put all your weight and strength on them. If knotted, as they should be, the sheets can't get adrift and will always be ready to hand. The large cockpit, too, is a great convenience when at anchor, as it can be covered in on wet days by a tent spread over the boom, thus making in effect another cabin, in which you can dress, cook or wash-up. And it provides that privacy which is so desirable when one is brought up in a crowded anchorage or harbour.

I know that many yachtsmen consider a large cockpit dangerous, as they think a sea might be shipped in it with disastrous results, but the risk of such an incident is very remote if one's cruising is confined to comparatively short coastwise trips, such as most of us engage in. Although I have been sailing for sixty years, the number of times when I have shipped heavy water in the cockpit could be counted on the fingers of one hand. Of course, in comparatively large yachts it is possible to have a cockpit that is both deep and self-draining, but in the little ships which most of us own, I can see no advantage in a self-draining cockpit, other than keeping rainwater out of the boat.

If a yacht engages in ocean cruising it is, of course, desirable that there should be some means of keeping the water out of the boat in heavy weather, but that can be effected equally well by the use of a watertight cockpit of ordinary type. It could be made watertight by lining it with sheet lead, but an independent pump would have to be provided for throwing out the water should a sea be shipped in it.

The views of the late Mr. A. G. H. Macpherson on this subject are interesting. When sailing *Driac I* home from the Mediterranean he found the self-draining cockpit so unsatisfactory that on building that wonderful little ship *Driac II*, in which he subsequently sailed all over the world, covering some fifty thousand miles, he went in for a deep cockpit. "As I like comfort," he wrote, "and prefer to take the chance of filling up to being washed out of, or smashed up in, a shallow self-drainer, the cockpit is a real deep one, but bulkheaded off from the saloon except for the flap which opens into it. If occasionally a little H_2O paid a visit to the cockpit, a plunger pump is there to attend to the matter."

With regard to the internal lay-out of the yacht, it is a mistake to cut up the space too much. If the fo'c'sle be divided from the cabin at all, it should be by means of a curtain or, at the most, a half-bulkhead. Some small yachts have a complete fore-bulkhead, fitted with a sliding door, but the latter is so small that a man of generous proportions has difficulty in getting through it. In my experience the cabin of a small yacht fitted with a fore-bulkhead is invariably stuffy, and the only excuse for dividing the cabin from the fo'c'sle is the presence of ladies, or a paid hand. You may thus secure a certain amount of privacy but will certainly suffer from lack of ventilation. If the fo'c'sle is divided from the cabin with a curtain, the latter can be looped back to the side of the boat, and if the fore-hatch be opened, a free current of air can pass through the yacht and thoroughly ventilate the cabin. In the absence of ladies, a w.c. is quite unnecessary. A bucket serves the purpose equally well, takes up but little space and is infinitely more sanitary. But for comfort you should have a loose seat that can be placed on top of the bucket. It must be remembered that the space below decks in a small cruiser is strictly limited, and if you have an enclosed w.c. you will probably not have room for a cooking galley and other desirable things.

If you do not have to study expense, you will be well advised to go to a leading firm, as you can then rely upon getting the very best that money can buy. British yacht-builders have a worldwide reputation for high-class workmanship, and the leading firms build up to a quality standard and not down to a price. Such construction is, of course, very expensive and beyond the means of the man with a comparatively small income. But there are lots of smaller firms who will build you a boat that will serve your purpose at a far lower price. She may not be constructed of such expensive materials or be so superbly finished, but there is no reason why she should not be strong and seaworthy.

A considerable saving can be effected by the use of an iron keel, which in some respects is preferable to lead in a cruising yacht. An iron keel makes for strength and is not so likely to be damaged should the yacht run aground on a rocky shore. I have always thought a lead keel an unnecessary extravagance in a small cruising vessel, and personally I should never have anything but an iron keel in such a craft. Of course, with lead the weight is kept lower and less of it is required to obtain the necessary stability, but as speed is not so important in a cruiser as in a racing yacht, I do not think it worth the extra expense. If the keel is of lead, yellow metal bolts must be used and they are expensive. If iron bolts were employed to fasten a lead keel they would soon be corroded by galvanic action. But if the yacht had steel floors, as some do, the yellow metal bolts would corrode the floors, as those metals are as bad shipmates as lead and iron. I remember the case of a racing yacht only two years old having to have new steel floors, as the original ones were so badly corroded by contact with the metal keel bolts! By the use of an iron keel such troubles are eliminated, as the bolts can be of iron, which will not be antagonistic to the steel floors. But in the case of inside ballast, I think lead worth the extra expense, as it takes up less room and tends to keep the bilge sweet and clean. Iron, even when coated with black varnish, soon rusts and makes for a dirty bilge.

With regard to the materials used in the construction of your yacht, much will depend upon the price you are prepared to pay. If cost is not of importance to you, I would recommend teak for the planking and decks, as it will last for a lifetime. Teak has a natural oil in it which prevents its shrinking or swelling, so it is an ideal wood for shipbuilding. But there is teak and teak, and the best, which I believe comes from Rangoon, is very expensive. If you can't afford teak, I would suggest pitch-pine planking, which is very durable and comparatively cheap. I know a yacht nearly fifty years old planked with pitch-pine and a recent survey showed her to be still as sound as the proverbial bell. Another good wood for planking, which comes midway between teak and pitch-pine in cost, is Honduras mahogany. Oak is pretty nearly as durable as teak, if cut in the autumn, but is apt to crack under the heat of the sun. Elm is cheap but unsuitable for planking, as when constantly wet and dry it is liable to rot, but is excellent for keels.

For timbers, crooks and knees, oak takes a lot of beating, but if the timbers are to be steamed, Canadian rock elm is perhaps better as it is more pliable. For stem, stern-post and floor timbers oak cannot be surpassed. Cedar is a nice wood for cabin lockers as it always smells sweet, but is unsuitable for planking on account of its absorbency. Uffa Fox, in one of his books, quotes the case of two dinghies, one planked with Honduras mahogany and the other with cedar. The planking of the cedar boat was $1/16$ inch thicker than the mahogany one and she weighed 8 lb. less, but after a few days sailing the cedar dinghy weighed 12 lb. more. If I were having a yacht built and did not have to study expense, my specification would include elm or oak for the keel, oak stem and stern-post, oak floor timbers, oak or Canadian rock elm frames and teak planking, decks, fittings and floorboards.

It is of the first importance that the wood used in yacht-building should be thoroughly seasoned, otherwise the vessel may be attacked by dry rot in a very few years. I remember a 10-ton cutter at Burnham which had to be entirely re-planked when only two years old! But seasoning by natural process takes a long time and, as the supply was practically exhausted during the war, I am afraid that builders will have to use kiln-dried timber for some years to come. The timber merchant, no doubt, will say that it is just as good, but I doubt whether yachts built of kiln-dried wood will last as long as those produced in the past.

A certain amount of money could be saved by having the vessel iron-fastened, but I don't think such fastenings suitable for yachts. I do not suggest that they are not durable, because many smacks thus fastened have lasted for fifty years and more.

But sooner or later they will rust and the vessel become what is termed 'nail-sick' and begin to leak. Rust-stains in a yacht, moreover, are very unsightly and if painted over soon reappear. Of course, the difference in cost between copper and iron nails is not very great, in the case of a small yacht, but the labour involved in copper fastening is very much greater. Galvanized nails can be driven, but those of copper are too soft for such treatment. A hole has first to be bored and the nail subsequently clenched over a copper roove, which of course takes a lot of time.

Builders persist in using galvanized chain and runner plates, but even if it costs a little more, it will be better to specify chain-plates of stainless steel, or some other non-rusting metal. Iron chainplates rust on the inside and the top-sides of the yacht are disfigured by unsightly stains. Nothing spoils the appearance of an otherwise smart yacht more than brown streaks below the chain-plates, but if iron is used for that purpose, they cannot be prevented, unless, of course, you have the chainplates taken off and re-galvanized from time to time.

The best time to order a new yacht is in the summer, or early autumn, when the yards are slack. At that season the firm will probably be content to accept a comparatively low price, as they are glad of the work to keep their hands employed. If you defer placing the order until after Christmas, prices are likely to rule higher and it is probable that the yacht will not be ready in time for the opening of the season. In the early months of the year most yacht-building yards are working at high pressure with new construction, repairs and fitting out, and if orders for racing craft are plentiful, it is possible that work on your little cruiser may be stopped for a time. If possible, you should see that there is a penalty clause in the contract to compensate you for late delivery, or, failing that, you should reserve the right to cancel the order if the vessel is not delivered on or before a specified date. A third of the contract price must be paid on signing the contract, a third when the yacht is planked up and the balance against delivery.

The designer's fee may be anything from 5 to 10 per cent on the contract price of the yacht, and he should supervise her construction. If she is to be built to a Lloyd's class, she must be constructed in accordance with their rules and scant-ling tables, and to the satisfaction of their surveyor. These rules, together with a scale of fees, can be obtained on application to the Secretary of Lloyd's Register, 71 Fenchurch Street, London, EC3.

If the yacht is to be registered, notice must be given to the Custom House, when she is completed, or approaching completion. An official measurer will then be sent to measure her and on payment of the prescribed fee, a carving order will be issued. The registered tonnage of the vessel and her official number must then be carved on her main beam. By the way, the tonnage must be indicated in tons and hundredths of a ton. I once had the tonnage carved as 3.63 tons and they would not pass it. I had to have it cut out and re-carved as $3\,{}^{63}/_{100}$ tons.

I would advise you to make the specification as comprehensive as possible, including every item of which you can think, and then strictly adhere to it. Yacht-builders thrive on 'extras,' and it is astonishing how they mount up if you don't keep a jealous eye on them. Any departure from the original specification, no matter how small, will rank as an extra, and a few trivial alterations from the original scheme may add pounds to the cost of the yacht. Although the designer is responsible for superintending the construction, I would advise you to visit the yacht yourself from time to time. You may not know much about the job from a technical point of view, but you will find it most interesting to watch your little ship growing. At first, progress will seem slow, but you must remember that much preliminary work has to be done. When she is in frame you will be able to form some idea as to what she will look like when completed. Your greatest interest will be aroused, however, when she reaches the planking-up stage, for you will see her suddenly develop from a mere skeleton into a real boat, and will probably get the impression that she is approaching completion. Not a bit of it. She is still in a comparatively early stage of construction and you will have to possess your soul in patience for a good many weeks ere she is ready to take her first plunge into her natural element.

A Yarn

❧

Wave's First Cruise

The first pocket cruiser I ever owned was, like the servant girl's baby in Captain Marryat's novel, 'only a little one,' being in fact but little more than a large dinghy. That was away back in the 'nineties, when as an impecunious youngster I had to buy not what I should like but what I could afford, which incidentally was precious little. I gave but £10 for her, and even that insignificant sum, I remember, had to be paid in two instalments. During the two years or more that I owned her she provided me with no end of fun, although on one occasion she gave me about the worst fright of my life. That was when I got ashore on the Buxey Sand one night in February, in a fresh breeze accompanied by driving sleet and rain – but I have told that story elsewhere.

I admit that *Wave's* appearance was not particularly prepossessing, and one evening at the Royal Corinthian Yacht Club, when, in the course of a lantern lecture, her photograph was shown on the screen, it was greeted with ribald laughter. But I did not care a hoot, because I knew that my 'little old tore-out' provided me with a good deal more sailing than most of their 'spit and polish' boats. And what was more, she had saved the lives of men, which they had never done. She had belonged to a collier brig which was wrecked one wild winter's night on the Gunfleet sands, and it was in this little boat that the crew got ashore. She was subsequently bought for the proverbial song by a working man, who fitted her with a false keel and built a tiny cabin. It was from him that I bought her, and that I got good value for my money will be gathered from the fact that in one season I sailed upwards of 1,200 miles in her.

Wave was only 16ft. long by 5ft. 2in. beam and her draught rather less than 2ft. The work of conversion had been very roughly carried out and nothing done but that which was absolutely necessary. The keel was merely an unshaped plank and most of the original thwarts were left in her. She had been 'riz on,' as the East Coast longshoremen say, and with the aid of a coachroof, the little cabin afforded just sufficient headroom to sit up on a bunk placed about 2in. from the floor. From the cabin bulkhead to the transom she was quite open. The mast was stepped through one of the thwarts, while another thwart across the doorway made it rather difficult to get in and out of the cabin. She was clinker built of larch and painted white, with a broad black topstrake. Sloop-rigged, her mainsail was old and dirty, and in light weather I set a small topsail that I had made myself. No! *Wave* definitely was not a smart yacht, but she was sound and made very little water. She sailed a good deal better than her appearance suggested and was an extraordinarily buoyant little sea boat.

Turning over the spray-stained pages of logs compiled forty years ago, I am able to remember the incidents recorded therein as if they had happened yesterday. In those carelessly scribbled notes, not always legible, I read of days of balmy breeze and brilliant sunshine when it was good to be alive, and of others when a biting north-easter chilled one to the marrow, that were not so good. Looking back down the vista of the years, I am inclined to think that was the best time of my life. I lived at Fambridge with three friends, who were brothers and old school-fellows of mine. We lodged at the Ferry Boat Inn, then kept by a retired barge skipper and his wife. We paid but twelve shillings a week each for our board and lodging, and our hostess fed us like fighting cocks; but, of course, in those days money would buy about twice as much as it does now. It is true that we spent three hours a day in the train going backwards and forwards to the City, but it was worth it, as we could sail and bathe in the evening and usually slept in our boats.

Hugh, the youngest of these boys, accompanied me when I set sail from Fambridge on my first cruise in *Wave*. As there was only one bunk in the cabin I procured a 'donkey's breakfast' for him to sleep on. This was spread on the floor at night and lashed to the side of the boat during the daytime. The other appointments of the cabin were equally Spartan, as the only stowage accommodation consisted of a box under the thwart in the cockpit and another in the cabin, which also served as a table. Our cooking equipment comprised a Primus stove, kettle and frying-pan, and we each had a knife, fork and spoon, enamelled plate and mug and an egg-cup. The cabin was lit at night by a tin lamp attached to the mast and a hurricane lantern served as a riding-light. I had arranged to cruise with my brother, who had recently sailed his canoe-yawl *Norah Creina* from Teddington to the Crouch. He had a fortnight's holiday and I three weeks, and we planned to go to Pin Mill. We had heard so much about the beauty of the Orwell that we had long wanted to visit those waters, but Pin Mill seemed a long way off and the passage in our little boats promised to be something of an adventure. However, we were determined to get there somehow, although I must confess that I had secret misgivings as to whether we should ever get back again.

The Saturday morning appointed for the start of our cruise was all that could be desired. I had slept on board overnight and turned out to find a thick mist, and the gear and decks wet with dew, sure signs of a fine day. By the time I had bathed and had breakfast, the sun had burst through the mist, which was rapidly dispersing, and a gentle breeze had filled in from the westward. When Hugh came on board an hour later, the breeze had strengthened sufficiently to carry us over the flood tide, so we wasted no time in getting under way. As we should have a fair wind down to Burnham, where we were to meet my brother, it seemed a favourable opportunity for setting the topsail. Owing to my lack of skill in the sailmaker's art, this homemade sail would not set for nuts on a wind, but when the breeze was aft it did good service and we used it quite a lot in the course of our cruise.

We brought up at Burnham for lunch and then went ashore to the club to wait for my brother, who was coming down from town. The Royal Corinthian Y.C. had a small timber-built club-house at the west end of the quay in those days, and a very jolly little place it was. There were comparatively few yachts at Burnham then – probably no more than a hundred – and most of the owners knew each other well, a fact that enhanced the social amenities. Burnham of to-day, with its fleet of a thousand yachts and palatial club-houses, may be the most popular yachting station in the kingdom, but for me it has lost most of its old charm and I seldom go ashore there now. When my brother arrived, we got under way and sailed down to the Roach, where we anchored near the coastguard ship *Frolic*. *Norah Creina* brought up close by and then sheared alongside of us and made fast. We often did this when the water was smooth, as it was more sociable, but of course had to part before the tide turned. On other occasions *Norah Creina* moored to *Wave* and we both rode to my anchor; we were thus able to join forces in the preparation of our evening meal. Presently we were joined by several other craft from Burnham and Fambridge, this being a favourite Saturday night anchorage at that time. There were often forty or fifty yachts brought up in Key Reach, but now one seldom sees more than eight or ten. I suppose the introduction of the auxiliary engine has enabled them to get further afield on Saturday afternoon; or is it that the owners are unable to resist the temptation of the social amenities ashore?

When we turned out the next morning at 6.30 a.m. we found an unpleasant cold day with a light breeze from north-east, the wind having chopped right round during the night out of pure cussedness. It seemed very certain that we should not be able to get to Harwich, so we decided to go to West Mersea and spend a day or two exploring the Blackwater, where none of us had been before. It was nearly eight o'clock before we were ready to start, and by then the wind had backed to the north. There was not much of it, but a few boards took us clear of Branklet Spit and we were then able to fetch down the Crouch. The breeze carried us to the Fishery Beacon and then it died away completely, leaving us becalmed. For the best part of an hour we drifted and then, just as we were debating whether we should turn back, a fine north-easterly breeze filled in and we were soon making good progress beating through the 'Raysan.' The breeze, however, knocked up a short sea, which made my brother very wet, but with the cover on the well he managed to keep his gear dry. Then it came over hazy and we lost sight of both the Fishery and Buxey beacons, and a little later *Norah Creina*, which had worked out a long lead, was also obscured. For a time we were in doubt as to our position, but presently the sun broke through and dispersed the mist and we could see Sales Point and the entrance to the Blackwater. With the aid of my glasses I also located a barn-like structure that I took to be St. Peter's-on-the-Wall, which at that time was actually in use as a barn, although it has since been reconsecrated and reverted to its legitimate function as a church. St. Peter's-on-the-Wall is all that remains of the ancient city of Othona, which now lies buried beneath the sea. It is said that at exceptionally low tides the founda-tions of the old Roman and Saxon buildings are ex-posed, but I have never come across anyone who has actually seen them. The church, or chapel, was built by the Saxon missionary Bishop Cedd in the seventh century, and is perhaps the oldest church in England in which services are still held.

There was more east in the wind now and we could lay our course to West Mersea, which was per-haps as well, as the flood tide was beginning to gather strength. *Norah Creina*, which had been a long way ahead, now ran back to us and we had a slashing sail in close company across the estuary of the Blackwa-ter. With the aid of the lead we managed to find our way into the Besom Fleet and brought up close by the church and King's hard. In the light of the westering sun West Mersea looked charming, with its square church tower backed by fine old trees, and that first impression was not belied when we went ashore. The cultivation of oysters was, and still is, the staple indus-try, and a long line of smacks at anchor extended up the creek. There were very few yachts and they were lying in another creek, which we subsequently learnt was known as the Thornfleet. But West Mersea has now, like Burnham, be-come a popular yachting station and is so crowded in these days that it is impossible for a visiting craft to find a clear berth, except in the Quarters, or Deeps, at a considerable distance from a landing hard.

Nass Beacon

After tea, we got a lad from one of the smacks to put us ashore, where we visited the White Hart Inn and did some shopping. Then we strolled down to the old village, which curiously enough is known as Mersea City. The road from the church, which stands on high ground, to the city runs by the side of the creek, affording a fine view of the estuary. And what a glorious stretch of sailing water it is; deep and clear as crystal and nearly two miles wide. There is no other river on the East Coast to compare with it from a yachting point of view, but when the wind blows strong against the tide it can be pretty rough for a little ship. At the city we discovered the old Victory inn, of which I had read in Baring Gould's *Mehalah*, where an old fisherman told us smuggling yarns over a glass of beer. When we returned on board, the sun was setting in a blaze of glory over Tiptree Heath and we lost no time in preparing our somewhat belated dinner. Before turning in we smoked a pipe in the cockpit and marvelled at the peace of our surroundings. West Mersea was shrouded in darkness, for its inhabitants, leading the simple life, had gone to bed and there was no sound but that of the lapping of the tide against the lands of our boat and the occasional plaintive cry of a curlew. We decided that West Mersea was one of the most charming spots we had ever visited, an opinion I hold to this day.

We awoke the next morning to find a lovely sunny day with a moderate north-easterly breeze, but as the wind was foul for going to Pin Mill we decided to run up the river and see something of the upper reaches of the Blackwater. As there was no hurry, we took our time over breakfast and it was nearly ten o'clock before we got under way. We both got out of the creek without trouble, although *Norah Creina*, which drew more water than *Wave*, once touched the mud, but she dragged her bulb through it and got clear. Having reached deep water, we bore up and ran up the river over the tide. The Blackwater was looking its best that morning. The water was of a bottle-green hue, flecked with white horses, and there was enough sea to make sailing exhilarating. On our port bow we could see the masts of craft in Bradwell Creek and away in the distance ahead was Osea Island, looking like an atoll in the Pacific, for the trees seemed to grow out of the water. The more we saw of the Blackwater, the better we liked it.

I had heard of the great Goldhanger flat but had no idea that it extended so far as it did. I consequently had something of a fright when, happening to look over the side, I saw the bottom. Promptly hauling our wind we went in search of deeper water, but when I hove the lead I found that there was more than a fathom. However, it was a warning and we stood farther out into the tideway. As we approached Osea Island we were surprised to see *Viper* anchored there, as she had sailed from Fambridge some days before, bound for Lowestoft. She was a 7-ton converted ship's life-boat, owned by Hugh's brothers, and like most boats of her type, would not sail to windward for nuts, as the saying goes. Meeting with foul winds, they had abandoned the idea of going to Lowestoft and run up the Blackwater. Although it was noon, the lazy blighters had only just finished breakfast, so we jilled about and waited while they got under way. Then we started to beat down the river in company with a view to finding a berth for the night in Bradwell Creek. The ebb had finished before we got there, but there was a fine breeze and we had no trouble in beating over the young flood. At this game we had no difficulty in beating *Viper*, but *Norah Creina*, of course, left us both far astern.

As she waited for us off the entrance to the creek, however, it fell to *Wave* to show the way in. The entrance is extremely intricate for a stranger as the narrow channel meanders through wide mud flats in the form of a letter S. As it was not long after low water, it was little more than a ditch, but as the mud was uncovered we managed to get in without running aground and brought up close to a smack that was riding to a mooring. This we subsequently found was one of the few berths where a boat can lie afloat at low water. *Norah Creina*, following close astern of us, was equally successful, but *Viper*, when she arrived, was not so fortunate and ran ashore twice. She, however, soon got off again as the tide was making, and brought up astern of us.

Bradwell Creek is a wonderfully snug berth, except perhaps at high water in a strong north-easterly wind, and one can land at any state of tide on a hard at the old quay. Ashore, the country is delightful, a special feature being an avenue of giant elms. The village is about a mile from the waterside, but in those days shopping facilities were poor. One could buy bread and other necessaries at the grocer's, but meat could only be procured on two days a week, when the butcher came over from Tillingham. After a shopping expedition ashore, we had tea and then I rowed over to the smack to pass the time of day with the old fisherman. He pointed out to me various leading marks for entering the creek and gave me a lot of other local information, of which I made notes when I returned to *Wave*. A fine leading mark was a tall tree, which one kept between the chimneys of a certain house; but it was cut down during the War and we have since had to find other guides.

For the next two days it blew hard from the north-east and we lay weather-bound in Bradwell Creek. Then the wind eased up a little, although still from the same quarter, and with a pair of reefs in the mainsail and the small jib, we beat across the Bench Head flat to Brightlingsea, getting nicely wet in the process. It was low water when we entered and, with vessels swung across the channel, there was precious little room. But we gradually worked up in short boards and anchored near the mouth of St. Osyth Creek. We had a rather checkered night, as several times I had to turn out in my pyjamas to fend off smacks that had come foul of us. That was no uncommon experience in those days, as there was then no harbour authority and the smacks brought up anywhere they fancied, without regard to the safety or convenience of small yachts. However, we managed to get to sleep at last and did not wake until eight o'clock. When I looked out I rejoiced to find that the north-east wind, which had persisted for so long, had at last changed. It was a cold grey morning, but there was a nice little breeze from the north, which seemed to give a fair chance of making Pin Mill. I therefore aroused my brother by throwing lumps of sugar at his boat and discussed the situation with him.

The conditions were certainly not ideal, but we thought we should be able to fetch most of the way through the Wallet and then pick up the young flood for the beat in to Harwich Harbour. Deciding that it was worth trying, we set about getting breakfast. *Viper*, which had brought up lower down the creek, had, we found, already left ❧

Part II: HEADQUARTERS

CHAPTER 12: *The Thames Estuary*

For those engaged in business, who have but little time to devote to yachting, the choice of headquarters is often something of a problem. That difficulty has been considerably enhanced of late years by the crowded state of the more popular anchorages, where it is now anything but easy to secure a berth for one's yacht within reasonable distance of a landing hard. The owner whose leisure is limited is loath to waste much of his all-too-short holiday in the train, and it is essential therefore that his yacht shall be stationed somewhere within easy access of town. But there are, of course, other considerations that must not be overlooked. It is desirable, for instance, that the anchorage he selects should have sufficient water at all states of tide to enable him to leave and return to his mooring at any hour that he wishes, and it must be sufficiently landlocked to afford adequate shelter from the elements. Then there is the financial side of the question. If his means are slender, he must choose a place where watermen's and shipwrights' charges are comparatively low.

The man of means and leisure is not faced by such difficulties and has a far wider range of choice. As time is not of much consequence to him, he can view with equanimity a railway journey that the week-end yachtsman would consider prohibitive; or, what is more likely, he will own a car and be independent of the railway altogether. In discussing this question, therefore, I shall confine my remarks to places within easy distance from London and suitable for the small yacht-owner who has but little leisure to devote to sport.

Thanks to improved railway facilities, the London yachtsman now has a fairly wide selection, but if a short journey and reasonable railway fare are matters of importance to him, he will naturally turn to the Thames Estuary and the East Coast, where there are numerous safe anchorages in tidal rivers and creeks, in which he can leave his vessel during the week in perfect security. Headquarters situated a few miles up a river are ideal for the week-end yachtsman, as he can be sure of getting a sail no matter how hard it may blow, but the anchorage should not be too far from the open sea or his cruising will be restricted.

The ideal anchorage, it seems to me, is one within easy reach of town on a railway system with a good service of trains and cheap fares. There should be a few good shops at which provisions and other necessaries may be bought, and efficient shipwrights and sailmakers whose charges are moderate. The anchorage should be situated away from traffic and where the tides are not unduly strong. It is, of course, desirable that the yacht shall be able to lie afloat at all states of tide, whilst a good hard for scrubbing purposes is essential. Shore attractions, such as a yacht club or a good hotel, cannot altogether be dispensed with, as the yachtsman sometimes requires a meal ashore, or perhaps to get his clothes dried after a 'dusting' at sea. There must, of course, be a good landing causeway available at all states of the tide, and if a dinghy can be left on the foreshore without fear of molestation by mischievous small boys, so much the better.

To discover a delectable haven possessing all these desiderata is wellnigh impossible; but by the exercise of a little discrimination, you will probably find a yachting centre that will fulfil your more immediate requirements. For those who can only get away from town from Saturday afternoon until the following Monday morning, the South Coast ports are rather too far afield. The Londoner's choice therefore usually falls upon some place in the Thames Estuary, or on the Essex and Suffolk coasts, and the tidal rivers that there abound afford capital sailing for small craft. Some fifty-five years ago, when I first commenced sailing regularly, the lower reaches of the Thames were the favourite venue, and at such places as Erith, Greenhithe, Gravesend, Grays, Hole Haven and Southend, a little fleet of yachts could always be found. Of late years, however, there has been a general exodus to places farther round the coast, such as Burnham-on-Crouch and Heybridge, of which the former has become a sort of Londoner's Cowes. The reason for this migration from the Thames is not difficult to understand. Owing to the enormous increase of steam tonnage, the London river has been rendered unsuitable for small yacht sailing. The never-ending procession of steamers has become a grave menace to the safety of small sailing craft, particularly after the shades of night have fallen, whilst the sails and gear of yachts are sullied by their smoke. Even in the early days of the Royal Corinthian Yacht Club, which was established at Erith in 1872, the Thames was anything but an Elysium for yachtsmen; but they made their headquarters there from necessity rather than choice, there being nowhere else within easy reach of London. But the extension of the Great Eastern Railway, as it was then called, to Burnham-on-Crouch opened up a new district of which they were not slow to take advantage. Since then Corinthian yachting has advanced by leaps and bounds. Few people realize what an important yachting centre Burnham has become. Just before the first world war some enterprising person, who apparently found time heavy on his hands, took a census of the sailing vessels lying in the anchorage at the height of the season, and the number of craft with masts reached the astounding total of upwards of 800, surely the largest pleasure fleet in the kingdom. Since then the number has increased and I think a thousand would be a conservative estimate. The anchorage extends for the best part of two miles and abreast the town the yachts are moored as thick as berries from shore to shore, with the exception of a narrow fairway on the south side of the river.

Although the increase of steam traffic was mainly responsible for driving yachts out of the Thames, there are other reasons why the lower reaches of the London river are not suitable for small craft. The tides run hard, and unless the yachtsman works them with judgment, he may not be able to get back to his mooring. To those who have business engagements which necessitate their catching a certain train that is a most important consideration. The mere thought of the possibility of missing the train home might be enough to mar the pleasure of the day. And these same tides may be responsible for more than mere inconvenience; they may be the means of placing the small boat sailor in a position of some peril. Should the little craft be caught in a strong wind down below the Nore, when wind and tide are unfavourable for her return, she has no alternative but to run for a distant port, as the average small cruising yacht has but little chance of beating over a Thames ebb, particularly when the tides are at the springs. This fact was brought home to me very forcibly many years ago, and as the incident was one of the closest calls I have ever had during my sailing career, I remember it well.

A young friend of mine had become the owner of a small boat, which was lying at Greenhithe, and as he had not had much experience he asked me to help him sail her round to Fambridge She was a little slip of a canoe-yawl, with about 9 inches of freeboard, and quite unsuitable for a trip round the Whitaker late in the year. Leaving Greenhithe one Saturday afternoon, we ran down to Hole Haven, where we passed the night ashore. When we went on board the next morning to resume our passage to the Crouch, there was a smart westerly breeze, but nothing to worry about, and so we got under way with light hearts. All went well until we were in the neighbourhood of the Maplin Lighthouse, and then the breeze began to pipe up. The tide was still ebbing hard, and as returning was out of the question there was nothing for it but to harden our hearts and face the music. Having stowed the mizzen, we pulled down a pair of reefs in the mainsail. A few minutes later a fierce squall of wind and rain caused us to tie down the last reef, and as we stormed along down Swin I wondered what would happen when we brought her on the wind to beat up the Whitaker Channel.

Although close reefed, the little yacht was over-canvassed when we came on the wind and as wet as a half-tide rock. She had a small lifting cabin-top, but it afforded but little protection, and quantities of water poured into the well. As there was no bailer on board, my friend cheerfully sacrificed his felt hat, and began bailing operations which were destined to extend over a period of some hours.

Then the flood began to make, and the tide meeting the wind knocked up a nasty short sea that threatened to swamp our craft. To add to our troubles, the boat began to work and leaked like a sieve. Despite my companion's vigorous bailing, the water soon rose above our ankles and our shore-going clothes washed out into the well as if in silent protest. On the Buxey side of the channel the yawl invariably missed stays, and I had to wear her every other board. Although we had a fair tide, we seemed to make no progress, and debated what we should do. If we turned tail and ran for it, it meant a trip to Harwich, as the boat would not have laid up for Brightlingsea, even had we succeeded in getting through the Wallet Spitway. With the yawl leaking like a basket, the prospect was not alluring, and so we decided to plug on to windward. I thought that if we could keep her afloat until there was water over the Buxey sands we might run across to Brightlingsea; but that if assumed larger proportions in my mind than I cared to think about. However, to cut a long story short, we ultimately succeeded in getting into the Crouch; but luck was the prime factor in the business. When the position seemed wellnigh hopeless, the wind suddenly backed to the southward, and we were able to make a long board on the port tack. This shift of wind also had the effect of smoothing the water, and although it blew harder than ever, we gradually drew in towards the land. We got into the Crouch none too soon, as we were both dead beat, and my friend's hat – our only bailer – was in the last stages of disintegration.

That trip convinced me once for all that the Thames Estuary is no place for little boats in any but the finest of summer weather, and I think owners of such craft have shown sound common sense in seeking headquarters in other districts. It is not that I have any particular prejudice against the Thames Estuary, as sailing in those waters has always had a peculiar fascination for me. Indeed, I often recall with pleasure the time when we made Hole Haven our headquarters and sailed about Sea Reach in old 'hookers,' which we pumped out in the dead of night, being ashamed of their leaking propensities. But that was in the golden days of youth, when all our geese were swans, and I doubt whether the few who are left of the old brigade would now care to brave the elements in the much-betingled 5-tonners, rescued from the knacker's yard, in which we enthusiastically served our apprenticeship to yachting.

It is, I think, essential that the week-end yachtsman, who has so little time to devote to his sport, should be able to go for a sail under almost any conditions of tide and weather, with a reasonable prospect of being able to return in time to catch his train home. In the Thames Estuary there is always some doubt about the matter, and, as I have pointed out, should the yachtsman be caught out in bad weather down below Southend, it is possible that he may have to run for a distant port and face an unpleasant, even perilous, experience ere he reaches a haven of refuge.

CHAPTER 13: *The Lower Thames*

Although the Thames above Gravesend has lost much of its popularity as a sailing ground for small craft of late years, a certain number of yachts are still stationed at such places as Erith, Greenhithe, Grays and Gravesend itself. Personally, I can see little attraction in those waters, as, apart from the everlasting procession of steamers, the smoke and dirt from numerous factories ashore and the vessels in the tideway sullies the sails and decks of yachts, while the congestion of traffic hampers their movements and menaces their safety. As, however, some owners still keep their craft in that part of the London river, probably from necessity rather than choice, I will give a few brief particulars of the places where yachts are stationed.

ERITH

Situated on the south side of the river, some sixteen miles from London, Erith was formerly the headquarters of the Royal Corinthian Yacht Club, which was established there in 1872. When the club migrated to Port Victoria, their old premises were taken over by the Erith Yacht Club, which continued to occupy them until a few years ago, when the club moved into its present premises. Erith has little to recommend it as a cruising centre, as a yacht has to cover something like thirty miles of the congested tideway before reaching open water. With an east wind and flood tide the yachtsman who sails from Erith cannot hope to get very far down the river, and when such conditions obtain he has no alternative but a trip in the direction of the metropolis.

Erith, however, is quickly reached from London, as there is a good service of electric trains, and there is plenty of water for a yacht to lie afloat at all states of tide. The anchorage is off the club, or off the old clubhouse, where water can be obtained by permission. There are good shopping facilities (early closing day, Thursday) and supplies of petrol and oil can be procured. The more convenient anchorage is that off the old clubhouse, as it is close to the station and shops, and the landing causeway is available at all states of tide.

Club: Erith Yacht Club, Entrance fee one guinea, annual subscription two guineas.

GREENHITHE

Although situated some five miles lower down the river on the same shore, most of the objections that attach to Erith as headquarters obtain at Greenhithe. It is, however, rather prettily situated, and Long Reach in the light of the westering sun has often struck me as quite charming on a summer's evening. There are frequent electric trains from London and bus services to neighbouring places. The best anchorages are astern of the training ship *Worcester* and near the causeway, just outside a buoy that marks the edge of the mud at low water. Good ground tackle is essential, as the holding is only moderate and the anchorage exposed to north-westerly winds, which blow straight down Long Reach. The local boat builders, Messrs. Tester Bros, take charge of yachts, and water can be obtained from a hydrant on the causeway, which is available at all states of tide. There are

adequate shopping facilities in the town (early closing day, Thursday) and supplies of petrol and oil can be obtained.

GRAYS

I believe that a few yachts are stationed at Grays, about a mile and a half below
Greenhithe on the north side. There is good anchorage to the eastward of the
training ship *Warspite*. Personally, I have anything but pleasant recollections
of Grays, where I once kept a boat for a short time, as almost every week when
I boarded her I found that something had been stolen. One foggy night nearly
every yacht on the station was broken into, the unwelcome visitors appropriat-
ing everything portable and much that could only be removed by force. As evidence of the brazen effrontery of these pirates I may mention that, not contented
with various articles of spare clothing and all the loose cabin gear, they lifted the
floorboards of my boat and extracted 11 cwt of lead ballast, which happened to
be in pigs of convenient size for portage. Their booty also included some tins of a
certain cheap brand of Irish stew from Chicago, which I had never had the pluck
to tackle myself, and I can only hope that they ate it. On another occasion some
courteous gentleman borrowed, without permission, my dinghy and I did not
see it again for a month, when I discovered it lying on the foreshore with the side
stove in. In consequence of these little amenities I took my boat away from Grays
and have never been there since.

GRAVESEND

Situated on the south side of the river abreast of Tilbury Fort, Gravesend is thirty-three miles from London Bridge. The anchorage is close in under the shore,
where the tide is comparatively slack. The safest place in which to leave a small
yacht during the owner's absence is in the Canal Basin, but, of course, one can
only get in and out of it at, or near, high water. Members of the Cruising Association, I believe, enjoy the privilege of keeping their yachts in the Canal Basin at
special rates, which are quite reasonable.

This is one of the busiest reaches in the London river, as it is here that the
Customs officers board inward-bound vessels. The Gravesend Sailing Club, established in 1894, is a sporting little club which promotes frequent handicap
races, and has a clubhouse pleasantly situated on the promenade. As Gravesend
is a town of considerable size, there are plenty of good shops, where anything
needed in the way of stores can be bought, and there are shipwrights and sailmakers. Gravesend would not be at all a bad place for yachting headquarters
were it not for the traffic and strong tides. It is sufficiently far down the river to
enable one to have a good sail, either towards London or seawards, according to
the tide.

The best anchorage for yachts is off the east end of the promenade, but as it
is usually very crowded, a yacht intending to stay for some time should go into

the Canal Basin, the entrance to which is close by. The Basin can be entered or left for about an hour on either side of high water. Of course, visiting yachts have to pay dock dues, but they are reasonable, and also a locking fee, which, if I remember rightly, is two shillings. Season tickets are issued to yachts permanently stationed in the Basin.

Yachtsmen can land at either the Town Pier or the Gravesend Causeway. Petrol and oil can be obtained in the town and water at the Terrace Pier. Early closing day is on Wednesday. There is a good train service from London and also a service of buses. A ferry plies between Gravesend and Tilbury.

Shipwrights:	G W Chaney & Co., F H Wells & Co., Brownfield and Parkinson Bros, and W D Inglis.
Club:	Gravesend Sailing Club. Entrance fee, one guinea; annual subscription, one guinea.

HOLE HAVEN

For ten miles below Gravesend there is not a single place in the London river where a small yacht can be stationed; but then we come to Hole Haven, on the Essex side, which in many respects is the best spot in the estuary for the purpose. Hole Haven is the entrance to the creek that runs round the back of Canvey Island, and there is good anchorage for small craft at all states of the tide. It is now more than half a century since I kept a boat there, but beyond the building of the Kynoch Hotel, the place does not seem to have changed very much since my day. Looking back down the vista of the years, I have nothing but pleasant recollections of sailing from Hole Haven, first as one of the syndicate which owned the *Two Sisters*, referred to in a previous chapter, and later as sole owner of a prehistoric 6-tonner. The Lobster Smack inn, commonly known as 'Becky's' in those days, was the feature of the place, and its fame for good fare having spread afar, it became the Mecca of all yachtsmen who sailed the waters of the Thames Estuary. On Saturday evenings, when the shades of night began to fall, small craft would follow one another into the Haven until the little creek was so congested that there was barely room for the yachts to swing clear of one another at the turn of the tide. Then, after stowing away the gear, the crews would repair to 'Becky's' to stow away a supper of wonderful home-cured ham and fresh eggs, to be followed by an impromptu concert. Should one feel disinclined to turn out into the night at closing time, one might climb up into a great four-poster bed and sleep like a prince beneath a canopy of the whitest curtains. We had great times in the Haven in those days, but for me they are beyond recall. 'Becky' died many years ago and I must be nearly the last survivor of the syndicate which owned the *Two Sisters*.

The resemblance of Hole Haven to Holland is very curious, but not, perhaps, altogether surprising when one comes to know its history. Early in the seventeenth century the island was in danger of being engulfed by the sea, when a Dutchman, one John Croppenburgh, offered to reclaim it on condition that he received a portion of the land as his remuneration. He brought over from Holland a number of his countrymen to assist him in carrying out the contract, and they built themselves little octagonal houses, after the Dutch fashion, and many subsequently settled on the island. John Croppenburgh did his work faithfully and well; the sea-walls he built are of great strength and look like standing for all time. The land reclaimed lies feet below the level of the sea, and is laced with deep dykes to carry off surplus water, and there are numerous little windmill pumps.

Since the days of Charles II, the Haven has been the venue, in this country of the Dutch *eel schuijts*, of which there are usually several lying in the creek. It is also the home of explosive hulks, and it is a common sight to see an outward-bound steamer brought up in the tideway taking in explosives from lighters. Hole Haven derives its name from the presence of a deep hole in the bed of the river, which causes a curious tide-rip. The surface here is never still, even on the calmest day, and outside the bar there is always a jabble of laughing water. There is another hole of a similar nature in the creek itself, about half a mile from the entrance, where a small island splits the channel, the soundings dropping from 4 to 23 feet in a few yards.

To a stranger the entrance to this delectable haven is somewhat of a trap, for at high tide it presents a wide expanse of water that invites a yacht to sail in with confidence. As a matter of fact, the entrance is extremely narrow, lying close along the island shore, where there is bold water. Perhaps the best spot to anchor is just above the first powder hulk, as the swell from passing steamers is not there felt to any appreciable extent. When sailing in or out of the creek it is advisable to keep a sharp look-out for several groynes of stones built out from the island shore, for they are rare traps for the unwary. I remember once piling up the *Two Sisters* on one of these and the receding tide left her perched up on top of the obstruction. Fearful that she might topple over, we passed the night on the sea-wall, not daring to venture on board until our vessel was once more water-borne. At low water spring tides there is barely 5 feet of water over the bar, but at the same condition of tide a vessel will find a fathom and a half inside the Haven.

There is plenty of good sailing to be had in the neighbourhood under almost any conditions of wind and tide. With a flood tide and easterly breeze one may run up the river to Gravesend and Greenhithe, and when the weather is suitable for a trip seawards, fine sailing may be had down below the Nore. Should you fancy a trip farther afield, it is an easy day's sail to Ramsgate, Burnham, the Blackwater, Brightlingsea, or Harwich. Those who are prevented by business engagements from joining their yachts until late on Saturday afternoon can sail across the river, through the Jenkin swatchway, to the Medway, where they can

Hole Haven, Benfleet and Leigh

bring up for the night at, say, Queenborough. On the Sunday they can enjoy a day's fine open-water sailing before returning to Hole Haven.

In the days when I sailed from the Haven one had to put up with many inconveniences. Unless one chartered a trap, which cost three or four shillings, one had to walk a matter of three miles across the island, no mean undertaking when laden with a bag and other luggage. And then there were no shops nearer than Benfleet and one had to carry all one's stores, except bread, to the Haven as best one might. Such articles as butter and meat, when wrapped in paper, do not travel well on a hot summer's day, and by the time we got our provisions on board they often looked anything but appetizing. Matters are nowadays much improved, as there is a service of motor-buses between Benfleet and Hole Haven. It is true that most of the buses go no farther than Canvey village, which is more than a mile short of the Haven, but some go right through to the Lobster Smack inn.

There is something indescribably jolly about sailing in the lower part of the Thames Estuary, and I can imagine nothing more exhilarating than a beat down Sea Reach with a weather-going tide. It is wet work, I grant you, but the strong tide sets the yacht over the ground so fast that it flatters her weatherliness and puts the helmsman in the best of tempers. To those who love the sea and ships the never-ending procession of passing vessels is fascinating in the extreme, as one sees craft of every type and nationality, whilst the red-brown sails of barges innumerable add a pleasing splash of colour to a scene that can never fail to delight the eye.

One can land at the causeway by the Lobster Smack inn or, if anchored higher up the creek, on one of the groynes. The nearest shops of any account are at Benfleet, more than three miles distant, although necessaries can be bought at Canvey village, which is about a mile and a half from Hole Haven. Permission to lay moorings must be obtained from the Port of London Authority and I understand that such permission is not readily granted. The nearest railway station is at Benfleet, and there is an excellent service to and from London.

BENFLEET

A few small craft, mostly sailing dinghies and half-decked boats, are stationed at Benfleet, round at the back of Canvey Island, but as there is only water there for about two hours on either side of high tide, and the creek is very narrow, these waters are not suitable for cruising yachts. There is a club there – the Benfleet Yacht Club – which promotes racing for dinghies and other small boats, besides making a feature of social entertainment. The annual subscription is only one guinea, and I understand that the club waterman looks after the members' boats without extra charge. The owner of a sailing dinghy could have a lot of fun when the tide served, pottering about in the creek. He could sail down to Leigh in under an hour, or to Hole Haven in about the same time, although the creek in the latter direction is much narrower. Benfleet is only about three-quarters of an hour's journey from London and has possibilities as a laying-up station for small yachts in the winter.

There are shopping facilities at Benfleet (early closing day, Wednesday) and the local shipwrights, H. Pask & Son, will take charge of a boat during the owner's absence.

Club: Benfleet Yacht Club. Annual subscription one guinea.

Chapman Lighthouse

CHAPTER 14: *Southend District*

LEIGH-ON-SEA

Proceeding seawards down the Estuary, the next place on the Essex shore where yachts are stationed is Leigh-on-Sea, the home of the Essex Yacht Club. The club is a very sporting institution which makes a feature of one-design and handicap racing. Established in 1890, this club has managed to flourish despite many natural disadvantages, of which the chief is lack of water. Yachts drawing 4 feet are only able to depart from or return to their moorings for about four hours at the top of the tide, and unless an owner keeps his craft out in the Ray, his vessel must take the ground every tide. At low water there is a wide expanse of hard mud, which I have no doubt the enterprising local house-agent would describe as sand.

In considering the possibilities of Leigh as headquarters let us first study the question from the point of view of the owner who has his moorings near the club. The tides only serve for leaving and returning to his moorings in the afternoon every other week, and unless he goes to the expense of having his craft laid off in the Ray in readiness for him, his sailing at alternate week-ends will be much curtailed. Then, his yacht, taking the ground every tide, is likely to be used as a playground by innumerable small boys when the tide is out. As one sinks into the black mud almost to the ankles when one walks on it, the state of the yacht when the aforesaid small boys have done with her will be readily imagined. This nuisance became so intolerable years ago that the yacht-owners clubbed together to employ a man to watch the boats at low tide, but I do not know if the practice is still continued. The fact of being able to walk out to the yachts on more or less terra firma opens up great opportunities for thieves to practise their profession during the dark hours of the night, and a prudent owner has no alternative but to take ashore everything of a portable nature when he leaves his boat. Although under normal conditions there is water at the moorings near the club for a craft drawing 4 feet 6 inches for about four hours at the top of the tide, there is often considerably less when strong southerly breezes obtain. The tides over the flats are slack and at high water excellent triangular courses can be laid off for small boat racing.

Should an owner elect to station his yacht out in the Ray, he can, to a large extent, overcome the lack of water difficulty, as he can use his mooring at any state of the tide. It is, I understand, possible to row a dinghy up the creek to the shore for about four hours on either side of high water, but on the last of the ebb and the young flood, there is no alternative but to walk across the flats. When one arrives on board after this pedestrian exercise, the footprints one leaves on deck are as clearly defined as those that startled Robinson Crusoe, and if the owner takes a pride in the appearance of his vessel, I am not sure that the effect on his mind is not equally disconcerting. Another objection to keeping a yacht in the Ray is the obligation of hoisting a riding light at night and in the owner's absence he has to pay someone to do it.

But apart from these natural disadvantages, the place has all the facilities that a yachtsman could desire. There is a fine train service, the railway fare is reasonable, and there are good shops, shipwrights, sailmakers, yacht-chandlers and every convenience. During the season the Essex YC in conjunction with the Westcliff and Southend clubs, hold a regatta week, at which some of the finest racing yachts afloat may be seen racing in the estuary. The good railway service – the journey from town only takes about fifty minutes – has attracted many sailing men to Leigh, where a large number of craft are stationed. They are, however, for the most part, small racing boats of the one-design order, for which the comparatively slack tide over the flats provides admirable racing courses. There are numerous shipwrights at Leigh and watermen to take charge of yachts in their owners' absence. Water, petrol and oil are readily obtainable and the shops near at hand (early closing day, Wednesday).

Clubs: The Essex Yacht Club. Entrance fee, two guineas; annual subscription, two guineas.
Leigh-on-Sea Sailing Club. Entrance fee, five shillings; annual subscription, twelve shillings and sixpence.

WESTCLIFF AND SOUTHEND

My remarks about Leigh-on-Sea apply for the most part to Westcliff and Southend, which are now merged into one great town. There is perhaps a little more water, and a craft drawing 4 feet 6 inches could lie afloat at her mooring for nearly three hours on either side of high tide. The principal clubs are the Westcliff, Nore and Alexandra, each of which has a clubhouse and gives frequent races for one-design and handicap classes. There is also inter-club racing, which has proved very popular.

The anchorage in this district is rather exposed to south and south-east winds, which knock up a nasty short sea in heavy weather. When such conditions obtain, a good deal of damage is sometimes done to small craft. There are a number of efficient shipwrights in the locality, but as facilities for hauling out yachts are rather inadequate, the larger vessels usually go to Burnham or Brightlingsea when extensive repairs are required. There is a fine train service, the journey taking only a few minutes longer than that to Leigh-on-Sea. Yachtsmen who sail from Southend have the benefit of two routes; from Fenchurch Street and Liverpool Street respectively. The former is rather the quicker but the latter perhaps more comfortable.

There are, of course, many good shops, both at Westcliff and Southend (early closing day, Wednesday), and every convenience that a yachtsman could desire, except lack of water near the shore. Yachts can lie afloat off the end of the pier, where one can land or embark at a charge of twopence per head, but the pier is a mile and a quarter long and the anchorage so far from the shore too exposed for small yachts to be left unattended for any length of time. An electric railway will convey one from the shore to the end of the pier for a small charge and water can be obtained on the pier at a charge of twopence per breaker.

Clubs: Alexandra Yacht Club. Annual subscriptions, three guineas, two guineas and one guinea.
Nore Yacht Club. Annual subscription, two guineas.
Westcliff Yacht Club. Entrance fee, one guinea; annual subscription, one guinea.

CHAPTER 15: *River Medway and The Swale*

PORT VICTORIA

Nearly opposite Southend, in the mouth of the Medway, is Port Victoria, at one time the headquarters of the Royal Corinthian Yacht Club. Although the club had a luxurious clubhouse, the place was never very popular with small yacht-owners, as the anchorage was too exposed. Small craft stationed there sometimes sank at their moorings, the tides ran hard and shopping facilities did not exist. It was, and I believe still is, a desolate spot, infested by mosquitoes of a virulent brand, which bite hard and often. The train service was very poor and I don't think it was with much regret that the Royal Corinthian Yacht Club abandoned their premises there and built their present fine clubhouse at Burnham-on-Crouch. I don't know whether any yachts are now stationed at Port Victoria and it has certainly nothing to recommend it as headquarters for small craft.

QUEENBOROUGH

Queenborough, on the opposite side of the Medway, affords a far more sheltered anchorage than Port Victoria, but as the mud uncovers for a considerable distance from the shore at low water, yachts should not anchor inside of a line between the pierhead and the red spherical buoy off the town causeway.

Care must also be taken not to bring up too far out in the tideway, as there is a lot of barge traffic. Many years ago I was run down in the night by a barge, while lying off Queenborough, and had my mast knocked out, a disconcerting incident I have not forgotten. The tides run hard, but the holding is fairly good. Harbour dues are charged if a yacht stays for more than one tide, the rate, if my memory be not at fault, being two shillings for a period not exceeding one week. I believe, however, that a yearly season ticket can be obtained at a very reasonable rate for a yacht permanently stationed there. Petrol and oil can be obtained in the town, where there are fair shopping facilities (early closing day, Wednesday). Yachts can be left in charge of a local waterman, from whom moorings can be hired.

GILLINGHAM

The best place on the Medway at which to station a small yacht is Gillingham, although it is rather a long way up the river. The anchorage is an excellent one and there is a landing pier and a convenient hard for scrubbing small craft. The anchorage is about ten minutes' walk from the station and there are shops near by (early closing day, Wednesday). Petrol and oil are obtainable and water from a hydrant on the dock quay. The train service is excellent, the best trains running up to town in a little over an hour.

For those who have to study economy, Gillingham seems particularly attractive, as I am told that the charge for looking after a small yacht is only about half a crown a week, or at any rate was before the war, and one can do one's own fitting out without interference. There are several local watermen who take charge of yachts and the railway fare from town is reasonable.

Club: Medway Cruising Club. Entrance fee, five shillings and ten
             shillings; annual subscription, twelve shillings.

CHATHAM, STROOD AND ROCHESTER

Although situated some thirteen miles up the Medway, a number of yachts are stationed at Chatham, Strood and Rochester, where four clubs are domiciled. Chatham is the home of the Royal Engineer Yacht Club, whose membership is, of course, confined to officers of the Royal Engineers. There are many cement works in the neighbourhood and the anchorage, near the Sun Pier, rather crowded. Water, petrol and oil are obtainable and there are shops of all descriptions (early closing day, Wednesday.) There is a good train service.

At Rochester, the yacht anchorage is above the bridges, on the Rochester side of the river. Owing to the bridges, Rochester is only suitable for small craft with lowering masts. The train service is good and the fare much the same as to Chatham. There are good shopping facilities (early closing day, Wednesday) and several shipwright firms and watermen to take charge of yachts.

Clubs: Royal Engineer Yacht Club. Annual subscription, ten shillings.
              Medway Yacht Club. Entrance fee, one guinea; annual
              subscription, one guinea and a half.
              Rochester Cruising Club. Entrance fee, ten shillings; annual
              subscription, one guinea.
              Maidstone and Upper Medway Cruising Club.

HARTY FERRY

Harty Ferry, in the East Swale, is a delightful anchorage for small yachts but unfortunately not very accessible. One has first to go by train to Faversham, then by bus to the village of Oare, from whence one has, to walk for a mile or more to the ferry and finally cross to the north side of the Swale. Although there is a good train service to Faversham, it would take the Londoner the best part of three hours to get on board his boat. But when once there, the anchorage is charming, as it is backed by a green hillside, dotted with little clumps of trees. It is, moreover, well sheltered from all except east to north-east winds, as it lies between a horse in the middle of the Swale and the shore. A small shop is attached to the inn, where such articles as butter, eggs and milk can be obtained, and the man at the inn will take charge of a yacht in the owner's absence. Of course, if you station your craft at Harty Ferry you will have to be a 'nose-bag' yachtsman and take most of your stores down from London, or purchase them at Faversham. One can land at the ferry, but, so far as I remember, the hard is one of the sea-boots order. There is a hard on which yachts can be scrubbed and repairs can be effected at Faversham, where, by the way, early closing day is Thursday.

WHITSTABLE

The chief objection to Whitstable as yachting headquarters is the lack of water. As at Southend, the foreshore dries out for a long way and a yacht has to take the ground every tide. The bottom, too, is neither one thing nor the other, for it is hard, with a thick coating of mud, and a yacht does not cut in. In the harbour, however, the mud is very soft, although it dries out at low water, and harbour dues have to be paid, according to the tonnage of the vessel. Water can be obtained from a hydrant on the quay. The railway station is close to the water and there is a good train service to and from town, the best trains taking about an hour and a half over the journey. Yachts may be left in charge of the local shipwrights, Messrs. Anderson, Rigden & Perkins.

Club: Whitstable Yacht Club. Entrance fee, ten shillings and sixpence, annual subscription, one guinea.

CHAPTER 16: *Rivers Crouch and Roach*

BURNHAM-ON-CROUCH

Since the migration from the Thames Estuary, the tidal rivers of Essex and Suffolk have become the most popular venue of the London yachtsman. That is not surprising, as they are comparatively easy of access and provide safe and convenient anchorage for small craft. Burnham-on-Crouch is nowadays a sort of East Coast Cowes, and if one gauged the importance of a yachting centre from the number of vessels stationed there, it would easily take first place. Formerly, Burnham was a sleepy little village, of which the staple industry was the cultivation of oysters, and prior to the opening of the branch line from Wickford to Southminster, about 1890, the nearest station was at Maldon, some ten miles away, and the only means of access the carrier's cart. Off the picturesque quay a small fleet of rather shapely smacks dredged over the oyster beds, whilst an occasional barge, with a stack on her deck, dropped down on the tide from the upper reaches of the river. In those days few people had even heard of the place and the yachts could almost have been counted on the fingers of one hand.

Now, Burnham is a thriving town, with yacht clubs, building yards, slipways, yacht-chandlers, stores, and in fact every requisite of a prosperous and popular

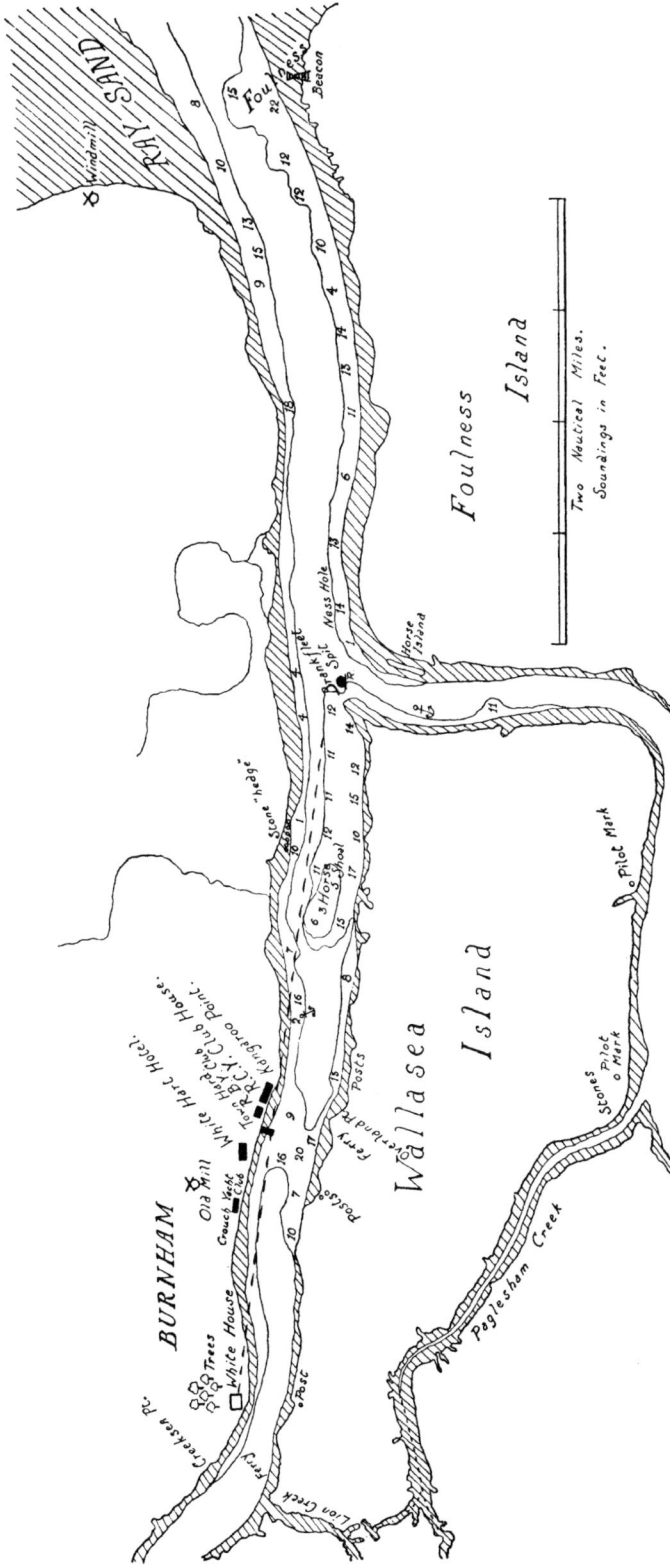

Burnham and the Lower Crouch

yachting resort. The anchorage is something at which to wonder. For more than a mile abreast the town yachts are moored so close together that there is barely room for them to swing clear of one another at the turn of the tide. Until comparatively recently the anchorage extended from shore to shore, but of late years a fairway about 100 yards wide has been maintained on the south side of the river. The yachts are for the most part small craft of under 20 tons, which leave their moorings only at the week-ends. For the rest of the week they are as the lilies of the field, for they toil not, neither do they spin.

My personal knowledge of the Crouch extends back to the beginning of the 'nineties, when after a miserable night spent at anchor in the neighbourhood of the Swin Middle Lightship, in a craft of more than doubtful seaworthiness, I one morning found my way into the river. I saw at once that here was the ideal yachting centre and have sailed from there ever since. At first I kept my boat at Burnham, but in 1895 moved farther up the river to Fambridge, which I have made my headquarters down to the present day. When I first came to the Crouch there were probably no more than twenty or thirty yachts stationed at Burnham, but its advantages soon became known and every season witnessed a large influx of new-comers. It has been estimated that at the height of the season there are now upwards of a thousand yachts on the station and it is difficult for a visiting vessel to find a berth within reasonable distance of a landing hard. But the whole river is a safe anchorage and if still more boats come to Burnham, as undoubtedly they will, further landing facilities are sure to be provided, for demand creates supply.

One of the best features of the Crouch is that blow high, blow low, the owner of a small yacht can always enjoy a good sail, for there are some twenty miles of good honest sailing water in the Crouch, and in addition there is its tributary the Roach, which is navigable at low water to Paglesham, and even farther on the tide. And there are few traps for the unwary. It is true that there is a bar at Creeksea and a horse below Burnham, but one soon gets to know where these obstructions are, and when a vessel runs aground on either, it is usually the result of sheer carelessness. Being situated but five miles from the mouth of the river, Burnham is within easy reach of the sea, and the cruising to be had in the neighbourhood is exceptionally good. One can sail round to the rivers Blackwater and Colne, or even farther afield to Harwich and Ipswich. Or if the owner prefers to direct his course to the southward, he can voyage round the Whitaker Spit to the Thames Estuary, across to the Medway and Swale, or outside the Island of Sheppey to Ramsgate.

Burnham is well provided with clubs, as it is the home of the Royal Corinthian YC, the Royal Burnham YC, the Crouch YC and the Burnham SC, the last mentioned having been established mainly for the benefit of the local watermen. The premier club is the Royal Corinthian, which has a palatial clubhouse at the east end of the quay. Although replete with every comfort and convenience, it is one of those modern buildings which suggest to my mind the work of a child

with a box of bricks and a meccano set, and situated at the end of that picturesque old-world quay, with its red buildings mellowed by time, it fairly hits me
in the eye every time I pass it. But that, of course, is only my personal opinion
and I have no use for what the rising generation is pleased to term art. As a matter of fact, the Royal Corinthian clubhouse is considered an exceptionally fine
building of its kind and, I believe, won for its architect a prize for the best design
of the year.

The Royal Corinthian YC is one of the most enterprising and progressive
yacht clubs in the kingdom and under the guidance of its Commodore, Mr. E. G.
Mitchell, has gone ahead in the most gratifying way of late years. It maintains
quite a number of racing classes, one design and otherwise, and every season
arranges a racing programme of gargantuan proportions. The Royal Corinthian,
believing in 'catching 'em young,' has sponsored a club for young boys and girls,
which is known as the Corinthian Otters. This club, however, is a separate entity,
managing its own affairs and having its own little clubhouse and hard. I often
see the youngsters sailing about in their little pram dinghies and sailing them
very well. Some are so young that one cannot help thinking that they occupied
prams of another kind not very long ago, but they all have to pass a swimming
test before being allowed to go afloat.

The Royal Burnham YC also has very comfortable premises and provides a
lot of racing. Their one-design class is perhaps the most popular in the district,
the boats, designed by Mr. Dallimore, being admirably suited to local conditions.

The Crouch YC, a very sporting institution, is mainly interested in cruising, but gives a good many handicap races in the course of the season and also
maintains a one-design class, for which races are provided almost every Saturday from Easter until September. One of this club's chief events is a race from
Burnham, round the Cork and Sunk Lightships and back, a distance of about
90 miles, which is said to be the longest race in the kingdom for craft manned
entirely by amateurs. The club has comfortable premises near the Coronation
hard, and close by is the clubhouse of the Burnham SC which gives races for the
local watermen and others on Wednesday afternoons.

Plenty of sport is thus provided for those whose fancy lies in the direction
of racing, and it should not be difficult for anyone to select a class to suit his
means. As the River Roach runs into the Crouch some miles below Burnham at a
right-angle, it is possible to lay off courses capable of testing the yachts on every
point of sailing, and every Saturday afternoon during the season, which opens
at Easter and lasts until the end of September the local waters are flecked with
the white sails of craft engaged in racing. In September all the clubs join forces
in the promotion of a great racing week, which has come to be regarded as an
outstanding event of the yachting season.

Burnham is well supplied with boat-builders, sailmakers, yacht-chandlers
and indeed everything that an owner can require. Many famous small racing

yachts have taken shape in Burnham yards and also some fine cruising vessels. There are slipways and adequate laying-up berths, and a crane capable of lifting a small yacht right over the sea-wall. There are also a number of reliable watermen to take charge of yachts in their owners' absence. There are good shops close to the water (early closing day, Wednesday) and water, petrol and oil are easily obtainable.

The best trains run down from town in a little over an hour, but it is a pity that there are not more through trains. In most cases one has to change at Wickford, which causes delay, but no doubt the train service will be improved in course of time. There are bus services from Burnham to Maldon, Witham, Southminster and Bradwell.

With a strong easterly or westerly wind against the tide the anchorage is inclined to be rather rough, but one can always find a quiet berth under such conditions by running up to Cliff Reach, or down to the Roach. The mouth of the Roach is a favourite anchorage, but does not seem to be used so much on Saturday nights as formerly. That is probably due to the advent of the auxiliary motor, which enables yachts to get farther afield; or it may possibly be due to enhanced amenities ashore.

Quite a number of owners live aboard their yachts during the summer months, going backwards and forwards to town every day. The cost of a season ticket is reasonable and, I believe, for a small additional payment it can be made available to and from Burnham, Maldon or Southend. Burnham station is about three-quarters of a mile from the quay, but a bus is available for the lazy.

Taking it all round, I know of no other place so suitable as headquarters for the London yachtsman. The anchorage, it must be admitted is now unduly crowded, but that is the only fly in the ointment, and if an owner desires a quieter berth, where there is more room for getting under way, he can find it higher up the river.

Clubs: Royal Corinthian Yacht Club. Entrance fee, three guineas; annual subscription, four guineas.
Royal Burnham Yacht Club. Entrance fee, two guineas; annual subscription, four guineas.
Crouch Yacht Club. Entrance fee, ten shillings and six pence; annual subscription, two guineas.
Burnham-on-Crouch Sailing Club. Annual subscription, five shillings; life membership, two pounds ten shillings.

CREEKSEA

Of late years the congested state of the anchorage at Burnham has driven some of the yachts up to Creeksea Ferry, about a mile above Burnham, and quite a fleet has now collected there. This is in some respects the pleasantest berth in

CREEKSEA

Ferry

20
20

The Cliff

Althorne Creek

24

20

16

18

12

Cliff Reach

18

9

Easter Reach

7

9

Canewdon
✝ Church

Bridgemarsh

Brick works

(disused) Island

8

20

18

15

Shortpole Reach

Great Breach

12

12

Longpole Reach

S. FAMBRIDGE

N. FAMBRIDGE

Tel. Cable

8

6

Ferry

Stow Creek

Landing

6

Brandy hole Reach

Clements Green Creek

Ferry

Quay

HULLBRIDGE

Three Nautical Miles.

Soundings in feet.

BATTLES—BRIDGE

Bridge

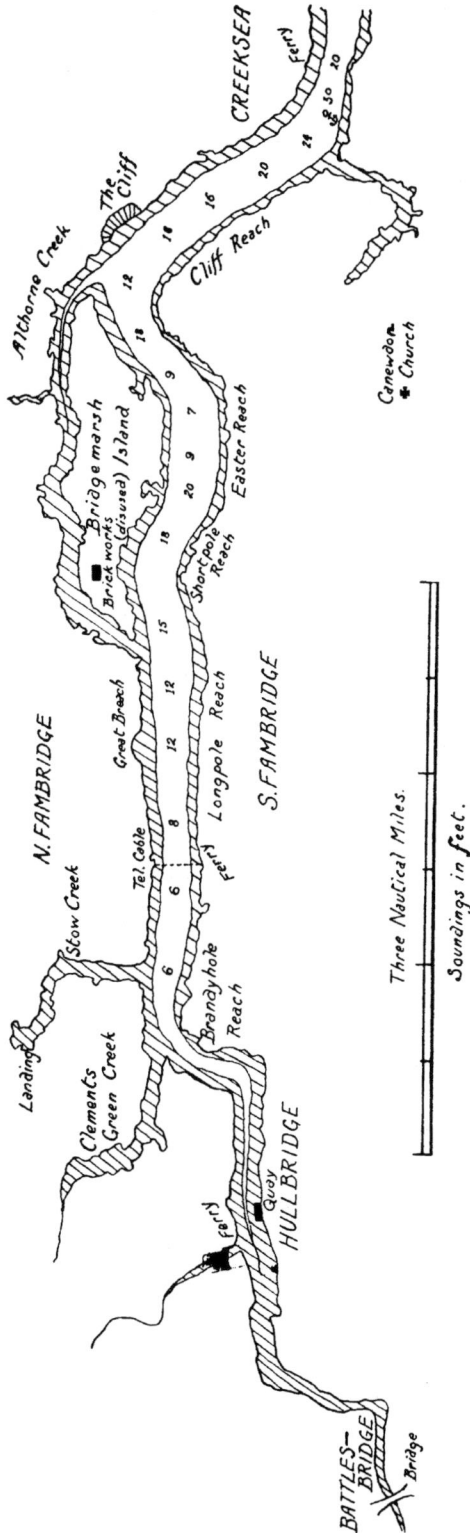

The Upper Crouch

the river, as the shore on the south side is steep-to and a yacht may lie within a few yards of the causeway. Cliff Reach, which derives its name from a rather picturesque wooded cliff on the north shore, lies northwest and south-east, and as the prevailing winds are off shore, yachts stationed there nearly always have a quiet berth.

A few years before the outbreak of the second World War, the place was developed as a yachting station, and a number of moorings were laid down, some just above the ferry, but mostly just below, in Wallasea Bay. There is an inn there and the hard is a fine one on which one can land at any state of tide. Yacht stores have been built and supplies of petrol, oil and water are available. There are, however, no shops, and provisions must be procured from Burnham or brought from town. Unfortunately Creeksea is not very accessible, being rather more than a mile from Burnham station, and as the anchorage is on the south side of the river, one has to cross by the ferry. If one has shopping to do, the best way is to go to Burnham and then take one of the motor-boats which ply between the town and Creeksea Ferry. Creeksea can also be reached via Southend, from where an occasional motor-bus runs to the ferry.

It seems to me that if some enterprising waterman were to establish himself there, there are possibilities of a yacht anchorage on the north side of the river, either just above the bar, or above Mr. Sabel's house. To my mind the latter is one of the most delightful spots on the river and being protected by Creeksea Bar, there is little or no tide on the flood. There is a fisherman's hard close by, and although of the sea-boots order, it could no doubt be improved. At the time I write the only yacht permanently stationed on that side of the river is Mr. Sabel's schooner *Daffodil*.

FAMBRIDGE

After Burnham, the most popular yachting station on the Crouch is at Fambridge, situated some seven miles higher up. I first discovered Fambridge in 1895 and was so struck with the place that I have never since kept a boat anywhere else. At that time there were only four other yachts stationed there, but others soon followed my example and in 1898 I was able to found the Fambridge Yacht Club, of which I was Honorary Secretary for many years. The club flourished until the outbreak of the Great War in 1914, when it was closed down, as nearly all of the members were on war service, and has never been revived.

One of the chief charms of Fambridge is that an owner can work on his boat without having to submit to the criticism of a crowd of loafers, and if he should need assistance there are plenty of other amateurs about to give him a hand. In the old days of the Fambridge YC one could have one's boat in a mud berth right alongside the clubhouse and work to one's heart's content. Many of the yachts are fitted out by their owners, and it is seldom that one walks along the saltings without seeing yachtsmen busily engaged in painting or renovating their craft in some way or other. Although Fambridge is some twelve miles from the sea, the river is about four hundred yards wide and there is more than a fathom of water at low water spring tides. And there is plenty of good sailing to be had. On a Saturday afternoon one can sail down to the Roach and bring up for the night in Key Reach. The following day a trip can be made down the Raysand or Whitaker channel, before returning to one's moorings. When wind and tide are right, one can go farther afield on Saturday afternoons, visiting such places as West Mersea, Bradwell and Brightlingsea, returning to Fambridge the following day.

It is possible for small craft to sail up the river as far as Battlesbridge on the tide, the upper reaches of the Crouch being not unlike the rivers of the Norfolk Broads. Fambridge, in my opinion, is a far better place for a novice than Burnham, as he has more room in which to practise the rudiments of seamanship. Provided that he has his moorings on the outskirts of the anchorage, he cannot very well come to much harm and the worst that is likely to befall him is a sojourn on the mud for a few hours, if he runs his craft ashore. And no better place for headquarters could be found by the owner who has to study economy, as the waterman's charges are extremely moderate.

The anchorage is on the north side of the river, although a few craft are now stationed on the south side. The train service is the same as that to Burnham, with the advantage that the journey to and from Fambridge takes nearly a quarter of an hour less time. There is a capital little shop near the water at North Fambridge, where one can obtain pretty well everything one wants, except meat, although one must order bread in advance. There is also an inn, where one can get a meal if desired.

We are fortunate in our waterman at Fambridge, for my old friend Mr. Flick is an honest conscientious man, who takes as much care of the yachts as if they were his own. He came up from Burnham as a lad in the late 'nineties to look after the few craft that were then stationed at Fambridge, and he has taken charge of all of my boats ever since. I may say that it has been his efficient and conscientious service more than anything else that has kept me at Fambridge for so long. Although there is no regular shipwright, one of W. King & Sons' men frequently comes up to do small repairs, while Flick keeps a large stock of yacht-chandlery and almost anything in the way of gear and fittings can be bought on the spot.

The main disadvantage of Fambridge as headquarters is its distance from the open sea, as one has to sail some twelve miles down the river before coming to Shore Ends. But splendid sailing can be had in the Rivers Crouch and Roach. Another objection is that the anchorage is apt to be rather rough when a strong wind blows against the tide. As Fambridge Reach is three miles long and lies east and west, there is a considerable drift to meet the prevailing westerly winds. I once rolled my decks under in a 7-tonner with a lot of freeboard when lying at my mooring; but, although uncomfortable at times, there is good holding ground and the anchorage a safe one. When such conditions obtain one can seek a quiet berth under a weather shore in Brandy Hole, about a mile and a half higher up the river, or by going down to Short Poles, or Cliff Reach.

HULLBRIDGE

A few small craft are kept at Hullbridge, some three miles above Fambridge. A small yachting station has been established there comparatively recently. The anchorage is a little way below Hullbridge, but there is not much water there and the boats have to take the ground at low water. There is a small club, and it would be a capital place at which to keep a sailing dinghy or half-decked boat. The station is at Woodham Ferrers, about a mile from the river.

PAGLESHAM

Paglesham, situated some four or five miles up the River Roach, has undoubted possibilities as a yachting centre, although at present it is not very easy of access. But demand usually creates supply, and if yachts assemble there in any numbers the present bus service from Rochford is sure to be improved. The worst feature of the place is the landing hard, which is rather muddy. A raised plank causeway has recently been erected, which has improved matters, but if you go ashore at high water and remain for some hours, you will have to push your dinghy for some distance over the muddy foreshore when you return. As a dozen or more yachts are already stationed at Paglesham, it must be assumed that their owners do not find the landing difficulties too bad. I feel sure that in the near future Paglesham will attain some measure of popularity as headquarters for small yachts, as it is one of the few places remaining on the East Coast where there is still plenty of room for new-comers. Although Paglesham Reach lies south-west and north-east, there is not sufficient drift to create a very rough sea when the wind is against the tide and it is consequently a more comfortable place at which to lie under such conditions than either Burnham or Fambridge. There is an excellent shipwright, Mr. Shuttlewood, who will take charge of a yacht in the owner's absence, but at present the only shopping facilities are such as are provided by a small shop in the village, where I think necessaries can be bought.

Situated about half a mile from the water, Paglesham is a very picturesque little village, of which the principal feature is the Plough and Sail, a delightful old-world inn which has not been spoilt by modern 'improvements.' I don't know the age of the Plough and Sail, but it has certainly stood there for several centuries and remains to-day as it has always been, with its snug little rooms in which one may sit on a high-backed settle at a well scrubbed table and drink beer that really tastes like beer. The old-fashioned country pub is now, alas, rapidly becoming extinct owing to the advent of the motor-car and charabanc; the tendency nowadays being to turn these delightful old-world hostelries into cheap imitations of the London tavern. A garish display of mirrors, cast-iron tables with marble tops, and bent-wood seats in such surroundings is apt to excite feelings of disgust, and it is distressing to anyone fond of the countryside and country institutions to see a homely old inn converted into a sort of inferior London pot-house. And the beer supplied at many of these places appears also to have been 'modernized,' for it tastes like nothing on earth. It may be all right as an aperient, but as a beverage it is positively futile. One can bring up anywhere at Paglesham, but I think the best anchorage is on the south side, where the shore is steeper-to. In some places the anchorage is none too good, as there is much stripweed which may cause an anchor to drag.

It is a pity that the bus service between Rochford and Paglesham does not dovetail into the railway service better than it does, but given sufficient demand, more buses are sure to be put on. There is an excellent train service from Liverpool Street to Rochford, most of the Southend trains stopping there.

CHAPTER 17: *Rivers Blackwater and Colne*

So far as actual sailing is concerned, the Crouch is quite eclipsed by the River Blackwater, situated a few miles farther north. The estuary of this river is a noble expanse of water, a mile and a half wide, and it would be difficult to imagine a more delightful cruising ground for small yachts. The water is deep and clear and below Tollesbury pier there are no obstructions. During the shipping depression that followed the first great war, more than forty big steamers were laid up there, which will give some idea as to the expanse and depth of the water.

MALDON

Unfortunately the Blackwater is not readily accessible from London, the only place in touch with the railway being Maldon, at the head of the river, where there is little water. Few craft, except small sailing boats and dinghies, are permanently stationed at Maldon, owing to the lack of water, but many go there for repairs and laying up at the yards of Dan Webb and May & Butcher. Dan Webb has a particularly well-equipped yard, with building sheds and slipways and many yachts are built there, notably the well-known Blackwater Sloops. There is a hole just below the bridge, where craft drawing up to about 5 feet can lie afloat at all states of tide, but I think it is usually occupied by barges going to Sadd's timber yard.

Clubs: Maldon Little Ship Club. Entrance fee,
two shillings and sixpence; annual subscription,
five shillings.
Blackwater Sailing Club. Entrance fee, one guinea; annual
subscription, two guineas; ladies, one guinea.

HEYBRIDGE

A number of yachts, however, are stationed at Heybridge, the home of the Blackwater Sailing Club. The nearest station is Maldon East, nearly three miles away, but there is a bus service to Maldon. Most of the yachts are berthed in Heybridge Basin, at the entrance to the Chelmer Canal, but some have moorings in the river, which dries out at low tide. The Basin affords a pleasant berth, as a yacht can lie against the bank, but it can only be left or entered for about an hour and a half at the top of the tide. There is indeed little water anywhere above Osea Island and it is essential for week-end yachts stationed at Heybridge to work their tides, which is apt to curtail their cruising activities. In these days of auxiliary engines, yachts do not often fail to save their tide home, but if they do they have to be left far from a railway station until the following week-end, which may be very inconvenient.

At Heybridge the Blackwater SC has a nice little clubhouse and the club gives frequent races, both for handicap yachts and dinghies. There is an inn close by and water can be obtained, but provisions must be bought in Maldon, or brought down from town.

OSEA ISLAND AND MAYLANDSEA

There is a charming anchorage off Osea Island, a little lower down the river, where one can lie off a sandy beach. There is deep water there but the tides run rather hard on the ebb. The best berth is a little below and about fifty yards outside a prominent black post on the foreshore. This post was driven in many years ago to facilitate the scrubbing of the famous *Jullanar*, a yacht that made history. Although designed by Mr. E. H. Benthall, a local manufacturer of agricultural implements, she revolutionized the science of yacht designing. She was a yawl of 126 tons, and in her design Mr. Benthall cut away her dead-woods both fore and aft to reduce skin-friction to a minimum and gave her a raking midship section, the greatest beam of each succeeding waterline being farther forward. With a clipper bow and short tucked-up counter over a vertical sternpost she was an ugly vessel but proved so successful when racing, particularly in hard winds, that the principles evolved by this amateur designer were almost universally adopted.

Osea Island is so inaccessible by land that it is never likely to be developed as a yachting station. So far as I know, the only yacht permanently stationed there is the 17-ton yawl *Dirk II*, owned by Mr. J. Bunting, who farms the island.

Up a creek opposite the island, however, is Maylandsea, where Cardonel & Co., have their building yard. There is also a small club there with a few yachts, which have to take the ground at low water. Lower down the river, on the same side, a few small sailing boats lie off the beach at Steeple Stone.

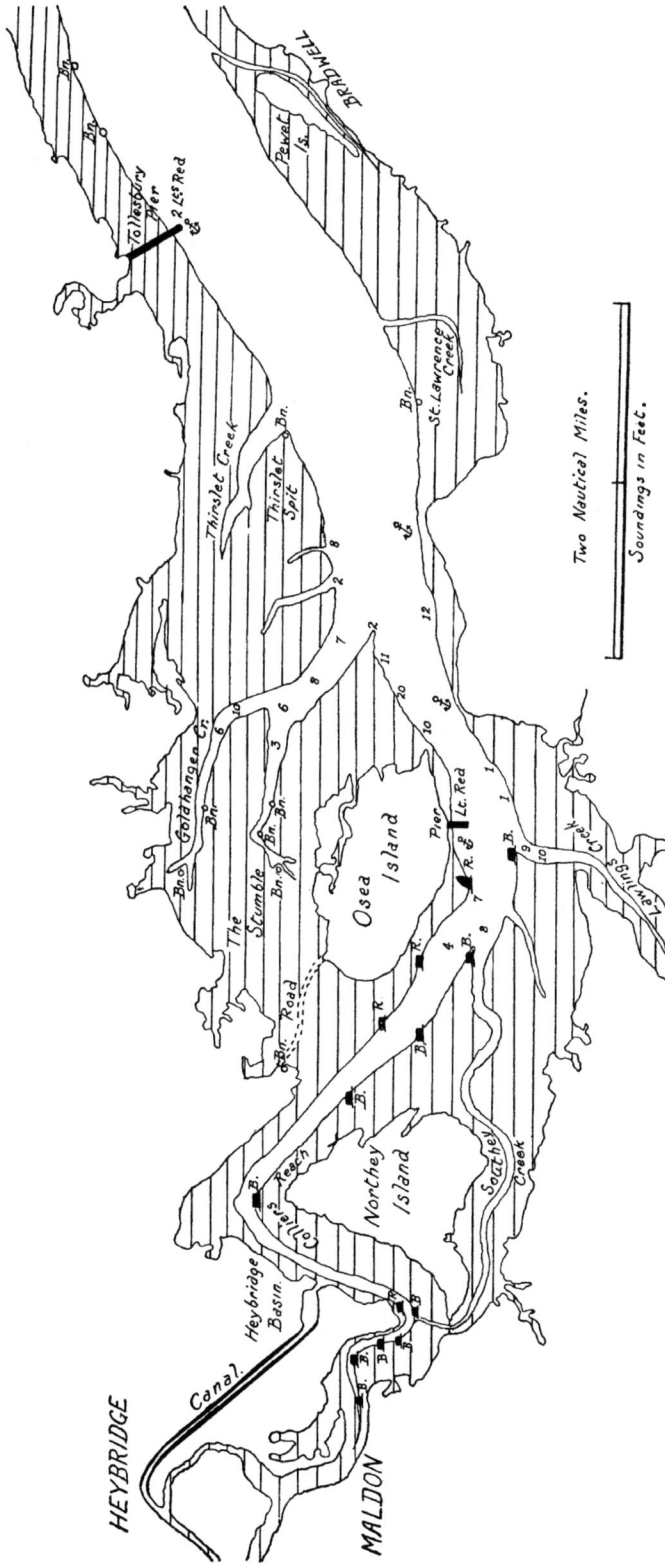

The Upper Blackwater

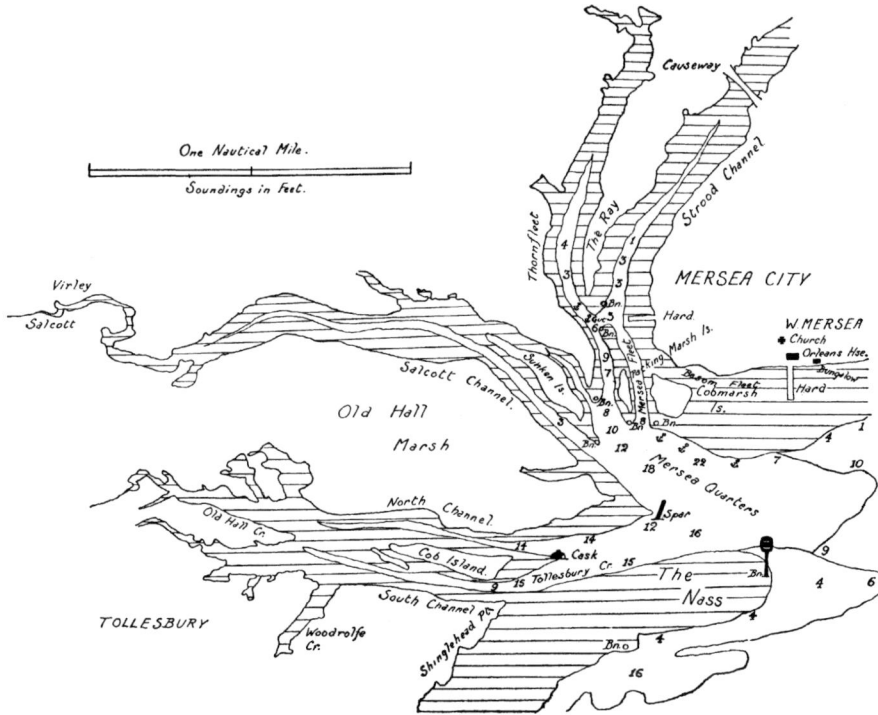

West Mersea and adjacent creeks

WEST MERSEA

But the only place on the Blackwater, other than Heybridge, worth consideration as headquarters is West Mersea, which in many respects approaches within
measurable distance of the ideal. Situated on the north side of the estuary, there
is fine open sailing water in the immediate neighbourhood, while to the dinghy
owner it is a veritable paradise, as there are innumerable creeks for him to ex-
plore. Although ten miles from Colchester, the nearest station, the bus service is
so good that one can be on one's boat in little more than two hours after leaving
Liverpool Street. The station at Colchester, being on the outskirts of the town, is
a mile or more from the bus park, and if one can't get a bus – they don't seem to
run very often – one has to walk, and as there is a devil of a hill up into the town,
it is something of an ordeal on a hot day, if one is carrying a heavy bag.

Of late years West Mersea has been developed as a seaside resort. Many houses have been built and scores of bathing huts are dotted along the shore, but the
yachting industry is still centred upon the old village, curiously known as Mersea
City. There can be found shipwrights, a sailmaker, a yacht-chandler and every
requisite of a yachting centre, and they are all quite close to the hard. There too
is a small shop where one can buy most things in the way of provisions. The best
shops, however, are near the church, about half a mile away (early closing day,
Wednesday). Water can be obtained either from a tap at Clarke & Carter's yard,
or from a natural spring by the roadside to the east of the Victory Hotel.

The best anchorages, indeed the only suitable ones for quite small craft, are in the Thornfleet and Mersea Fleet, but they are both so crowded nowadays that it is impossible for a new-comer to find a clear berth. There is still plenty of room in Mersea Quarters, locally known as the 'Deeps,' but the anchorage there is rather exposed to easterly winds and a very long way from the landing hard.

The West Mersea Yacht Club is a nourishing organization, which maintains several racing classes and also provides sport for yachts sailing under handicap conditions. It has comfortable premises close to the hard.

Club: West Mersea Yacht Club. Entrance fee, one guinea;
               annual subscription, three guineas.

BRADWELL

A few yachts are also stationed in Bradwell Creek, on the opposite side of the river, but it is eight miles from the nearest station at Southminster. There is, however, a bus service which makes it more accessible than in the days when I used to frequent it. Then one had to get there on one's legs, or by the carrier's cart, which took nearly as long, as it stopped in every little village to deliver parcels. Like Mersea, Bradwell is now crowded to congestion and there is no room there for any more craft. The entrance to the creek is very intricate for a stranger and unless one knows exactly where to bring up, the yacht will take the ground at low water. There are, however, several holes in which a craft drawing not more than 4 feet can lie afloat at all states of tide, but local knowledge is necessary to find them. One is just above the old wharf and another in the bay on the mainland side, just inside the entrance. Barges often come into the creek to load or discharge cargo at the quay, and the way their crews handle them is something at which to wonder. If a yacht is in the way, the bargee gently pushes her aside with a long quant. The country round Bradwell Quay is delightful and the creek

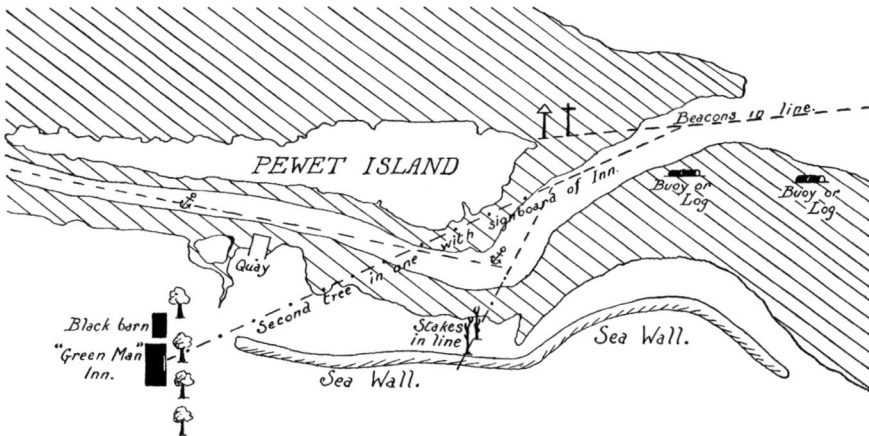

Bradwell Creek

affords a comfortable berth under most conditions, if you are able to bring up in one of the holes. With a strong wind, however, it may be anything but comfortable at the top of the tide and one of the worst nights I ever spent in a small yacht was in Bradwell Creek under such conditions. It blew a hard easterly gale and I spent an hour or more shivering in my pyjamas, fending off other craft that dragged their anchors.

Water can be obtained from the Green Man inn at the Quay, where there is a shipwright – a branch of the Tollesbury Yacht & Boatbuilding Co. Ltd. There is a very good grocer's shop in Bradwell village, about a mile from the waterside, where one can get pretty nearly anything but meat (early closing day, Wednesday).

Going northwards, the next river is the Colne, which is only navigable at low tide as far as Alresford Creek, a distance of some three miles from the entrance, although small yachts can sail as far as Wivenhoe, or even right up to Colchester, on the tide.

BRIGHTLINGSEA

Brightlingsea, situated on the east side of the river, near the entrance, is an important yachting station, as many large yachts lay up there in the winter and others go there for repairs. Brightlingsea, too, is the home of many of our smartest racing hands, most of the men in the big racing yachts hailing from this town, Wivenhoe or Tollesbury. There are also a great many small yachts stationed there and there is a good deal of racing in the course of the season.

Personally, I am not fond of Brightlingsea as I have in the past spent many uncomfortable nights there. There were formerly a number of large smacks out of commission, which rode to a big scope of chain, taking the ground at low water. When the tide made sufficiently to float them, they came charging down on top of you when you least expected it. Even the smacks in commission had no compunctions about giving you a foul berth, and if you spent a night in Brightlingsea Creek in those days without losing some of your topside paint you were very lucky.

Once, when lying there, I was awakened early in the morning by the sound of the water rippling along the sides of my boat, and on turning out to investigate, discovered that I was outside in the Colne, about half a mile below Brightlingsea Creek, and being towed along by a smack.

"Where are you taking me to?" I shouted.

One of the hands on the smack looked over the side and exclaimed: "Lord lumme, Bill, we've got the little bwot's anchor."

And sure enough they had, for they had pulled it up with theirs. Having cleared my anchor, they dropped it and left me anchored half a mile from the entrance to the creek. And before I could have breakfast I had to row ashore in my tiny Berthon dinghy to buy bread!

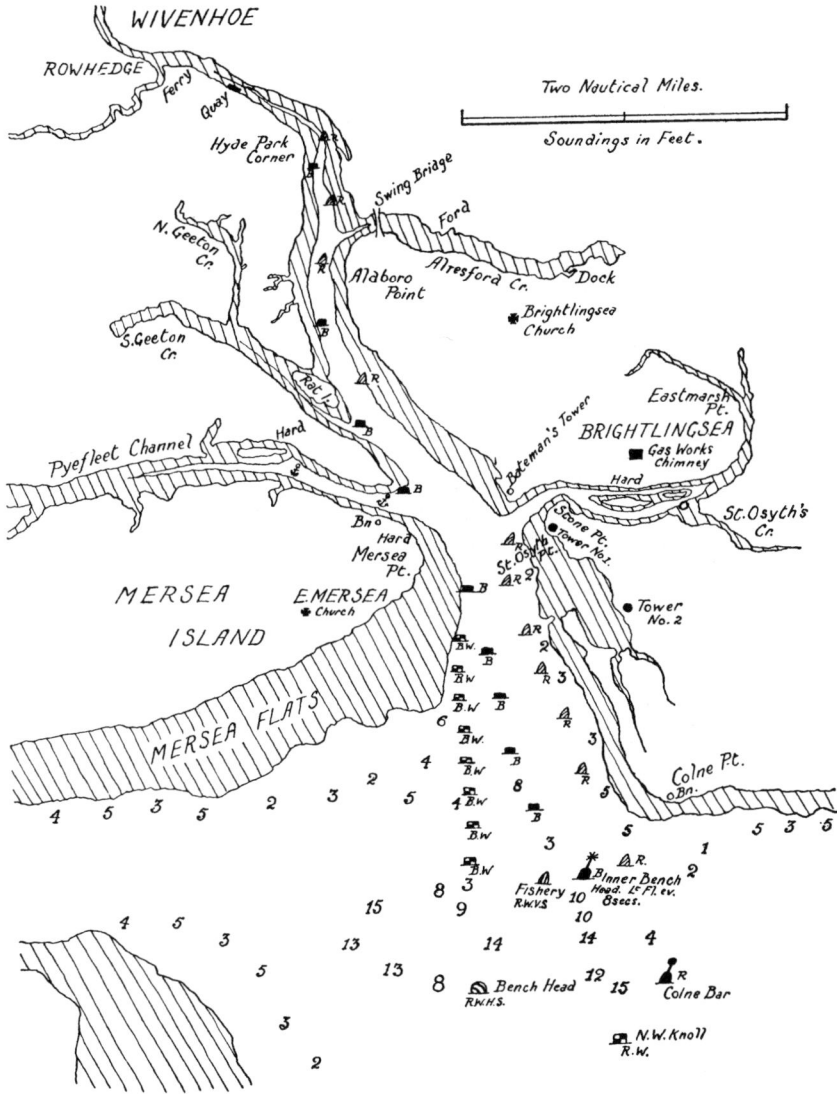

River Colne

Episodes of that sort do not endear a place to one, and so I am afraid that I am rather prejudiced against Brightlingsea.

I understand, however, that Brightlingsea Creek has been much improved as a yacht anchorage of late, as there is now a harbour master and moorings have been laid down for the use of yachts, away from the smacks, but the creek is very crowded. I looked in there recently, but the congested state of the anchorage did not appeal to me; so I came out again and sought a more comfortable berth in the Pyefleet, on the opposite side of the Colne.

There are, of course, all the facilities in the way of shops, yacht yards, slipways, etc., that one could want, but the journey from Liverpool Street is slow and tedious, the best trains taking nearly two hours. There is a fine hard on which one can land at any state of tide, good hotels and a yacht club. Moorings are laid down by the Harbour Commissioners, the rent charged for them ranging from three shillings to nine shillings per week, according to tonnage. Permission to lay private moorings must be obtained from the Commissioners, who charge a rate of one shilling per foot, over all length, for the season. Water, petrol and oil are obtainable and shopping facilities are adequate (early closing day, Thursday).

Club: Colne Yacht Club. Entrance fee, one guinea; annual subscription, two guineas.

CHAPTER 18: *Walton to Lowestoft*

THE WALTON BACKWATERS

Journeying northwards along the coast the next favourable place for yachting headquarters is Walton-on-the-Naze, which in some respects is unique. Walton itself is a popular seaside resort, with a fine sandy beach, a pier and all the usual amusements in the season; but the yachts have their moorings in the Creek which runs round the back of the Naze up to the town. The place therefore combines the amenities of a watering place with a fine natural harbour, which could hardly be improved upon for yachts up to about 15 tons T.M. Such a place has exceptional attraction for a family man, as the children can disport themselves on the beach while father goes yachting. The train service is excellent, the best trains running down from London in rather less than two hours. Some of the yacht-owners spend the summer at Walton, travelling to and from town every day.

The extensive backwaters round about Walton form a fine cruising ground for little boats, whilst the anchorage in the Creek is about the snuggest to be found on the East Coast. No matter from what quarter the wind may blow, you can always get a quiet berth with an off-shore wind. If the wind is easterly or westerly you can bring up in Walton Creek, and when northerly or southerly, in the Twizzle, which runs at right-angles to the former. Those who have experienced the annoyance of a dinghy bumping into the yacht – and who has not? – will appreciate this feature, as it is never necessary to remain in a berth in which the wind meets the tide. Should the wind change during the night, it is merely a matter of running round the corner into the other creek. In either of these anchorages there is about 15 feet of water at low tide and there are two hards near by. The lower of these is rather muddy when the tide is down, but the upper one, which belongs to the club, is quite good. Both, however, are about a mile from the town, and if one has shopping to do it is better to row up to the town in the

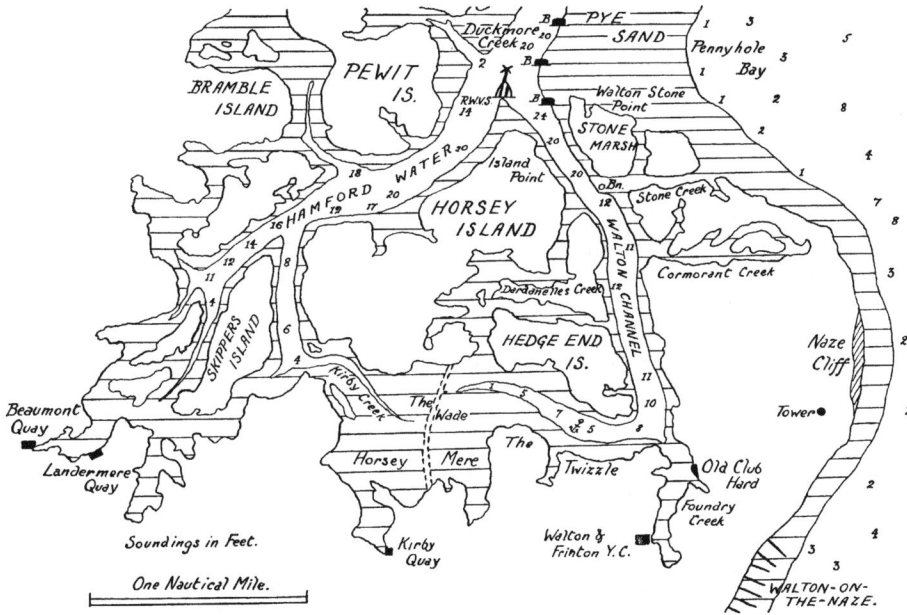

Walton Backwaters

dinghy and land at the club. At about two hours flood there is sufficient water to row a dinghy right up into the heart of the town, which is a boon when one has a lot of parcels. Water can be obtained at the club from a tap on the landing-stage. This is very convenient as one can fill one's cans and put them straight into the dinghy. Once, when I landed on one of the lower hards, I tipped a small boy to fill my breaker while I was ashore and it was only the next morning at breakfast that I discovered that the little brute had filled it with sea-water to save himself the trouble of taking it to one of the cottages, as he had promised to do.

There are any number of sheltered mud berths available for laying-up purposes in the winter, excellent shops in the town (early closing day, Wednesday), shipwrights, facilities for scrubbing, and garages where oil and petrol can be obtained. It is not surprising that, despite the distance from town, small yacht owners are making the place their headquarters in ever-increasing numbers.

When I first found my way into Walton Creek nearly fifty years ago the entrance was extremely difficult, as there was little to guide one but the hand lead and the 'look of the land.' Thanks to the enterprise of the Walton and Frinton Yacht Club, who have buoyed the approach to the creek very efficiently, the entrance is now as easy as walking down the Strand.

It needs but a glance at a map to see that Walton is situated in the very centre of the Essex and Suffolk estuaries, most of which are within an easy afternoon's sail, and the cruising to be had in the neighbourhood is exceptionally good and varied. Although Walton Creek is not very wide, the banks are for the most part fairly steep-to, and there is plenty of room for a small yacht to work up and down the creek, particularly as the tides do not run very hard. The anchorage, moreover, is much nearer to blue water than that of Burnham, for it is not much more than three miles to the tail-end of the Pye Sand, which shelters the approach from the North Sea.

The Walton and Frinton Yacht Club has gone ahead by leaps and bounds since it was established in 1920, and now has a large number of members. It provides plenty of racing and has a comfortable clubhouse in the town, where members of other recognized yacht clubs are always made welcome. The club is a successor to an older institution, known as the Walton-on-the-Naze Yacht Club, which first began the good work of buoying the channel and providing facilities for yachtsmen. For an owner with a fair amount of leisure Walton would be a capital place at which to station his craft, as he would have a safe, convenient anchorage and any amount of good sailing in the neighbourhood.

It is advisable when bringing up in Walton Creek to attach a tripping line to the crown of one's anchor, as the creek is a graveyard of lost anchors and chains. Many a time my anchor has got foul of an old anchor or chain. Moreover, the moorings are laid athwart stream and constitute a trap for the unwary.

Club: Walton and Frinton Yacht Club. Annual subscription, two guineas, outport members one guinea.

HARWICH

There is no more charming sailing ground on the East Coast than the waters in the immediate neighbourhood of Harwich. As a base for the yachtsman's operations, Harwich Harbour can hardly be improved upon, as he can always make a fair wind of it, no matter what the conditions may be. Should it be too rough for a trip to sea, he has the choice of a sail up the Orwell to Ipswich, or up the Stour to Wrabness and Mistley. When the weather is fine, a delightful cruise can be made up north to Aldeburgh, Southwold and Lowestoft, all within a day's sail; or he can go down south to the Colne, Blackwater, Crouch or Thames. Harwich, moreover, is a splendid racing venue, as exceptionally fine courses can be laid off for small craft in the harbour, and for larger vessels outside.

Harwich itself, however, is not a particularly good place as headquarters, as the journey from town is tedious and there is no suitable anchorage in which a small yacht may be left unattended. There is, too, much steam traffic to and from Parkeston Quay, from where the continental steamers depart. Suitable anchorages for small craft are not plentiful or easily accessible. At a pinch, one might leave a small craft in the pound for a night, but it is rather crowded and there would be a risk of the vessel's paint being scratched by the watermen's boats, which are constantly coming in and going out. Another anchorage is in the Upper Pound, but the holding ground is poor and the mud very black and offensive. An owner who takes pride in the appearance of his yacht must, when

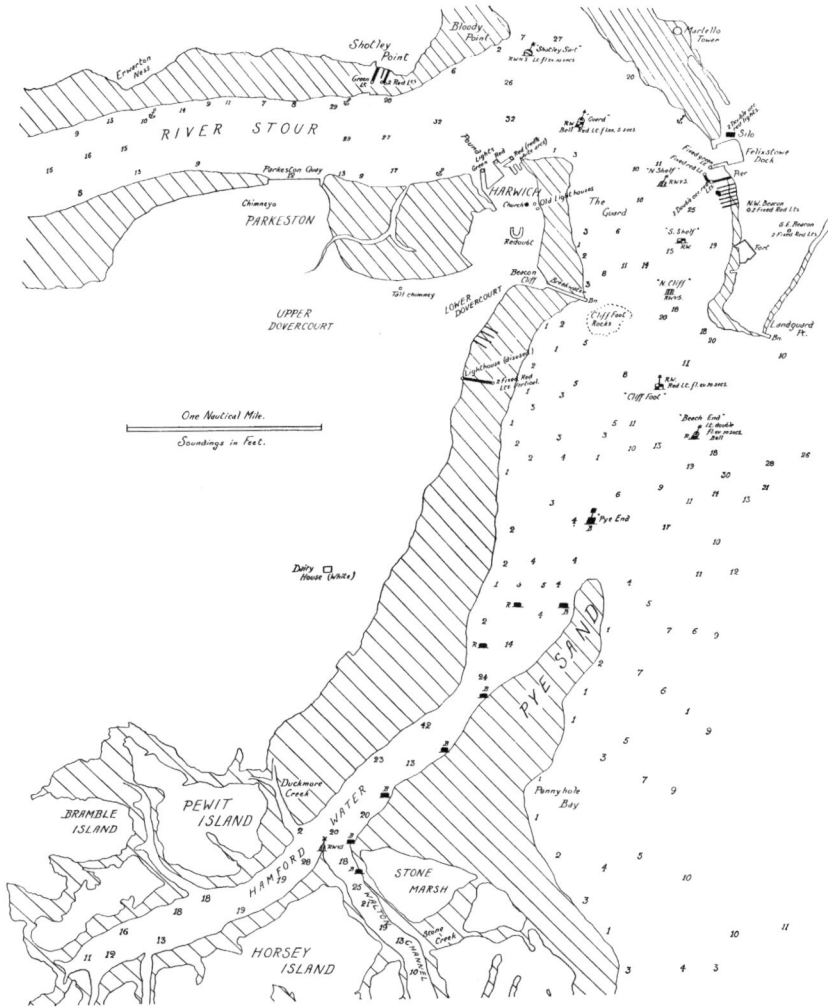

Harwich Harbour and Approaches

weighing anchor, scrub every foot of the cable as it comes inboard, a tedious operation likely to try his temper. Another anchorage is on the other side of the Stour, off Shotley Pier, but as there is a lot of traffic, it would not be wise to leave a boat there unattended for very long. Another berth is in the Orwell, just above Shotley Spit. The shore is steep-to there and a yacht can lie close in to the shore, out of the traffic. There is a hard of sorts near by, but landing entails the use of sea-boots.

Harwich is a town of great historical interest, but its glory has departed. The last time I was there, the wharves looked neglected and dilapidated, the Great Eastern Hotel, formerly the home of the Royal Harwich Yacht Club, had stood empty for years and the town had a dead-alive appearance that was depressing in the extreme. The fact is that most of the trade of Harwich has been transferred to Parkeston Quay, while such social amenities as formerly existed have been swamped by the development of near-by Dovercourt as a seaside resort. But the harbour remains and it is undoubtedly a fine cruising centre.

The Royal Harwich Yacht Club, established in 1843, gives a two-day regatta every year, which usually marks the opening of the first-class racing season. It attracts many of the finest racing yachts afloat and is the principal yachting event of the East Coast. It was the Royal Harwich YC that backed the first challenge for the America's Cup, that of Mr. James Ashbury's *Cambria* in 1870. There is also a local sailing club, the Harwich and Dovercourt SC, which gives races for small craft in the harbour. There are fair shopping facilities at Harwich (early closing day, Wednesday) and petrol, oil and water can be obtained.

The best place at which to station a small yacht in this neighbourhood is Felixstowe Dock, on the other side of the harbour, but I believe it is now largely used for commercial purposes and often very crowded. I think the minimum charge is half a crown a week, or at any rate it used to be. At one time I frequented the dock a good deal, having a season ticket, for which I paid, if I remember rightly, ten shillings for the season. Water can be obtained on the quay, but there are no shops nearer than Felixstowe town, some three miles distant. There are a few trains which run to the dock, but they are very few indeed, and in my day one usually had to walk from the town station. Another way of reaching Felixstowe Dock is by going to Harwich and taking the ferry across the harbour, but in either case the journey is a very slow one. Taking it all round, I think a London yachtsman who wishes to keep his boat in this neighbourhood, will be well advised to make his headquarters at Pin Mill.

Clubs: Royal Harwich Yacht Club. Entrance fee, one guinea; annual subscription, one guinea.

              Harwich and Dovercourt Sailing Club.

PIN MILL

The favourite anchorage in these parts is at Pin Mill, some five miles up the Orwell. This spot is the gem of the East Coast, the scenery being not unlike that of the River Dart. Sailing up the Orwell, the first mile or two are rather uninteresting, but on rounding Collimer Point one suddenly sails into a land of enchantment. The river meanders through a densely wooded valley of surprising beauty, trees extending from the water's edge as far as one can see. In Butterman's Bay the big grain ships discharge a portion of their cargo before proceeding to Ipswich, and there is a row of large iron mooring buoys placed there for their special benefit. Soon after passing these buoys, one comes to Pin Mill, the Mecca of East Coast yachtsmen. It is a charming little waterside village, situated on the bank of a small bay, in which yachts may lie out of the way of traffic. At high tide the water laps the walls of the Butt and Oyster inn, where the beer is good and cheap. Water can be obtained from a pump in the yard of the inn, but you must be careful not to waste it when filling your cans as the supply is none too plentiful in a dry summer. The landlord recently complained to me that yachtsmen were very careless in this respect and by neglecting to use a funnel wasted far more water than necessary. He remarked that he would always lend anyone a funnel who had not got one, and I hope that any of my readers who visit Pin Mill will bear this in mind. In periods of drought the well sometimes runs dry and then all of the water for the inn has to be fetched from Ipswich by road. My remarks, of course, apply to other places also, as when a well is the sole source of supply water is apt to be scarce in dry weather.

The hard is a good one and landing can be effected at all states of tide, but it is of great length – 367 yards, I believe, at low water. This makes it very inconvenient when you go ashore, for if you remain for some time you may experience difficulty in getting away. Should it be near low water when you land and you remain ashore for some hours, you will find your dinghy far from the shore when you return; or, if you land at or near high water, you may have to push the boat down the hard for perhaps two hundred yards ere you can get afloat. At weekends and holiday times, however, there are always boys about who will keep the dinghy afloat during your absence for a small tip, and it is money well spent. Down one side of the hard is a row of posts against which yachts can rest for scrubbing purposes, and near by is Mr. King's yacht-building yard. He is an excellent shipwright who puts in good work at a reasonable price and

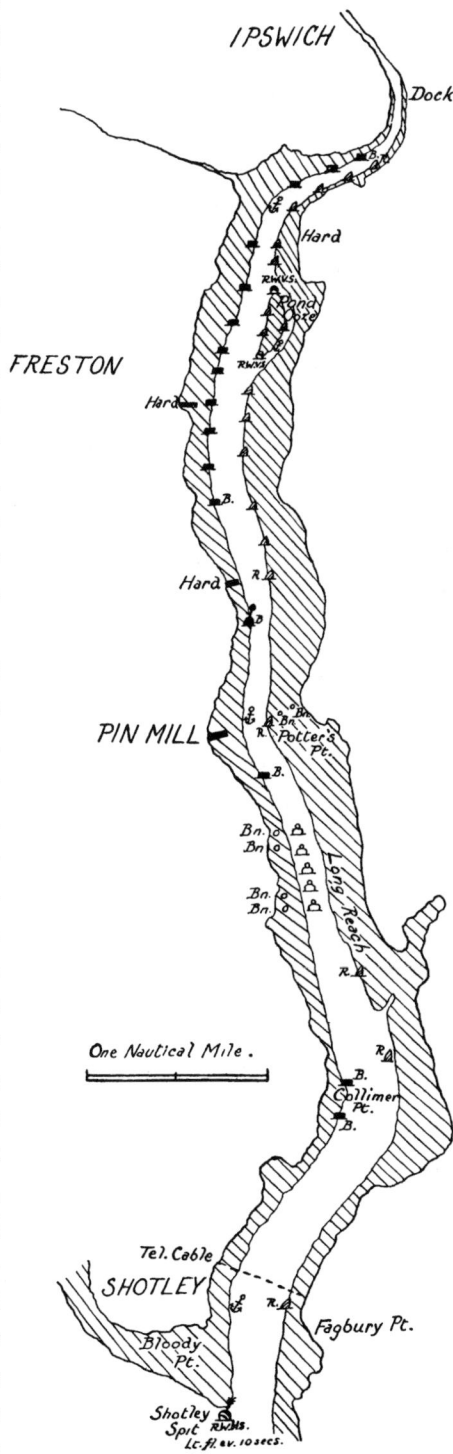

River Orwell

155

also takes charge of yachts during the owners' absence. There are a few shops at Chelmondiston, about half a mile from the waterside (early closing day, Wednesday). Vegetables can be obtained from almost any of the cottages at the side of the road that leads to the village. The cottages are in a deep hollow and as their gardens are well protected from the wind, one can get new potatoes earlier here than at most places. The nearest station is Ipswich, but there is a good service of buses and it is possible to get to Pin Mill from Liverpool Street in rather less than two hours. Formerly steamers plied between Ipswich and Harwich, calling at Pin Mill, but the service was discontinued some years ago, its place having been taken by the motor-buses. I have always regretted the passing of the steamers as the trip down the river was delightful. The steamer, moreover, dropped you into the ferryboat at Pin Mill and the ferryman would put you straight on board your craft, if she were not very far away. The bus is perhaps a little quicker, but as it puts you down at Chelmondiston, you have a walk of half a mile to the waterside, so there is not much in it in the matter of time. Supplies of petrol and oil can be obtained at Pin Mill and a yacht can safely be left in the care of either Messrs. Harry King & Son or Harry Ward. There is also a sailmaker on the spot.

Nowadays the anchorage at Pin Mill is very crowded during the season, but if you do not mind a fairly long row to the hard, you can usually find a clear berth. My favourite berth is some little way below the hard, where the barges used to lie, and I usually manage to get it. The shore is wooded to the water's edge and at night the nightingales sing fit to burst their little hearts. Although I have frequented Pin Mill since the late 'nineties, the place never palls upon me. For one thing the surrounding scenery is so lovely, and then there is always something to interest one. Ipswich is now an important grain port, and one sees big steamers, sometimes as large as 12,000 tons, passing up and down the river. Almost every summer I have seen one or other of the big sailing vessels that bring grain from Australia, and a barque of some 3,000 tons, with her tall masts towering above the trees, is a sight to remember.

IPSWICH

Although there is a fine train service to Ipswich and every convenience, few London yachtsmen keep their vessels there, as it is too far up the river and owing to the trees, which keep off the wind, it takes a long time to sail down to Harwich, some eleven miles distant. A number of small locally-owned craft, however, are stationed a little lower down the river in a creek by the Ostrich inn. The channel, as it approaches Ipswich, becomes very narrow and tortuous and as there is a lot of traffic to and from the docks, the Orwell is not suitable for sailing much above Freston. Of course every requisite for yachting is easily obtainable at Ipswich, where there are many good shops (early closing day, Wednesday).

Club: Orwell Yacht Club. Annual subscription, ten shillings.

We are now getting rather far from London, and ports farther north on the East Coast could hardly be considered suitable as headquarters for the metropolitan yachtsman. As, however, a few yachts are stationed in such rivers as the Deben and Alde, a few passing remarks about those waters may not be out of place.

THE RIVER DEBEN

Felixstowe Ferry, also known as Bawdsey Haven, situated at the mouth of the River Deben, is a delightful anchorage for small craft when once inside, but the entrance, under certain conditions of wind and tide, can be a perfect hell for a stranger. This river, like the Alde (or is it the Ore? I can never remember which) has a shingle bar at the entrance that frequently shifts, and the tide runs like a millrace. On the first of a spring ebb it probably attains a speed of more than six knots and I have seen quite a smart yacht with a fresh fair wind pinned against the tide so that she took the best part of an hour to cover a hundred yards. Even to those who have an intimate knowledge of the entrance the navigation is not free from difficulty, as the shingle banks shift their position so often that one can never be sure that the channel is in the same place two days running. There are certainly beacons on the shore to mark the way in, but as the pilots do not always shift them at once, one cannot rely on them. It is essential therefore to take a pilot when entering or leaving; even the local craft do that.

When once inside, however, there is a delightful anchorage just above the steam ferry. The shore is there quite steep-to, so that a small yacht can lie afloat within a few yards of the beach. On the flood she will be in almost slack water and lie wind-rode, but on the ebb the tide, even in the anchorage, runs fairly hard. Taking it all round, however,

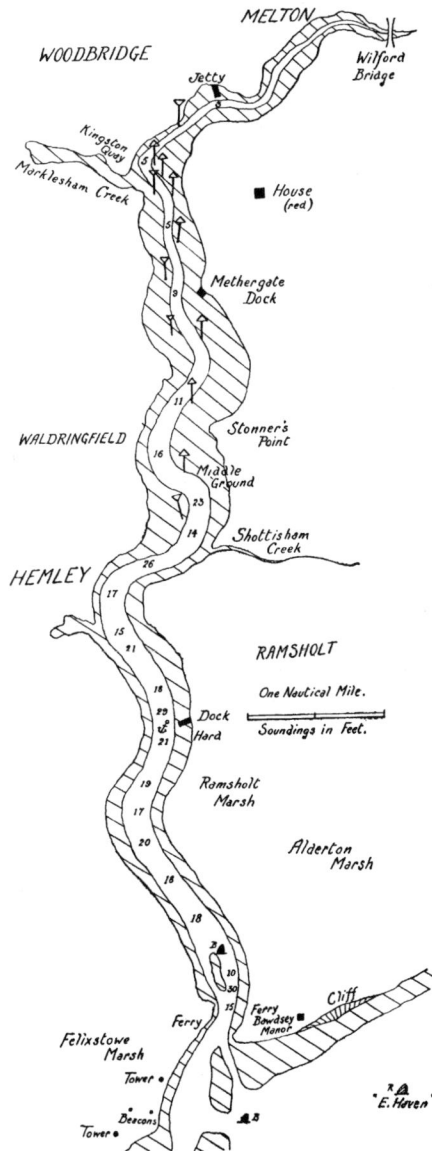

River Deben

it is a capital anchorage, as, being protected by a horse in the middle of the river, there is but little fear of the yachts being damaged by passing barges. There is an inn, and tradesmen's carts come in from Felixstowe every day and one can procure from them such articles as meat, bread, vegetables and other necessaries. The chief drawback to the place is its inaccessibility, the nearest station being at Felixstowe nearly three miles away; but as holiday headquarters for a family man it is a most delightful spot. There is a nice sandy beach for children to play on and a capital golf course, whilst good sailing can be had in the river for those who do not fancy negotiating the difficult entrance. The river is extremely pretty, the scenery up by Ramsholt and Waldringfield being but little less attractive than that of the Orwell. It is, however, a rather tricky river for a stranger to navigate as the mud flats are wide and the channel none too well marked. One can sail right up to Woodbridge on the tide, but it is prudent to make the trip on the young flood, when the flats will be for the most part uncovered.

Club: Deben Yacht Club. Annual subscription, ten shillings.

ALDEBURGH

The next river, going north, is the River Alde, which is of very similar character to the Deben, although most people consider the entrance even more difficult. An extraordinary feature of this river is that after proceeding for some miles at right angles to the coast, it turns off sharp at Aldeburgh, and for a distance of ten or twelve miles runs parallel with the coast and so close in places that anyone on board a yacht in the river could almost throw a stone into the sea. Between the sea and the river there is nothing but a narrow strip of shingle, and it certainly seems strange that the river has never succeeded in breaking through this extremely narrow obstruction at Aldeburgh. The River Alde is a capital sailing river, as there are few obstructions to trap the unwary, and the

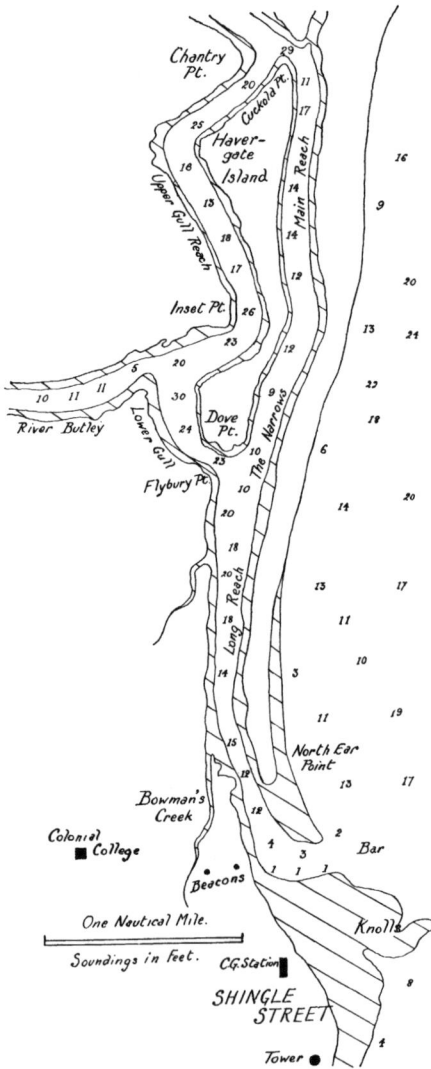

Orford Haven

banks are for the most part steep-to. Near the mouth the tide runs very hard on the ebb, even more so than that of the Deben. I have heard it stated that the velocity of the ebb exceeds seven knots and from my personal observation I do not think that is an exaggeration. Half-way up the river is Orford, a delightful little place where a few yachts are stationed. A visitor to Orford should make a point of inspecting the ruins of Orford Castle, in which there still remains a room that is fully furnished.

Aldeburgh is a capital place for dinghy sailing, as one can either go seaward, past Orford, to Shingle Street, or else inland up the river to Iken. It would be an ideal place for holiday quarters for a dinghy sailor, as he could easily take his boat there by train. There is an exceptionally good golf course and all the attractions of a seaside resort.

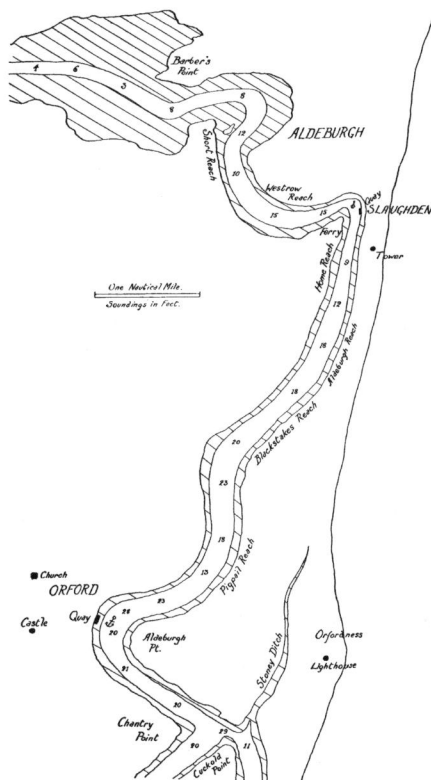

Rivers Ore and Alde

Club: Aldeburgh Yacht Club. Entrance fee, one guinea; annual sub., yachts under 2 tons, one guinea; over 2 tons, two guineas.

SOUTHWOLD

Proceeding up the coast the next port is Southwold, or rather Walberswick, about a mile to the southward of Southwold town. Some years before the first World War a sum of £65,000 was expended on reconstructing the harbour with the idea of using it as a relief port to Lowestoft for the North Sea fishing fleet, but the harbour failed to attract the fishermen and has been allowed to go to wrack and ruin again. The planking of the piers has rotted away and the channel silted up, although I am told that it is still navigable for small craft with care at certain states of tide. It is a great pity that the harbour has not been better cared for, as Walberswick is one of the most picturesque spots on the East Coast and would have been a convenient refuge for small craft that failed to save their tide to Lowestoft.

LOWESTOFT

Lowestoft is about twelve miles farther north and, as every one knows, is one of the most popular watering-places on the East Coast. It is one of the few artifi-

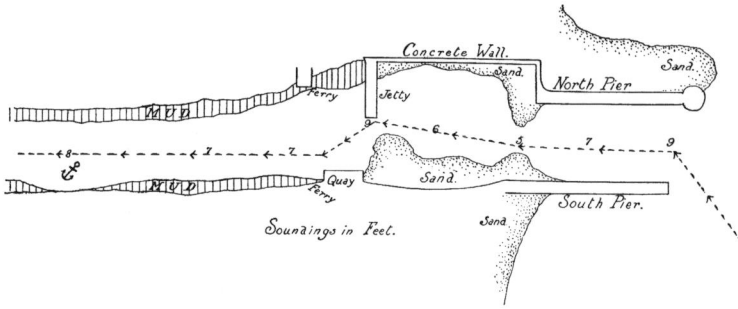

Southwold Harbour

cial harbours that I know in which a yacht can lie with any degree of comfort. The railway company, who own the harbour, seem to have gone out of their way to make things attractive to yachtsmen, charging them no dues and placing at their disposal during the season a large basin situated just under the promenade pier. One can spend a few days very pleasantly in the yacht basin at Lowestoft. Morning, afternoon and evening a good band performs on the pier, whilst the innumerable smacks coming in and going out of the harbour are a source of never-failing interest. Looking out over the yacht basin is the commodious club-house of the Royal Norfolk and Suffolk YC, which extends a cordial welcome to all members of recognized yacht clubs.

Lowestoft is, of course, a long way from London, and those with only the week-ends at their disposal would not care to sacrifice so much time in travelling to and from their vessels; but for those who can get away from, say, Friday to the following Tuesday every week the place would make very pleasant headquarters. In addition to fine open-sea sailing, the famous Broads are near at hand, as one only has to go a matter of two or three miles through Lake Lothing to reach Oulton Broad.

Club: Royal Norfolk and Suffolk Yacht Club. Entrance fees, six guineas, four guineas or three guineas; annual subscriptions, six guineas, four guineas, or three guineas; ladies, two guineas and one guinea.

A Yarn

ぞ♥

A Night on the Buxey

The miniature cruiser has her limitations and it is imprudent to put to sea in such a craft if the weather looks threatening. I think I mentioned in a previous chapter that when I was a boy I had a little converted ship's boat named *Wave* in which I cruised upwards of 1,200 miles in one season. She was only 16 feet long by 5 feet beam and half-decked, the after part of the boat being quite open. I had a lot of fun in her and incidentally the fright of my life. As it may serve as a warning to other enthusiastic but inexperienced youngsters, I will tell you about it.

Having been rather lucky in the way of Christmas tips, I bought a little binnacle and compass that I had seen in a yacht-chandler's window and coveted for some time. It was a pretty dome-shaped toy of shining brass, with a lamp at the side-the sort of thing that nobody but a silly kid would buy. Having mounted it on the cabin-top, where it was rather suggestive of a brass knocker on a pigsty, I was, of course, all agog to try it, but did not get an opportunity until early in February.

It was late when I arrived at Fambridge, having missed my train, and then much time was wasted in getting on board. To reach the river-bank in those days was a difficult matter, as, owing to a breach in the sea-wall, the marshes were flooded at high water and the tide swept rapidly across what was left of the road. As a rule we crossed the floods in an old shooting punt, but that night it was not there and I had no alternative but to remove my trousers and wade. As the road was full of holes, I had, like Agag, to walk delicately, but feeling my way carefully I contrived to cross in safety. I was miserably cold, however, when I arrived on board, as a handkerchief is a poor substitute for a towel.

Having set the sails, I made the dinghy fast to the mooring, as *Wave* was too small to tow a dinghy, and got under way, bound for Brightlingsea. The tide had just begun to ebb and, with a fair wind, the little boat made good progress. It was beastly cold, but with a blanket wrapped round my legs and another over my shoulders I managed to keep fairly warm. As I ran down the river with a fresh north-westerly breeze, I ate some sandwiches I had brought with me from town.

It was a dark night, with low driving clouds, and sailing down the river was a rather nervy business, as the loom of the sea-wall made it difficult to judge the distance from the shore. Well as I knew the river, I frequently had to heave the lead, and handling the wet line numbed my hands. But I contrived to keep

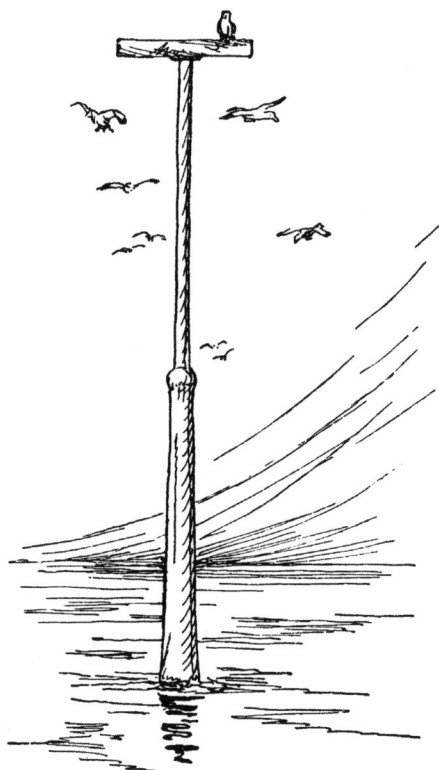

Buxey Beacon

off the mud as far as the Roach, and then the lights of some barges brought up at Shore-ends were a useful guide.

When clear of the river, I had nothing to guide me but the compass and lead, for in those days the West Buxey buoy was not lighted. Now was the time to try my new binnacle. After several attempts I lit the lamp, but in a few minutes it went out. Time after time I relit it until, having used up a whole box of matches and exhausted my patience, I came to the conclusion that it was a futile toy of no practical use. Then it occurred to me that perhaps a bit of candle might burn, so, lashing the helm, I went into the cabin to get one.

But I could not remember where I had stowed the candles, and as I frequently had to return to the cockpit to re-adjust the tiller, it was quite a long time before I found what I wanted. While thus occupied I had lost touch with the edge of the Dengie Flat and it was obvious that I should have to rely entirely upon the compass.

Substituting a short length of candle for the binnacle lamp, I was glad to find that it burnt pretty well and kept alight for quite long periods. But then I was faced with another difficulty. The compass was not a spirit one and the card oscillated like a thing demented with the motion of the boat. To steer a reliable compass course under such conditions would have tried a far better navigator than I, and after a time I was forced to the conclusion that I had fairly lost myself.

I continued to sail on a north-easterly course as nearly as I could and hoped for the best, thinking that sooner or later I should see the lights of some vessel coming through the Raysand Channel. But I saw nothing and every minute became more and more anxious. The wind had freshened considerably and the sea was getting up. Moreover, the visibility was reduced to a few yards by a mizzle of rain intermingled with sleet. I carried on in this way for a time and was just thinking that I should have to reef when there was an ominous scrunch, and *Wave* was hard and fast on the Buxey Sand. As I had been travelling fast, with a fresh wind on the quarter, she had run on good and proper, as they say. Of course, I should have at once jumped overboard and pushed her off, but jumping into icy water on a cold winter's night was not a form of entertainment that appealed to me. So I lowered the sails and then tried to push her off with an oar. But she would not budge and the tide was running off fast. Having no dinghy I could not lay out the anchor, so I abandoned the attempt to refloat her and retired to the cabin to think things out.

I reckoned that it was about four hours ebb when she struck and so it would be at least four hours before there would be sufficient water to float her again. I knew that I must be on the Buxey, but whereabouts I had not the haziest idea. It was now snowing and altogether the prospect was about as cheerless as it well could be. Having lit the Primus stove, I brewed a large jug of coffee and, lighting a pipe, lay down on the bunk to think what I should do.

A feeling of impending disaster obsessed me. Here was I, three miles from the nearest shore in a half-decked boat with no dinghy. The wind sang a mournful song in the rigging and the halyards played a devil's tattoo on the mast. The breeze had freshened into quite a strong wind and I could hear the surf breaking on the sands. As I lay on my bunk thinking of these things I wondered what would happen to me when the flood tide made. It seemed that there was a good chance of the boat either being swamped or dashed to pieces, and a feeling of unutterable desolation and despair slid into my soul.

But these were the thoughts of a 'rabbit,' and feeling ashamed of myself, I began to turn my attention to action. First, I took down two reefs in the mainsail and then set the small jib in stops. When I reckoned it was low water, I took off my trousers and carried out the anchor as far as I could by wading. Having hauled the chain taut, I dried my legs thoroughly, put on my trousers again and then ran about on the sands until I was warm. There was nothing more that could be done until she floated, and so I returned to the cabin to think out a plan for getting her under way.

It seemed to me that if I got under way in the ordinary manner, the boat would drive ashore again as soon as I got the anchor, and so I decided to try the method frequently adopted by McMullen in *Procyon* and other yachts when single-handed. I had often read of it in his *Down Channel*, but had never yet had occasion to try it. The idea was to sail out the anchor, thus making the boat do the work. While doing it, she would be sailing farther from the sands all the time and if I failed to get the anchor, I should be no worse off than before, as I could pay out chain again and have another try.

But somehow or other I had to pass the best part of two hours before there would be sufficient water to float her, and, wrapped in blankets, I tried to read, but with indifferent success. At first I looked out every few minutes to see what the weather was like, but the prospect was so disheartening that I came to the conclusion that the less I looked at it the better and vowed that I would not do so again until the water was round her. To kill time, I brewed some more coffee and had a meal.

At long last the advancing tide slapped her sides and presently she began to lift. Putting on my oilskins, I went out into the well, prepared to battle with the elements. It was still blowing hard but the snow had ceased. The waves as they struck the side of the boat sent up clouds of spray which fell on board and into the cockpit. Then she began to bump and every bump sent my heart into my mouth. Gradually she slewed round until she was head to wind and sea and the bumping began to get less violent. At last she was afloat, pitching into the seas and taking spray freely over her bows. Pulling up the floor-boards in the cockpit, I rejoiced to find that she was not leaking to any appreciable extent. The time had now come for action.

Having set the reefed mainsail and coiled the halyards, I went aft and, breaking out the jib, which I had set in stops, hauled it a-weather. The boat at once took a wide sheer and I dashed forward. Snubbing at her chain, she came round on to the port tack and began to sail towards her anchor. As she sailed, I rattled in the chain as fast as I could and, snatching a turn round the bitts as she came over the anchor, sailed it clean out of the ground. In a moment I had hauled it up to the stemhead and, as she came up into the wind, I jumped to the tiller and shoved it over, at the same time letting the jib sheet go. Round she came on to the starboard tack and was fairly away. It had worked like a charm and I had thus learnt a method of getting away from lee shore that I have practised with invariable success ever since. Having sailed some distance from the sands, I hove-to and got the anchor on board.

I had now to decide whether to go on to Brightlingsea or return to the Crouch, but I felt so elated at having extricated *Wave* from such a 'tight' place, that I determined to adhere to my original plan and go to Brightlingsea. I was still uncertain as to my position, but felt pretty sure that if I kept the wind on the beam, or thereabouts, I should go clear of the Buxey Sand, provided of course that the wind remained steady. So I resumed my journey to Brightlingsea, taking the precaution to heave the lead every now and then.

After sailing for some time, I picked up a flashing light, which I identified as the Knoll buoy. Taking a rough bearing of it, I hove-to and went into the cabin to look at the chart. It was now quite half-flood and I saw that there was plenty of water over everything with my light draught, and as the buoy seemed a long way off, I decided to haul my wind and cut across the sands. I did not expect to be able to fetch right into the Colne, but the flood would be pushing me up to windward all the time and I should at least be able to get into comparatively smooth water. It would be light before I reached the Colne, as dawn could not be far distant. Indeed, I thought I could already distinguish a lightening of the darkness to the eastward.

Close-hauled, the boat had as much sail as she could carry in the rough water, but she was a buoyant little sea boat and nothing but spray came aboard. And so I sailed on, gradually getting smoother water, while the eastern sky grew lighter and lighter. Soon I was able to distinguish in the uncertain light the ghostly forms of smacks and barges coming out of the Colne, and with a procession of vessels to guide me, had no longer to worry about navigation. It was broad daylight when I entered the Colne and had no difficulty in finding my way into Brightlingsea Creek. There I brought up alongside of a yacht belonging to a friend, whose invitation to breakfast I was jolly glad to accept after my trying adventure.

Well, that is the sort of silly thing that kids do in boats, and one cannot help thinking that they are looked after by a special Providence, for they seldom come to grief ❧

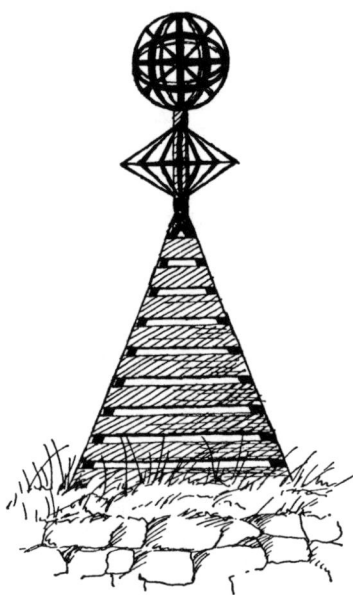

Our Lady of Canvey

Part III: CRUISING DESIGNS

CHAPTER 19: *Design Commentaries*

LONA
(Drawing 3) by J. Pain Clark, c1900

LOA	31ft	Headroom	4ft 7in
Beam	6ft 7½in	Mainsail	359 sq ft
Draught	4ft	Foresail	108 sq ft
Ballast, lead	28 cwt	Rating	23 Linear

Lona is a particularly handsome little ship. She was designed for himself by Mr. J. Pain Clark, and built by the Burnham Yacht Building Company. Her principal dimensions are given on the drawing, but she has recently had some slight alterations effected, which have proved quite satisfactory. Her lead keel has been increased by some 5 cwt., and lowered 4in. This has permitted a considerable increase in her sail-area, and she is now cutter-rigged with a jackyard topsail. Although her sail-area is now rather inclined to be of the generous order, she carries it like a little ship, and, being fitted with Turner's roller reefing gear, sail can, if necessary, be speedily reduced. She has a commodious cabin, which is very tastefully fitted, and is altogether a jolly little craft. *Lona* is a good sea-boat, and, for her size, remarkably fast; indeed, last season, she held the best record in the Royal Corinthian Yacht Club's under 6 tons class. The illustration shows shows the yacht as a cutter, but before her sail-area was materially increased.

GRANUAILE
(Drawing 4) by Doyle, Kingstown, 1901

LOA	33ft 2½ in	Forward overhang	2ft 10½in
LWL	23ft	Counter	7ft 4in
Beam	7ft 5½in	Displacement	4.72 tons
Draught	5ft 6in	Ballast on keel	2.7 tons
	Sail area	745.5 sq ft	

The best 6-tonner I have seen of late years is Messrs. H. & C. Becher's *Granuaile*. She was designed and built by Doyle, of Kingstown, in 1901. Beautifully kept up and capitally sailed by her owners, she has proved to be the fastest boat in the six tons and under class of the Royal Corinthian Yacht Club. The photograph by Ambrose of Burnham, will give the reader a good idea of the general appearance of this pretty little cutter when under way. Her total Y.R.A. sail-area, as designed, is 745.5 square feet, which is apportioned as follows: Mainsail

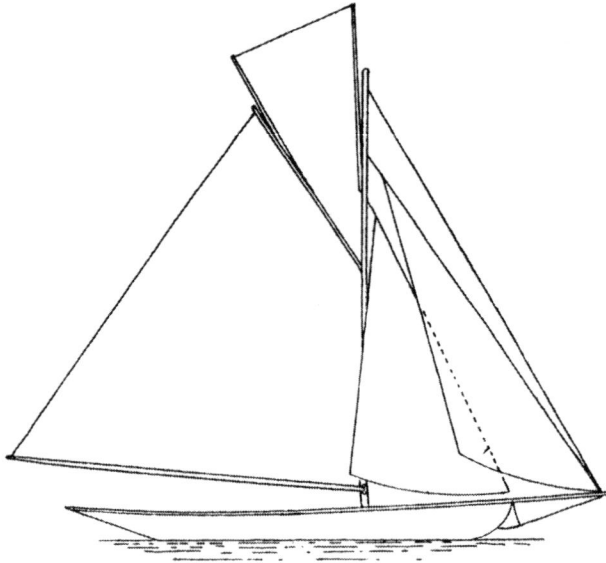

Granuaile sail plan

401.35 square feet; Headsails 261.95 square feet; Topsail 83 square feet. In addition to above, she also sets a small jib topsail. The yacht is flush-decked, with a 3ft. skylight, and has 4ft. 9in. head-room under the beams, whilst a man of average height can stand upright beneath the skylight. The boat is fitted with a self-draining cockpit 3ft. 4in. in length. Fast, weatherly, and a capital sea-boat, *Granuaile* is an ideal little cruiser for two men who know their business. There is no fore bulkhead, the fo'c'stle being divided from the cabin by means of a curtain. There is good head-room in the fo'c'stle, which is fitted with two cots. The majority of the running gear is of flexible steel wire, which has proved so satisfactory that her owners have fitted their 21-ton cutter *Zulu* in a similar manner. Such a craft as *Granuaile* could probably be built, with pine planking, for about £330, inclusive of lead ballast, sails, spars, blocks, and all necessary gear.

MERCIA III
(Drawings 5 & 6) by G. Umfreville Laws, c1903

LOA	29ft 3in	Draught	4ft 3in
LWL.	20ft 8in	Ballast	28 cwt
Beam	7ft 2in	Sail area	550 sq ft

The next design is that of *Mercia III*, a 5-ton cutter from the board of Mr. G. Umfreville Laws. This design is almost identical with that from which *Leonore* was built by the Burnham Yacht Building Company, for Mr. N. M. Robins, the only difference being that, in the design here illustrated, Mr. Laws has drawn the lines slightly finer aft, and given her a few inches more counter. *Mercia III* was built in London by her owner, Mr. J. Jarvis, jun., in 1905. He had previously had some little experience of amateur boat construction, having built the 2-ton sloop

Mercia II in 1901 which, I regret to say, went ashore near Orford Haven during the great gale of September 10th, 1903, and became a "constructive total loss". Although *Mercia III* was a considerably larger job than Mr. Jarvis had before tackled in the building line, his previous experience stood him in good stead and the yacht when completed would have done credit to a first class professional builder. She has proved an excellent little cruiser and her internal accommodation is noticeable for several ingenious fitments. One of these is a lavatory basin fitted below one of the bunks, and supplied with fresh water from the tank. *Mercia* has done a good deal of cruising on the east coast and is a capital sea-boat with a good turn of speed.

ARIMA
(Drawing 7) by H. C. Smith, c1903

LOA	25ft	Draught	3ft 8in
LWL	18ft	Ballast	0.95 tons
Beam	6ft 6in	Sail area (w/o topsail) . . .	408 sq ft

The design of the 4-ton sloop *Arima* is by Mr. H. C. Smith, of the Burnham Yacht Building Company, by whom the boat was built. The dimensions are stated on the drawing, but in actual building there were one or two slight modifications. The cockpit was reduced in length by 5in., giving 7ft. length of berth in the cabin and 5in. extra length in the fo'c'stle. The balance-rudder was also replaced by a sternpost one. *Arima* is an excellent single-hander, and strikes me as being a nice little craft of very suitable size and type for a novice to commence his sailing career with.

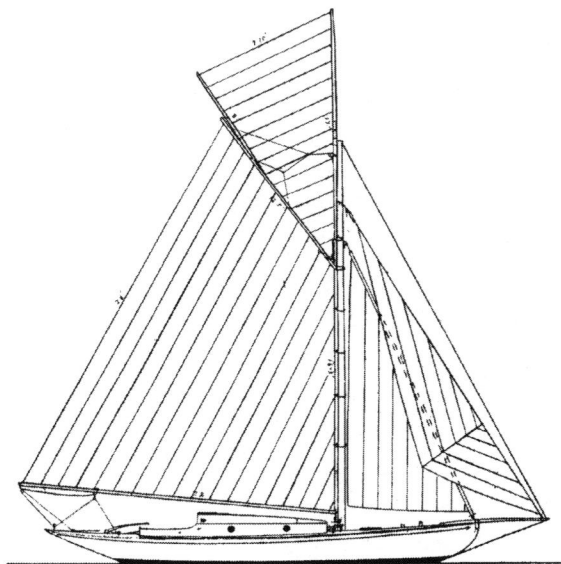

Mercia III sail plan

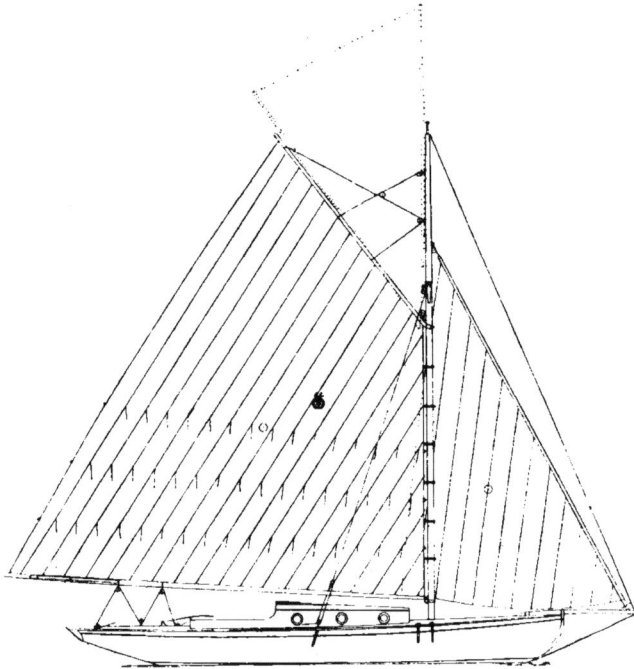

Arima sail plan

SKATE
(Drawing 8) by Howard Messer, c1904

LOA . . . . 34ft 6in   Draught . . . . 1ft 4in / 4ft

LWL. . . . . 27ft   Beam 8ft 3in

Year built 1904

I reproduce the design of *Skate* for the especial benefit of yachtsmen in search of a craft suitable for shallow waters, where it is necessary for her to take the ground at every tide. This remarkable little boat was built at Maldon in 1904 from the design of Mr. Howard Messer, and is planked with 1-inch Kauri pine (Riband carvel construction). In addition to her iron plate, which is ¾ inch thick, she carries 15 cwt. of lead ballast inside. Her decks are of white wood, covered with canvas, and she has a coach-roof of moderate height, under which there is some 4 feet 6 inches headroom. A drip-piece is placed over all ports and others below (inside), so they are doubly protected. There are two sofa berths in the cabin and a cot in the fo'c'sle. Between the cabin and the fo'c'sle there is a w.c. on the port side and a pantry opposite on the starboard side. Her present owner, Mr. J. Manning Prentice, uses an Evinrude detachable motor in a compartment in the after deck, and although of only 1½ h.p., it propels her easily.

One of the chief objections to a centre-plate in a yacht that has to take the ground is that there is a risk of stones jambing between the plate and the sides of the case, with the result that the former can be neither hoisted nor lowered. Mr.

Messer has entirely eliminated such a risk by the following ingenious method: The case is made much wider than necessary, but iron bands project beyond the edges of the case and reduce the width of the slot to about the normal. Any stones or mud that find their way through this entrance are soon washed aft, and drop out through a hole left for the purpose. In addition to her centre-plate, the yacht has a small iron fin, or skeg, just forward of the rudder, the latter being of the drop variety. *Skate* is sloop-rigged with a gunter mainsail, the total sail area being 550 square feet. The foresail is fitted with a light boom and the mainsail with roller reefing gear. By the greatest stretch of the imagination *Skate* could not be termed a handsome vessel, but she is an eminently useful craft, having all the virtues of the barge yacht without the disadvantages of that type. She will work to windward under either mainsail or foresail alone, and has quite a remarkable turn of speed for such a boat.

Mr. Messer twice crossed the North Sea in her, and cruised in Dutch waters, for which her shallow draught and handiness render her particularly suitable; and her present owner, Mr. Prentice, went 'foreign' in her last year. She is of a type that is very cheap to build, and without any exact information on the subject, I should guess the cost of *Skate* as in the neighbourhood of £130. For wildfowling purposes such a vessel could hardly be improved upon, as she can sail in shallow, narrow creeks and lie on mud flats almost upright, whilst her comparatively small sail area and handy rig render her easy to sail single-handed.

12-TON YAWL
(Drawings 9 & 10) by Harold Clayton, c1904

LOA	40ft 6in	Sail area	1,123.5 sq ft
LWL.	28ft 9in	Displacement	9.44 tons
Beam	9ft 4in	Lead keel	4 tons
Draught	5ft 4in	Year built	1904

Builder . Penarth Yacht Building Co.

By the courtesy of Mr. Harold Clayton I am able to reproduce the lines of an exceedingly pretty 12-ton yawl he designed for Mr. R. McNeil, Commodore of the Penarth Yacht Club. She has been built by the Penarth Yacht Building Company in capital style, nothing but the very best selected materials having been employed, and all her fastenings are of copper or yellow metal. With the exception of the top plank, which is of oak, her skin is of pitch-pine. The timbers, beams, carlines, shelf, bilge stringers, knees, deadwoods, aprons, etc., are oak, and her keel English elm. The deck is of yellow pine, laid in narrow planks, whilst the coamings, coach-roof, bulwarks, covering boards, etc., are of teak. The internal decoration scheme is carried out in polished cedar and canary, and the cabins are lighted with electric light. The yawl was designed with a special view to comfort, but with a fairly liberal sail area she should have a useful turn of speed. With good headroom and nice wide floor, the cabin is exceedingly com-

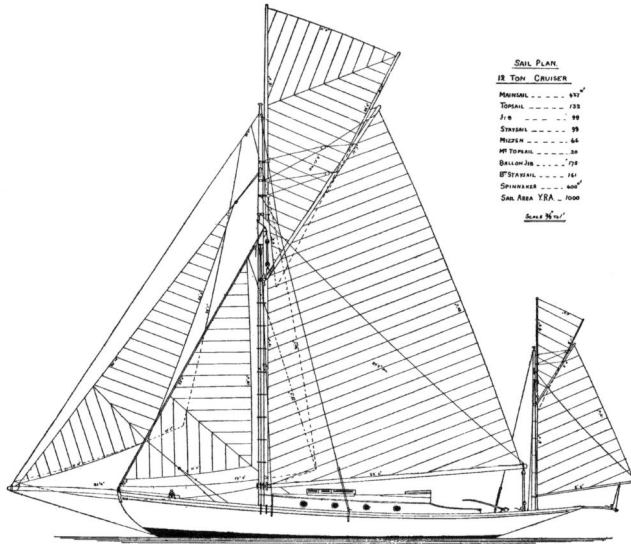

12-ton Yawl sail plan

fortable, and the accommodation below decks very conveniently arranged. A notable feature is the w.c, which has two doors – one from the saloon and the other from the sleeping-cabin – a washing-stand being placed behind the w.c. The well has been made water-tight by means of a piece of deck about a foot wide between it and the cabin. There is plenty of room below the well floor for a motor, and it is probable that a 5-h.p. engine will be installed. The saloon sofas have upholstered backs, and should be comfortable both for sitting and sleeping purposes, and there is a good-sized table in the centre of the cabin. In most yachts of this tonnage the sleeping-cabin is placed aft, but here we find it forward of the saloon. Between the sleeping-cabin and the fo'c'sle is the cooking galley to port and pantry on starboard side. There is a cot for a paid hand in the fo'c'sle. With a moderate overhang forward and a long, graceful contour, the yawl is a very handsome little vessel. Personally, I would sooner have her as a cutter, and in any case her mizzen topsail of only 20 square feet strikes me as bordering upon the absurd; but it certainly gives a finishing touch to the yacht's appearance, and, after all, the rig is a matter that must be left to the individual fancy of the owner.

LONA II
(Drawing 11) by J. Pain Clark, 1905

LOA.	32ft	Draught	4ft 6in
LWL.	22ft 3in	Lead keel.	2½ tons
Beam	7ft	Displacement.	4.75 tons

Lona II was designed by Mr. J. Pain Clark, for his own use as a single-handed cruiser. Beautifully constructed of teak by William King & Sons, of Burnham-on-Crouch, she has proved in every way an excellent little craft, with over 5ft.

headroom under a flush deck; her internal accommodation is exceptionally good for a five tonner, and she sleeps three with comfort. When sitting upon a nice high bunk, one can lean back under the deck, and the sofas feeling slightly concave are particularly comfortable for sleeping purposes. At the ends of the bunks are sideboards fitted below with drawers which are secured with spring latches to prevent them sliding out when the yacht is heeled in a breeze. A skylight, which is really watertight, affords both light and ventilation. There is a water tank under the cockpit floor, and a small cooking galley fitted with a 'Salamander' oven stove and a 'Primus.' *Lona II* is cutter rigged and has a moderate sail area, the mainsail and foresail being fitted with roller-reefing gear. Her running gear is of flexible wire, and anchor work is rendered easy by the aid of a powerful winch. The yacht is fast and weatherly and easily sailed single-handed. Mr. Pain Clark has done a good deal of single-handed cruising in her, and in 1906 won the Royal Corinthian Yacht Club race from Burnham to Port Victoria entirely unassisted.

Lona II sail plan

5.75 TON CANOE YACHT (DAWN II)
(Drawing 12) by G. Umfreville Laws, c1906

LOA 28ft	Sail area . . . . 500 sq ft
LWL 22.12ft	Displacement . . . . 5 tons
Beam 7.66ft	Headroom 5.5ft
Draught 4.5ft	Iron ballast . 2½ tons outside, 5 cwt in

Another attractive design is that of a 5.75 ton canoe yacht, designed by Mr. G. Umfreville Laws for Mr. H.S. Algar, and now being built by Thomas of Fal-

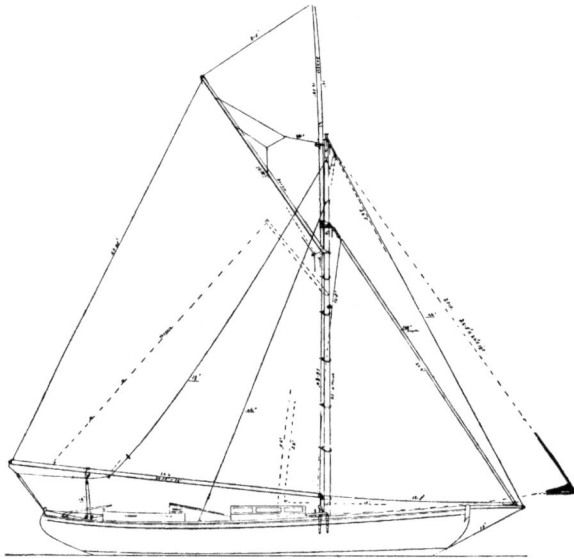

Laws 5.75 ton Canoe Yacht sail plan

mouth. The yacht will be sloop rigged and fitted with roller-reefing gear. Her internal arrangement is excellent and she will sleep three, two in the cabin, and one in the fo'c'astle. She has a flush deck and a lifting skylight. The cabin is lined with ¼-inch Kauri pine, and the bunks fitted with Kapok cushions. To avoid spoiling the profile of the keel, 400 lbs weight of iron has been placed inside in the form of a cast iron mast step.

DESIGN NO 130
(Drawings 13 & 14) by A. R. Luke, c1906

LOA. 26ft 6in	Beam 8ft
LWL. 19ft	Draught 4ft

Sail area . . . . 401.4 sq ft

I am indebted to Mr. A. R. Luke, of Hamble, for two nice designs. The first is a single-hander. The boat has a modified spoon bow, a handsome counter and good freeboard. The accommodation below is excellent, comprising a comfortable and compact cabin 6ft. 6 ins. in length with 5ft. headroom. There are the usual cushioned bunks on either side and a folding bed on the starboard side. At the after end of the cabin is one of Sand's patent under-waterline closets, and a washing basin is fitted below the cockpit floor. When in use this latter is drawn out and stands on top of the W.C., the waste water being drained into the pan to be pumped out subsequently. Moveable steps lead from the cabin to the cockpit which is water-tight and self-draining. Forward of the cabin, on the port side, is a pantry fitted for plates, cups, etc., and opposite is the cooking galley. Forward is the chain locker and the remaining space is devoted to shelves for cooking utensils and hooks for hanging clothes, etc. The boat has a sail area of 401.4 sq. ft., both mainsail and foresail being fitted with roller reefing gear. The halyards lead aft through fairleads near the foot of the mast so that the craft can be worked almost entirely from the cockpit. Several yachts have been recently built from this design and have proved good sea boats, stiff and handy. They are in every way able little cruisers and pleasing to the eye.

DESIGN NO 137
by A. R. Luke, c1906

LOA	30ft 6in	Beam	7ft 8in
LWL	26ft	Draught	3ft 6in
Headroom	5ft 9in	Sail area	412.43 sq ft

The second design by Mr. Luke is for a small auxiliary cruiser fitted with a paraffin motor of 8 B.H.P. She is a canoe sterned boat, with moderate forward overhang. In order that she may be sailed comfortably singlehanded the sail area is small and the boat yawl rigged. Personally I should prefer the yacht rigged as a sloop, but that is merely a matter of taste. The accommodation below decks is very comfortable; there is a sofa each side of the cabin, and sideboards with cupboards and drawers beneath. Forward of the cabin to starboard is a pail W.C. hidden by a curtain and opposite is the cooking galley. A skylight is fitted at the fore end of the booby hatch, with the sashes divided, so that one half opens over cabin and the other, at the fore side, to ventilate and give light to the galley, etc. The fore peak is fitted with a pantry and chain locker, and there are hooks round the sides on which to hang clothes, etc. As the boat is intended to be worked without professional assistance, no accommodation has been provided in the fo'castle for a paid hand. The paraffin supply tank will be fixed on port side of

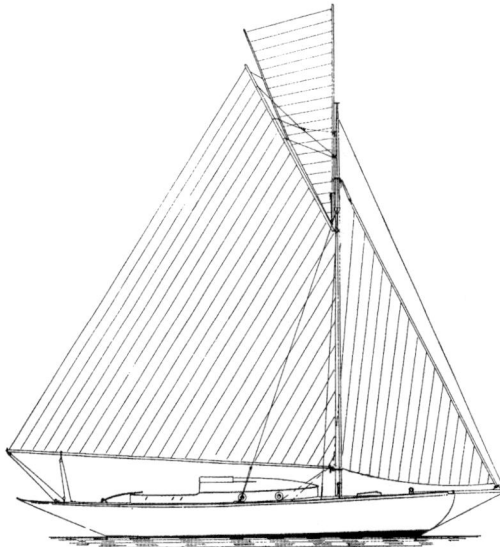

A. R. Luke single-hander sail plan

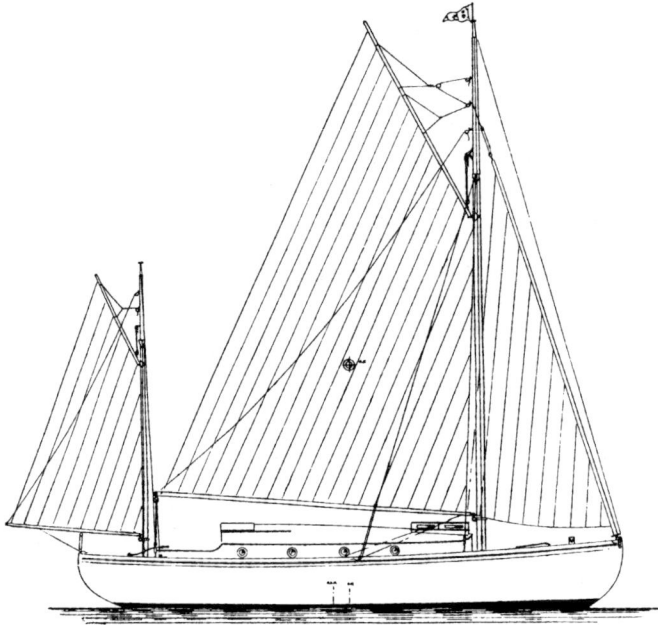

A. R. Luke auxiliary yawl sail plan

the cockpit, and opposite will be fitted a drop-down bunk, so that if required the yacht will accommodate three persons. The cockpit is both watertight and self-draining. Between the cabin and the cockpit is the engine room from which steps lead to the cockpit.

LONA III
(Drawing 15) by J. Pain Clark, c1906

LOA.	35ft 6in	Tonnage	approx 7 tons T.M.
LWL.	24ft	Sail area	812 sq ft
Beam	7ft 7in	Builder.	Wm King & Sons, Burnham
Draught	4ft 6in	Year built.	1907

Of Mr. Pain Clark's able little cruisers, *Lona III* is one of the best. The over-hang forward is moderate, and a handsome counter and graceful sheer enhance her pleasing appearance. Under the skylight she has about 5 feet 6 inches head-room, and the bunks are wide and comfortable. The yacht is planked with pitch-pine to the water-line, and the topsides are of teak, the latter wood being also employed for deck furniture, such as skylight, coamings, covering boards, etc. At the after end of the sofa, on the port side, is placed a cooking galley, and at the forward end a neat chest of drawers. The decks are laid in narrow planks, shaped to the contour of the boat, and are of 1¼-inch Kauri pine. She has sleeping ac-commodation for two in the cabin, and there is a folding cot in the fo'c'sle for a third person. The water tank is placed below a step in the cabin doorway, and is within handy reach of the cooking galley. Designed for single-handed work,

Lona III is altogether a jolly little vessel, and in the hands of her present owner, Mr. Richard Manders, C.B., K.C., has met with considerable success racing in Ireland.

LONA IV
(Drawing 16) by J. Pain Clark, c1907

LOA.	32ft 6in	Sail area	550 sq ft
LWL.	24ft	Displacement	4 tons
Beam	9ft	Tonnage	approx 9 tons T.M.
Draught	3ft 6in	Year built	1908
	Aux engine	Kelvin 16hp	

Lona IV, built this year for Mr. Pain-Clark from his own design, is a craft of quite a different type to *Lona III*. Intended for cruising in shallow waters, such as are found in Holland and the French canals, her draught is light, but sufficient to enable her to get to windward respectably. She has a canoe stern – a feature for which her designer, who was formerly a canoe sailor of note, has always had a predilection. A Kelvin paraffin motor of 16 h.p. is installed below the cockpit floor, and is expected to give the vessel a speed of about seven miles per hour in calm weather. The yacht is rigged as a sloop, with the very moderate sail area of 550 square feet. Although displacing but 4 tons, her great beam gives *Lona IV* a Thames measurement tonnage of nearly 9 tons. Under the skylight, which is fitted on a teak cabin-top, the headroom is about 5 feet 6 inches, and her generous beam gives her a very roomy and comfortable cabin. The fuel tank is placed right aft, whilst the water tank is forward of the engine. On the port side of the well is an engine store, and opposite, on the starboard side, the larder. At the forward end of the port sofa there is a sideboard, and the cooking stove is fitted in the fo'c'sle, in which there is also a folding cot. The mast is stepped in a tabernacle, to enable the yacht to pass under bridges, and the lowering and hoisting of the mast is facilitated by the aid of a sheerpole forestay – a device much used in Dutch waters. At the time I write *Lona IV* has not been launched, but she has all the appearance of a comfortable little shallow draught cruiser.

ROYAL CORINTHIAN YACHT CLUB "SEABIRD"
(Drawing 17) by J. Pain Clark, c1908

Length over all	22ft	Sail area	300 sq ft
LWL.	17ft	Displacement	33 cwt
Beam	6ft	Iron keel	1,800 lb
Draught	3ft 3in	Builder	W. King & Sons, Burnham

I have included this boat as, although designed mainly for racing, she is admirably adapted to modest cruising if the crew sleep under a tent. Adopted by the Royal Corinthian Y.C. in 1909 as a one-design class, the boats proved very popular and, although now nearly forty years old, most of them are still in good condition. They are planked with ½-inch mahogany on an oak frame. The original rig, as designed, was that of a gaff sloop but as the owners were permitted by the rules of the class to choose their rig, provided that the total area of 300 square feet was not exceeded, several of the boats were rigged with gunter mainsails. As I have already written about these Seabirds earlier in this book, further comment is unnecessary.

10-TON CENTRE-PLATE CUTTER
(Drawings 18 & 19) by Linton Hope, c1909

LOA	38ft 6in	Sail area	930 sq ft
LWL	30ft	Displacement	4 tons
Beam	9ft	Lead keel	4.24 tons
Draught (plate up)	4ft	Centre-plate (⅝-in gunmetal)	450lb

The next design comes from the board of Mr. Linton Hope, and represents a 10-ton centre-plate cutter, which should prove a very useful vessel in districts where there is not a great deal of water. The yacht has a short forward overhang and a counter of moderate length.

She has an elm bottom and pitch-pine planking on American elm timbers. Decks are of 1-inch Kauri pine, with teak covering board, whilst the bulkhead and cabin fittings are of pitch-pine. The cabin-top is of 1-inch spruce, covered with canvas, and the floor of the cockpit water-tight, but not self-draining. There are two sofas in the cabin and a cot in the fo'c'sle, and between the cabin and fo'c'sle there is placed a w.c. on the port side and a pantry opposite on the starboard side. The yacht is of an eminently useful type, and one that could be built for a reasonable price.

ALETHEA II
(Drawings 20 & 21) by A. R. Luke, c1910

LOA	31ft 6in	LWL	25ft
LBP	29ft 3in	Beam	8ft 6in
LWL	25ft	Draught	5ft 6in
Beam	8ft 6in	Year built	1910
	Builder	Luke & Co.	

Alethea II is an 8-ton ketch, with canoe stern, designed by Mr. A. R. Luke, and built by his firm at Hamble in 1910 for Mr. J. G. H. Cockburn. She is a particularly comfortable little ship below decks, having 5 feet 10 inches headroom under the skylight in her saloon. There is also sufficient room in the fo'c'sle for a cot for a paid hand, but the yacht is invariably sailed by Mr. Cockburn and his wife without professional assistance of any kind. There is a lavatory on the starboard side of the cockpit, and a cooking galley and pantry are placed opposite on the port side. The vessel has a snug sail plan, and as both mainsail and mizzen are fitted with roller reefing gear, and the foresail also has a roller, she is very easily handled. The steering well is of the water-tight, self-draining type, which, personally, I do not care very much about; but the floor seems to be placed sufficiently high above the water-line to prevent water slopping in through the drainpipe.

There is a locker in the well for oilskins, and a large fresh-water tank is placed below the cockpit floor. The cabin is fitted with two sofa bunks, and there is a wardrobe on the forward end of that on the port side. At the after end of the starboard bunk is a sideboard, with a cupboard above, and a bookcase at the forward end. *Alethea II* is a capital sea-boat, and, for a vessel of her rig, has quite a good turn of speed.

In 1911 she won the Romola Challenge Cup – one of the most coveted trophies of the Royal Cruising Club. In the course of the cruise, for which Mr. Cockburn was awarded this cup, *Alethea* got caught out in heavy weather whilst crossing from Cherbourg, and had to run for Poole, where she arrived safely after a rather exhausting passage of twenty-five hours' duration. In the course of this run of over seventy miles, with a heavy following sea, the ketch behaved splendidly, and her owner, in his log of the cruise, speaks very highly of her capabilities as a sea-boat. I have only to add that she is strongly built, carries all her ballast in the form of a lead keel, and below decks is most tastefully finished in polished woods.

LADY BELLE
(Drawings 22, 23 & 24) by Harley Mead, c1910

LOA 28ft	Draught 6ft 2½in
LWL. 26ft 8in	Displacement . . . . 9.13 tons
Beam 9ft 2½in	Sail area . . . . 750 sq ft

Year built 1910

The next design I give is that of the 28-feet Falmouth Quay punt, *Lady Belle*, whose lines come from the board of Mr. Harley Mead. One sees many pseudo Falmouth Quay punts nowadays, but this yacht is the real thing, being modelled on the lines of the boats used by the Falmouth watermen who get their living 'seeking.' She has the usual yawl rig of the quay punt, but the mizzen is of a more serviceable size than is usually found in small yawls. The internal accommodation of *Lady Belle* is particularly well arranged. The roomy saloon has a settee on either side, with a folding berth above, and there is a folding table in the centre. There are shelves above the berths, and at the after end of the port settee is a wardrobe; whilst opposite, on the starboard side, is a sideboard with bookcase above. Between the cabin and the fo'c'sle the pantry is placed on the port side, and a toilet-room and lavatory on the starboard side. There is a folding cot in the fo'c'sle, where also the cooking galley is situated. Under a coach-roof of moderate dimensions there is plenty of headroom for comfort; and below the cabin floor is placed a 30-gallon fresh-water tank.

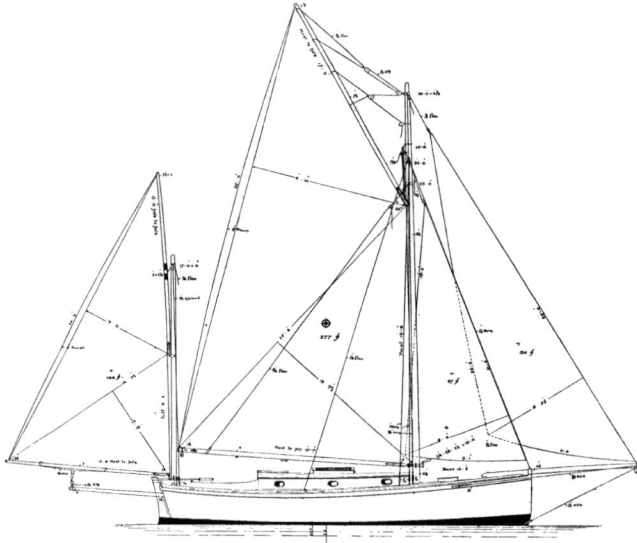

Lady Belle sail plan

CHERUB III
(Drawings 25 & 26) by Albert Strange, 1910

LOA	28ft 6in	Draught	3ft 9in
LWL	22ft 11in	Displacement	4 tons 12 cwt
Beam	8ft 2in	Sail area	483 sq ft
	Builder . . . . . . A Dickie & Sons		

Cherub III is a beamy shallow-draught canoe yacht, specially designed by Mr. Albert Strange to fulfil certain conditions. She was wanted for rather a large party, comprising the owner, his wife, and two sons. Intended mostly for sketching, an easy draught was essential, so that she might lie in shallow harbours, enter the mouths of small burns, and use the harbours of the East Coast with comfort. It was also desirable that she should be light enough to be shipped abroad if required.

During two summers she has fulfilled her purpose satisfactorily. These two seasons were spent on the West Coast of Scotland, and all sorts of weather and sea were encountered. The boat proved stiff, dry, and, in fresh winds, fast for her length; her best day's work being a cruise from Tarbert to Inverary and back to Loch Gair – forty-one miles in eight hours five minutes, rather less than a third of the distance being a turn to windward with a failing breeze. Her small sail plan is against good performance in light winds, but is a great comfort in a strong breeze, the short, slight spars adding to her stiffness. The yacht will lie to very steadily, and sail to windward with the tiller lashed a trifle to weather.

Another yacht built from the same lines has had an addition of 12 per cent, made to her sail area, and 4 inches extra draught aft – alterations that will doubtless be found improvements so far as general speed is concerned. *Cherub III* was built by Messrs. A. Dickie and Sons, Tarbert-Loch Fyne, whose work is well known for thoroughness, good material, and care in carrying out the designer's ideas.

Illness having incapacitated Mr. Strange from cruising single-handed, the yacht was purchased by Mr. W. Murdoch, and is now known as *Redwing. Cherub III* has a generous freeboard, which makes her dry in a seaway, and has enabled the designer to obtain 5 feet 7 inches headroom in the cabin. She is planked with pitch-pine ⅞ inch finished, and her decks are of 1⅛-inch Kauri pine. The timbers are all steamed, being 1½ by 1¼ inches, spaced 6 inches from centre to centre. Her floors are of oak and galvanized iron, and the ballast on her keel weighs 1 ton 12 cwt., whilst a further 15 cwt. is carried inside. The yacht's best point of sailing is to windward, as compared with other yachts of the same size, her extreme stiffness making up for her light draught. She also runs well and steadily, but on a broad reach in strong winds carries a good deal of weather helm. This is doubtless due to her great proportional beam.

GRANUAILE (II)
(Drawing 27) by Frederick Shepherd, c1910

LOA.	40ft 6in	LWL.	28ft
LBP	32ft 10in	Beam	9ft 9in
	Draught.	6ft 4in	

By the courtesy of Mr. Frederick Shepherd, I am able to reproduce the cabin, sail, and midship section plans of *Granuaile*, a particularly nice cruiser of about 11 tons that he designed for Mr. Harry Becher a couple of years ago. The boat has proved a most able craft, with a good turn of speed, and plenty of comfort below decks. The internal accommodation of *Granuaile* is exceptionally good for a yacht of her tonnage. The saloon is 7 feet 4 inches long, with 5 feet 6 inches headroom. The sofas, which have upholstered backs, with shelves and lockers behind, are 2 feet wide, and at the forward end of each is a sideboard with cupboard above. The after-cabin has two berths, with drawers below, and space has been found at the end of each seat for a wardrobe.

Between this cabin and the saloon there is a large cupboard for oilskins on the port side, and a w.c. opposite. A washbasin and large mirror are also placed in this part of the boat, and there is a useful cupboard over the w.c. The pantry is in the fo'c'sle, with the cooking range near by. A folding cot affords sleeping accommodation for a paid hand, and the fo'c'sle is fitted with the usual seats and lockers. The freshwater tank is fitted below the cockpit, which is roomy and comfortable, and there is a large sail locker in the vessel's counter. In chilly weather the saloon is warmed by one of Pascall, Atkey and Son's bulkhead stoves. *Granuaile* was built to the scantling rules of Lloyd's 'R' class (9 metres rating), the topside planking being of mahogany and the bottom of pitch-pine. Her keel is of American elm, 5-inch moulded, and timbers of English oak, 2⅝ by 2⅜ inches,

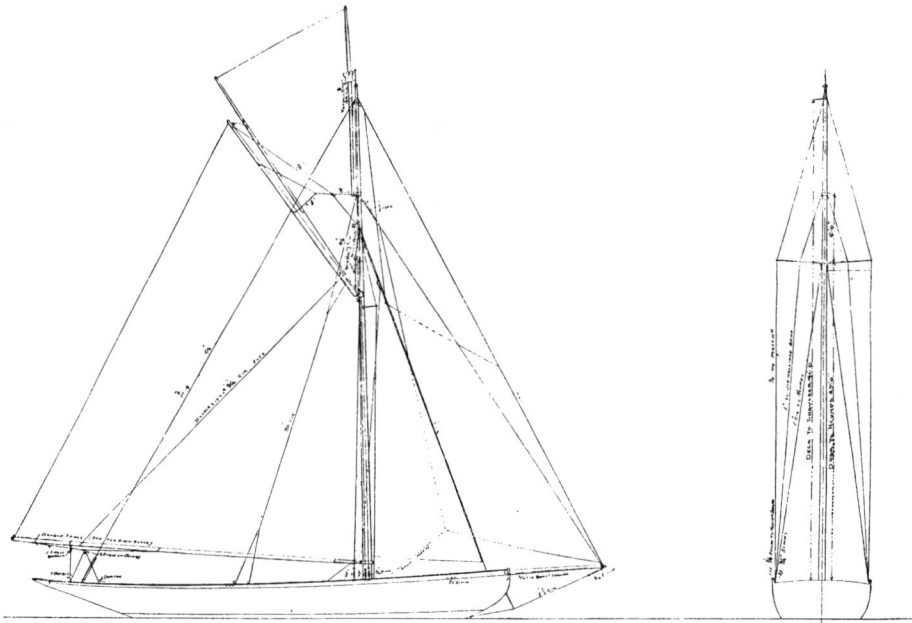

Granuaile (II) sail plan

spaced 23 inches from centre to centre. She is fastened throughout with copper or yellow metal. Her sail plan is that of a snugly-rigged cutter, and she is very stiff in a breeze.

LAPWING
(Drawing 28) by J. E. Doyle, Kingstown, c1910

LOA	22ft	Beam	6ft 10in
LWL	20ft	Draught (plate down)	4ft 6in

Sail area . . . . 260 sq ft

The next design I give is that of *Lapwing*, a very nice centre-plate day boat, designed by the late Mr. Doyle, of Kingstown, and owned by Mr. Becher. She has proved a most useful little knockabout craft for estuary sailing, shooting, and fishing, and her owner keeps her afloat all the year round. She has a moderate sail area of about 260 square feet in a sloop rig, and is a fast, handy little boat.

FANCY (*EX-NORTHSEAMAN*)
(Drawing 29) by Archie Watty, Fowey, c1910

LOA	26ft	Depth	5.9ft
LWL	25ft	Sail area	475 sq ft
Beam	8.65ft	Builder	Archie Watty, Fowey
Draught	5.7ft	Year built	1910

Aux engine . . . . Kelvin 7hp 2-cyl

I have reproduced the lines of my own yacht *Fancy*, as I think she is a good example of the Falmouth Quay punt, a type of craft that has become very popular of late years. *Fancy* is a true Falmouth Quay punt, designed and built by Watty at Fowey in 1910. She was converted into a yacht three years later. The lines reproduced at the end of the book were, I believe, taken off the boat by a previous owner, and unfortunately I have neither a sail plan nor a plan of the internal arrangement. I have, however, described the lay-out of the cabin, etc., elsewhere, and she carries the yawl rig common to this type of vessel, the mizzen mast being stepped within a few inches of the transom. She has 6 feet headroom in the cabin and about 5 feet in the fo'c'sle, and there is plenty of room in the engine-room to get all round the motor, a 7-H.P. twin-cylinder Kelvin, which runs on paraffin. *Fancy* is one of the most beautifully balanced boats I have ever steered, showing no tendency to gripe, even with a fresh wind on the quarter. She is a fine sea boat, although perhaps a trifle slow in stays, and below decks is the most comfortable craft that I have hitherto owned. Falmouth Quay punts are famous for their sea-going qualities and many long voyages have been made in small vessels of that type. Mr. W. E. Sinclair's 4-ton *Joan*, for instance, sailed round Great Britain in 1923, to Madeira in 1925, the Baltic in 1926 and was finally lost in 1927, while crossing the Atlantic. In the course of her cruises she carried her owner through a lot of bad weather, but during that last fatal voyage to Newfoundland, via Iceland, she was dismasted and had to be abandoned. If you have not read Mr. Sinclair's book, *Cruises of the Joan*, you should certainly do so.

5-TON CANOE YACHT (NEREID II)
(Drawings 30 & 31) by G. Umfreville Laws, c1913

LOA	29.5ft	Sail area (yawl rig)	500 sq ft
LWL	22.25ft	Displacement	5.2 tons
Beam	7.7ft	Iron keel	2.25 tons
Draught	4.5ft	Centre-plate (⅝-in gunmetal) .	.450lb

Builder . Wm King & Sons, Burnham

The lines of the 5-ton canoe yacht from the board of the well-known East Coast designer, Mr. G. Umfreville Laws, show a particularly nice example of this type of vessel. Personally, I do not believe in this rig for so small a yacht, and I think my views on the subject are shared by the designer. The owner, Mr. J. Boyd Buckle, however, has a fancy for a yawl, and the man who pays the piper is entitled to call the tune. At the time I write the yacht is in course of construction at Burnham-on-Crouch, in the yard of Messrs. William King and Sons, and with her nice easy lines she should be a capital sea-boat. In the matter of displacement Mr. Laws seems to have just struck the happy medium that is so often difficult to attain, for she has sufficient body to afford comfort below decks without killing her speed. The yacht is planked with teak, and carries an iron keel of 2¼ tons weight. In connection with her sail and rigging plan, the arrangement of the main sheet is somewhat novel. There is a single block on the boom and a similar block on either quarter, but in addition there is a purchase on one end of

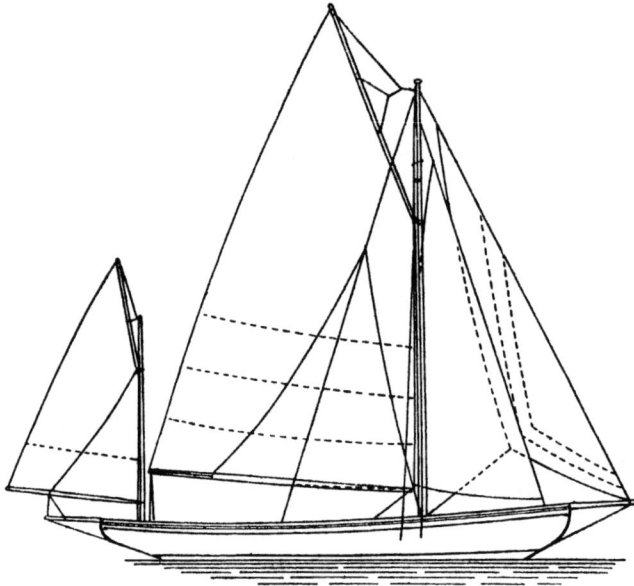

Nereid II sail plan

the main sheet. As the mainsail is small – having an area of only 290 square feet – this additional purchase would only be required in strong winds, and under ordinary conditions the other end of the sheet would be worked. The advantage of this arrangement is that in light breezes the sheet renders freely through the blocks, and the boom can be hauled in or eased off very quickly, whilst the extra power can always be obtained by means of the deck purchase when wanted. The double span on the gaff for the peak halyard is also a good idea, as it distributes the strain nicely along the spar – a feature that not only makes for strength, but also assists the set of the sail. Other interesting features about this yacht are the chain bollard and method of anchor stowage – ideas of Mr. Laws, to which I refer in another chapter. Below decks the accommodation is all that could be desired in a yacht of this size. The headroom is ample and the bunks comfortable. There is sleeping accommodation for two in the cabin and a folding cot in the fo'c'sle. It is the intention of the owner to cook in the fo'c'sle, which I think rather a mistake, as the smell of cooking in a yacht is unpleasant and apt to hang about for a long time. It is, moreover, a rather inconvenient place to have a stove should a single-handed passage be contemplated, as it is too far from the helm.

VENTURE
(Drawings 32 & 33) by Albert Strange, 1917

Length over all	29ft 6in	Headroom	5ft 3in
LWL.	22ft	Displacement	4.3 tons
Beam	6ft 7in	Tonnage	4 tons T.M.
Draught	4ft 3in	Builder	A. Wooden, Oulton Broad

The design of *Venture* is of particular interest as it was the last ever made by Albert Strange. He was, in fact, engaged upon it at the time of his death and had made no accommodation plan. It was therefore left to her present owner, Mr. P. T. Walsh, to draw the accommodation plan here reproduced, and Mr. Walsh has altered her rig from gaff-yawl to that of Bermudian yawl. She was built by A. Wooden, of Oulton Broad, for Mr. H. J. Suffling, and had passed through several hands before Mr. Walsh bought her. An auxiliary engine has been removed by her present owner.

Venture is a very lovely little ship, with easy lines and the graceful sheer characteristic of all Strange-designed boats. Her original sail plan consisted of gaff mainsail, jackyard topsail, thimble-headed mizzen and one headsail. This Mr. Walsh has changed to Bermudian mainsail and mizzen with a single headsail, fitted with the Wykeham-Martin gear. According to Strange's own formula of 100 square feet of sail to each ton of displacement, the yacht is under-canvassed with her area of 350 square feet and she is consequently rather slow in light airs, but a moderate breeze wakes her up and she then has quite a good turn of speed. She is perhaps a trifle narrow according to modern ideas, but is a fine sea boat and her owner tells me that she is very comfortable for two people to live in.

When Mr. Walsh bought *Venture* she was in very poor condition, owing to neglect by some of her previous owners, and he therefore handed her over to a local

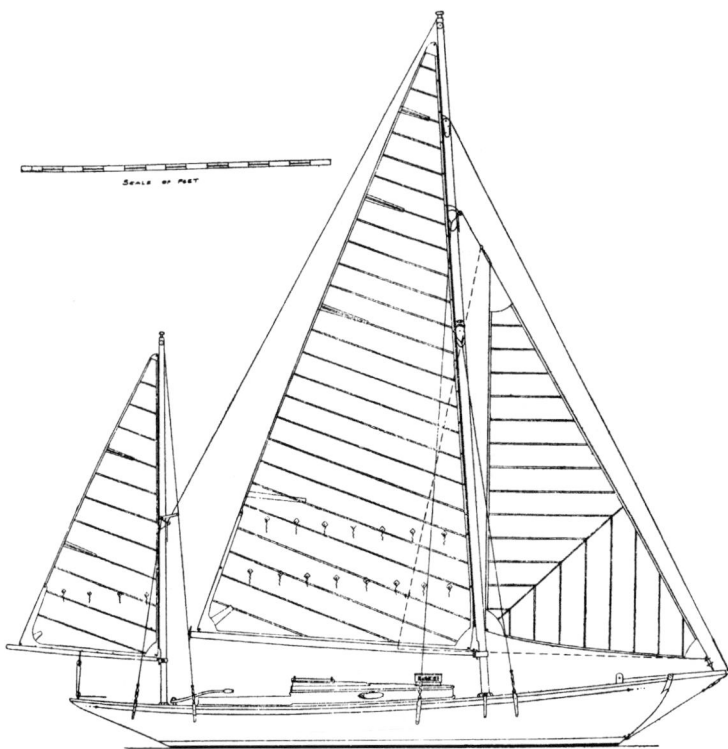

Venture Bermudian sail plan

shipwright to be reconditioned. All the deadwood under the wood keel was re-newed and the new wood is protected with galvanized iron shoes. The old canvas was stripped off her deck, which was re-covered with masonite, screwed down over thick paint, the edges being covered by varnished canvas put on under the rail and rubbing strake, and a stout teak beading fitted round the coamings. This masonite deck-covering has proved a great success and should last indefinitely with reasonable care.

A new mahogany blade was fitted to the rudder, and after the engine had been removed the hull was thoroughly overhauled. "I christened the space lately occupied by the engine the 'Glory-hole,'" writes Mr. Walsh, "and it took me two years to clear away the filthy accumulation underneath and to restore cleanliness and a condition healthy for boat and owner. I will not attach blame to previous owners, as only a serpent could have wriggled under the engine and its bearers for cleaning purposes, but it was a shock to find that certain bearers supporting the cockpit floor had been sawn away to permit the engine to go into place and no sane attempt had been made to provide alternative support."

When she was re-rigged the only original spar retained was the oak bowsprit, and *Venture* was given a new hollow silver spruce main mast and a Bermudian mainsail with a hoist twice the measurement of the foot, a Bermudian mizzen and single headsail. In lieu of runners she has a permanent backstay. The main-sail track is of the enclosed 'C' type with bronze slides, which, with an occasional spot of vaseline, run perfectly. Mr. Walsh gutted the yacht's interior and put in new mahogany bulkheads, seats, etc., replanning the accommodation. As the accommodation plan here reproduced does not show the cross sections, it may be as well to supplement it with a brief description of the lay-out. In the cabin are the usual port and starboard sleeping berths, over 6 feet long, with kapok mattresses covered with Willesden canvas, and stowage space beneath. There is a net rack, 2 feet 6 inches long on each side and food lockers port and starboard. Stowage space for a Primus stove, crockery, etc., is provided on the starboard side. There is a bucket w.c. under the fore-hatch in the fo'c'sle and on the star-board side a quarter-round shelf for side lights, with the riding light beneath. Just aft of this shelf is a blanket locker. The chain locker is below the floor and the second anchor is also stowed in the fo'c'sle, where the second and spitfire jibs are slung to the shelf. Two oars and the spinnaker boom are kept under the deck between the stem and fore side of the cabin. In the cockpit, which is 4 feet 6 inches long, there are four lockers on seat level and two at floor level. Water cans are stowed under the floor. The sail locker is right aft, with access by a shifting door. Here are stowed the trysail, mizzen staysail, deck brush, spare rope, etc. The spinnaker and reaching jib are kept in a bag in the cabin and the kedge, warps, bucket, washing-up bowl, sponges, etc., in the cockpit lockers.

Some time ago Mr. Harrison Butler worked out *Venture's* metacentric analy-sis and found the shelf completely crossed at 30 degrees of heel. He said that theoretically she ought to pull hard on her helm, especially when reaching rail down, but, in fact, she did nothing of the sort when he sailed her in a gale of wind on Breydon Water years ago, and Mr. Walsh tells me that he has found her very light on the helm under all conditions, whether under her original gaff rig or her present Bermudian, which goes to show that theory and practice do not always walk hand in hand. Although I have attributed the design of *Venture* to Albert Strange, it was, as a matter of fact, based on plans made by her first owner, Mr. H.J. Suffling, and so it would perhaps be more accurate to describe it as a joint effort.

TALISMAN II
(Drawings 34 & 35) by Norman E. Dallimore, c1924

LOA.	27ft	Displacement.	6 tons
LWL.	24ft	Sail area	460 sq ft
Beam	7ft 9in	Builder.	Wm King & Son, Burnham
Draught	4ft 9in	Year built.	1924

The next design is that of *Talisman II* by Mr. Norman E. Dallimore, the well-known Burnham-on-Crouch designer, who has created many desirable small cruisers. *Talisman II* was built by William King & Sons at Burnham in 1924 for Lord Ruthven as a single-handed cruiser. She is rigged as Bermudian sloop, the area of her sails being: Mainsail, 350 square feet, and foresail, 110 square feet, giving a total area of 460 square feet for her working canvas. In addition she has a trysail of 210 square feet and a storm jib of 50 square feet. The mainsail is fitted with roller reefing gear and the foresail also has a roller. With an iron keel of 2½ tons the yacht stands up to her canvas well. A point to which I particularly wish to draw attention is the cabin-top, which is of the all-over type such as I have described elsewhere. This cabin-top, without being in the least unsightly, adds enormously to the comfort below and very materially to the strength of the vessel.

There is full 6 feet headroom under the skylight and 5 feet 6 inches under the cabin-top, or deck, for in effect this all-over cabin-top is a flush deck as far as the after-bulkhead. All of the advantages of a cabin-top of this type, to which I drew attention in the last chapter, are apparent in this yacht, and the internal accommodation is quite exceptional for a craft of her size. The internal lay-out strikes me as admirable. Between the cockpit and the cabin, under the bridge deck, is a cooking galley, fitted with an oven stove and Primus on the port side, whilst on the starboard side the auxiliary engine is installed. The engine shown in the drawing is a Kelvin, but, as a matter of fact, an Ailsa Craig motor was actually installed to suit the requirements of the owner. Below the galley, space is provided for the cooking utensils, and beneath the cabin step is fitted a W.C. On the port side, as one enters the cabin, are the pantry and sink, and below, a drawer and a locker. Opposite, on the starboard side, is a hanging cupboard for

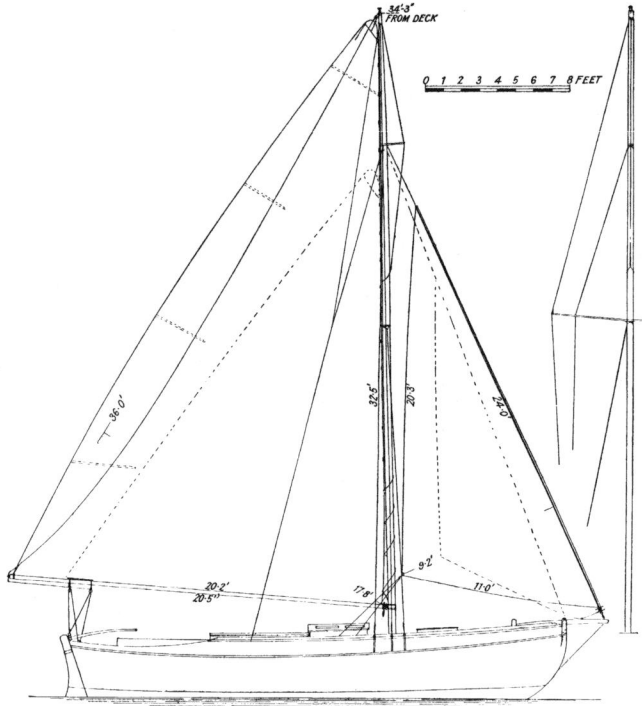

Talisman II sail plan

clothes. Folding cots are fitted above the sofa bunks, and between the cabin and fo'c'sle on the port side is a bookshelf with drawers below. In the fo'c'sle there are racks for gear, the chain locker and, right forward, a large locker. The headroom in the fo'c'sle under the fore-hatch is about 5 feet, with 3 inches less under the deck. There is a locker in the stern right aft and a sliding hatch to draw over the cockpit in bad weather. Altogether, *Talisman II* strikes me as a very useful boat which reflects credit on her designer.

MARIE MICHON
(Drawing 36) by Bevil Warrington-Smythe, c1926

Length over all	28.0ft	Sail area	623 sq ft
LWL.	25.7ft	Headroom	4.75ft
Beam	8.7ft	Tonnage	8 tons T.M.
Draught	5.5ft	Builder.	Gilbert & Pascoe, Porthleven

Those who favour yachts of smack type will be interested in the design of *Marie Michon*, which is a fine example of such craft. She was designed by Mr. Bevil Warrington-Smyth for Mr. F. R. H. Swann in 1927. If she lacks something of the finish one associates with smart yachts, there can be no question as to her strength, for her construction is exceptionally substantial. I am inclined to think that the average owner panders too much to mere appearance and devotes time to 'spit and polish' which otherwise could be spent in sailing. That, in my opinion, is foolish, for the *raison d'etre* of a yacht is to be sailed and not to be looked at.

The requirements of the owner were a vessel in which he could cruise in safety and which would provide reasonably comfortable accommodation for three people. Seaworthiness was to be the chief aim of the design, and as the lay-out of the cabin and deck were not even considered until the vessel was actually in course of construction, there are no plans that I can reproduce. I must therefore fall back on a description of those features, which I hope will give the reader a good impression of the boat. But first a word or two about her construction. The keel is of elm and the frame of oak, similar wood also being used for the transom and beams. The planking is pitch-pine, with a thick strake of oak, and the decks of yellow pine. The cockpit, companion and deck fittings are of teak. She is galvanized-iron-fastened and the ballast consists of an iron keel weighing 2 tons and 2½ tons of iron inside. It is no doubt due to this distribution of the weight that *Marie Michon* has proved such a comfortable ship at sea.

For the sake of strength and appearance the vessel was given a flush deck and the cabin is lighted by a skylight and four prism decklights. The 8-foot pram dinghy, which has a removable middle thwart, can be stowed bottom upwards over the skylight. The cockpit, 5 feet long, is of the self-draining type, and as the vessel has generous freeboard, it was possible to make it deep enough to afford protection from wind and water and comfortable to sit in. The objections to a self-draining cockpit to which I have referred in another chapter, do not therefore exist in this yacht. At the fore end of the cockpit is a stand for the binnacle and pins for the headsail sheets. A bridge-deck is laid on two stout beams, 3 inches by 3 inches, and beneath it is the water-tank of 30 gallons capacity. The companion, forward of the bridge-deck, is small and of pilot-boat type.

On entering the cabin, the cooking galley is on the starboard hand and opposite on the port side is a compartment for hanging oilskins. In this compartment the w.c. is also situated. The remainder of the boat is entirely open, thus forming a cabin approximately 16 feet long. On the port side is a large chart table, with a bookshelf above and a locker beneath; then comes the skipper's cot, a clothes cupboard and a rack for sails. On the starboard side are two cots, which, like the skipper's, are of the usual pipe-frame type, fitted with horsehair mattresses. The locker seats are uncovered, loose cushions being used, which are stowed away when at sea. As the cots and bedding are protected with waterproof covers, there is nothing to get wet in bad weather. Forward of the mast are a coal stove and the chain locker, and right forward lockers for the lamps and coal. The headroom below the deck is 4 feet 9 inches and there is standing headroom under the companion and skylight.

With her transom stern and deep draught, *Marie Michon* is 'all boat' and an exceptionally powerful vessel for her size. Her heavy displacement calls for a generous sail plan, but the boom-end is plumb with the transom, so that roller

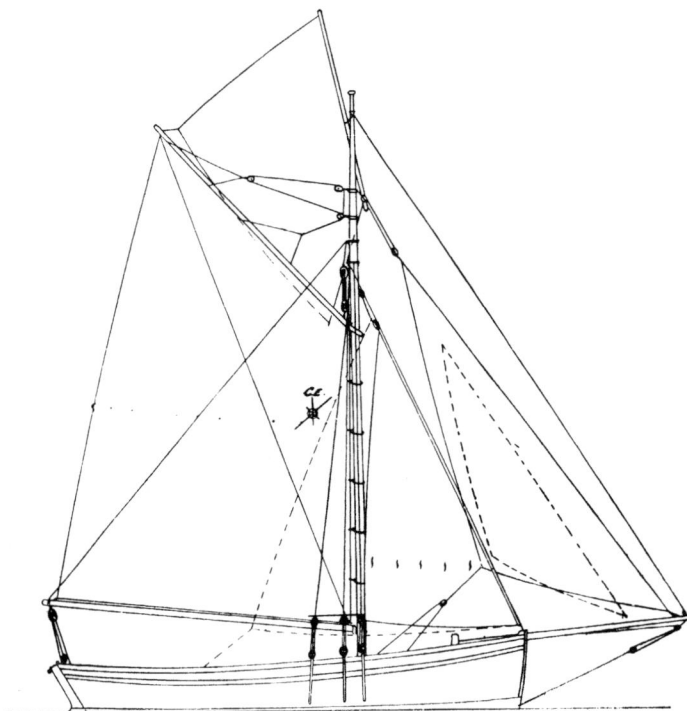

Marie Michon sail plan

reefing gear can be used without that abominable contrivance a claw-ring. The gaff is nearly as long as the boom, after the style of the French fishing boats, and the mast, 34 feet from deck to truck, is a Norway spruce spar, supported by three shrouds each side. The mast is of substantial size, being almost the same diameter (6½ inches) from deck to hounds and over 5 inches at the topmast band. No bolts pass through the masthead, the gear being attached to iron bands, and there are no cross-trees. As the mast is well supported by the shrouds, of which one pair leads to the masthead, runners are not necessary, while the sturdy bowsprit needs no shrouds. The shrouds are fitted with dead-eyes and lanyards of 1¼-inches hemp bolt-rope, which is dressed occasionally with Stockholm tar. They seldom need setting up more than once a season. All of the spars and also the deck are painted. The reefing gear, gooseneck and mastband are of the pattern advocated by the late Mr. Claud Worth, and on the mast is a powerful winch, which can be used for breaking out the anchor and setting up the halyards.

Marie Michon carries a bower anchor of the Worth pattern weighing 50 lb., and a spare bower of the same pattern with disconnecting crown for easy stowage. The main and peak halyards lead to pin rails inside the shrouds, one on each side. The yacht's equipment of sails is very complete, comprising, in addition to the mainsail, a trysail, balloon jib made of very light material, a working jib, second jib and storm jib, balloon staysail and topsail. The sails are dressed, the topsail and reaching staysail being blue and the rest red.

Marie Michon is a fine sea boat with quite a good turn of speed, even in light weather, when with her flying kites aloft she slips through the water very easily. Like most vessels of this type, her initial stability is not very great, but when she has heeled a little she stiffens up and goes no farther. Her motion at sea is very easy and when hove-to through stress of weather she is dry and comfortable.

Mr. Swann has done a deal of cruising in *Marie Michon*. After her launch in 1927 he sailed her to Belle Île and back to Helford, whilst in 1932 he won the Romola Cup of the Royal Cruising Club with a fine cruise from Helford to Marie-hamn, a distance of 1,349 miles, covered in 16 days 1 hour sailing time. That the yacht is no sluggard will be gathered from some of her passages, as, for instance, the 136 miles from Helford to Poole Bar in 24 hours 10 minutes. On another occasion she sailed from Le Fret, in the Rade de Brest, to Morgat, 25 miles, in 4 hours, and from Morgat to the Manacles, about 130 miles, in 26 hours. Another good run was from Anvil Point to St Anthony's, 128 miles, in 25 hours.

I have described this little yacht at some length as she seems to me to approach within measurable distance of the ideal for off-shore cruising. She is fast enough for all practical purposes, an exceptionally good sea boat and economical to maintain. What more could anyone desire in a small cruising yacht?

CYCLONE II
(Drawings 37 & 38) by T. Harrison Butler, 1928

LOA .	25ft	Displacement .	5.7 tons
LWL.	22ft 6in	Tonnage	6.5 tons T.M.
Beam	8ft 7in	Iron keel	2.2 tons
Draught	4ft 2in	Mainsail	250 sq ft
Foresail	80 sq ft	Jib.	75 sq ft
	Sail area	405 sq ft	

Cyclone II is an enlarged edition of Dr. Harrison Butler's well-known Cyclone design. The latter has been extensively built to, and is quite famous amongst cruising yachtsmen. Dr. Butler has very kindly prepared these lines of a larger boat for me and I feel confident that she would prove as successful as the smaller vessel. The design strikes me as ideal for coastwise cruising and the accommodation is extremely well thought out. The generous beam would make her very comfortable both to sail and live aboard and she is altogether a jolly little ship. I append Dr. Butler's own notes on the design:

The lines of Cyclone II were drawn with the idea of obtaining the best possible sea boat for the size which has been selected as most suitable for general work round the coast. A large number of yachts have been built to the design all over the world and they have been most satisfactory. *Kandoo*, with a L.W.L. of 20 feet and a largish Bermudian sloop rig, was caught in a moderate gale half-way across the Channel. Her tiller was car-

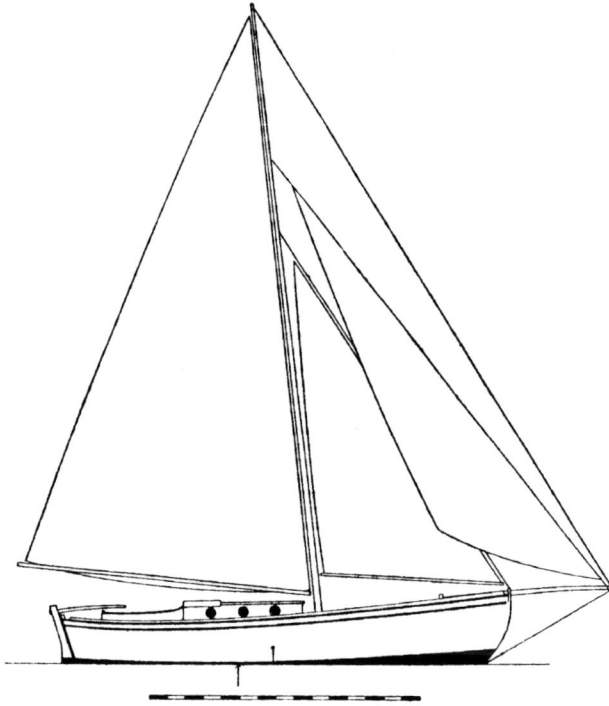

Cyclone II sail plan

ried away and the decks swept. The mainsheet block came out of its strop and the masthead shrouds came out of the notch in the spreaders. She got involved in Alderney race and her crew, tired out, hove her to and let her sail herself back to England while they slept. They awoke to find her inside the Dartmouth Mew-stone! The mast did not carry away and the boat brought her crew home in safety. Another, with a 19-feet L.W.L., was built in Sweden and rigged as a yawl. While out fishing in winter she was caught in what her owner described as a cyclone, hence the name chosen. Two 40-ton yachts were blown ashore and another 60-tonner dismasted; *Cyclone* rode out the gale and came home safely. I mention these facts to show that the model is eminently seaworthy.

The draught has been kept low to render the yacht suitable for the East Coast. The large beam allows the boat to sail at a small angle of heel, so that all the draught is available, and in consequence the boat goes well to windward. The freeboard is generous and enables the cabin plan to be arranged under a flush deck. It is necessary to give the deck a large camber, but this furnishes a safer platform to windward when the boat is heeled. A flush deck is a valuable asset in a small yacht and gives plenty of deck room to walk on.

Sail Plan: The Bermudian rig has been adopted, but the yacht is suitable for the ordinary cutter, the sloop or the yawl rig. The Bermudian rig gives a 10 per cent efficiency over the gaffsail and the area is accordingly 10 per cent less than would be necessary with a gaffsail. The mast is kept well aft, in the old-fashioned position, to obtain a large foresail. The head-sails of a yacht, area for area, are twice as effective as a sail behind a mast and therefore I get as much headsail as I can. The small mainsail makes for easy handling, and the yacht would work in a strong wind with staysail alone. The sail works on a boom.

The drawing shows the sail rigged without a runway. The lower part below the crosstrees is attached to ordinary mast-hoops or, better, to parrels. The upper half is shackled to a jackstay which passes within the hoops and is set up to the deck. To prevent the sail from sagging aft when reefed two travellers are fitted on the pole. To each is attached a light line which is cleated to the mast at the deck. The upper traveller comes into play when the sail is reefed, the lower keeps the full sail up to the mast.

Deck Plan: The anchor will be got by hand, but a small capstan is fitted for breaking out when necessary. A metal roller leads the chain fair to the fairlead on the stem. The chain pipe is well aft and leads to a self-stowing chain box. There is plenty of room to stow the chain under the forecastle floor, but the further aft the weight can be got the better and, for single-handed work, a self-stowing arrangement is essential.

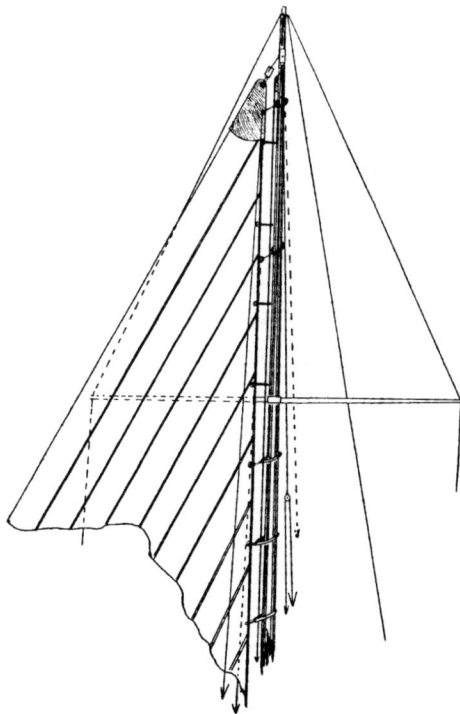

Cyclone II Bermudian sail

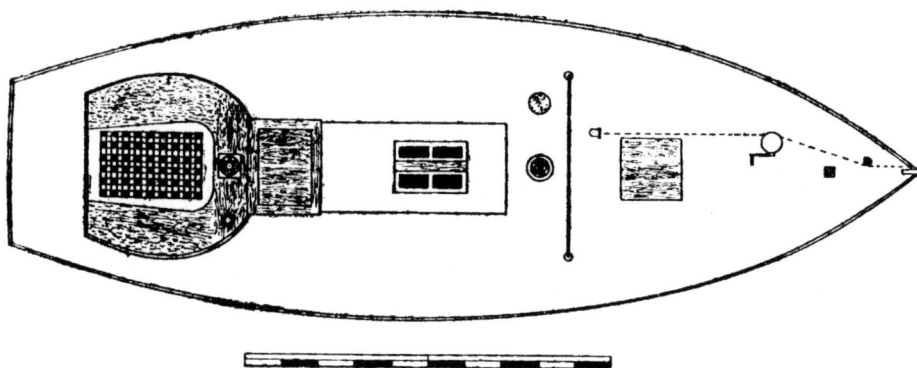

Cyclone II deck plan

The foresail horse is shown and aft of it, to the port side of the mast, is the stove pipe and cowl. This stows away below when not in use and the hole is covered with a watertight plate.

The central deckhouse has four opening ports in the sides and one forward. In addition, a small skylight can be fitted. This gives 6 feet headroom when the table is stowed away. The skylight can be stowed below in bad weather and a hatch fitted. The deckhouse is shown wider in the mid-section plan, and either dimension can be adopted, according to the individual taste of the owner.

The compass is shown in the half-deck. It can, if desired, be seen through an angled plate-glass window. This seems to be the only place for it, but it is very near the engine and it will be well to have a standard compass on the forward end of the deckhouse, so that any deviations can be allowed for. A deviation card is a nuisance in a small yacht.

The cockpit is shown with artistically curved coamings. Probably straight sides with a sharp turn-in at the fore-end would be more comfortable. All sheets and the fore halliard and down-haul lead to the cockpit, or to cleats on deck within reach of the cockpit. The main halliard and purchase can come aft too if desired and I certainly should like this arrangement.

Cabin Plans: The *en echelon* arrangement is unusual but has its advantages. There is a suggestion of privacy for two sleepers. The galley and pantry are together and there is a seat free of the table, but, if desired, the pantry can go forward and the starboard seat can come aft by the width of the pantry.

Forecastle: From forward aft: The side lights, which are not often used, stow in the eyes of the boat. On the port side of the forecastle there is a pipe cot of full size. The unusual shape gives the maximum space. A bucket, or a mechanical toilet, is found at the fore-end of the seats. On the starboard side there is a folding wash basin and a shelf for the riding light of full size and for a paraffin tin. Aft of the basin is a large food cupboard opening into the cabin.

Main Cabin: In front of the mast, on the port side, we find a heating stove. When not in use it is covered up and we get a useful sideboard. A heating stove is a great asset in a small yacht that is used in the spring and autumn. In front of the stove is the chain locker, nearly amidships. The port side has no padded swab, although one is shown in the elevation. Forward, the backboard can be removed to allow both doors of the cupboard to open, and aft, its place is taken by the folding chart table, which must be turned down to allow access to the cupboard D. Right aft is a hanging space for oilskins. The starboard sofa has a comfortable stuffed back, as shown on the port side in the elevation. The cushions are Vi-springed and are used for bunks.

There is plenty of room in the forecastle to stow the sleeping-bags. If desired, folding berths, or better pipe cots, can be fitted. Right aft, on the starboard side, is a gimballed stove of approved pattern and behind it a space to stow the cooking gear. There is a locker under the galley. The pantry is forward of the galley and in front of it is a cooking table, or side-board, as occasion may dictate. Two tanks are shown under the cockpit seats. One, or both, can be used for water. If an engine is fitted, one tank will be arranged for the fuel; but it need not be as large as shown in the

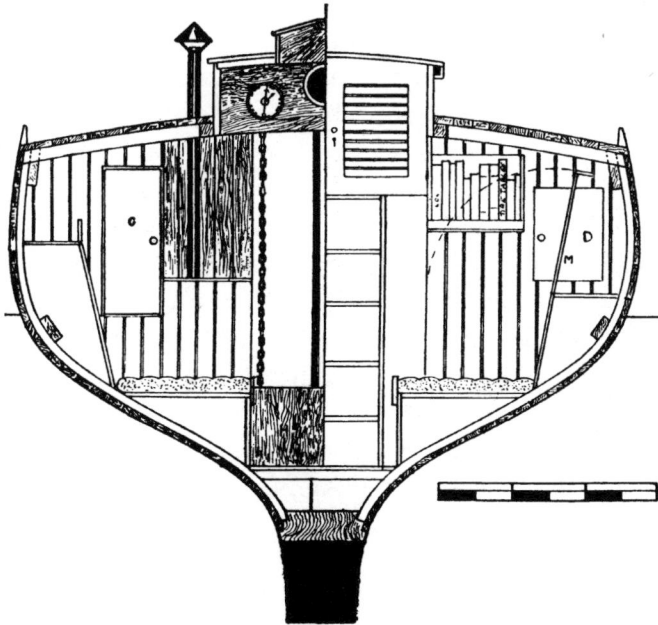

Cyclone II midship section

drawing, thus leaving a larger locker aft. Two small lockers are shown aft of the tanks, one for bosun's stores the other for meat. In the transom is the sail locker. Warps will be stowed under the cabin seats. We find, in *Sandook*, that they are instantly available when so stowed. Smaller warps and spare gear will find room in the sail locker.

The engine could be fitted a little further aft, but its weight is undesirable there, and I have brought it well forward where it is perfectly accessible. A Brook's 'Dominion' would be most suitable. The pump, of the force pump variety, is fitted at the fore-end of the cockpit, where it can be worked with comfort. It is shown in the deck plan too far from the midline.

RONA
(Drawings 39 & 40) by W. Easton, 1929

LOA.	24ft	Displacement.	2.56 tons
LWL.	18ft	Iron keel.	1 ton
Beam	7ft	Centre-plate	1 cwt
Draught (natural).	3ft	Inside ballast.	2 cwt
(with plate)	.6ft.	Tonnage.	4 tons T.M.
	Sail area (ex light canvas)	. 333 sq ft	

Rona was designed by her owner, Mr. W. Easton, and partially built by him in the Philippine Islands with the assistance of Chinese carpenters. When planked up and decked he brought her home and the yacht was subsequently completed by William King & Sons, of Burnham-on-Crouch. *Rona* was designed as a sturdy day-boat, capable of holding her own in such waters as the Swin and Wallet in ordinary summer sailing weather, and of running safely if the sea got up too much for her to face it. She proved such a comfortable and able little ship all round, that she was eventually fitted out for short cruises.

Sail can be reduced in a moment by lowering the mizzen and furling the jib, and she is then left under a snug sloop rig and perfectly balanced, as the centre of effort of the mainsail and foresail is the same as for the whole sail area. She is very fast under whole sail in light weather and a grand little vessel in a hard wind and rough sea. She runs very steadily before a strong wind and following sea, and in moderate weather is fast, both reaching and running, under her light canvas, which includes a big balloon jib, reaching foresail and mizzen staysail.

The housing of the centre-plate is enormously strong, and being all in the iron keel does not encroach on the cabin space so much as most centre-plates. The small case for the lifting arm is for the most part in the fo'c'sle and an extension of it forms the chain locker. The cabin lay-out was planned to suit the requirements of the owner, who, before the war, often cruised in her with his two sons. Personally, I do not care for the self-draining cockpit, for reasons stated elsewhere in this book, but that, of course, is a matter of opinion, and it is only

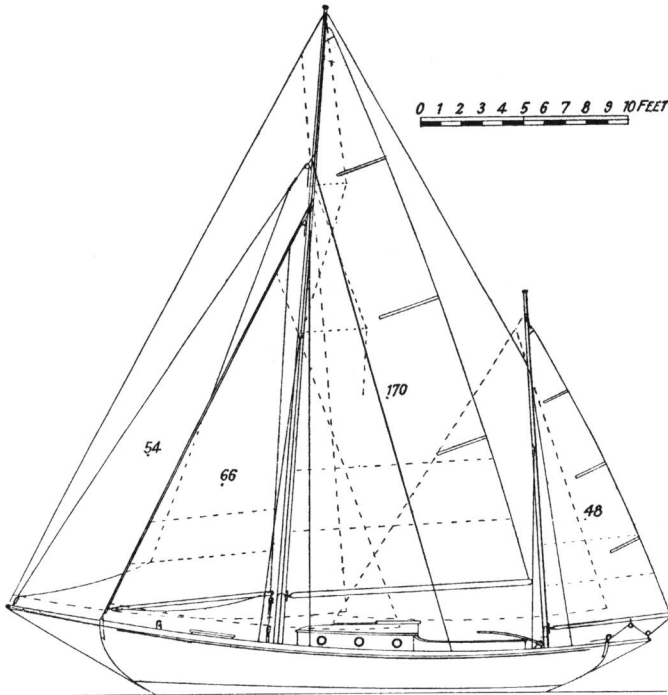

Rona sail plan

fair to say that the views of many small yacht owners on this subject are dia-
metrically opposed to mine.

Mr. Easton has designed several other extremely attractive yachts, but I have
selected *Rona* for reproduction here, as she is one of the few really satisfactory
small centre-plate cruisers that I know. That in her case the centre-plate is not
a source of weakness will be gathered from the fact that, although she has been
sailed hard in all sorts of weather, she has never leaked a drop since she was
built in 1929. All the same, if she were mine, I should drop her keel 6 inches
and remove the plate, for although the case is comparatively small it does cut
into the cabin accommodation. As it is, she sails quite well to windward with the
plate housed and I feel sure that with an additional 6 inches natural draught her
weatherliness would be all that one could desire.

2½-TON BLACKWATER SLOOP
(Drawings 41 & 42) by Dan Webb, c1930

LOA.	18ft	Draught	2ft 9in
LWL.	16ft 6in	Sail area (gaff)	193 sq ft
Beam	6ft 6in	Sail area (Bmdn)	.173 sq ft

Last summer [c1937] I decided to sell my 7-ton Falmouth Quay Punt *Fancy*.
She was in many respects a nice old boat, but owing to lack of time and advancing age my days of serious cruising are over and it seemed a waste to keep a craft

197

of that size just for sailing in the river and short trips to neighbouring waters. I found, too, that her draught of nearly 6ft. was inconvenient, as I often had to jill about waiting for water before I could get through the Ray Sand Channel. I came to the conclusion that a little pocket cruiser would be more suitable for my purpose and cost comparatively little to maintain, so I advertised *Fancy* and she was sold within a week.

Previously when I have sold a boat, and I have sold more than a score, I have been able to replace her within two or three weeks, but on this occasion it proved a very different matter. There seemed to be a dearth of small craft in decent condition in the market and although I inspected quite a number, I could find nothing suitable. Some were little better than old junk, long overdue for the scrap-heap, whilst others were nothing like what I was led to expect from the particulars supplied to me. After spending more than three months in a hopeless quest, I came to the conclusion that there was no alternative but to build.

As I could not afford to spend a great deal on a boat, my thoughts turned to those of standard design. As I remarked in a previous chapter, there are now a number of firms producing little cabin boats to standard designs and specifications, but the one that attracted me most was the 2½-ton Blackwater sloop built by Dan Webb, of Maldon. The design seemed to me a good one and the specification quite adequate.

The first time I ever saw one of these little ships under way was one afternoon at Fambridge, when it was blowing like hell. My son and I had tried to get on board *Fancy*, but had to put back as our dinghy, which rather lacked freeboard, was in danger of being swamped. While waiting for the tide to ease up a little, we noticed two girls trying to reach this Blackwater sloop in a pram dinghy. For half an hour or more they battled with the elements, one rowing and the other bailing, and making practically no progress, they eventually returned to the hard with the water nearly up to the thwarts. Later, when the tide had slackened a little, we and they took advantage of a short lull to get on board. Shortly after, I was surprised to see these girls get under way, and concluded that they were merely going to run down to Burnham under a jib. But not a bit of it. They set the mainsail with a pair of reefs in it and after running some distance down the reach, hauled their wind and began to beat up against the tide. I watched the boat closely through my glasses and noticed that she stood up well to her canvas and made excellent progress over the tide. This performance impressed me a good deal and I remembered the incident when I came to consider getting a standard boat for myself. As I had never been on board, or examined one of these boats closely, I decided to go over to Maldon. There I found that Dan Webb had a well-equipped yard with a fine slipway. It was early in October and a number of yachts had already been hauled out. I noticed that they were well shored up and the covers securely fastened, a fact that impressed me, for little matters of detail are usually a reliable index to a man's general methods.

147 Sq. ft.

46 Sq. ft.

173 Sq. ft.

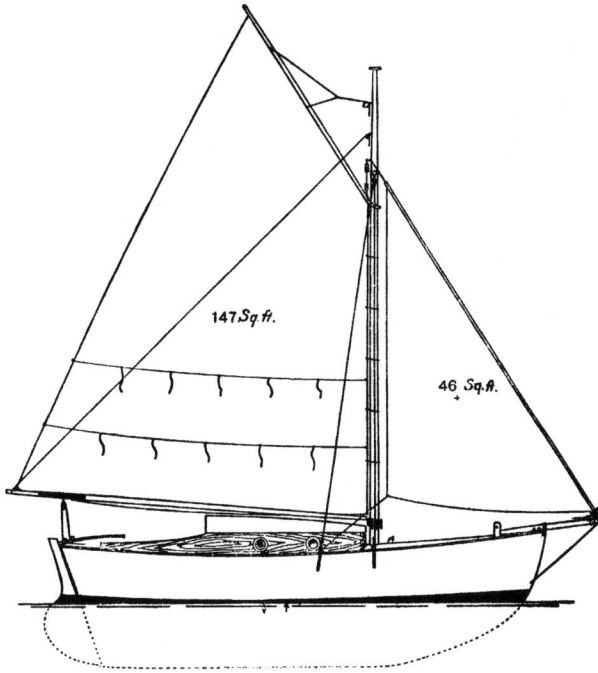

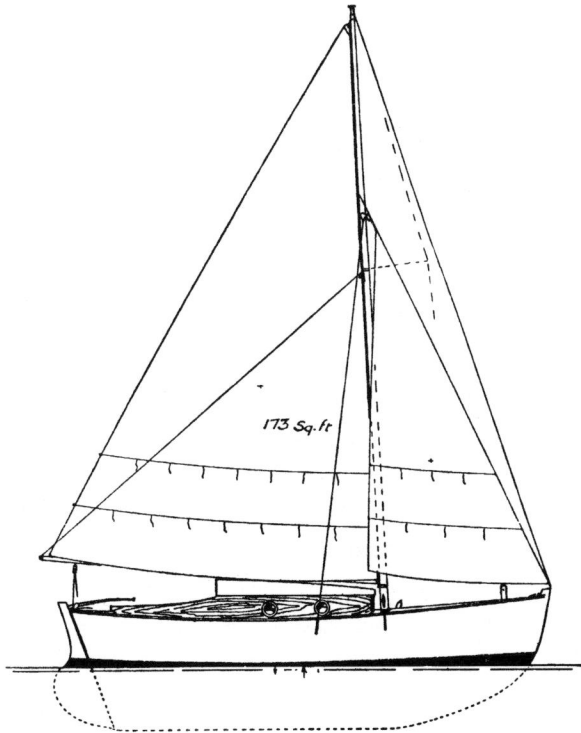

2½-ton Blackwater Sloop sail plans, gaff and Bermudian

One of the Blackwater sloops was lying alongside, waiting to be hauled out, so I went on board. I found that she had a roomy comfortable cockpit, deep enough to afford good protection from the weather and with the seats at a convenient height. This particular boat had an auxiliary engine and as its case was raised but a few inches from the floor, it did not encroach unduly on the well. On opening the cabin doors, I was astonished at the amount of room in her cabin. The usual bunks were fitted with good cushions, covered with velvet corduroy, and there was a pipe cot on either side. Under the cabin-top there was 4ft. 6in. headroom and up forward any amount of room for stowage. Then I went into Mr. Webb's office to study the lines and specification. With a rounded bow and sloping transom stern, she is a shapely little ship. The price complete was originally £115, but owing to the advance in the cost of labour and materials it has been found necessary to increase it to £135. A Stuart Turner auxiliary engine can be fitted at an additional cost of £47 10s., or £52 10s., with reverse.

The standard specification includes ⅝-in. British Columbian pine planking, and timbers of oak or American elm, steam bent, 1in. by ¾in. finished thickness, spaced 6in. from centre to centre. The stem, sternpost, deadwood and deck-beams are of oak, transom of elm or oak and keel of elm. The deck-beams are 1½in. by 1¾in., planked with ⅞-in. pine, canvas covered. The planking is copper-fastened, the other fastenings being of galvanized iron. The iron keel weighs rather more than 9 cwt. and the inside ballast consists of iron pigs. With generous beam and stiff midship section, she heels but little, thus reaping the full benefit of her draught. The cabin-top and cockpit coamings, seats and doors are of British Columbian pine. The standard specification also includes sails and gear, bunk cushions, anchor and 15 fathoms of ¼-in. galvanized chain, riding light, brass pump, a pair of sweeps and rowlocks, a boathook, mop and bucket, and the cabin floorboards are either stained or painted. *Iolanthe*, as I have named her, is however an edition *deluxe*, so to speak, as I have had her planked with pitch pine, and the cockpit seats, doors, bulkhead and coamings of teak. I have chosen the gaff rig, as I think it better suited to a boat of this kind, and the lay-out of the cabin has been planned to suit my own ideas.

Mr. Webb is a thoroughly conscientious craftsman who takes a pride in his work and nothing is scamped. The frame has been admirably put together and there are no butts in the planking, which is of specially selected pitch pine. The extra cost of the pitch pine planking and teak fittings is about £11 and I think such refinements are well worth the money, as they will enhance the selling value of the boat should I wish to dispose of her at any time. Altogether, I think *Iolanthe* will be a jolly little ship. She has a really comfortable cabin and her light draught will enable me to nip across the flats between the Crouch and Blackwater at practically any state of tide. Of course, there are lots of things one wants beyond the equipment supplied with the boat and I reckon that a craft similar to *Iolanthe*, with a new 8-ft. dinghy and everything in the way of equipment that one could desire, would cost at the present time about £175 or £180. That seems to me an extremely reasonable price for a well-built yacht of this size, completely equipped in every detail. Built to the standard specification and with a rather more modest equipment, she would cost about £20 less and that price would include, say, £10 for a new dinghy.

CENTREBOARD BLACKWATER SLOOP
(Drawings 43 & 44) by Dan Webb, c1930

LOA.	18ft	Draught (plate up).	1ft 8in
Beam	7ft	Draught (plate down)	4ft 5in
	Sail area (gaff).	193 sq ft	

Mr. Webb has recently standardized a very similar craft, fitted with a centre-plate for the benefit of those who keep their boats at places where they have to take the ground every tide. This boat draws only 1ft. 9in. with the centre-plate housed and about 4ft. 6in. when it is lowered. To secure the necessary stability the beam has in this model been increased to 7ft., which gives her a fine roomy cabin, with 4ft. headroom under the beams. She is planked with ⅝-in. Columbian pine on bent oak timbers 1in. by ¾in., spaced 6in. from centre to centre. The decks are canvas covered, as in the other boat, and the cabin-top is of two skins of oak and canvas covered. The buyer has the option of either a gaff rig with an area of 193 sq. ft. or a Bermudian of rather smaller area. The iron keel is slotted in way of the galvanized-iron centre-plate, of which the case is securely fastened. Owing to the additional cost of the centre-plate and casing it is not possible to build this little yacht quite so cheaply as the keel boat, and the price is £130 complete. An auxiliary motor can be fitted at an extra cost of from £37 to £50 according to the type of engine selected.

The headroom of these Blackwater sloops is surprisingly good considering their extremely light draught. It, of course, has only been secured by the use of a fairly high coach-roof, but owing to its cambered top it is not at all unsightly. Indeed, they are both handsome little ships and strike me as being almost ideal for, say, a couple of youngsters who have just left school. As a matter of fact they are admirable craft for those who have only the week-ends to devote to their sport, for there is plenty of room in the cabin for two people and the cost of upkeep would be almost negligible.

3-TON BLACKWATER SLOOP
(Drawings 45 & 46) by Dan Webb, c1930

LOA.	20ft 3in	Draught	3ft 6in
LWL.	18ft	Sail area (Bmdn)	230 sq ft
Beam	6ft 9in	Iron keel	14 cwt

In addition to the 2½-ton Blackwater sloop, Dan Webb produces a 3-tonner built to a standard design and specification. As I write [c1937], one of these

3-ton Blackwater Sloop sail plans, gaff and Bermudian

boats is taking shape alongside of my own craft and a very jolly little ship she is. She has a rounded bow and sloping transom stern, very like those of the smaller boat, but has rather less displacement in proportion to her size.

The keel, stem, sternpost and deadwoods of the standard 3-tonner are of English oak and the planking of Russian larch or Norway spruce, all plank fastenings being of copper, clenched on roves. The decks and cabin-top are of tongued and grooved pine, canvas covered. The timbers are steam-bent oak or American elm of ample scantling and her spars of Norwegian spruce, with American elm crosstrees. The internal accommodation provides the usual settee berths in the cabin, a cooking galley, and a large rack in the fo'c'sle for the stowage of spare sails, etc. There is a fore-hatch and room beneath for a bucket w.c. The extra length should make her faster than the 2½-tonner, and of course her cabin and fo'c'sle are more commodious. The buyer has the choice of either Gaff or Bermudian rig.

The equipment supplied with this boat is similar to that of the smaller vessel, and built to the standard specification, the price complete is £178 10s., but she can be built with pitch pine planking for an additional £5 15s., and a further £6 10s. 6d. will cover the cost of teak fittings. The yacht that is being built next to mine is being planked with cedar, a lovely wood with a fine straight grain, but I believe cedar is rather experimental for planking purposes, although it has occasionally been used for small boats. This particular cedar comes from abroad and certainly looks very nice, but I know nothing of its durability. The extra cost of an auxiliary engine is the same as in the smaller boat.

FIDELIS
(Drawings 47 & 48) by F. J. Welch, c1930

Length over all	34ft	Headroom in cabin	5.6ft
LWL.	24ft	Sail area	585 sq ft
Beam	8.5ft	Tonnage	8 tons T.M.
Draught	.4.75ft	Builder. Hugh McLean & Sons, Govan	

The lines of this 8-ton cutter are of particular interest as she was the first yacht designed on Admiral Turner's metacentric-shelf system. I am not going to attempt to describe this system as, to be quite frank, I know little about it. It is, I believe, claimed for it that it ensures perfect balance, and there can be no doubt about *Fidelis* being beautifully balanced. In many yachts, indeed most, the weather helm increases as the boat heels and in some cases, where the ends are not well balanced, the vessel gripes so badly in a fresh quartering breeze that she needs a great deal of helm to keep her on her course. That, of course, is extremely tiring to the helmsman. There is no trouble of that sort with *Fidelis*, which steers easily in wind of any weight and from any quarter. She is a fast, handy yacht and a fine sea boat.

Writing of her in the *Yachting World*, Mr. Welch remarked:

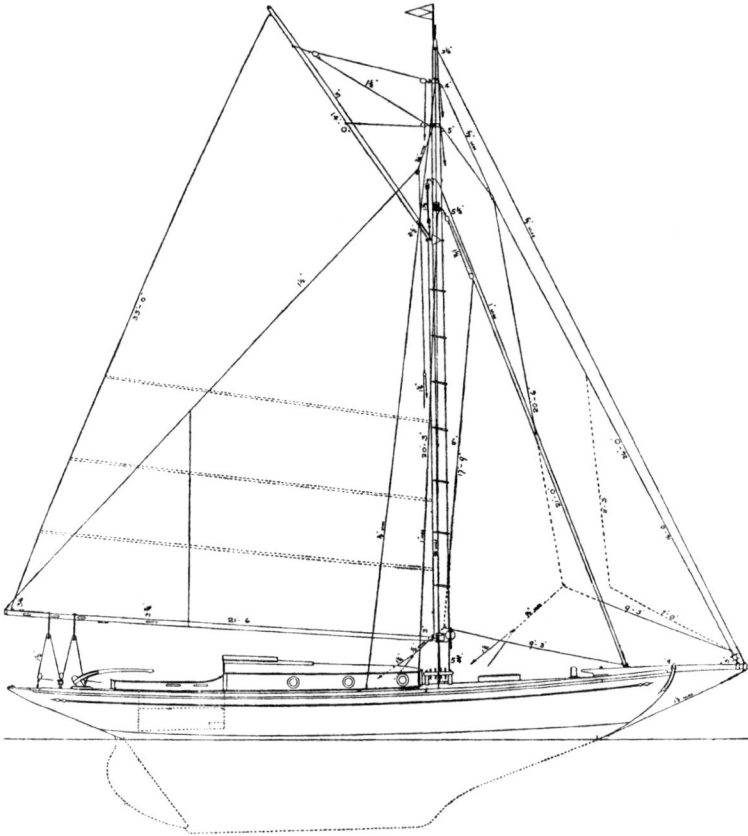

Fidelis sail plan

As our fifth boat, and as the result of over twenty years' cruising between North Wales, Morecambe Bay and the Clyde, she was, I suppose, our 'dream ship.' But not the dream ship beloved of those who propose to heave-to in winter gales for pastime, but a capable little lady with some pretensions to good looks and speed, to give us the maximum amount of pleasure in the sailing of her during limited summer holidays and week-ends, with moderate draught and straight iron keel for easy beaching, and moderate displacement for easy driving, with ample reserve buoyancy to keep the sea off the deck, she is just a normal cruiser – but with a distinction.

We wanted a boat easy on her helm in light winds or hard squalls on any point of sailing, a thoroughly sweet-tempered biddable boat in calm or storm ...

A few fittings not found on all 8-tonners may be mentioned. An inverted stainless steel rudder pintle in which the sand cannot lie to form a grinding medium. An ample sized rudder-head bearing to keep the rudder quiet. A light non-geared mast winch for anchor chain or warps.

Oversize stemhead rollers that really roll. Drop-nosed pins instead of screw shackles for speed with security. Hook blocks with home-made spring mousings (why are these not in the catalogues?). Jam cleats for head sheets with a central hole to keep the end handy on a dark night. A deep cockpit for comfort (not the footbath variety), but self-draining just the same. Conor O'Brien's throat block chock, Weston Martyr's cabin stanchion, F. B. Cooke's chain stopper, and oversize Wykeham-Martin gear on headsails and a 'Tiercel' boom gooseneck. Lastly, an 80-lb. dinghy stowed on deck.

All of these fittings are to be found in *Fidelis* and make for ease and comfort in handling her. Below decks she is very comfortably arranged. There are two berths in the cabin and a cot in the fo'c'sle, but details of the accommodation will be gathered from the plans. The auxiliary engine, a twin-cylinder Ailsa Craig, is installed amidships, but the propeller is under the starboard quarter.

Some years after her launch, Mr. Welch sailed her from the Clyde to the Crouch, making a fine passage via the West Coast and Channel, and she has since been stationed at Creeksea, on the Crouch. A year or two before the War, Mr. Welch converted *Fidelis* to Bermudian rig, which I understand he finds quite satisfactory. The illustration shows the original sail plan.

ENGLYN
(Drawings 49 & 50) by T. Harrison Butler, c1932

LOA	.26ft 1in	Displacement	.5.5 tons
LWL	22ft 6in	Tonnage	7 tons T.M.
Beam	8ft 6in	Iron keel	1.5 tons
Draught	4ft 6in	Lead keel (same mould)	2.36 tons
Sail area	393 sq ft	Mainsail	255 sq ft
Staysail	88 sq ft	Jib	50 sq ft

Area of lateral plane . . . . 83 sq ft

When heeled to 20 degrees the centre of buoyancy moves forward 1 in

In 1928 Mr. Harrison Butler prepared a special design for reproduction in the fourth edition of my book *Cruising Hints*, which he named Cyclone II. She was a yacht of 6½ tons, a very handy size for coastwise cruising, and its publication aroused a good deal of interest among yachtsmen all over the country. Quite a number of vessels were built from the design and proved admirable cruisers. Mr. Butler, however, was not quite satisfied with the design, as he thought the boat was inclined to carry rather too much weather helm when reaching with a fresh breeze on the quarter, although the owners of the yachts built from the design appeared to be quite satisfied.

With a view to eradicating what he considered a fault, Mr. Butler prepared an improved design, which he called Yonne. As the first yacht build from the design and named *Yonne* has been stationed at Fambridge for some years, I know her well and can testify to her admirable qualities.

The Englyn design is a refined edition of Yonne and I do not think I can do better than quote at length Mr. Butler's own description, which he sent me with the lines of the yacht:

Size: This has proved to be the most useful and popular. It is just large enough to allow a flush deck with comfortable sitting headroom under the beams, and a large area of deck for getting about with safety and comfort. She is large enough to look after herself, and for this reason would be an ideal single-hander. There is ample room to get at the gear in a seaway, and there is no sail too large to be handled with comfort.

Design: This is the result of evolution. The original small Cyclone has been built in considerable numbers, and has proved to be satisfactory. I enlarged that design proportionately to a L.W.L. of 22.5ft. This drawing will be found in *Cruising Hints* (fourth edition). Six of these yachts have been built and I have had the opportunity of sailing two of them. They are handy and seaworthy and will heave-to under headsails alone, and in smooth water will turn to windward with this combination of sails. But all of them have a tendency to pull hard with a strong wind on the quarter. As an improvement I designed Yonne, which was published in the Yachting World. This yacht is practically an enlargement of the design which won the competition held by the *Yachting Monthly* for a yacht of 18ft. on the L.W.L. Three Yonnes have been built, but I am not yet in a position to speak about their performance. *Yonne* herself has made one passage from Portsmouth to Poole in a strong N.W. wind. With full headsail and trysail she tended to carry lee helm, so we conclude that the hard-headedness has disappeared.

Englyn is a development of Yonne. On the same dimensions and displacement the stern has been fined down to give a better balance between the fore and aft bodies. The transom is narrower and the quarters finer. When heeled to 20 degrees the centre of buoyancy moves forward only 1in., which is negligible. The design has been made on a log keel with parallel sides. This is to give greater strength and to make the yacht easier and cheaper to build.

The keel shown can be either of iron or lead. If lead is chosen, some adjustment may be necessary according to the weight of the engine. With a light engine a little will probably have to be cut off the forward end, because the weight is close to the total amount of ballast necessary with ordinary robust construction. I shall be glad if anyone contemplating building to the design will communicate with me, for I shall shortly have information about the behaviour and balance of Yonne, and it might be desirable to make minor alterations in the relation of centre of effort to centre of lateral resistance. One Englyn is already laid down.

Lay-out: This speaks for itself. The cockpit can be made deeper if desired, and the galley can come aft without any material alteration in the bulkheads.

Starting from the stern, there is a moderate-sized after locker for sails and warps. On the port side there are two lockers under the seat. The after

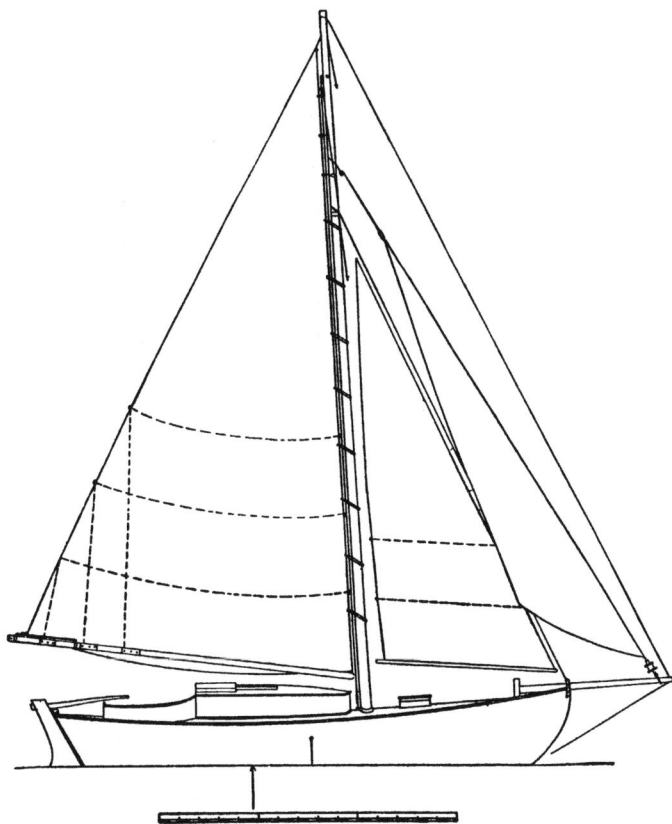

Englyn sail plan

one is a bosun's store and is shown containing lead-line and fog-horn. The forward one is the meat locker and will be zinc-lined. The compass is under the bridge deck and is viewed through a sloping window, which can be covered by a hinged flap. It will be electrically lighted. It is rather near the engine, but this cannot be avoided.

The petrol tank is under the starboard seat, and forward of this is a large locker opening from the cabin. To port is a large hanging locker with hooks and coat-hangers. I have found these most satisfactory on my *Sandook.* In the cabin, we have to port a folding chart box and table and in front of it a blanket bin that forms the back of the seat. We sleep on the cushions to port and let them be Vi-sprung. On the starboard side there is a side table with a large locker under it. A folding pipe-cot is provided on this side. Forward there is a heating stove and a pantry to port, and a food locker-to starboard. These both open into the fo'c'sle as well. In the fo'c'sle there is a swinging double Primus galley, with ample shelf space behind it for all the cooking utensils. The navigation lights are stowed ahead of this. To starboard there is a folding pipe-cot. In the eyes there is a large clothes locker for the guest. There is also a clothes locker under the pantry and food locker. There are five of these lockers in all. Right aft on the starboard side there is a cupboard for small articles, medicine bottles, etc. A simple bucket 'toilet' has been shown forward; there is not room for a mechanical apparatus, but if such is desired it can be placed behind the food locker and under the folding cot.

Engine: A 6 h.p. Watermotor, or Stuart Turner, is shown, but there is ample room for a larger model. No attempt has been made to hide it away under the cockpit; it is completely accessible and does not have the evil effect on the moment of gyration that it would have if further aft. Again, there is ample room for a large water tank under the cockpit. The pump is in the cockpit and discharges through the topsides; it can easily in this position be fitted with a brake.

Extra sails: Trysail, 2nd jib, storm staysail, balloon foresail and spin-naker.

It will be noticed that instead of the usual mast track and slides, Mr. Butler attaches the luff of the mainsail to the mast with mast hoops as far as the cross-trees, and above that it is hanked to a wire jackstay. To keep the head of the stay close to the mast when reefed there is a ring on the jackstay, which is free to travel above the hanks on the head of the sail, and to this is attached a line which leads through a fairlead at the side of the mast, just below the crosstrees. By set-ting up this line taut when the sail is reefed the jackstay, and, of course, the head of the sail, will be kept close in to the mast. But a glance at the illustration will show the method of working more clearly than I can explain it. Nowadays, how-ever, such expedients are hardly necessary, as trackways and slides have been so much improved of late years that they seldom give trouble. I have never seen a yacht built from the Englyn design, but if she is an improvement on Yonne, she must be a fine little ship. The only criticism I have to offer is that I doubt whether the cable would automatically feed down into the chain locker in view of the dis-tance of the navel hole from the windlass, but that is a trivial matter that could be easily rectified. Altogether, Englyn strikes me as a jolly little cruiser and I feel sure that anyone who built to the design would have a vessel of which he could be proud and which would be a joy to sail.

DRIAC II

(Drawings 51 & 52) by S. N. Graham, 1932

LOA.	32.2ft	Headroom in cabin	6.1ft
LWL.	25.5ft	Sail area	546 sq ft
Beam	8.5ft	Builder. . . H. Feltham, Portsmouth	
Draught	5.5ft	Year built.	1932
	Aux engine . . . Thorneycroft 4 cyl		

I am particularly pleased at being able to reproduce the lines of *Driac II*, as she is perhaps the most famous small ocean cruiser in yachting history. Her owner, the late Mr. A. G. H. Macpherson, did an immense amount of cruising in her and she has proved a wonderful little sea boat. In 1932 he won the Royal Cruising Club Challenge Cup, the highest honour a cruising man can attain, for a voyage in the Bay of Biscay and to the Azores, and the following year captured the Romola Cup of the same club for a cruise to Iceland and the Gulf of Finland. After that Mr. Macpherson competed no more for the club's trophies, but continued to contribute accounts of his cruises to the club journal.

And what cruises they were! The little ship was his home and in her he cruised all over the world without mishap, covering some fifty thousand miles. Throughout his voyaging he was accompanied by Bill Leng, who, joining the ship after her launch as paid hand, soon became Mr. Macpherson's intimate friend and trusted companion. Year after year they sailed the seven seas together in perfect harmony, and when at long last advancing years and bad health compelled Mr. Macpherson to give up his wanderings afloat, he gave the yacht to Leng. In an early chapter of this book I made some rather scathing remarks about yacht hands of a certain type, but Leng was an outstanding example of the best type, than which no finer class of men could be found.

I don't think I can do better than quote *in extenso* the description of *Driac II* which Mr. Macpherson wrote for the Royal Cruising Club Journal of 1932, for it not only conveys a good impression of the yacht but is also amusing.

Driac II – 8-ton auxiliary cutter, [Mr. Macpherson wrote] is a younger sister to *Driac*, now *Marlin*. She has much of the family resemblance in her Bermudian mast and bumpkin, and in her very pronounced sheer and freeboard. Her sawn-off counter may lack the other's elegance, but it has proved a very workmanlike proposition when running in heavy weather. She was built during the winter of 1931-2 by Harry Feltham, of Portsmouth; designed by Sidney N Graham, AMINA, who not only took infinite pains in working out her design and arrangements to my requirements, but devoted a great deal of time to supervising her construction. The main feature of this is her steel frames. The horrors of galvanic action have been dinned into me by the Hearts of Oak Brigade, but modern methods are very different from old, and as regards strength I don't think the question admits of argument. The object aimed at was a small, deep-water cruiser of modern type, easy underwater lines and moderation in everything. Dimensions, 32 feet O.A., 25.5 feet W.L., 8.5 feet beam, and 5.5 feet draught. The only excessive proportions, perhaps, are sheer and freeboard. These may be detrimental to speed, but they have provided me with the driest little ship I ever sailed in. Reliability in coming round is essential for a cruiser, and, though D-II is quick in stays for her type, she has sufficient length of keel to heave-to and be left to herself under any conditions of weather. She is inclined to be a bit hard-headed, and this is mainly due to a small cruising jib with which she balances when reefed down.

Her motor is a 10-16 horsepower, and works on petrol. My knowledge of engines is confined to their going or not going; and as most of my former engines have preferred not to go, and this one seems to want to go, it ranks as the blue-haired boy of the class. But, of course, this type of gasbag will be pre-Ark in a few years. I could have grown oysters inside my magneto and carburettor returning from the Azores.

To permit of an 8-foot pram dinghy being carried on the cabin-top, the boom, which is solid and well inboard, has a sliding gooseneck. Turner's reefing gear is fitted, with a swivel the other end. No claws this time, thank goodness, and as the fore end of the boom is slightly tapered to permit of even rolling, I have never experienced my former troubles, either in reefing or of the boom dropping down during the process. In the event of the reefing gear misbehaving, there are two rows of eyelets, with cringles, in the mainsail. A portable steel crutch, about 2½ feet high, takes the boom on the quarter when the trysail is set.

The hollow mast, 41 feet from the deck, as well as all the other spars, came from McGruer. The sail area is only 546 square feet, which is inadequate in light airs, but a big ballooner and a reaching foresail prove very useful allies under these conditions. The other spares include a trysail, squaresail, flax storm staysail, and storm jib – the lot stowing in the sail locker aft. Having experienced the benefit of a roped leach, I got the sailmakers who supplied the canvas to rope round everything except the light stuff.

The staysail is boomed, and my first venture in Wykeham-Martin for the jib proved entirely satisfactory. The squaresail hanks on to the yard and runs up on the forestay. This arrangement permits of the sail being set very quickly, but is apt to chafe on the stay and would be unsuitable for prolonged running. The runners are on a slide which works up and down a tramway; the same as in the smaller racing craft. A mast-winch is under the gooseneck, so that cable stows where it ought to and not in the eyes of the boat. We invariably got the anchor up by hand and only once seriously called on the winch, when it proved most efficient.

On the ground floor, as they say, there is the saloon, fo'c'sle, and usual offices – with a special line in cupboards for the owner's trousers, of which he never takes less than two dozen pairs on a cruise, and never wears more than two pairs. Headroom of over 6 feet under the cabin-top; ports – no skylight. Anyone who has enjoyed the privilege of hearing the ocean unload overhead will recognize the vital necessity of strength in this piece of furniture. Can't be bothered with any more swing-tables which are either knocking out your teeth or hitting you in the stomach. A settee is recessed on the port side under a bookcase and cupboard, and it makes an excellent marine bed, the main essentials for which are depth and moderate beam, so that one can wedge in. I intended having a leather-backed cot on the other side for my own use, but this developed into a colossal panelled four-poster which weighs about 5 tons and was responsible at times for a perfect orgy of language. To appreciate its virtues one had to be a Hercules to lift it up and down, as well as a sardine to fit in when the bed closed up. This performance actually took place on several occasions when the Atlantic was particularly active, the sleeper experiencing the soothing sensation of first turning turtle and then going back to earth with a bang that woke everyone in the ship.

A fo'c'sle is a necessary evil if one carries a paid hand, but in a small yacht in bad weather, with everything battened down and two Primuses going, it is literally 'anellovaplace' and unfit for human habitation. At sea, only the saloon is used for sleeping; when all turned in, the odd man took his turn on the floor.

The brutes, however, have to be fed, and on returning from the first cruise I installed an additional gimballed Primus in a locker by the companion. This proved a tremendous asset, as not only cooking, but washing-up operations, could be conducted in comfort from it, and we never went a day without our two hot meals. Also, I bought specially large cooking pots so that they could be left unattended in the fo'c'sle without the contents slopping over. Another most welcome addition was a set of the deep, round enamel dishes that the good dog Tray eats his Spratt out of. Why one never thought of these before I can't imagine.

There are 3½ tons of lead on her keel, as well as a bit of inside trimming. Inside ballast may make for easier motion, but it is messy stuff in the bilge and takes up invaluable water space. In this direction, apart from 5 gallons emergency in tins, there is a 40-gallon tank under the saloon floor, as well as a 20-gallon tank (with a tap in the lavatory) under the cockpit seat. On the other side is a 20-gallon petrol tank.

As I like comfort, and prefer to take the chance of filling up to being washed out of or smashed up in a shallow self-drainer, the cockpit is a real deep one, but bulkheaded off from the saloon except for the flap which opens into it. If occasionally a little H_2O paid a visit to the cockpit, a plunger pump is there, as well as one in the lavatory, to attend to the matter. In addition to the after dodgers, which are very useful in keeping out the merchant that goes down the back of your neck, I had a life-line rigged on the fore-deck running through a couple of stanchions. This proved a gilt-edged security and no small cruiser ought to go to sea without it. The compass (E.L.) is fixed rather high for reading, and on the last cruise we screwed on a small box compass well below it for steering purposes. Being just over the engine, there was considerable deviation on some points, but it enabled one to snug down and steer without dislocating one's neck in the process.

A small 4-valve wireless set gave excellent results the first cruise. We got the time right across the Bay and heard Daventry quite plainly at Santander. Unfortunately, damp got into the set during the last cruise and it packed up.

ARISTENE
(Drawing 53) by T. Harrison Butler, c1933

LOA.	38ft	Draught	6ft
LWL.	30ft	Displacement	10.67 tons
Beam	10ft 3in	Iron keel	3 tons
	Inside ballast	approx 1 ton	

Although personally I do not care for the schooner rig in a yacht as small as 14 tons, it may be an advantage when the vessel has to be handled by a small crew. Anyhow, rig is largely a matter of personal choice and does not affect the design of *Aristene*, which seems to me a very useful boat, which could be rigged according to the owner's fancy. In sending me her lines for reproduction, Dr. Butler writes as follows :

The leit-motif of this design is ease. Her long easy lines should give an easily driven hull, her softish bilges make for ease in a sea-way, and her schooner rig for ease of handling. We can regard her for home cruising as a 60-40. For this purpose she could have a 15- to 20-H.P. engine, and then she would be ideal for handling with a small crew. A similar design of mine, *Fastnet*, is run all the year round in British Columbia by the owner and his wife. For ocean cruising, for which I think she is very suitable, I would give her a 7-H.P. Thorneycroft Handy Billy engine. On the other hand, she could be rigged up to her capacity as a Bermudian cutter or yawl. Another alternative would be the Bermudian ketch, which is now so popular in America. The lines and the plans speak for themselves. A suitable lay-out has been sketched in, but many alternative plans could be adopted.

CORBIE

(Drawings 54 & 55) by T. Dennis Jacobs, c1933

LOA.	22ft 6in	Displacement	5.8 tons
LWL.	20ft 6in	Sail area	215 sq ft
Beam	8ft	Builder. . Alexander Costelow, Boston
Draught	3ft	Year built.	1934

Aux engine . . . . Kelvin 3hp

This cutter is a little ship that appeals to me strongly, as within the limits of 5 tons Thames Measurement, Mr. Jacobs has contrived to provide everything that could reasonably be desired for comfort without undue crowding. In order to obtain the necessary stability on a light draught, Mr. Jacobs gave her a rather generous beam, but as the turn of her bilge is easy she is not unduly lively in a seaway and has proved an excellent sea-boat.

Her rig is very simple and effective, a noticeable feature being the short mast-head. In this, Mr. Jacobs evidently followed smack practice, thus saving unnecessary weight and windage aloft. The after-shrouds lead from the masthead, and being set up well abaft the mast, the necessity for runners is avoided, whilst the sturdy short mast needs no cross-trees. Like myself, Mr. Jacobs has no use for roller reefing gear and the loose-footed mainsail is reefed with tackle and pendant in the old-fashioned way. The jib is fitted with the Wykeham-Martin furling gear and the foresail has a boom, which travels on the sheet in the manner I describe in the chapter on sails.

Corbie is substantially built, the keel being of wych elm, the deadwood of English elm and the rest of the frame of English oak. The planking is red pine and the coamings, hatches, etc., of teak. An unusual feature is that the bitts, instead of being fastened to the keel, are oak crooks fastened to one of the frames. By adopting this method room was made in the fo'c'sle for a pipe cot. The auxiliary engine is installed at the after end of the cabin on the port side and drives a 12-in. propeller under the port quarter. The top of the removable casing forms a very convenient sideboard just inside the cabin.

The lay-out of the cabin strikes me as extremely well planned. There is 4ft. 6in. headroom under a very low flat cabin-top and ample headroom under the side-decks to enable one to sit back comfortably. The galley and pantry are at the after-end of the starboard bunk, and on the other side, behind the engine, are a locker and hanging space. A bookshelf is placed on the fore bulkhead on the port side and in the corner on that side is a small bogey stove for heating the cabin in cold weather. The table is placed a little to port of the centre-line and large enough for four people to sit comfortably at meals. Although instantly detachable, it is very firm when in use, being secured to a standing tubular leg from the floor to the cabin-top. Far from being in the way, this post affords good handhold when at sea. In the fo'c'sle, just forward of the bulkhead, is a clothes locker on the starboard side and just abaft the mast is the chain locker, the chain running

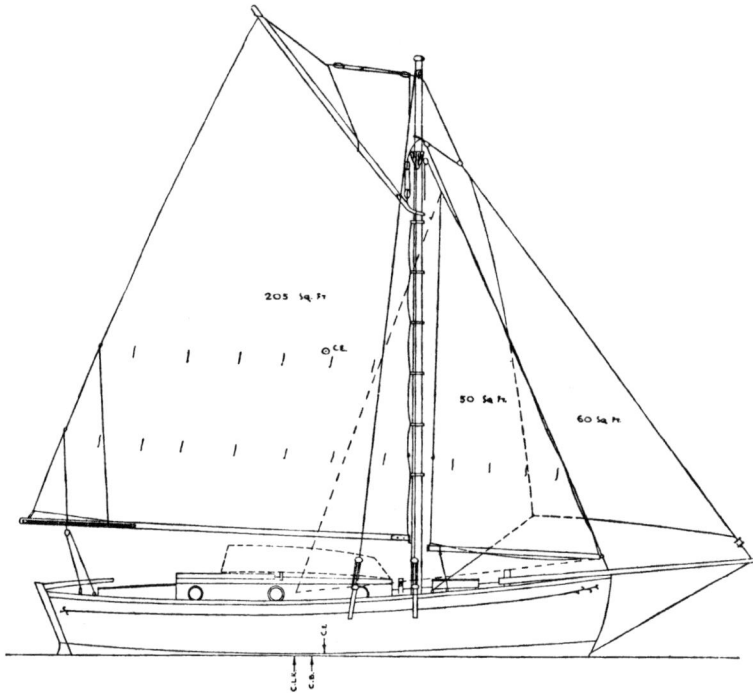

Corbie sail plan

down a chute into it from the hawsepipe, the weight of the cable being thus in the right place from a ballasting point of view. The folding cot is on the port side and there is a locker for bosun's stores under the seat. In addition to the working sails, dressed with red ochre and oil, *Corbie* carries a large balloon jib, which can also be used as a spinnaker. As this sail is 17ft. long on the foot and hoists to the masthead, it pulls her along grandly with a fair wind. Being dressed with green Cuprinol, this sail strikes a rather unusual note, but affords a pleasing contrast to the red sails and black hull.

I frequently came across *Corbie* cruising on the East Coast and she seems to me a very attractive little ship. She conveys the impression of having been designed for use rather than ornament, and her internal accommodation has been so admirably planned that she is as comfortable to live in as many 7-tonners.

After she was launched in 1934, Mr. Jacobs sailed her from Boston to the Crouch, where she is stationed, and has since done a lot of cruising in her. Her light draught enables her to make use of low-ways and short cuts across the sands that would not be available to yachts drawing more water, and to find snug anchorages in the creeks that abound on the East Coast. And she is equally satisfactory at sea. Last summer she cruised to Holland and the return passage from Veere to Harty Ferry was made in a very hard northerly breeze. For several hours during the night she was hove-to off the Galloper and her owner tells me that the little ship lay-to very quietly and steadily.

ALETHEA III
(Drawings 56 & 57) by A. R. Luke, c1934

LOA.	34ft 4in	Headroom in cabin	. 5ft 10in
LWL.	26ft	Total sail area	490 sq ft
Beam	.9ft	Aux eng Kelvin-Ricardo 2 cyl, 7/9 hp	
Draught	5ft	Builder.	Luke & Co

I have always admired the designs of the late Mr. A. R. Luke, of Messrs. Luke & Co., of Hamble, and this 9-tonner seems to me an excellent example of his work. She was built for Mr. J. G. H. Cockburn, who required a vessel that could be handled easily without paid hands. A Bermudian ketch rig was therefore chosen, and she was given a canoe stern for the sake of its sea-kindly qualities. Canoe sterns, by the way, are becoming increasingly popular and quite a large proportion of the small cruisers one sees nowadays have sterns of that description. After experience of the ketch rig Mr. Cockburn seems to have become dissatisfied with it, for in 1938 he converted the yacht to a Bermudian sloop.

Messrs. Luke & Co. made a fine job of building *Alethea III*, which is planked with pitch-pine on double oak natural grown frames, spaced 2 feet apart from centre to centre, with two steamed timbers of rock elm between each set of grown frames. The deck fittings are all of teak, and the internal fittings of waxed oak. The sails were made by Ratsey & Lapthorn, and the auxiliary engine runs on paraffin.

As Mrs. Cockburn liked to keep the cooking and food well away from the engine, the pantry and galley were placed at the fore end of the cabin. This is a point that many designers seem to overlook, and in my opinion it is an important one, for there is always a certain amount of smell from an engine, no matter what the makers may say on the subject. When I owned *Fancy*, which had a paraffin engine, the bilge got so dirty and smelt so offensively, that to keep it sweet I frequently had to pour in many buckets of water and pump it out again. Sometimes it took twenty or thirty buckets before the bilge was clean and sweet. Both the main and mizzen sails of the original rig were fitted with roller reefing gear. The area of the mainsail was 303 square feet, that of the staysail 112 square feet, and the mizzen 75 square feet, and she carried no sail forward of the stemhead.

The accommodation below decks is admirably arranged. Between the cockpit and cabin, on each side, are a 15-gallon water-tank, a cupboard and a large bin, with hinged lid, the engine being installed amidships. In the cabin there is a Pullman berth on each side with a shelf above. At the aft end of each berth there is a cupboard and at the forward end a sideboard and a cupboard on either side of the vessel. Forward of the cabin, on the port side, is the lavatory, with a wash basin that folds down over the w.c., and a toilet cupboard. Opposite, on the starboard side, is the pantry, with cupboards for crockery, drawers and a cupboard beneath. In the fo'c'sle the chain locker is situated close to the mast on the port side, the weight of the cable being thus well inboard. The cooking galley is also on the port side, with a locker for navigation lights near by. On the starboard side of the fo'c'sle there is a folding cot, with a seat below, fitted over lockers and a bin. The headroom in the cabin is 6 feet 6 inches under the skylight and just short of 6 feet under the cabin-top. The cockpit is lead-lined and there are lockers beneath the seats. The yacht is fitted with a steering wheel, and the engine controls, on the port side, are within easy reach of the helmsman. Like most of Mr. Luke's creations, *Alethea III* is an extremely shapely craft, with a particularly nice midship section and graceful sheer.

SUNART
(Drawings 58 & 59) by W. Easton, c1934

Length over all 28ft 6in	Sail area (ex balloon canvas) 400 sq ft
LWL. 22ft 6in	Displacement . . . . 5.38 tons
Beam 8ft 3in	Tonnage . . . . 6½ tons T.M.
Draught 4ft 8in	Weight of lead keel . . . . 2.25 tons

Earlier I reproduced the lines of a 4-ton Bermudian yawl named *Rona*, designed by Mr. W. Easton, of West Mersea, one of the best little cruisers that I know, and am now able to reproduce the design of a larger yacht from his board, which is equally interesting. A feature of Mr. Easton's designs is that they are always perfectly balanced. When sailing *Rona*, for instance, one can let go of the tiller when on a wind and she will keep steadily on her course for quite a long time. Even in a strong breeze the weather-helm is no more than sufficient for safety. This seems to me an important point, for the more helm a yacht carries, the greater the retarding influence. *Sunart* should be fast and handy and with her nicely balanced ends and easy lines, a kindly sea-boat. The mast is perhaps a trifle on the tall side, but it is well stayed and should give no trouble. The yacht has a canoe stern and a permanent backstay is provided.

She is fitted with a watertight self-draining cockpit, which you will gather from my remarks in another chapter I do not care much about, but as this yacht has generous freeboard, the well should be deep enough to afford some protection from wind and water. Although the boat has no auxiliary engine, space has been provided for a motor, with propeller shaft through the port quarter, which in my opinion is the best place for it, as it eliminates the necessity for cutting an aperture in the rudder for the propeller, which often upsets the steering. A trysail is provided for use in heavy weather, and it should be noted that the centre of effort of trysail and foresail is in the same fore-and-aft position as that of full sail. To relieve the masthead of strain a special halyard is provided for the trysail. The foresail is fitted with a boom and the sheet works on a horse. The accommodation below decks is commodious, there being 6ft. headroom under the cabin-top, which, not being very wide, leaves fine deckroom. Three bunks are provided, two on the starboard side and one on the port. Between the bunks on the starboard side is a wardrobe and forward of the bunks on that side are a

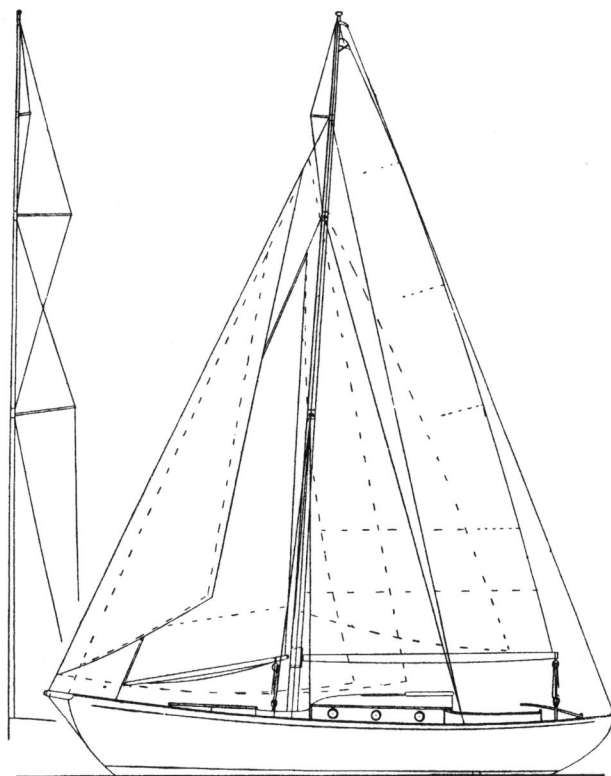

Sunart sail plan

bookcase and sideboard. On the port side, abaft the bunk, are situated a hanging cupboard, a sink, with a table over it, the galley and pantry. At the fore-end of the cabin is a coal-stove, with a drying locker in the fo'c'sle. On the starboard side of the fo'c'sle, opposite the drying locker, is a chest of drawers, and forward of that a bin for sails. Stowage space for lamps is provided in the eyes of the boat. Between the cockpit and cabin is a place for oilskins and under the cockpit, on the port side, a fresh-water tank. There is another fresh-water tank under the cabin floor. On the starboard side there is a chart table to fold down over the bunk at the after-end of the cabin. Altogether *Sunart* strikes me as a most desirable little ship.

In designing *Sunart*, Mr. Easton was considerably restricted. The yacht was to be 6 tons T.M. and no more, the waterline, beam and draught were definitely stipulated and the forward overhang was to be very small and the forefoot not unduly cut away. She was to have a short canoe stern of good shape for running in broken water and providing a useful locker aft. The headroom in the cabin was to be sufficient for a 6-foot man to walk about freely and good sitting head-room under the side-decks. Three good bunks were to be provided, galley and pantry aft, wardrobe and hanging locker, space for oilskins, a small engine, a chart table and the fo'c'sle fitted as dressing-room. Above all, she was to be thoroughly seaworthy and able to heave-to steadily and look after herself, and finally she must have a good turn of speed. To provide all of these features in one yacht presented a difficult problem, which I think it will be agreed Mr. Easton has very satisfactorily solved.

VINDILIS
(Drawings 60, 61 & 62) by T. Harrison Butler, c1934

LOA.	30ft	Displacement.	5 tons 5 cwt
LWL.	22ft 6in	Lead keel.	2 tons
Beam	8ft 6in	Sail area	410 sq ft
Draught	4ft 4in	Headroom in cabin	6ft

Builder . . . . . A. H. Moody & Son

There has been no more popular designer of small cruising yachts of late years than the late Mr. T. Harrison Butler. Although by profession a distinguished surgeon, he devoted his leisure to designing yachts, a hobby that engrossed him for the greater part of his life. How many small cruising craft he created I cannot say, but upwards of fifty appear in the current issue of Lloyd's Yacht Register, and as many more are not included in that volume and others were built abroad, I should say that the total number of yachts built from his design must have run well into three figures. Having himself cruised in little ships for many years, he learnt from practical experience just what was necessary for comfort and convenience afloat. Added to that ripe experience was unbounded enthusiasm and exceptional talent, and he gradually evolved a type of vessel that approached within measurable distance of the ideal. His death in 1945 was a great loss to the sport, as he not only freely lent his drawings to potential builders but gave them valuable advice as to where to get a yacht built and the best materials from which to build her. *Vindilis* was built for Mr. Butler in 1935 for his own use, and he cruised in her until the outbreak of the World War, when he sold her to Mr. F. R. Hole, who owns her at the time I write. The following is his own description of the yacht:

I designed this 6-ton yacht for a competition in which she was placed second. She was slightly modified for my own use and was built by Messrs. A. H. Moody & Son, of Swanwick Shore on the Hamble River. The original design was called *Davinka*, but the new yacht will have the name *Vindilis*, the Roman equivalent for Portland. In choosing this design from others I had to keep in mind two considerations: the yacht must be the smallest that satisfies our needs as a family, and she must to some extent be an investment; a craft that one could sell without undue depreciation. My experience is that a craft of 6 to 7 tons is the most useful and popular size, and with good reason. It is the smallest size in which one can obtain 6 feet headroom in the main cabin, with sitting room under the main deck, giving wide and safe side-decks. Such a yacht is not large enough to be expensive to build or maintain, and yet she can sleep four in comfort and another on the cabin sole on an air bed, although three would be the best number for cruising. She is quite able enough to make long cruises – a yacht of her dimensions has just completed a long voyage from America to the Pacific Islands and back – and yet she is the ideal size for single-handed work. The design was built to eight years ago by Dr. Enroth of Helsingfors. He still owns her and has covered about 8,000 miles in the Baltic. He tells me that she is an ideal yacht; she will sail herself all day long to windward, and runs with remarkably little attention, if the wind freshens the mizzen is furled and the yacht still balances well. He regards her as a dry and able sea boat.

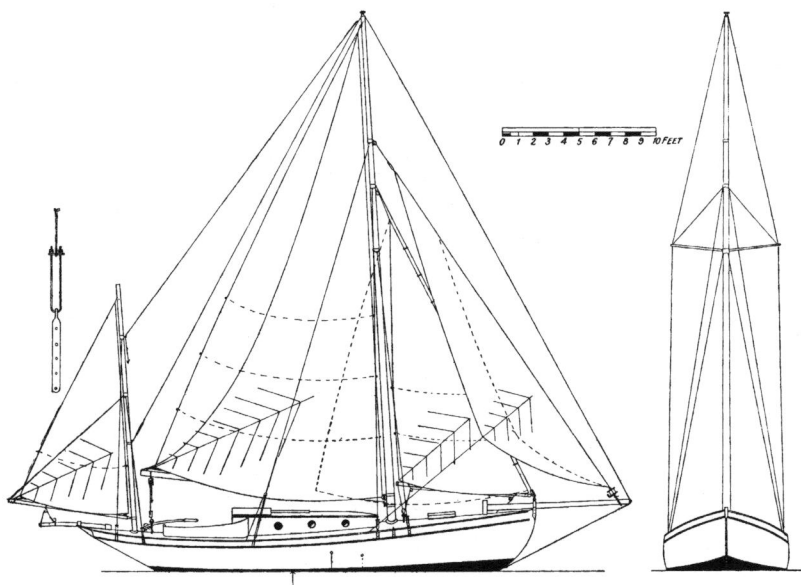

Vindilis sail plan

My reasons for adopting a counter are: first, that I wanted to have a yawl; secondly, that a counter stern is the best-looking of all types; and finally, that from the investment point of view a counter stern is more popular than a transom. My reasons for wishing to own a yawl are quite definite. My experience is that most yachts tend to pull on the helm with a strong wind on the quarter. This is especially marked with the Bermudian rig. Many yachts get hard-headed when close-hauled in a strong wind. These evil habits are at once cured by furling the mizzen. The yawl rig enables one to reduce canvas in a few seconds. By pulling on the Wykeham-Martin furling line the jib disappears, and a second pull on the mizzen topping-lift furls the mizzen. In a few seconds 100 square feet of canvas, 25 per cent of the total area, have disappeared and the yacht is now a handy well-balanced knock-about, with a highly effective if small sail area. Finally, the yawl rig brings the boom-end inboard over the cockpit, and reefing becomes easy. When running in a strong wind the mizzen is furled, and then the yacht will go down the wind sweetly and safely. I hold no brief for sailing a yawl in a strong wind with headsails and mizzen; this practice throws an unfair strain upon the mizzen mast, and tends to strain the hull. Sixty-five years ago Edwin Brett in a small book, *Notes on Yachts*, pointed out that the main driving force of the sail plan ought to be as far as possible over the centre of effort. In any case in heavy weather the sails should be concentrated over the centre of the yacht, where they will effect a steady drive and not yaw the vessel about.

Although it is bad practice to sail a yawl or ketch under headsails and mizzen in strong winds, it is often very convenient to do so in ordinary weather. Most of my designs will go to windward as cutters under headsails alone and in ordinary conditions will come about with certainty. They will heave-to under staysail and jib, and even under staysail alone. I expect that the addition of the mizzen will enable *Vindilis* to do these things even better. It has been said and repeated that a yawl is a foolish compromise between a cutter and a ketch, with the faults of both and the advantages of neither. This is true of the orthodox yawl, a mere abbreviated cutter with a flag-pole mast perched precariously at the end of a long counter.

Vindilis has a submerged counter and her stern-post a moderate rake. In consequence, her mast is able to have a sound stepping well inboard. It is well stayed and has a spring stay from the head to the mainmast. As the mainsail is a Bermudian, its after leach is well away from the luff of the mizzen, and in consequence the mizzen can get an undisturbed wind; at any rate I imagine that this will be the case. I hope that my yawl will have many of the advantages of both cutter and ketch and that it will have lost some of their disadvantages. The lower 2 or 3 feet of the mainsail will not be attached to the track, but will be kept to the mast by a lacing. This will avoid girting the sail from clew to mast if the sail settles, or if the halyard is eased before the weight of the boom is taken by the quarterlift. The upper and lower rows of reef-points are of cotton rope, the middle row of manila. The reason for this is obvious.

The lay-out has been thought out in inches. The crew, having sailed on *Sandook* for many years, know exactly what they want and hope that they have got it. We can sleep four in comfort, and a fifth can use an air bed on the cabin sole. Each of the four has his own clothes locker. The door of the pantry falls down to form a large chart table.

The engine is a 6-h.p. Stuart Turner two-stroke, driving a 16-inch propeller through a two-to-one reduction gear. We had this engine on *Sandook* for two years. It had some faults, but the makers went into them thoroughly, and in the new engine they have been eliminated. The original installation passed the cooling water into the exhaust pipe. Under certain conditions water could flow back from the pump and enter the engine. Now there is a water-cooled silencer and this trouble cannot occur. After considering several makes of engine, we came to the conclusion that the S.T. best supplied our needs.

In the actual yacht some alterations have been made from the plans. By making templates of the bunks, we found that if we shortened the port one 3 inches we could run the bulkhead straight across and still have room for hanging clothes. This gives us a more symmetrical cabin, and 9 inches more room. The lead keel came out at exactly 2 tons.

NORAH CREINA
(Drawing 63) by W. Easton, c1934

Length over all 21ft	Draught . . . . 2ft 9in / 5ft
LWL. 16ft 3in	Sail area . . . . 225 sq ft
Beam 6ft	Tonnage . . . . 3 tons T.M.

Builder . . Clark & Carter, W. Mersea

Hitherto my remarks have been mainly confined to keel boats, and I will now tell you of an extraordinarily attractive little ship with a centre-plate, in which most of the disadvantages of that type of craft to which I drew attention in a previous chapter have been successfully eliminated.

I refer to the 3-tonner *Norah Creina*, designed by Mr. W. Easton and built by Clark & Carter, of West Mersea, in 1935. She is a miniature edition of Mr. Easton's 4-ton Bermudian yawl *Rona*, described earlier, and has proved very fast and weatherly. As originally designed, she carried a Bermudian cutter rig and had an auxiliary engine, but as my son, R. L. Cooke, who has recently bought her, dislikes motors as much as I do, the engine has been removed. He has also substituted a gaff mainsail, peaked high, for the Bermudian sail. She has moderate overhangs fore and aft, the stern being of canoe type. The sail area is 225 sq. ft. in a gaff cutter rig, the mainsail having considerable hoist and a high peak, which should make for weatherliness. The stump bowsprit is very short, the jib overlapping the foresail in accordance with modern practice. The foresail has a boom, with the sheet working on a horse, so that it looks after itself when going to windward. When a reef is taken in the mainsail, the jib is rolled up with the Wykeham-Martin gear, with which it is fitted, and the yacht is then under a snug stemhead-sloop rig.

My son is rearranging the cabin accommodation, which will include pipe-cots over the bunks, a clothes locker, a cooking galley at the after end of the port bunk, and a fine range of lockers under the bridge deck. The centre-plate is L-shaped and housed in the iron keel, only the arm being in the case, which is consequently not very large. But even the smallest centre-plate case encroaches

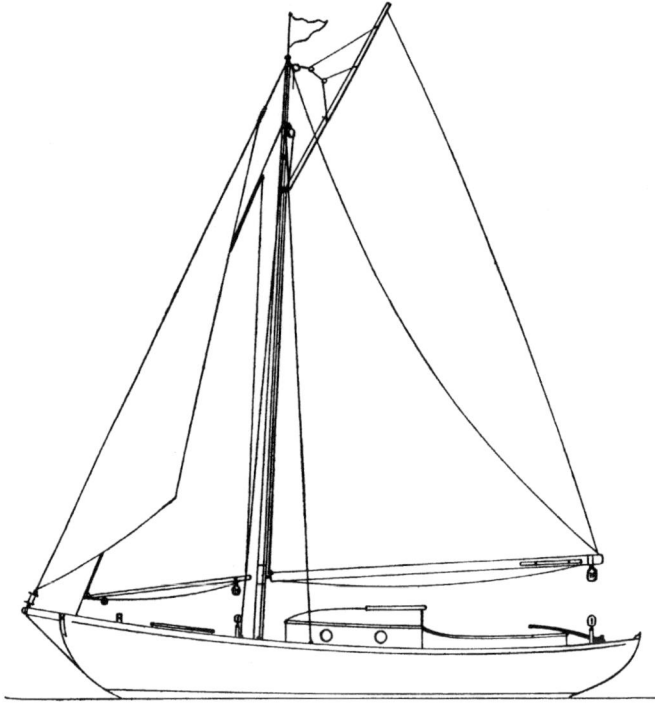

Norah Creina sail plan

seriously on the cabin space and it is possible that the plate may be removed later on. The boat sails to windward very well without the plate and if the keel were dropped about 3in. the loss of weatherliness would probably not be very great, whilst the absence of the plate-case would make a lot of difference to the comfort of the cabin. However, my son intends first to try her with the plate for a time to see how he likes it.

Like all of Mr. Easton's creations, *Norah Creina* is perfectly balanced and very fast and weatherly for a craft of her size. She is beautifully built of the very best materials. The planking is of specially selected mahogany, the original owner having been something of a timber expert, and the cockpit and cabin fittings are of teak. She is, of course, copper fastened and the chainplates are of stainless steel; the other metal fittings being either of brass or bronze.

As the designer lives close to the builders' yard he was able to give the construction his constant supervision and it would be difficult to imagine a better built boat. What a similar yacht would cost to-day I cannot say, but it would be a pretty penny – probably upwards of £300 fully equipped for cruising – but the owner would have a vessel that, properly cared for, would last a lifetime.

HILLYARD 2½-TON SLOOP

(Drawings 64 & 65) by David Hillyard, c1935

LOA . . . . 18ft   Beam 6ft 6in

Draught 3ft

Mr. David Hillyard commenced the production of small cruising yachts to standard designs and specifications some years ago, and they have proved extremely popular. In the course of my cruising I have seen many of these craft and they strike me as well-built and eminently serviceable little vessels. Since he adopted these standard designs a very large number must have been built, and at the time I write he has no fewer than twelve on the stocks, all building to order. He has standardized six boats, ranging in size from 2½ tons to 12 tons, which he is able to produce at most reasonable prices.

The little 2½-ton sloop is the latest addition to his schedule, having been introduced last year. This craft is of the same dimensions as the keel yacht supplied by Mr. Webb, namely, 18ft. long over all by 6ft. 6in. beam, but she has 6in. more draught. As will be seen from her lines, she has a stiff midship section and should stand up well to her sail area. She is substantially built of the best materials, the pine planking being copper fastened to a frame of oak. The keel is of elm or oak and the stem, sternpost and deadwood of oak. The cabin coamings and deck fittings are of mahogany and the decks covered with canvas and painted. There is sitting headroom in the cabin of which the arrangement is optional, but usually comprises two sofa berths, cooking space, lockers, shelves, etc. If the purchaser prefers them, I understand that folding cots are fitted in the cabin to let down over the bunks, and he is given the option of either a gaff mainsail or Bermudian rig. The iron ballast is mainly in the form of a keel, but a certain amount of trimming ballast is carried inside. This excellent little craft, with an equipment including sails, spars, running gear, anchor and 15-fathom warp, is sold for the remarkably low figure of £100. As the price does not include such items as cabin cushions, riding light, sweeps, boathook, chain cable, bucket and mop, the cost of the yacht fully equipped for cruising would be much about the same as that of the Blackwater sloop produced by Mr. Webb. Fitted with a Stuart Turner auxiliary engine, this Hillyard production is sold for £149.

Whether it is advisable to fit an engine in these little tabloid cruisers is, of course, a matter of opinion, but personally I think they are too small. The cockpit of the Hillyard boat is 3ft. 3in. long, just large enough to accommodate two people, but if an engine were installed I think they would be unduly cramped. It must be remembered, too, that an engine means also a fuel tank, for which it would be difficult to find room without encroaching on valuable locker space. But it cannot be denied that an auxiliary engine extends the cruising range of a week-end yacht enormously. When one is solely dependent upon sails one is more or less at the mercy of wind and tide, and in order to make sure of getting back to one's moorings in time to catch the train on Sunday evening, it is necessary to work the tides. This often means the sacrifice of many hours' sailing, to say nothing of a certain amount of anxiety. If, on the other hand, the boat has an engine, the owner can always be sure of getting back in time, whether there is any wind or not, and he can thus defer his return until a later hour.

The other standard yachts produced by Mr. Hillyard are as follows:

4-ton sloop costing £220, or with a Brooke Empire engine, £330. 5-ton sloop, with transom stern, £250, or with canoe stern, £276. 7-ton sloop £420, or with a Thornycroft Handybilly engine, £535. 9-ton sloop £460, or with a Thornycroft Handybilly engine, £575. 12-ton ketch £600, or with a Thornycroft Handybilly engine, £720.

I have seen most of these yachts under way and they appear to sail well and also have a good turn of speed under power. The yachts of from 4 to 12 tons have a much fuller equipment than the 2½-ton sloop. Each is fitted with a patent W.C. and has bunk cushions, roller reefing gear on the mainsail and Wykeham-Martin furling gear on the foresail, whilst the rig is optional; that is to say, the buyer can select either the gaff mainsail or Bermudian, as he fancies. It would, of course, be impossible to produce yachts of the same quality from individual designs at anything like the price, but by the adoption of a standard design and specification a considerable saving can be effected in the cost of materials and labour.

ANDANTE II
(Drawings 66 & 67) by Norman E. Dallimore, c1935

Length over all	38ft	Draught	5ft 6in
LWL.	27ft	Headroom in cabin	6ft
Beam	9ft	Sail area	725 sq ft
Aux engine	Morris 4 cyl	Tonnage	10 tons T.M.

The small cruisers designed by Mr. Norman Dallimore, of Burnham-on-Crouch, are very popular on the East Coast and elsewhere. Having sailed such craft himself since boyhood, he knows just what is needed in a small cruising vessel, and being based on sound practical experience his creations have a deserved reputation for good sailing qualities, convenience and comfort. *Andante*, whose lines I reproduce, is a typical example of his work and has proved a very able little ship. She has a good turn of speed, is extremely weatherly and dry, and, as her long keel makes her very steady on the helm, she will sail herself and heave-to perfectly. She was built in 1936 by William King & Sons for Mr. Harold C. Smith.

With moderate overhangs and graceful sheer, she is a handsome vessel, and with a lead keel of 5 tons weight, stands up well to her canvas. With a powerful midship section and buoyant ends, she is a fine sea boat and her generous displacement affords roomy accommodation below decks. The arrangement has been admirably thought out and there are several features not usually found in

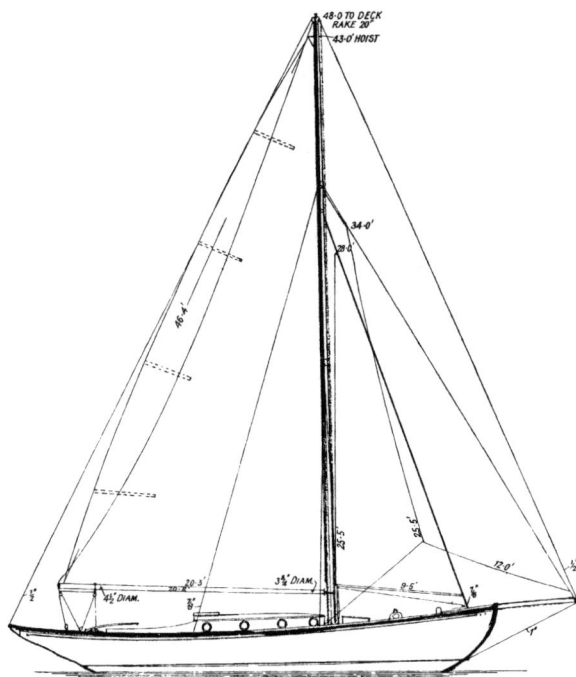

Andante II sail plan

a yacht of this size. Of these I would draw attention to the fo'c'sle, or fore-cabin, as it might be termed, which has proper built-in berths, with drawers and lockers beneath. Between the fo'c'sle and main cabin is a toilet room, extending right across the ship, fitted with hanging cupboards, drawers, mirrors, w.c., etc. This apartment has doors leading into both fo'c'sle and cabin and can be entirely shut off. The cabin is roomy and comfortable, with the usual bunks and a table in the centre. The galley is at the after end, on the starboard side, and there are sideboards and lockers at the ends of the bunks. At the fore end of the cockpit, on the port side, is a hanging locker for oilskins, and the coamings are carried round the sailroom hatch, thus protecting it from water. This hatch much facilitates access to the sail locker and is, I think, an improvement upon the usual door opening into the cockpit, which entails a good deal of stooping and interferes with the helmsman. The cockpit is roomy, and although of the self-draining type, affords reasonable protection from wind and water.

The auxiliary engine is a Morris Navigator, giving a speed of about 7 knots, and so tucked away that it does not encroach upon the accommodation. It is installed in a manner that provides for accessibility when the steps are removed, and the taps and controls are so arranged that the engine can be started, either by hand or with the starter, without removing the steps.

The sail area of 725 square feet is split up as follows: Bermudian mainsail, 475 square feet; Jib, 130 square feet; and foresail, 120 square feet. The foresail has a boom and the sheet travels on a horse. The height of the mast, from deck to truck, is 48 feet and it rakes aft 20 inches. The yacht is fitted with a roller-boom for reefing the mainsail, the spar tapering to prevent dropping when the sail is reefed.

As regards construction, the keel, stem, stern-post and horn timber are of English oak, the floors and knees are oak crooks, timbers of American elm, planking of pitch-pine, copper-fastened, and the decks and fittings of teak. The ironwork is heavily galvanized and the chainplates internally fitted, which should effectively eliminate the unsightly iron rust-stains that so often mar the appearance of a yacht's topsides. She is built to the high standard of finish which one has come to expect from W. King & Sons.

ZYKLON
(Drawings 68 & 69) by T. Harrison Butler, c1935

Length over all	21ft	Sail area	260 sq ft
LWL.	19ft	Displacement	3.3 tons
Beam	7ft 2in	Iron keel	1 ton
Draught	4ft	Tonnage	4 tons T.M.
	Speed under power.	5kts	

Many years ago I reproduced in one of my books the lines of a delightful little cruiser by Dr. T. Harrison Butler named 'Cyclone', and a number of boats were built from the design. Although admirably adapted to the requirements of a couple of youngsters, she was a real 'tabloid' and very small. Dr. Butler has now got out the lines of a larger Cyclone, measuring approximately 4 tons T.M. and re-designed on the metacentric shelf principle, to which he has recently become a convert.

By the courtesy of Dr. Butler I am able to reproduce the design of this little ship, which is of a size and type likely to appeal to a great many of those who delight in cruising in small craft. As I think it likely that a good many people will want to build to this design, I give below the specification, as drawn up by the designer:

Keel: Wych elm. Sided 4in., moulded to drawing.
Stem, Stern-post and Dead-woods: Sided 3½in., moulded as in drawing; fastened with galvanized-iron bolts.
Transom: Mahogany, 1½in.
Planking: Pitch pine, ¹³⁄₁₆in. finished;
Garboards: Wych elm, ⁷⁄₈in.
Stringers and Shelf: Pitch pine, 1½in. by 4in.
Timbers: American elm, oak or ash, 1in. by 1³⁄₈in.
Decks: ⁷⁄₈-in. pine, T. and G., covered with canvas and painted.
Coach Roof: ⁵⁄₈in. T. and G., covered with canvas and painted.
Coamings: ¾-in. teak.

Sliding Hatch, Fore Hatch, Cockpit Seats, etc: Teak.

Deck Beams: Oak. Through beams, 1½in. by 2½in.; Main beams, 2¼in. by 2½in.

Interior Fittings: Seat fronts, cupboards, etc., spruce, with mahogany or teak beading.

Cabin Sole Boards: Teak. (Note: It is very important to have these of teak and is well worth the extra expense.)

Knees: Galvanized iron.

Floors: Galvanized iron with 18-in. arms.

Iron Keel: 1 ton, to be fastened with galvanized-iron bolts.

Fastenings: Centre fastenings to be of galvanized iron. All other fastenings to be of copper.

Spars: Mast and boom of solid Norway spruce. Mast to be fitted with Laurent Giles track and shackles. (Note: A silver spruce mast would be better and well worth the extra cost.)

Anchor: 30 lb. Kedge, 20 lb.

Chain: Short-link tested chain, ⁵⁄₁₆in.

Warp: 15 fathoms, 2-in. bass. Bilge Pump.

Engine: Stuart Turner, 4 h.p. with reduction and reverse gear.

The name Zyklon is the German for Cyclone, and Dr. Butler considers that this design is an improvement upon the original Cyclone lines, which were extensively built to all over the world. All the owners of that little ship were enthusiastic about her. Dr. Butler tells me that he never had an opportunity of sailing one of them and is obliged to depend upon the reports of others, some of whom may have been of an optimistic temperament. The boat was said to be well balanced, very fast for her type and a fine sea boat. The new design was made with three objects in view, namely, to provide a modern version of a design which, judging by its wide adoption, is a popular size and type; to make her as cheap as possible without any sacrifice of efficiency; and finally, to prove that a yacht can be designed of the old-fashioned quay-punt type, which is a metacentroid and has a perfect metacentric shelf and curve of moments. The designer, judging by the perfect balance of *Edith Rose* – an improved *Vindilis* – and by the good reports he has had of the original Cyclone, hopes that Zyklon, combining as she does, a perfect metacentric analysis, with the orthodox long keel with good drag aft, will be self-steering on all points of sailing, and will probably run even for long periods unattended. The design can be drawn out and then enlarged proportionately to produce a larger craft up to 12 tons or so.

Zyklon is, in Dr. Butler's opinion, the smallest and cheapest yacht that can be built for Channel cruising. The specification is based on one drawn up by a firm of repute, who are willing to build her for £220. She would be an excellent single-hander, or a two-men, or man-and-wife boat. Designed for off-shore work, she is perhaps a trifle under-canvassed, but Butler boats are easily driven and do not need much sail. The sail-plan is simple and easily handled, the area of the mainsail being 190 sq. ft. and that of the jib, 70 sq. ft. A large balloon jib could be used in light winds, and boomed out with the boathook to act as a spinnaker. For the luff of the mainsail, a female track should be used, although it costs rather more, as the other pattern is pretty certain to give trouble.

Now, as regards the lay-out of the cabin. The internal fittings should be kept light and oak and teak avoided to eliminate unnecessary weight. Some light wood such as spruce would be best. It must be remembered that every pound of weight put into the fittings is lost in ballast and a small yacht needs all the stability she can obtain. Starting from forward, there is in the fore-peak a shelf for light stuff. Aft of this is the chain locker and then a bucket 'toilet.' This is better in a small boat than the mechanical variety, which is expensive and heavy. There would, however, be room for, say, a Baby Blake Minor, and sufficient headroom under the hatch. On the starboard side is a bin for the balloon jib and the second jib, and under the seat a locker for shoes. To port, there is a large clothes locker and a shelf for the riding-light. In the cabin there is a food locker to port, and at the after-end a sideboard, with clothes-locker below. The galley is to starboard. Possibly the starboard cot would house further forward, in which case the galley could come further forward, leaving room aft of it for a hanging locker. Or, as an alternative, the galley could remain where it is and a chart table, with drawers beneath, placed in front of it. If the yacht were intended for single-handed work, the starboard bunk could be omitted and then there would be ample room for the chart table. On the port side of the sideboard there is a small cupboard for bottles and such small stuff.

The engine is a 4-h.p. Stuart Turner. Dr. Butler had one of these engines in *Sandook* and another in *Vindilis* and says that the latest improvements have rendered it a fool-proof, reliable engine and he considers it the most suitable in the market. He prefers to off-set the propeller as with a central propeller the aperture in the deadwood and rudder has in a small yacht a devastating effect upon the speed and handiness of the vessel. This was proved in *Vindilis*. Until the aperture had been greatly reduced in size, her speed and handiness left much to be desired. The alterations made her about a knot faster and she is now perfectly handy.

No provision has been made in the plan for a water-tank, as a tank is rather expensive and heavy for a 4-tonner. Fresh water can be conveniently carried in galvanized-iron cans of the same size as, or rather larger than, a petrol tin. I myself use cans that hold just short of 4 gallons and find that they stow quite well under the side-decks aft. In a 4-tonner, however, it might be better to have 2-gallon cans, which could be stowed beneath the cockpit seats, or forward by the side of the mast.

I have reproduced a good many of Dr. Butler's designs in my books, and cannot remember any that took my fancy more than that of Zyklon.

THE 'Z' CRUISER
by T. Harrison Butler, 1935

Length over all	21ft	Sail area	260 sq ft
LWL.	19ft	Displacement	.3.3 tons
Beam	7ft 2in	Iron keel	1 ton
Draught	4ft	Tonnage	4 tons T.M.

Speed under power 5kts

I paid a visit, just before the war, to the yard at Brentford where the popular 'Z' cruisers were built. There I saw what I should think must be the last word in the mass-production of small cruisers and it was certainly a revelation to me.

The 'Z' cruiser is a 4-tonner built from Mr. Harrison Butler's 'Zyklon' design. Although designed on the metacentric shelf system, of which Mr. Butler is an enthusiastic advocate, I am told that she carries a little weatherhelm. I saw a number of the yachts in various stages of construction and was astonished at the speed with which they are built. One commenced that morning was in frame in the early afternoon, and yet the frame seemed admirably put together, the work not having been scamped in any way. It seemed incredible until I went round the works and saw just how it was done.

In one department men were engaged in turning out oak keels, stems and sternposts to accurate templates; in another, oak frames of exactly the right dimensions for each station were taken from the steam-box and set in steel jigs to the correct curve and bevel. As jigs are extensively used in the preparation of the various parts of the vessel, a perfect fit is ensured. Planks for a number of yachts are prepared ready for fitting; hatches, doors and cabin furniture are produced in quantities in the joiners' shop and metal work in the blacksmiths' department. Elsewhere, iron keels and engine beds are cast in the foundry, while the spar-makers are busily employed in the production of hollow masts and spars. The actual building is thus mainly a matter of assembling the prepared parts and progress is very rapid.

A complete steel mould of the design is the basis. The shelves and stringers are first put in and then the stem, keel and sternpost are fitted, welded steel knees making a good strong job of it. The timbers, already bent to the required shape, are now fitted and fastened to the keel and stringers. Planking up is then commenced and as each plank has already been cut to shape it fits exactly. The work for a time is now slowed down, as the copper fastenings have to be put in and clenched in the usual manner. In the early stages the yacht is built upside down, but when planked up she is wheeled out into the yard, lifted off the steel mould by a crane and turned over. The iron keel is then fitted and eight galvanized steel floors put in. Then she is decked and the interior work completed.

This 'Z' cruiser, being built up to a standard of quality and not down to a price, could hardly be described as a cheap boat. I don't know what the price would be now, but just before the war she was sold for £339, complete, with a 6 h.p. Watermota engine with reverse, neutral and feathering propeller, and a certain amount of equipment. The figure may seem rather high for a 4-tonner built to a standard design and specification, but a similar yacht of like quality built to an individual design would at that period probably have cost from £50 to £100 more. Without an engine the 'Z' cruiser was sold for £289.

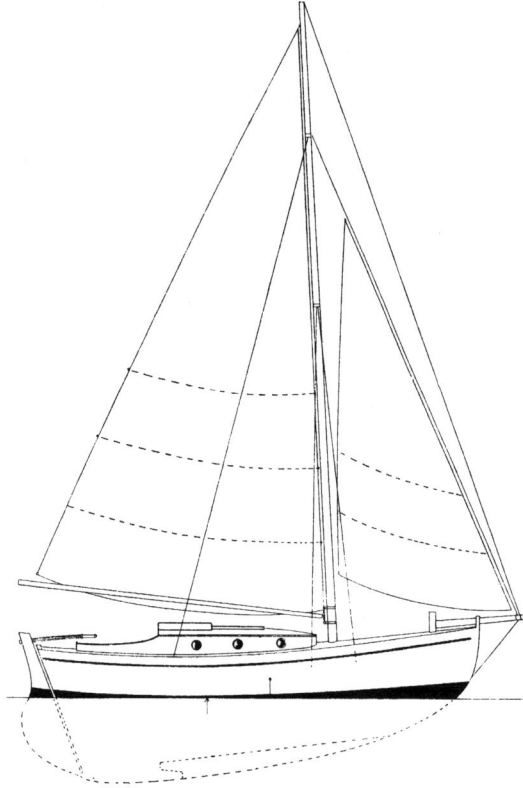

'Z' Cruiser sail plan

The 'Z' cruiser was deservedly popular before the war and is undoubtedly a fine little ship, admirably adapted for single-handed cruising. Her planking is of $7/8$-inch larch and all hatches, cockpit fittings, cabin floor, etc., of teak. The internal accommodation is particularly good for a craft of this size. In the fo'c'sle are two shelves, the chain locker and a bucket 'toilet,' covered by a neat teak box; on the starboard side there is a locker and on the port side a cupboard, or a locker. The cabin has the usual settee bunks, fitted with sprung mattresses, with lockers beneath. Forward of the port bunk is a locker with three shelves facing aft and a shelf below for boots, while at the after end is a sideboard with locker beneath. On the starboard side a roomy galley is fitted close to the cabin door, and shelves and lockers wherever possible. There is a fore-hatch, and the cabin is lit and ventilated by means of opening portlights and a mushroom ventilator. To facilitate entrance and assist ventilation a sliding hatch is fitted at the after end of the coachroof.

The yacht possesses several unusual and interesting features. The mast, for instance, is stepped on deck in a steel tabernacle, which is securely bolted to a steel frame going right round the boat. The shroud-plates are also bolted to this frame and as no trouble has been experienced it must be assumed that the arrangement affords adequate strength. The absence of the mast below decks renders the fo'c'sle easy of access from the cabin and also tends to enhance the comfort of the latter. The engine is installed on a massive steel bed, cast to fit the boat. I do not know what the weight of this casting is but should think it must be something like 4 cwt. and it forms part of the ballast. As it is bedded down in bitumen there should be no risk of water settling below the casting and rotting the planks. It is claimed that by this method of installation vibration is completely eliminated. Another unusual feature is the laminated stem, but I do not know what advantage, if any, it has over the ordinary solid stem. Both mast and boom are hollow, the gooseneck of the latter sliding on a short rod, so that the luff of the sail can be set up by a purchase on the tack, which seems a sound idea, and there is a permanent backstay leading to a bumpkin aft. When I was at the yard I was shown a 'Z' cruiser with a raised deck, or over-all cabin-top, which they had built as an experiment and the difference it made in the vessel's internal accommodation was astonishing.

I have dwelt at some length on this 'Z' boat because I think she represents mass-production at its best, but she must be regarded as a standard cruiser *de luxe*.

MONIE

(Drawings 70 & 71) by J. Laurent Giles, 1938

LOA 25ft 3in	Draught 4ft 6in
LWL 21ft 6in	Headroom in cabin 5ft
Beam 7ft 2in	Sail area . . . . 380 sq ft

Mr. Laurent Giles, designer of *Maid of Malham* and other well-known ocean racing yachts, has long been recognized as the creator of exceptionally able small cruising craft, and I am pleased at being able to reproduce the lines of one that I think he regards as the best boat he has yet designed. A large number of yachts have been built from these lines, and although in some cases minor modifications have been introduced in the accommodation and sail plans, the hulls of all are similar to that of the pioneer *Andrillot*, 5 tons T.M., which was built by Moody & Son at Swanwick in 1936 for Mr. R. A. Kinnersly. As *Andrillot* was a gaff cutter and her cabin plan, designed to suit the wishes of the owner, rather unorthodox, I have selected her sister ship *Monie* for reproduction in this book.

Monie was built by the Berthon Boat Co. at Lymington in 1938 for Mr. D. Milner Deighton, and is rigged as a stemhead Bermudian sloop. These yachts have sweet lines and are beautifully balanced. Experience has proved them to be fine sea boats, and although intended solely for cruising, they have a good turn of speed. In 1946 one of them, *Francolin*, was third in the Round the Island race, competing against the best the Solent could produce in the way of racing craft. The latest edition is fitted with a 'dog-house,' which gives 6ft. headroom at the after end of the cabin and enables one to stand up and look around through

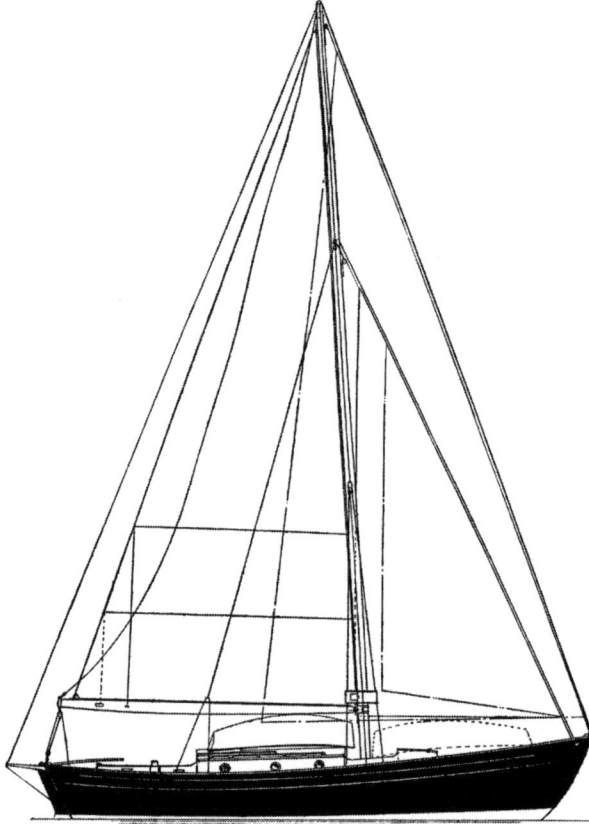

Monie sail plan

the armour-plate glass windows at the sides. The dog-house fits there extremely well and gives no trouble, but necessitates carrying the dinghy on the fore-deck instead of on the cabin-top.

In 1937, Mr. H. D. E. Barton, a member of the firm of Laurent Giles & Partners, borrowed *Andrillot* for a short cruise and accompanied by his wife, sailed to Concarneau and back. The following year he sailed *Monie* to Pwllheli, via the Caledonian Canal. He says it was a most interesting comparison of rigs on identical hulls, the Bermudian proving preferable on every point, particularly in heavy weather, of which he had more than his fair share, encountering two gales on the north-east coast and two on the west coast of Scotland. Nevertheless, the yacht covered the 1,056 miles in 25 days. She made the run from Ryde to Dover, 104 miles, in 15½ hours giving an average of 6¾ knots, a fine performance for a vessel measuring only 21ft. 6in. on the waterline. The next day she made Lowestoft, was in Filey Bay four days after her departure and reached Scotland in less than a week from the time she sailed from the Solent.

The lay-out of *Monie's* cabin is admirably planned, provision having been made for everything that one could possibly want for comfort and convenience. There can be no doubt that she and her sister-ships are eminently desirable little yachts, fast and weatherly, fine sea boats, beautifully balanced and possessing admirable accommodation below decks, as shown in the plan. There is comfortable sleeping accommodation for three, or four at a pinch, and an auxiliary engine is housed under the bridge deck.

THE BURNHAM SLOOP
(Drawings 72 & 73) by Norman E. Dallimore, c1939

Length over all	21ft	Sail area	265 sq ft
LWL.	18ft	Displacement	2.75 tons
Beam	6ft 8in	Headroom	5ft
Draught	3ft 9in	Tonnage	3.2 tons T.M.

Builder . . . . R. J. Prior & Son Ltd.

This is another attractive little yacht from the board of Mr. Dallimore, which particularly appeals to me as she has a very nicely designed raised deck. Mr. Dallimore has prepared an alternative design with a coach-roof cabin-top, but I have selected the former for reproduction as, apart from the enhanced accommodation below decks, it is in my opinion the more pleasing to the eye. Indeed, I consider it confirms my contention that a raised deck, if well designed, does not in any way mar the appearance of a small yacht, as many people seem to think.

The Burnham Sloop was designed for Messrs. R J Prior & Son, of Burnham-on-Crouch, just before the war, as a standard yacht, and although several keels for the boats had been cast, production was stopped by the outbreak of hostilities. I understand, however, that work will be resumed as soon as circumstances permit. There is likely to be a big demand for these little ships in the future as they are admirably adapted to week-end sailing in the Crouch and adjacent waters. Having lived at Burnham and sailed on the Crouch for many years, Mr. Dallimore knows the type of boat best suited to the district, and I shall be surprised if the yacht does not prove extremely popular. The Burnham Sloop has pleasing lines and a graceful sheer, and with her short forward overhang should prove a good sea boat. With a good length of straight keel she should be steady on the helm and take the ground well. Her sail area in a snug Bermudian rig should be adequate, as it conforms approximately to Albert Strange's rule of 100 square feet for each ton of displacement, and the height of the mast – 29 feet from deck to truck – is not excessive. She should be easy to handle and with the Wykeham-Martin furling gear on the foresail would make an admirable little single-hander.

Below decks, the boat is exceptionally roomy, sleeping accommodation being provided for three people – two on the bunks in the cabin and one on a pipe-cot in the fo'c'sle. The bunks are 1 foot 9 inches wide and the cabin sole 1 foot 11 inches. The raised deck affords about 6 inches more headroom in the fo'c'sle, where

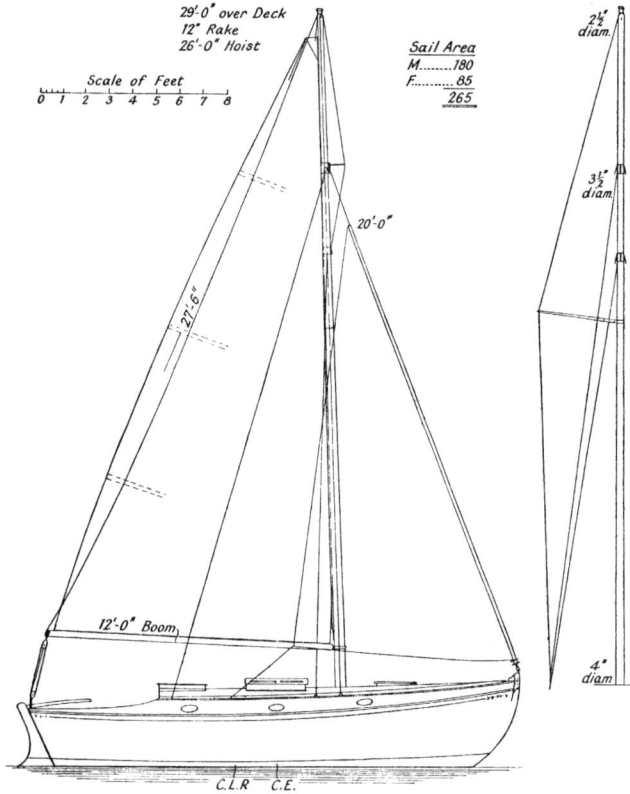

Burnham Sloop sail plan

the sanitary bucket is installed, and she is well-found in cupboards and lockers. Exception might be taken to the position of the chain locker, which is perhaps rather nearer the bow than desirable. Even a C.Q.R. anchor and 20 fathoms of ¼-inch chain weigh 1 cwt, a load that would be better carried nearer the mast, but a little ship like this must of necessity be something of a compromise and I think it will be agreed that Mr. Dallimore has laid out the available space to the best advantage. Thanks to the raised deck, there is ample headroom to allow one to sit back on the bunks and rest against the side of the boat, a feature that makes for comfort.

There is a small galley, large enough to take a gimballed Primus, under the side-deck, near the companion on the starboard side, with a locker in front of it. Opposite, on the port side, are placed a cupboard and a sideboard, with another sideboard at the fore end of the port bunk. Space has been left beneath this sideboard for a sleeper's feet, thus ensuring a bed 6 feet in length. Forward of the starboard bunk is a large hanging clothes locker, and another locker is provided forward of the port bunk. There are also lockers under the bunks and in the cockpit.

At the time I write the price of the yacht has not been fixed, but is expected to be from £400 to £450, which seems a reasonable figure in view of the big advance that has taken place in the cost of construction since the war. As the yacht will accommodate three people, the cost to each, if they owned the boat in partnership, would be quite moderate. Altogether, the Burnham Sloop strikes me as a jolly little ship in which one could have any amount of fun and cruise from port to port in reasonably fine weather.

The specification drawn up before the war included pitch-pine planking, with American elm timbers and English elm keel; the stem, stern-post and deadwood of oak, and decks of fir, covered with canvas and painted. The covering boards, hatches, skylight, cockpit were to be of teak or mahogany and internal fittings of mahogany. This specification will be followed as closely as possible, but will of course depend upon what materials are available.

There is room for a 4 hp Stuart Turner engine, but it is possible that an outboard engine would be a more popular form of auxiliary power.

MOWGLI
(Drawings 74 & 75) by Ian C. Bridge, c1943

Length over all	.18ft 6in	Headroom	. 4ft 3in
LWL.	16ft	Displacement	.1.9 tons
Beam	6ft 3in	Iron keel	1,900 lb
Draught	3ft 3in	Sail area	180 sq ft

Designed by Mr. Ian C. Bridge, *Mowgli* is one of the most attractive little pocket cruisers I have come across for a long time. She was designed to provide comfortable accommodation for two persons for limited periods on the Clyde, where sheltered anchorages are plentiful and never very widely separated. She would, however, be good enough, I think, for coastwise cruising in reasonably fine weather; but, of course, in a craft as small as this a long passage should not be attempted in any but settled weather. The specification is as follows: Keel, oak, 3 inch moulded; stem and sternpost, oak, 2½ inch sided; floors, knees, etc., oak; timbers, American elm, 1⅛ inches by ¾ inch spaced 7½ inches; planking, Columbian pine, ¾ inch copper fastened; beams, 1⅜ inches by 2 inches-1½ inches, Oregon pine, spaced 12 inches; deck, ¾-inch t and g pine, canvas covered; shelf, 3 inches by 1½ inches, Oregon pine; mast and boom, Oregon pine.

A feature of this little yacht that particularly pleases me is the over-all cabin-top, as it makes an enormous difference to the comfort below decks and adds materially to the strength of the boat. The raised sides and end would be of mahogany, as would the bulkhead, cockpit coamings, seats and lockers. By carrying the cabin-top right across the vessel it has been possible to fit a galley at the after end of the cabin on the port side and lockers for clothes and blankets opposite, which would not have been practicable with the ordinary coach-roof and side decks. Then again, it affords sufficient headroom over the bunks to enable one to sit back comfortably and lean against the side of the boat. Unless one has a back to rest against there can be no real comfort in a small craft.

In describing his design in the *Yachting Monthly*, Mr. Bridge remarked:

> The displacement is about the minimum required to accommodate crew and gear, and the lines are of necessity somewhat chubby. A fairly full mid-section is combined with reasonably clean ends, the run in particular being finer than usual in this type of craft. The centres of heeled and upright buoyancy practically coincide and the centre of gravity of the iron is slightly forward as shown. This, with about 150 lb. of inside ballast, which should be available, will make it possible to avoid excessive trim by the stern when the crew are aft in the cockpit – always a difficulty in a small craft.

I should think this trimming ballast would hardly be required when the boat was sailed single-handed, as the weight of one man aft would not put her down by the stern to any great extent. The cabin has been admirably laid out and should provide everything one could reasonably desire for comfort and convenience. The galley, at the after end of the port bunk, is large enough to house a Primus or two-burner pressure stove, with shelves above for crockery and space below for cooking utensils. On the opposite side is a large lined locker for clothes and sleeping-bags with a cupboard above. The step at the cabin entrance houses the sanitary bucket and makes a convenient seat when cooking. The bunks are long enough for sleeping purposes, but the two forward cushions would be stowed away when sailing, thus leaving a convenient platform under the fore hatch. Imperishable stores could be stored under the bunks and there are several shelves forward which would be useful for stowage. The locker for the cable, which runs through a tube, is below the fo'c'sle floor. Three lights are fitted in each side of the raised cabin, as shown in the drawing, with an opening port forward and two in the bulkhead aft. Two ventilators in the cabin doors could, Mr. Bridge says, remain almost permanently open. I would suggest that if a 'shop-blind' ventilator, such as I have in *Iolanthe*, were employed it could always be left open, when no one was on board, without fear of rain driving through into the cabin. The cockpit is fitted with fore-and-aft seats, leaving the door of the sail locker aft freely accessible. There are lockers under the waterways behind the seats for stowage of small gear, and below there is room for water cans on the port side and a food locker, with zinc gauze panel, on the starboard side. A cockpit tent for use in wet weather would make for enhanced comfort.

The sail area of 175 square feet in a Bermudian stemhead sloop rig seems adequate, although slightly less than Albert Strange's estimate of 100 square feet for each ton of displacement. It must be remembered, however, that Strange's allowance was based on the gaff rig and as the Bermudian is about 10 per cent,

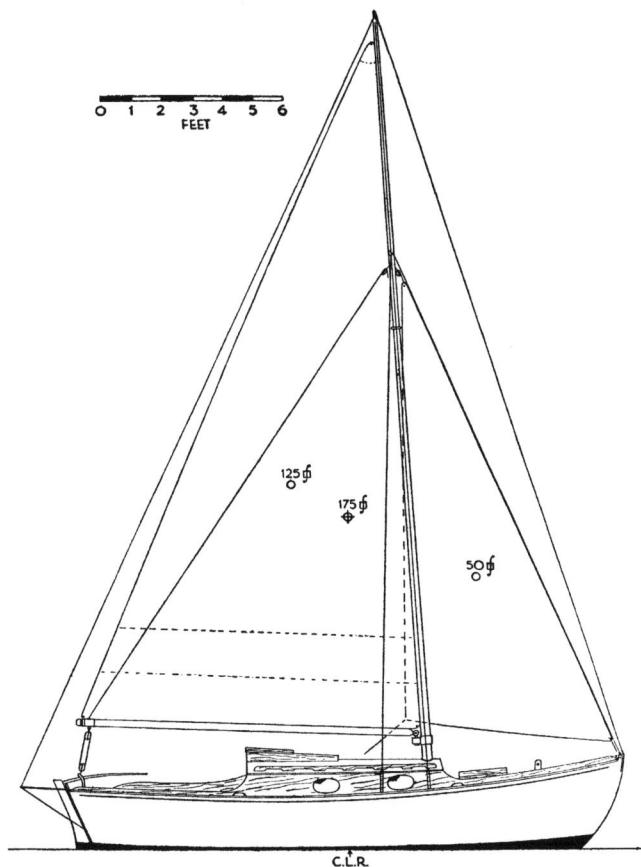

Mowgli sail plan

faster to windward, rather less sail is needed. As a permanent backstay is set up to an outrigger aft, runners are not required. No provision has been made for an auxiliary engine, for, as Mr. Bridge very truly says, the cost would be out of all proportion in so small a craft and it is doubtful if room could be found for it. I agree with him, as to fit an engine would completely ruin the accommodation and the drag of the propeller seriously affect her sailing qualities. A little boat like *Mowgli*, too, can be propelled quite well with a sweep in case of need.

Altogether, I think *Mowgli* as jolly a pocket cruiser as one could desire. She would make a capital little single-hander for estuary cruising, while for a couple of youngsters she would be a thing of joy.

THUELLA

(Drawings 76 & 77) by T. Harrison Butler, 1945

Length over all	23ft 6in	Displacement	3.6 tons
LWL.	20ft	Lead keel	1.15 tons
Beam	6ft 1in	Tonnage	4.4 tons T.M.
Draught	4ft	Sail area	245 sq ft
Mainsail	165 sq ft	Foresail	80 sq ft
Second staysail	50 sq ft	Storm staysail	15 sq ft
Genoa	160 sq ft	Trysail	58 sq ft
Headroom	4ft 3in	Turner's Stability Factor	19

At the time I write *Thuella* is Mr. Harrison Butler's latest design and in my opinion one of the most delightful little ships he has yet produced. I am indebted to Mr. Butler for the following description of the design:

Thuella, the Greek for a whirlwind, was designed with definite objects in view. It seems certain that after the war yacht-building will be very expensive and upkeep far greater than it was formerly. Therefore yachts will be smaller, simpler and in consequence cheaper both in first cost and maintenance. I think that many more will be built by amateurs than has been the case in the past, and so in designing *Thuella* I have tried to make the construction as easy and economical as possible.

An over-all length of 24 feet is about as much as the ordinary amateur will be able to undertake. Having decided that a Thames tonnage of about five or less is suitable, the next consideration is what is the best type to choose, one that will have the maximum sea-keeping ability combined with comfortable cruising accommodation for a crew of two, say a man and his wife. My conception is not a mere day-boat or estuary cruiser, but a ship capable of real Channel cruising in reasonable weather. She must have good stability, be weatherly, handy and as fast as she can be, keeping the other demands in view. On the whole the Norwegian type seems the best. The sharp stern is easy to build, does not add weight in the wrong place and is eminently sea-kindly. I think that *Thuella*, with a couple of warps towing astern, would be able to run under her storm jib, or storm spinnaker, with safety in heavy weather. My Zyklon design, published in Mr. Cooke's earlier book "Small Yacht Cruising" and subsequently reproduced as the standard 'Z' 4-tonner, has run before a 70-mile-an-hour gale in the Channel, from Beachy Head to Dover, and her owner told me that he had perfect confidence in her, as she ran easily and shipped no solid water. The only drawback to the Norwegian stern is that it contracts the cockpit. This can be overcome by giving an extra foot on the waterline – Zyklon has 19 feet and *Thuella* 20 feet. The extra foot would be an advantage in every way, adding speed and easy running power.

It may be urged that the cut-away forefoot and stern will render her wild on her helm, and that a straight keel would run better. This is of course the orthodox view, but model sailing shows that the long keel type will not run at all, whereas the fin-keel type, with little or no deadwood aft, runs straight and so wins races. A Montague whaler is said to be perfect on the run. Give her a central fin and you have in no wise altered

Thuella sail plan

her running power, and the same is true of the ordinary yacht. If the hull proper is balanced metacentrically she will run well, and the addition of the fin appendage will not be detrimental. The profile of *Thuella* is well cut away fore and aft but not unduly. The stem below the waterline is straight so that it can be easily fashioned by the amateur and it cuts into little wood. Both stem and sternpost drop down on to a keel that is almost straight. This shape is not only easy to build but gives a flat surface when the yacht takes the ground and it brings the ballast keel as low as possible. I am not certain that I would not have liked to give the yacht a little more sheer, but this would have added considerably to the difficulty of planking. The topsides are carried up amidships to form a central turret. This construction is not continued to the stemhead, for we do not want our yacht to resemble a motor-boat, nor to carry a lot of extra weight and windage forward, where the extra headroom is useless. This method of building has every advantage and I cannot see any disadvantage. If the upper strakes are left bright, or painted a different colour to the actual topsides, and if there are two widely-spaced, broad rubbing strakes, the appearance is quite good. This form of hull is easier to construct than one with an orthodox cabin-top, with all its short half-beams and carlines; it is lighter, stronger and safer; gives a noble deck and adds immensely to the room inside. It is worth quite a foot more beam.

The lines are metacentrically balanced and the centres of the curves of upright and heeled areas coincide. The hull is not quite a metacentroid, but I do not think that is a matter of great importance. The rudder is small and does not come down to the heel of the sternpost. The shape of the hull and its good balance does not call for a large rudder and the heel had to be well rounded off to complete the metacentric balance. The rudder is well out of the way should *Thuella* take the ground. The body plan shows easy bilges and a log-keel. The easy turn of the bilge makes for sea-kindliness, as does the absence of flaring topsides.

The Lay-Out: The drawings are self explanatory. There is room for a crew of two on bunks and another can sleep on the cabin sole. Five water-cans are provided. They are of the exact size of a petrol-can and made of galvanized iron. The ordinary commercial size, such as the 'Gem,' is too large. There are clothes lockers to port and starboard aft, that to starboard, having two shelves, under the food locker. There is ample locker space on the port side of the cockpit, and in the stern locker for warps and bosun's gear. Sails are carried in the fore-peak, and here too is ample locker space.

The Sail Plan is somewhat unusual. The mainsail is fitted with ordinary mast-hoops. This plan has worked well in many yachts I have designed with Bermudian rig. All that is necessary is to make the mast a shade thicker, but as it should be a hollow spar the slight extra weight would not matter. At the top of the sail is an extra hoop that can be detached and if necessary reattached to the head of the sail. This will prevent a reefed sail from sagging to leeward, and might be useful if the sail were hoisted ready reefed. The single-handed spinnaker is set on a pole fitted with a jackstay that is attached to the mast. Double guys are fitted so that the sail can be set amidships for running without the mainsail, or alternatively to port or starboard. A special sail of stout material might be carried for heavy running. There is a large Genoa, second and third jibs and also a trysail. It will be noted that a downhaul is fitted to the staysail that leads aft and bunches up the sail at the foot of the forestay, making an immediate temporary stow. I used that plan in an 'X' boat with great success.

Thuella seems fit for any weather, although a hinged hatch to cover the after two feet of the cockpit might at times be useful, when sailing single-handed in bad weather. By this I mean when one hand is below, or sitting in the companion way.

Mr. Butler's description is so complete that it calls for no amplification, but there are one or two comments I should like to make. I think his remark that "model sailing shows that the long keel type will not run at all" is rather too sweeping. I have not sailed models for many years, but when I was a small boy I had a long-keeled model with a straight stem that would run steadily before the wind, without a rudder, under a sail I invented, which I called a kite sail. It was shaped like an old-fashioned kite, stretched on a horizontal spar, from which guys were lead aft to the stern. It was cut very baggy and bellied out ahead something like the modern parachute spinnaker. It was very effective when set without the mainsail and under it she would run fast and steadily straight across the pond. That model would certainly run and I have no doubt that many others will also.

I also do not agree with his remarks about a raised deck. If well designed it is not at all unsightly. I do not think that the slight extra weight would materially affect the yacht's performance and I doubt whether the windage would be any greater, if as great, than that of the fore-coaming of a cabin-top. Mr. Butler suggests that extra headroom is useless in the fo'c'sle, but I do not agree. It seems to me that in a little ship the fo'c'sle is useless unless one can get into it, and 2 or 3 inches additional headroom may make all the difference. The 3-ton *Sirius* has a useful cot in the fo'c'sle, which would have been impracticable in the absence of the raised deck. But these are minor points that do not affect *Thuella*, which, in my opinion, is one of the most delightful designs produced for a long time.

Since writing the above I have learnt with great regret of the death of Mr. Harrison Butler, which occurred on January 29th, 1945. Although I never had the pleasure of meeting him, we had corresponded for many years, and some of his most successful designs were made specially for inclusion in my books. Although an eminent eye surgeon, he had devoted his leisure to yacht designing for something like half a century, striving to evolve an ideal type of small cruising yacht, and the scores of delightful little ships to be seen all round the coast are evidence of the success he achieved in that direction. The design of *Thuella*, reproduced in this book, if not actually his last, must have been nearly his last creation as he sent me the lines shortly before he died.

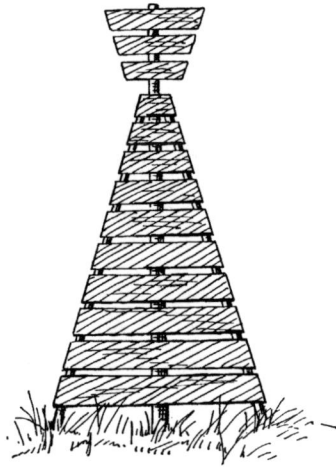

Foulness Beacon

CHAPTER 20: *Design Drawings*

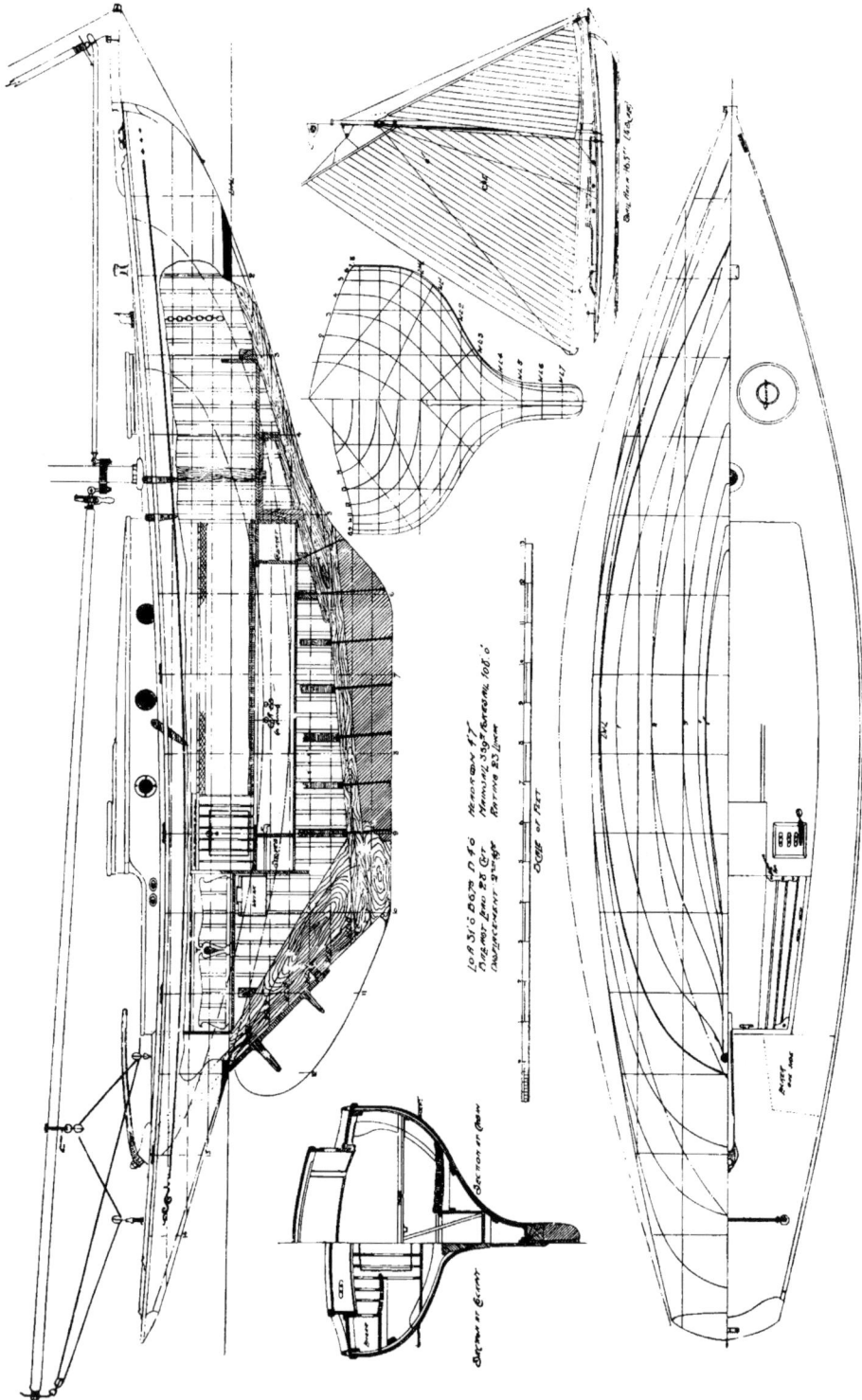

Drawing 3: Lona by J. Pain Clark

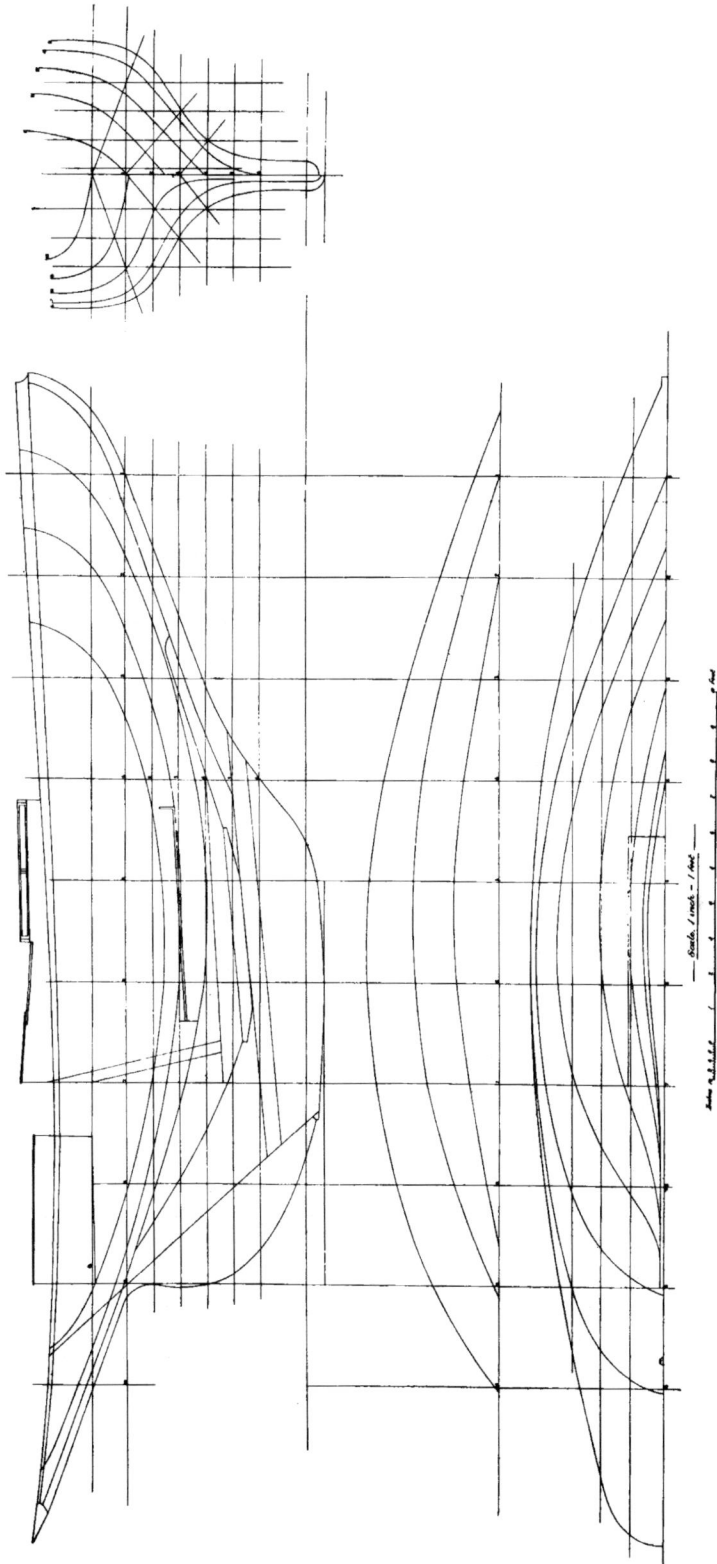

Drawing 4: Granuaile by James E. Doyle — Lines

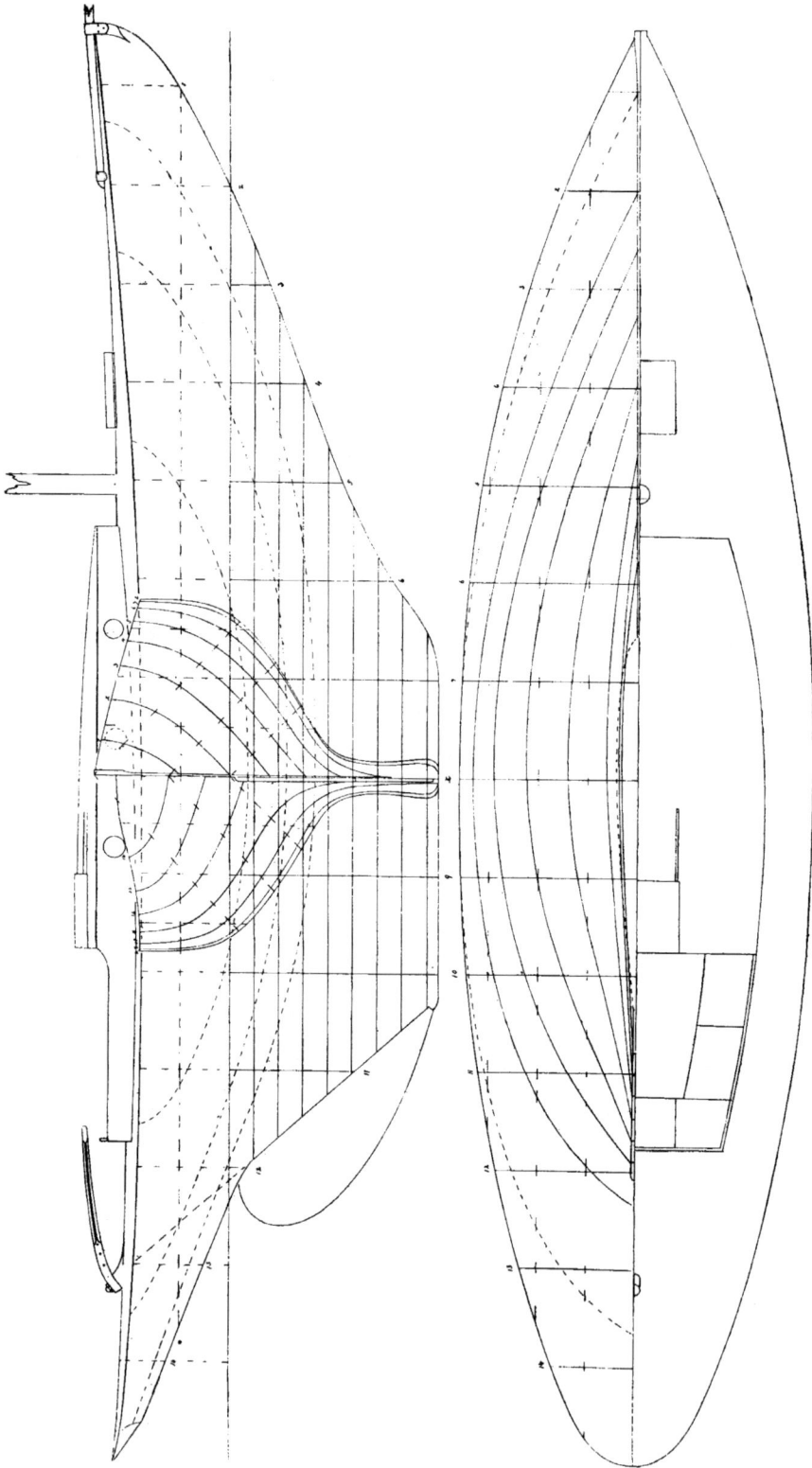

Drawing 5: Mercia III by G. Umfreville Laws — Lines

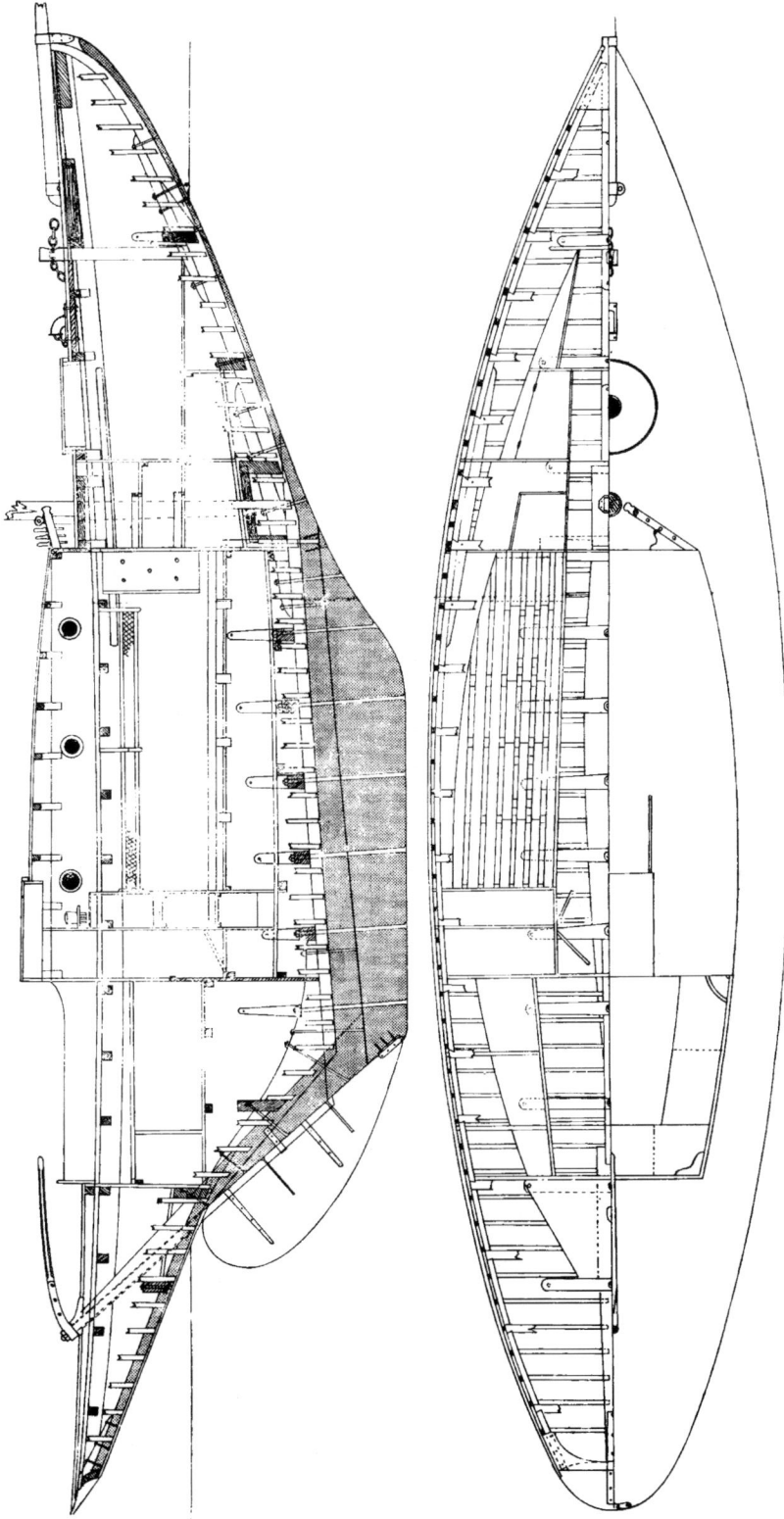

Drawing 6: Mercia III by G. Umfreville Laws — Construction and Accommodation

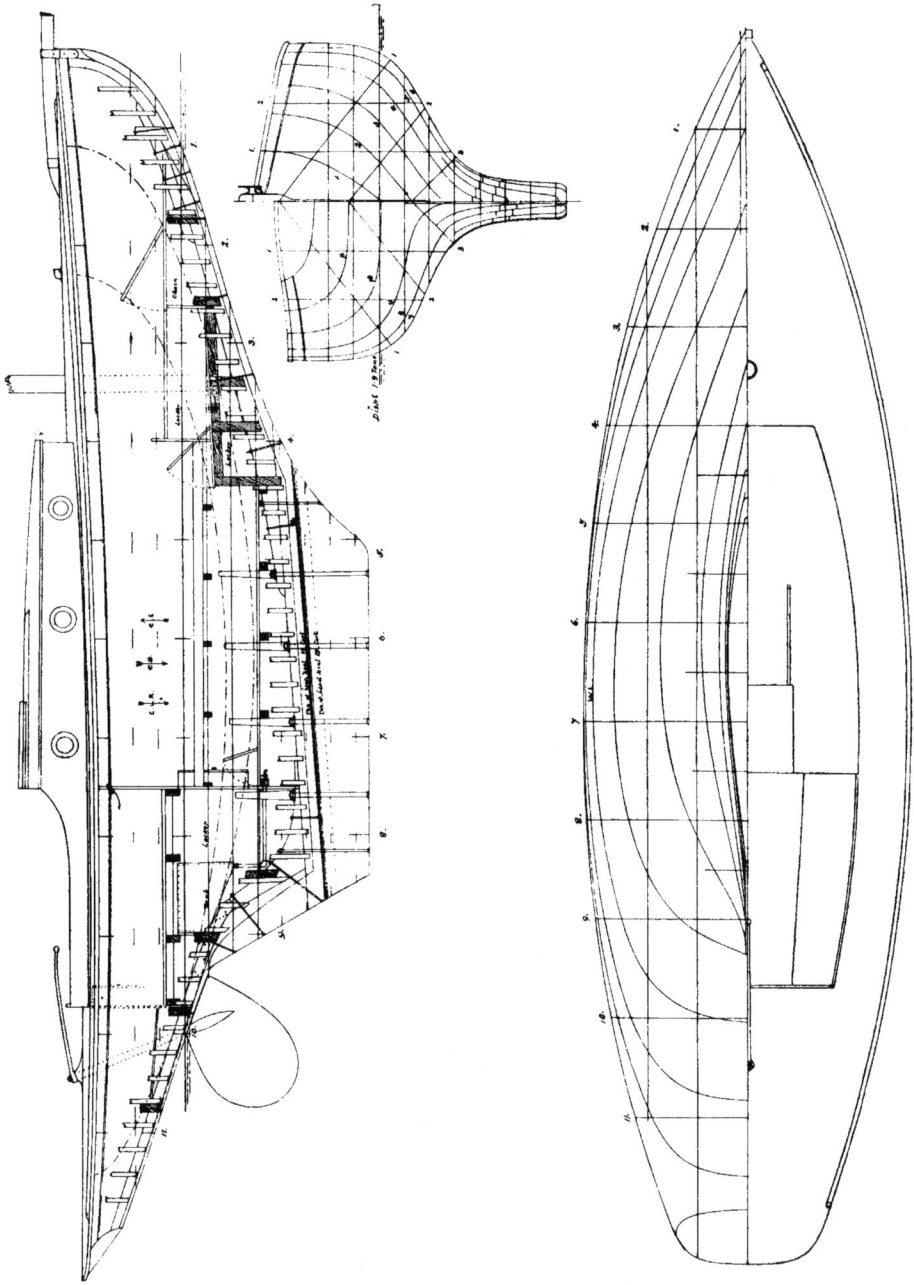

Drawing 7: Arima by H.C. Smith

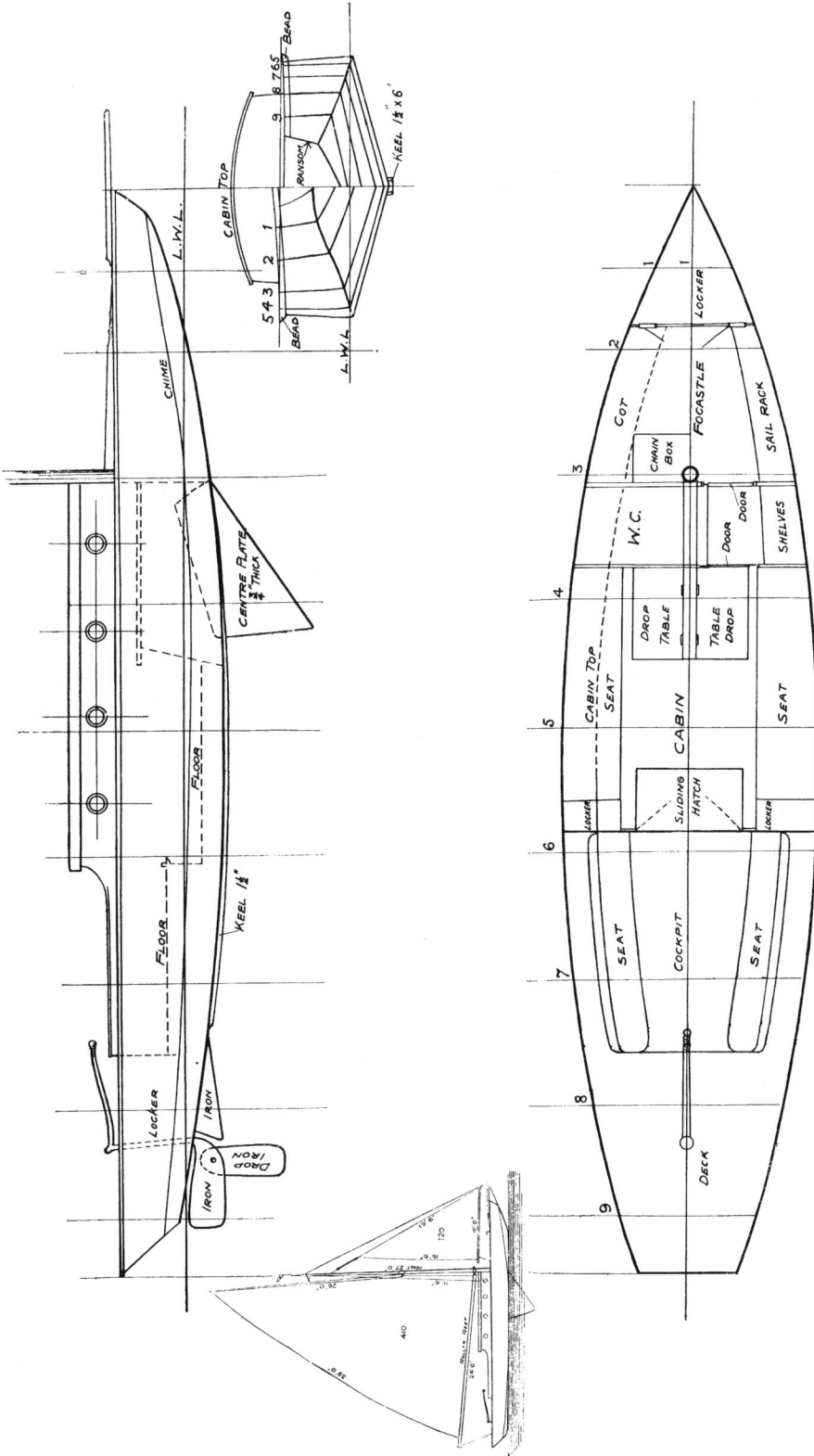

Drawing 8: Skate by Howard Messer

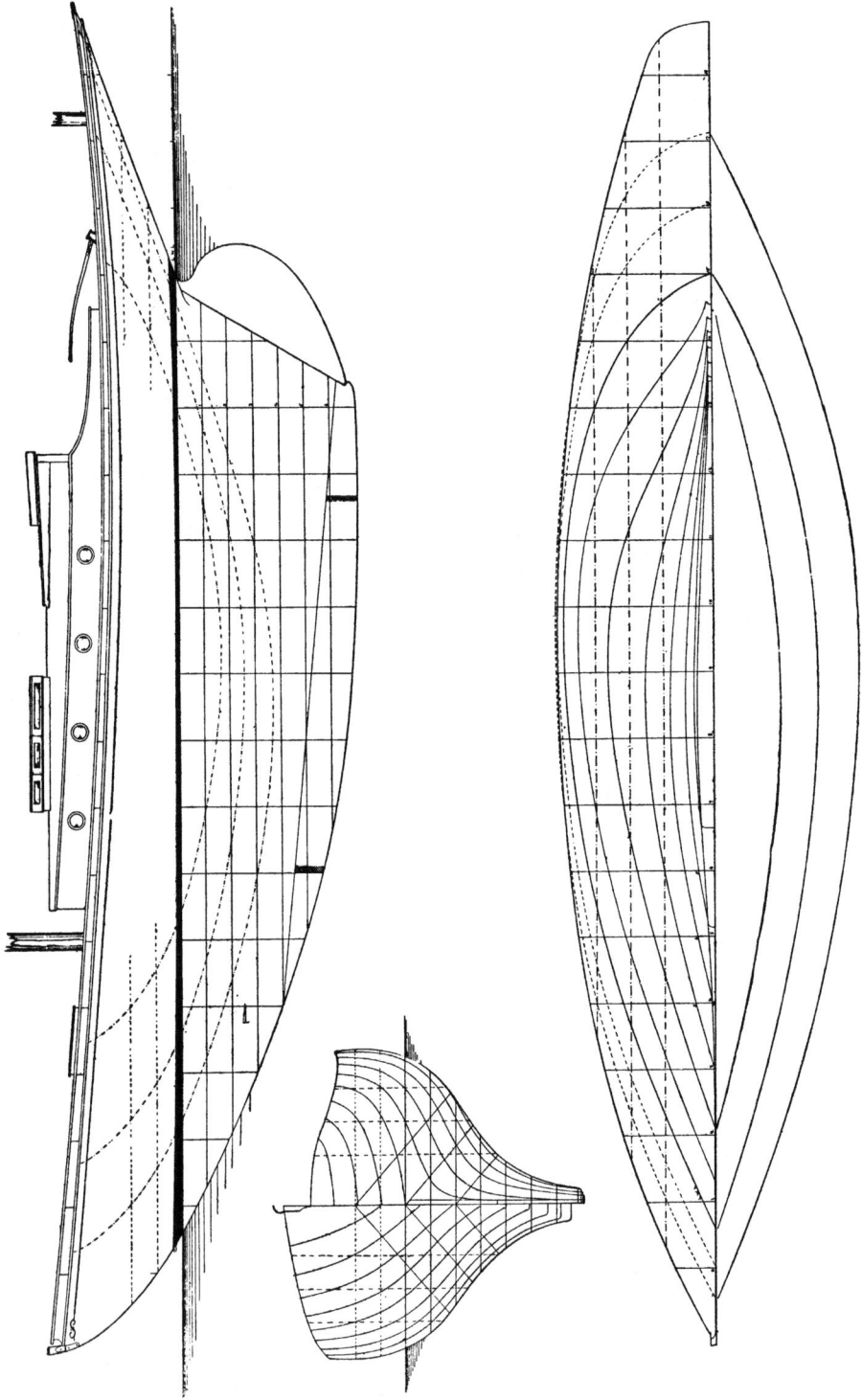

Drawing 9: 12-ton Yawl by Harold Clayton — Lines

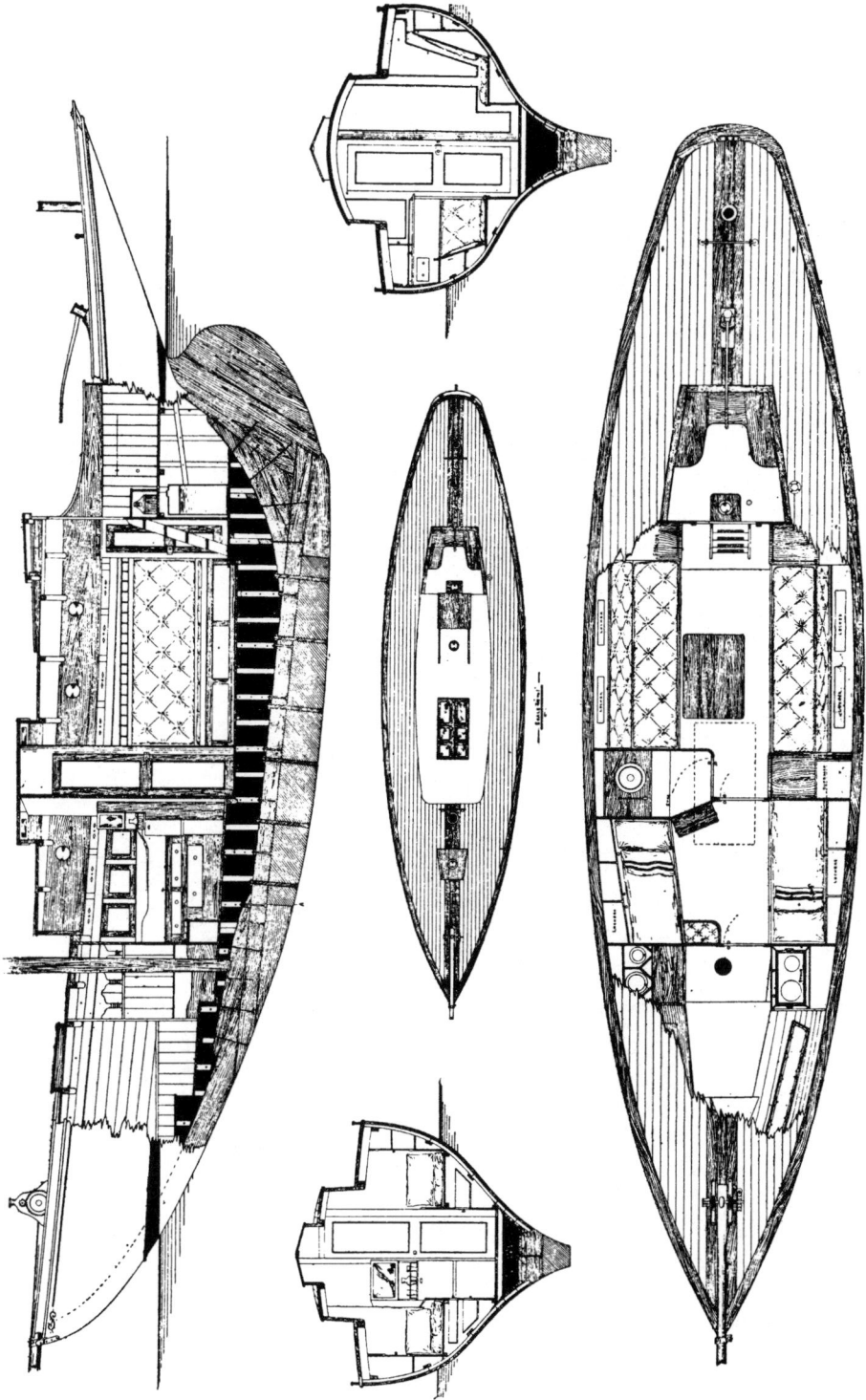

Drawing 10: 12-ton Yawl by Harold Clayton – Construction and Accommodation

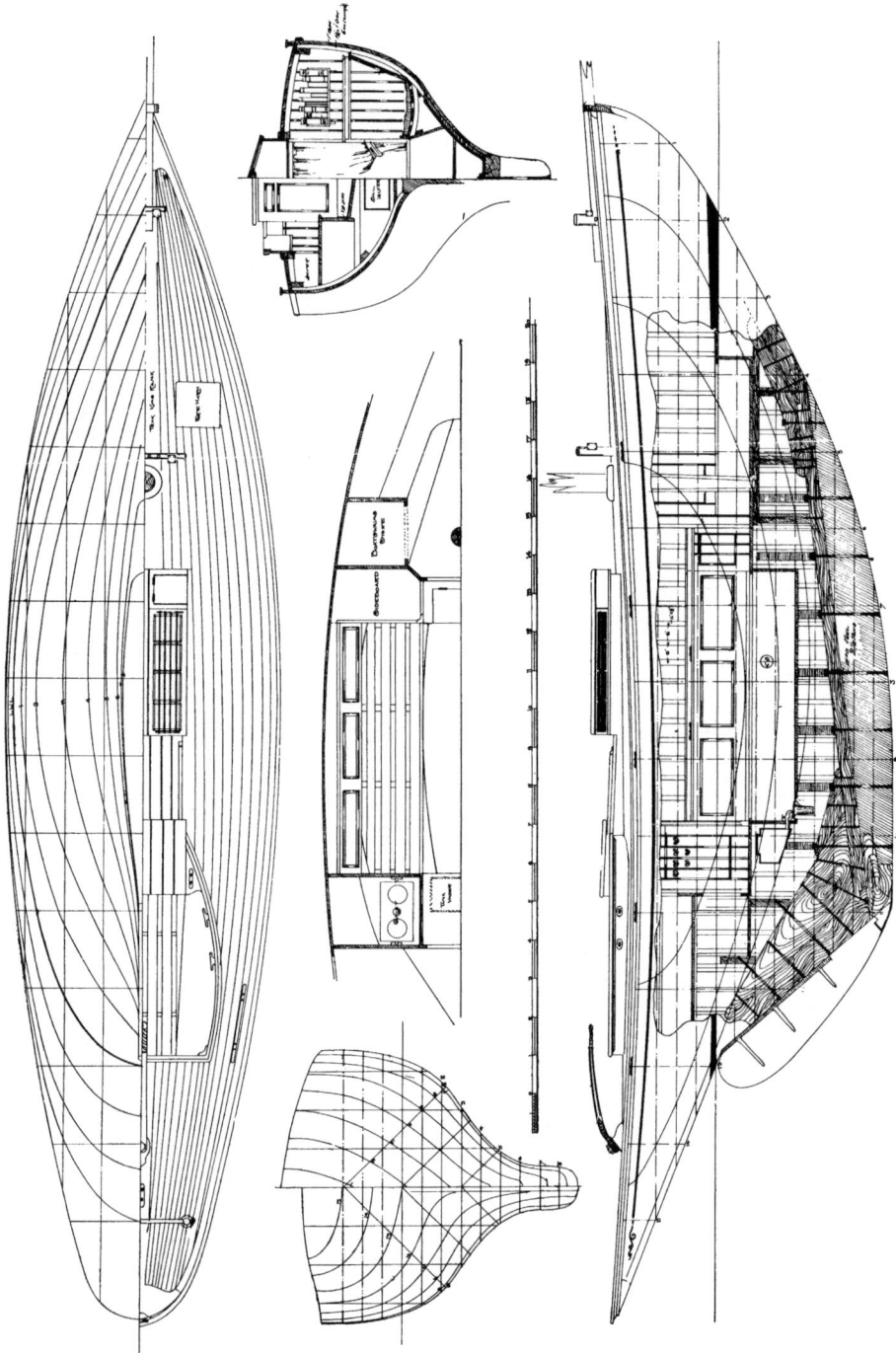

Drawing 11: Lona II by J. Pain Clark

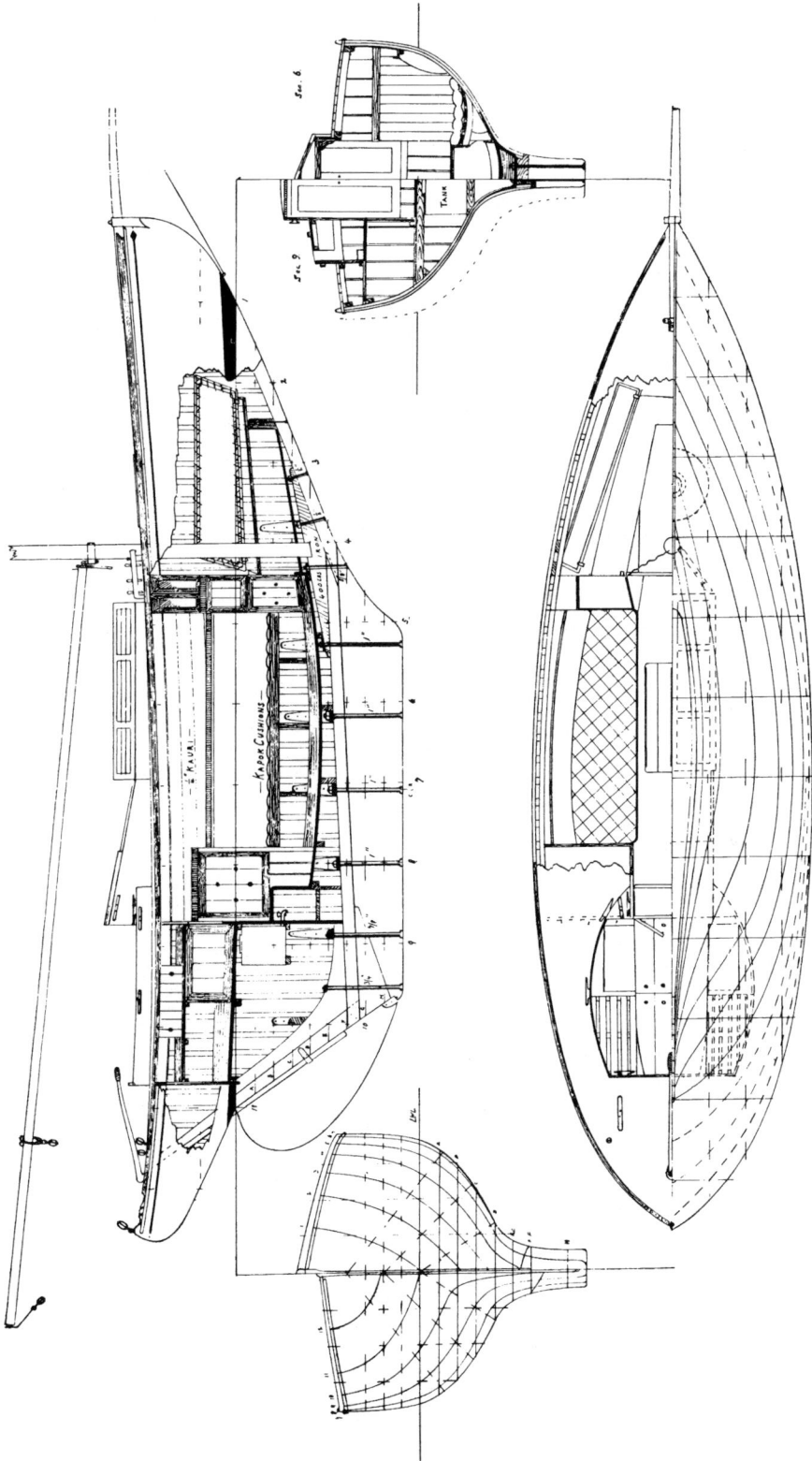

Drawing 12: 5.75-ton Canoe Yacht (Dawn II) by G. Umfreville Laws

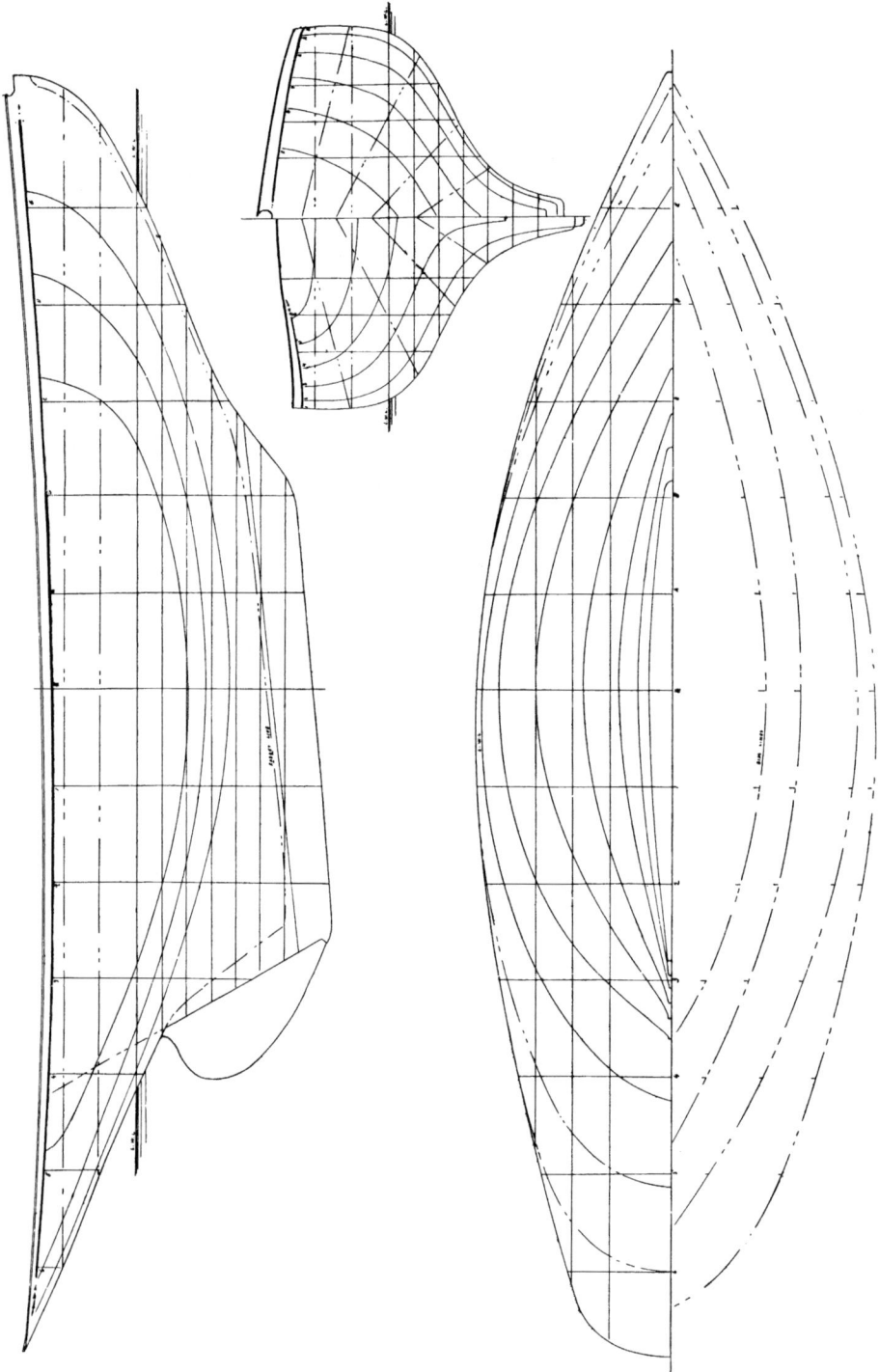

Drawing 13: Single-hander by A. R. Luke — Lines

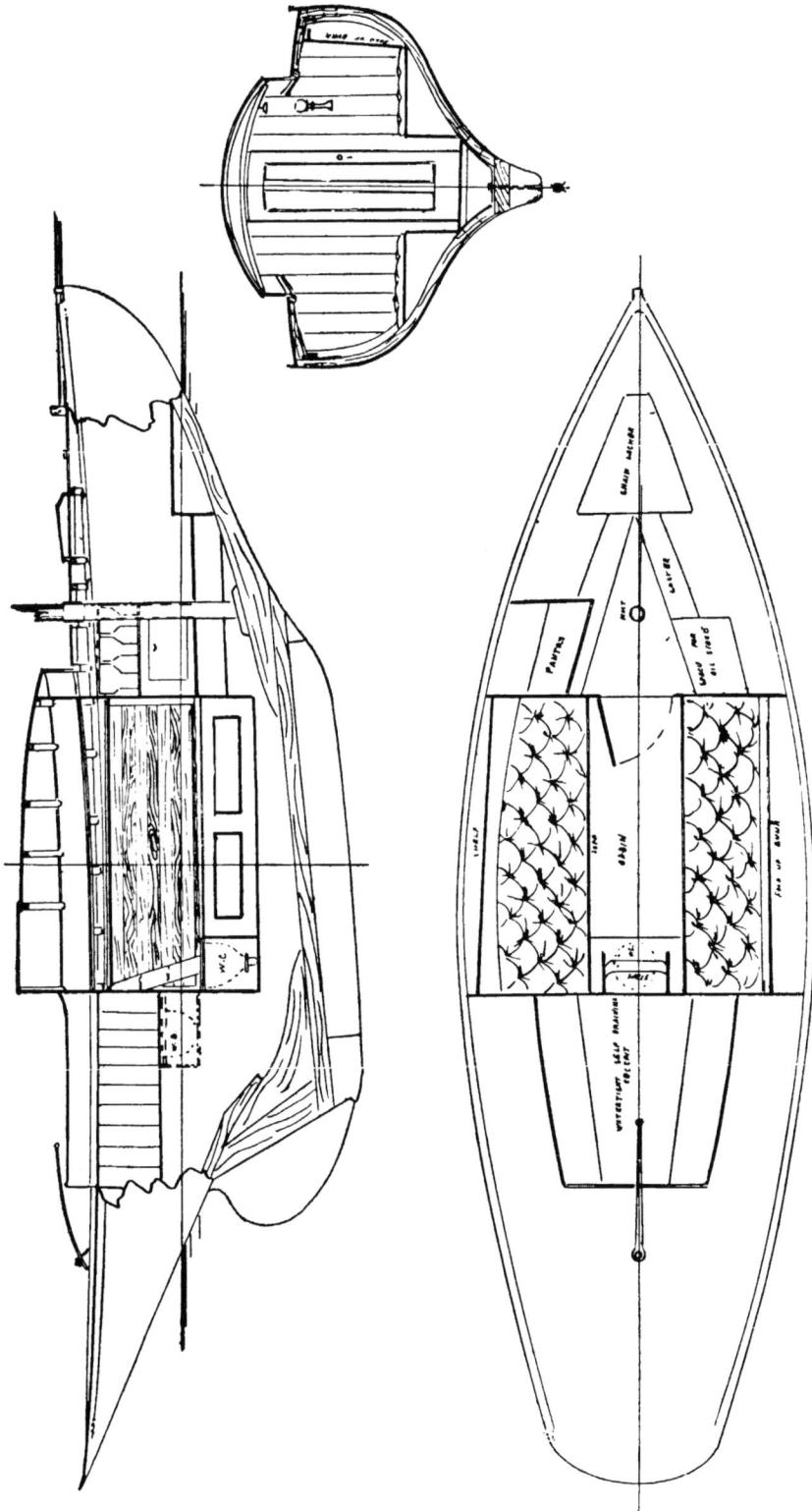

Drawing 14: Single-hander by A. R. Luke — Accommodation

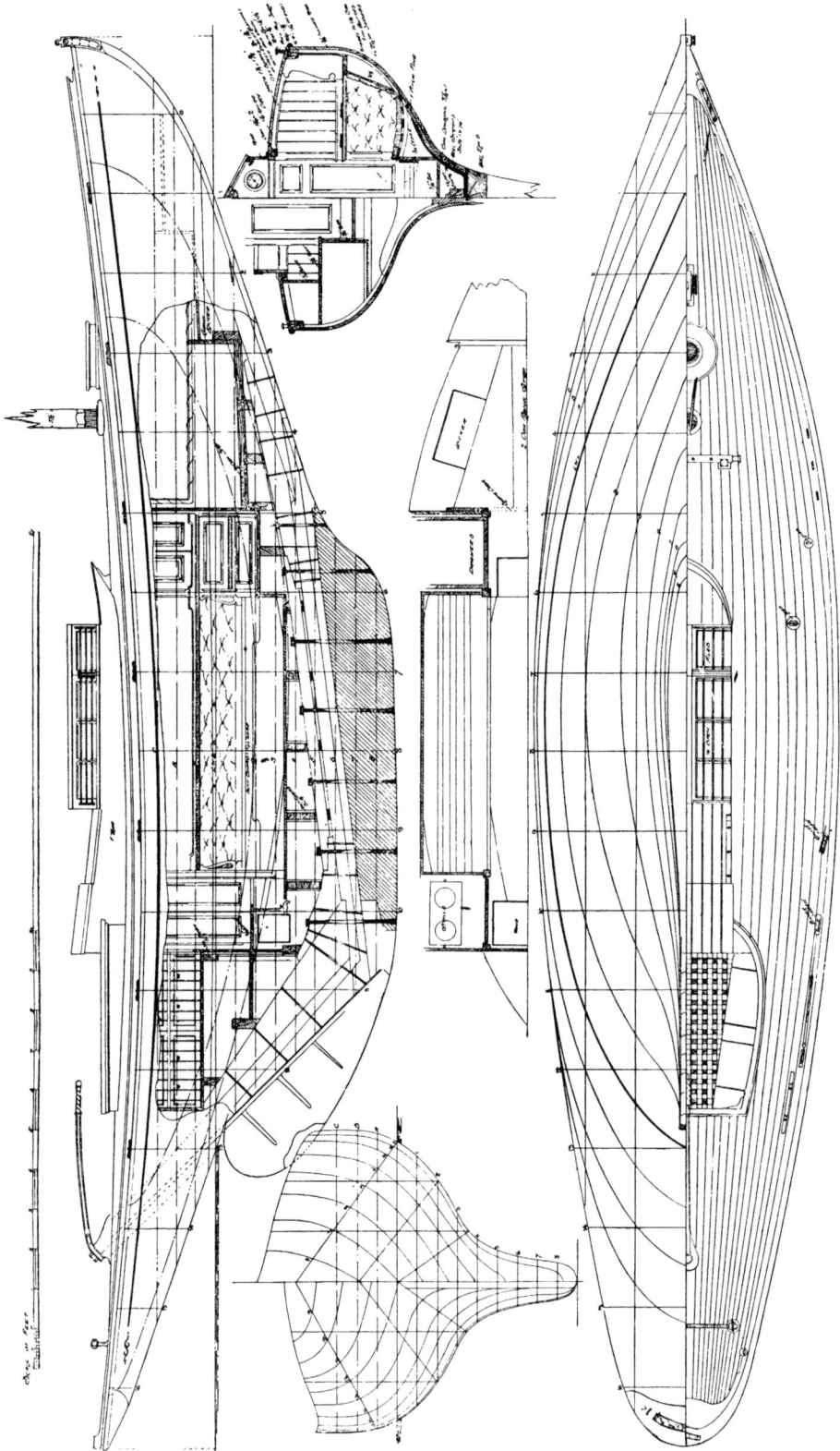

Drawing 15: Lona III by J. Pain Clark

Drawing 16: Lona IV by J. Pain Clark

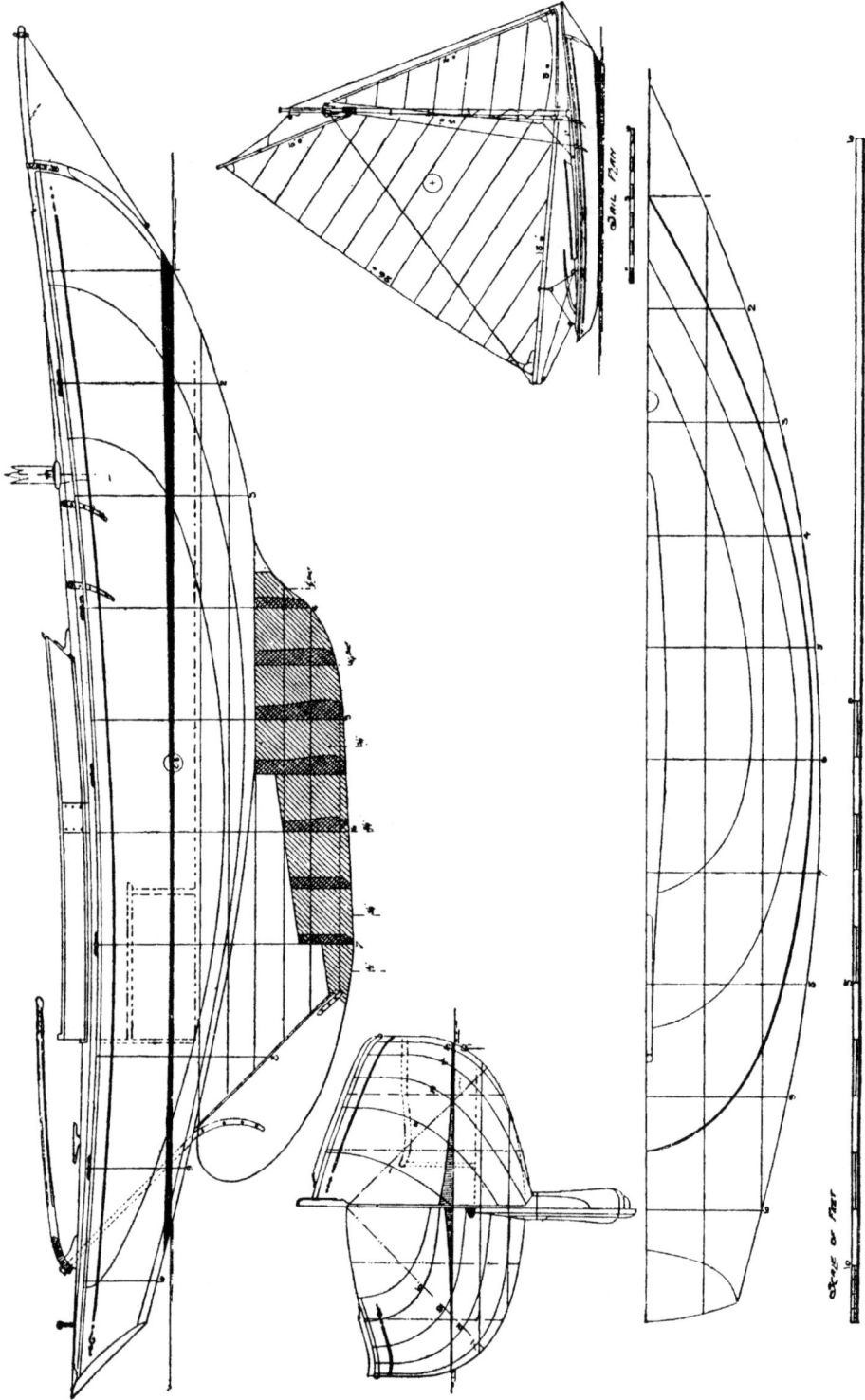

Drawing 17: RCYC Seabird by J. Pain Clark — Lines

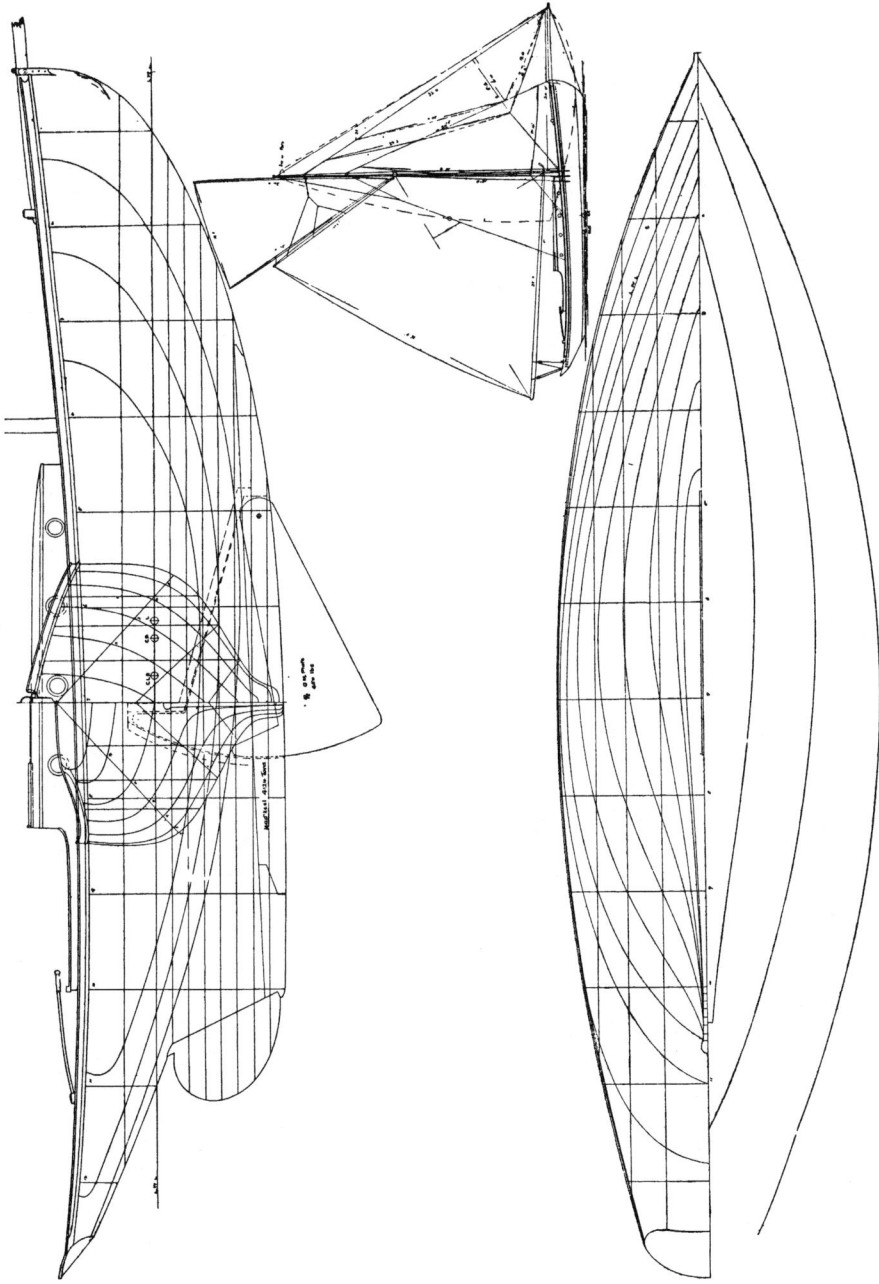

Drawing 18: 10-ton Centre-plate Cutter by Linton Hope — Lines

Drawing 19: 10-ton Centre-plate Cutter by Linton Hope — Construction and Accommodation

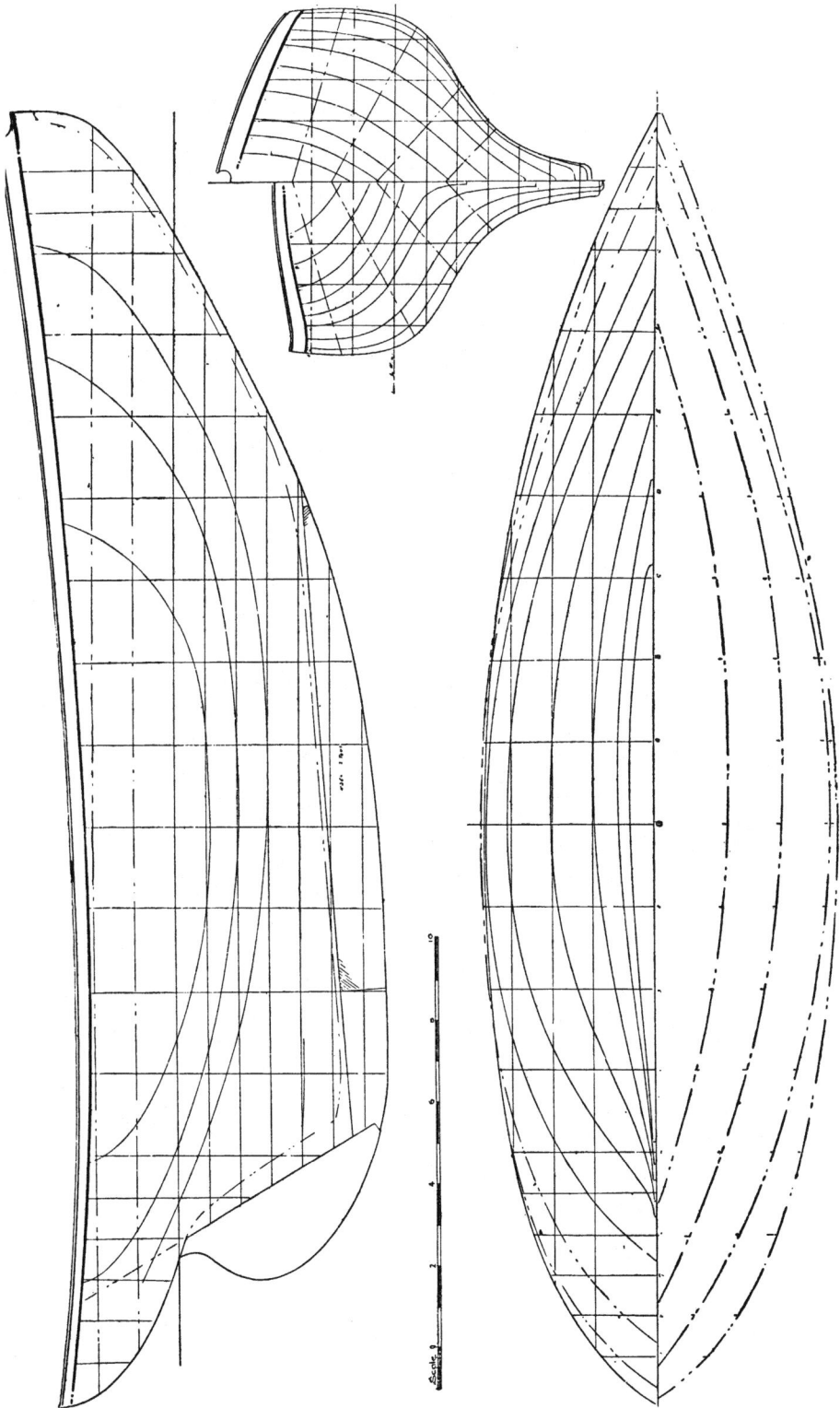

Drawing 20: Alethea II by A.R. Luke — Lines

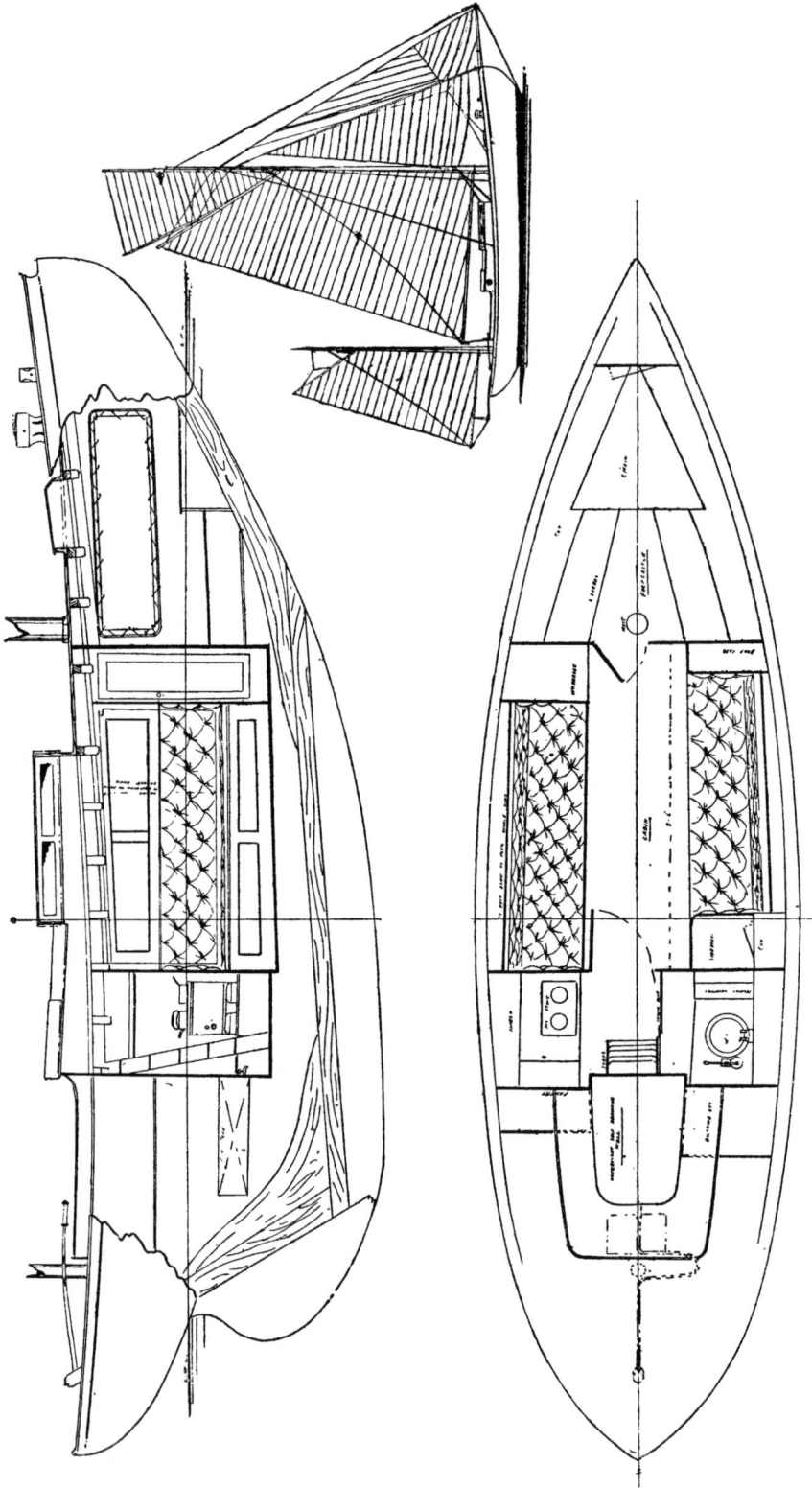

Drawing 21: Alethea II by A. R. Luke — Accommodation and Sail Plan

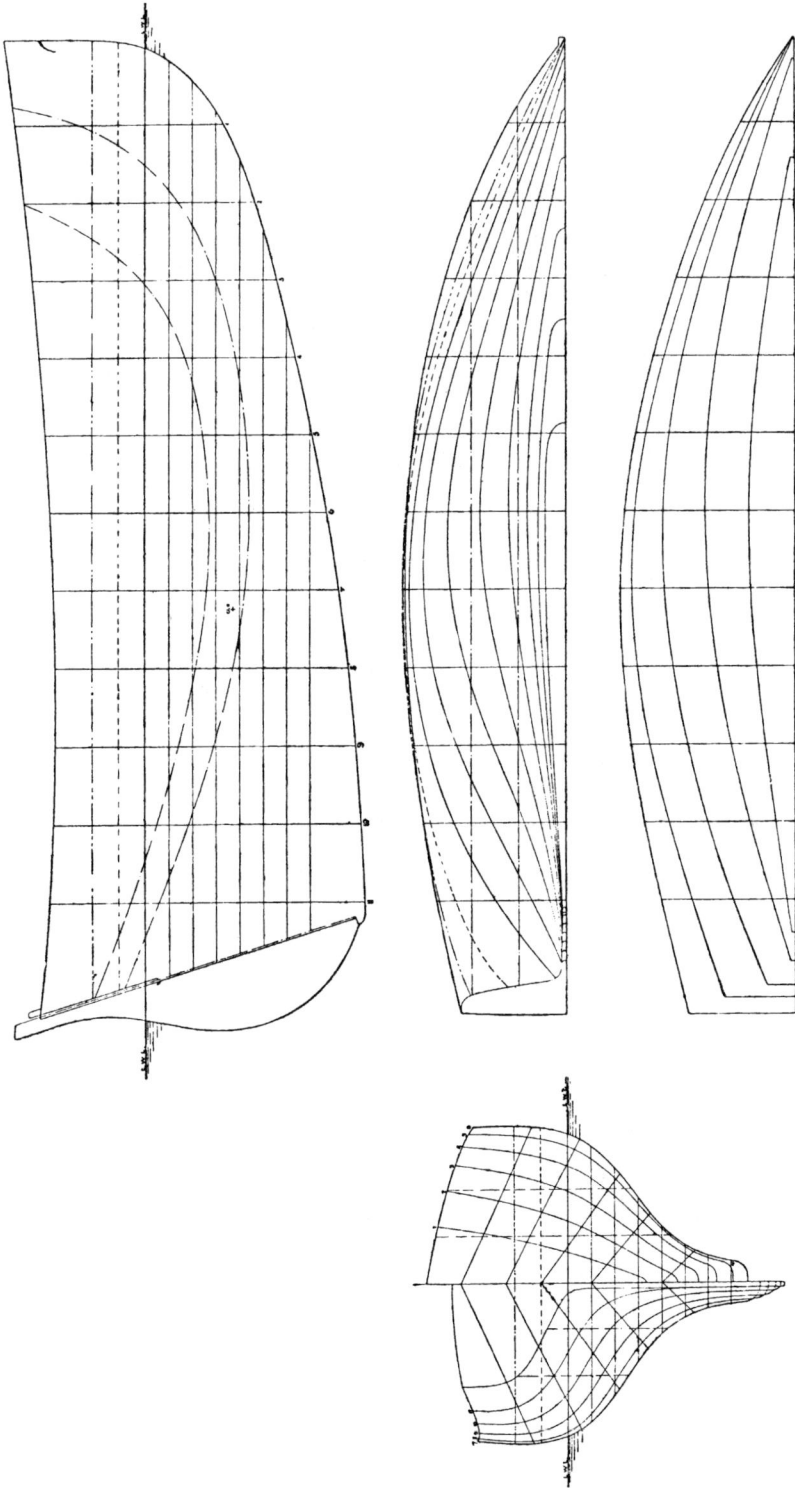

Drawing 22: Lady Belle by Harley Mead — Lines

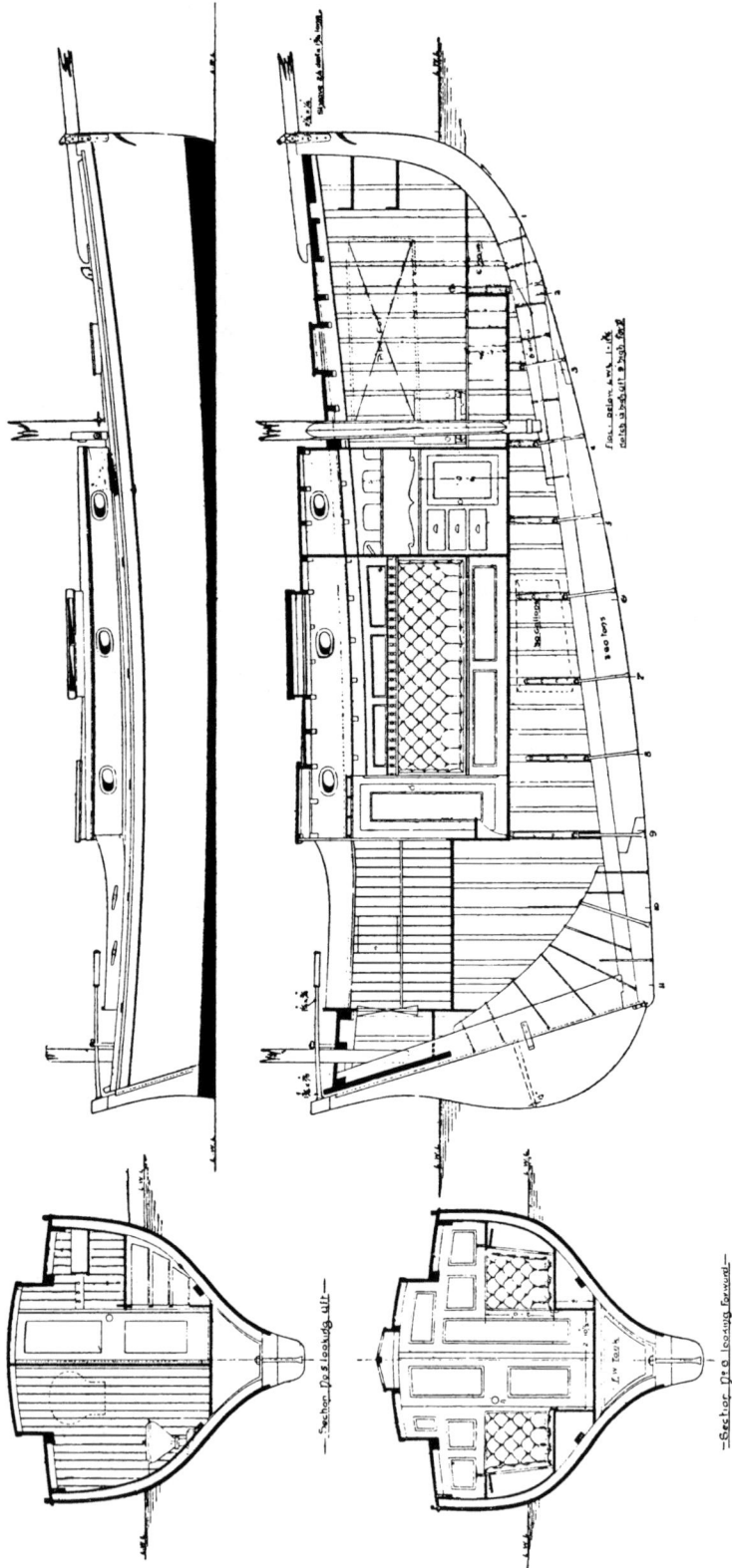

Drawing 23: Lady Belle by Harley Mead — Construction and Accommodation — 1

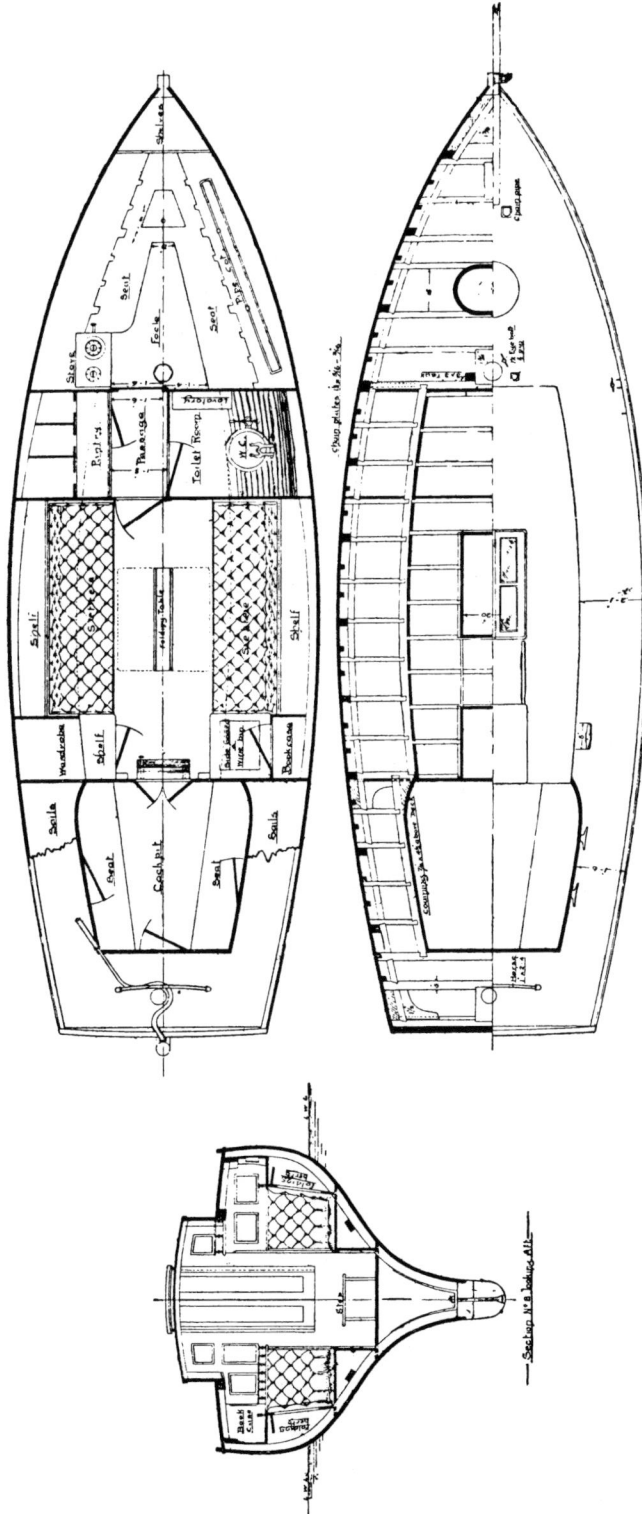

Drawing 24: Lady Belle by Harley Mead — Construction and Accommodation — 2

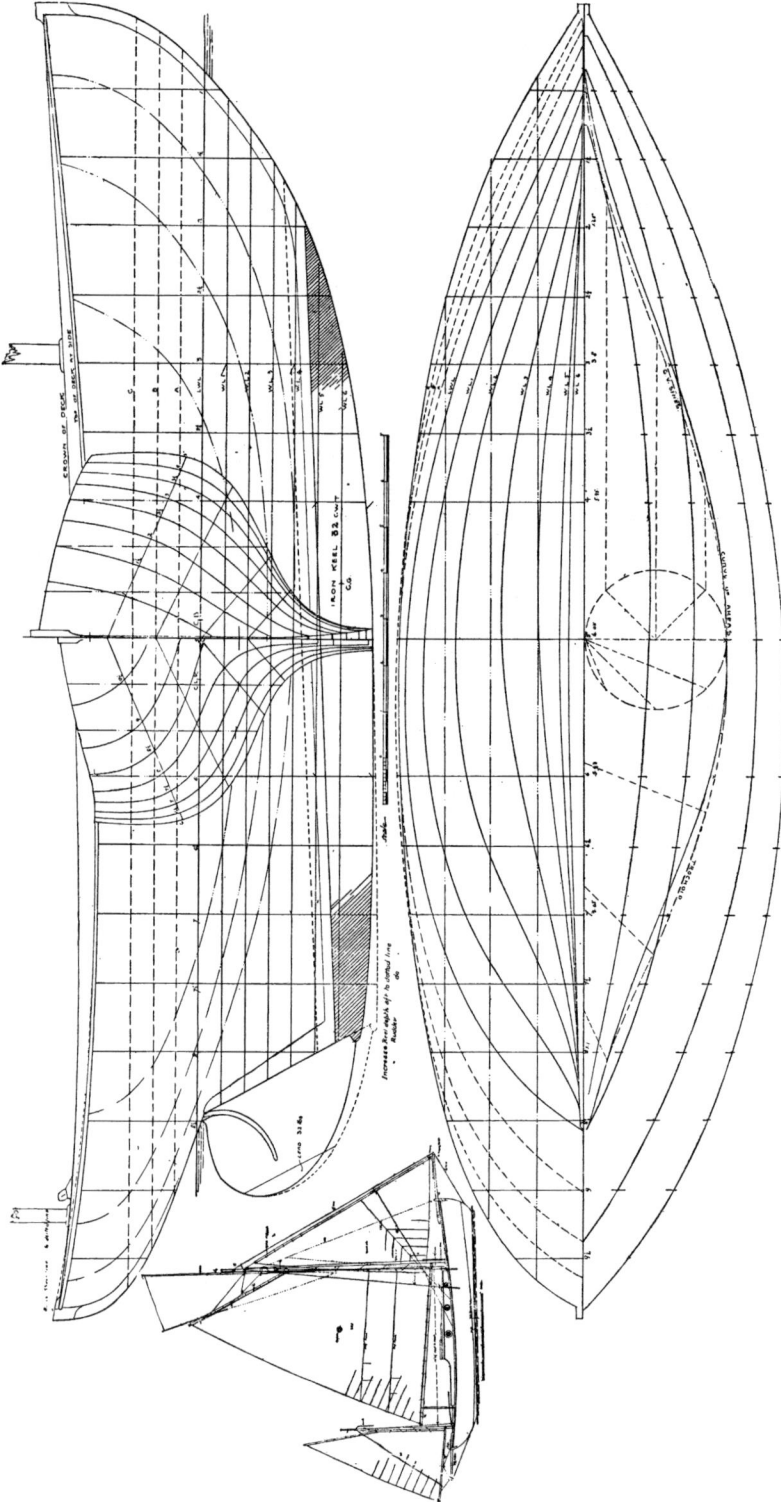

Drawing 25: Cherub III by Albert Strange — Lines

Drawing 26: Cherub III by Albert Strange — Construction and Accommodation

Drawing 27: Granuaile (II) by Frederick Shepherd — Construction and Accommodation

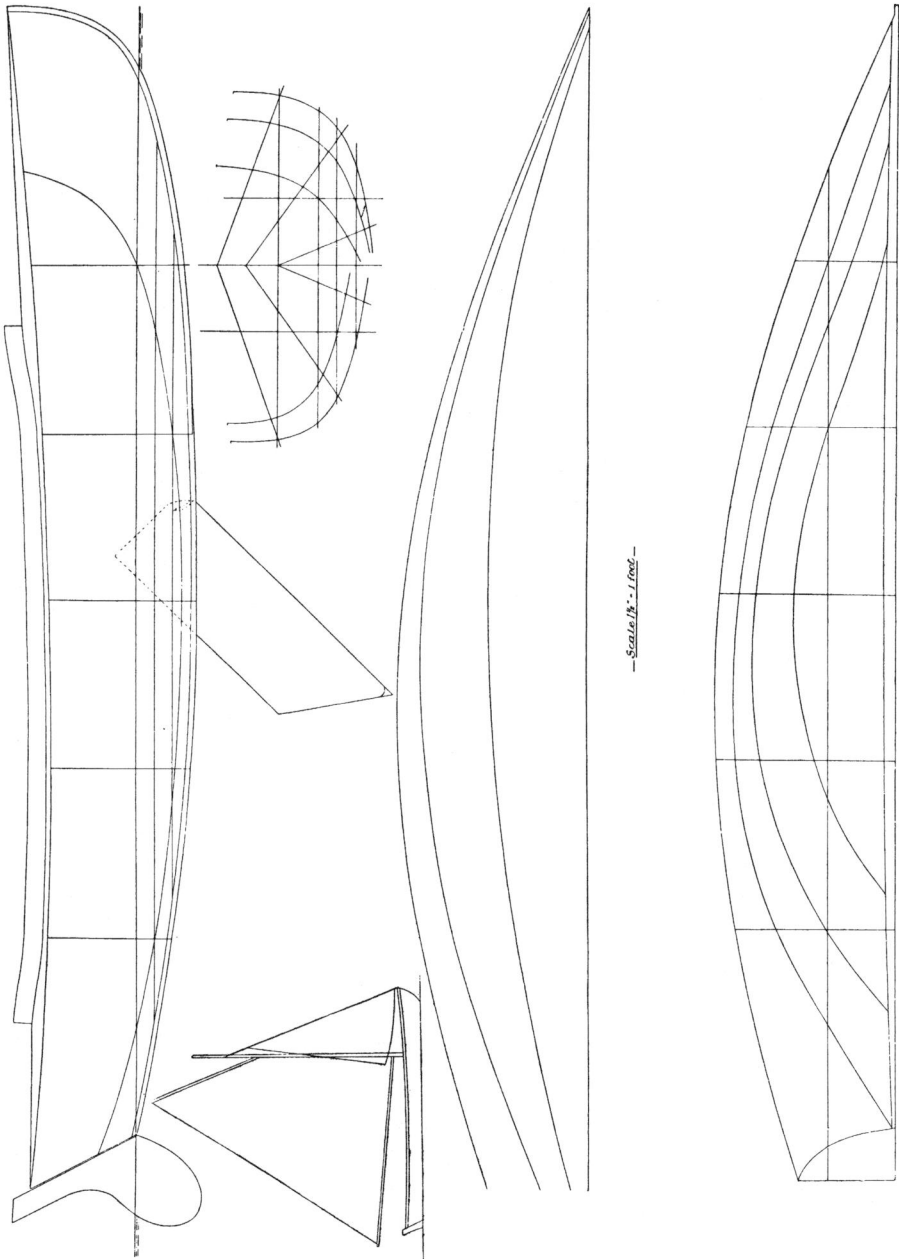

— Scale 1¼" = 1 foot —

Drawing 28: Lapwing by James E. Doyle

AUX. YACHT "FANCY"

Dimensions: L. on W.L...26'-6"
Beam........8'-6"
Draught......5'-9"

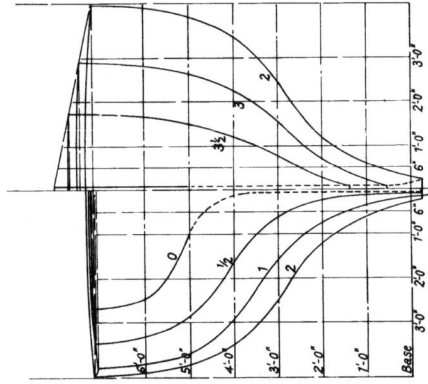

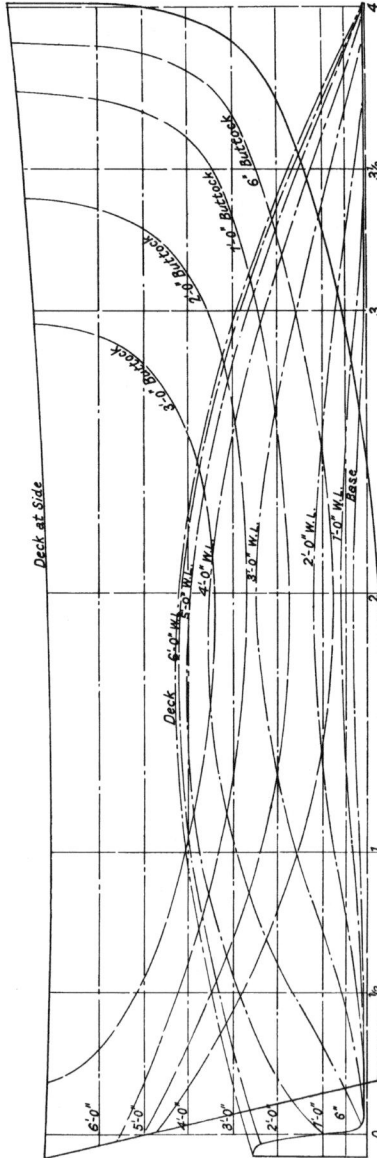

Drawing 29: Fancy by Archie Watty — Lines

270

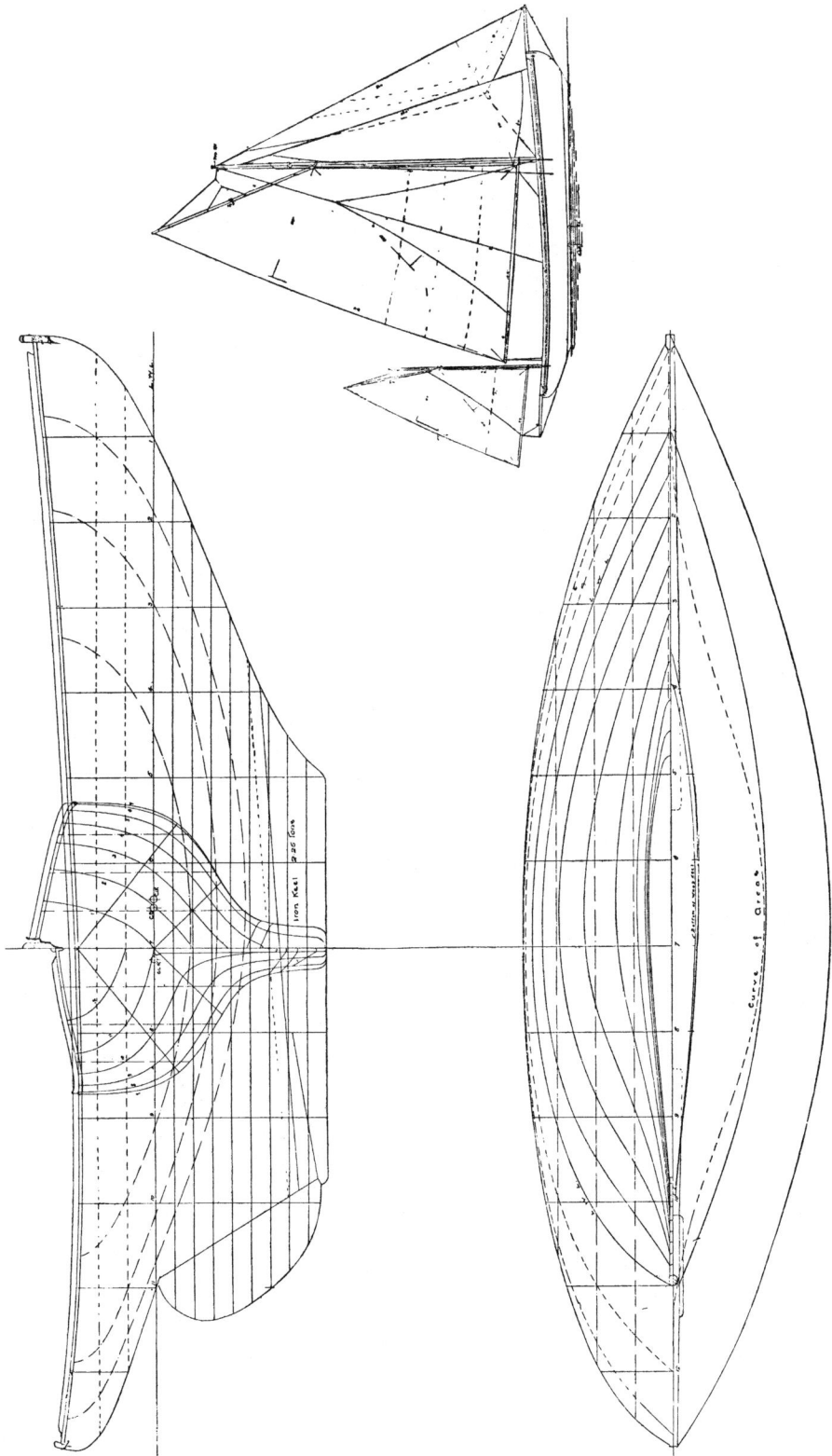

Drawing 30: Nereid II by G. Umfreville Laws — Lines

Section N° 8
looking forward

Section N° 9
looking aft

Iron Keel 2.25 Tons

Timbers 1⅞ x 1¾ Spaced 6" etc

Main Sheet Buckles

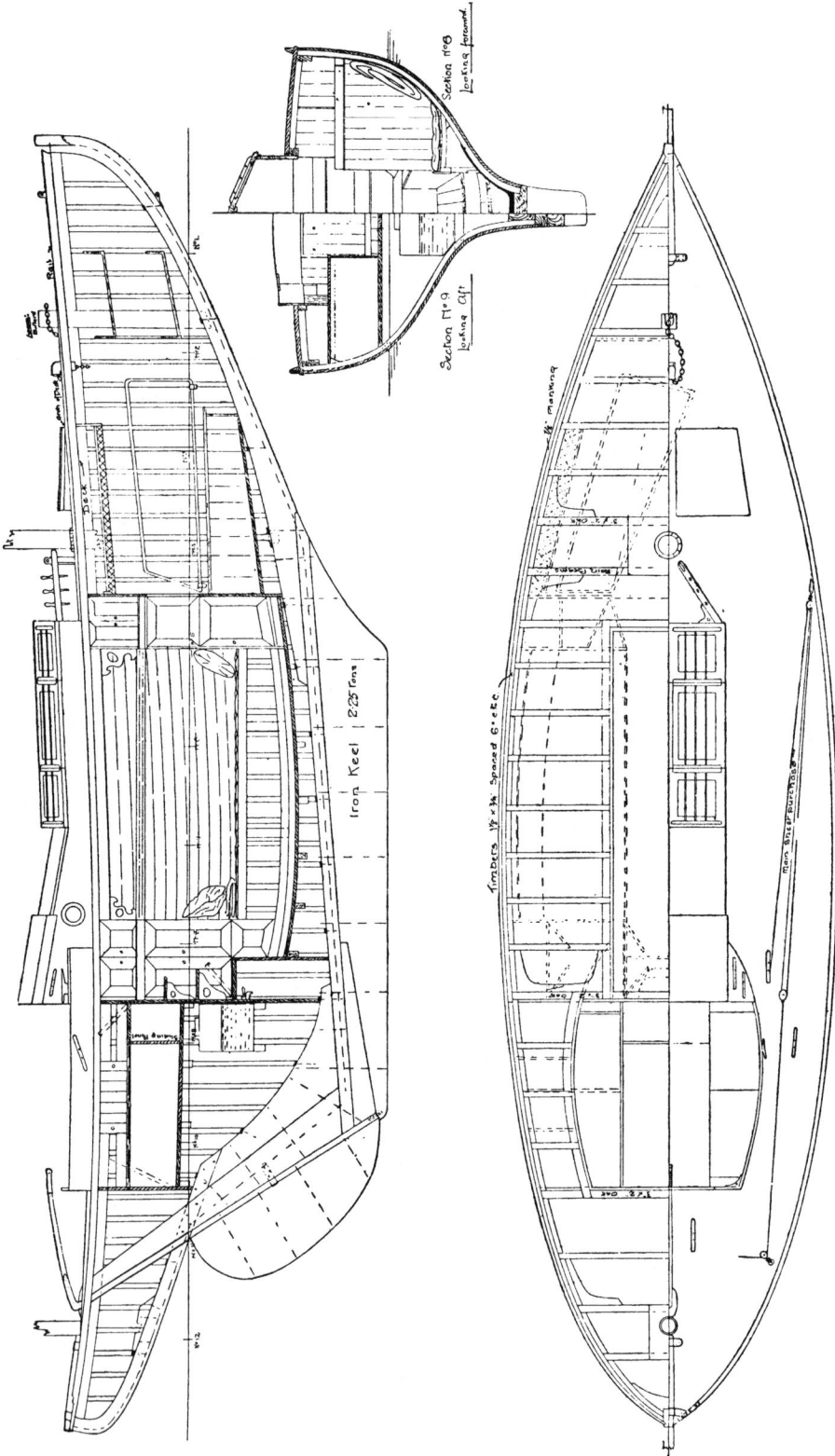

Drawing 31: Nereid II by G. Umfreville Laws — Construction and Accommodation

Drawing 32: Venture by Albert Strange — Lines

SCALE OF FEET

SHELF

3"×1½"

STRINGER

MAST STEP

36 K.B.

LEAD KEEL 2 TONS

CHAIN LOCKER FLOOR

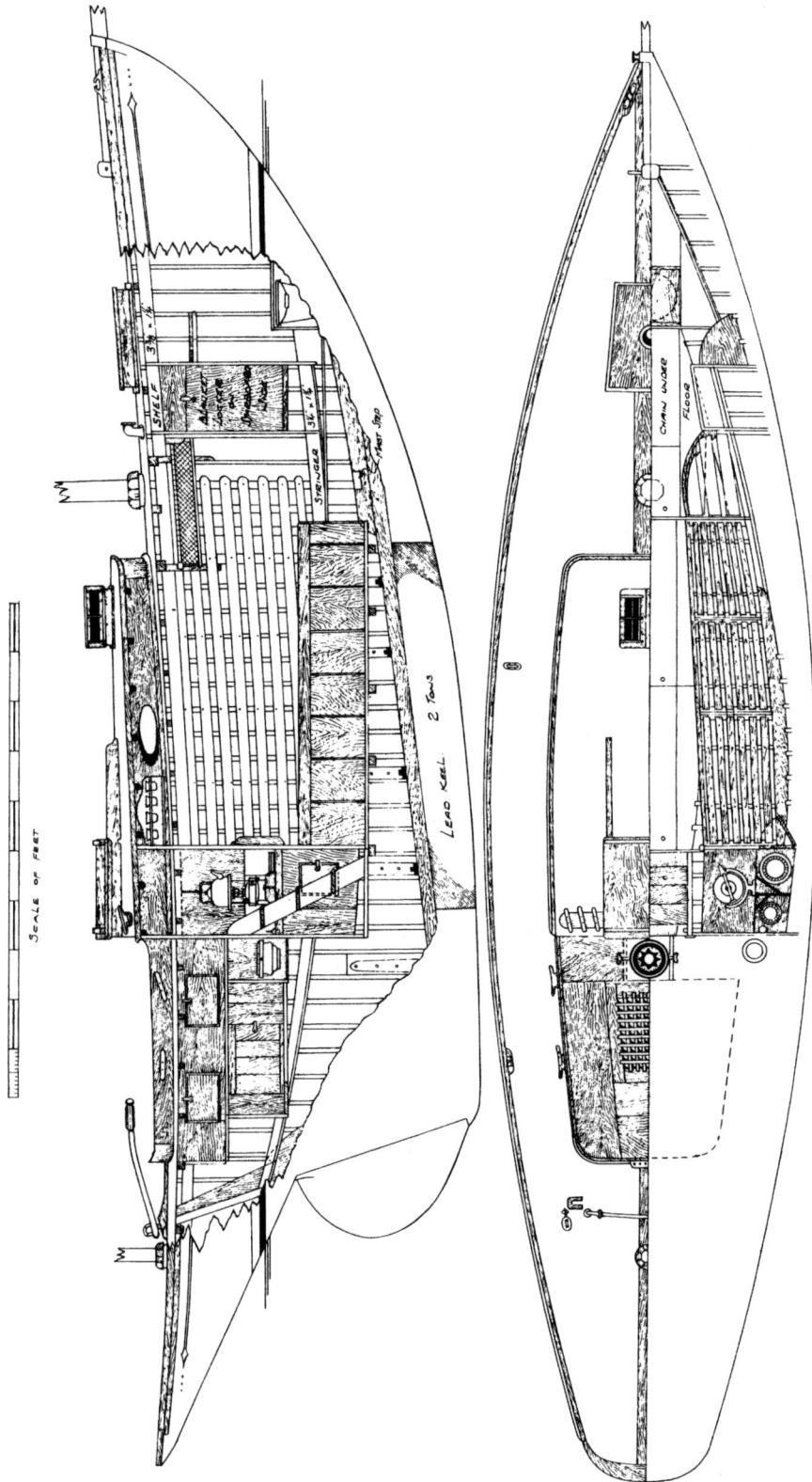

Drawing 33: Venture by Albert Strange — Construction and Accommodation

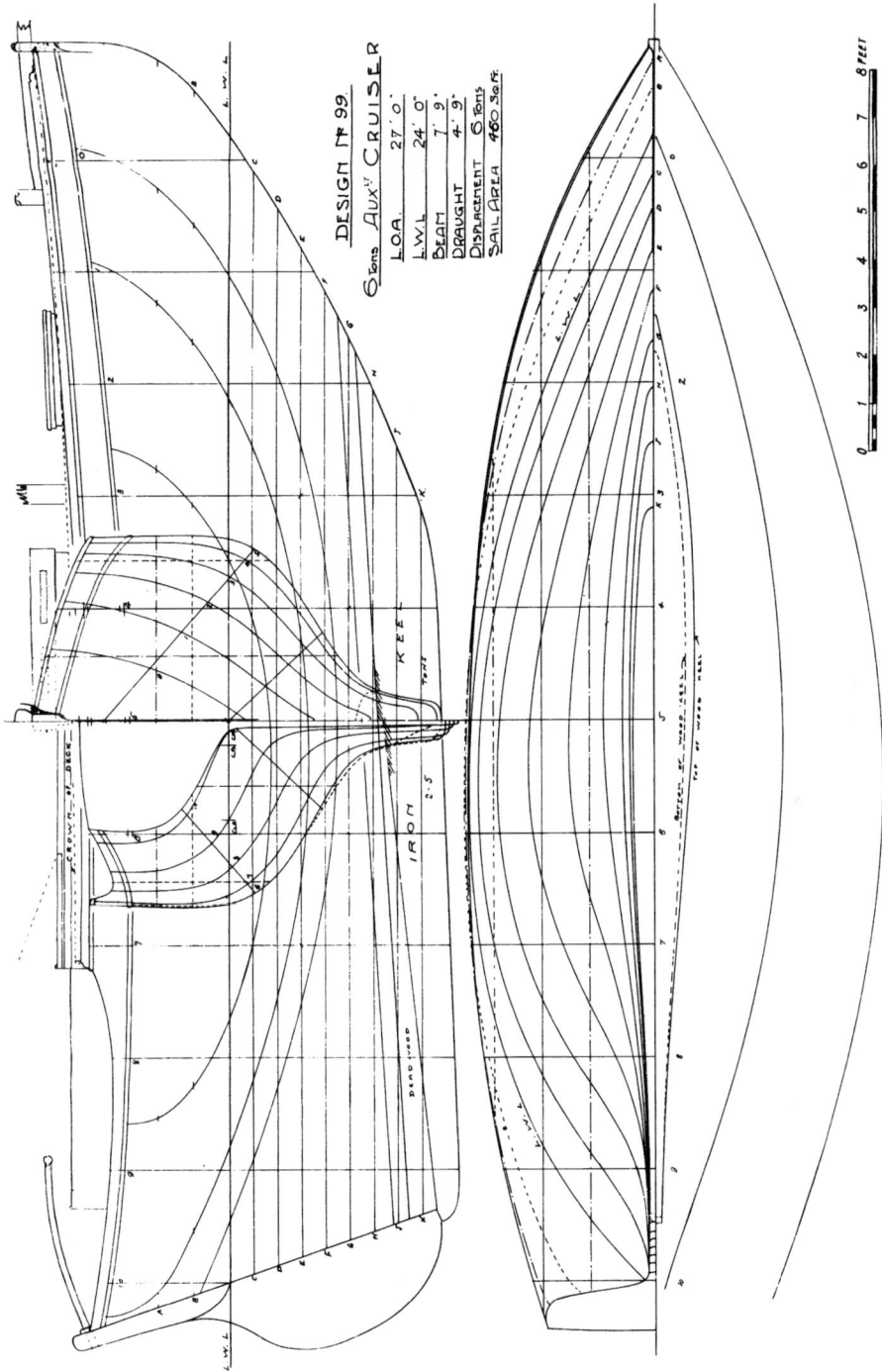

DESIGN № 99

6 Tons AUX.ˡʸ CRUISER

L.O.A.	27' 0"
L.W.L.	24' 0"
BEAM	7' 9"
DRAUGHT	4' 9"
DISPLACEMENT	6 Tons
SAIL AREA	460 Sq.Ft.

Drawing 34: Talisman II by Norman E. Dallimore – Lines

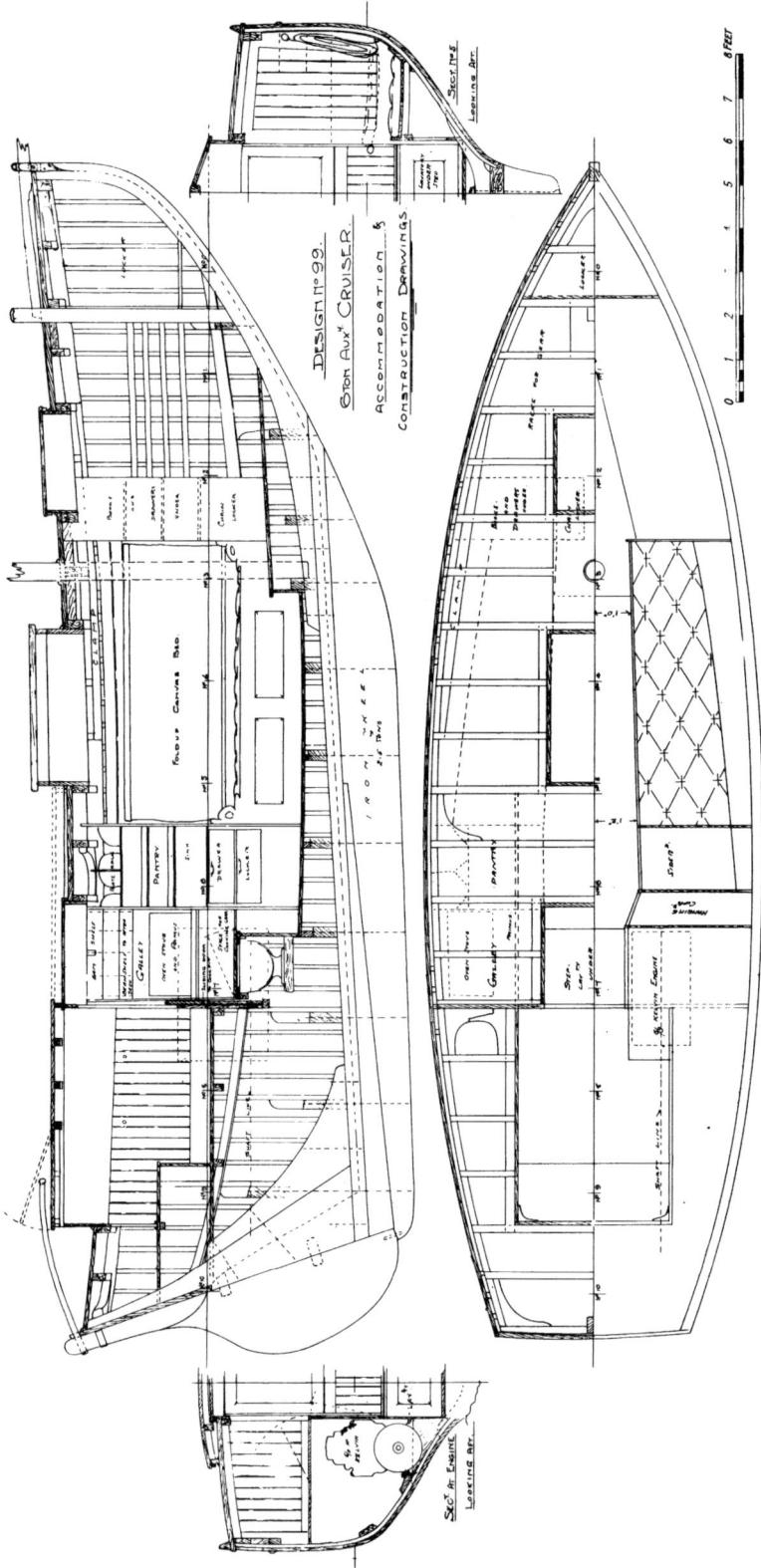

Drawing 35: Talisman II by Norman E. Dallimore — Construction and Accommodation

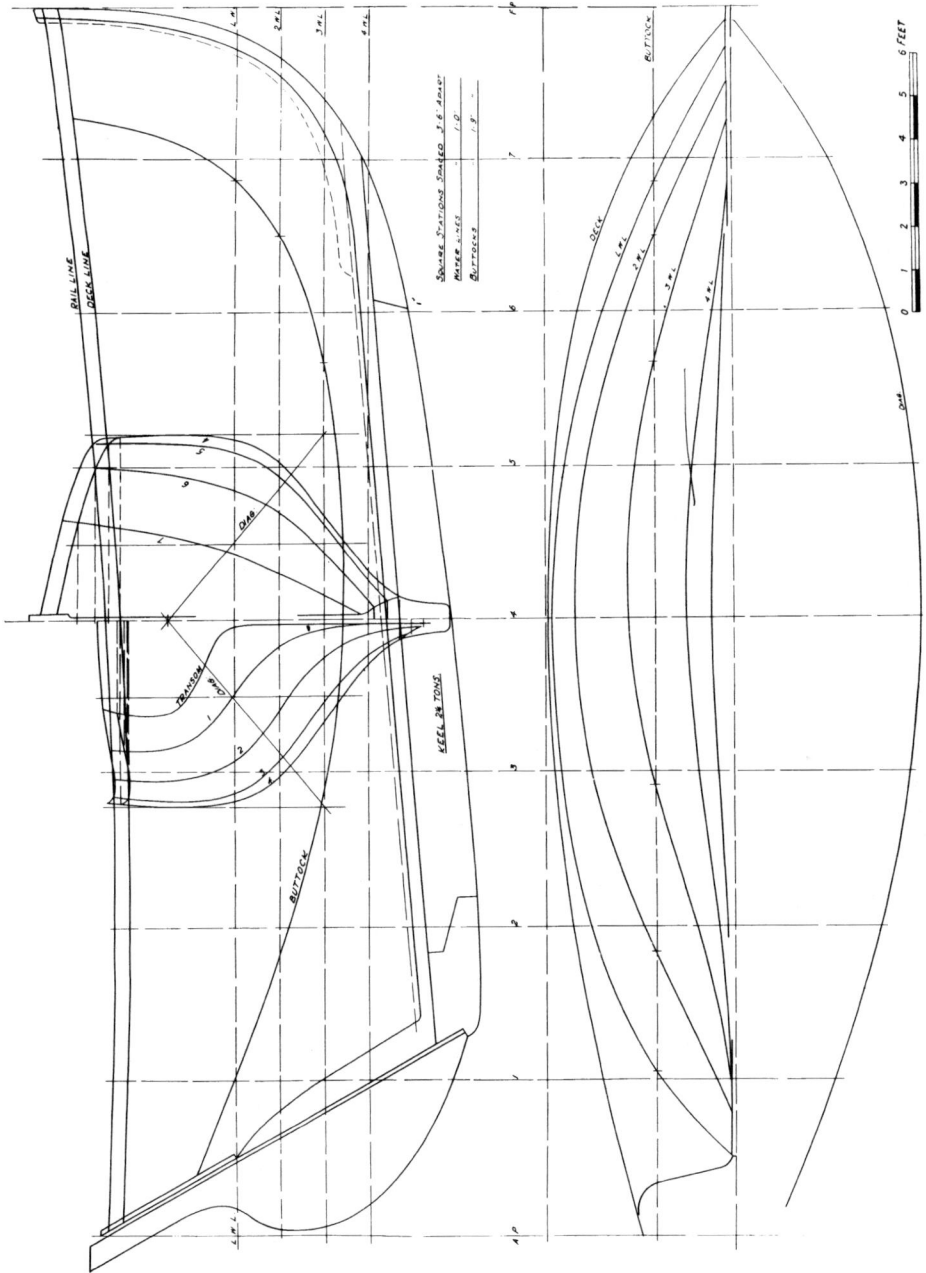

Drawing 36: Marie Michon by Bevil Warrington-Smythe — Lines

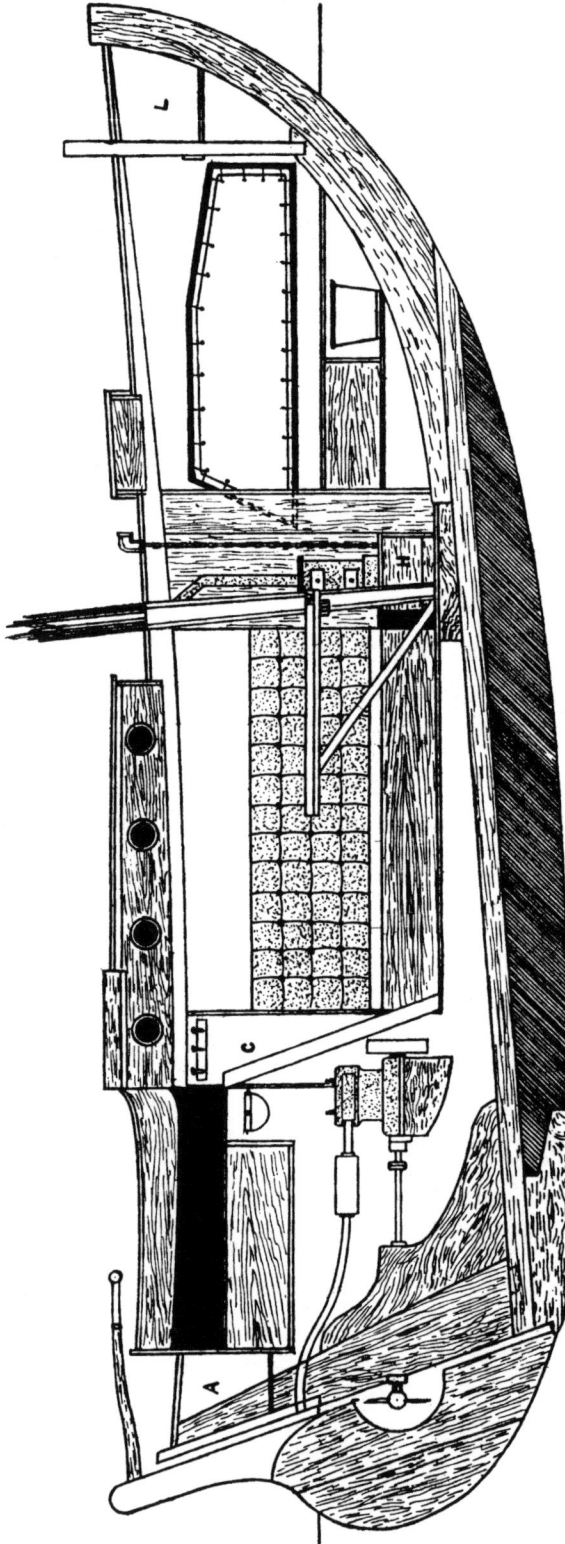

Drawing 37: Cyclone II by T. Harrison Butler — Accommodation

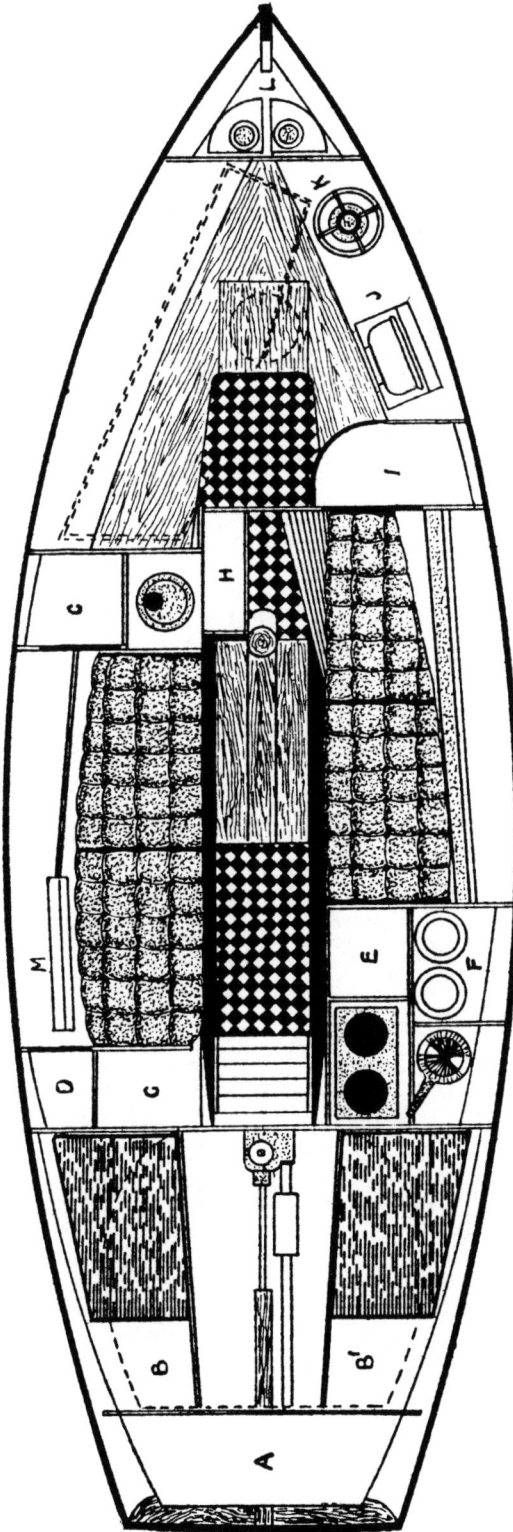

A – Stern locker for sails, warps, etc; B – Locker under seat for bosun's stores; B' – Locker under seat for meat; C – Hanging space for oilskins; D – Locker opening into cabin; E – Table with bread locker under; F – Pantry; G – Clothes locker behind heating stove opening into H – Chain box; I – Locker for food opening into cabin; J – Folding wash basin; K – Riding light; L – Side lights; M – Folding chart table.

Drawing 38: Cyclone II by T. Harrison Butler — Cabin Plan

Drawing 39: Rona by W. Easton — Lines

"RONA"

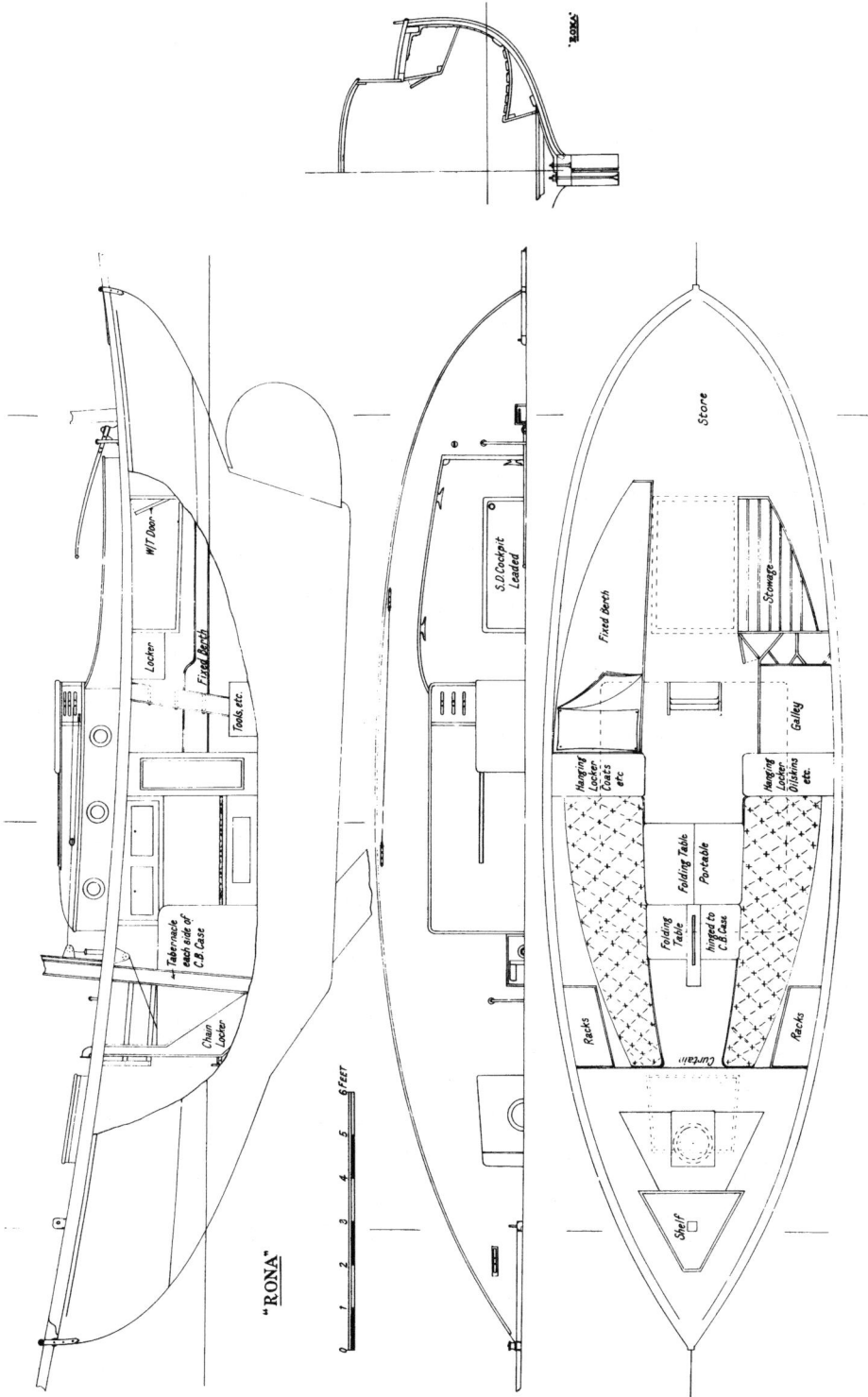

Drawing 40: Rona by W. Easton — Accommodation

IOLANTHE
2½ TON SLOOP

(Note: Since these lines were drawn the keel has been dropped 3 inches and increased in weight by about 1 cwt.)

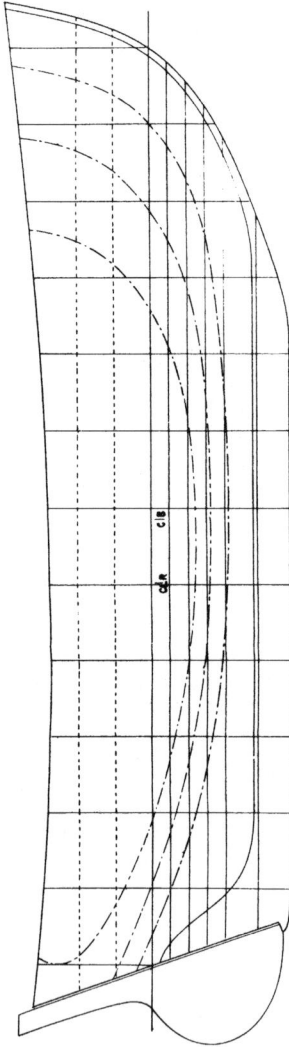

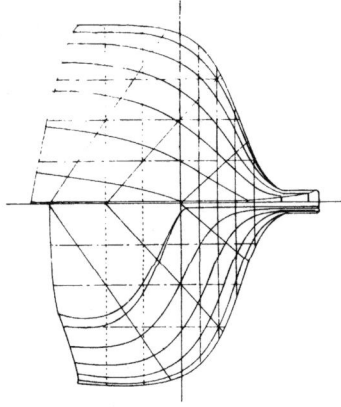

D.WEBB.
—YACHT & BOATBUILDER.—
MALDON

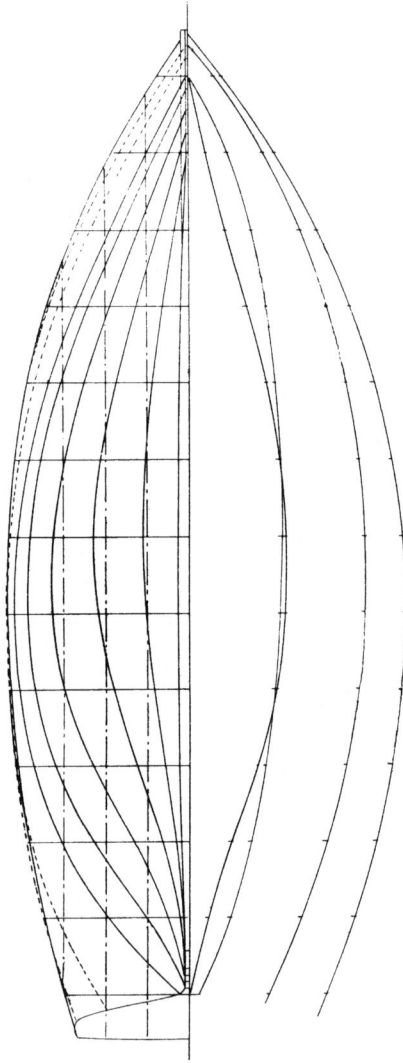

Drawing 41: 2½-ton Blackwater Sloop by Dan Webb — Lines

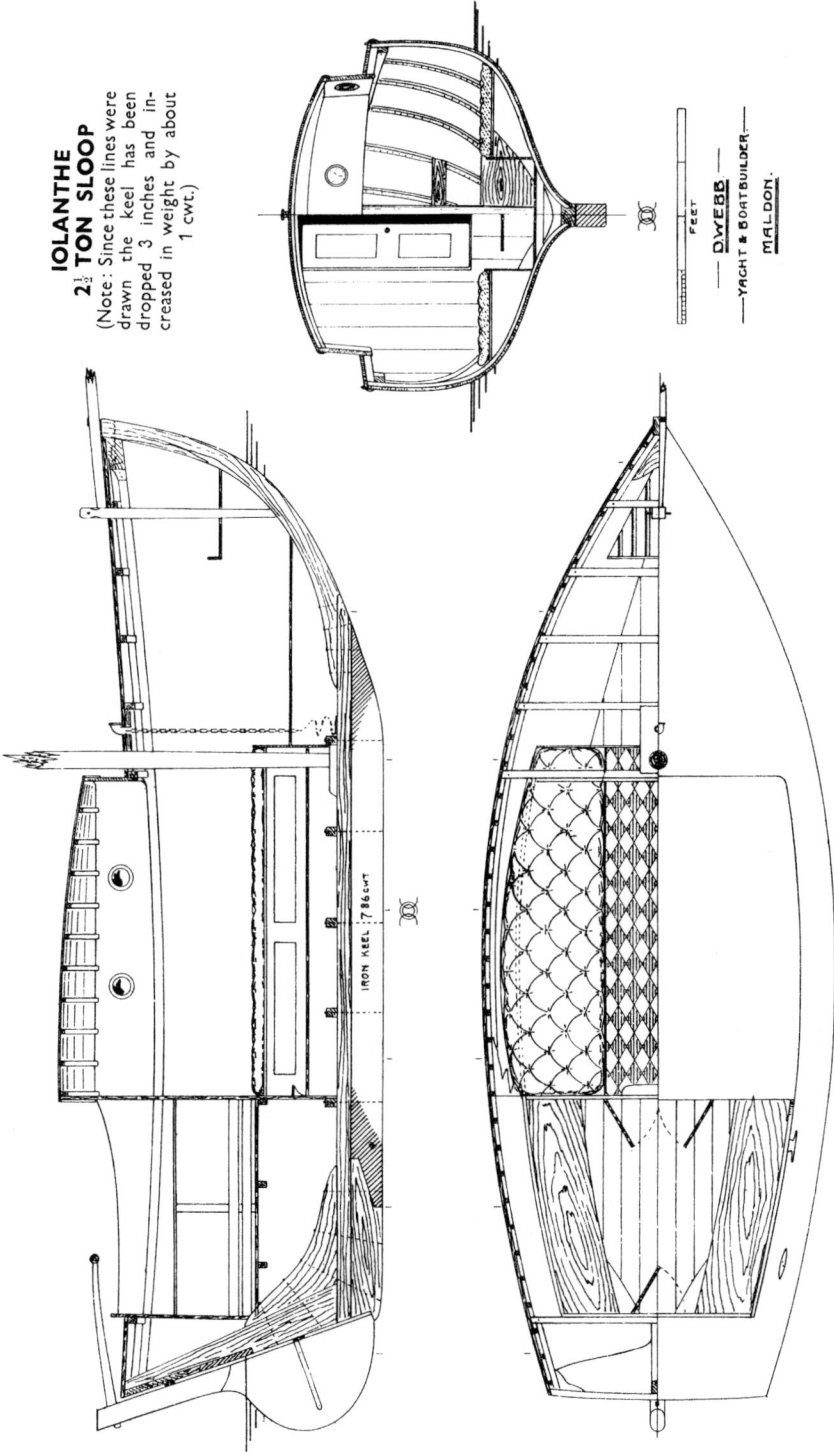

IOLANTHE
2½ TON SLOOP
(Note: Since these lines were drawn the keel has been dropped 3 inches and increased in weight by about 1 cwt.)

IRON KEEL 7.86 CWT

DWEBB
—YACHT & BOATBUILDER—
MALDON.

FEET

Drawing 42: 2½-ton Blackwater Sloop by Dan Webb — Construction and Accommodation

"BLACKWATER"
— CENTRE BOARD SLOOP. —
18' x 7' x 1'8" – 4'5':

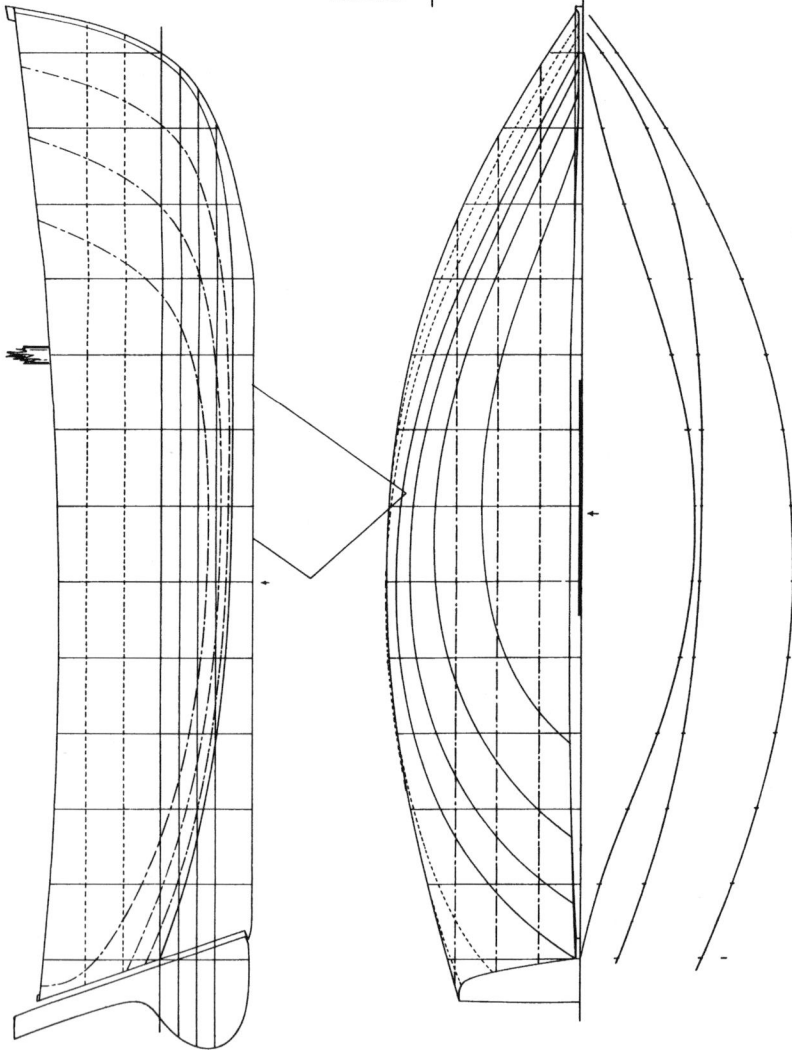

— D.WEBB. —
— YACHT BUILDER—
MALDON.
ESSEX.

Drawing 43: Centreboard Blackwater Sloop by Dan Webb — Lines

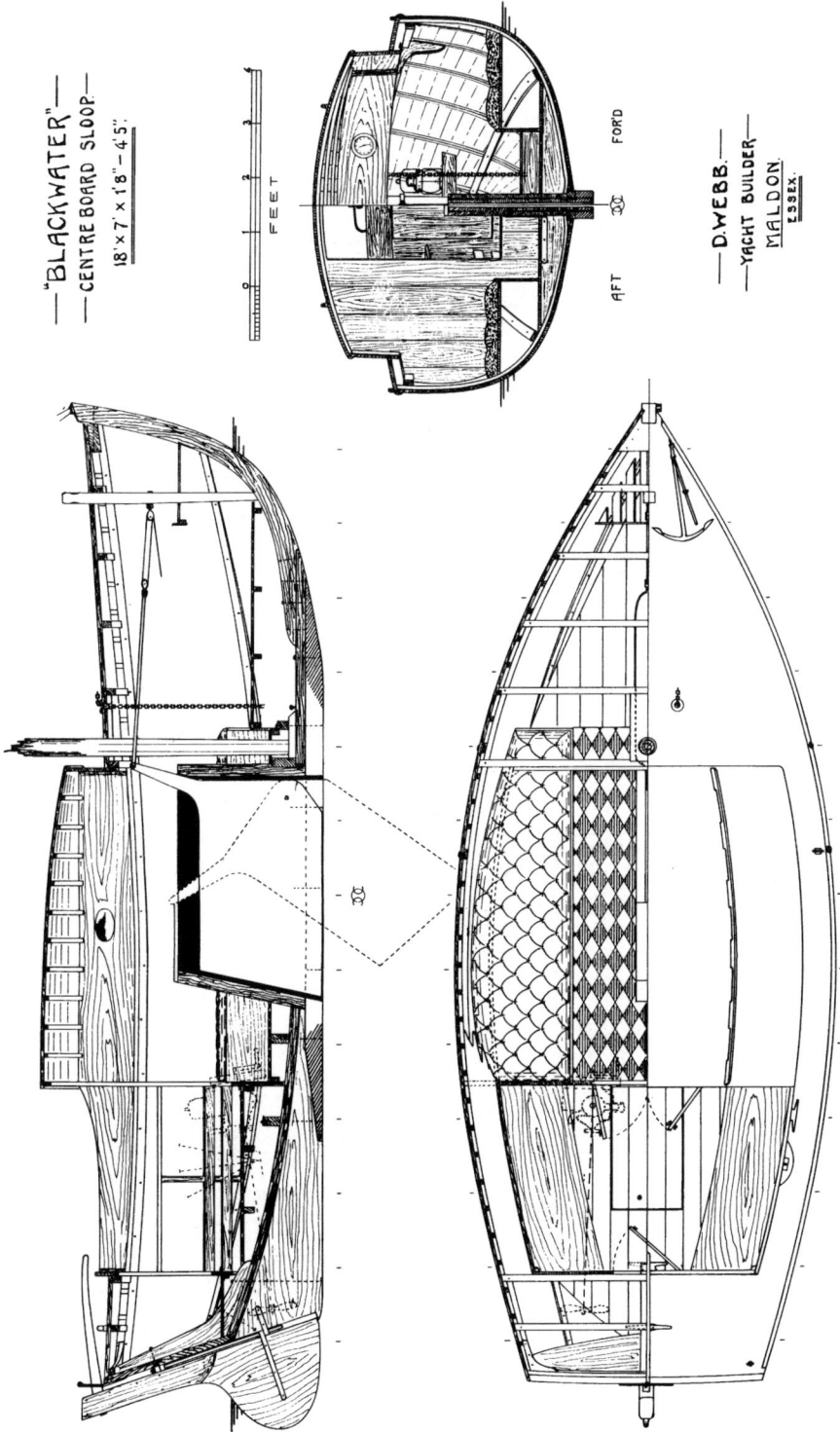

"BLACKWATER"
CENTRE BOARD SLOOP
18' × 7 × 18" − 4'5"

FEET

FOR'D

AFT

D. WEBB.
YACHT BUILDER
MALDON
ESSEX.

Drawing 44: Centreboard Blackwater Sloop by Dan Webb — Construction and Accommodation

3 TON BLACKWATER SLOOP

LENGTH O.A. 20'3"
" W.L. 18'1"
BEAM 6'9"
DRAUGHT 3'6"

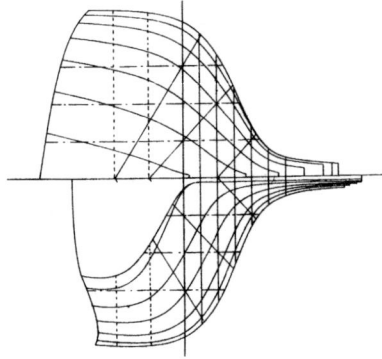

D.WEBB.
YACHT BUILDER
MALDON
ESSEX

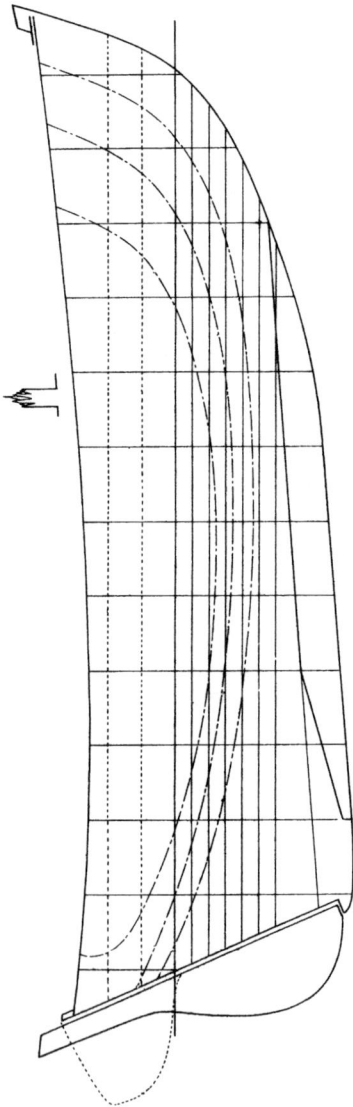

Scale of Feet

0 1 2 3 4 5 6

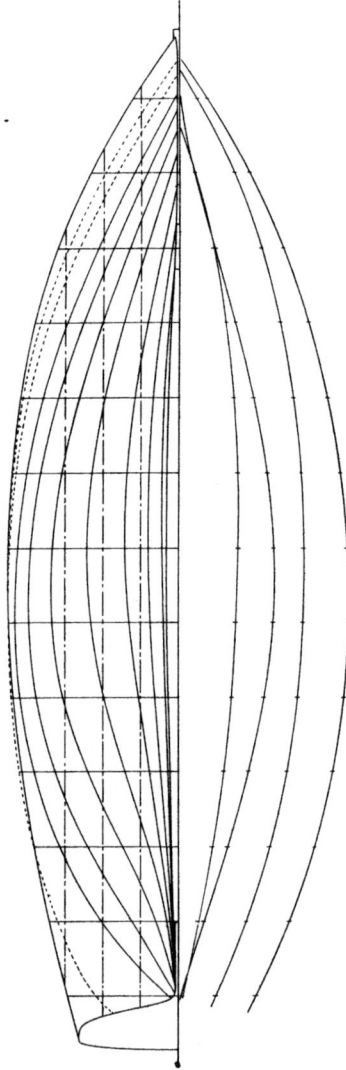

Drawing 45: 3-ton Blackwater Sloop by Dan Webb — Lines

3 TON BLACKWATER SLOOP

LENGTH O.A. 20'3"
" W.L. 18'1"
BEAM 6'9"
DRAUGHT 3'6"

D. WEBB.
YACHT BUILDER
MALDON
ESSEX.

B

A

Scale of Feet

0 1 2 3 4 5 6

Galley

Iron 14 cwt.

B

A

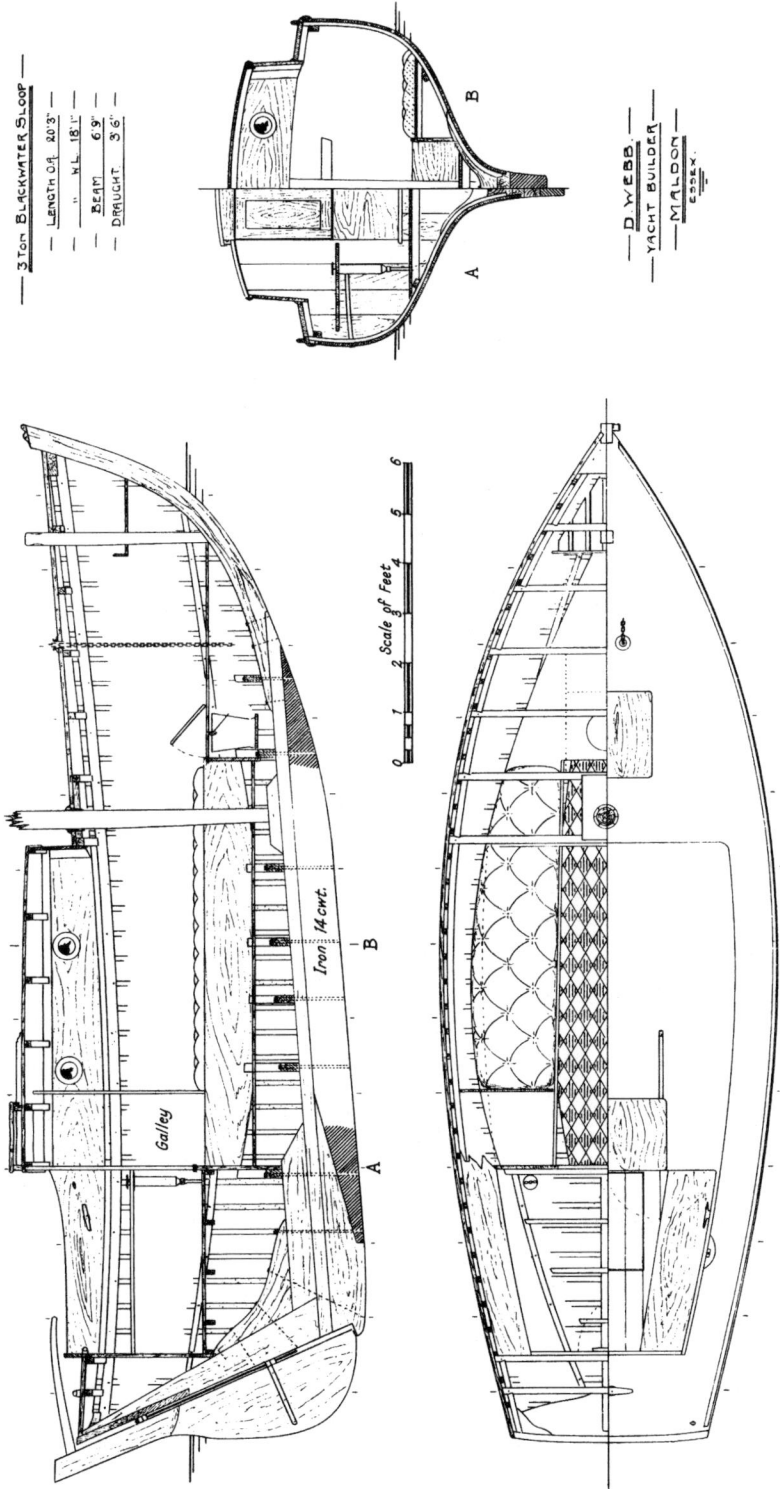

Drawing 46: 3-ton Blackwater Sloop by Dan Webb — Construction and Accommodation

SCALE OF FEET

0   5

1 2 3 4 5 6 7 8 9

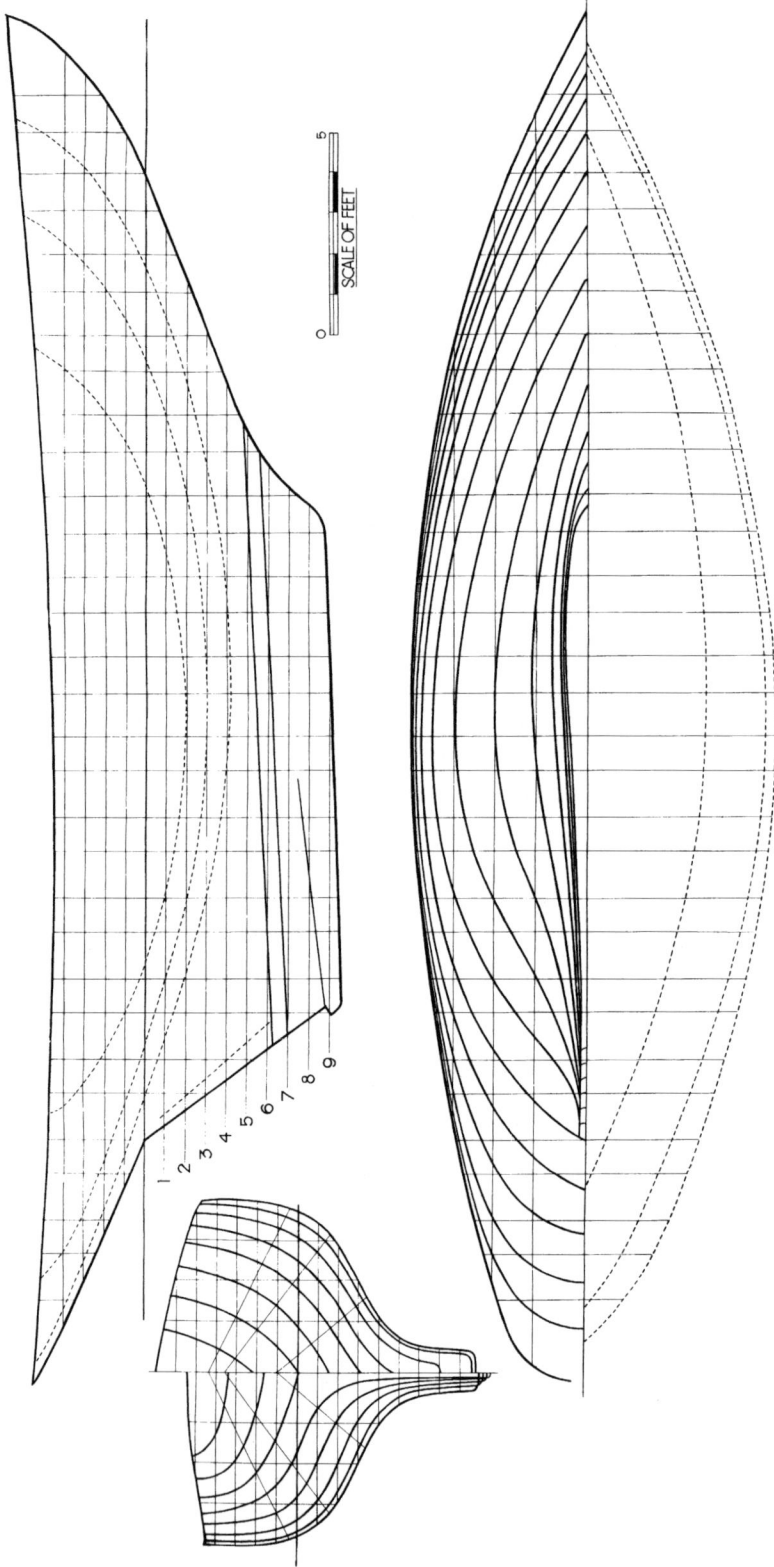

Drawing 47: Fidelis by F.J. Welch — Lines

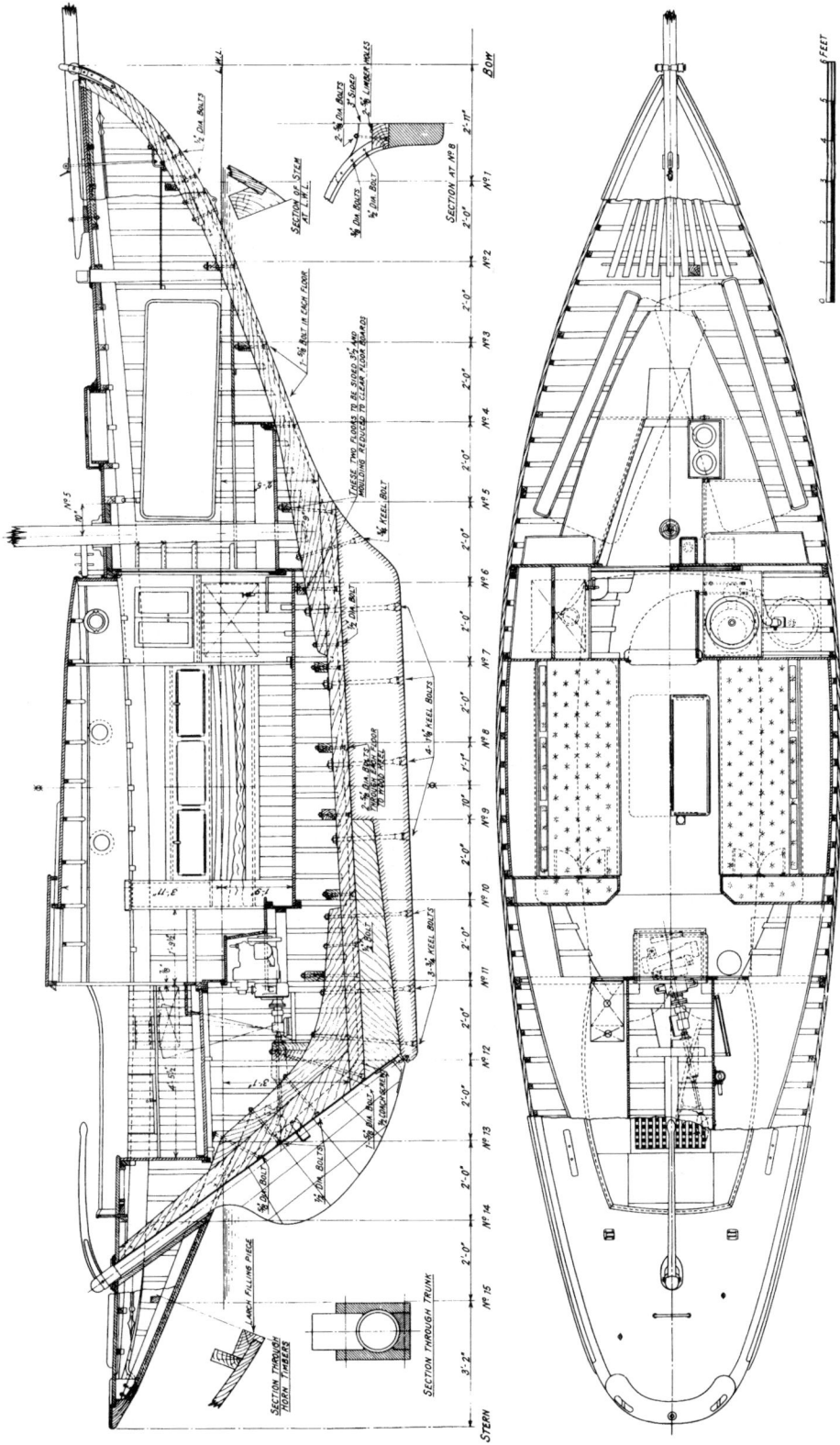

Drawing 48: Fidelis by F.J. Welch — Construction and Accommodation

ENCLYN

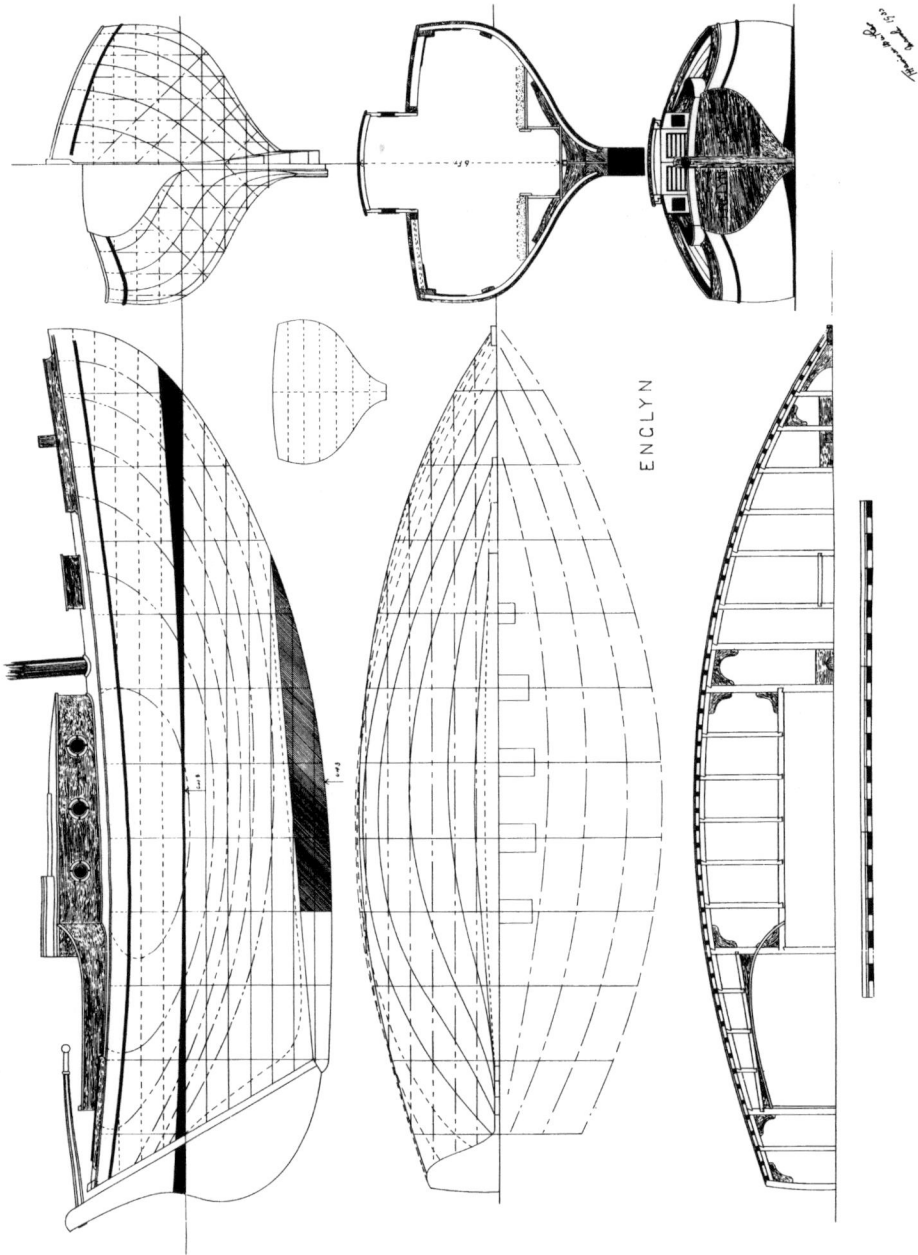

Drawing 49: Englyn by T. Harrison Butler — Lines

ENGLYN

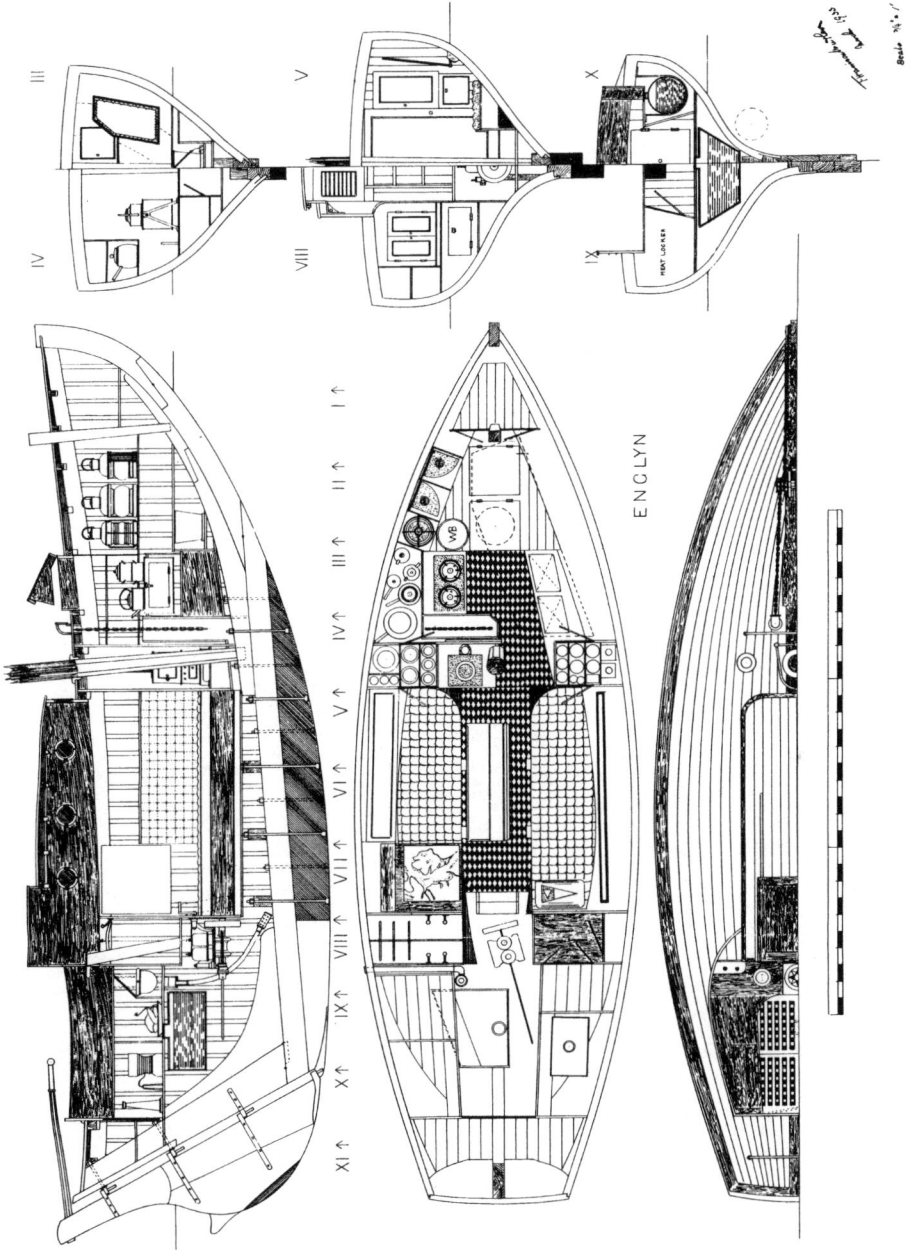

Drawing 50: Englyn by T. Harrison Butler — Construction and Accommodation

AUX. CUTTER YACHT
"DRIAC II"

Length overall	32'·3"
" B.P.	28'·9"
" Waterline	25'·6"
Breadth	8'·7"
Depth (Top of beams at side to top of lead keel amidships)	6'·6"
Draught extreme	5'·6"
Thames measurement	8 tons

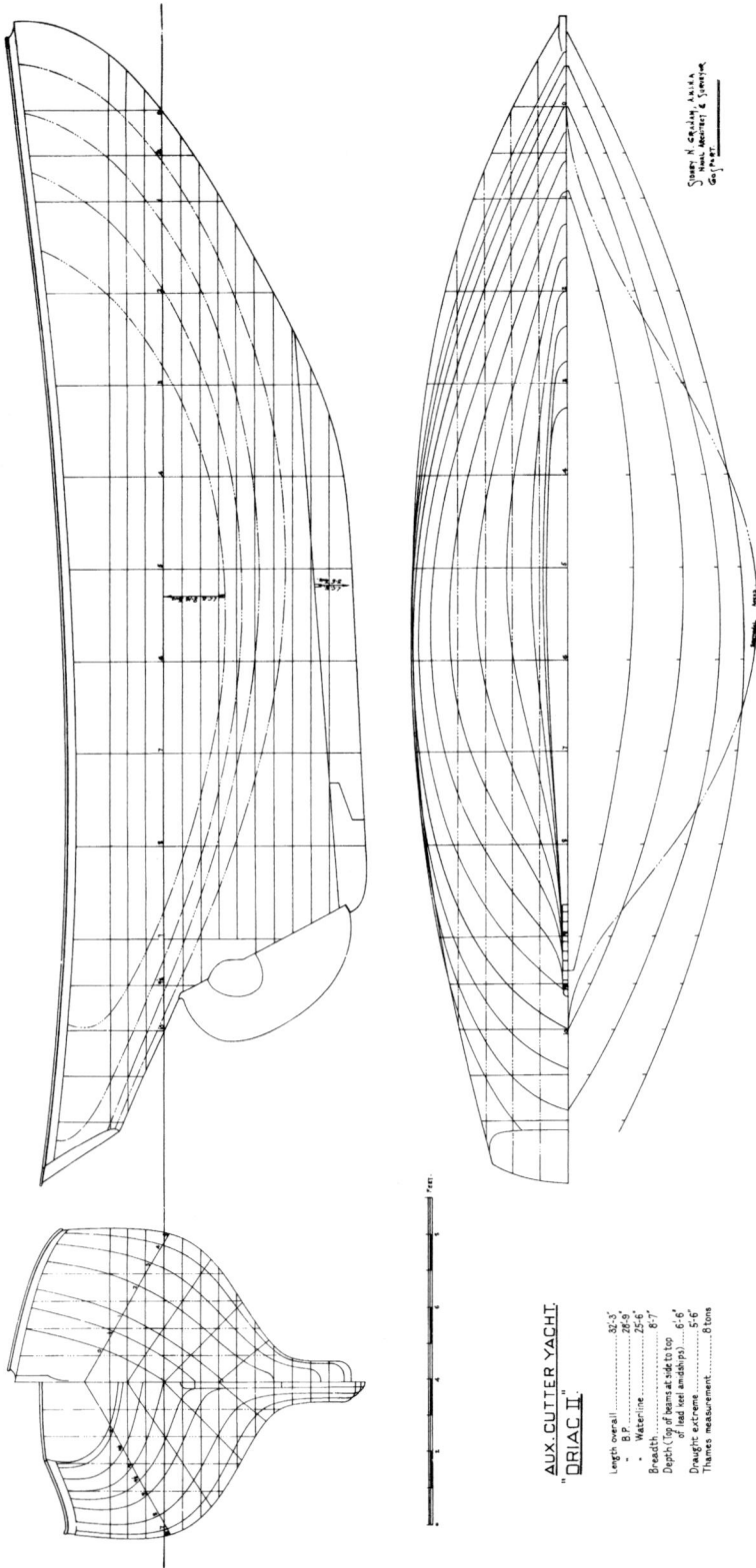

Drawing 51: Driac II by S. N. Graham — Lines

Drawing 52: Driac II by S. N. Graham — Construction and Accommodation

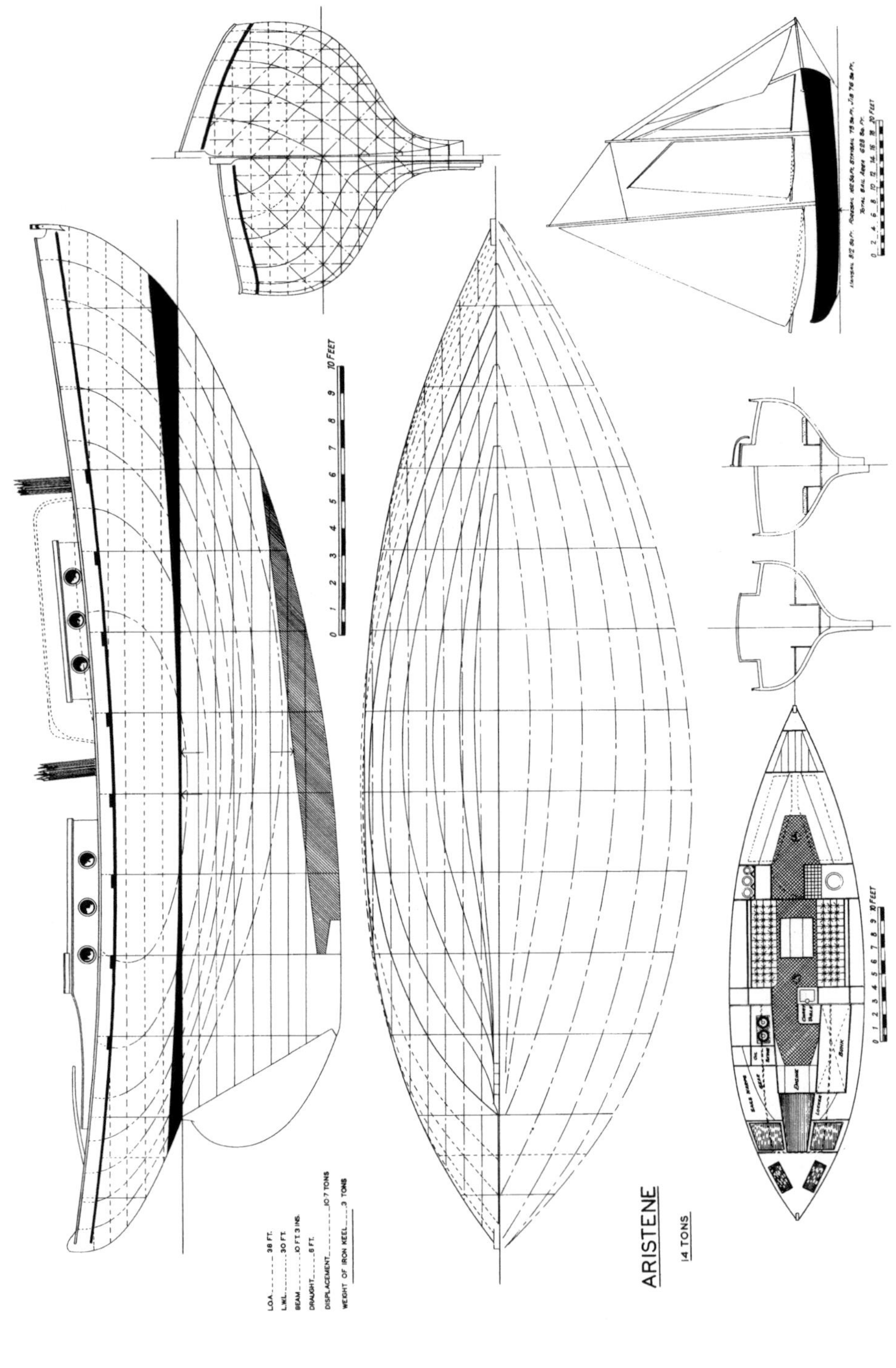

LOA............38 FT.
LWL............30 FT.
BEAM............10 FT 3 INS.
DRAUGHT............6 FT.
DISPLACEMENT............10.7 TONS
WEIGHT OF IRON KEEL............3 TONS

ARISTENE

14 TONS

Drawing 53: Aristene by T. Harrison Butler

DISPLACEMENT · 5·8 TO
THAMES · TONNAGE · 5 ·
LENGTH · W.L · 20'6'
LENGTH · O.A · 22'6'
BEAM · 8'0'
DRAFT · 3'6'

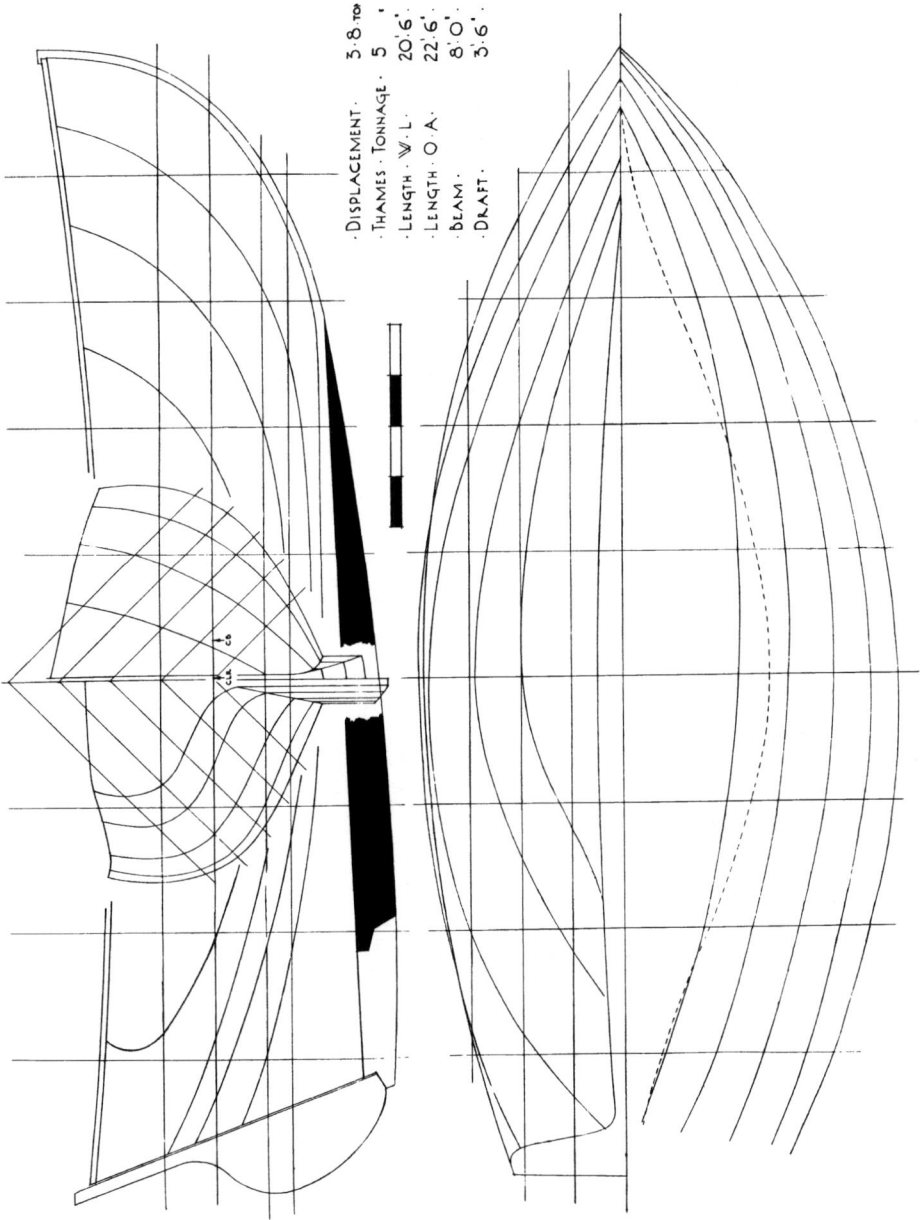

Drawing 54: Corbie by T. Dennis Jacobs – Lines

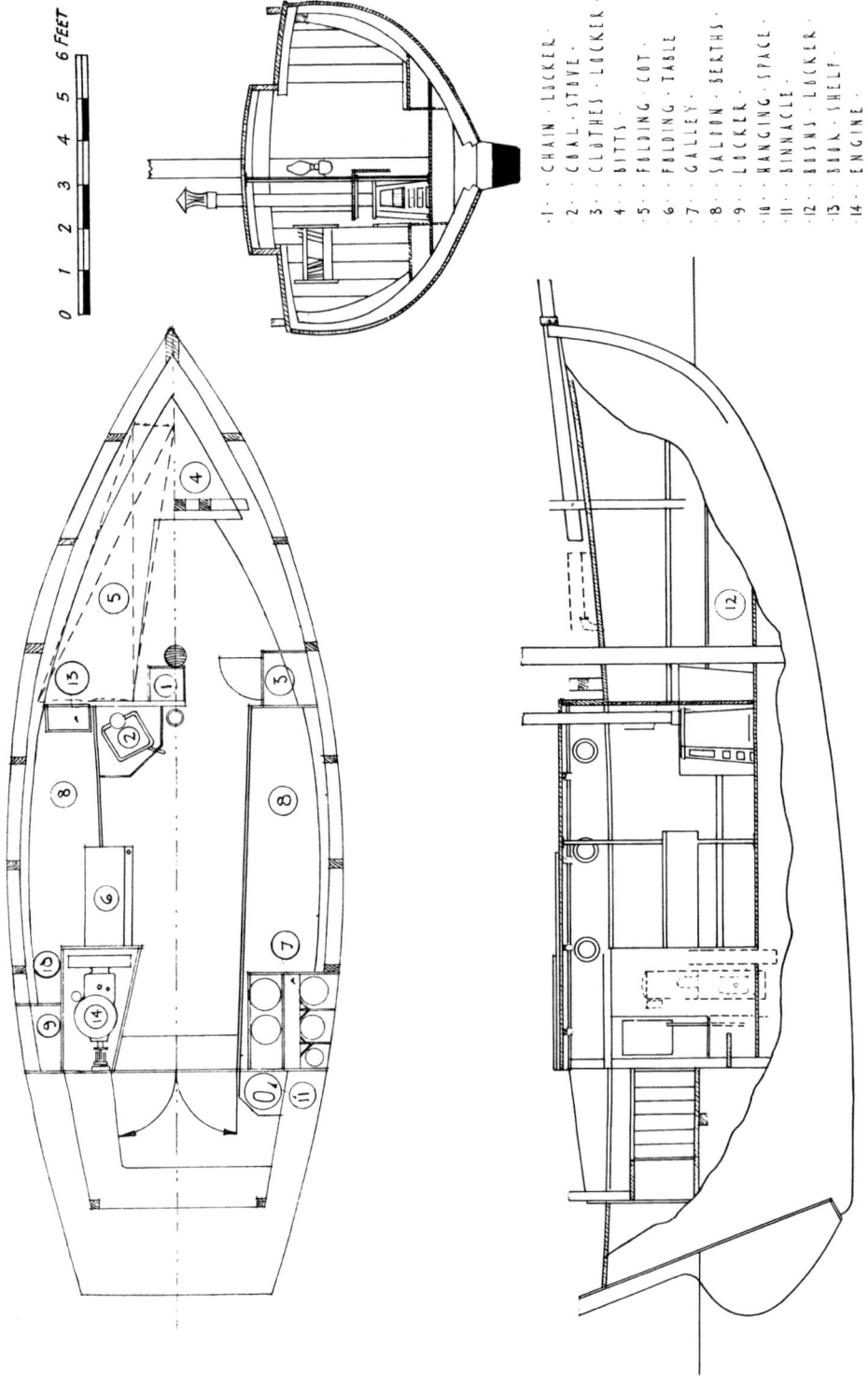

·1· CHAIN·LOCKER·
·2· COAL·STOVE·
·3· CLOTHES·LOCKER·
·4· BITTS·
·5· FOLDING·COT·
·6· FOLDING·TABLE·
·7· GALLEY·
·8· SALOON·BERTHS·
·9· LOCKER·
·10· HANGING·SPACE·
·11· BINNACLE·
·12· BOSNS·LOCKER·
·13· BOOK·SHELF·
·14· ENGINE·

Drawing 55: Corbie by T. Dennis Jacobs — Accommodation

296

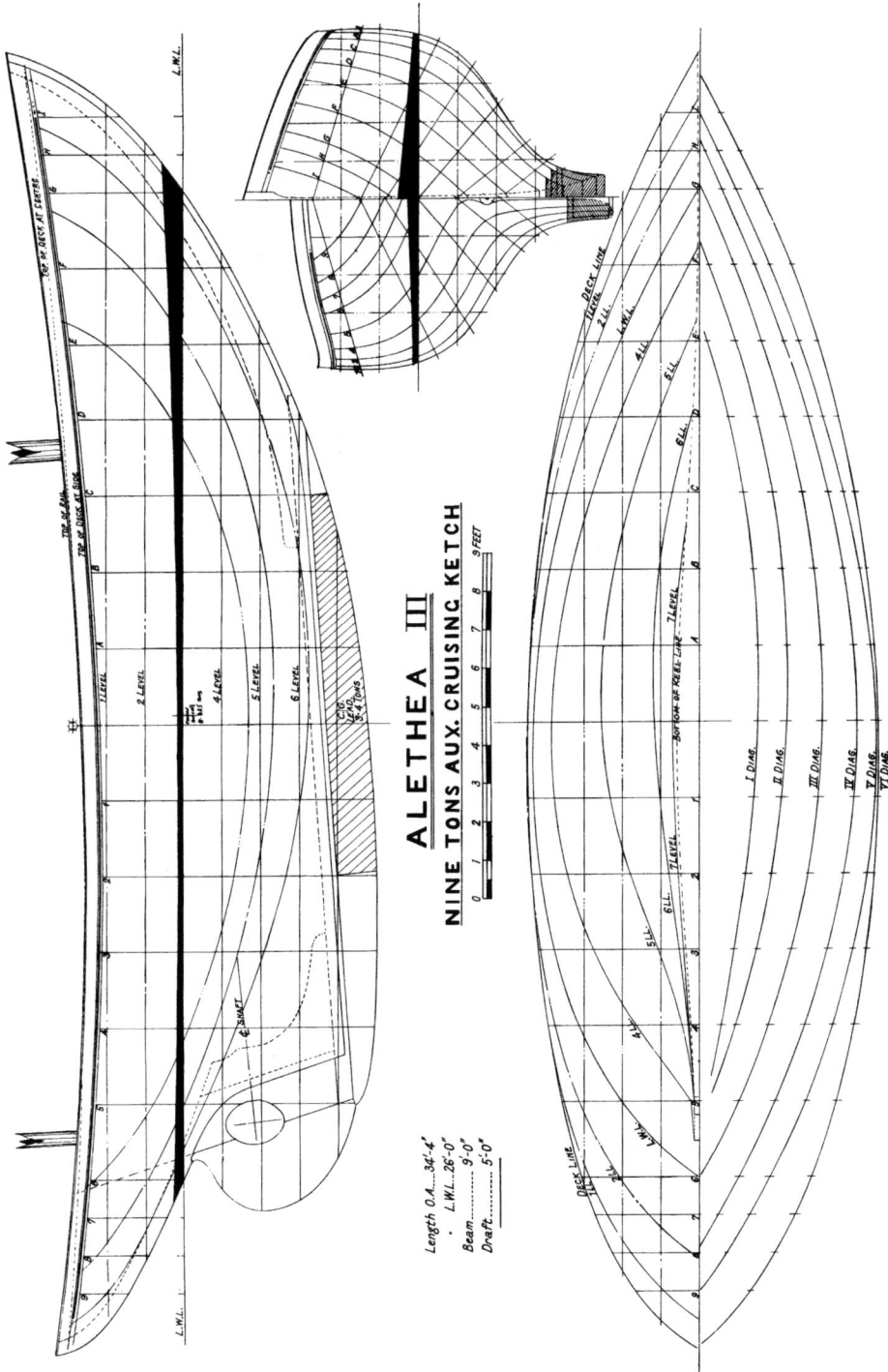

ALETHEA III

NINE TONS AUX. CRUISING KETCH

Length O.A...34'-4"
     "   L.W.L..26'-0"
Beam .... 9'-0"
Draft .... 5'-0"

Drawing 56: Alethea III by A. R. Luke – Lines

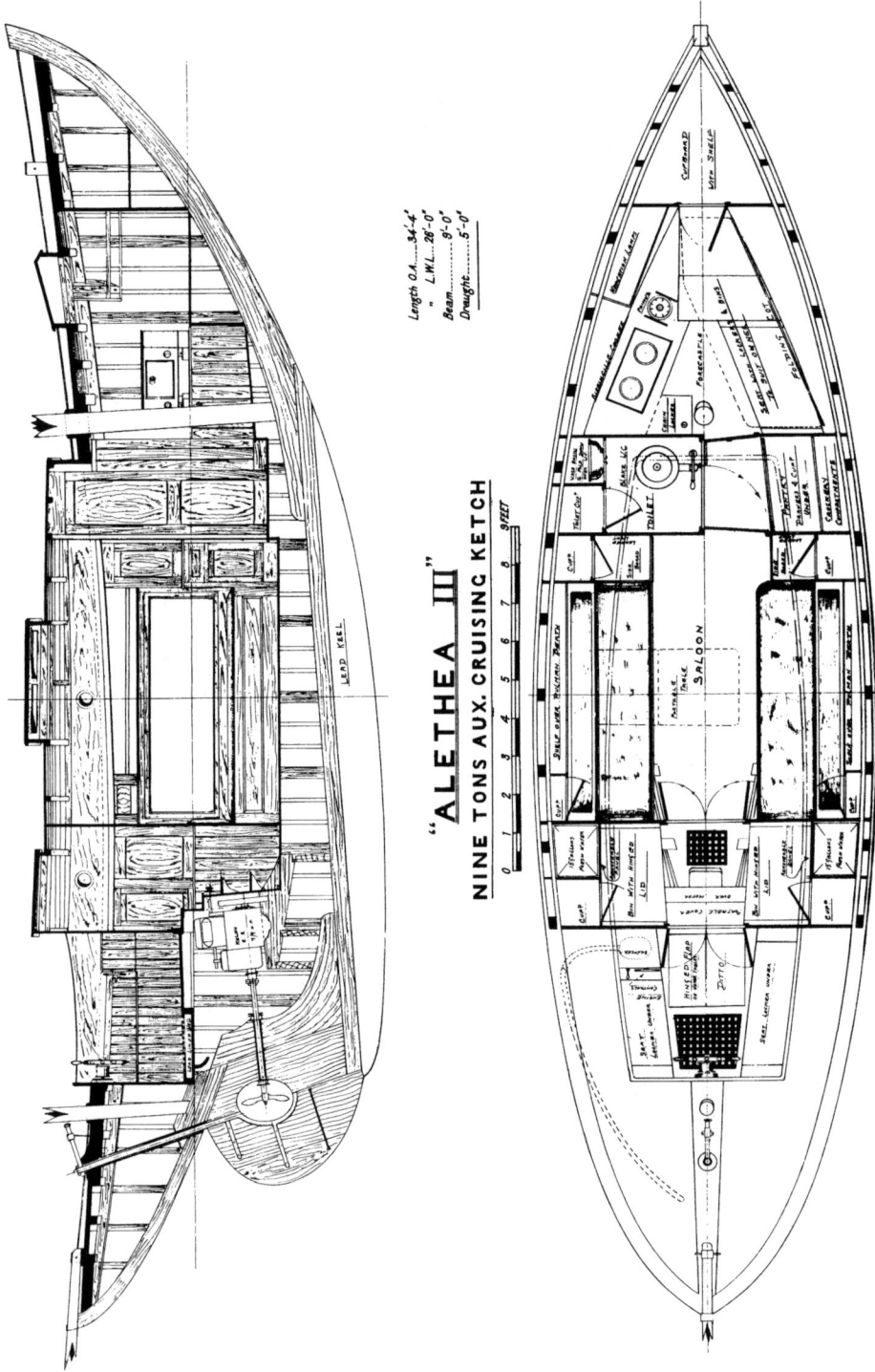

"ALETHEA III"

NINE TONS AUX. CRUISING KETCH

Length O.A. ..... 34'-4"
" L.W.L. 26'-0"
Beam ..... 9'-0"
Draught ..... 5'-0"

0 1 2 3 4 5 6 7 8 9 FEET

Drawing 57: Alethea III by A.R. Luke — Construction and Accommodation

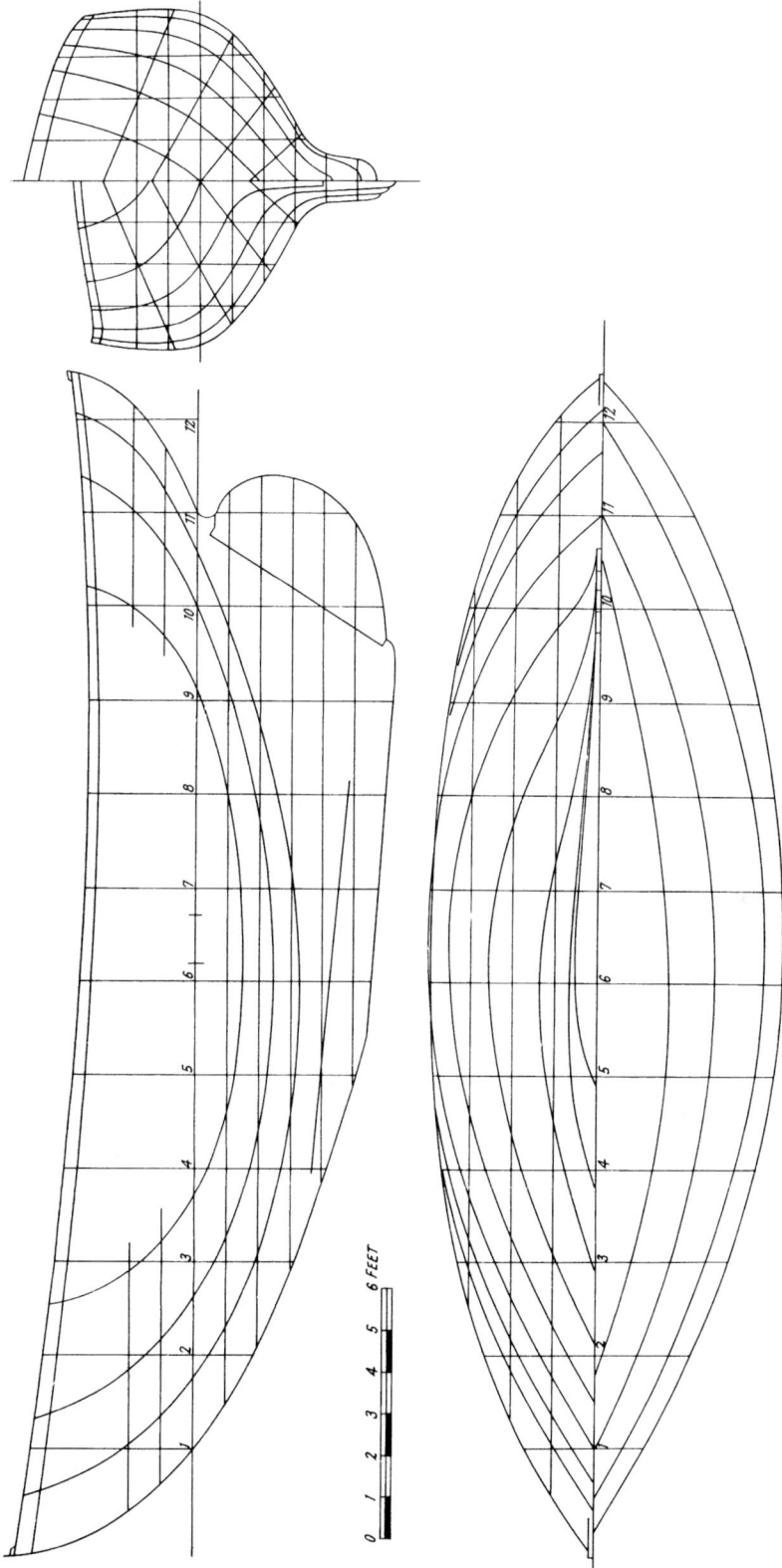

Drawing 58: Sunart by W. Easton — Lines

6 FEET

REFERENCE

A. Locker for navigation lights.
B. Bins for sails.
C. W.C.   Wash-basin over.
D. Drawers on shelves.
E. Drying locker.
F. Bookcase.
G. Sideboard.
H. Coal stove.
I. Shelf.
J. Fold-up bed.
K. Sofa.
L. Wardrobe.
M. Hanging locker.
N. Oilskin   "
O. Galley and pantry.
P. Sink. Table over.
Q. Fixed berth.
R. Chart table to fold down.
S. Motor casing.
T. F.W.Tank – Pipe to galley.
U. Paraffin tank.
V. F.W.Tanks – fitted between floors.

6'0"

3'3"

0   1   2   3   4   5   6 FEET

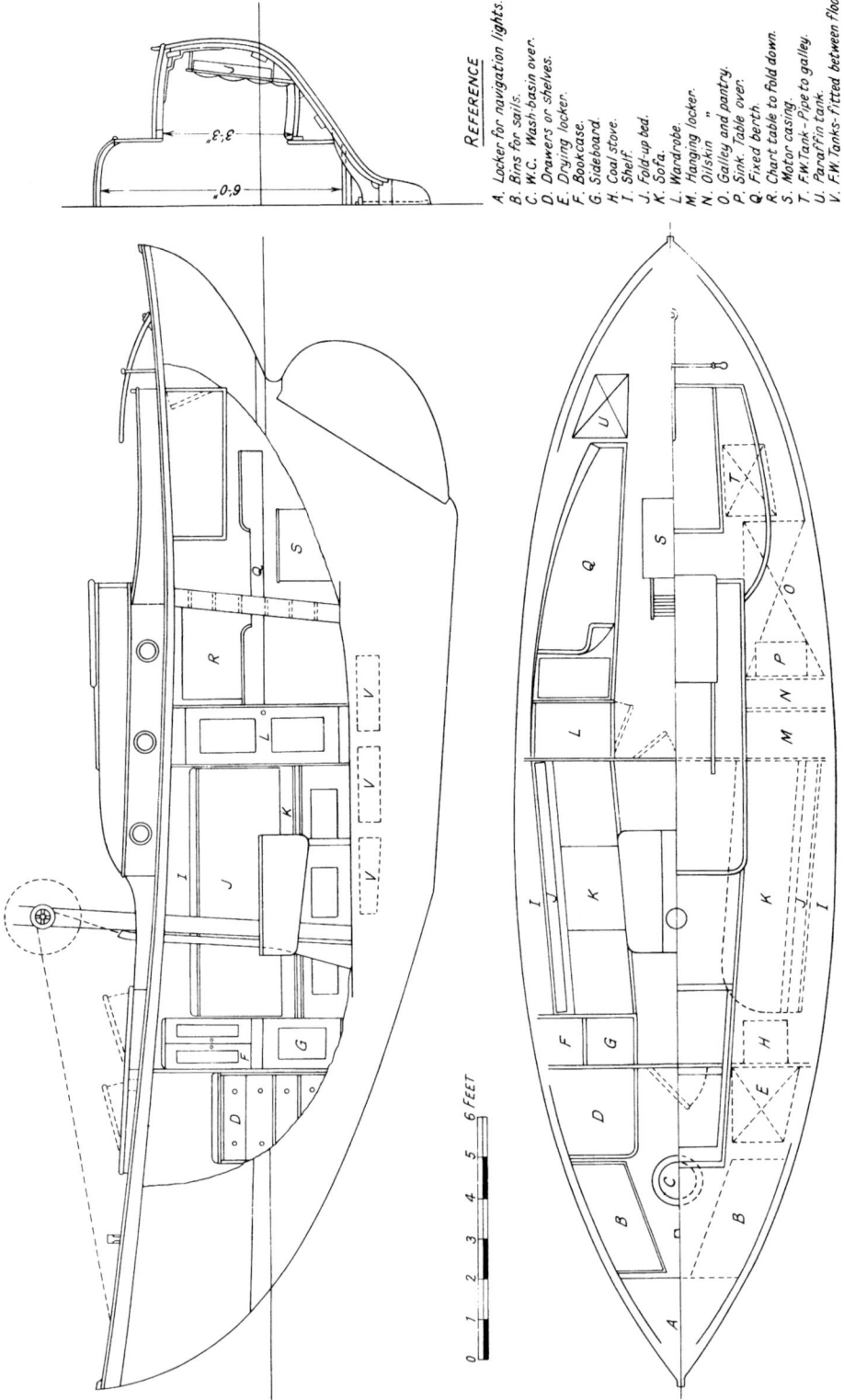

Drawing 59: Sunart by W. Easton — Accommodation

VINDILIS   (DAVINKA)

L.O.A. -------- 30FT.
L.W.L. -------- 22FT. 6IN.
BEAM -------- 8FT. 6IN.
DRAUGHT -------- 4FT. 4IN.
DISPLACEMENT. 5·26 TONS.
T.M. -------- 6·5 TONS.

C.L.R.   C. of B

C. of G of KEEL

LEAD KEEL 16 CWT.

0 1 2 3 4 5 6 7 8 9 10 FEET
SCALE ¾ INCH = 1 FOOT.

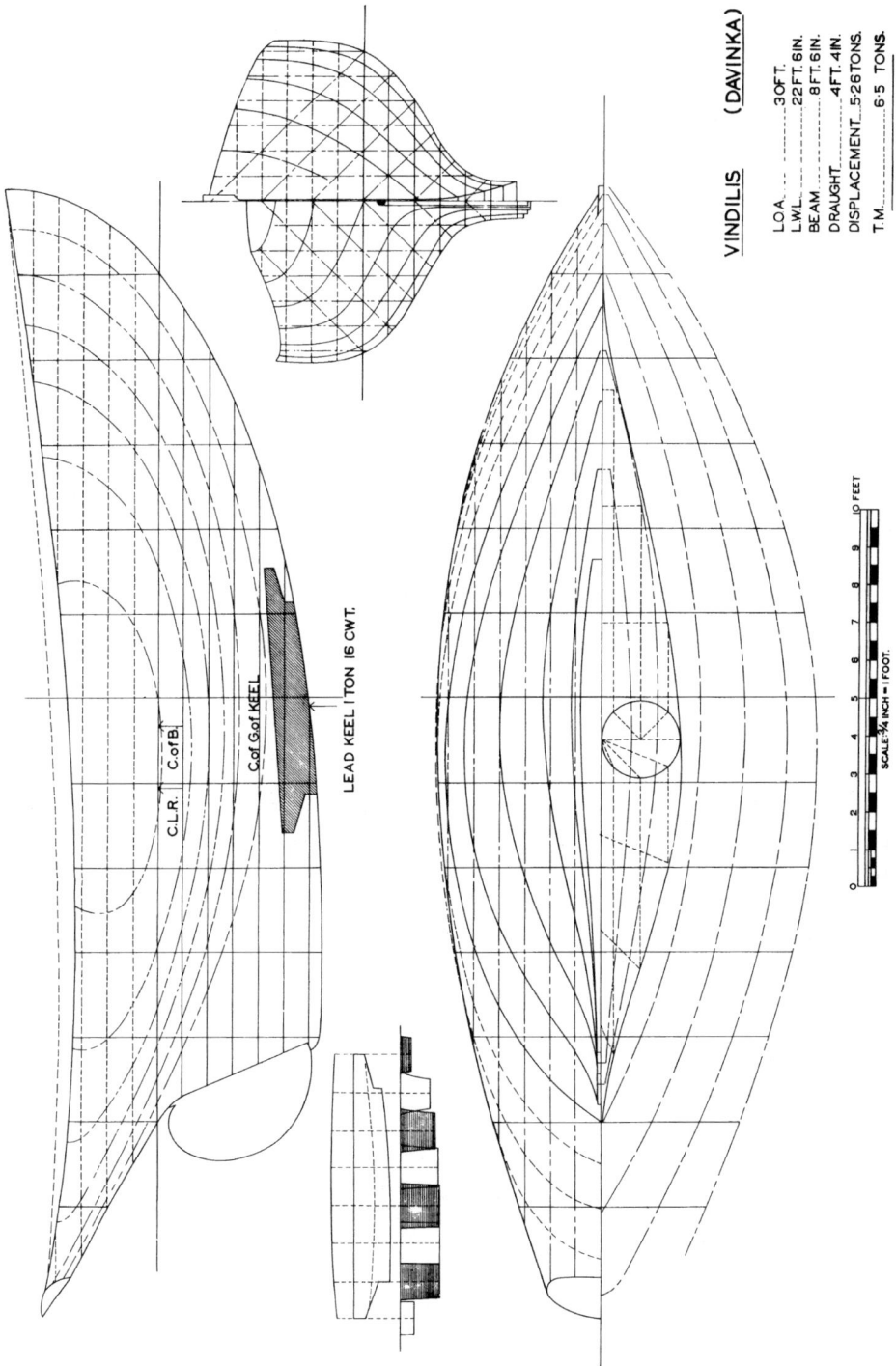

Drawing 60: Vindilis by T. Harrison Butler — Lines

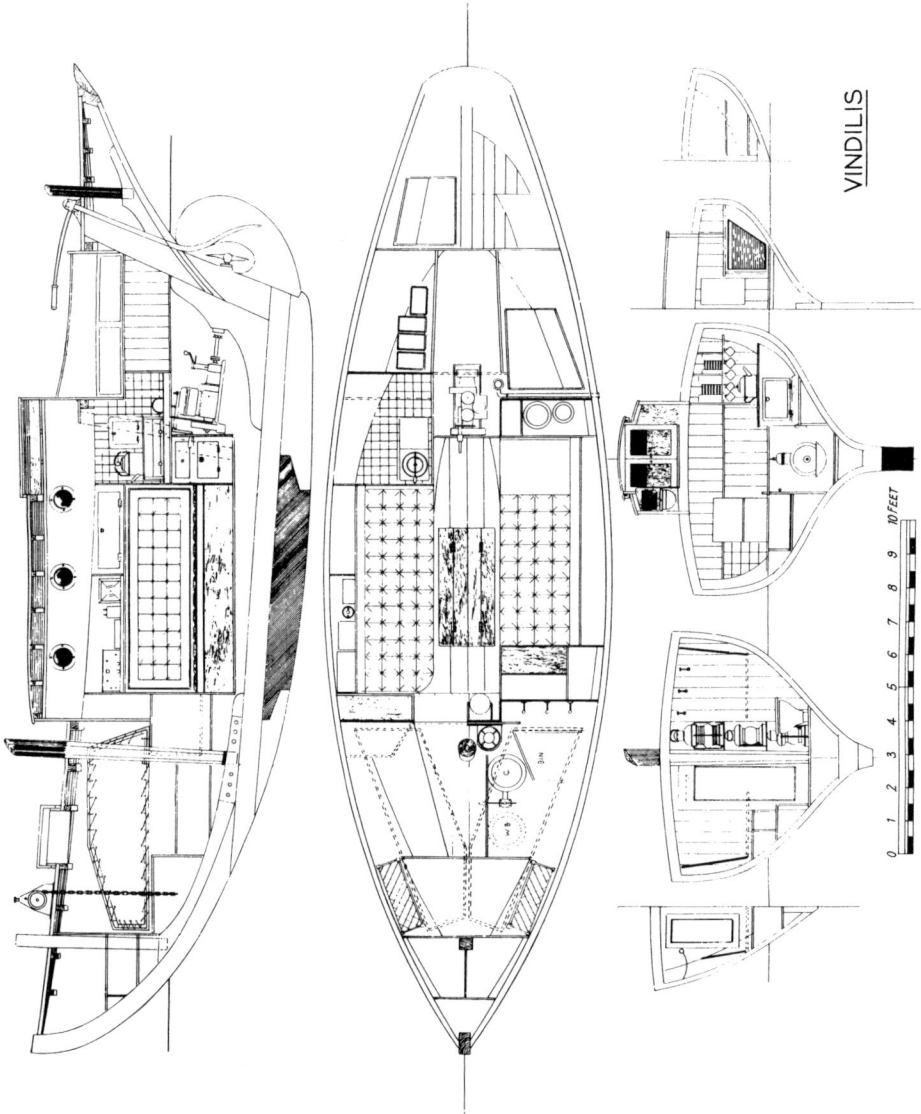

VINDILIS

Drawing 61: Vindilis by T. Harrison Butler — Construction and Accommodation

VINDILIS

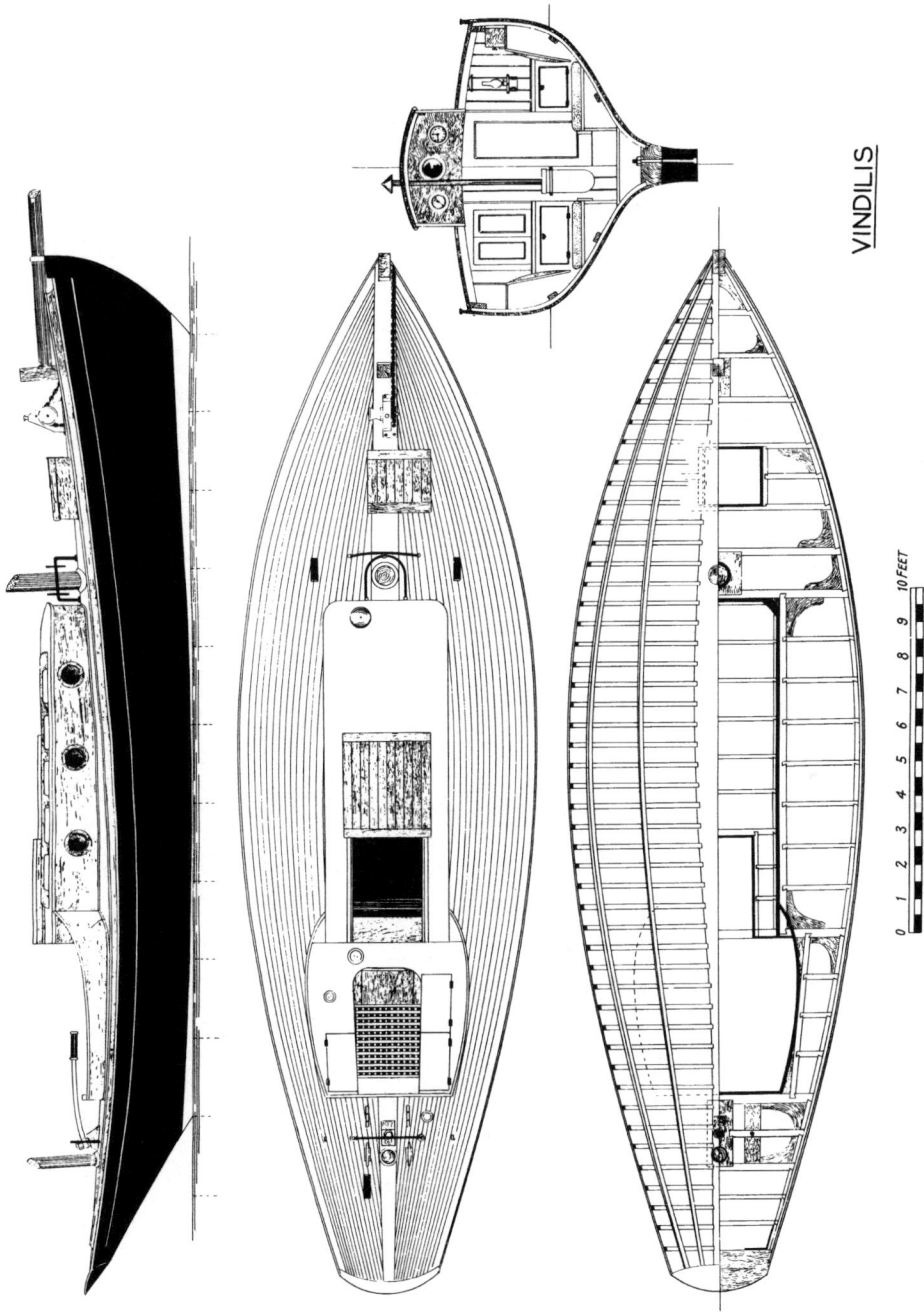

Drawing 62: Vindilis by T. Harrison Butler — Deck and Sheer Plan

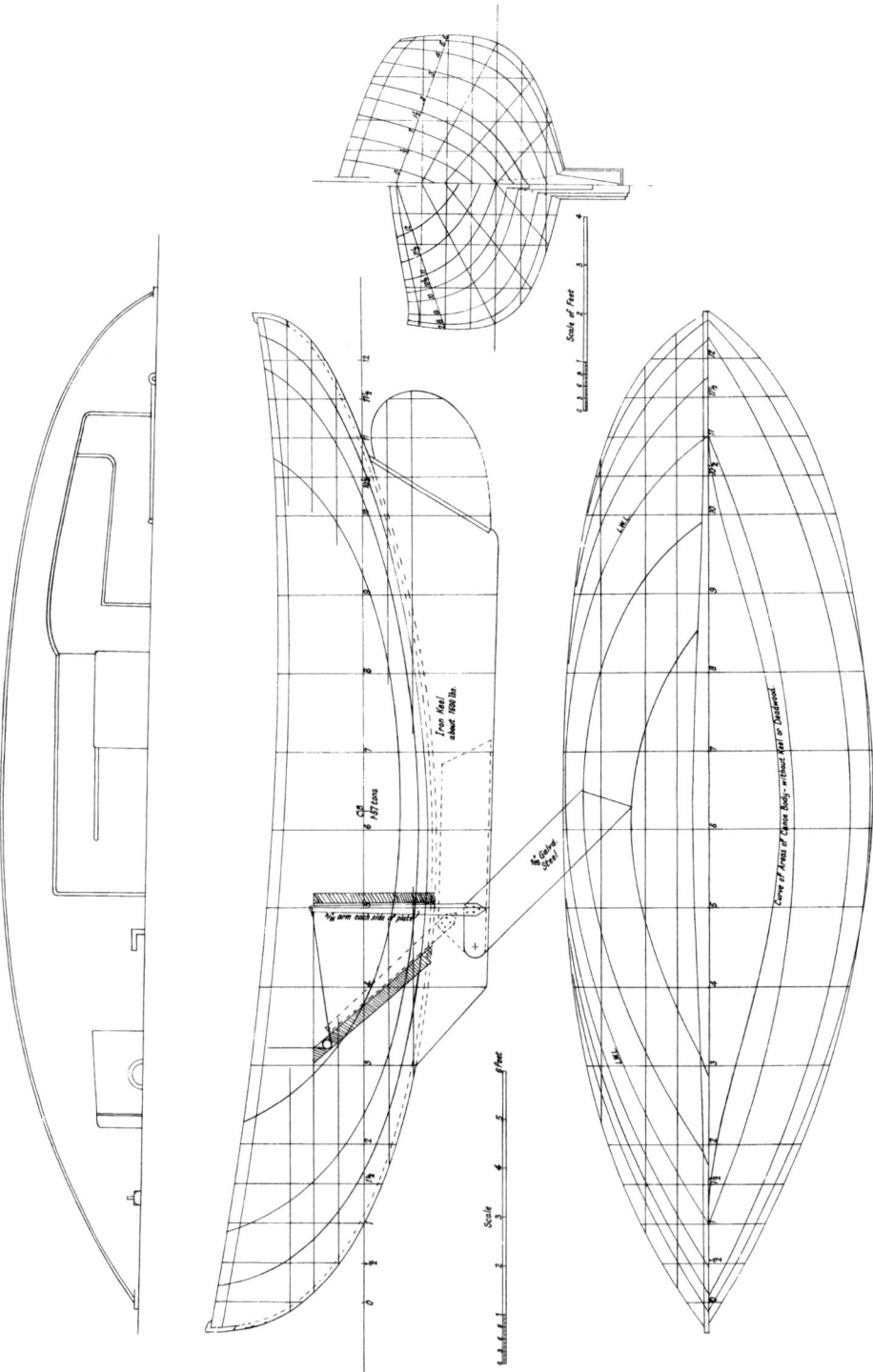

Drawing 63: Norah Creina by W. Easton — Lines

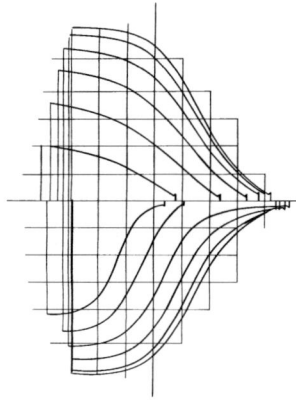

LINES OF 18 FT SLOOP

BEAM 6 FT 6 INS

DRAFT 3 FEET

DAVID HILLYARD
LITTLEHAMPTON

Drawing 64: 2½-ton Sloop by David Hillyard — Lines

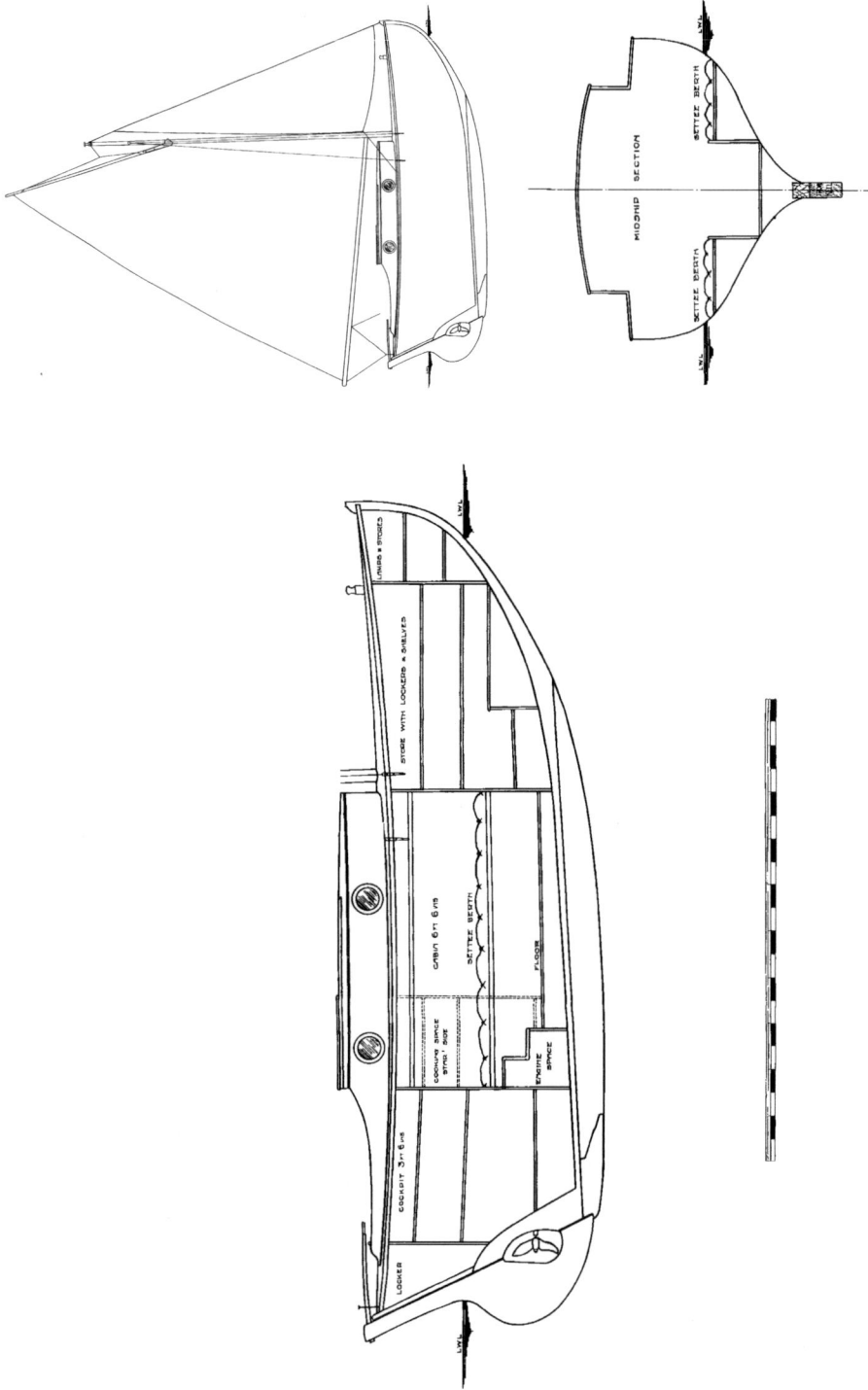

Drawing 65: 2½-ton Sloop by David Hillyard — Accommodation and Sail Plan

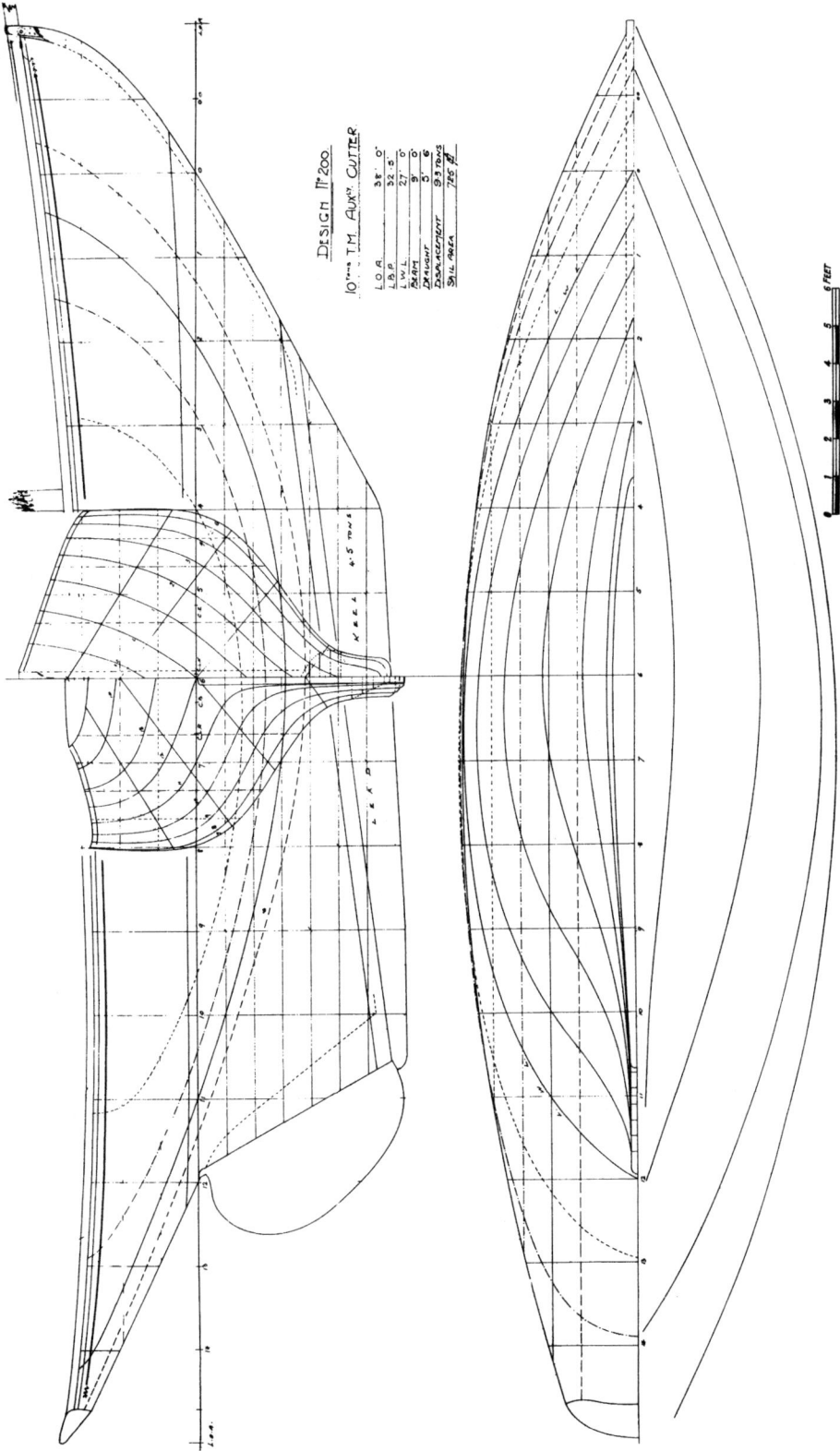

DESIGN N° 200

10 TON T.M. AUX. CUTTER

L.O.A.	38′ 0″
L.B.P.	32′ 5″
L.W.L.	27′ 0″
BEAM	9′ 0″
DRAUGHT	5′ 6″
DISPLACEMENT	9.9 TONS
SAIL AREA	725 □

Drawing 66: Andante II by Norman E. Dallimore — Lines

Drawing 67: Andante II by Norman E. Dallimore — Construction and Accommodation

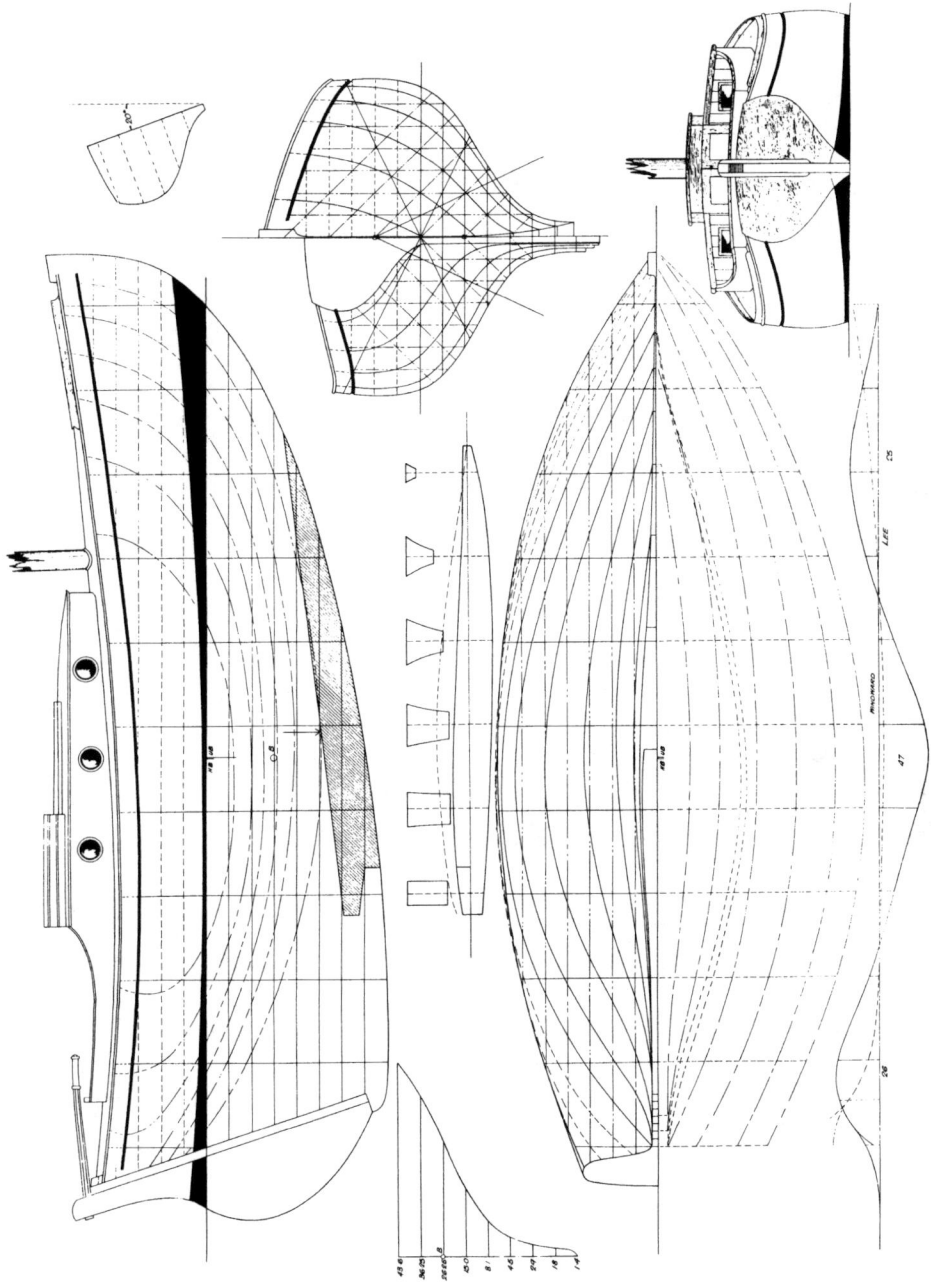

Drawing 68: Zyklon by T. Harrison Butler — Lines

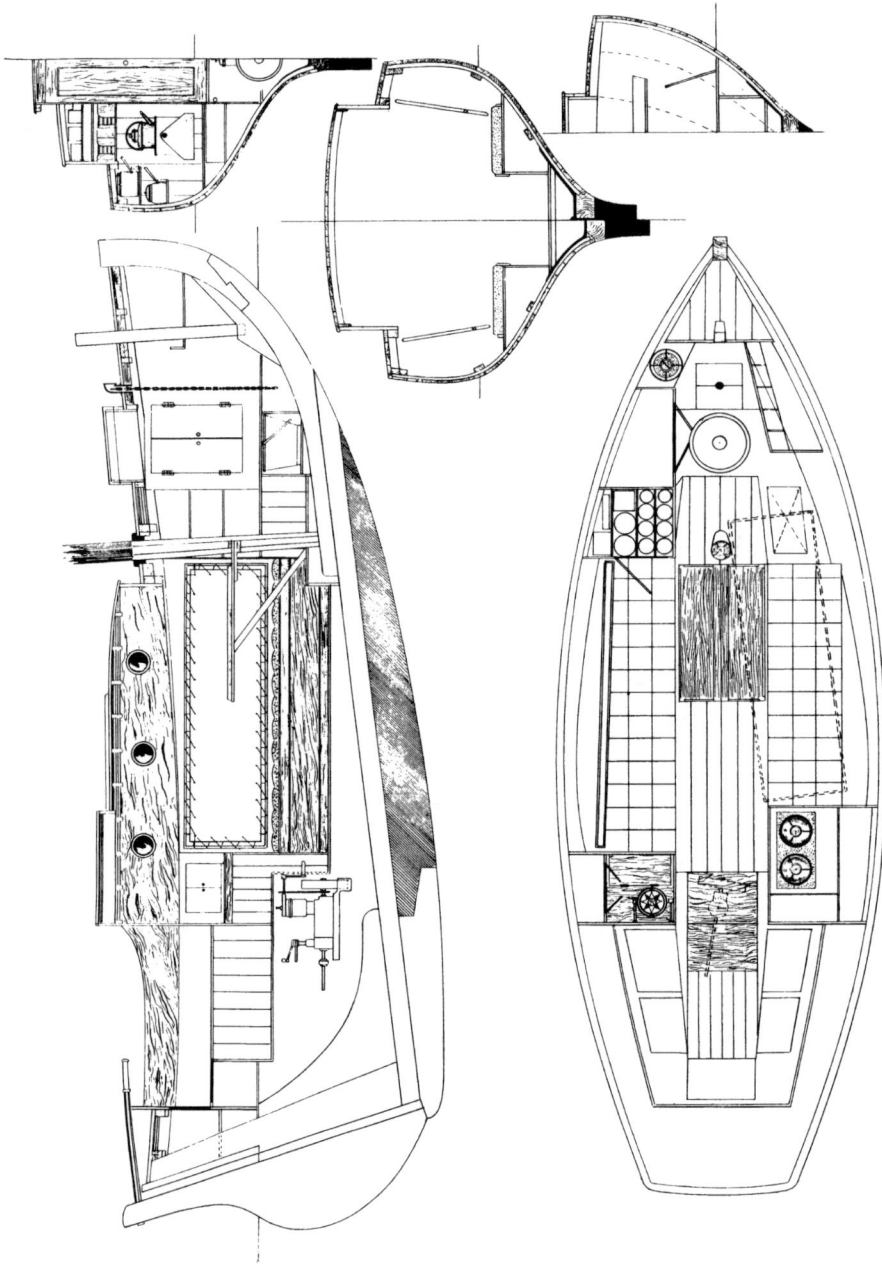

Drawing 69: Zyklon by T. Harrison Butler — Accommodation

Drawing 70: Monie by J. Laurent Giles — Lines

311

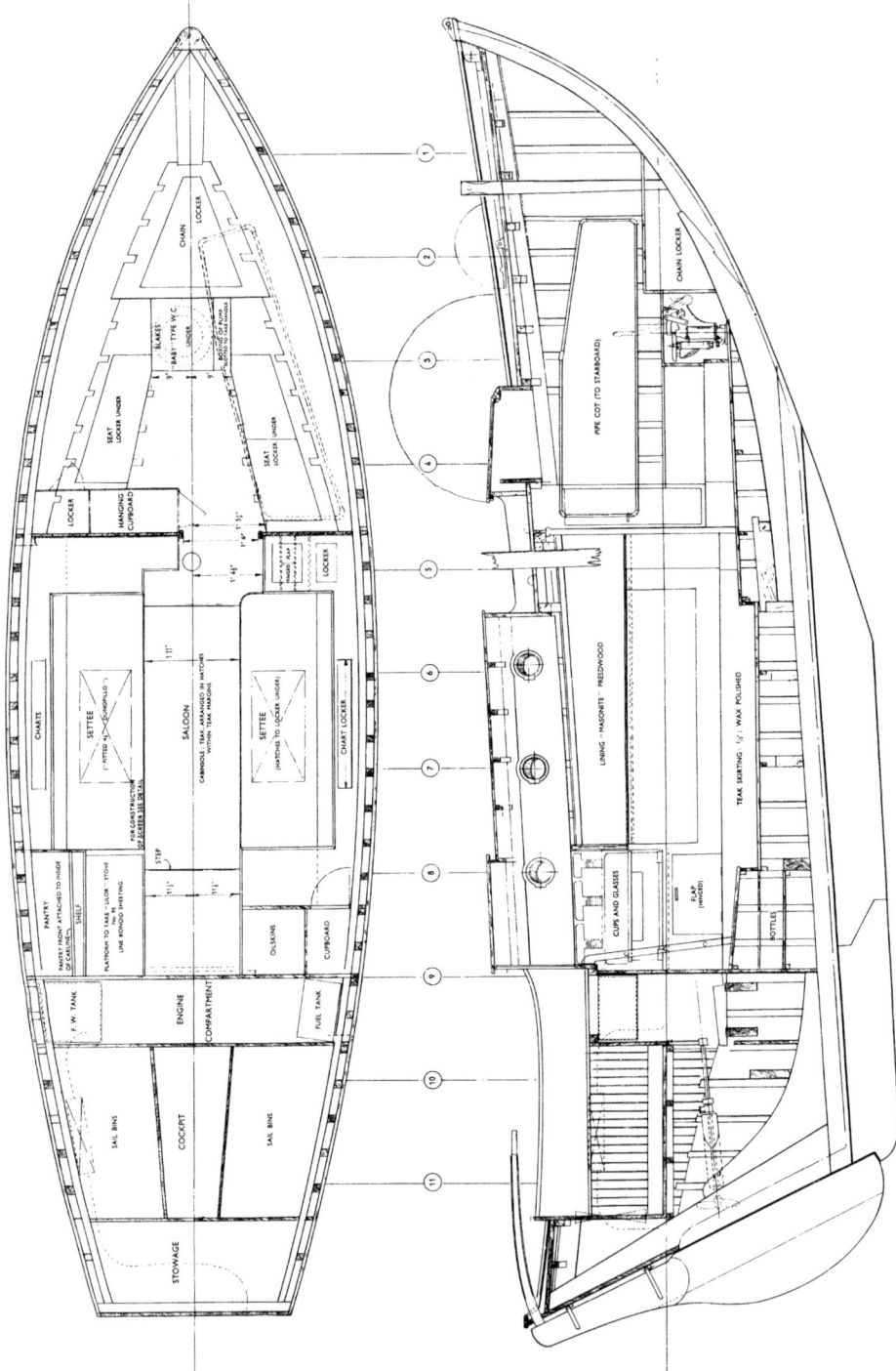

Drawing 71: Monie by J. Laurent Giles — Construction and Accommodation

L.O.A.

SCALE

L.O.A.	21'0"
L.W.L.	18'0"
BEAM	6'8"
DRAUGHT	3'9"
DISPLACEMENT	2·75 TONS
SAIL AREA	265 SQ.FT.

INS./2

IRON KEEL

C.B. CH.K.

C.L.R.

1 TON

L.O.A.

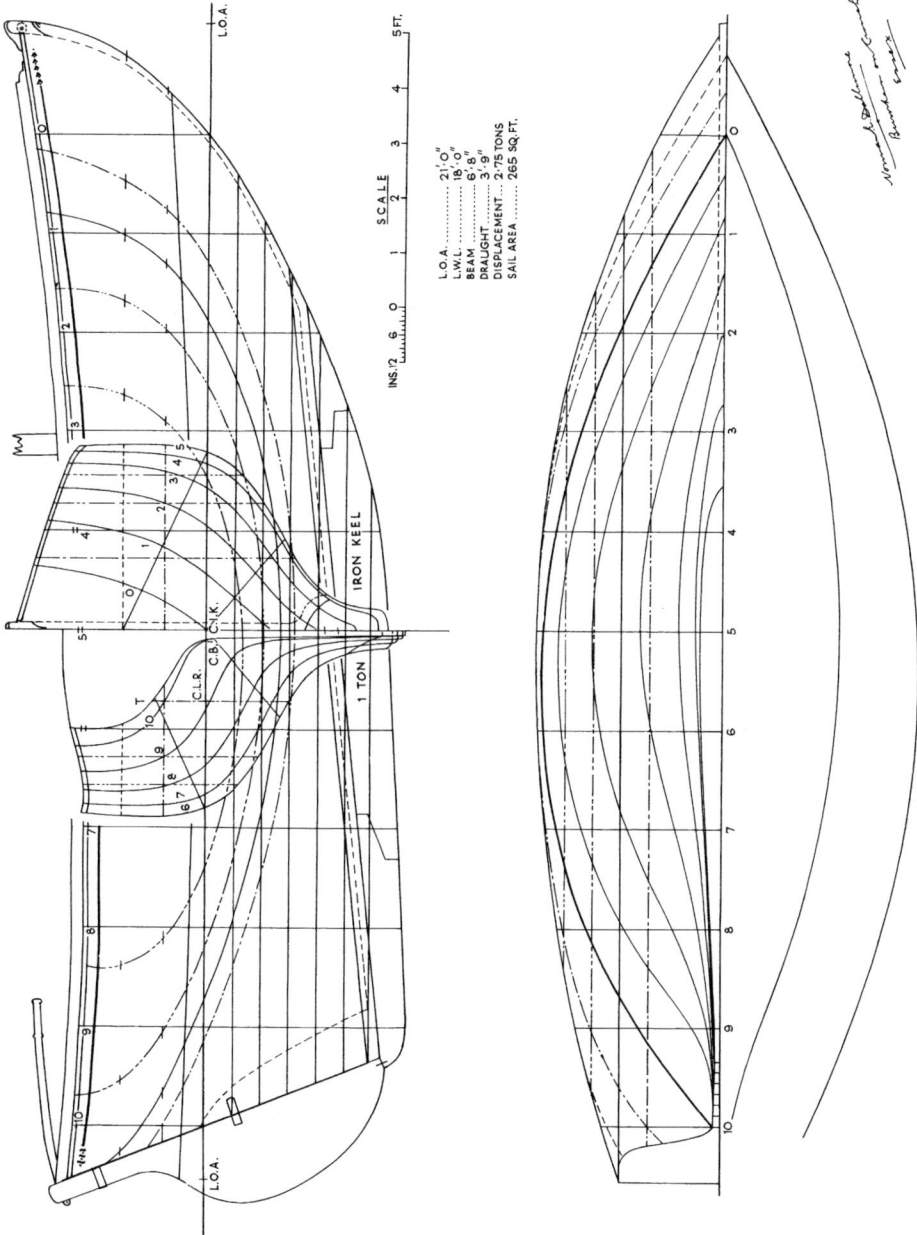

Drawing 72: Burnham Sloop by Norman E. Dallimore — Lines

Drawing 73: Burnham Sloop by Norman E. Dallimore — Construction and Accommodation

DIMENSIONS:-
Length O.A. = 18'6"   Length W.L. = 16'
Beam " = 6'3"   Draft " = 3'5"
Displt. = 1·89 tons. Iron Keel = 87 tons

WINDWARD

LEEWARD

Scale in Feet

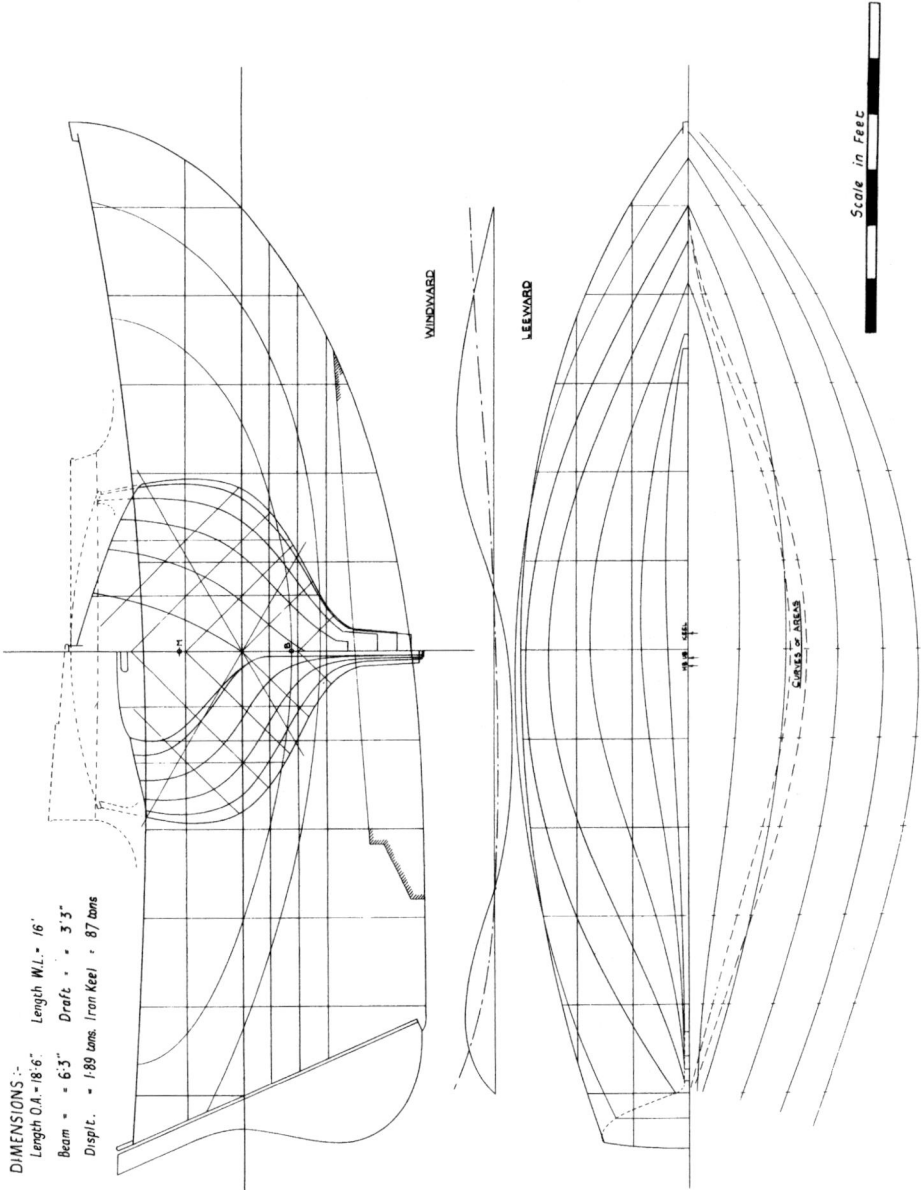

Drawing 74:   Mowgli by Ian C. Bridge — Lines

GALLEY

LK⁰

LK⁰

STOWAGE

CHAIN PIPE

SHELF P.&S.

SEAT

CUPBOARD

FOOD LK⁰
UNDER

SHELF

LOCKER

KEEL

IRON

BUCKET

WATER CANS

SCALE

FEET

0   1   2   3   4   5

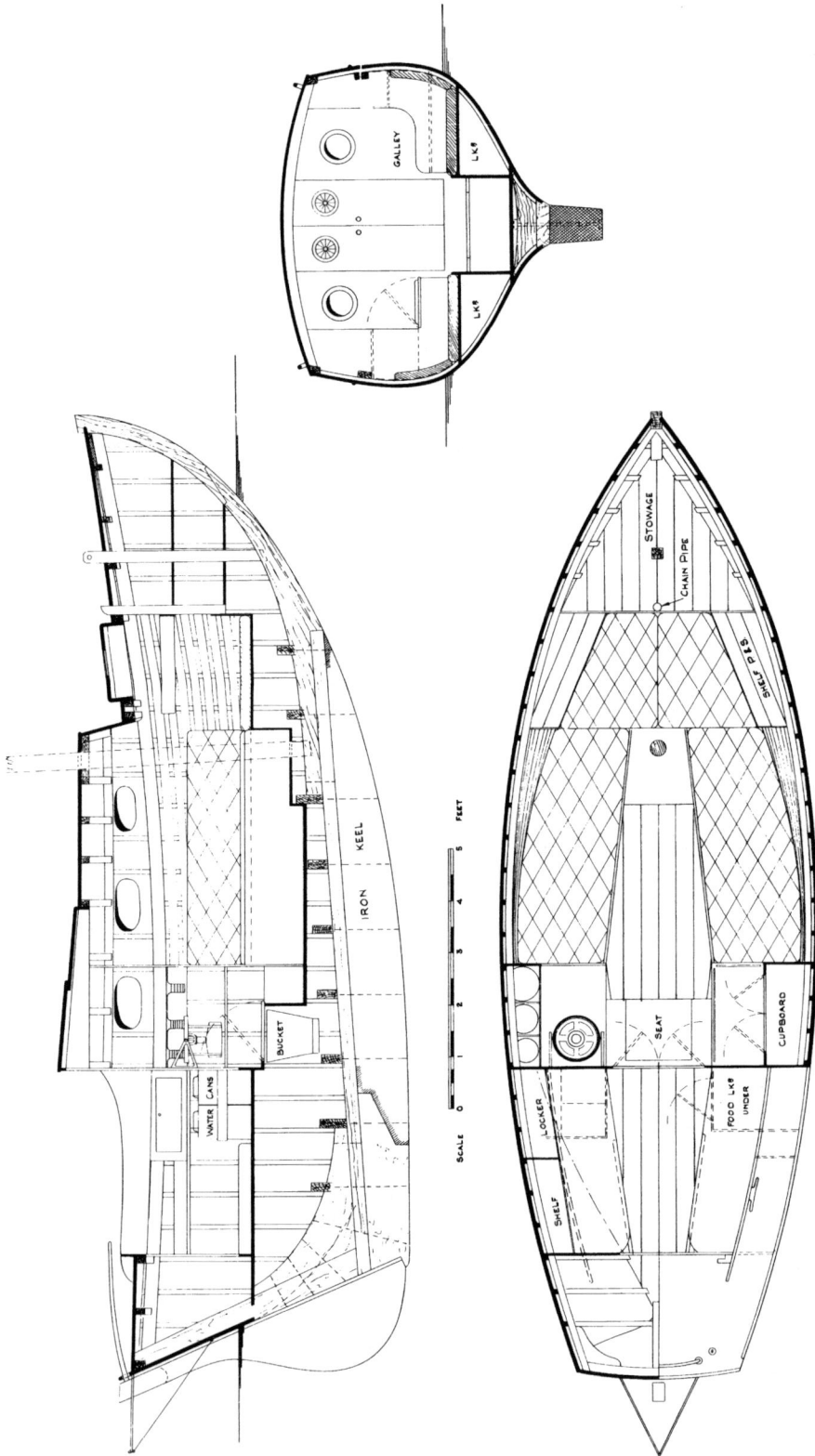

Drawing 75: Mowgli by Ian C. Bridge — Construction and Accommodation

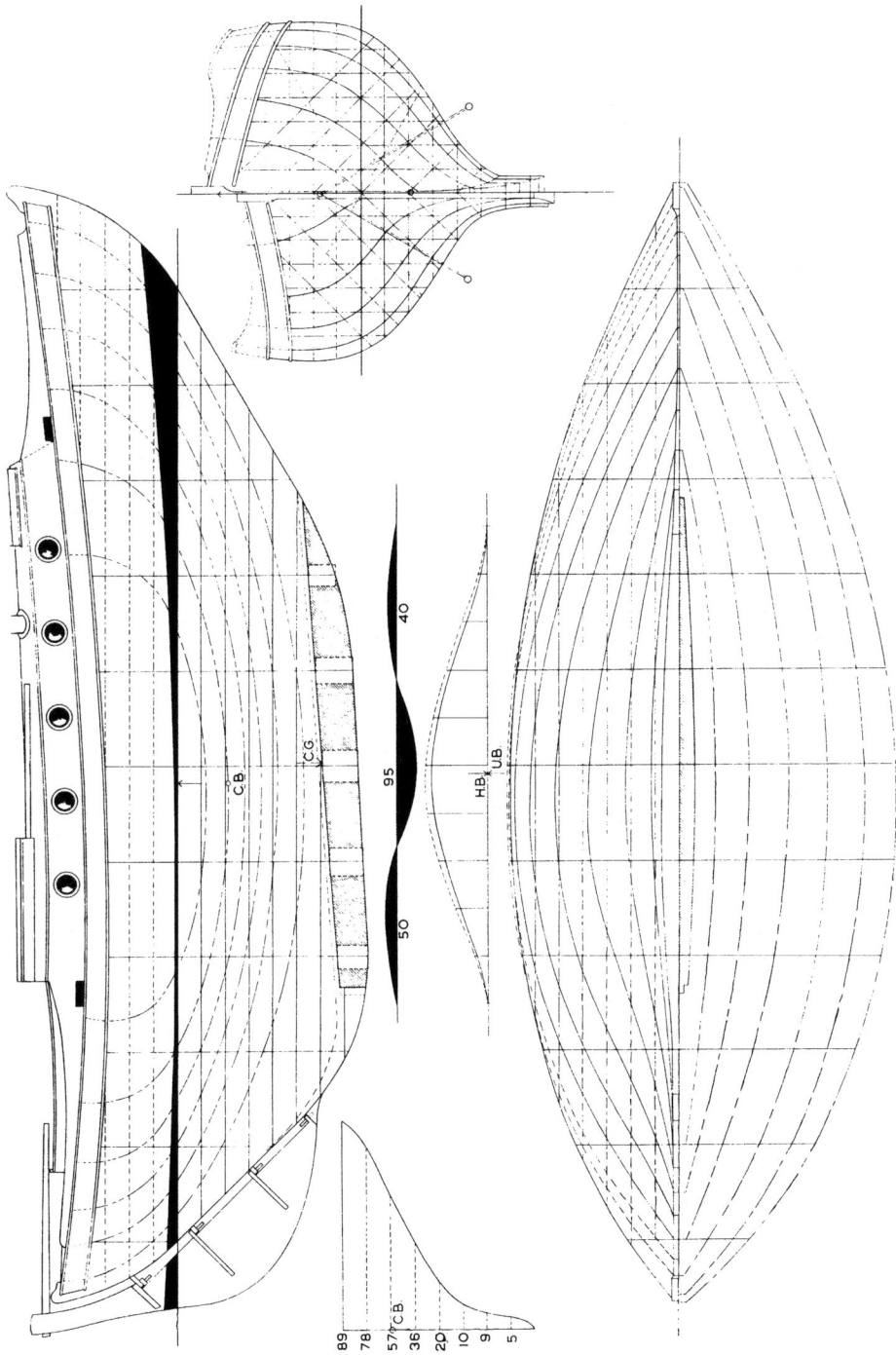

Drawing 76: Thuella by T. Harrison Butler — Lines

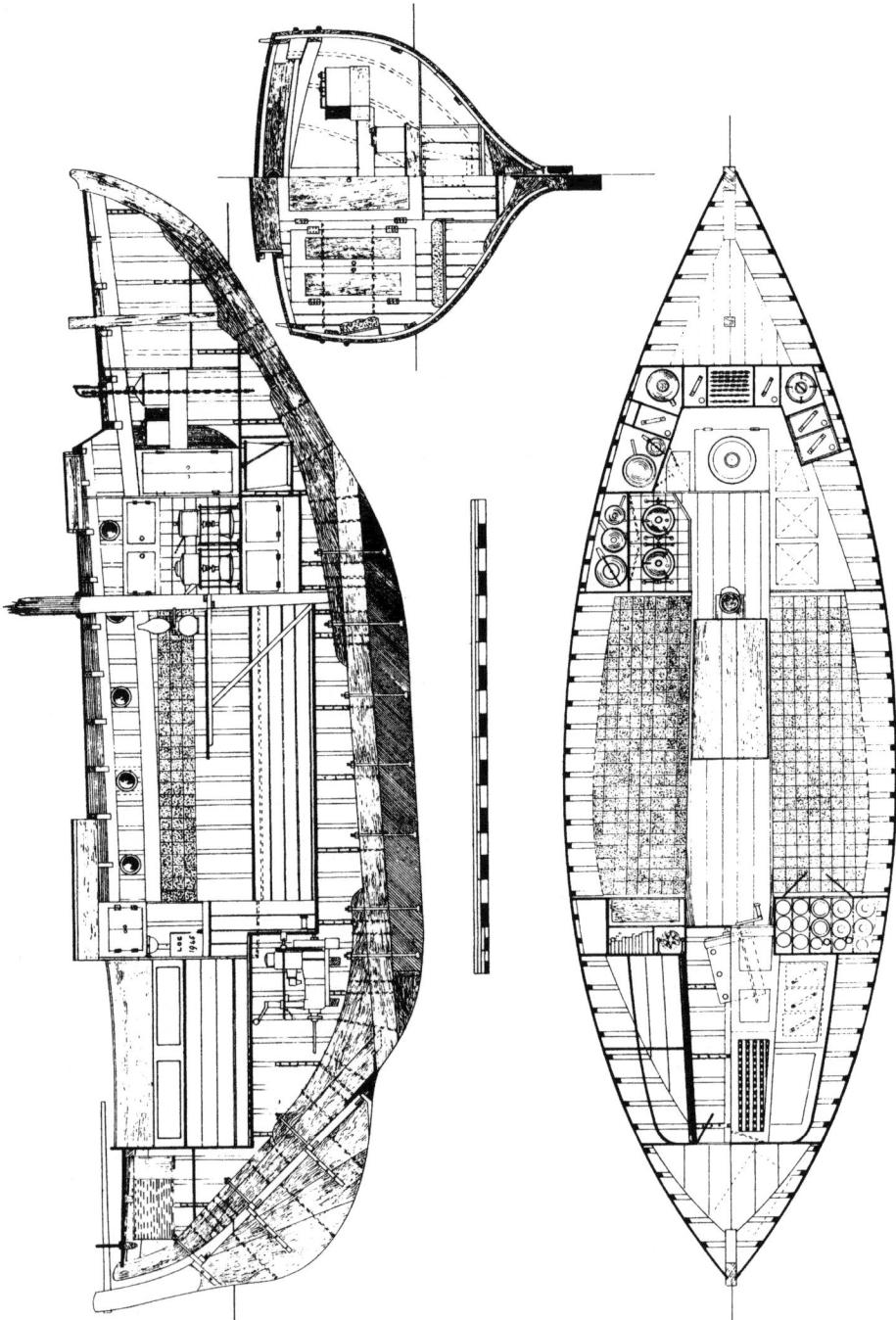

Drawing 77: Thuella by T. Harrison Butler – Construction and Accommodation

A Yarn

❧

Dirty Weather in the Wallet

We were anxious for *Wave* to get away as soon as possible as the ebb tide had already been running for some time, but things went wrong. First, we upset the kettle just as it boiled and had to fill and boil it again, which delayed breakfast. Then, when we came to get under way, we found that our anchor was foul of a smack's chain and we had a good deal of trouble in clearing it. Owing to these mishaps two valuable hours of ebb tide had been lost ere we left the creek, and by the time we got out into the Colne, *Norah Creina* was rounding Colne Point.

With fair wind and tide we did not take long to run down to Colne Point and, hauling our wind, we crossed the Bar fairly close to the shore. *Norah Creina* was a mere dot in the distance and soon we lost sight of her altogether and saw her no more that day. There was a smart breeze, and I was sorry to notice that it had veered a little and there was now a distinct touch of east in it, but at present we could fetch comfortably along the coast and as the wind was off shore the water was quite smooth. We made good progress as far as Clacton, but all the time the wind was drawing round more towards the east and we had to get in our sheets gradually until we were close hauled. After passing Clacton Pier we could no longer lay our course for, apart from the wind breaking us off, the coast there begins to trend more towards the north-east. We were now heading towards the Gunfleet Sands and, as it was likely that we should soon find rougher water, took the opportunity to have lunch. As we drew away from the land we lost the shelter of the shore and the sea got rougher and rougher. It was nothing much really, but for a little boat like *Wave* it was quite a big sea, and as we drew near to the Gunfleet Sands we began to ship water in the open well. I came to the conclusion that it would pay us better to work the shore, where we should find smoother water, although, of course, we should not have such a good tide. We therefore put about on to the starboard tack and headed for the shore.

At the end of that board we were off Holland Gap and the ebb tide had about finished. With a foul wind and the flood tide against us, our chance of getting to Pin Mill began to look a trifle thin and we discussed the question of turning back. But having come so far, we hated the idea and decided to carry on. "We can always run back if we have to, and the wind may change," I said, with the optimism of youth, and we began to work along the shore in short boards. But the only change in the wind was in its strength and soon we had to pull down a reef and shift jibs.

Being close to the shore we were able to mark our progress. Every board we made a little ground, but as the flood gathered strength the gain became less and less. We were off Frinton by tea-time and then it took us nearly two hours to get round Walton Pier. Then it began to blow really hard and we had to take down the second reef, but still we struggled on. There was now a heavy sea and we were taking more on board than was pleasant. It was mainly spray, but a gallon or two of spray shipped at frequent intervals makes its presence felt in a little boat and the water was swishing about on the cabin floor.

At eight o'clock we were off the Naze and then had to give the position serious consideration. We had spent about six hours in getting from Holland Gap and it was now almost high water. We were wet through and miserably cold, with the prospect before us of a long beat into Harwich Harbour against the ebb. Under the most favourable circumstances we could not hope to get in before dark and we had no navigation lights. There could be no doubt about it; the game was up, and we had no alternative but to run back to Brightlingsea or West Mersea. It was all very well to talk glibly about running back, but when we bore up, we found it hell. *Wave* rolled like the devil. At one moment her boom-end soared towards the sky and the next was buried in the water and she was pursued by a wild sea. Every now and then water lapped over the gunwale, for abaft the bulkhead she was an open boat. We should have done better with the mainsail off, but did not care to risk going forward to lower it, as the weight of a man on the foredeck would have put her head down and probably caused her to broach-to. She was storming along like a frightened stag and we were scared stiff.

We seemed to be back at Walton in next to no time and seeing some watermen on the pier as we passed, I decided to bring up and try and get ashore. Luffing round the pier, we let go the anchor, running out our full scope of 20 fathoms of chain. Lying head to wind, *Wave* pitched abominably and it was with great difficulty that we managed to lower the sails and make a rough stow. Then we shouted and waved to the men on the pier. After a time we saw, to our relief, that they were manning a boat, and presently they came and took us off.

Having got ashore we did not quite know what to do, but good fortune directed our steps to the Portobello Hotel. I shall never forget the kindness of the proprietor, who lent us dry clothes, prepared a hot meal and lit a fire for us in his private sitting-room. Moreover, he dried our clothes for us during the night. We turned in early, being dog-tired, and as I lay in bed, listening to the roaring of the wind without, I thought that I had seen the last of *Wave*, as it seemed impossible that she could ride out such a blow in her exposed position.

The next morning was a complete contrast to the day before. The sun shone brilliantly and the genial warmth suggested that the summer had at last come to stay. After breakfast we went down to the pier, and to our joy there was *Wave* lying where we had left her, but looking rather bedraggled, with her mainsail lashed up like a bundle of washing and some of her halyards adrift. There was a flat calm and the sea smooth, save for a slight ground swell, the aftermath of the previous night's blow.

The cabin, when we went on board, was a sorry sight. Almost everything in the boat was lying on the floor in about 2in. of water. Clothing, cushions, books and various other things were in a heap, and pots of jam and marmalade and a tin of condensed milk had shed their contents indiscriminately. It was an appalling mess, which took us two hours to clear up, but thanks to the hot sun we were able to get our clothes and cushions dry and at noon were ready to resume our journey to Pin Mill.

In the absence of wind, we had to row her round the pier with the sweep and then let her drift with the ebb while we had lunch. Then a nice little breeze filled in from the south-east and we had a delightful sail to Harwich. The harbour was full of interest in those days as it was an important naval station, and as we sailed past the Stour we saw a battleship and a flotilla of destroyers; higher up the training-ship *Ganges* – a picturesque old three-decker – lay at moorings. The harbour, indeed, seemed full of shipping and we noticed two large barques, a barquentine, a brig and several square-topsail schooners.

How different is Harwich to-day. The harbour is usually comparatively empty, save for a few small craft, and ashore the old town wears a dilapidated appearance, for the trade has moved higher up the Stour to Parkeston Quay. The wharves are rotting and the Great Eastern Hotel, formerly the home of the Royal Harwich Yacht Club, is derelict. But if the glory of this historic old port has diminished, the fine natural harbour affords splendid sailing for small yachts and its picturesqueness remains unimpaired, although one misses the *Ganges*, long since broken up. H.M.S. *Ganges* is now an establishment ashore, where the masts from the fine old ship have been erected. I suppose it is better for the boys, who now have the benefit of modern buildings and a sports ground, which includes a running track, but all the same I think the passing of the old ship is in some respects a matter for regret.

We soon passed Bloody Point, which separates the Stour from the Orwell. I wonder how this point got its sanguinary name. Probably, I should think, from some disgruntled mariner who piled up his ship on it. As we sailed up Sea Reach, the Orwell seemed rather disappointing, as I had heard so much of its scenic attractions, but when we rounded Collimer Point, the beauty of the river fairly staggered me. Densely wooded to the water's edge on both banks and as far as the eye could see, the wonderful wealth of foliage was unbroken. As we sailed through Butterman's Bay, where a big barque was discharging a cargo of grain into barges, it seemed to me that the scenery of this lovely river was not unworthy to rank with that of the Dart or Fal, and it was difficult to believe that we were on the East Coast.

And so, after much trouble and tribulation, we came to Pin Mill, the Mecca of East Coast yachtsmen. The anchorage is in a delightful little bay, sheltered by the trees of Wolverstone Park, where the nightingales sing at night and where one can lie out of the way of the traffic which passes to and from Ipswich. On the other side of the river is the equally beautiful Orwell Park and away in the distance Freston, with its red towers peeping out from midst the trees. Here indeed was a yachtsman's paradise and we came to the conclusion that the passage, despite its alarms and discomfort, had been well worth the making.

The only fly in the ointment is the hard, which is of inordinate length, being no less than 367 yards at low water spring tides. It is quite a good hard, but its length and flatness make it difficult to dispose of the dinghy when you land in such a way that you can get it when you return. Should you go ashore when the tide is flooding, your boat may be far from the shore on your return, and if at high water you may have to pull her down the causeway for perhaps a hundred yards or more. The only satisfactory solution to this problem is to tip a boy to keep the dinghy afloat for you, but during the week, when the youngsters are at school, such assistance may not be available. But if the Pin Mill hard has this disadvantage, it is an uncommonly good place for scrubbing purposes, as at the side there are some stout posts against which yachts can rest without being legged. There were formerly two inns at the waterside, the Butt and Oyster and the Alma, but the latter was closed years ago.

Another institution that has disappeared is the service of steamers that used to ply between Ipswich, Harwich and Felixstowe Dock. They were rather curious little vessels, being sharp at both ends and having fore and aft rudders. They were so designed because there was insufficient room at Ipswich to turn them, so what was the bow during the journey up the river became the stern when she came down. At Pin Mill the steamers slowed down and passengers were embarked or discharged by means of large ferry-boats. It was a delightful trip from Ipswich to Pin Mill and back, and if I remember rightly the return fare was only ninepence. The present service of motor buses may be rather quicker, but the journey by road is not so pleasant and costs more. There are shops at Chelmondiston, about half a mile from the waterside, and a shipwright and sailmaker at Pin Mill.

We found *Norah Creina* and *Viper* lying in the anchorage and brought up close to them, but their crews were absent. As the larder needed replenishing, we got the ferryman to put us ashore and walked up to the village, where we were able to buy everything we wanted. On returning to the hard, we met the others, who had just landed from the Ipswich steamer, and learnt that they had saved their tide round the Naze the previous day and got into the Orwell before the bad weather set in. They were rather anxious when we failed to arrive, but concluded that we had put back to Brightlingsea.

As Hugh was due back in the City on Monday morning, he transferred to *Viper*, which was returning to Fambridge, and his brother Ernest joined me in *Wave*. When we turned out the next morning *Viper* had already sailed. After a leisurely breakfast, we got under way and ran down to Harwich with a fine breeze and then beat up the Stour almost to Wrabness. With a weather-going tide the water was choppy and we got pretty wet with spray, so decided to return to Pin Mill. On rounding Shotley Spit we found that the wind had freshened considerably and we were rather over-canvassed with the whole mainsail, but had a grand reach up to Collimer Point, fairly holding

Whitaker Beacon

Norah Creina. When we came on to the wind in Butterman's Bay, however, she soon left us. We brought up in our old berth at Pin Mill and *Norah Creina* sheered alongside, so that we could have dinner together, but while the meal was in progress we experienced a violent thunderstorm with a lot of wind and had to part company. My brother had a rather bad time, as he was compelled to take down his tent and it rained cats and dogs.

Having spent a day at Ipswich, we came to the conclusion that it was time that we got nearer home, so decided to sail to Brightlingsea on the morrow. We therefore turned out the next morning at the unholy hour of 3.30 a.m. and half an hour later, after a very scratch breakfast, got under way. There was a flat calm and we did little more than drift down to Harwich, pulling with the sweep occasionally to keep steerage way on the boat. In the Harbour, however, we found a nice little breeze from about south-west by west, which enabled us to lay our course to the Naze, but from there we had a head wind, which gradually increased in strength, whilst the sea began to get rough. Off Frinton it became necessary to take down a reef, and so quickly did the wind increase in strength that we had hardly got it down before we had to take in another and shift jibs. As the little boat was simply standing on her head, this was no easy job and took a long time. But at last it was done and we let the jib draw and filled on her. *Wave* immediately buried her gunwale and gallons of water poured into the well. It was obvious that she was over-powered, and so we hauled the jib a-weather again and lay-to. With the boom eased off she rode the seas buoyantly, and nothing but spray came aboard.

As we lay there, tossed about like a pea in a whistle, we felt particularly sorry for ourselves and the position certainly seemed pretty desperate. We did not know what to do. I knew that the boat would not handle in that heavy sea under a close-reefed mainsail, yet she was over-canvassed as she was, and we did not fancy running back after our previous experience of running in a heavy sea. *Norah Creina* was miles ahead, almost out of sight, and we wondered how she was faring. She seemed to be working along the shore near Clacton and was probably finding smoother water – at least I hoped so, for in any case my brother must have been having a very juicy trip.

Having had but little breakfast we were now ravenously hungry and so, with some difficulty, cut hunks of bread and cheese, which we devoured in the well. The weather fortunately did not seem to be getting any worse and so we hoped it might get better. And sure enough it did, for 'the Lord tempered the wind to the shorn lamb'; or, to put it in less poetic language, Providence looked after a couple of young fools. After being hove-to for nearly two hours, we were able cautiously to resume our journey. But owing to the delay we had wasted much valuable fair tide and it was evident that our passage would be a long one. We made a board in towards the shore, where we found smoother water, and all the time the wind was taking off. Presently we were able to shake out a reef and soon after set the whole mainsail and working jib. We lost the flood tide off Clacton and then, having the ebb to contend with, began to work the shore in short boards, taking frequent soundings. In this way we were able, with our light draught, to stand in so close that we found ourselves mixed up with the bathers, our unexpected appearance leading to several bathing-machine doors being hastily and violently slammed.

The wind had now fallen very light and progress was painfully slow, but we crawled along until about a mile short of Colne Point, when the wind dying away altogether, we had to anchor. This seemed a favourable opportunity for another meal, but on opening a tin of sardines that we had bought at Pin Mill we found they were bad and the butter was also rancid. So our meal consisted of dry bread and jam, as we had nothing else.

It was nearly low water before a light air enabled us to get under way again. We had only made three short boards when we struck some submerged piles and bumped heavily four or five times on them. As soon as we had got clear, we dropped the anchor and pulled up the floor-boards to investigate the extent of the damage, if any. We were glad to find that she was apparently making no water and came to the conclusion that *Wave* must be jolly strong, as we had bumped really hard. At the same time the parrel line had parted and a shower of wooden balls fallen on deck. We managed to grab three of them, but the rest were lost overboard. Having fitted a new parrel, we made another start and, as the young flood was now making, *Wave* at last got into the Colne. We crossed the Bar with barely a foot of water under our keel and seemed to be sailing over a sort of marine garden, so luxuriant was the growth of sea-weed of all kinds and colours. There were also many 'five-fingers' and crabs, which Ernest tried to stab with the boathook.

Having got into the river our troubles were over, for with the aid of the flood tide and a light breeze we soon sailed up to Brightlingsea. As we sailed into the creek, the skipper of a barge, which had passed us in Harwich Harbour, sung out, "You've 'ad a tidy bit of sailin' to-day, ain't you, mate?" And we readily agreed that we had – sixteen hours of it and no food worth mentioning. As soon as we had anchored and stowed away, we went ashore and hastened to the Swan hotel for a much-needed meal and there found my brother, who had just finished dinner. He also had had a good 'dusting,' and although he had covered up the cockpit of *Norah Creina* until there was only just room for his legs, the water was over the floor and his gear all awash before he reached Brightlingsea.

After this very unpleasant passage from Pin Mill, the clerk of the weather turned over a new leaf and it was gloriously fine for the remainder of my holiday. It was, indeed, the sort of sailing weather which we dream of and so seldom get. Brilliant sunshine all day long and a nice sailing breeze after the early morning. And every day it came from the same quarter, the south-east, which is ideal on our coast. We spent a couple of days sailing about the Blackwater and then had a nice trip back to the Crouch. *Norah Creina* remained at Burnham, as my brother was going up to Town, but *Wave* sailed on to Fambridge and picked up her mooring.

The rest of my holiday was spent in the Crouch and Roach, and one day I sailed right up the Broomhill River, as the upper part of the Roach is called, on the tide to Stambridge Mills, near Rochford. Above Paglesham there seemed to be withies all over the place and, not understanding what they indicated, I ran ashore more than once. The only other incident worthy of note that I find in the log was the capture of a huge fish at Fambridge. There was nothing heroic about it, as we found it stranded on the mud, the deed being done with the aid of a large meathook on the end of a rope. I was told that it was a 'devil fish,' or 'sea devil,' the local cognoscenti arguing hotly as to which was the correct name. It measured 4ft. 6in. long by 2ft. 9in. in breadth and weighed over a hundredweight. It was a horrid-looking brute with an enormous mouth and some of the 'natives' who ate part of its tail declared that it tasted very like a pork chop.

This first cruise in *Wave* led me to the conclusion that she was quite unsuitable for sea work in her present state, and I determined to have waterways and coamings fitted to the well as soon as I could afford it. Barring that trait of shipping water aft, she sailed very well, but for the next year or so I confined my activities to the Crouch, with an occasional dash round to the Blackwater when the weather was fine ❧

Part IV: EQUIPMENT

CHAPTER 21: *Hollow Spars*

Although hollow masts and spars have been extensively used in racing yachts for a good many years, it is only comparatively recently that they have been employed in cruising craft. Anything that tends to save weight aloft is of course beneficial, but for a long time owners of cruising yachts were inclined to look askance at such spars, regarding them as unreliable and very expensive. Since those days, however, the manufacture of hollow spars has been vastly improved and, being now as reliable as solid ones, the prejudice that was felt against them has ceased to exist.

There is nothing particularly novel about hollow masts, for they were first introduced in this country as long ago as 1870, when *Cambria*, the first challenger for the America's Cup, was equipped with them. And such masts were used in America twenty years before that date. The big sloop *Maria*, which was employed as a trial vessel for the America before the latter was sent on her triumphant visit to this country, had a hollow mast.

There are two kinds of hollow mast in common use, that which is known as a 'dug-out' and the McGruer. In the former, a solid spar is split from end to end and, after the middle has been scooped out, the two halves are glued together with a special waterproof glue. The McGruer is made on quite a different principle, being in effect a wooden tube. The wood used is Pacific Coast spruce, which is particularly suitable for the purpose on account of its clearness and even growth. Boards of any thickness between 0.1 inch and 0.4 inch are bent breadthwise, the edges being made to meet in a scarf joint and stuck together with a thoroughly waterproof glue known as 'Certus'. One or more layers may be used, the glue being employed between the layers as well as at the joint. Only wood that is quite free from knots and swirls is used and the fibres must all lie parallel with the length. The result is a spar that is very light, strong and in

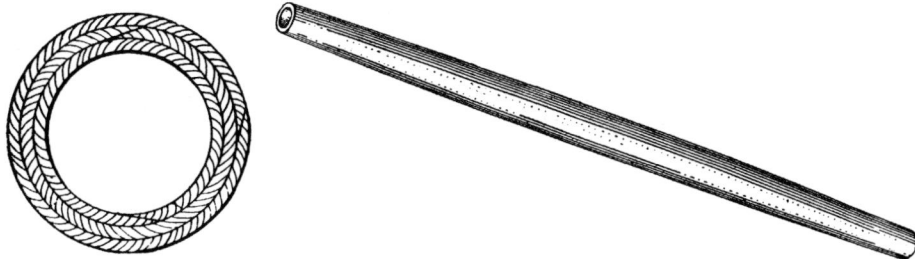

McGruer hollow spar

every way reliable. One of the advantages of the McGruer type of spar is that any form of straight or curved taper can be obtained, whether the cross-section be circular, oval or pear-shaped. Another feature is that the continuous radial grain prevents shakes or sun-cracks, and it is immune from splintering.

To clear up several points that occurred to me, I some years ago put three questions to the McGruer Hollow Spar Co., and as the replies are both interesting and instructive, I cannot do better than quote them *in extenso*:

Question 1: "What percentage of the diameter should the wall be in the case of mast, boom, gaff, and topsail yard respectively for an average 5-ton cruising yacht?"

Answer: "For McGruer construction this figure is 15 per cent, or one-seventh, which should be taken at the maximum diameter. The walls of hollow spars are generally kept about the same thickness throughout the length of the spar, but in specially designed spars the walls may taper at the ends as the spar decreases in diameter, although the thickness is usually greater in proportion to the diameter there than it is at the middle. For 'dug-out' construction the thickness should be not less than one-sixth of the diameter, and one-fifth is a safe figure. In McGruer construction a spar of a given diameter and wall thickness, formed with four layers, will *ceteris paribus* be stronger than one formed with only three layers. The layer system thus gives great latitude in the designing of spars to meet varying conditions."

Question 2: "Is the McGruer spar as strong as a solid spar of similar diameter; if not, how much would the diameter have to be increased to obtain equal strength?"

Answer: "A McGruer or dug-out hollow spar is not as strong as a solid spar of similar diameter and of same material. To obtain the same strength the hollow spar would require to be approximately one-fifth greater in diameter. In the case of a mast, however, the saving in weight is greater, which will be explained in the answer to question 3 on weights."

Question 3: "What are the comparative weights of a McGruer spar, a dug-out hollow spar, and a solid spar?"

Answer: "The average saving of weight in a hollow spar of the kind under review is 45 per cent. The McGruer spar is very slightly heavier than a dug-out when the diameter and wall thickness are exactly the same. This is due to the fact that the McGruer absorbs more glue and the wall is of greater density owing to the pressure to which the timber is subjected during manufacture. For ordinary calculations both may be taken at the same weight. To get a comparison, take the mast of a 5-ton yacht as specified. For actual strength of material a mast (of silver spruce) would only require to be about 4 inches diameter if solid, but at that diameter it would be too whippy and would need extra staying. The diameter of the solid mast for such a vessel is therefore usually from 4½ inches to 5 inches. Now, when a hollow mast is used, the diameter need only be one-fifth greater than the 4-inch solid measurement; but as it is customary to employ a 4½-inch or 5-inch solid spar, the actual increase in diameter is only one-sixth to one-seventh.

"McGruer hollow spars are reinforced at all places where there is a crushing strain or where bands are fitted. Such reinforcement is effected by means of solids and sleeves made of silver spruce which are accurately fitted inside the walls. It may be noted than an internal sleeve is better than a solid where there is a crushing strain. In this case the spar tends to go oval without damage to the wall, where an internal solid would prevent the wall giving and the whole strain would be thrown on the wall thickness itself."

I would particularly commend to the attention of owners of Bermudian-rigged yachts these notes on hollow masts and spars, as the advantage of saving as much weight as possible in the top-hamper of a vessel carrying such a lofty rig cannot be overestimated. A hollow boom robs a heavy gybe of half its terrors and is particularly desirable when roller reefing gear is used. In this latter connection it may be remarked that it removes some at least of the difficulties usually experienced with such gears when used in conjunction with a solid spar. Unless the boom be of the same diameter throughout its length the sail will not roll up evenly, and if the spar bends much when the sail is full of wind it cannot be revolved without first bringing the vessel to the wind. As a hollow boom can be of the same diameter throughout and is far stiffer than the average solid spar, it is more efficient than the latter when used with roller reefing gear. When a McGruer boom is to be used for this purpose, a grooved strip of spruce is fitted along it.

Appended is a complete specification of a set of hollow spars for an average 5-ton gaff-rigged cutter used for cruising purposes.

Hollow Mast: 37 feet over all. Maximum diameter, 5½ inches (this at heel and spider band); diameter at the position of jaws, 4¾ inches, and at top shoulder, 3 inches. Walls to be ¾ inch thick, formed with four layers. The spar to be reinforced at the heel, deck, mastband, hounds and head with internal sleeves and solids, the heel and head solids being shouldered over the ends of the walls.

The head solid to be formed into a short pole fitted with truck and sheave. A metal-lined mortice with sheave provided at top shoulder for topsail halyard. A galvanized steel ferrule of lipped type fitted on top shoulder taking chafe of rigging and securely covering ends of layers at joint of head solid; a galvanized steel band over joint of heel solid with ends of layers. Other galvanized steel bands to be of 'divided' type, bolted together and supported with small galvanized steel or hardwood cleats. No through bolts to be used. Approximate weight of mast with internal reinforcements would be 87 lb.

Hollow Boom: 22 feet over all. Parallel diameter 3¼ inches for roller reefing. Walls to be ½ inch thick formed with three layers. Solids fitted at the ends and shouldered over ends of layers; centre holes bored accurately to take spindles of reefing gear; grooved strip fitted for foot-rope of sail. Approximate weight (spar only), 21 lb.

Hollow Gaff: 14 feet over all. Maximum diameter, 3 inches; throat diameter, 2¾ inches; peak diameter, 2¼ inches; walls $7/16$ inch thick, formed with three layers. Metal-lined lacing hole at peak, also sheave for topsail sheet. Approximate weight, 12 lb.

Hollow Topsail Yard: 15 feet over all. Maximum diameter, 2¾ inches; ends, 1¾ inch. Walls to be $3/8$ inch thick, formed of three layers. Metal-lined lacing hole at each end. Approximate weight, 7½ lb.

Hollow Jackyard: 8 feet over all. Maximum diameter, 2⅛ inches; ends, $1^3/8$ inch. Walls $5/16$ inch thick, formed of three layers. Metal-lined lacing holes at ends. Approximate weight, 2½ lb.

Note: Both yards would be reinforced at ends with shouldered solids through which the lacing holes would pass. Solids must always be provided in a hollow spar where through holes are to be made.

All McGruer spars are made of the best selected silver spruce, and are highly finished and varnished before leaving the factory.

As it is essential that hollow masts and spars should be reinforced in the correct places, a sail plan should be supplied to the makers when ordering. The importance of this will be obvious to the reader, for if the spar is not blocked to take the crushing strains where they come, it is pretty certain to collapse. Quite recently a case came under my notice of the owner of a small yacht who bought a second-hand hollow mast and stepped it in his boat, the result being that it broke soon after getting under way. A hollow mast from one yacht should never be stepped in another, unless, of course, both are of the same design and sail plan.

Bamboo is sometimes used in very small yachts in lieu of hollow spars, but it is a poor substitute, as it is apt to split. This trouble can be obviated to a certain extent by whipping the cane between every joint. The whipping should be laid on very tightly, and then varnished. Some users of bamboo spars also drill tiny holes between each joint, as it is thought that splitting is partly caused by the expansion of imprisoned air. As it is almost impossible to procure a bamboo of sufficient stoutness for a cruising yacht's mast, the use of the canes is practically confined to such spars as booms, gaffs and yards.

CHAPTER 22: *Standing Rigging*

The shrouds of a yacht should be of the best plough steel and the splices well turned in. Small craft, up to about 8 tons, if of gaff rig, usually have three shrouds each side, two from the hounds and the other from the masthead, but little 'pocket' cruisers of 2½ or 3 tons sometimes have only two aside, leading from the hounds. If, however, it is proposed to carry a spinnaker, or Genoa jib, I think there should be masthead shrouds to support the pole of the mast.

With the Bermudian rig a more complicated system of staying may be necessary. If the mast is a very tall one, two and sometimes three pairs of cross-trees may be used, augmented by other struts, known as 'parrot perches,' and there may be a permanent backstay from the masthead to the counter, or set up to a bumpkin. This elaborate system of staying is necessary, not only to support the tall mast but also to keep it from bending and thus affecting the set of the sails. Small cruising yachts, however, do not as a rule carry excessively tall masts and one pair of cross-trees and three shrouds aside are adequate. When two pairs of cross-trees are used, the masthead shrouds may be in the form of a diamond, leading from the masthead, over the upper cross-trees and back to the mast at the hounds.

If the yacht has a gaff mainsail and the after shrouds are set up slightly farther aft than usual, runners can be dispensed with, but in Bermudian-rigged craft, I think they are necessary. In small beamy yachts the spread of the shrouds is usually sufficient to support the mast without the assistance of cross-trees, but if the mast is a tall one, they are essential. Steps must be taken to secure the shrouds in the cross-trees, either with wooden pegs or seizings, for if the shroud gets adrift from the cross-tree it can no longer do its work and the mast maybe lost.

Each shroud should have a separate eye. Sometimes the shrouds of small yachts are made in pairs for the sake of neatness and seized at the hounds; but that is bad practice, for if the seizing should happen to carry away both shrouds are placed out of action. I once lost a mast through the seizing giving way.

As the forestay is the sole support of the mast forward it must be a substantial one and well set up. Sometimes it is led through a hole bored through the stemhead in a fore-and-aft direction before being set up, which strikes me as a good plan. In a sloop the forestay, of course, is set up to the bowsprit-end, which, as I think I pointed out in a previous chapter, is the weak part of the sloop rig with a fairly long bowsprit. In a 7-ton sloop I formerly owned, I rigged an inner forestay, set up to the heel of the bowsprit to support the mast in the event of the bowsprit being carried away. Far from being in the way, it served to keep the foresail sheets clear when the yacht was in stays and was useful to hang on to when working on the fore-deck in rough weather.

In these days of short bowsprits, the bobstay can be permanently set up, and it should be a metal rod or of galvanized chain. Many small yachts are fitted with wire bobstays and I cannot imagine anything more unsuitable. As the bobstay is constantly in and out of the water, the wire rope of which it is composed soon rusts and cannot be trusted for longer than a couple of months or so. A chain bobstay, on the other hand, will last for years. It should be shackled direct to the stem and bowsprit-end and be quite taut. If, when fitting it, you get someone to sit on the bowsprit, you will have no difficulty in securing the shackles.

If the yacht has bowsprit shrouds they should be of iron wire, which does not rust so soon as plough steel. As, however, it is not so strong, rather stouter wire should be employed. The bowsprit shrouds can be set up to the bow plates with lanyards, preferably of tarred hemp, although hambro-line will serve very well for the purpose.

If the yacht is a yawl, the mizzen mast should have two shrouds aside to support it. The bumpkin shrouds should be set up to plates fitted midway between the rail and the waterline, so that they will take the strain both horizontally and vertically. They should be of iron wire, as they are often wet.

I think most yachtsmen will agree that runners are an infernal nuisance, but if the mast is a fairly tall one they are indispensable. The most convenient form of runner for a small yacht is that which travels on a rod fitted to the deck. To set up the runner all one has to do is to pull the slide aft by a rope attached to it,

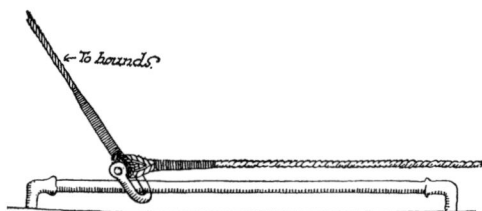

Runner on slide

which takes far less time than setting up a purchase. With a tall Bermudian rig the runners usually have to be tended both when gybing and staying, for if the weather runner is not set up when on a wind, the luff of the jib cannot be kept taut; and if the lee runner is not let go the sail will be girt across it.

Like the shrouds, each runner must have its own eye at the hounds, for my remarks about shrouds put on in pairs applies also to runners. The eyes of all shrouds, stays and runners must be parcelled and served to protect them from wet. The services should be thickly coated with varnish. An alternative method is to cover the eye and splice with leather, or painted canvas. If leather is used, it should be sewn on when wet, as leather stretches when wet and shrinks when dry. The splices at the lower ends should be treated in a similar manner.

Various methods are employed for setting up the rigging. Nowadays rigging screws are frequently used for the purpose and although convenient, I, personally, don't care about them. When a shroud can be set up by merely giving a bottle-screw a turn or two, there is a great temptation to set them up too taut and I am sufficiently old-fashioned to believe that the mast should be allowed to take the initial strain. I am not alone in that belief, for many of the older generation of yachtsmen hold similar views. William Fife – the second of that name – always declared that one of the *Shamrocks* owed her defeat in a contest for the America's Cup mainly to the fact of her being screwed up too much, and another well-known designer, the late G. U. Laws, maintained that the shrouds should be allowed a little play. At one time he crewed for me in a small racing yacht of his design, and when coming on board the first thing he always did was to test the tension of the shrouds to make sure that they were not too taut. And I have read that in the old slave-trading days when a slaver was pursued by a warship, it was the custom to slacken the rigging in order to get the utmost speed out of the vessel.

I know that such views are now considered out-of-date and I am not prepared to say whether there is anything in the theory that slack rigging makes for enhanced speed, but I feel pretty sure that if a yacht's rigging is set up as taut as fiddle-strings an undue strain is thrown on her topsides and mast-step. When I see a yacht that is 'hogged' I always attribute it to this cause and I don't think I am often wrong.

With rigging screws it is almost impossible to get the same tension on both shrouds and one

'U' rigging screw

consequently has to do more than its fair share of work, but with lanyards the rope stretches sufficiently for any difference in tension to adjust itself. Rigging screws, too, are not by any means reliable. When a mast is lost it is seldom due to a broken shroud, but usually to a hidden flaw, or the stripping of the thread, in a rigging screw.

A more reliable form of rigging screw is that in the shape of a letter U. They don't seem to be stocked by yacht-chandlers but are easily made at trifling expense. A length of brass rod of suitable diameter is bent to the required shape and threads put on the ends for the nuts. The cross-bar must be stout and a score made in the middle for the thimble of the shroud to rest in. With rigging screws of this kind nothing is concealed from view; but of course they are more trouble to manipulate, as four nuts have to be operated with the aid of a spanner. If you use rigging screws of the ordinary type, you will be wise to have them of generous size, and the screws should be kept well greased, otherwise they may get set up and you will have trouble in unscrewing them when you come to lay up.

Taking it all round, I think lanyards are safer and there is enough stretch in them to allow the mast to take the first of the strain. For small yachts, up to about 5 tons, dead-eyes are not necessary. If you use small tarred hemp rope, or hambro-line, for the lanyards they are quite easy to set up, but you will have to unreeve most of the lanyard first. In larger craft dead-eyes must be employed and stout tarred hemp for the lanyards. Such a lanyard is easily set up, if well soaped, with the aid of the main halyard. By the way, the lanyard should be spliced round the shroud just above the dead-eye and not secured to the latter with a wall-knot, as they often are. Wall-knots have been known to draw through the dead-eye.

Many yachtsmen say that they don't like rope lanyards as they have to be set up so often, but if they are short they will not need attention oftener than, say, twice in the course of the season. If there is a drift of about 18 inches between shroud and chain-plate, they will, of course, stretch a good deal and require fre-quent setting up, but if the drift is no more than 4 or 5 inches, there is little rope to stretch. Anyhow, it is a job that only takes about ten minutes in a small yacht.

Shackle key

An alternative to rope lanyards is those of thin flexible steel wire, which will not stretch to any ap-preciable extent; but they are not to be recommend-ed, as the tiny wires of which the rope is made soon rust. If you use wire lanyards, they should be renewed every season.

When rigging the yacht, a rope grommet should be fitted round the mast on the hounds for the rig-ging to rest on, in order to reduce the risk of chafe.

If you use the spike on your knife for unscrewing a stubborn shackle-pin you may either bend or break the spike, or, what is worse, jab it into your hand. A shackle key will be found much more serviceable for the purpose. To make one, take a strip of hard brass, or stainless steel, of fairly stout gauge, about 5 inches long. Cut in each end a slot large enough to fit over the pin of the shackle, the slots being of different width so as to accommodate small and large shackle-pins. The slot at one end should be open, so that it can be used for shackles in a rather inaccessible position. Such a key will fit most of the shackles of your running gear and can be carried in your pocket. A small adjustable spanner would also serve the same purpose but as it would have to be adjusted every time, would be more troublesome to use. Another alternative is the top of an old-fashioned latch-key, which would fit most small shackle-pins.

CHAPTER 23: *Running Rigging*

Opinions are by no means unanimous as to the best material for running gear. Most of the old brigade still remain faithful to manila rope, but many of the younger generation, particularly those who have had some experience of racing craft, favour flexible wire rope. Each has its advantages and it is largely a matter of personal preference. I myself use manila for everything except the jib halyard, because it is more pleasant to handle than wire and can easily be repaired in the event of accident. If you carry away a manila halyard, you can repair it with a long splice that will render through the blocks, but if you should happen to break a wire halyard when at sea you will be 'up against it,' as they say, for it is next door to impossible to make a satisfactory temporary repair. As a matter of fact you are not in the least likely to carry away a wire halyard in decent condition, for it is customary to use far stouter wire than is actually necessary to withstand any strain likely to be imposed upon it. The reason for this is that the very small sizes of wire rope are composed of such fine wire that it soon rusts.

The chief objection to manila for halyards is that it stretches and one has occasionally to re-set the sails. When one gets under way in the morning the halyards are often damp with dew and stretch as they dry, and after one has been sailing for a few hours it becomes necessary to take a pull on all the halyards. But that really is not much trouble and, after a good deal of experience with both, I have come to the conclusion that I prefer manila for all but the jib. Other objections to manila halyards are that when new they are apt to kink and when wet are inclined to swell and will not then render freely through the blocks unless the latter are of ample size. All the same, I think they are better for a small yacht, as a much more simple system of purchasing can be adopted and there are fewer ropes round the mast.

Flexible wire halyards do not stretch to any appreciable extent and having set your sails when you get under way, they remain properly set all day without attention. Wire, too, is unaffected by wet and will always render freely through the blocks. For the jib halyard I consider wire essential, even in the smallest boat, as no yacht will sail decently to windward unless the luff of the jib is kept as taut as an iron bar. If you use manila for the purpose you will constantly have to set up the halyard to keep the luff of the sail taut. Particularly is this the case when a small jib is set. The luff of the sail is so short that there must be a considerable drift of halyard and if it is of manila it will stretch so much that it will be almost impossible to keep the luff taut. In such circumstances the only way of satisfactorily overcoming the difficulty is to inset a wire span between the halyard block and the head of the sail.

Yachtsmen sometimes complain that the parts of the jib halyard twist when the sail is set, but this is almost invariably caused by an unsatisfactory halyard arrangement. The two parts of the halyard should be some distance, say 18 inches or 2 feet, apart, and then it is impossible for them to twist together. If the jib halyard has a purchase it can be arranged as shown on the right in the drawing.

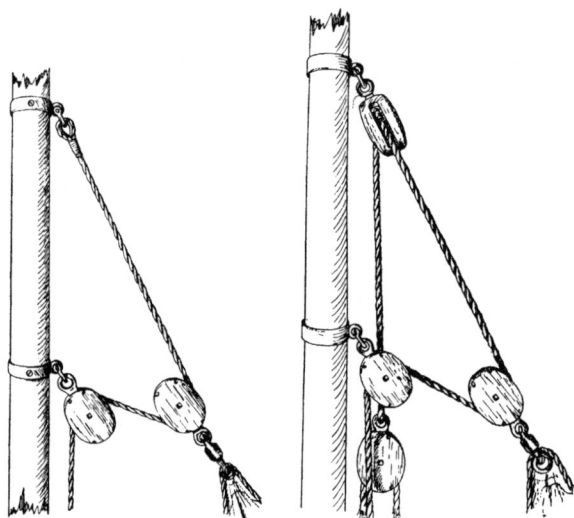

Jib halyard arrangement, without and with purchase

For sheets and purchases either manila or Italian hemp, lightly tarred, is generally used and personally I prefer the latter, as I do not think it so likely to kink; it is said to be rather stronger and is, I believe, much the same price. Some of the racing yachts use flax rope for sheets as it is very supple and enormously strong. You will glean some idea of the great strength of this flax rope when I tell you that its breaking strain is approximately three times that of the best white yacht manila. It is, however, very expensive. Even before the war it cost, I am told, 4s. 6d. per pound, and as the best flax rope was manufactured in Germany from Irish-grown flax, it is not likely to be procurable for some time to come.

As regards cost, I don't think there is much difference between that of manila and wire. The wire rope costs more in the first place, but if properly cared for, has a longer life. Manila halyards cannot be trusted for more than three seasons, while flexible wire rope, if occasionally rubbed over with tallow, should last for five years. I, myself, replace manila halyards after two seasons' use. That may be rather extravagant, but it is a great comfort in heavy weather to know that your running gear is thoroughly sound. Some owners do not even think of renewing their gear until it carries away, but that is a very foolish policy that may lead to serious trouble.

Many small cruisers are over-blocked and, in consequence, their sails do not come down as freely as they should. A gaff mainsail should run down by its own weight when the yacht is head to wind, and if it does not do so, it must be assumed that the blocks are either too small, or in an unsatisfactory condition, or there are too many of them. No more purchase should be employed than is absolutely necessary, for the greater the purchase the longer it takes for the sail to go up or come down. You can only obtain additional power by the sacrifice of speed – you can't have it both ways. The secret of sweetly running gear is the use of large blocks with patent sheaves, adequately lubricated. The blocks for manila rope should be at least one size larger than absolutely necessary and the patent sheaves should be lubricated from time to time.

If you have wire running gear the blocks should be of metal and have large sheaves in order to avoid anything like a sharp nip of the wire. It is important that the sheave should be a good fit in the shell of the block, for if it be a sloppy fit, there will be a risk of the wire rope coming off the sheave and getting jammed between shell and sheave. Should that happen you will be betwixt the devil and the deep sea, as it will be practically impossible to clear it, even if you go aloft. The more you pull the tighter the wire will be jammed and you will find yourself in the awkward predicament of being unable to get the sail either up or down. In such circumstances all you can do is to go aloft, unhook the blocks and get the whole caboodle on deck. Then, if you attack it with a screw-driver and hammer, you may be able to clear it, although the wire is likely to suffer in the process. If you would avoid such misadventures, you will be wise to see that the sheaves of your blocks fit sufficiently well to render it impossible for the halyard to get jammed in this way.

The best blocks for manila gear have internal metal strops, but they are rather expensive. Wire strops, however, serve very well, provided that they are protected from the weather. They can be either covered with leather, sewn on when wet, or they can be parcelled and served, the service being well coated with varnish. If your halyard blocks have ordinary sheaves, I should recommend you to remove them and substitute patent ones; they do not cost very much and make an enormous difference to the efficiency of the running gear.

Many years ago I used a set of very beautiful blocks for wire gear, designed by the late Mr. G. U. Laws. They were known as the Burnham blocks and made of bronze, with patent sheaves. For the sake of lightness the shell was perforated, but they were very strong and the patent sheaves ran very sweetly. I have not seen any of these blocks for a long time and do not know whether they can now be procured.

Below I give a specification of running gear for an average 4-ton cutter with gaff mainsail using manila rope for all halyards except that of the jib, which should be of flexible wire rope. The size of rope is the circumference, as all ropes are thus measured.

RUNNING GEAR FOR 4-TON POLE-MASTED CUTTER

Main Halyard: 1¼-inch rope. Double block on mast and single on gaff.

Peak Halyard: 1¼-inch rope. Single block on mast and single block on gaff, the latter attached to wire sling.

Jib Halyard: Flexible steel wire rope, ⁵⁄₈-inch; single block, with large sheave on mast, and purchase (2 single blocks and 1¼-inch manila rope) on end of wire halyard.

Foresail Halyard: 1¼-inch manila rope. Single block on mast. Luff of sail hanked to the forestay.

Mainsheet: 1¼-inch manila rope. Double block on boom; single block on horse, or attached to an eye-bolt in deck if there is no main horse; and two single quarter-blocks. An alternative, if the yacht has a main horse, would be a double block on boom and a single on the horse, the fall of the sheet being led through a bull's-eye attached to the shackle of the lower block.

Runners: Two single blocks on each. The runners should be of ⁵⁄₈-inch wire rope and the purchases of 1¼-inch manila. If the runners are of the type travelling on rods, there is no purchase, the wire runner being attached direct to the slide. A single part of 1¼-inch manila is attached to the slide for pulling it aft.

Topsail Halyard: 1¼-inch manila rope, led over a patent sheave in masthead.

Topsail Sheet: 1¼-inch manila rope, rove as follows: From the deck, up through a single block on the under side of the gaff near the jaws; then through a sheave at the outer end of gaff, reeving the sheet from beneath the spar, and bringing the end down to the deck again. When not in use the two ends of the sheet should be knotted together, one having first been passed through the lowest mast-hoop. This will keep the sheet from being unrove accidentally.

Topsail Tack: 1¼-inch manila rope. Two single blocks.

Spinnaker Halyard: 1¼-inch manila. One single block stropped to pole of the mast, or if no topsail is carried, over a sheave in the masthead.

Spinnaker Guy: 1¼-inch manila rope, led from end of spinnaker boom, through a single block, or bull's-eye, attached to the runner plate. This lead will prevent the boom skying, particularly if the boom is attached to the mast a foot or two higher than the outer end of the spar.

Spinnaker Sheet: 1¼-inch manila rope.

Topping-lift: 1¼-inch manila rope. Single block at masthead, fitted above that of the peak halyard. If it is fitted below the peak halyard, the mainsail can only be set on one side of the topping-lift, which is a nuisance.

Jib Sheets: 1¼-inch manila rope.

Foresail Sheets: 1¼-inch manila rope.

Signal Halyards: Hambro-line. The ends should be knotted together.

As the tonnage of the yacht is increased and the sails become larger and heavier, more power and stouter rope will be needed. For example, if the yacht were of 7 tons, the halyards would have to be of 1½-inch manila, or even 1¾-inch, and the peak halyard would need a single block on the gaff and two singles on the mast; the standing part of the halyard would be shackled to the gaff and the middle block of the purchase attached to a wire sling on the gaff. The jib halyard purchase would need a double block and a single, and the foresail halyard two single blocks.

In little miniature cruisers of less than 4 tons, however, the size of rope for halyards and sheets should not be decreased, as 1¼-inch manila is the smallest size that can be handled with any degree of comfort. Two single blocks would suffice for the main halyard and 1-inch rope would serve for the purchase. Many of these little 'pocket' cruisers have sheets of 1-inch manila, but one cannot get a good grip on rope as small as that and it is better to use 1¼-inch. It is not extravagant, as the larger rope will last longer.

The size of rope and number of blocks I recommend must only be regarded as approximate, as they are based on the requirements of an average cruising yacht. It is not the size of the vessel that has to be considered but the strain that is imposed upon the gear, and if the yacht has a very large sail area she will need stouter gear and more power. In making the above suggestions I have assumed that only the best quality rope will be used and it will be discarded before it becomes untrustworthy.

I give below a table of sizes of wire suitable for the gear of small cruising yachts of various size, but as much depends upon the area of the sails and the power of the vessel, they must only be regarded as approximate.

APPROXIMATE SIZES OF FLEXIBLE STEEL WIRE FOR RUNNING GEAR

	3- to 4-ton Sloop	5-ton Cutter	7-ton Cutter	10- to 12-ton Cutter
	inch	inch	inch	inch
Main halyard	5/8 (1 part)	3/4 (1 part)	3/4 (1 part)	7/8
Peak halyard	5/8 (1 part)	5/8 (1 part)	5/8 (2 part)	3/4 (2 part)
Jib halyard	5/8 (1 part)	5/8 (1 part)	5/8 (2 part)	3/4 (2 part)
Foresail halyard (hanked to stay)	5/8	5/8	5/8	5/8
Topsail halyard	5/8	5/8	5/8	3/4
Topsail sheet	1/2	1/2	1/2	5/8

The sizes indicated are, of course, the circumference of the rope.

The purchase is usually attached to the end of the wire, and so arranged that when the sail is set the blocks are as close together as practicable, as the less manila there is in operation the less there is to stretch. When a two-part wire halyard is employed, the arrangement is as follows: The purchase is attached to one end of the wire and a manila downhaul to an eye in the other end. When setting the sail this eye is hauled down and hooked to a strong hook in the deck. The sail will then be more than half-way up and the rest of the work is done by hauling on the purchase. When lowering the sail the purchase should always be let go first, as it will not then be necessary to overhaul it when next setting the sail.

With a Bermudian sail there is of course only one halyard, which in small yachts usually is of wire with a purchase on the end. In larger craft the wire halyard may wind on the drum of a winch at the foot of the mast, in which case there is no purchase. Still another method is to purchase the tack instead of the halyard. The sail is hoisted to the masthead and then the luff is hauled taut by means of a purchase on the gooseneck fitting, which slides on a short metal rod attached to the mast. An advantage of this method is that there is no purchase block aloft to foul the cross-trees when the sail is lowered, and as the rod is secured to the mast by two metal bands, the thrusting strain of the boom is distributed.

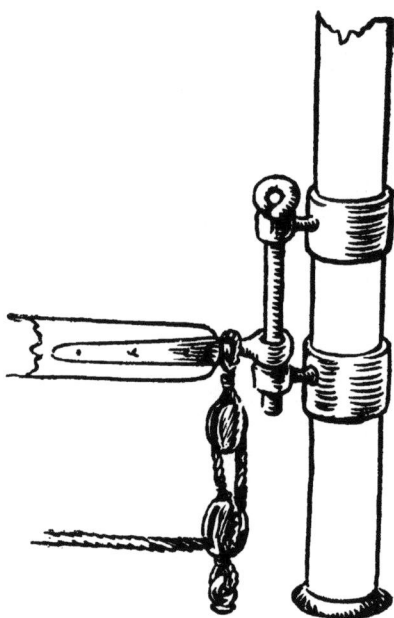

Bermudian tack purchase

If the fullest benefit is to be derived from the use of wire halyards, the blocks of the purchase should be as close together as practicable when the sail is set. If there is a wide gap between them, the manila rope of the purchase will stretch and the tautness of the halyard be impaired. Now, it is the usual practice for the fall of a purchase to lead from the upper block and some yachtsmen maintain that it is essential that it should do so. But that is all bunk. If the purchase blocks of a wire halyard are only a few inches apart when the sail is set, as they should be, how the deuce are you to put any power on the purchase if the fall leads from the upper block? If you are to get any power on the fall by pulling down, the block must be above your head, and that would entail a long drift of manila which would stretch and thus defeat your object in using wire gear. The obvious thing is to reverse the usual method and arrange the purchase so that the fall, or hauling part, leads up from the lower block. When pulling up from the deck you can use all the strength of your legs, arms and back and get far more power than you possibly could by hauling down.

Reefing a Bermudian mainsail, of course, would bring more manila rope into operation, but even so the drift between the blocks of the purchase would not be excessive; and it must be remembered that the greater part of one's sailing is done under a whole mainsail. These remarks also apply to a wire jib halyard, but in that case there never need be more than a few inches drift between the blocks of the purchase, even when you set a smaller jib. The luff of

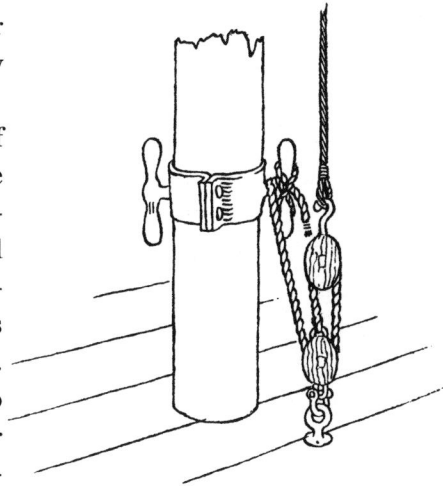

Bermudian wire halyard purchase

the smaller sail is, of course, shorter than that of the working jib, but a wire span can be inserted between the head of the sail and the halyard to make it equivalent to the larger jib. The span can either be shackled to the sail or spliced direct into the cringle, preferably the latter as it makes for a neater job. When led from the lower block, the fall of the purchase can be conveniently belayed to one of the belaying pins on the mast.

In my own boat the jib halyard is merely a length of flexible steel wire rope, led through a block at the masthead, with a thimble spliced into each end. As when one end is on deck the other is aloft, it is necessary to attach a downhaul to the latter. When setting the sail I haul it up by pulling on the down-haul until I can shackle on the purchase, and then purchase it until the luff is bar-taut. Finally I remove the downhaul, which is attached to the halyard with a spring hook, and stow it away. There is then nothing left to clutter up the foot of the mast but a few feet of the purchase fall. Before lowering the sail, the down-haul must of course be hooked on to the end of the halyard, for otherwise the latter would go aloft like the late Tom Bowling.

Earlier I referred to a form of sliding runner much used in small racing yachts but seldom employed in cruising craft. As it is a very handy contrivance a little further explanation may be desir-

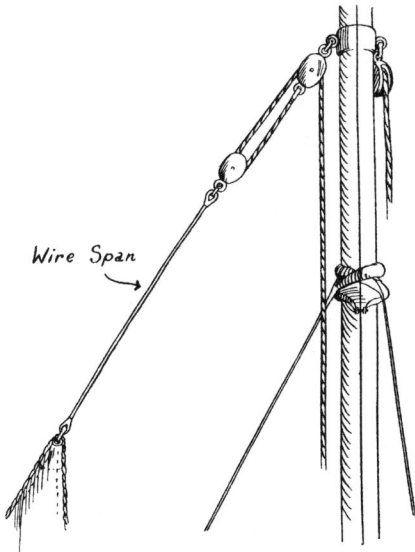

Wire Span

Wire span at head of small jib

able. A strong metal rod is fitted on the covering board on either side, extending from near the after shroud to the usual position of the runner plate. The runner consists merely of a wire stay attached to a shackle, which is free to travel on the rod. A short rope is spliced round the foot of the runner, between the thimble and the shackle, by which the traveller can be hauled aft, and the length of the runner is such that it is fully stretched when the traveller is a foot or so from the after end of the rod. To set up the runner, all that one has to do is to pull the traveller aft, until it will come no farther, and make fast the line. By this method the runner can be set up taut without the employment of any purchase. When the mainsail is gybed, the runner line is released and as the boom comes over, it carries the runner forward with it. This kind of runner, although extremely simple, strikes me as more efficient than the usual purchase which, unless overhauled, often hinders the boom from going forward sufficiently. It also enables one to dispense with four blocks (two on each runner).

If you want to try this type of runner without going to the expense of having rods fitted, I think that spans of wire rope would serve the purpose equally well and they could be shackled to the after shroud plates and the runner plates. The spans would have to be set up as taut as possible and the runners, of course, cut to just the right length, so that they became taut before the traveller was at the end of the wire span.

The form of mainsheet employed must depend a good deal upon the type of yacht. If the boat has a counter, a double-ended mainsheet leading through quarter-blocks can be used, and it is certainly an advantage being able to work either end. One cannot lay down any hard and fast rule as to the amount of purchase required, as it will depend upon the area of the mainsail and weight of the boom. For most yachts of from 5 to 10 tons, canvassed for single-handed work, a double block on the boom, and a single in the centre of the counter, or travelling on a short horse, will give ample power if the ends of the sheet are led through quarter-blocks. For yachts of less than 5 tons so much power will not be necessary and a single block can be substituted for the double one on the boom. With only a single block on the boom, however, a double-ended mainsheet will not be practicable, and the best method is to secure the standing part of the sheet to the upper block, and lead the fall through a bull's-eye fairlead stropped to the becket of the lower block. This will give a neat lead, and enable one to put plenty of power on to the sheet when hauling in the boom.

Many small yachts, particularly those with transom sterns, are fitted with a main horse, but the lead of the sheet is apt to impede the movement of the tiller, unless the fall is made fast with a hitch round the other parts of the sheet, which is rather inconvenient. In a yacht with a canoe stern, the arrangement of the mainsheet is usually a matter of some difficulty. Neither a horse nor quarter-blocks are quite satisfactory, as either will impede the action of the tiller and prevent the helm from being put over as far as it should be. In my 7-tonner

Seabird I got over the difficulty by the use of an oval-shaped iron hoop bolted to the sternpost. The tiller worked inside of this hoop, which, being within a few inches of the rudderhead, allowed plenty of play for the tiller. In effect it was a miniature horse, the lower main-sheet block having about a foot of travel ere it was pulled up by an iron collar shrunk on to the hoop in such a position as to prevent the block traveller from getting foul. This fitting, I admit, was rather unsightly, but eminently practical. In my little canoe-yacht *Snipe* there was a main horse just abaft the well coaming which answered fairly well, but as the horse restricted the movements of the tiller the boat required a good deal of water in which to come round.

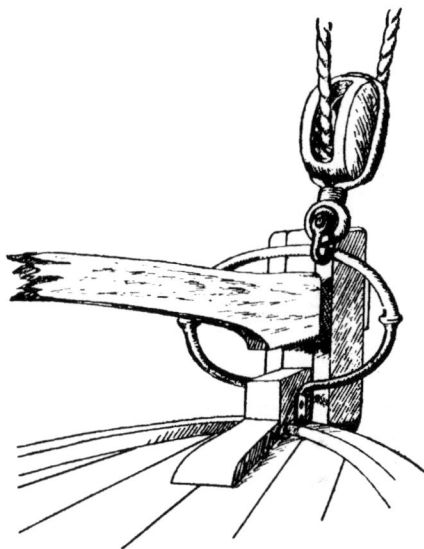

And now I want to say a few words about the lead of headsail sheets. In many small yachts, indeed, in most, the cleats for the headsail sheets are fitted either on deck or on the outside of the

Mainsheet horse on *Seabird*

cockpit coamings, in which position it is impossible to put much power on to the sheets; and when the vessel is in stays the sheets are often dragged forward as far as the fairleads and are out of reach. That entails climbing on deck to re-cover them. Now, if the sheets are led through holes in the coamings and belayed inside, you will be able to put all your weight on them, and if the ends are knotted, as they should be, it will be impossible for them to get adrift. And if you use wooden jam cleats, such as I shall describe later, you can belay the sheet with a single turn. The difference this makes to easy handling cannot be realized until you have tried it.

Of course, if you have one of those silly little self-draining cockpits like a foot-bath, you cannot lead the sheets inside, but with a cockpit of reasonable depth it is a great convenience to have them where you can put your weight on them and where they are always ready to hand.

The holes in the coaming should be of ample size and bored straight through, not at an angle. When my present boat was built, the builder, with a view to obtaining a fairer lead for the sheets, drilled the holes through the coamings at a sharp angle, and although the idea was correct in theory, it did not pan out well in practice, as the wood was so thin at the edges that it soon began to break away. If the holes are bored at right-angles to the coaming and of sufficient size, the sheets will render quite freely. For 1¼-inch (circumference) rope, the holes should be, say, of ¾-inch diameter.

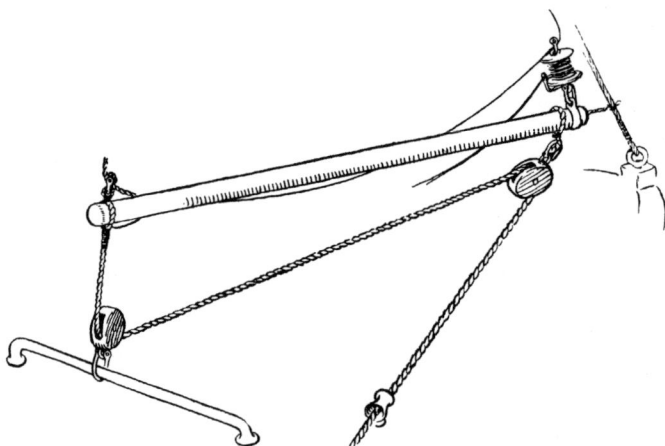

Boom foresail sheet lead

When I bought the 7-ton *Fancy*, she had two-part sheets on both jib and foresail and they were belayed on deck. I told the late owner that the first thing I should do would be to scrap the two-part sheets, which were always getting foul, and substitute single-part ones, led through the coamings and belayed inside. He replied that if I did so I should never be able to handle the sails, but being a pig-headed sort of cove I put my ideas into practice. The result was a revelation. The single sheets never fouled, were quite easy to handle and in light winds I no longer had to go forward to overhaul the weather sheet after going about. When hauling my wind I certainly found the foresail a bit of a handful, but could always get it in by giving the boat a 'shake-up.' Two-part sheets are an infernal nuisance. They foul everything it is possible for them to foul when in stays, and in light winds the friction is too great for the weather sheet to clear

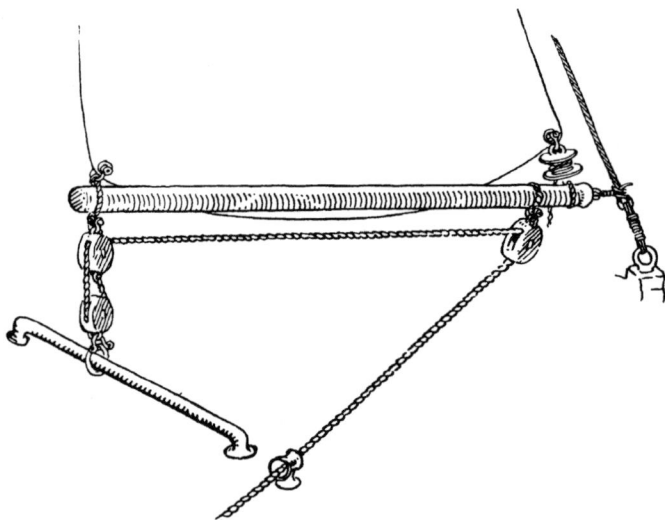

Boom foresail sheet lead — alternative

Wave (top left) and *Snipe*

PLATE 1: Wave and Snipe

Clockwise from top: *Granuaile*
(by Doyle), *Corbie, Marie Michon,
Nola* (RCYC Seabird conversion).

Marie Michon was sold to an
owner in Northern Ireland and
was lost when she parted her
mooring in a gale and drove
ashore, in the 1940's

PLATE 2: Granuaile, Corbie, Marie Michon, Nola

Falmouth Quay Punt *Fancy*,
Iolanthe in the 1930s,
Iolanthe in 2001 following a refit by
Nick Gates including new teak toerails
and rubbing strakes, replacing the
top 3in of rotten stem, repairs to the
forehatch and paint and varnishwork
nickgates.co.uk

PLATE 3: Fancy and Iolanthe

Mercia III by G. U. Laws, built 1903, was discovered languishing in a boatyard in 1988 by her present two owners, based in the North of England. They write: Over the years we have replaced all 64 steamed oak ribs, made a new stem post and fitted a new enlarged stern post and horn timber (to take the prop shaft as she was not originally designed to have an engine). All new deck beams with the addition of a sailing beam, the top two hull planks and a sub deck fitted, the coach roof and companionway and hatch fitted to the coach roof. A redesigned self draining cockpit, in keeping with the original lay out, and several new floors fore and aft were fitted. Keel bolts were replaced. The keelson had so much rot in the stern post joint we had to graft in a new after end. The hull planks are of New Zealand Kauri pine and 90% have survived. We were fortunate to find a supply of Kauri Pine to complete repairs from wine vats which were dismantled in the late 1990s at Kingston on Thames where she was originally built. (Kauri pine is now a protected species). Every copper and bronze fixing has been replaced. A new rudder has been made and fitted. She still needs her new deck covering - this is intended to be teak laid planks on the 10mm sub. The caulking has been paid up, ports fitted and she will then be ready to be dipped in for her first sea trials. Then she will return back to the yard to fit the topside sailing gear, mast and rigging.

PLATE 4: Mercia III

Dawn II by G. U. Laws, built 1906, has been in her owner's family for fifteen years and is undergoing restoration in the South of England. He writes: A lot of the stern planks, ribs and structure were replaced. Unfortunately due to work and time constraints she was put on hold for a good 10 years. This is where I stepped in and was offered the project by my father. Unfortunately roughly 80% of the deck planks and deck beams had become structurally unsound so the first job was to remove every plank one by one to reveal the beams. (I didn't find out that the beams were beyond repair until they were revealed!) I have now replaced every deck beam. Originally larch now they are all laminated oak. As with the deck the doghouse was also beyond repair so I'm currently fabricating a new coach roof using as much of the same joint techniques as possible and getting through a massive amount of mahogany in the process.

Nereid II by G. U. Laws, built 1913, was spotted as an available 'project' on the Albert Strange Association website by a French boatbuilder then working in the U.S. A year later she was still at Maldon, Essex and in need of restoration when he returned to France, and 'roped in' his brother to share the task. Today she has a purpose-built shed in Brittany and work is about to start. He writes: We already gathered some oak from Jura (couldn't find rock elm) for her backbone. I also found a nice log of teak 24 feet long for a new deck. Everything is to be rebuilt except the teak planking and a really few pieces. So we will reframe her, change the keel, the forefoot, stem. The stern has been rebuilt so we might keep that also it will be nice to have a real engine inboard and not a side shaft like she had. I believe she had an engine installed in 1925 (one cylinder internal combustion), then another one, two cylinder paraffin in 1930. That would explain why her ballast has been cut aft, which isn't the way it looks on the original plans of 1913, with a full length ballast keel. Otherwise we will change all the remains of steel floor timbers. The cabin will be redone like she was originally, with round portholes (Now they are square). The idea is to do a rebuild as close as the original as possible with the same techniques.

PLATE 5: Dawn II and Neried II

Lona II by J. Pain Clark, built 1905, spent many years in the South of England, where she was a familiar face with the Old Gaffers, before being sold to an Italian enthusiast in 2006, who undertook the latest of a number of restorations, bringing her rig back to the original designed specification and, it seems, excellent balance. She is now active on the Italian classic racing scene.

PLATE 6: Lona II

Lona III, built 1906, spent some years ashore in the U.K. before being rescued in 2010 and shipped to Belgium, where she is undergoing restoration.

This boat, photographed by the editor in 2005 on the East Coast of England, appears to be Pain Clark's *Lona IV*, built 1907, or a sister, now with Bermudian rig and possibly another name. Efforts to track her down have been unsuccessful.

PLATE 7: Lona III and Lona IV

Lady Belle by Archie Watty, built 1910, saw service with the Sea Scouts in the 1960s and was lived aboard on the Hamble in the 1970s. She was acquired as a near wreck by her present owner in 2003,. He writes: She had been neglected for several years and could barely float from Polruan to Fowey for loading on to the lorry. The centreline (including the elm keel) had to be replaced. She had a new deck, rigging, sails and engine over a three year period. We have only raced her occasionally, but she has clocked up two seconds in class IIA in the Solent race - once in light winds, and last year in 30-35 knots (when we lost some time at one point because I got the course wrong!). In OGA terms she is acknowledged to be competitive. She won a Channel Race (small class) in heavy weather in 1936.

PLATE 8: *Lady Belle*

Redwing, formerly Albert Strange's own *Cherub III*, was built for the west of Scotland, and there she lives today. Her owner writes: Three pictures from a gentle weekend's cruise to Oronsay, as in Colonsay, in 2006. The first has Islay in the background and the second has Jura. The third illustrates the tail of the Corryvrechan on a calm day. *Redwing* is currently undergoing an overhaul as she is showing signs of her age. Stripped right down as I write, the cause has been identified as metal rotting the feet of the 8 frames attached to the iron floor straps. Otherwise, apart from needing a new stern tube and rudder column reinforcement, she is as sound as a bell and will be fit again soon for another century. Ed Burnett is on the case giving good advice on how to replace the floor straps in wood to add new and extra strength to the hull/keel with minimum metallic interference. The last cruise we had in her was the year before last, circumnavigating Skye via the coastline, and islands facing Skye.

PLATE 9: Redwing, ex-Cherub III

The design of *Venture* was conceived by H.J. Suffling and executed, apart from accommodation and coachroof, by Albert Strange, who died in 1917 with her still on his drawing board. The Suffling brothers completed the design and had her built in 1920, and she proved a very successful and well-balanced cruiser. She was meticulously restored by Jamie Clay and Jim Maynard in Essex and relaunched in 2005. She is pictured here by Den Phillips on her trial sail with her new owner on the River Blackwater. She now lives on the west coast of Scotland. *www.denphillipsphotos.co.uk*

PLATE 10: Venture

The Sufflings scaled *Venture* up to 33ft (*Charm*, top, 1921) then 40ft (*Charm II*, Centre, 1922) before concluding that 33ft was the perfect size for two-person cruising, and building *Sea Harmony* in 1937. After many years in need of care, *Charm* was acquired and restored, being relaunched in 2005, and lives on the East Coast of England. *Charm II* is being restored in Spain. *Sea Harmony* was sailed to the U.S. in the 1970s and since 1999 has lived in Massachusetts in the care of a boatbuilder.

PLATE 11: Venture family

Fidelis by F.J. Welch, built c1930, lives in the south-west of England. Her owner has written: It is some time since I read my collection of books by Francis Cooke and I had forgotten how fully *Fidelis* is described in *Small Yacht Cruising* (pp42-45). All the information there is correct and I would only add that in her design Mr. Welch and his brother were much influenced by the West Solent Restricted Class, but they gave *Fidelis* a greater beam and a counter of reduced length to improve her at sea. Many of her original drawings survive, having been passed down through successive owners.

As Francis Cooke says, it is claimed that *Fidelis* was the first yacht to be designed to Admiral Turner's 'metacentric shelf' principle, which is intended to ensure a balanced helm whatever the angle of heel. Mr. Welch wrote two articles about this for *Yachting Monthly* in November 1933 and February 1934. Whether it is due to Admiral Turner, or for some other reason, *Fidelis* exhibits near perfect balance when sailing. If we need more than two fingers on the tiller, we know we have something wrong with our sail trim!

Frank Welch kept *Fidelis* all his life and took her wherever he went. Later in life he wrote an account of *Fidelis* and his sailing in her, which was privately printed. Mr. Welch moved from Glasgow to Essex in 1935 and *Fidelis* was kept at Burnham-on-Crouch. In 1937 he changed the rig from a gaff cutter (as she had been built) to a bermudian cutter, retaining the bowsprit. He fitted a boomed staysail and later adopted a seven-eighths rig and this is how we have restored her. Mr. Welch envisaged the possibility of having a bermudian rig at the design stage and so the change was made without altering the position of the mast.

In 1962 Mr. Welch moved, with *Fidelis*, to the Isle of Wight and took up a serious interest in racing. Rather sadly from the traditional point of view, he disposed of the wooden spars and converted her to a sloop with a single large foresail, aluminium mast and boom. In photos of her at that time her rig looks most incongruous on her beautiful hull. However, Mr. Welch was highly successful racing her in this form in the Round the Island races during the 1960s and 70s.

Frank Welch died, I believe, in 1976 and *Fidelis* remained with the family until 1980. My wife and I bought her in 1989, there being two other owners between the Welch family and ourselves. We undertook a complete restoration including refastening, the fitting of new grown oak floors and new wooden spars. She now has her cutter rig, bowsprit and boomed staysail back again and is as she was in the late 1930s.

In *Small Yacht Cruising*, Francis Cooke includes an account by Mr. Welch of some of Fidelis's fittings. We have reinstated many of these and I would mention, in particular, 'F.B. Cooke's chain stopper'. Cooke refers to this himself as a 'chain-grip' in his book *Hints, Tips and Gadgets* (pp60-61). The fitting we have on *Fidelis* is rather more sophisticated than that shown by Cooke, in that it is an integral part of the inner forestay deck fitting, the whole being made as a casting. It is positioned just inboard from the stemhead and the chain is simply locked in the slot and secured with a pin. Bringing the chain aboard and casting could not be easier. There is no hauling across the deck to get it over, or off, a cleat. Of all *Fidelis*'s special fittings, this is undoubtedly the best.

PLATE 13: Fidelis

Vindilis by T. Harrison Butler, built 1935, lives in western Scotland and recently underwent a structural overhaul with boatbuilders A & R Way. Adam Way writes: The main body of the work was reframing, with up to 70% of the steamed oak timbers replaced. All other fastenings were replaced: Garboards, hood ends, etc., and all keel bolts and structural fastenings through the deadwood and stem. New bronze floors were cast, and all steel hanging knees were removed, inspected and re-galvanised. The cockpit was converted to be self-draining (while remaining satisfyingly deep) and was rebuilt using the original teak. All caulking, fairing, painting and brightwork was restored to a high standard. *www.aandrwayboatbuilding.co.uk*

Her owner writes of *Driac II* (opposite): *Driac II* first came in to my life on a cold winter's morning in February 1999. I travelled the long road up to Ardfern, a beautiful marina nestled in the heart of the west coast of Scotland. . . . I asked David the yard owner if he had any other boats available to view and he led me to the other side of the yard where she stood, *Driac II* back home from 10 years in the Caribbean under the careful ownership of Gary Brown who nursed her back across the Atlantic (see *Yachting Monthly* Aug. 1997). She spent another 2 years under new ownership and eventually she was hauled onto the hard standing after nearly sinking on her mooring, and at hearing that most people would have walked away, but I always have been up for a challenge. She looked magnificent in her full standing rig and standing aboard her with the sea as a back drop I could imagine her every roll, her every pitch and every response to the squalls as they came across the loch towards us, and at that point I was hooked, she had me like a fish in the bottom of the boat taking its last breath. The owner would sell to recover yard costs and so I had myself a beautiful classic at a fair price. It was only in the coming months would I find out her true history and what a famous little boat she actually was.

Driac II was recently relaunched following a substantial rebuild by Patterson Boatworks at Hawkshead in the English Lake District. She has a 28hp Beta Marine engine, and at the time of writing awaits finishing of her interior. *www.pattersonboatworks.co.uk*

PLATE 14: Vindilis and Driac II

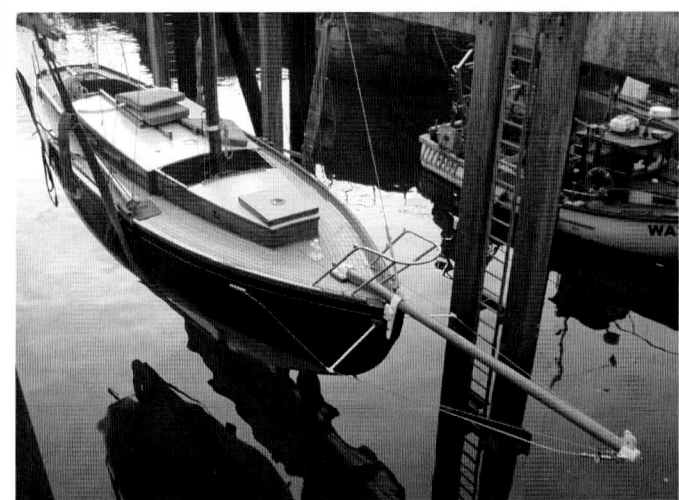

PLATE 15: Driac II

Aged 4 c1876

Aged 34 in 1906,
with Kathleen

FRANCIS B. COOKE

1872 - 1974

Aged 90, c1962

Probably c1950,
with wife Alice

PLATE 16: Francis B. Cooke

itself when the yacht goes about. That means that you have to go forward and overhaul it every time. You know what I mean by a two-part sheet, don't you? The end is shackled to an eye-bolt in the deck and then the sheet is led through a bull's-eye, or block, on the clew of the sail; then through a fairlead, and so aft to the cockpit, or thereabouts. It is true that you have a sort of whip purchase on the sheet, but the friction is so great that you don't derive very much benefit from it.

In many yachts nowadays the foresail is fitted with a light boom, and the sheet travelling on a horse looks after itself when the vessel goes about. In a small yacht the best lead for the fore-

Boom foresail without horse

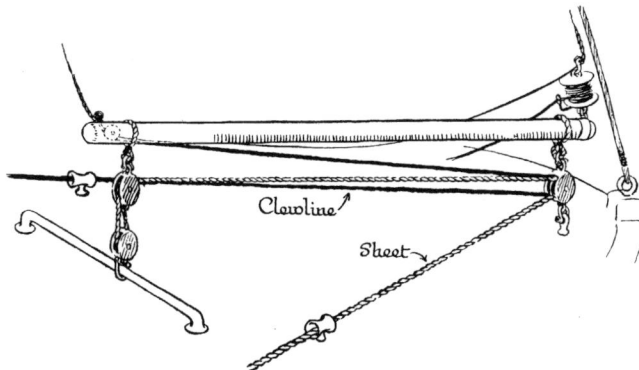

sheet is from the boom, through a block on the horse, then through another block on the deck, near the stemhead, and so aft to the cockpit. It is possible to use a boom foresail without a horse if the sheet be arranged as follows: One end is attached to the deck on one side of the yacht and led through a block on the clew of the sail, and finally through another block on deck on the other side of the boat. In this way the sail travels on its own sheet instead of on a horse. It is a simple arrangement but I don't think the sail sets so well as when a horse is used, as the clew is inclined to lift and slack up the leech.

Some years ago I devised a method by which the Wykeham-Martin furling gear can be used in conjunction with a boom foresail. It is extremely simple, the only extra gear required being a sheave in the boom and a double block at the tack. Instead of the clew of the sail being lashed to the boom in the usual way,

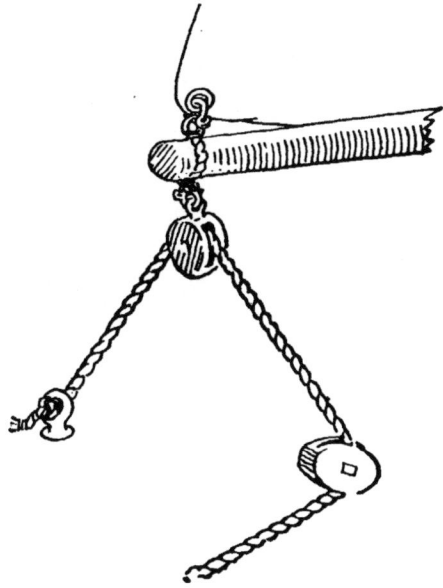

Clewline

Sheet

Boom foresail with Wykeham-Martin gear

345

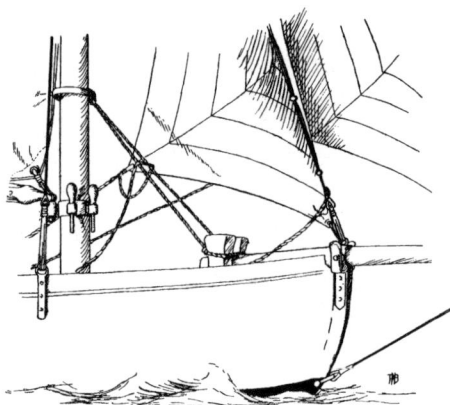

Headsail sheet guide-line

it is fitted with a clew-line, which leads over the sheave in the boom and then forward through the double block at the tack, from where it is led to the cockpit through a fairlead attached to one of the chainplates, or on the deck. The sheet leads over the other sheave of the double block at the tack and aft through a fairlead on the other side of the boat. To set the sail, one hauls on the clew-line, slacking up the rolling line; and to furl it one hauls on the rolling line, slacking up the clewline. The sheet must be made fast before setting or furling to prevent the boom lifting. The advantages of being able to set or furl a boom foresail without leaving the helm are so obvious that it is not necessary to enlarge upon them.

In some yachts the headsail sheets are apt to foul when the vessel is in stays, particularly the foresheets which catch on belaying pins on the mast. This annoyance can be mitigated in the following way. A line should be made fast round the mast, about two feet above the spider-band, led between the sheets and set up taut to the bitts. The line will keep the sheets clear of the belaying pins and any other excrescences they might otherwise foul. The jib sheets, too, are sometimes inclined to catch on the forestay when the yacht is in stays. This tendency to foul can be eliminated by fitting a rope span between the sheets as shown. When splicing the span into the sheets, the splices should be tapered down so that they offer little or no resistance when passing across the forestay.

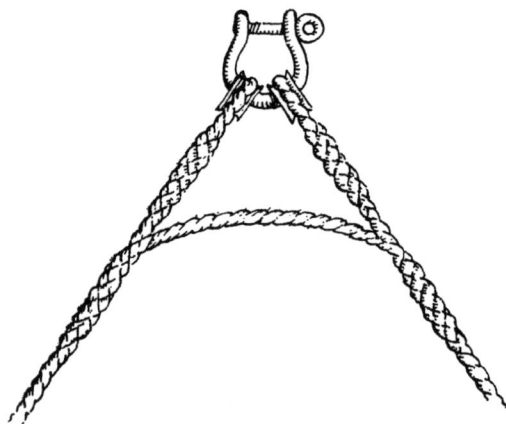

Span on jib sheets

CHAPTER 24: *The Sails*

Prior to 1851 the sails of yachts were made of loosely woven flax canvas, very baggy in cut, and the foot of the mainsail always loose. To make such sails stand on a wind it was necessary to wet them, and various expedients were adopted to facilitate the operation, which was termed 'skeeting.' Buckets were freely used for the purpose, and for the upper portions of a sail, that could not be reached with a bucket, bullocks' horns mounted on long poles were employed. That such drastic measures were not altogether desirable is suggested by a remark of "Vanderdecken" in his *Yacht Sailor*, a book published nearly a century ago.

> With new and well-cut canvas [he wrote] wetting is not, I think, productive of such great results as are generally attributed; ill-cut and bagged sails may be immensely improved by shrinking up the useless slack canvas. But it is probable that more well-cut and setting sails are twisted out of shape, and rendered useless, from the too indiscriminate use of the bucket and skeet, than that any beneficial results are uniformly obtained in speed or windward going qualities of a vessel.

The advent, in 1851, of the schooner *America*, which wrested from us the historic trophy that now bears her name, led to a revolution in sailmaking in this country, for she proved immeasurably superior to our yachts to windward. The America's sails were made of light closely woven cotton duck and cut to set flat, both mainsail and foresail being laced to the booms. Such sails set perfectly on a wind without wetting and being superior in every way to the canvas of our yachts, soon displaced the old-fashioned baggy flax sails. The laced foot, too, came into general use for racing and for that purpose has endured down to the present day. It is, however, since the first Great War that the greatest advance has been made in sails. The coming of the aeroplane led to a closer study of the science of aerodynamics, and as many of the principles involved apply equally to sails, much has been learnt. It has been discovered, for instance, that a yacht sailing on a wind is not pushed along by wind pressure as was previously supposed, but sucked along by the partial vacuum on the lee side of the sails. This has been conclusively proved by experiment, startling as it may seem, and Manfred Curry, a leading authority on aerodynamics, remarks in his well-known book *Yacht Racing*:

> ... the yachtsman was confronted with a phenomenon that seemed entirely incredible at first thought. It was that this negative pressure, namely,

the suction effect in the lee of the sail, amounted to three to four times the positive pressure on its windward side. In other words, we yachtsmen sail, properly speaking, not with the pressure which arises from the impact of the wind on the sail, but chiefly with the 'suck,' which acts on the lee side of it. A sail boat is sucked, not driven forward.

The yacht designer has always played the sedulous ape to nature, for even as he bases the shape of the hull on that of a fish, so does he model a sail on the shape of a bird's wing. The modern Bermudian mainsail follows very closely the wing of a bird, and it has been discovered that when the headsail overlaps the luff of the mainsail, the efficiency of the latter is greatly increased. Let me quote Manfred Curry once more:

As in thousands of other cases, man does not invent; he only observes casually that Nature presents in her creations the most ingenious mastery of a certain problem. The bird possesses on the fore edge of its main wing a narrow, tiny wing, which acts as a conducting surface in throwing the air on to the main wing. Although with our small birds this fore wing is, if at all, only slightly developed, many of the large birds of prey, such as the eagles, possess it in a marked degree. This conducting wing on the fore edge of the main wing, which we may imagine as replacing the thumb, projects somewhat beyond the latter. Hitherto no explanation has been offered for the function played by this small conducting wing, nor has even any attempt been made to attribute any function whatever to it. In the insect world, with the June bug for example, the stationary fore or so-called protecting wing appears to possess an air-guiding function. With most flying insects the fore wings are also smaller and, curiously enough, always overlap the hinder wings somewhat.

The theory of overlapping sails is that an effective wind funnel is formed between them which increases the suction and thus enhances the speed of the vessel, but the sails must be so sheeted that the wind out of the one ahead does not impinge on the lee side of the one behind. Overlapping headsails are now extensively used, and it is probable that the discovery of the benefit of overlap was at least partly responsible for the introduction of the now popular Genoa jib, although I suspect that the main attraction of that sail for racing is the large area of canvas that escapes taxation.

There seems a tendency now to revert to old ideas, for sails are cut with more flow than the flat-setting form of sail introduced by the schooner America. It is now generally agreed, too, that the foot of the sail should be allowed to take its natural parabolic curve, and booms of various kinds have been adopted to achieve that end. Nowadays, large racing yachts carry either what is known as a

Park Avenue boom, or a flexible boom, the object in both cases being identical. The Park Avenue is a triangular hollow spar, with the apex downwards. On the broad upper side the foot of the sail is attached with transverse slides, which permit the foot to take the desired curve.

With the flexible boom the amount of curve is regulated by means of struts, stays and tackles, but such devices are too complicated for adoption in small cruising yachts. Much the same effect can be obtained by the use of a loose-footed mainsail, although it may entail a rather stouter boom. As I pointed out in a previous chapter, the loose-footed mainsail possesses certain definite advantages, and with it one can slack up the foot of the sail a little in light winds, which will enhance the performance of the yacht.

The foot of a Bermudian sail is usually laced to the boom, but there seems no reason why it should not be left loose. Indeed, I know several yachts with loose-footed Bermudian sails, which seem quite efficient. Of course, if you have a loose-footed sail, you cannot use roller reefing gear, but to me that is no disadvantage, as I prefer to reef by the old-fashioned method of tackle and pendant.

Although most yachts' sails are now made of Egyptian cotton duck, it is, I think, better to use flax canvas in a yacht intended for extended cruises, as it is stronger and has a longer life. Sails of cotton duck probably owe their popularity to the fact that they retain their shape better, are lighter and, I believe, rather cheaper.

Formerly all sails were made with vertical cloths, but nowadays practically all racing sails and many used for cruising are crosscut, or in other words, with the cloths put in at right angles to the leach. The wind is supposed to flow off the latter easier and for that reason they are better for racing. For a cruising yacht, however, I think cross-cut sails a mistake, for in the event of a tear it will spread right across the sail. Some time ago I saw a cruising yacht with a cross-cut mainsail foul another craft which was at anchor. Her mainsail just touched the latter's mizzen and in a moment it was split right across, and as the leach-line held and the wind was light, she continued sailing under the upper part of the mainsail, which looked like a big topsail with no mainsail beneath it. Now, if the mainsail has vertical cloths, a tear seldom spreads very much and can be repaired with a small patch. A tear in a cross-cut sail, on the other hand, usually entails a whole new cloth. For ocean cruising it is advisable to have the whole of the leach roped, instead of only a few feet at the clew, as is usual.

Good sails cost a lot of money, but if properly cared for last for a long time. One of the old Solent one-design class yachts used her original Ratsey mainsail for just on thirty years and it set well to the end. Another yacht I knew had her sails stolen after nineteen years' use. Few owners keep their sails for such long periods, but with reasonable care the canvas of a cruising yacht should last for seven or eight seasons. But much depends upon their treatment when new. A sail should never be reefed until thoroughly stretched, for premature reefing is almost sure to stretch it out of shape and spoil it. For stretching new sails fine weather is essential, or at any rate desirable, and as it is a slow process the owner is likely to watch the weather with anxiety for some weeks. The inexperienced yachtsman is apt to think that his new sails are thoroughly stretched after sailing for a few hours with a good breeze, but that is not the case. They will not be fully stretched to the limit of the spars for some weeks and the longer reefing can be postponed the better. If the sail is a Bermudian and you have an old sail on board, the stretching period will be considerably shortened, as you will not fear to sail on doubtful days. If, when under way, the wind pipes up strong, or a shower of rain threatens, you can unbend the new sail and substitute the old one to get you home. With trackways on both mast and boom the change can soon be effected. If the sail is a gaff one and you have a trysail, you can set the latter to return to your moorings should the conditions render it undesirable to use the new sail. On no account reef the new sail unless it is absolutely unavoidable. Sail-stretching in an uncertain climate like ours is always a chancy business and there is a lot of luck about it. I was particularly lucky when my present boat was built, as I did not have to reef until I had had three months' sailing; such a spell of fine weather, however, is rare indeed.

Select a fine sunny day for bending the new sail. If it is a gaff mainsail with laced foot, do not pull it out more than hand-taut on the spars or lace it too harshly. When set it should not be peaked too high, nor yet too low. Peak it until wrinkles just begin to show in the throat; they will disappear as soon as the topping-lift is slackened and the sail takes the weight of the boom.

As it will be your aim to get the sail stretched as soon as possible, do not neglect any fine day. Get under way as often as you can and sail as long as you can before the dew begins to fall. Should you be caught in a shower, slack up the outhauls and ease the lacing; also lower the peak a trifle to allow a margin for shrinkage. Before coating the sail, ease up the clew outhaul. The sail will stretch inch by inch and you should take up the slack on head and foot from time to time, but do not pull them out more than hand-taut. If the sail has a loose foot, do not haul it out too much at first. After the initial stretch has been taken out of the canvas you can peak up the sail a little more, but you should treat it with care for some months. Stretching a new mainsail is undoubtedly a tedious business, but you must remember that it has to last you for a good many years and if it is to set well throughout its life, the stretching process must not be hurried. Above all, defer reefing it as long as you can, for the almost certain result of premature reefing is a flapping leach which will impair the yacht's sailing to windward and be an intolerable nuisance. By the way, a flapping leach, if not very bad, can sometimes be cured by easing up the head lacing a little.

When ordering new sails it is advisable to let the maker take the measurements himself, as then he will be responsible for any mistake. He will know, too, how much allowance to make for stretching according to the quality of cloth used. That, of course, is only possible when the sails are made by a local sail-maker. If you order them from a distant firm, you should send him a sail plan, drawn to scale, for his guidance. Failing that you will have no alternative but to take the measurements yourself, warning the maker that no allowance has been made for stretching. The measurement should be as follows:

Mainsail (Gaff): Exact measurements of boom, gaff and hoist. Those of the boom and gaff should be from the outhaul sheave and lacing hole respectively. The measurement of the hoist can be taken from the old sail.

Mainsail (Bermudian): The boom measurement from gooseneck to outhaul sheave, or hole. The hoist from gooseneck to halyard sheave.

Jib: Measurements of luff and foot, and also that from bowsprit-end to jib-sheet fairlead.

Foresail: Measurements of luff and foot, and from stemhead to sheet fairlead.

Topsail: Measurements from throat of mainsail, when the sail is set, to topsail-halyard sheave, and also the length of gaff and topsail yard. If the sail is to be a jackyarder, the length of the jackyard from lacing hole to lacing hole must also be given.

Mizzen (Yawl): The measurements given should be those of the hoist and of the boom and gaff, from lacing hole to lacing hole. I should advise you, however, to have a mizzen of the Bermudian type, even if it involves a rather longer mast, in order to get the necessary area. A mizzen with a gaff, or yard, is an infernal nuisance to stow, but a jib-headed sail can be set or stowed very quickly, as the boom can be triced up to the mast by hauling on its topping-lift. That places the sail out of action at once and then all you have to do is to roll up the slack and take a few turns round it with the fall of the topping-lift. To set the sail, you have merely to unwind the turns and let the boom drop into place. To stow a gaff mizzen, on the other hand, one must lower the sail and make it up like a mainsail, a job that necessitates going out on the bumpkin shroud.

To select a very cheap sailcloth is false economy, as it soon stretches out of shape and the sail will probably develop a flapping leach long before it is worn out. Choose a good quality of closely woven material, stout enough to stand hard wear. The sail-cover should be made of waterproof canvas, as painted covers soon begin to leak – at least that is my experience.

The yachtsman who can only use his craft at the week-ends is rather badly placed as regards the care of his sails, as he often has to trust to others to air them. If they are not bone dry when coated they are liable to mildew and it often happens, when he brings up on Sunday evening, that they are damp, either from rain or dew. In such circumstances it would be folly to coat them and it is far better to stow the mainsail loosely, so that the air can get to it, and leave it to the caretaker to air and coat the sail next day. The other sails, too, must be quite dry before they are stowed away in the locker.

It is not every waterman who can be trusted to air sails, and if you should have to leave your boat at a strange port in the care of a man you do not know, he may neglect to do it. I once had a new spinnaker completely ruined in that way. I think it advisable therefore to have the sails of a week-end yacht tanned, or treated in some way that will tend to eliminate the possibility of mildew. They can be either boiled in cutch, dressed with oil and ochre, or mildew-proofed.

Tanned sails may not look very 'yachty,' but they are not by any means unsightly and certainly save the owner a good deal of anxiety. It is the custom in the Thames Estuary and on the East Coast to dress sails with oil and ochre, and of late years I have had my canvas treated in that way. It is a job best left to a professional sailmaker, as it is important that the correct ingredients be used, for otherwise the treatment may have the effect of rotting the sails rather than preserving them.

Dressed sails are usually of the red-brown tint favoured by the Thames barges, but a yacht I know, the cutter *Hirondelle*, has her mainsail and jib a darkish blue, similar to that of the sails of the French sardine boats and the effect is very pleasing. Her topsail and foresail are brown, which makes an effective contrast. In the West of England the sails of the fishing boats are boiled in cutch to preserve them and the colour is a very dark shade of brown. One method is probably as good as the other from the preservative point of view, but in my opinion the colour of the oil and ochre treated sails is much the more attractive. Dressing the sails in this way adds something to their weight and makes them rather stiff to handle but, apart from its preservative value, it saves a great deal of time and labour. If your sails are dressed, you can view the weather with equanimity and do not have to bother about sail-covers. The foresail can be left hanked to the forestay, and the jib, if fitted with the Wykeham-Martin furling gear, left *in situ*. Getting under way is then merely a matter of a few minutes and much time and trouble are also saved when you bring up. The only disadvantage of dressed sails is that they do not draw so well in light airs and for that reason balloon canvas such as a balloon foresail, spinnaker and Genoa jib, are better left white.

I would warn the reader against having his sails dressed with any alleged preservative unless he has definite and reliable information that it really does what it professes to do. A friend of mine some years ago had his new sails treated with a much-advertised sail preservative which completely rotted them within three months! If you decide to have your canvas dressed, you can't do better than have them done with the oil and ochre process used by Thames barges and fishing smacks for many years.

If you do not fancy having your sails dressed, I would strongly advise you to have them mildew-proofed. The cost is trifling and you can, if you wish, do it yourself. Here is a recipe, adopted by the Admiralty and recommended by Ratsey & Lapthorn:

2¼ lb. Sugar of Lead
2¼ lb. Alum
Mix with 10 gallons of water,
and soak the sail in the mixture for 24 hours.

I do not suggest that sails treated in this way are absolutely immune from mildew, but I have had my white sails thus proofed for many years and have never had one mildewed.

I will conclude this chapter with a few notes on sails of various kinds:

Gaff Mainsail: Personally, I prefer a high-peaked mainsail with a short gaff, as I think it stands better on a wind. In yachts of yawl and ketch rig, the gaff is often as long as the boom, in order to get adequate area, and the gaff sags away to leeward and robs the vessel of a good deal of her weatherliness. The windward work of such vessels might be improved by the use of vangs on the gaff, as sometimes adopted for the foresail of a schooner, but they would probably be more bother to handle than they are worth. It is the custom to lace the head of the sail to the gaff with one long continuous lacing, but it is much better to attach it to the spar with a separate stop at each eyelet – stout marline will serve for the purpose if five or six turns be used. A long lacing is apt to chafe through and then the whole of the head of the sail comes adrift. If separate stops be used, as I suggest, it will be of little consequence if one carries away, as it will not affect the set of the sail to any appreciable extent and can easily be renewed at the first convenient opportunity. The parting of a head-lacing is a fairly common mishap, as it is apt to be chafed by contact with the runners, topping-lift, etc.

Bermudian Mainsail: The Bermudian sail is more effective when there is considerable roach on the leach, but that entails the use of battens, which are a nuisance, as they get foul of the rigging when the sail is set or lowered. Many owners of small cruising yachts consequently dispense with battens, the slight sacrifice in efficiency being more than compensated for by ease in handling. I have referred to reefing Bermudian sails in a previous chapter.

Headsails: Headsails are now what is known as 'diagonally' cut; that is to say the cloths are put in at right angles to the leach and foot respectively. Cut in that way they keep their shape better and in comparison with those of the old-time yacht the jib used to-day is small and narrow. A jib should be cut high in the foot and when set the luff should be as nearly parallel to that of the foresail as practicable. The luff-rope of the modern jib is usually of flexible steel wire, and when the sail is stowed away, it should be rolled round the luff-rope and then coiled to prevent kinks in the wire.

The foresail is, for its size, the most powerful sail in the ship and usually cut lower on the foot than the jib, but it should not be so low that the helmsman cannot see under it. As it is hanked to the forestay it has a hemp luff-rope. By the way, the luff-rope, when of hemp, of any fore-and-aft sail is always sewn on the port side of the sail, a useful guide when bending it. As a wire luff-rope is inserted in a pocket, you cannot always tell which is the head and which the foot without spreading out the sail; but if you tie a bit of marline to the head cringle you will have no trouble in identifying which is which.

Many owners of small yachts have adopted the boom foresail and there can be no doubt that a sail that looks after itself when the vessel is in stays is a great convenience, particularly when one is single-handed. It seems to me, however, that with such a sail there must be a certain loss of efficiency. Not only must it be rather smaller to allow the boom to clear the mast, but the absence of overlap tends to reduce the effectiveness of both foresail and mainsail.

As I pointed out earlier in this chapter, it has been discovered that when a headsail overlaps the mainsail, the wind funnel thus formed enhances the power of both sails and it is mainly due to this fact that the Genoa jib is so extraordinarily effective. Since the foresail is for its size so powerful, if you reduce its area in order to fit a boom, there must be some sacrifice in speed and weatherliness. But the handiness of the sheet travelling on a horse and requiring no attenion cannot be denied. In considering whether you will fit a boom or not you must decide whether you are likely to gain more on the swings than you lose on the roundabouts, so to speak.

A common fault of the boom foresail is that the traveller is apt to stick on the horse and needs a little persuasion to make it go to the end. In larger craft, such as smacks, that persuasion is usually applied by one's boot, but in small yachts a light auxiliary pair of sheets are often used. It only needs a slight pull after the yacht is on her new tack, and the extra sheets are also useful for holding the sail to windward when heaving-to.

I have been shipmates with fore-horses composed of iron rod, wire rope, and a length of mast-track, but the traveller showed the same sticking propensity on all of them. On the whole I think an iron rod makes the most satisfactory horse, the sheet block being attached to an iron figure-of-eight traveller. The auxiliary sheets can be hitched round the waist of the traveller and need not be very stout, as their purpose is merely to trim the sail.

The only objection to an iron horse is that it sticks up above the deck for two or three inches and you might trip over it, but you soon get used to traps of that sort and come to avoid them by intuition. A wire-rope horse has the advantage of falling down on to the deck when not in use, but I don't think the sheet travels so freely on it. A strip of a large yacht's Bermudian trackway makes a very neat fore-horse for a small boat, a sail slide being used for the traveller, but the latter is inclined to stick unless the trackway is kept well greased, and there is also a risk of the track being dented, thus preventing the slide from functioning.

A boom foresail can be used without a fore-horse if the sheet is arranged in the manner I indicated in an earlier chapter, but I don't think it is to be recommended. It works quite well but, instead of the pull coming all on the lee side, it is distributed between the weather and lee sides. The tension is insufficient to make the sail stand well on a wind, as the boom is inclined to lift and slack up the leach.

If you use a boom foresail the sail should not be laced to the boom, as that would prevent the foot taking its natural curve.

Topsail: Topsails are not often carried in small cruising yachts nowadays as owners of such vessels seem to think the sail not worth the extra gear and trouble it involves. It is not much trouble, however, to set a topsail fisherman fashion and the yard is short enough to stow comfortably on the side-deck when not in use. A rope is rove through a bull's-eye fitted to the upper side of the gaff a few inches from the jaws. When setting the sail the lower end of the yard is attached to this rope and the yard mastheaded. Then the tack is brought into position by hauling on the rope on the gaff, and the clew hauled out by the sheet in the usual manner. The yard is the same length as the luff of the sail. The illustration in Part VIII clearly shows this method of setting.

Genoa Jib: This sail, a comparative new-comer, is mainly used in racing yachts, but sometimes employed in cruising craft. Its main attraction for racing is that it enables a very large area of untaxed sail to be carried. It extends from the masthead to the end of the bowsprit, or stemhead if the yacht has no bowsprit, and far aft past the runner. As the chief object is to get as much untaxed sail as possible, the foot of the sail is cut very low, almost to the deck, thus completely shutting out the helmsman's view to leeward. It is the modern equivalent of what we used to call a balloon jib in the old days, but is cut to set flatter and can be used with effect on the wind in light weather.

Balloon Foresail: This is a most useful sail in a cruising yacht as it pulls the vessel along grandly on a reach, and if well cut can be used with effect in light weather when the wind is several points forward of the beam. When used on a wind the sail should be sheeted as far aft as possible, so that it will make an effective wind funnel and carry the 'dirty' wind clear of the lee side of the mainsail. If sheeted at the fore end of the cockpit, as it often is, the back-draught may impinge on the lee side of the mainsail and do more harm than good.

A balloon foresail can be usefully employed when running before the wind, in lieu of a spinnaker, if set fisherman fashion across the yacht. The tack is secured to a shroud plate on one side and the sheet led outside the shrouds on the other. Thus set, it will belly out almost to the forestay and pull the boat along well, although, of course, being of smaller area, it is not so effective as a spinnaker. It is not necessary to touch the sail when gybing, as it is immaterial which side the tack is made fast. I always use my balloon foresail in this way when single-handed, as it is far easier to set or hand than a spinnaker.

Spinnaker: While admitting its utility, the spinnaker is a sail for which I have a particular aversion, probably because I usually sail alone and it is a most unsuitable sail for single-handed work. Every time the mainsail is gybed the spinnaker has to be shifted over to the other side; it entails extra gear, and the boom, although usually not very long in these days, is another spar to clutter up the side-deck. Still, if you elect to carry a spinnaker there are one or two points to which I would call your attention.

Wooden jaws on the boom are a better means of attaching the spar to the mast than any gooseneck-cup arrangement, as you are able to fit it on the mast at any position you like. If the inboard end is higher than the outboard end, and the guy be led on board at a fairly sharp angle, say, through a bull's-eye attached to the runner plate, the sail is less likely to 'sky'. Indeed, if you use a fore-guy as well, it is impossible for the boom to lift.

Squaresail: Although extensively used for ocean cruising, the squaresail is not very suitable for sailing in estuaries and round the coast, as it is less efficient than a spinnaker and more difficult to handle. In running down the trade winds the sail comes into its own, for then the wind comes strong and true from the same quarter day after day. When used in conjunction with the mainsail, half the area of the squaresail would be blanketed if steps were not taken to prevent it. This is done by pushing out the windward clew with a long pole, thus increasing the effective area.

The squaresail yard should be in length about four-fifths the hoist of the mainsail and have a row of reef points by which its area can be reduced by about a third. The sail is usually set on a wire jackstay, from the hounds to a strong eye-bolt on deck, just forward of the mast. The halyard should be attached to a wire sling on the yard. It is a brute of a sail to handle in a strong wind unless provided with brails.

Perhaps the best plan is to attach the head of the sail to the yard with wooden hoops, such as are used for the luff of the mainsail. The sail could then be extended on the yard by means of outhauls, led through blocks on the yard-arms. Inhauls, through blocks at the centre of the yard, would also be required for stowing it. By hauling on the inhauls, the sail would be bunched up in the centre of the yard and then one of the falls could be passed round the sail a few times and made fast.

Trysail: A trysail is seldom needed in a small cruising yacht, but if you do want it you may want it very badly, so it is well worth carrying. It may be particularly useful if you have a new and unstretched mainsail which you do not care to reef. Being intended for use in heavy weather, it is made of stout canvas and has a loose foot, which is sheeted to quarter-blocks. The luff is attached to the mast with toggles, or a lacing.

There are two kinds of trysail in use in small yachts, one being thimble-headed and the other having a short gaff. Of these I prefer the latter as the thimble-headed variety tends to throw the centre of effort farther forward, like a close-reefed Bermudian, and in my experience many small craft will not handle in heavy weather under a trysail of this form. The gaff of a gaff trysail should not be more than half the length of her usual gaff and should be fitted with strong jaws and a parrel.

The well-known sailmaker, Mr. T.C. Ratsey, recently made some very instructive remarks, in the course of a lecture, on the subject of sails. Coming from such an authority, his advice cannot be ignored, so I take the liberty of passing on a few of the more important points of his lecture, culled from the report that appeared in the Journal of the Royal Corinthian Yacht Club:

> The question of a full or flat sail is guided by all sorts of factors, but primarily by the speed of the boat. The faster a boat, the flatter the sail must be. For instance, a scow, which will go at over 20 knots off the wind, cannot have its sail too flat, and the same applies to an ice boat. In very light weather a full sail is necessary to start a boat with, and, were it possible to adjust the flow, the sail should be flattened as the speed of the boat increases. A Thames barge will hold an extraordinarily high wind, with her foresail blowing right out and the sprit sagging away to leeward, but were she to go faster in order to hold the same wind, she would have to have a much flatter sail. This point may be interesting in deciding what type of sail is needed for different kinds of weather, but in any one boat it is a great mistake to have too many sails, because as likely as not, if one starts with a light-weather sail, before the end of the day the wind will freshen. What is wanted is an adjustable sail, or at least a sail with an adjustable flow, and we are approaching that with the Park Avenue boom.

I take it that Mr. Ratsey means by this that as the wind increases in strength the sails should be flattened and vice versa, and it is partly for that reason that I have always advocated the use of a loose-foot mainsail for cruising purposes. With such a sail the clew outhaul can be eased up in a light breeze and easily hauled out again should the wind freshen. It is difficult to understand why loose-foot mainsails are not more often used in racing craft, for it seems to me that much the same results can be obtained in that way as with a flexible or Park Avenue boom. It is now generally accepted that the mainsail should be allowed to take its natural parabolic curve, and if that is the main object of flexible and Park Avenue booms, as I believe it to be, then why not secure it by the simple means of leaving the foot of the mainsail unlaced? I suppose, however, that it would call for a rather heavier boom, and the extra weight might be detrimental in a racing yacht.

Mr. Ratsey's remarks on the subject of the stretching of sails were also very illuminating:

> As regards the stretching of sails, it is an absolute fallacy to suppose that the sail, after leaving the sail loft, ever gets any bigger. True, it may, and will, stretch on the foot and luff and in the head if it is a gaff sail, but what it gains one way it is bound to lose the other way, so it is not cause for concern if a sail does not go out to the end of one's spars, even if a hated rival's sail in a sister ship seems much bigger. Of course, this does not refer to a badly-roped mainsail. If the rope is put on too tight, it will obviously never stretch out. Roping plays the most important part in sailmaking.

That certainly never occurred to me, and in the past I have usually waited until my sails were thoroughly stretched before having them tanned, being under the impression that if I had them treated when new some of the threads would be insufficiently coated when the canvas was stretched. What art (or is it science?) there is in sailmaking! It is far more difficult than making, say, a coat, for in the latter case the tailor tries on the garment and prances round you with a piece of chalk, marking the places where it is necessary to take in the slack. The sailmaker, on the other hand, has no such adventitious assistance to guide him, for he can't try on a sail and mark defects with chalk. He has to rely solely upon his brains and experience, and yet it is seldom indeed that a sailmaker who knows his job is at fault in his calculations. It is not surprising that good sails cost a lot of money, for apart from the skill needed in making them, Egyptian cotton sailcloth of the best quality is very expensive. It behoves the owner therefore to take the greatest care of his sails.

Mr. Ratsey pointed out that although canvas will dry in perhaps an hour on a fine sunny day, it will take as long as six hours to dry the heart of the rope. I don't think this fact is generally appreciated, and most owners stow away their sails in the locker, or coat the mainsail as soon as the canvas feels dry, without giving a thought to the condition of the roping. But that, it seems to me, may lead to the generation of mildew, and it is therefore advisable to have all white sails mildew-proofed. He deprecated what he described as "the pernicious practice" of drying headsails by hoisting them and leaving them to flap in the breeze for two or three hours.

"That not only affects the setting of the sails in the future, but perforates the cloth just as surely as if it had been shot at.

"Roller reefing headsails and mainsails are the sailmaker's best friends. Those who must have a roller headsail should always take it off at night time, otherwise the leach and luff will become slack through being continually rolled up, added to which the outside of the sail gets very dirty. A roller boom is almost as bad."

It is interesting to note that Mr. Ratsey himself uses a loose-footed mainsail.

CHAPTER 25: *Reefing Devices*

Anything that tends to accelerate the operation of reefing the mainsail of a yacht, or reduce the labour to a minimum, is, of course, much to be desired, and with that end in view various patent reefing gears have been introduced from time to time.

Most of them, however, work on the same principle, that of a revolving boom, round which the foot of the sail is rolled like a blind. The difference between them is mainly in the method of operating the boom. This may be done either by a small ratchet winch, as in the Turner gear; by a worm gear as in the Woodnutt; or by a wire rope wound on a drum on the boom.

The oldest, and certainly the most popular, of these gears is the Turner, which consists of a ratchet winch on the gooseneck end of the boom and a swivelled plate on the other end, to which the topping-lift and mainsheet are attached. If the boom extends much beyond the stern of the yacht, one or more claw-rings must be used to carry the upper block, or blocks of the mainsheet; and let me say at once these claw-rings are an infernal nuisance. They are shaped something like a pair of calipers, the ends of the claws being fitted with rollers of hard wood to protect the sail. Theoretically speaking, when the boom is revolved the sail rolls up neatly round the boom, travelling between the claws. In practice, however, it seldom does anything of the sort. When the boom is revolved the claw-ring as often as not fails to 'do its stuff' properly, and is wound up in the sail together with its attendant block. That is not good for the sail, which may even be torn and, of course, puts the mainsheet out of action. One then has no alternative but to let the boom unwind and start all over again.

Various expedients have been tried to overcome this defect but none that I know of has been entirely successful. The most common is a metal rod connecting the claw-ring with the topping-lift swivel, but far from curing the fault, the rod, as well as the claw-ring, may be wound up in the sail. A method I adopted in several of my yachts which were fitted with roller reefing, was simpler and I think on the whole more effective. It was merely a line from the topping-lift plate to the claw-ring and then set up taut to the mast below the gooseneck. That

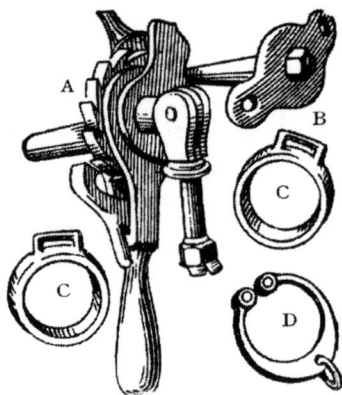

Components of Turner's
roller reefing gear

it was by no means infallible, however, will be shown by the following incident.

One morning my son and I were in the neighbourhood of the North Buxey buoy in the 5-ton sloop *Spray*, which we then owned. She had a rather long boom, which necessitated the use of a claw-ring. It was a dull forbidding morning with a fresh breeze and we were just able to carry the whole sail. We noticed, away over Mersea Island, that the sky had become as black as ink and it was evident that we were in for something special in the way of squalls and decided that the sooner we got the main-sail close-reefed the better. Well, I went forward to operate the boom, while my son, then a lad not long from school, stood aft to guide the sail into the claw-ring. I had got down about four turns, when he shouted, "Hold on, Gov'nor, it's foul; slack up a bit." Throwing back the pawl of the winch with my right hand, I attempted to ease the boom sufficiently to clear the sail; but owing to a physical defect I am only able to use two fingers and the thumb of my left hand, and I could not hold it. Consequently, the whole of the reef I had taken down was unrolled and we had to start all over again. The same thing happened time after time and the squall was coming nearer and nearer. Then, to create a diversion, the wildly kicking boom caught my boy a wallop on the backside and knocked him overboard.

Fortunately we were hove-to at the time and the dinghy having come alongside, he fell into it and was back on board in next to no time; but his remarks on the subject of roller reefing gear would have done the inventor a power of good, if he had heard them.

Then the squall struck us and it was the mother and father of a squall. The wind shrieked in the rigging and the rain was of the order usually termed torren-

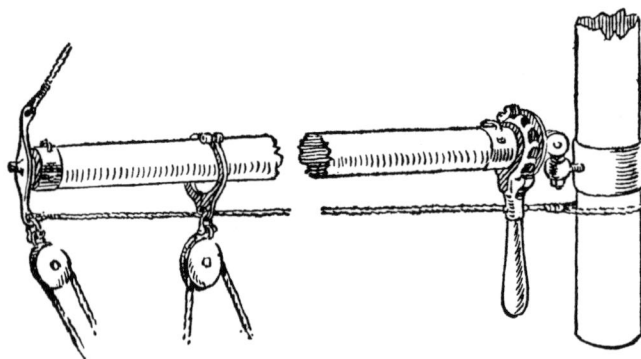

Turner's roller reefing gear

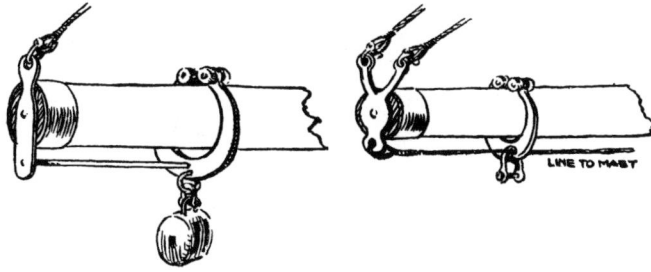

Roller-reefing claw-ring arrangements — rod and wire types

tial. The yacht was buried to her coamings and we had a rare struggle to get the mainsail off her, but at last we succeeded and made all secure. As we had been far too busy to think about oil-skins we were soaked to the skin and looked and felt like the proverbial drowned rats. When the worst of the squall had blown over, we managed to get the sail reefed and eventually arrived at West Mersea with several inches of water on the cabin floor. After that experience I vowed that never again would I use roller reefing gear, and I never have.

In any case there must be either a rod or line to connect the topping-lift swivel to the claw-ring, otherwise the latter will slide inboard along the boom when the yacht is running. The claw-ring is the bugbear of the whole contrivance and needs as much looking after as a child at the Zoo.

If your boom is short and you can dispense with a claw-ring, there is no reason why the gear should not work satisfactorily, but, apart from the objections to which I have referred, roller reefing possesses certain inherent disadvantages. Of these, the most serious is that the whole sail must first be set ere a reef can be rolled down neatly, a fact that may place you in an awkward predicament. Suppose, for instance, that you are brought up in a narrow creek, or a crowded anchorage, and the conditions are such that you have to get your anchor before setting any sail. In such circumstances you would have neither the time nor the room first to set the whole mainsail and then reef it. The only way in which such difficulties could be avoided would be by making a practice of always reefing the sail before stowing it: then you would be ready for any emergency. But I don't

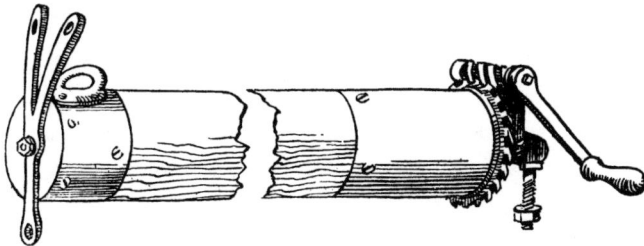

Woodnutt roller reefing gear

361

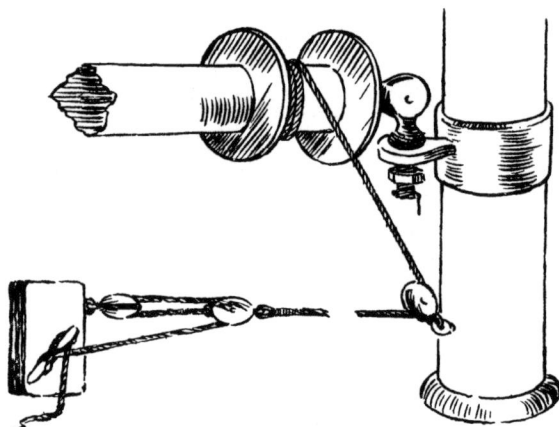

Wire-and-drum roller reefing gear

think any owner would keep that up for long. It would seem absurd to reef over-night when there was not a cloud in the sky and the weather appeared to be set fair; but this climate of ours is as fickle as the love of a film star and the weather might completely change before dawn.

If you decide to adopt roller reefing there are a few points to which I would call your attention. The boom must be of the same diameter throughout its length, if the sail is to roll up neatly, and should be a very stiff spar, for otherwise it will bend when the sail is full of wind and be very difficult to revolve. A Mc-Gruer hollow spar would probably fulfil these conditions better than any other. Then the boom must be at right angles to the mast, otherwise the luff of the sail will come away from the latter as it is rolled up. The lower part of the luff must not be attached to mast-hoops, but laced; and the lacing must of course be cast off before reefing. Finally, if the boom is at right angles to the mast it is likely to be unpleasantly close to your head, and as when reefing a Bermudian sail with a roller boom the spar has a tendency to drop, that trouble is aggravated. In some Bermudian-rigged small yachts the boom, when the sail is close-reefed, is almost on the coamings. In such circumstances every time you go about or gybe you will probably have to kneel in the cockpit to avoid a biff on the head, and although your attitude may appear devout, I am inclined to think that you will be saying more than your prayers. Sometimes, to eliminate this dropping tendency, which is mainly due to the turns of the luff rope overriding, the boom is tapered, or has splines of wood fitted near the end, but that must surely in course of time stretch the sail out of shape. In one respect roller reefing has an advantage over the old-fashioned method of reefing with pendant and tackle, for with it you can roll down just as much as you wish, while with the latter the size of your reef must be determined by the positions of the cringles and points of the sail. All the same I personally prefer the old-fashioned method, for although it may take a little longer there is nothing that can go wrong.

Before leaving this subject I should like to quote the views of Mr. H. D. Barton, a yachtsman of wide experience who in 1938 won the Founder's Cup of the Royal Cruising Club. In the log of his prize-winning cruise, which appeared in the Club's Journal, he made the following remarks about reefing:

Although desirable, but not really necessary, I decided to reef the mainsail. I was interested to discover whether a Bermudian sail can be reefed when running in a strong wind. The boom was broad off to port. The pendant was already rove and the reef-tackle hooked on and stopped along the boom. I eased up the main halyard and the sail slid down the track of its own free will. I lashed the first cringle down to the tack and then hauled away on the fall of the reef-tackle. There was not the slightest difficulty in bringing the leech cringle down to the boom and in less than two minutes the area had been reduced by over 50 square feet. I then tied every reef point (there are only about ten) except the outer two, which were just beyond my reach. When I compare the simplicity of this operation with the struggles I have had with roller reefing – gear that has seized up and leeches that will run forward – I cannot help feeling that some owners are prejudiced against the old-fashioned method. But the most serious objection to roller reefing is that it eventually ruins the set of any sail.

To which I would add that although in theory a sail is reefable with a roller boom when running before the wind, in practice it seldom is ; for unless the boom is an exceptionally stout and stiff spar, it is apt to be buckled by the strain of the wind in the sail and cannot be revolved.

Provided that you have everything ready, reefing with pendant and tackle does not take very long. The tackle should be in its place stopped to the boom and at least two pendants rove. You should also keep handy a short length of suitable rope for use as a preventer lashing. It should be kept in one of the cock-

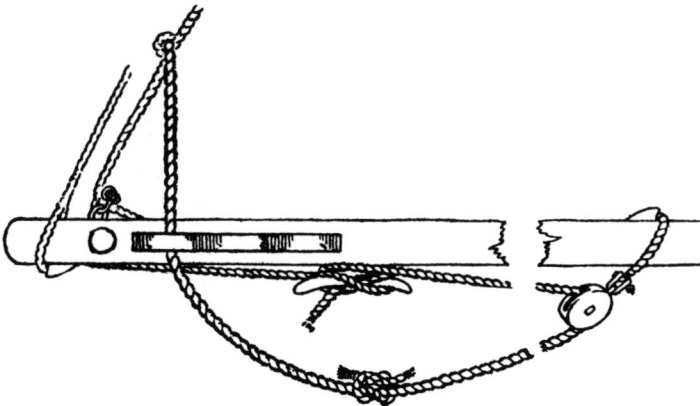

Main outhaul and reef tackle

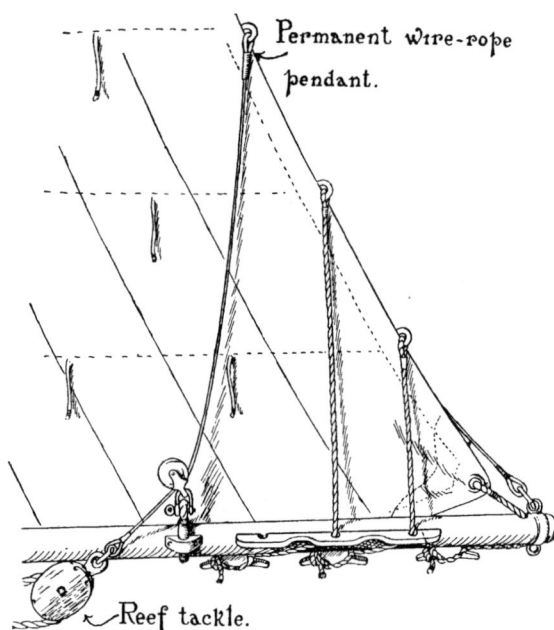

Harrison Butler reefing device

pit lockers and never used for any other purpose. There should be two strong cleats on the boom, one for the main outhaul and the other for belaying the reef pendant after it has been pulled down. As soon as the tack has been secured and the pendant bowsed down to the bee-block and made fast, the sail can be re-set and the yacht got under control. The points can be tied and the preventer lashing put on at your leisure. If the tack of the sail is secured by sister-hooks, stropped to the gooseneck, the hooks can be transferred to the appropriate reef-cringle in a few seconds. I am sure that a sail reefed with pendant and tackle sets better than with any roller boom device and is not so liable to be stretched out of shape.

Of course, if you have nothing ready, reefing may take the deuce of a time. The tackle will have to be bent on to the boom and then you may have to search for a reef pendant and suitable piece of rope for the preventer lashing. Such casual methods are to be deprecated, as reefing is a job that must be done expeditiously. It is important, too, that the pendant should render freely through the bee-blocks. I went for a sail some time ago with a friend in his 8-ton cutter and we had occasion to pull down a reef. He had all the necessary gear rove but the pendant was such a tight fit in the bee-blocks that we only succeeded in getting it hauled down by clapping a handy-billy on to the fall of the tackle.

Now here is another point and in my view an important one, although those who write books on yachting seldom, if ever, refer to it. The pendant must be hauled down on the weather side if the sail is to be reefed without trouble. If it is pulled down on the lee side the clew of the sail is likely to be trapped, or even drawn into the bee-block and torn. Yet it is common practice for a reef pendant to have a fancy knot, such as a double-wall-and-crown, on one end so that the other is the only one available. Very often, too, when sheaves are fitted in the bee-blocks they are only on one side. In my opinion, a reef pendant should be merely a length of rope with the ends whipped, rove through both bee-blocks and the reef cringle of the sail. A figure-of-eight knot in each end will keep it from getting adrift. With such a pendant either end can be used at will and you can always pull it down on the weather side.

In small yachts of 3 tons or less a reef-tackle is unnecessary as the pendant can very well be pulled down by hand, but there should be a strong cleat on the underside of the boom to which it can be belayed. If this cleat is fitted near the centre of the spar, you will not have a lot of superfluous rope to dispose of, and it will be within easy reach from the cockpit.

The older I get the more I crave for simplicity in the gear of a yacht, and for the life of me I cannot see much wrong with the old-fashioned method of reefing by means of a tackle and pendant, particularly when used in conjunction with a little device, for which I believe Dr. Harrison Butler can take credit. It is a wire rope pendant permanently attached to the third reef cringle and led through a block attached to the boom. The reef tackle is permanently attached to this wire pendant and when taking down the first or second reef, you haul first on the wire pendant and belay the tackle. Then you can easily pull down the first or second reef pendant, as the case may be, by hand and secure it. When that has been done you have merely to slack up the wire pendant again. It is desirable to have two strong cleats on the boom, one for the reef tackle and the other for the pendant of the reef you take down. Only one cleat will be necessary for the pendants, for as you will always take the strain on the wire before pulling down another reef, you can cast off one pendant before making fast the other. In the accompanying illustration, Mr. Brooks has shown three cleats under the boom, but only two are really necessary at that end of the spar. One is, of course, for the outhaul and one other cleat would suffice for the pendants. The cleat for the tackle (not shown in the drawing) would be nearer the in-board end of the boom so that it could be reached comfortably, even if the boom were well over the quarter.

CHAPTER 26: *Roller Headsails*

Any contrivance that enables one to set or reef a headsail without leaving the cockpit is an inestimable boon, particularly to those who sail alone, provided that it is not attended by undesirable traits. The first roller headsail was invented many years ago by the late Major E. du Boulay and soon attained a considerable measure of popularity for small craft. For open and half-decked sailing boats it is a very useful form of sail, but in a cruising craft I regard it as an unseamanlike contraption. The luff of the sail is attached to a wooden roller, which revolves round a wire stay, and there is a flanged drum at the foot of the roller which carries the line by which it is operated. Pulling on the line causes the roller to revolve and roll up the sail like a roller blind. To set the sail, you haul on the sheet, at the same time easing up the rolling line. The sail can be reefed by partially rolling it up and belaying the line. You will probably say, "That seems a jolly good idea," and so it is in theory, but when it comes to practice it is not so good, as the device has many bad points. It makes for weight and windage aloft, which is undesirable, and it entails the use of a sail cut very low on the foot, which I regard as an abomination

du Boulay roller jib fitting

in a cruising yacht. When it is reefed the clew of the sail rises and then the lead of the sheet is not fair. No yacht can be expected to sail decently to windward if her headsail sheet fairleads are incorrectly placed, and so the advantage of being able to reduce the area of the sail by merely pulling a string is discounted by the faulty lead of the sheet. Another objectionable feature is that the sail, being always left *in situ* when the craft is at anchor, gets very dirty on the leach cloth, and when set has a sort of mourning band round its edge, as repulsive to the eye as the dirty finger-nails of a young schoolboy. And the leach cloth, being always on the outside when the sail is furled, is constantly wet and dry, which causes it to stretch, and a napping leach is the result. Moreover, the leach cloth soon rots and the life of a roller headsail is seldom very long.

du Boulay roller jib fairlead

A particularly serious fault of the du Boulay roller headsail is its liability to carry away unexpectedly. The foot of the roller chafes the wire stay, which soon rusts, for the wet trickles down the stay and settles at the foot. Being hidden from sight, the owner has no idea that there is anything wrong until he sees his jib flop over the side. When that happens he is in the deuce of a mess, as the sail cannot be set again until the stay has been renewed. In some cases the stay is shackled direct to the masthead and the owner has no means of setting another sail. The prudent owner who uses a roller headsail, however, sets up the stay with a halyard and is thus in a position to substitute a headsail of ordinary type in the event of the stay breaking.

Another frequent source of trouble with this form of headsail is that of the rolling line coming off the drum and getting jammed beneath the foot of the roller. When that happens the sail can be neither furled nor reefed until the line has been cleared and replaced on the drum. And that, let me tell you, is not an easy matter, particularly in the case of a jib on a fairly long bowsprit.

Major du Boulay must not be blamed for these defects, as he provided means to prevent them. Unfortunately, however, he did not patent his invention and as any shipwright is able to supply the gear, the inventor's special fittings are often omitted. As a rule the shipwright places a ball of hard wood at the foot of the roller for it to turn on, and although the roller may revolve freely enough, wet settles on the splice and rusts the wire stay. Then again, Major du Boulay provided a special fairlead for the rolling line to prevent its coming off the drum. That is often omitted, a screw-eye being substituted in its place. When fitted according to the inventor's instructions, a short piece of brass tubing with a bell mouth is driven over the splice and soldered to the stay. That makes a fine bearing for the roller to turn on and effectually prevents the settlement of moisture at the foot of the stay. His fairlead for the rolling line was fitted just under and close up to the foot of the roller, and with reasonable care the line seldom got adrift.

The drum fitting is secured to the wooden roller with small screws, which are apt to be drawn out, or sheared off. When that happens, the roller turns in the drum and places the gear out of operation. As the sail cannot then be reefed, you find yourself in the predicament of having to carry the whole headsail in heavy weather, with, perhaps, a pair of reefs in the mainsail, thus completely destroying the balance of the yacht. And when you bring up you will be unable to furl the sail and probably have to get the whole caboodle down on deck.

Now the Wykeham-Martin furling gear is a very different proposition, for it possesses all the advantages of the du Boulay and none of its disadvantages. Indeed, I consider it one of the most useful contributions to yacht equipment ever devised, and for single-handed sailing almost indispensable. I was one of the first to use it, as Major Wykeham-Martin sent me a set of the fittings to try out when he first placed them on the market, some forty years ago. I found the gear so extraordinarily useful that I have used it in all of my boats ever since and would not willingly be without it.

The Wykeham-Martin gear consists of two small ball-bearing fittings which are shackled to the head and tack of the sail, that at the tack having a drum on which the rolling line is wound. When you pull on the line, the sail rolls up neatly round its own luff rope. As there is no roller, the sail can be taken down and stowed away in the sail locker, and if you wish to change the jib for a smaller one, you unshackle it from the fittings, leaving them on the halyard and outhaul respectively, and substitute the sail you wish to set. Although I have used the gear for so many years, I have never known it fail to function, and it is a great boon being able to set or stow a headsail in a moment without leaving the cockpit. The gear can be employed on any thimble-headed fore-and-aft sail, although it is used on the jib more than any other. Major Wykeham-Martin gives the following directions for fitting and using the gear:

> Shackle the top swivel to the head of sail with the opening downwards to keep out wet, and shackle the drum swivel to tack of sail and bowsprit traveller or stem head.
>
> Wind the roller line on the drum so that the sail will be rolled up in the same direction as the lay of the luff rope.
>
> Before hauling the drum swivel out to the bowsprit-end, hitch the roller line round the drum with a hitch which will come adrift when pulled.
>
> If the parts of the halyard twist when hoisting, these should be unrove and well stretched until they can be hoisted clear.
>
> If, when first hoisting, turns appear in the head of the sail, the luff rope has turns in itself, and the last eighteen inches or so should be resewn on to the sail. This may also occur with light sails having wire luff ropes, owing to the fact that wire twists under strain, but this can be rectified by resewing the luff rope.
>
> NOTE: For a new sail we recommend that the top swivel be sent to the sailmaker, who can then hoist it up and alter the luff rope stitching if required.

For jib topsails the sail should have a wire luff rope, the top swivel must be shackled to the head of the sail, and the drum swivel fitted at the bowsprit-end, a wire pendant being taken from top of drum swivel to tack of sail. The working

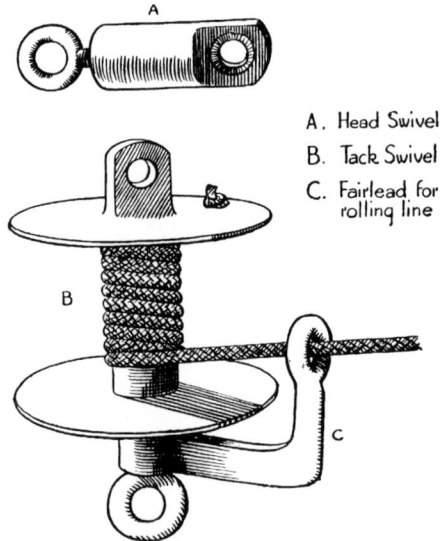

A. Head Swivel
B. Tack Swivel
C. Fairlead for rolling line

Wykeham-Martin furling gear

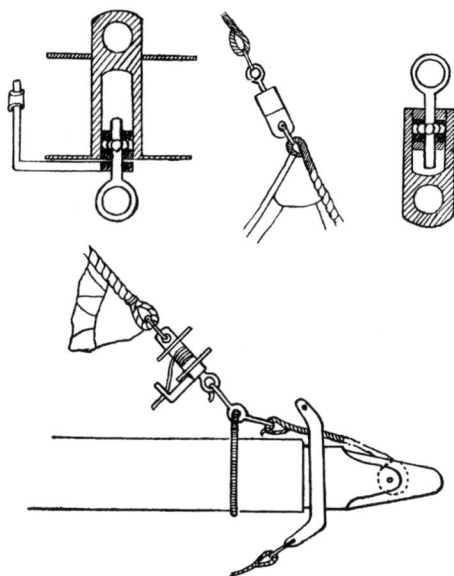

Wykeham-Martin gear detail

parts, being of steel, should be kept well lubricated with motor grease, which can be run in warm without opening the fittings. The bearings will last a long time if kept well lubricated; but to replace them the screw plugs closing one end of the fittings can be unscrewed in a vice. See that these screw plugs are kept well screwed up; the sizes above No 2 have a set screw which has to be removed before unscrewing the plugs.

There are one or two hints which I would add to Major Wykeham-Martin's instructions. As headsails nowadays usually have a wire luff rope, they should be stowed away rolled up and coiled, in order to avoid nips in the wire. When a sail is removed from the furling swivels there will be no line on the drum, the necessary turns being put on automatically when it is next set. As a sail is sometimes furled more tightly than at others – it depends upon the conditions under which it is rolled up – it may happen that when you next set it there are insufficient turns of line on the drum completely to roll it up and a little bit of the clew may be left unrolled. This can be avoided by giving a couple of turns anti-clockwise to the tack-fitting before bending on the sail, so that you have a margin of line in hand. Should the sail not roll up neatly it is due to the lead of the sheet not being fair and it should be corrected. With reasonable care the rolling line should never come off the drum; a slight strain should be kept on it as the sail is unrolled. A new form of tack-fitting, however, has recently been introduced which is 'fool-proof.' It takes the form of an aluminium cup in which the swivel revolves, the line being led through a hole in the cup. There is another small hole in the bottom of the cup to allow water to escape. With this new tack-fitting it is impossible for the line to leave the drum.

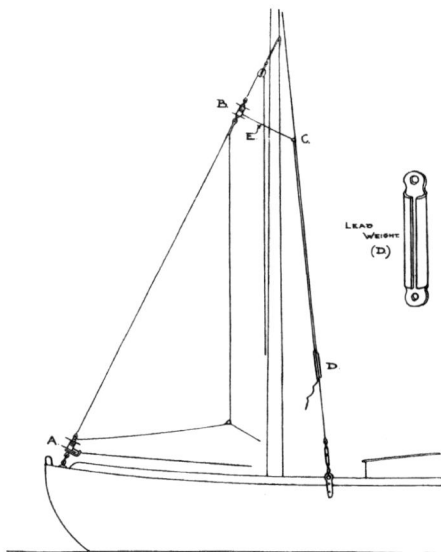

A: Ordinary tack swivel

B: Special swivel for head of sail fitted with flanges and no line guide

C: Small fairlead seized on shroud

D: Piece of lead pipe about 5 in long, ½ in bore, split and closed round shroud so as to move easily up and down; ends of tube formed into eyes

E: Extra line from head swivel through fairlead to lead weight, and a short length of line from lower end of weight

The fairlead C must be seized on the shroud in such a position that the line E is at right-angles to the luff of the sail. It is absolutely necessary to get the position correct or the line will not stay between the flanges.

Wykeham-Martin gear for reefing

Originally the Wykeham-Martin gear was designed for furling only and could not be used for reefing purposes. You could, of course, roll up part of the sail and belay the line, as with the du Boulay gear, but in the absence of a roller there was nothing to prevent the head of the sail from unrolling. Various dodges were tried by owners to make the gear serve both purposes, such as substituting a twisted chain for the wire luff rope in the sail, or rolling up part of the sail and then lowering it and tying up the head with a length of lamp wick. Although fairly successful they could only be regarded as clumsy expedients.

As there seemed to be a demand for a gear that would both furl and reef, Major Wykeham-Martin set his wits to work to solve the problem and succeeded in doing so in a very simple way. For the ordinary head swivel he substituted one with a flanged drum, from which a line was led through a fairlead attached to one of the shrouds to a piece of lead pipe, which was free to travel up and down the shroud. A line was attached to the lower end of the pipe, which was split to facilitate fitting on the shroud. (After the pipe has been put on the shroud the slot is closed by pressing the edges together.) When it is desired to reef the sail, it is partially rolled up and the line on the foot of the weight secured to one of the chainplates. That effectually prevents the head from unrolling.

Before placing the new model on the market, Major Wykeham-Martin sent me an experimental set to try. After I had found by trial and error the correct position for the fairlead on the shroud, I found that it worked perfectly. The new furling and reefing gear has now been available for some years, but I don't use it myself as I prefer to change to a smaller jib when necessary. I don't think that a headsail reefed by any form of rolling device can set as well as a smaller sail unreefed, but the lazy yachtsman who objects to the trouble of shifting jibs will no doubt welcome this clever invention. When the correct position on the shroud for the fairlead has once been found, this reefing device is quite automatic, but the upper rolling line should be of plaited cord, for otherwise when wet it may coil itself round the shroud and prevent the weight from travelling freely. As a matter of fact both rolling lines should be plaited, as hawser-laid rope is apt to kink when wet. A hank of plaited sashline cord, as used for windows, serves the purpose admirably and can be bought almost anywhere at trifling cost. Of course, when it is desired to set the whole sail again, the lead weight must be released before unrolling. The accompanying illustration shows the device and method of fitting.

The utility of the Wykeham-Martin furling gear has long been recognized and it is used in small cruising craft all over the world. Indeed, in my own district, most yachts seem to have it on the jib and many on the foresail as well. It has in fact quite superseded the du Boulay gear for cruising, although the latter is still used in little day boats and some small racing craft.

Some owners who employ the Wykeham-Martin gear on the jib leave the sail up throughout the season, just putting a tyer round the clew when the yacht is at anchor. That, however, is not to be recommended, as the leach cloth gets dirty and stretched out of shape. To leave the sail *in situ* for a night or two is all very well, but for longer periods it should be removed and stowed away. If the fittings are left on the halyard and bowsprit respectively they will be ready for use with any size of jib you want to set.

CHAPTER 27: *Ground Tackle*

There is no part of a yacht's equipment more important than her anchor and chain, for on their efficiency depends the safety of the vessel and that of other craft brought up in her immediate neighbourhood.

When I began cruising, more than half a century ago, one seldom saw a good anchor, but in these days one seldom sees a really bad one. In the old days the anchors produced for yachting purposes were modelled upon the Admiralty pattern, which combined all the faults an anchor could have. They were short in the shank, inordinately heavy, and had blunt spade-shaped flukes, that might have been specially designed to foul the cable. Notwithstanding its great weight, such an anchor could not be trusted to hold a yacht in anything more than a fresh breeze.

In course of time the Admiralty type of anchor was superseded in yachts by the 'fisherman,' which was much lighter and of better shape, for it had been discovered that it was not so much the weight as its proportions which gave an

Admiralty and fisherman's anchor types

anchor its holding power. Most writers on yachting are agreed that the shank should be long in proportion to the chord (i.e. the measurement from fluke to fluke), which is very true, but few have cared to venture into the realm of figures. Having taken measurements of a good many anchors which I knew to be good holders, I am of the opinion that the length of the shank should not be less than one and a half times that of the chord and not more than one and three-quarters. The stock, which in the case of a bower anchor should be fixed, should be almost as long as the shank, and the flukes sharp and of leaf, or spear, shape. Those are the proportions of the Nicholson, the best anchor of conventional shape yet devised. The shank and arms of the Nicholson anchor are of flat section to enhance its strength. In the 7-ton cutter *Seabird*, which I owned many years ago, I had a bower anchor which weighed but 32 lb., and it was a rare holder. The shank was almost twice as long as the chord measurement, but was evidently too long, as on one occasion when I had anchored over a stiff clay bottom, the shank was badly bent. I should think that anchor must have been specially made for a previous owner, as I have never seen any other with so long a shank.

With regard to anchor stowage, if the anchor be light enough to lift bodily on deck, the following method – which I believe was first adopted by Mr. G. Umfreville Laws – will be found to answer admirably: Close to the mast a tube, sealed up at the lower end, and just long enough to take half the stock of the anchor, is inserted through the deck, whilst the other half of the stock, standing up and down the mast, will not foul the headsail sheets. The shank rests in a chock screwed to the deck for the purpose, and is secured by means of a button. When bringing up all one has to do is to lift the anchor from its resting-place and drop it overboard.

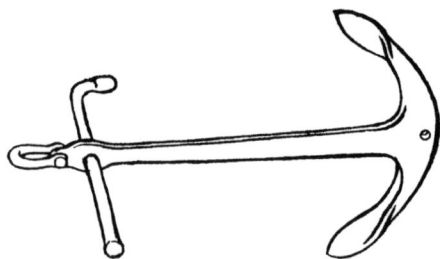

Nicholson anchor

A method I have personally employed for many years is as follows: The anchor is placed on deck in such a

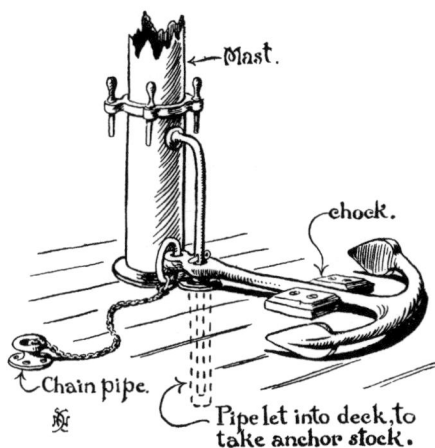

Laws' method of anchor stowage

position that half the stock lies up and down the foremost shroud, whilst the arms are flat on deck, the shank near the crown resting in a chock screwed to the deck. As the other end of the shank, resting on the rail, is raised a few inches it will usually be found that the stock lies nicely against the shroud, to which it is secured by a short line permanently attached to the shroud for the purpose. If this line be placed in such a position that it lashes the end of the stock, it is impossible for the foresail or jib sheet to jam between the stock and shroud and thus get foul. I think this method is quite as good as that of Mr. Laws, and does not entail boring a hole through the vessel's deck.

If either of these systems be adopted the anchor should, when lifted on deck, be passed outside the bowsprit shroud, for then, when bringing up, it can be dropped clear over the side. It is desirable in either case to protect the deck from being chafed by the flukes of the anchor by means of brass plates. Should the anchor be too heavy to lift comfortably it will be necessary to use a purchase consisting of two single blocks attached to the masthead. When the anchor has been hove up to the stem head, the lower block of the purchase can be hooked on to the ring, the purchase being passed outside the bowsprit shroud; then, as the chain is slacked away, the anchor is lifted by hauling on the purchase. To keep the anchor clear of the bowsprit shroud and the topside of the yacht a boat-hook will be found useful. When the anchor has been raised above the deck level, it can easily be guided into its place and stowed. An owner who takes a pride in the appearance of his vessel will often be annoyed by the paint on the bow being scraped by the anchor chain; this can be avoided by the use of a piece of half-round hard wood temporarily placed over the bow to protect the paint. The wood should be about 2 inches thick. At one end there should be a hook by which it may be attached to the bobstay shackle, and at the other end a piece of

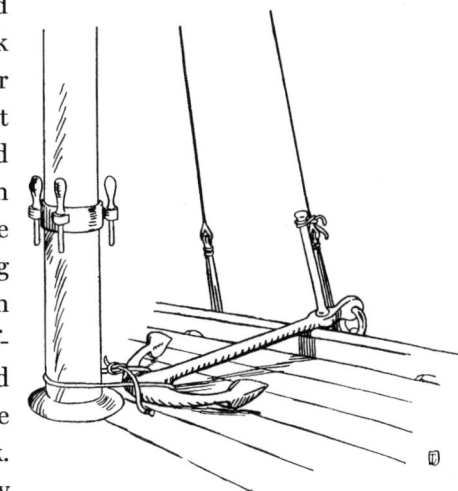

Author's method of anchor stowage

373

line with which to secure it to the shroud. Lying vertically across the bow of the yacht, this batten of wood will take the chafe of the chain. If painted the same colour as the yacht's topsides, it will not be at all unsightly.

Some owners are extremely casual about their ground tackle and seem to think that anything will hold a yacht. Some time ago a yacht of about 30 tons was brought up close to my craft and her cable struck me as absurdly light for a vessel of such size, and when she got under way, her anchor was so small that one of her crew easily lifted it on board with one hand. I was not surprised to hear some time later that she had dragged her anchor in a breeze and damaged another yacht. On another occasion, when I was at Pin Mill, a small converted ship's boat of about 3 tons was anchored near me. She was manned by three lads of the working class, who had sailed her down from Ipswich, and from the sounds of revelry that came from her cabin it was evident that 'a good time was being had by all.' She was riding to a warp that seemed no thicker than an average clothes line and when the tide began to ebb she began to drag her anchor. When informed of the fact, her crew emerged from the cabin and proceeded to get the anchor. Curious to see what sort of anchor it was that dragged in a flat calm, I watched them. When it came to the surface the 'anchor' proved to be the end of an old iron bedstead!

Many different forms of anchor have been introduced in my time and perhaps a few notes on those of which I have had personal experience may be of interest. One that attained some degree of popularity was the Trotman, which, although of 'fisherman' shape, had the arms hinged to the crown, so that when one arm was in the ground the other folded along the shank, thus reducing the risk of its being fouled by the cable. The Trotman, although quite a good holder, was rather slow to grip and awkward to handle, as the arms waggled about and were apt to trap one's fingers.

I don't think the Trotman anchor is often used nowadays as I have not seen one for a good many years. In another small yacht I bought the bower anchor was in the form of a grapnel, one pair of arms being made to slide up the shank, being kept in position by a pin to form the stock. As the sliding arms could be turned on a rounded portion of the otherwise square shank, the anchor could be stowed flat on deck. That was its only redeeming feature, for it would not hold the yacht in any but the finest weather.

Of stockless anchors I have had several, not from choice but because they

Trotman anchor

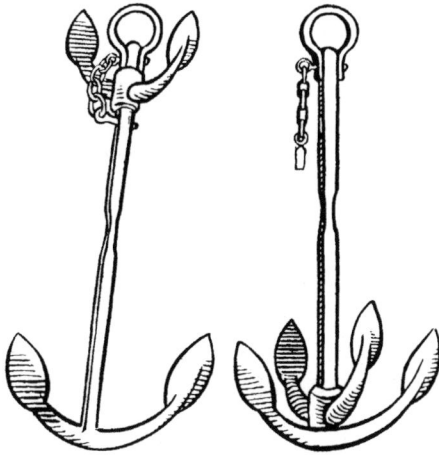

Grapnel anchor

happened to be in the yachts when I bought them. In every case I found the stockless anchor quite useless and scrapped it at once. A friend of mine had a stockless anchor weighing 1 cwt in his 12-tonner and it dragged so often that he discarded it in favour of a Nicholson weighing only 65 lb., which held his vessel securely.

I once carried out some experiments with a small stockless anchor to ascertain why it dragged so easily. At low water I dragged it through the mud, watching carefully to see what happened. I found that the flukes failed to clear themselves and in a few yards were encased in a ball of mud, which slid over the surface as easily as a stone.

None of these patent anchors showed any improvement on the old 'fisherman' type, but a few years before the outbreak of the second great war, a new form of anchor, known as the C.Q.R., was invented by Professor G. I. Taylor, F.R.S., of Cambridge, which has revolutionized all preconceived ideas. It is a radical departure from the anchors of earlier pattern, being shaped like a double ploughshare. It has no stock, but when dropped falls on its side and then turns over and begins to dig itself into the ground. The greater the strain imposed upon it, the farther it buries itself until the whole of the anchor is in the ground. It is thus impossible for it to be fouled by the cable. As the head is hinged to the shank and free to turn within an arc of a circle, the head is not disturbed by the ranging of the vessel. The C.Q.R. anchor has extraordinary holding power, more than twice that of any known anchor of traditional shape, and one can therefore use one of half the weight of a 'fisherman' type with perfect security.

When the C.Q.R. anchor first made its appearance I heard such good accounts of it that I decided to substitute one of only 20 lb. weight for the fisherman anchor, weighing close on 70 lb., in my Falmouth Quay Punt *Fancy*. It was almost unbelievable that such a light anchor would hold *Fancy*, which drew almost 6 feet of water and had a lot of freeboard, but I was assured that it would. *Fancy* was put afloat before Easter and, as the moorings had not then been laid, she rode to the C.Q.R. anchor for three weeks at Fambridge in strong easterly winds, which more than once reached gale force, and she never budged a yard.

Stockless anchor

C.Q.R. anchor

Later that summer the anchor was even more severely tested. I was lying in the Colne when there was a violent thunderstorm, accompanied by one of the worst squalls I can ever remember. For about ten minutes the wind was of hurricane force and it was impossible to stand on deck without holding on to the rigging. A yacht of 140 tons near by dragged her anchors and drove ashore, picking up a couple of smacks on the way. Most of the craft in Brightlingsea Creek were in trouble and a large schooner coming into the river travelled fast under bare poles. Yet *Fancy* held on securely. The next morning I had difficulty in breaking out the anchor with the aid of a powerful windlass; it must have buried itself feet deep in the mud.

In ordinary circumstances, however, the C.Q.R. is weighed as easily as any other anchor, as when, by hauling on the cable, the shank is lifted to a certain angle, the anchor begins to cut its way out of the ground. Given a proper scope of chain, I am convinced that a C.Q.R. anchor will never drag in any weather likely to be experienced in the course of the yachting season and it seems to me to approach within measurable distance of perfection. That a light reliable anchor is a great boon there can be no doubt and it is not surprising that the C.Q.R. should be rapidly superseding all other types for yachts. As it has to be made for the most part by hand, it is not cheap, but as one can use one of less than half the weight of one of conventional pattern, the extra expense is not so great as might be imagined.

Comparative tests of the C.Q.R., stocked (fisherman type) and stockless anchors, carried out on various kinds of bottom, yielded results which demonstrate the extraordinary holding power of the C.Q.R..

The anchor is so light that it can easily be lifted on board without the aid of a burton and stowed anywhere on deck that is convenient. In *Fancy* I stowed my C.Q.R. just abaft the mast and in my present boat it rests on teak chocks on the fore-deck. I have dwelt at some length on the C.Q.R. anchor because I regard it as one of the most important yachting discoveries of my time, and I think most yachtsmen will agree that it is the best yacht anchor yet devised.

For easy and safe riding the chain must be a comparatively heavy one. In ordinary weather the cable extends from the yacht to the anchor in a festoon and the weight of the chain acts as a spring. As long as this curve is maintained, she will ride comfortably and is not likely to drag her anchor, but if the chain be pulled out taut the yacht will 'snub,' and this snubbing, if violent, may lead to trouble. Let us consider for a moment what happens when a vessel is brought up in rough water. Every wave that comes along increases the depth of the water by the height of the wave. If there is a curve in the cable the vessel merely stretches out the chain a little and rides the sea with ease, but if the chain is already taut she must leap forward in order to accommodate herself to the increased depth of water. In doing this she meets the wave with tremendous force and one of several unpleasant things may happen. She may pull her anchor out of the ground, ship the sea, break the chain, or carry away the bitts, or samson-post, to which she is riding. If the chain be a light one it is probable that it will be quite taut in heavy weather, but if it be heavy there will always be sufficient margin of curve to permit the yacht to ride any sea that she is likely to encounter.

If your cable is unduly light the effect of a heavy chain can be obtained by lowering a weight down it. A round 56-lb weight with a ring on it is best for the purpose and it should be attached to the cable with a large shackle. It should be lowered for a few fathoms by means of a rope fastened to the ring. To shackle a heavy weight to the cable when the yacht is pitching into a head sea is not an easy matter and many years ago Mr. W. Etty Potter devised a special hook for the purpose, which he called a 'Sentinel.' Attached to the hook was a handle and a

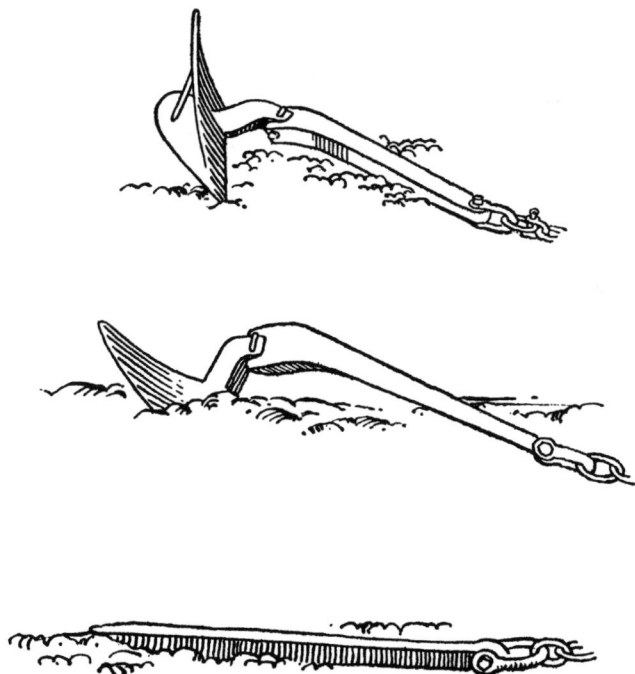

C.Q.R. anchor in operation

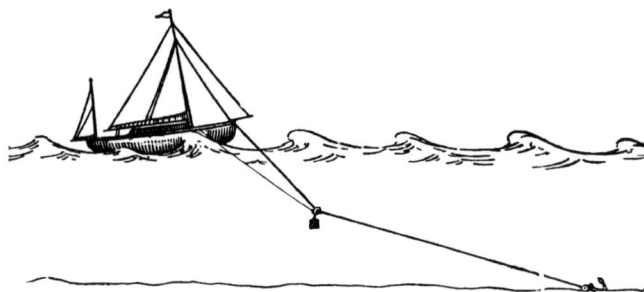

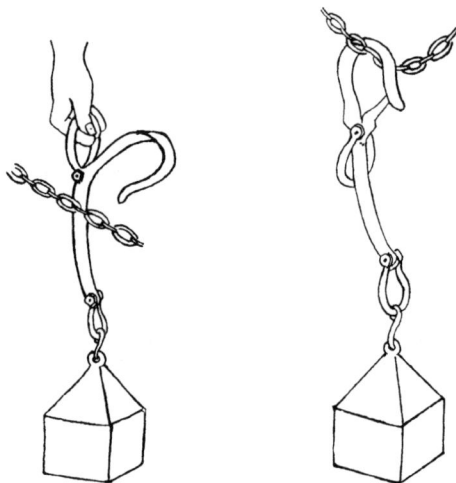

Anchor sentinel

tongue, which closed the hook when the latter bore the weight. Having attached the weight, you had merely to place the hook over the chain and release it. The weight was then securely hooked to the cable and could be lowered to the desired depth with a rope.

It was an ingenious contrivance, which I believe can still be procured from Pascall, Atkey & Co. of Cowes. An ordinary shackle, however, will serve the purpose quite well if it be sufficiently large to slide easily down the chain. When attaching it, the weight can be hooked on to the cable fairlead by its ring, which will then be lying against the cable. In that position there should be no difficulty in securing the shackle, and then the weight can be lifted off the fairlead and lowered.

The following table of weights of anchors and sizes of chain suitable for small yachts may be of use to those buying new ground tackle. The table, however, must only be regarded as approximate, as much depends upon the vessel's draught and windage. The chain should be the best galvanized short link and a certificate of its tested breaking strain supplied with it.

The kedge should be of about two-thirds the weight of the bower anchor, and if of the fisherman pattern it should have a loose stock to facilitate stowage. The reader may wonder why it is not necessary for a kedge to be as heavy as the bower anchor. The explanation is that it is generally used with a warp, which has a certain elasticity and is usually a good deal longer than the scope employed on the bower anchor, which makes for easier riding. McMullen, in his single-handers *Procyon* and *Perseus*, habitually rode to rope when lying in an open roadstead, which no doubt made for comfort but must have been extremely inconvenient when getting under way. Just fancy having to coil down and dispose of perhaps 40 or 50 fathoms of warp every time the anchor was weighed!

Tonnage of Yacht	Weight of Anchor	Size of Chain
2	23 lb	¼-in (15 fathoms)
4	30	5/16-in (20f)
7	42	3/8-in (30f)
10	56	7/16-in (40f)

The cable fairlead on the stemhead should be fitted with a large roller of not less than 2 inches diameter, even for a little boat of 3 or 4 tons, and preferably rather larger. It is important that it should be kept well lubricated and in good working order. I am afraid that many owners never give it a thought and I have frequently noticed in small yachts the roller set up solid with rust. You should keep an oil-can on board and use it frequently, for if the roller runs freely it will lighten your labour when getting the anchor and save the chain from undue wear. Why is it, I wonder, that the makers of these cable rollers never think of providing a hole for lubricating purposes? It would greatly facilitate oiling and save a deal of waste. Still, it is not a difficult matter to remove the roller and drill a hole.

For some reason or other which is incomprehensible to me, cable fairleads are usually made with an outward curve, with the result that the chain, or warp, is apt to jump out. Should the yacht take a sheer when you are hauling in your mooring, the buoy rope will probably come out of the fairlead, causing you to sit down hard on the windlass, or samson-post. Such an incident is not only disconcerting but may be exceedingly painful. A good fairlead should curve inwards a little, and I am pleased to see that some yacht-chandlers are now supplying them in that form.

The chain-pipe may be curved, or just a navel-hole in the deck, and personally I prefer the latter, as the chain is not so liable to jam in it. Sometimes a curved chain-pipe is fitted facing aft, the idea probably being that in that position water will be less likely to get down it. But a chain-pipe fitted in that way is an in-

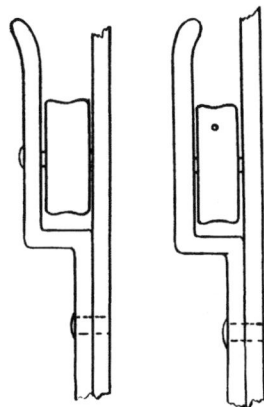

Chain leads,
bad and good

fernal nuisance, as the cable will not run down into the locker of its own weight. When getting the anchor the chain piles up on deck and must subsequently be fed down the pipe by hand. And if you are using a windlass, the heap of chain on deck will foul the drum, causing much delay and annoyance. The chain-pipe, if of the curved variety, should be fitted to face forward, so that the chain will run down into the locker as you get it in. Covers are usually supplied, but they soon get lost. A rag stuffed into the pipe will keep most of the water out and any that soaks through will merely trickle down the chain into the bilge and do no harm.

In yachts of over 4 tons Thames measurement a windlass is often a great convenience, particularly for single-handed work. The old-fashioned ratchet windlass, with the drum between the uprights, is very powerful, but gives slow delivery, and as the chain cannot be removed is quite unsuitable for such work. In craft under 10 tons most of the chain can be got in by hand, and a windlass is only required to break out the anchor; it is therefore essential that the drum

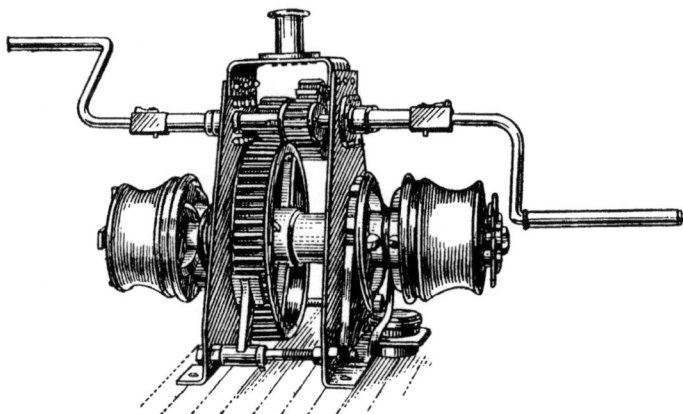

Reid's crank-handle windlass

should be at the side, so that the chain can be put on or taken off in a moment.

The windlass we had on *Fancy* was one of Reid's crank type and it proved very efficient, although, as I say, one has to operate it in a rather cramped and uncomfortable position. It is made of steel plate, with a brass bitthead on top, and fits over the heel of the bowsprit. The drum, which is of steel, with whelps cast on, is on the side, and on the other side are two forged-steel belaying pins, which are very useful for the jib out-haul and bobstay fall. The windlass is beautifully made and quite efficient, but a newer model, A9, strikes me as an infinitely better proposition. This particular windlass is operated by a double-acting ratchet lever and the cable-lifter is made suitable for $5/16$-, $3/8$- or $7/16$-inch chains. The cable-lifter is fitted on the starboard side, with warping drum on port side, having whelps cast on to grip a second chain when required. There is a foot-operated band brake and a forged steel chain redder is fitted to lead the chain to the locker. The framing consists of polished gun-metal box cheek, the sides being covered with polished sheet brass, and all steel and iron parts are galvanized.

This windlass is operated in a standing position, and as the ratchet lever gives a hoisting movement with both forward and backward strokes, the movement of the chain is practically continuous. It is quick in operation and very powerful and the brake controls the speed when letting go the anchor. The windlass is self-locking, one pawl holding against the other when the load is on the chain. The yacht can ride to the windlass. In the more recent models the gear case is totally enclosed, with a lid on top for access. The gear case contains a small quantity of oil which

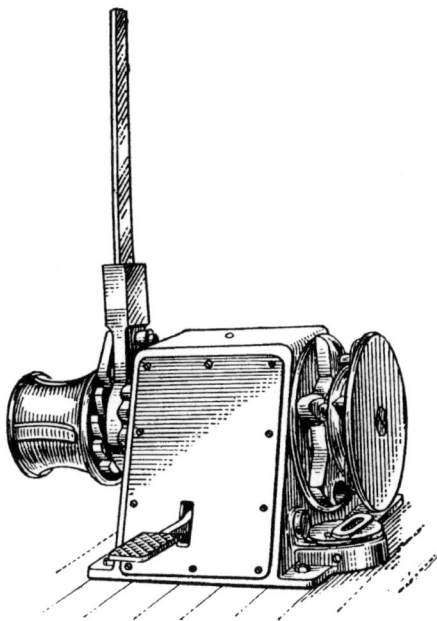

Reid's ratchet-lever windlass

lubricates the internal mechanism and it thus requires a minimum of attention. In the $5/16$-inch size the gear case is made of Birmabright Aluminium Alloy, which is non-corrosive and very light, the total weight being 50 lb. In the $3/8$-inch size the gear case is of gun-metal and the weight 84 lb.

Mr. Reid tells me that he once had a foul anchor in Oban Bay in seven fathoms of water, and single-handed managed to bring up to the surface a 200-lb. anchor with $\frac{1}{2}$-inch chain attached to it The load lifted was therefore approximately 370 lb., plus friction in the stemhead roller. That experience, I think, will convey some impression of the power of this windlass.

As in small yachts the services of the windlass are seldom required for anything but breaking out the anchor, a very good substitute is a mast winch. This can either have a single drum or two, working independently of each other. As the drums are fitted with whelps, the winch can be used for breaking out the anchor, or for a variety of purposes, such as warping and setting the sails. If you have a mast winch you can dispense with a reef-tackle as, by attaching a rope to the pendant, the latter can easily be hauled down.

The usual type of mast winch is not geared but has a long handle sliding into sockets on the drum. If more power is needed, the handle can be lengthened by drawing it farther out of the sockets, while if speed is called for, the handle can be shortened. The winch can be fitted to the mast at a convenient height from the deck and used whenever a little extra power is needed. It, of course, weighs much less than a windlass, the weight of one with a single wooden drum, suitable for a 5-tonner, being only 22 lb.

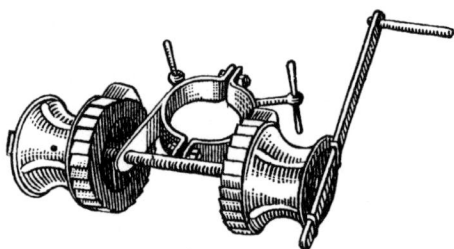

Mast winch

Messrs. Pascall, Atkey and Co., of Cowes, supply a useful mast winch with drum to take the chain, and Dr. Worth speaks very highly of the efficiency of this form of winch, which he had fitted in his 21-ton ketch *Maud*. The chief advantage of such a windlass is its central position, enabling it to be pressed into service for a variety of purposes; it can also be placed at a height from the deck that gives one plenty of power. The chain drops down through a hawse pipe near the mast, and ranges itself in a deep, narrow locker, the weight being in an excellent position from a ballasting point of view.

In a yacht of less than 5 tons it is only in heavy weather that any difficulty might be experienced in getting the anchor by hand, and even under such conditions the boat can be made to do the work herself. As she pitches into the trough of the sea it is easy to grab a few feet of chain, and if you can hold it as she rises to the next sea, you are that much to the good. By continuing the process you will in time be able to get in all of the cable and break out the anchor without any great exertion. But the difficulty is to hold the chain while the bow rises, for if you try and take a turn round the bitts, or samson post, you will probably lose most of what you have gained. There follows an answer to this problem.

For small yachts that carry no windlass a chain pawl on the stem head is a most useful fitment. It is, I believe, the invention of Dr. Claud Worth, who has kindly given me permission to reproduce the illustration and description that appears in his fine work *Yacht Cruising*. Dr. Worth, who had such a pawl fitted to his yacht *Foam*, gives the following description of it:

Foam had a ratchet windlass with the barrel between the bitts. It was powerful, but extremely slow. We could generally get the chain in by hand, so that the windlass was only wanted for breaking out the anchor; but in order to get the chain on or off the windlass the whole length of it had to be passed twice round the barrel.

We devised a sort of open hawse pipe, with a pawl in it to hold the chain, and got it made by a smith at Southampton. The hawse-pipe was made of sheet iron about 1 inch thick, and was bolted to the starboard side of the stem. The pawl was 1½ inches wide and ½ inch thick. The pin of the pawl was a ⅞-inch bolt passed through the stem.

When the pawl was lifted, the chain ran through in the open hawse pipe. When the pawl was dropped, the chain could still be hauled in, but was prevented from running out. In getting the anchor, if there was much chain out, we beat up to it in short tacks. During each tack the chain could be hauled in hand over hand. When the chain came taut, it was held by the pawl, and pulled the vessel's head round on the other tack until finally she sailed right over the anchor and lifted it out of the ground.

In a strong tide and light wind, if the chain had to be got in with a tackle, the pawl held it while the strop was being shifted. After we fitted this chain pawl the windlass was never used except for the bobstay tackle.

Worth's chain pawl

On a small craft that has no bowsprit, and consequently no bitts, it is often a matter of some difficulty to find anything on the fore deck to which the mooring or anchor chain can be securely fastened. To meet this difficulty Mr. G. U. Laws some years ago invented a special chain bollard. A glance at the illustration overleaf will explain the principle of this bollard. It will be noticed that the aft side of the bollard is faced with a stout plate of hard brass or galvanized iron. All one has to do when using this bollard is to drop the chain into the cleft, and a link engages on the metal plate and is securely held. This is a far better arrangement than a large unsightly cleat on the fore-deck, as it is more reliable and not so likely to foul the headsail sheets.

It is advisable to have a permanent mooring for your yacht at your headquarters, as it facilitates getting under way and ensures a berth within reasonable distance of a landing hard. The latter is no mean consideration in these days of congestion. At most yachting centres moorings can be hired, but I think it is more economical in the long run to have your own. If you have no mooring, you will probably have to moor with your kedge, as it is unlikely that there will be sufficient room to permit of your riding to a single anchor, and you will soon find weighing a kedge every time you get under way and laying it out again when you return, an intolerable nuisance.

The best form of mooring is composed of two heavy anchors connected by a stout chain, to the centre of which is attached another chain, known as the riding scope, to which the yacht rides. The mooring should be laid up and down stream so that the yacht rides first to one anchor and then to the other, according to the tide. The length of the ground scope will depend upon the depth of water at high tide and should not be less than four times the depth. The length of the riding scope should be about one and a half times the depth of water at high tide and it should be attached to the ground scope with a strong swivel. The buoy rope should be of bass, rather longer than the depth of water at high tide, and as the yacht may have to ride to it before the chain is hauled aboard, it should be fairly stout. If the mooring chain has to be led through a hawsehole in the bulwark, the buoy rope should be attached about a fathom from the end so that the loose end may be passed through the bulwark and belayed to the bitts, whilst the buoy is lifted over the rail and the buoy rope coiled down on deck. Should the riding scope merely have to pass over an ordinary snatch fairlead on the stem-head, the end of the chain can be shackled back so as to form a bight large enough to pass over the bitts or windlass, the buoy rope being attached to the chain just below the bight.

The chain for moorings need not be galvanized as it will not rust very much under water, particularly if it be tarred before the mooring is laid, but there should be a fathom or two of galvanized chain at the top of the riding scope, or otherwise the decks would be stained with rust. Any old anchors will do for moorings, provided that they be heavy enough, but the chain must be of the best quality and in good condition. A pair of condemned barge's anchors would answer admirably and could probably be picked up cheap from some marine store dealers, but one arm of each must be either bent down or cut off to eliminate the possibility of fouling.

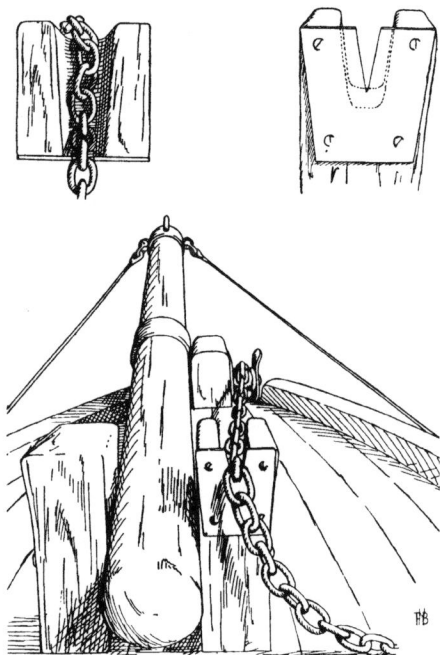

Laws' chain grip

The best form of mooring buoy is a small oak barrel. It should be fitted with two strong strops of tarred hemp, to which the buoy rope is attached on one side of the barrel and a handle of tarred hemp on the other. The barrel should be painted and bear the tonnage of the yacht on the ends as a warning to owners of larger vessels that the mooring is of insufficient weight and strength to hold them. The small iron nun buoys sometimes used are rather apt to wash under in a strong tide and are not so easily picked up, as one has to scoop under the buoy with the boathook to catch the buoy rope. I have occasionally seen optimistic yachtsmen endeavouring to hook the tiny ring on the top of the buoy, a diverting sight which suggests angling rather than yachting.

Moorings should be laid at low water spring tides if possible, and before laying, care should be taken that the shackle pins are secured with copper wire.

If you keep your yacht in an anchorage that dries out at low water and the bottom is of mud, you can use a simpler and less expensive form of mooring known as a 'windmill.' Get two pieces of stout plank, each about five feet long and bolt them together in the form of a cross. Make fast the mooring chain to the centre of the cross, the length of the former being about twice the depth at high water, and attach the buoy rope and

Barrel mooring buoy

buoy to the other end. Then dig a deep hole in the mud at low tide and bury the cross and you will have an efficient mooring at very small cost. There should be a strong swivel on the chain to prevent its being wound up by the vessel swinging to the tide. These windmill moorings are extensively used at such places as Leigh and Southend.

In order to protect the yacht's paint from being chafed by the mooring or anchor chain, a bow fender is often used. It takes the form of a long sausage, tightly packed with kapok, which is passed beneath the bobstay when the yacht is at anchor. The ends are secured by lanyards made fast to the covering board on either side. A bow fender can also be made of two pieces of half-round hard wood, joined by a rope grommet, and painted the same colour as the topsides of the vessel.

Iron nun mooring buoy

Before leaving this subject of ground tackle, I should mention that chain cables are usually made up in 15-fathom lengths and joined together with D-shaped shackles. The round end of the shackle should face forward when the chain is running out, as otherwise it may jam in the hawse-pipe. The big shackle

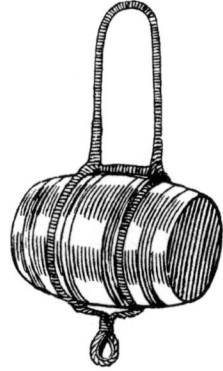

Bow fender

by which the cable is connected to the anchor should have its pin secured with copper wire. It is prudent, indeed, to secure all shackle-pins of ground tackle in a similar manner.

CHAPTER 28: *Fittings*

In this chapter I propose to ignore fancy fittings such as sheet winches and High-field levers, as they are seldom found in small cruising yachts. They are no doubt very useful for racing purposes, but the owner of a cruising craft can very well do without them. My remarks will therefore be confined to such fittings as are normally used in small yachts up to about 7 or 8 tons Thames Measurement.

Cleats and fairleads: For most purposes ordinary cleats, either of wood, galvanized iron or brass, will serve and call for little comment, except as regards the manner of fitting. Sometimes they are put on with screws, which is a mistake, as sooner or later a cleat thus fastened is pretty sure to come adrift. Cleats should be fitted with bolts and nuts, through a beam when possible. If there is not a beam handy, the deck should be reinforced by a chock of hard wood below and the bolts passed through both deck and chock and secured by a washer and nuts. The same thing applies to the fitting of headsail sheet fairleads, and as these must be placed in exactly the right spot to give the sheet a fair lead, it is unlikely that there will be a deck-beam just where it is wanted. The bolts and nuts should be of brass and they are seldom stocked by the ordinary ironmonger. They can be obtained, however, either from Simpson, Lawrence & Co., of Glasgow, or Carter & Aynesley of Middlesex Street, London, EC. If you cannot procure them of the exact length you want, get them rather longer and saw off the surplus with a hacksaw. The best kind of fair-lead for headsail sheets is that lined with lignum vitae as it does not chafe the rope. They can be procured from Simpson, Lawrence & Co., or Captain O. M. Watts Ltd. of Albemarle Street, London, W.1.

In the last chapter I drew attention to the convenience of jam cleats for the headsail sheets. Those stocked by yacht-chandlers are usually of brass, which are expensive and fail to 'do their stuff' properly when the rope is slightly worn. A jam cleat which requires more than one turn of the sheet to make the latter hold is no better than an ordinary one. Personally, I prefer jam cleats made of hard wood, such as teak or oak, but as they are seldom stocked, one usually has to have them made specially. Some years ago, when I owned the 7-ton *Fancy*, I could not obtain wooden jam cleats at any of the shops I visited and was induced to buy brass ones, which cost me ten shillings apiece. They looked very nice, but as jam cleats they were next door to useless. So I sent a sketch of what I wanted to Simpson, Lawrence & Co., and they made me a set to my own design. The feature of this cleat is that the business side of the jamming horn is not bevelled off

Wooden jamb cleat

but left perfectly flat. In most jam cleats the edges are rounded off for the sake of neatness and their gripping qualities impaired. With my cleat a single turn jams the sheet and although I have now used them for a good many years, I have never known the rope to slip.

The cleat should be fitted to the inside of the coaming, about nine inches abaft the hole through which the sheet is led, with the jamming horn forward and slightly raised. By the way, brass bushes for the holes in the coamings can be procured from Woodnutt & Co., of St. Helen's, Isle of Wight, who also stock a roller sheet lead, which can be let into the coaming. The addition of the roller assists materially in getting in the sheet.

Mainsheet buffer: A mainsheet buffer robs a heavy gybe of half its danger and is a refinement well worth the money, if you can afford it. An excellent buffer can be procured from Messrs. Pascall, Atkey & Son. It is of the double-action type and the fixing bolts can be made so as to bring the buffers any height from the deck, or the buffer can be made upon a horse so that the tiller may operate beneath it.

Main horse chocks: When the mainsheet travels on a horse trouble is often experienced through the block falling over the end of the

Mainsheet buffer

horse and getting jammed. To prevent this, turksheads of hambro-line are often put on the ends of the horse, but they are seldom very satisfactory and soon get worn by chafe. A better plan is to fit rounds of hard wood on the ends of the horse. Turn the pieces of wood up on a lathe and then split them in halves. After

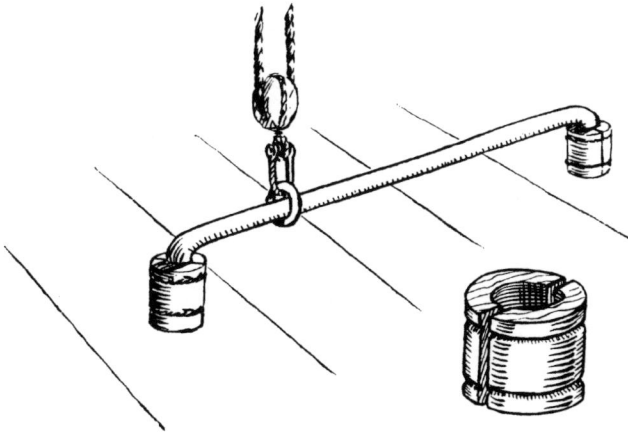

Wooden chocks on mainsheet horse

scooping out sufficient of the middle to fit round the horse, they can be seized on with copper wire. A disc of old motor-car tyre on top of the wood would serve as a buffer. Similar stops can be fitted to the fore-horse, if your foresail has a boom.

Cockpit tent: A cockpit tent is a great boon in a small yacht on a wet day, as it provides one with the equivalent of a second cabin, in which one can carry on such domestic operations as washing-up after meals. The tent will also provide much-needed privacy when lying in a harbour, or crowded anchorage. The usual well-tent is just an oblong piece of

Worth mast band

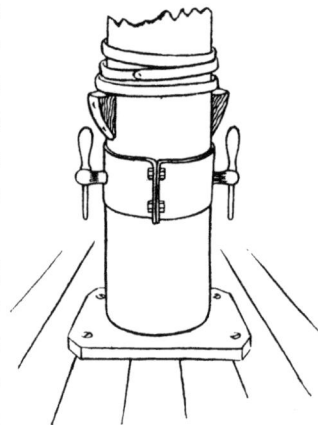

waterproof canvas spread over the made-up mainsail and boom and fastened down to screw-eyes on the outside of the coamings. Such a tent keeps the cockpit dry, but affords little headroom, except under the boom.

Its comfort would be much enhanced if the tent were laid over three or four spreaders shaped like a coat-hanger but as long as the width of the cockpit. It would, of course, have to be slung beneath the boom by lines from the hangers, passed through eyelets in the tent. Such a tent would provide adequate head-room over the whole cockpit, enabling one to sit up comfortably on the seats, and when not in use could be wrapped round the spreaders and stowed away in the sail locker or fo'c'sle.

Fife-rail or spider-band: Whether it is better to belay halyards to a fiferail on deck or to belaying pins in the mastband is a matter of opinion, but personally I prefer the latter. I admit that a fiferail is more convenient, but it seems to me that a great strain must be thrown on the deck when all of the halyards are set up to it. Now, if the halyards are belayed to a spider-band the whole of the strain is taken by the mast. Most owners, I think, object to a spider-band as the mast-hoops, when the sail is lowered, fall down on to the belaying-pins and get in the way. But that can very easily be avoided by fitting a couple of chocks on the mast, about a foot above the spider-band. The chocks should be fitted on either side of the mast and be large enough to catch the hoops and keep them clear of the pins when the sail is lowered.

Mast band: The usual type of mast-band, being single and narrow, has to be screwed up very tightly or otherwise it will turn. That is bad for the mast, as the wood may be crushed in the process and lead to the mast breaking at that point. To avoid this, Claud Worth designed a double band, joined together by plates of mild steel. This has a comparatively wide

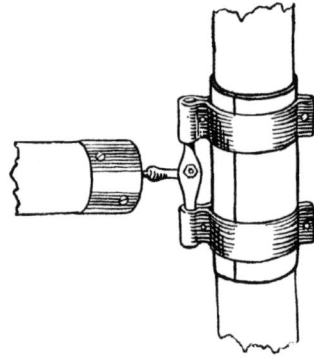

Mast hoop chocks

388

bearing and need not be screwed up so tightly.

The boom is attached to a stout pin fitted between the bands and is much more able to withstand the heavy shearing strain engendered by the vessel pitching into a head sea, than the ordinary gooseneck joint. Like most of Mr. Worth's ideas, this strikes me as very sound. I had such a mast-band in *Fancy* and found it most efficient.

Gaff jaws: The old-fashioned gaff-jaws made of wood are not often used

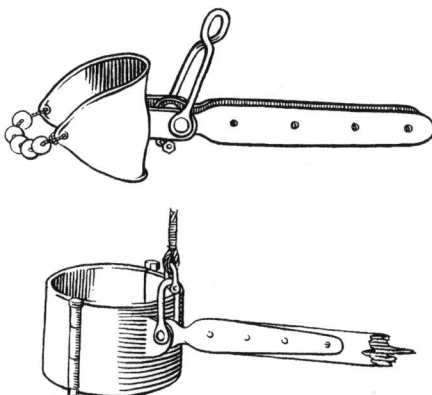

Gaff jaws, saddle and collar types

in yachts nowadays, but one sees them occasionally. I had them in several of my early craft and found them most inefficient, as they were easily broken and were apt to trap the halyards. Another objection was that the main halyard had to be attached to the gaff several inches from the jaws. When setting the sail, if it were peaked after the main halyard had been set up taut, the mere act of peaking caused the jaws to slip down the mast a few inches and slack up the luff. The only way in which this could be avoided was to peak the sail well above the horizontal before setting up the throat.

The present-day saddle jaws made of galvanized iron, covered with leather, are far preferable, as the main halyard is attached to the jaw fitting itself and is not affected by the position of the gaff. But even with a saddle jaw a halyard may be trapped if you don't watch it. A very satisfactory form of gaff-jaw consists of a leather-covered iron collar, about 6 inches deep, to which the gaff is hinged. If greased occasionally it will travel up and down the mast very easily and there is no possibility of the halyards being trapped in it.

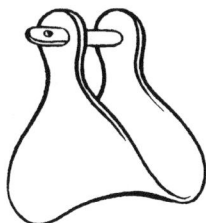

Gaff sling: The peak halyard should not be attached direct to the gaff but to a wire sling in order to distribute the strain. As an ordinary shackle might nip the wire sling unduly, the halyard should be attached by a special shackle of saddle shape, as supplied by Simpson, Lawrence & Co.

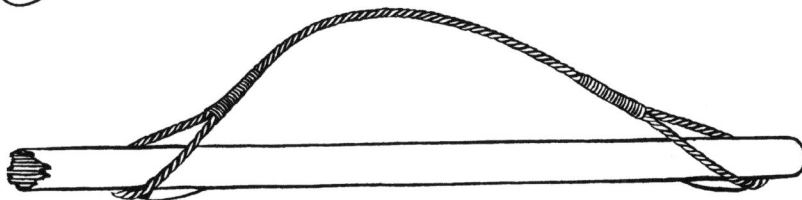

Wire gaff sling and shackle

Halyard bolts: The halyard bolts should be of galvanized iron, driven right through the masthead and secured with nuts and washers. That for the main halyard should protrude about 3 inches, otherwise the block will chafe the mast. Bolts through the masthead, of course, tend to weaken the spar a little, but if iron bands are used there is a risk of the beckets breaking off, and on the whole I prefer through bolts; at any rate for the halyards.

Pump: Every yacht should be equipped with a good pump. Most small craft have a pump of the ordinary plunger type fitted on deck at the side of the cockpit, but there are several objections to that sort of pump. Unless it is fitted with a brake, which it seldom is, it strikes me as dangerous in that position, as you have to stand either on deck or on the cockpit seat to operate it. As you have nothing to hold on to except the pump handle, your stance is somewhat precarious in rough weather, and a sudden lurch of the yacht might easily throw you over-board. A deck pump of that type, too, has to be fed with water before starting to work, and it is about the most back-breaking job I know. It does not throw a great deal of water and after you have been pumping for about a quarter of an hour your muscles ache inordinately, and you feel inclined to give up yachting and take up a less strenuous hobby, such as keeping silkworms.

A good semi-rotary pump, mounted on the bulkhead and discharging through the topside, is a much better proposition, as you can work it comfortably and in perfect safety while seated in the cockpit, and it needs no feeding to start it. The pump should be of useful size and capable of discharging ten or twelve gallons a minute. Semi-rotary pumps made of iron are quite cheap, but as they soon rust they are not suitable for yachting purposes. A brass one, although fairly expensive to buy, is cheapest in the long run. The brass semi-rotary pump fitted in my old *Snipe* when she was built more than fifty years ago is still, I believe, in perfect working order – at any rate it was a few years ago when my son owned her.

Another excellent pump is the SL Diaphragm, supplied by Simpson, Lawrence & Co. I have one in my present boat and find it very satisfactory. The 1¼-inch size will discharge ten gallons a minute and is very easy to work. It is fitted to the bulkhead and discharges through the topside. The rubber diaphragm will last for several years and can be renewed in a few minutes at trifling cost. The bilge pipe of any pump should be protected by a filter, otherwise the pump may get choked with dirt. And if you stow tinned food in the lockers under the bunks, remove the labels first; otherwise they may soak off and clog the pump.

Tiller: The tiller of a yacht should be made of oak. An iron tiller is an abomination, as it whips and sooner or later works loose on the rudder-head. I had an iron tiller in *Forsitan* and it worked very loose. I suggested to a shipwright that perhaps a stout spring washer under the nut would cure the trouble, but he scoffed at the idea and packed it with strips of brass. They worked out the very first time I sailed her, so I decided to try my washer idea. I screwed the tiller tight down on to a stout spring washer and it made the tiller perfectly rigid; and what is more it remained so all the time that I owned the boat. This tip may be of service to others who experience similar trouble.

Boom crutch: There are few more unsatisfactory items of equipment than the X-shaped boom crutch, commonly seen in small yachts. With the legs resting in small chocks on deck, or on the cockpit seats, it is extremely unstable, while the boom being in the middle of the boat is horribly in the way when the vessel is at anchor. You may set up the mainsheet quite taut when you bring up, but it is sure to stretch in a little while and then the crutch is liable to go adrift if the water is at all rough. Then the boom will bang about from side to side to the detriment of the gear, and if you have not taken the precaution to make it fast with a lanyard, you may lose the crutch overboard.

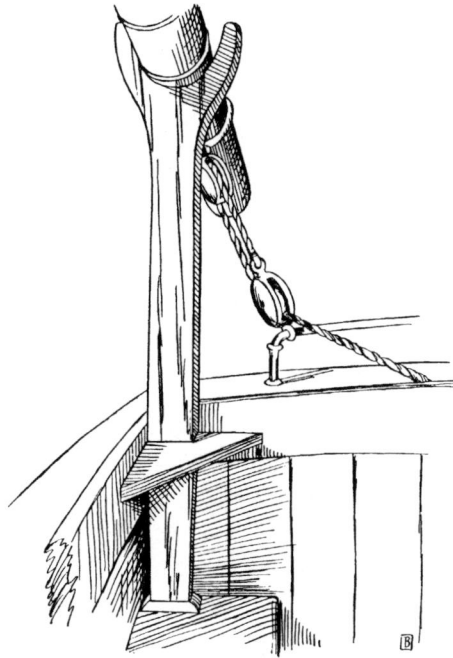

Y-shaped boom crutch

The simplest and best form of crutch for a small yacht is Y-shaped as used in fishing smacks. Stepped on the quarter, through the deck, it is quite firm and cannot get adrift, while it keeps the boom clear of the cockpit. It is usually made of wood, but there is no reason why it should not be of galvanized iron and stepped into a short length of galvanized water-pipe. An alternative method would be to step it in chocks in the corner of the cockpit, or on the outside of the coaming. In my own craft the crutch is stepped in a chock mounted on the outside of the after cockpit coaming, at the side. There is another chock on the coaming amidships, for use when the cockpit tent is erected.

CHAPTER 29: *Navigation Equipment*

Sailing at night is delightful in fine weather, when the moon is full and the heavens hung with stars, but all the same I think the best place for a small yacht during the hours of darkness is in some snug anchorage. I have never forgotten the loss of the 10-ton *Vesta*, nearly half a century ago, when three of my friends and a paid hand were drowned. It happened on a night such as I have described and the yacht was run down by some unknown vessel in the neighbourhood of the West Rocks and sunk with all hands. Still, there are times when you cannot avoid being under way after dark, but now that we have summer-time such occasions are comparatively rare for those who cruise round the coast. All the same the owner of a cruising vessel should be prepared for night sailing.

The regulations ordain that a sailing vessel under way between sunset and sunrise shall carry:

On the starboard side a green light so constructed as to show an unbroken light over an arc of the horizon of 10 points of the compass, so fixed as to throw the light from right ahead to 2 points abaft the beam on the starboard side, and of such a character as to be visible at a distance of at least 2 miles.

On the port side a red light so constructed as to show an unbroken light over an arc of the horizon of 10 points of the compass, so fixed as to throw the light from right ahead to 2 points abaft the beam on the port side, and of such a character as to be visible at a distance of at least 2 miles.

She must also show a white light from her stern should another vessel be overtaking her. Should the yacht have her auxiliary engine running, she ranks as a steamer, even if she is sailing as well, and must show a white masthead light at a height from the hull of not less than 20 feet, so constructed as to show an unbroken light over an arc of the horizon of 20 points of the compass, so fixed as to throw the light 10 points on each side of the vessel, viz. from right ahead to 2 points abaft the beam on either side, and of such a character as to be visible at a distance of at least 5 miles.

Those are the regulation lights to be carried when under way after sunset. When at anchor, between the hours of sunset and sunrise, the yacht must show a white light, forward where it can best be seen, visible all round the horizon for a distance of at least a mile.

It is a popular delusion that the size of the navigation lanterns should be based on the size of the yacht, but, far from that being the case, they should be in inverse ratio to the size of the vessel. The beams from a small yacht's lights are so close to the water that even if visible for the prescribed two miles, which they seldom are, they are not easily seen from the deck of a big steamer. It is advisable therefore to have some extraneous means of attracting attention. The light from a powerful electric torch flashed on the white sails is much more likely to be seen than the navigation lights, or a flare can be burnt. In my young days I was one of a syndicate owning an old 20-ton smack, which we sailed all the year round in the Thames Estuary. We were often under way after dark and it was our practice to keep a handful of cotton waste, steeped in paraffin, in a bailer. When a steamer came dangerously near, we put a match to the flare, and it never failed to do the trick.

Apart from the question of visibility, I am inclined to think that the navigation lights of small yachts seldom, if ever, conform to the regulations. The screens are fitted on the shrouds and when the yacht is sailing to windward, the lee shrouds are so slack that the screen waggles about with the motion of the vessel, with the result that at one moment the light is showing across the bow

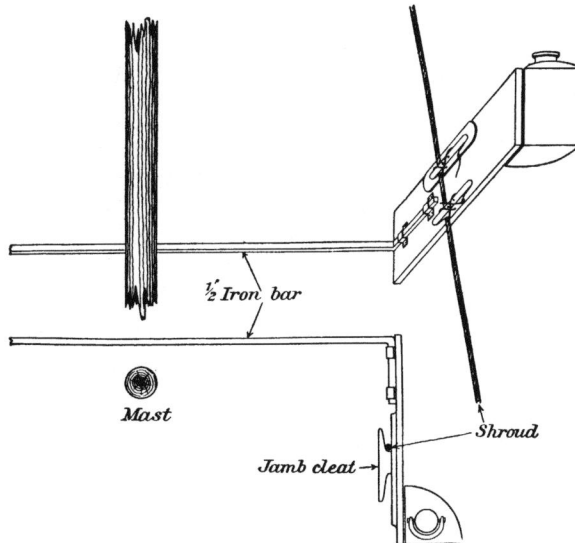

½ Iron bar

Mast

Shroud

Jamb cleat →

Laws' sidelight screen attachment

and the next it does not show right ahead and can be seen for more than the prescribed 2 points abaft the beam.

To overcome this difficulty, the late Mr. G. U. Laws devised a rather ingenious method of screen attachment. It is merely an iron bar with the ends bent back at right angles, to which the screens are attached. Each screen has two metal jam cleats on the back, which fit on the shroud, being secured there by lines. The illustration shows clearly the method of attachment. The screens should be fitted high up on the shrouds so that the bar will clear your head when going forward. As, when the yacht is sailing to windward, the weather shrouds are as taut as fiddle strings, both lights are held rigidly in their proper positions, while the lanterns are in a much higher position than customary.

The side-lights of small yachts are very difficult to keep alight in rough weather, as they either blow out or are shaken out by the motion of the boat, while the visibility, particularly of the starboard light, leaves much to be desired. They usually have paraffin burners and I don't think it would need much ingenuity to convert them to electric. A small bulb, fed by a dry battery, would serve the purpose, but it would be prudent to carry on board several spare batteries and bulbs. The beam, too, would be much intensified by mirror reflectors, as used in motor-cycle headlights. The best lenses for navigation lights are prismatic. They are not so powerful as dioptric, but the dioptric lens is not suitable for a sailing yacht, as when the vessel is heeled, the light shines on to the water instead of far ahead. For riding lights the dioptric is the best.

Fortunately, vessels under 20 tons are not compelled by the Board of Trade regulations to carry the specified navigation lights. They may instead use a lantern with a green glass on one side and a red one on the other, which must be displayed in time to prevent a collision in such a manner that the red light cannot be seen on the starboard side or the green on the port side. If you have no intention of sailing much at night, such a lantern will serve your purpose, particularly if you supplement it with an electric torch, or keep a flare handy. Your riding light will do very well for a stern light. You should keep it alight in a bucket, within easy reach of the helmsman, but the light should be screened from his eyes.

I would warn the inexperienced owner of a little cruiser against being persuaded to buy the miniature navigation lights often to be seen in yacht-chandlers' show rooms. Made of highly burnished copper, or brass, they look very pretty, but they usually have colza burners, which won't burn, and are altogether useless toys.

The only form of riding light worth a damn that I know is that having a windproof burner, such as that made by Davey & Co., Ltd., 88 West India Dock Road, London, E14. This has an inner glass of inverted cone shape and, provided

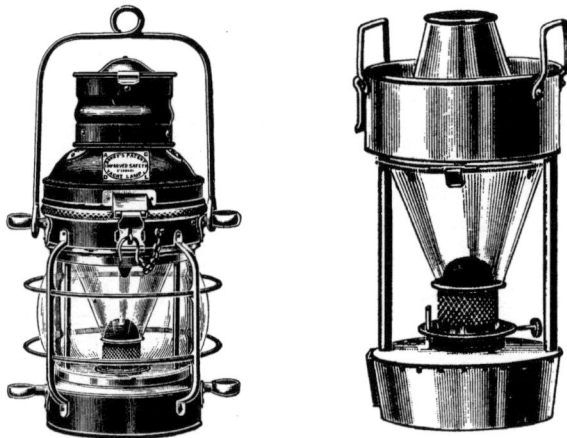

Windproof riding light and lamp assembly

that it is properly trimmed, it will burn brightly in almost any weather and will not be jerked out by the motion of the boat, however violent. The Davey lamps are most substantially made and will last for many years. A friend of mine has had one in constant use for more than thirty years and it is still in good order. A riding light of this type may cost you thirty shillings or more but is a good investment as it will save you from anxiety. It is a mistake to use a cheap hurricane lantern for this purpose, as some small yacht owners do, for it cannot be trusted and if you cannot rely on your riding light you will have many a sleepless night.

On a cutter, the best way of hoisting the riding light is with the foresail halyard. A spring hank should be seized to the ring of the lamp and snapped on to the forestay when hoisting. Lanyards should be led from the sides of the lamp and set up to the bowsprit shrouds, or rail if the yacht has no bowsprit shrouds. Thus hoisted, the lamp cannot swing about and will not be damaged by knock-

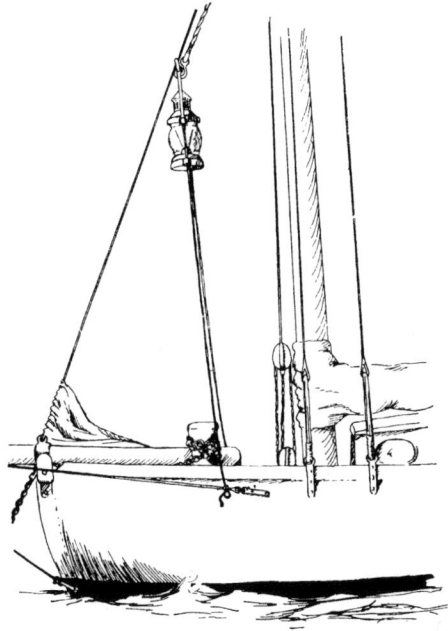

Hoisting riding light on a cutter

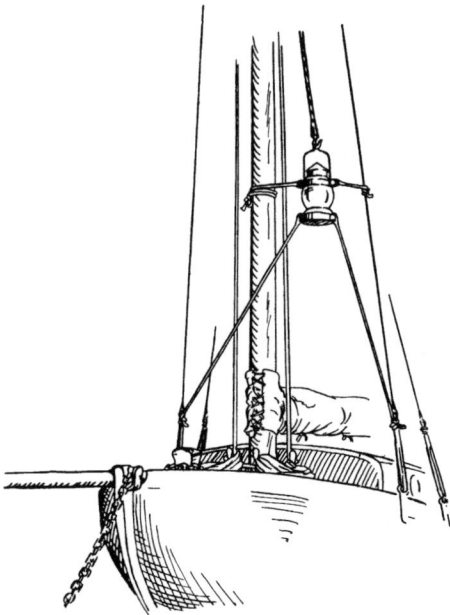

ing against anything. In a sloop with a bowsprit, the lamp can be hoisted in the same way, but instead of a spring hank, use a short length of line with a spring hook on the end, as shown in the illustration. The lanyards can be set up to screw-eyes in the covering-board, or to the rail. Another way of hoisting the riding light on a sloop is to suspend it between the rigging and the mast, with lanyards to both to keep it equi-distant.

The yachtsman whose sailing is confined to cruising round the coast, with perhaps an occasional trip across the Channel or North Sea, does not require much in the way of navigating instruments as he is not often out of sight of land, and if he is, can find his way very well by dead reckoning. You don't need

Hoisting riding light on a sloop

a sextant to find out where you are when you can see with your naked eye the girls bathing off Clacton beach – what you want then is a good pair of binoculars!

But even for coastwise cruising there are instruments that are indispensable, and of these the most important is a compass. Nothing but a spirit compass is of any use in a small yacht, as the card of an ordinary compass oscillates violently in a seaway, and it takes a skilful helmsman to steer an accurate compass course when he has to watch the limits of the oscillations and gauge the mean. In a spirit compass the card floats in glycerine, rendering the movement sufficiently sluggish to keep the needle comparatively steady in rough water.

I have bought my compasses from Messrs. Hughes and Sons for a good many years, and know no better firm for such goods. Even in a miniature cruiser it should be large enough to read easily without eye-strain, and I would suggest

Compass mounted in cabin

one with a 5-inch card. The binnacles supplied for small yachts are seldom very satisfactory, as the small oil lamps with which they are usually fitted will not burn reliably in rough weather. Electrically lit binnacles are of course obtainable, but they are usually too large for a small yacht and rather expensive.

The best plan is to mount the compass inside the cabin, behind a small window in the bulkhead. In such a position you can see it quite well from the helm by day and at night it can be illuminated by an electric bulb or candle mounted at the side. The compass should be installed as far away as possible from anything of iron, such as an auxiliary engine and water-cans, as such may cause considerable deviation. If the yacht has no engine and the compass is not very near such things as water- or oil-cans, or the kedge, it will probably be accurate enough for the sort of cruising in which you engage, but otherwise you should have the vessel swung and a deviation card prepared. It would be prudent to have that done in any case if you are going for a long cruise far from the land, for even a slight deviation might completely upset your reckoning.

Then you must have a hand-lead and line, properly marked, for taking soundings. The lead-line should be cable-laid, as such rope is not so liable to kink as the usual hawser-laid. You must remember, however, always to coil it anti-clockwise.

A proper lead-line is 25 fathoms in length, and marked as follows:

At	2 fathoms	Leather, with two ends
	3	Leather, with three ends
	5	White calico
	7	Red bunting
	10	Leather, with hole in it
	13	Blue serge
	15	White calico
	17	Red bunting
	20	Strand, with two knots in it

Those depths are called marks, and the depths in fathoms which are not marked are known as deeps. Thus, in 7 fathoms, the leadsman would call out, "By the mark seven," or in 9 fathoms, "By the deep nine." If the sounding shows the fraction of a fathom, the fraction is always called first, thus "And a quarter seven," when the depth is 7¼ fathoms, or "And a half six," for 6½ fathoms. For 5¾ fathoms he would sing out, "A quarter less six." That at least is the way in which it should be done, but as a matter of fact, the yachtsman would probably say, "About three fathoms," or "Two and a half," as the case may be.

The lead used by yachtsmen usually weighs about 5 lb. or rather less. Its heel is hollowed out, so that it can be armed (i.e. filled) with tallow or grease of some kind, for getting a specimen of the bottom. Particles of mud, sand, or shingle will adhere to the grease and by reference to the chart, it may be possible to locate the position of the vessel. When the coastwise cruiser takes soundings, however, it is usually in shoal water and a shorter line will be found more convenient.

The lead-line I use is a much more primitive affair, being only 6 fathoms long and having the fathoms marked with knots – one knot at 1 fathom, two close together at 2 fathoms and so on, and it serves the purpose well enough. For those who spend most of their time in estuaries and exploring creeks – mud-crawling it is usually called – a bamboo rod will be found a quicker and more convenient implement, as soundings in shoal water can be taken very quickly. A ring should be painted round the rod at each foot, in different colours.

If you intend to cruise out of sight of land, you will also need a patent log. There are various kinds on the market, but the most convenient is that which has the dial on deck, such as the Cherub, and a rotator at the end of the line, as you can read it at a glance. If your log is of the harpoon type, you must haul it on board before you can read it and it is more liable to get damaged, although cheaper. The log line should be about 40 fathoms in length and it is advisable to carry a spare rotator, as they are sometimes bitten off by sharks and other large fish.

A rough and ready way of calculating the speed of a vessel through the water is by means of what is known as the 'Dutchman's Log.' Two marks are made on the rail, or covering board, one near the bow and the other near the stern. To ascertain the speed, a bit of wood, a cork, or a ball of paper is thrown overboard ahead of the bow mark and the time taken of its travel between the two marks. The speed in knots is found by multiplying the length in feet by 6 and dividing by 10 times the time in seconds, thus :

$$6L / 10T = \text{knots (nautical miles per hour)}.$$

The distance between the marks should be a convenient round number, so that the speed can be calculated mentally. This method, of course, could only be employed when single-handed if the yacht were travelling very slowly.

Then you will need parallel rulers for laying off a course on the chart and a pair of dividers for measuring distances.

And now a word or two about charts. You must, of course, carry on board charts of the waters you propose to sail and it is important that they should be up to date. Changes are frequently made in the character and positions of buoys and an old chart may be misleading. As notice of buoyage changes are only published in the shipping papers, the average yachtsman is not in a position to keep his charts up-to-date himself. Most firms who issue charts, however, will make the necessary corrections for a trifling charge. It is important, too, that charts be kept clean and in decent condition. A story is told of the skipper of a collier brig caught in a heavy gale in the North Sea. After poring over a filthy chart for some time he turned to his mate and said, "Well, mister, if that is the Shipwash we are all right, but if it's a fly-blow, Gawd 'elp us."

The Admiralty and Blue Back charts are no doubt indispensable to the professional navigator, but I don't think them suitable for the requirements of the small yacht owner. They contain such a wealth of detail that the amateur cannot see the wood for the trees. Moreover, they are too large and unwieldy. The yachtsman often wants to consult the chart while at the helm and the large Admiralty charts are as intractable as a clock spring. With only one hand available, much time and temper are lost in futile struggles to keep the thing open, and as it is unprotected the chart may be damaged by rain or spray. Such charts, of course, are admirably adapted to the requirements of the professional navigator, who has a regular chart-room and can pin them down on a table, but to the owner of a little yacht they are a source of much inconvenience and annoyance.

Recognizing these facts, Messrs. Imray, Laurie, Norie & Wilson Ltd., some years ago brought out a series of charts for the special use of yachtsmen, which are known as the 'Y' charts. They contain all the essential information and are printed in colour. Sands that uncover at low water are printed in buff, waters with a depth up to three fathoms in pale blue, and deep channels in dark blue. In addition to the coast charts, there are large-scale plans of harbours and rivers, and they strike me as about the best charts for yachtsmen that have yet been produced. They are of uniform size, measuring 20 by 15 inches, and lie flat. The publishers also supply a special holder, known as the Rawlinson for these charts, which consists of a polished board on which the charts lie flat and are protected by a sheet of celluloid from rain or spray. Non-rusting metal clips hold the lot together and the whole series can be kept in the holder, with the chart in use on

Rawlinson chart holder

top. A canvas case is supplied in which the holder and charts can be slung on the bulkhead when not in use. No matter how good your charts may be, you will not derive the greatest benefit from them unless you know how to read them. Those who lack experience in that way should get an excellent little book by Lieutenant Luard, RN, published by Imray, Laurie, Norie & Wilson Ltd, called *The Yachtsman's Modern Navigation and Practical Pilotage*. One could not have a better guide than Lieutenant Luard, who possesses the art of being able to make a rather dry subject quite interesting to read.

Finally, you will require a book, or books, of pilotage directions to assist you in navigating the various channels and when entering harbours. If you sail on the South or East Coasts you could not do better than get one, or both, of the books compiled by Mr. W. Eric Wilson, of Messrs. Imray, Laurie, Norie & Wilson Ltd., entitled respectively *The Pilot's Guide to the English Channel* and *The Pilot's Guide to the Thames Estuary and Norfolk Broads*. They are the most complete works of the kind yet issued and have the advantage of being kept up to date by the yearly issue of supplements containing information as to alterations in buoyage, etc. They are illustrated by aerial photographs of the principal harbours, a very valuable feature, and contain a vast amount of information of just the kind that a yachtsman needs, and I consider them indispensable to anyone sailing those waters.

With these two books, which are published by Imray, Laurie. Norie & Wilson, and a set of 'Y' charts, you will be able to cruise anywhere between Land's End and Lowestoft, but if you sail for the most part in the Solent district, I would recommend you also to get Adlard Coles's admirable *Creeks and Harbours of the Solent*, published by Edward Arnold & Co. For cruising on the French and Belgian coasts Charles Pears's *Going Foreign* can be recommended; it is also published by Edward Arnold & Co. Your library should also include a nautical almanack, from which you will be able to ascertain the time of high water at practically any port on any day of the year and also glean much valuable information as to the lightships, buoys, etc. all round the coast.

A wireless set is a very desirable item of equipment in a yacht, particularly when making a long voyage, as it enables you to obtain the weather forecasts and Greenwich Mean Time several times a day. An ordinary portable set, however, is not likely to give satisfaction, as it is not designed for the severe conditions under which a radio set has to work at sea in a small craft. The highly polished case would soon lose its pristine beauty and some of the parts would probably corrode. Captain O. M. Watts Ltd., of Albemarle Street, London, W1, stock a range of reliable instruments, and I hear very good accounts of the receivers made for such work by Schooner Sets, 7 York Buildings, Bridgwater, Somerset.

The Schooner set is very substantially made, the case being of half-inch teak, oil polished, and all of the fittings are of brass or bronze. All parts of the receiver can be inspected and batteries changed without removing the set. The loudspeaker, which is of the moving-coil type, is housed in a separate case, so that it can be installed in the cabin, when the set itself is fitted in a locker.

The range of the Schooner receiver is extensive, and yachts cruising in the Baltic, North of Scotland, West of Ireland and down the Spanish coast have been able to receive signals from British stations. A 7-ton cutter, which crossed the Atlantic some years ago, managed to keep in touch with our transmitting stations for 1,200 miles and then picked up the station at St John's, Newfoundland. The dimensions of the Schooner, Models IIIA and IIIB, are 14 inches × 15 inches × 5 inches and either can be fitted by mirror-plates or lugs to a bulkhead. The weight is about 23 lb., and the set being readily portable can be used ashore during the winter, when the yacht is out of commission. The IIIA model is identical with the IIIB, but the former uses a small output valve, whilst the latter has a low consumption Pentode. All wavelengths are covered from 200 to 2,000. For small craft, where there is not room for a Schooner, the firm market a smaller set known as the Sloop, which measures only 12½ inches × 7 inches × 4 inches. It is sufficiently powerful to work a loud-speaker when the yacht is at anchor, but when at sea the makers recommend the use of headphones. Lt.-Commander Douglas Dixon, however, used a Sloop receiver in his cutter *Dusmarie* when cruising recently and received the time signals and weather forecast on the loudspeaker all the way from the Thames to Ushant. Full particulars and prices can be obtained from the makers of these sets, whose name and address I have mentioned above.

Apart from being able to get the weather forecast and time signals, an efficient wireless set is a great boon when cruising, as it enables one to keep in touch with the news of the day, to say nothing of its entertainment value. To the man who cruises alone it is an inestimable boon. The best results are obtained with an outside aerial, although the Schooner and Sloop sets can also be worked with an aerial of thin insulated wire arranged below deck. It is quite an easy matter to rig up an aerial of insulated wire from the masthead, leading it to the set through a tiny hole bored through the deck, whilst the earth wire can be attached to one of the keel bolts. Schooner wireless sets, by the way, were used by Mr. A. G. H. Macpherson in *Driac II*, which cruised all over the world, and by Commander Graham in *Emanuel* during her transatlantic voyages.

CHAPTER 30: *Auxiliary Engines*

[1928] Even the smallest cruising yacht is nowadays considered incompletely equipped if she has not an auxiliary engine, and it cannot be denied that a motor is often a great convenience. It enormously simplifies such problems of seamanship as getting under way in a congested anchorage, entering and leaving harbours, berthing against a quay, and picking up moorings, whilst in the event of the wind failing, it will often enable a vessel to make a port instead of spending the night at sea. To an owner engaged in business, who has to catch certain trains, a motor is almost a necessity, for in the absence of auxiliary power he is dependent upon the wind, which may fail him. It is essential, however, that the engine should be absolutely reliable, for a motor that cannot be depended upon at all times to start up and run without trouble, is worse than useless.

An auxiliary engine, however, should only be used in calms and when sail cannot be carried to advantage, or, of course, if you are seriously pressed for time. I think it a deplorable sight to see a yacht under power when she has a fine fair wind, for it can only be attributed to sheer laziness; but some owners seem to make a practice of using the engine most of the time when they are under way. One wonders why, if they take so little interest in sailing, they do not go in for motor cruisers pure and simple.

Ailsa Craig "Pup"

In selecting a motor for installation in your yacht, there are several points that call for consideration. In the first place the engine must be compact so that it will not occupy too much space. Secondly, it must not be too complicated. Thirdly, the working parts must be easily accessible. Fourthly, it should be capable of driving the vessel through the water at a speed of not less than four miles an hour; and lastly, it should be economical in its consumption of fuel. There are no doubt many engines on the market that more or less fulfil these conditions, but as I have not much space at my disposal I will confine my remarks to the Ailsa Craig engines that have long enjoyed a reputation for handiness and efficient service.

For a small cruiser, up to about 5 tons Thames Measurement, the Ailsa Craig "Pup" would be difficult to improve on, as it is so compact that in many vessels it could be installed under the cockpit floor, or in one of the lockers. Its overall measurements are only 22 inches long by 12¾ inches high, although it is a 4-6 h.p. engine with two cylinders. It is a two-stroke engine running on petrol, with petroil lubrication, or in other words the lubricating oil is mixed with the petrol in the tank. Lubrication is thus automatic and starts and stops with the engine. It has a sturdy reverse gear and reduction gear, swinging a large propeller at moderate revolutions, and is extremely easy to start and control. The design of the engine ensures the crank-case compression being maintained, a very important feature in a two-stroke motor, whilst a Bosch magneto and Zenith carburettor make for reliability.

As this engine has been specially designed for installation below the cockpit floor, care has been taken to render all parts accessible from above. The magneto is conveniently placed high up so that the contact breaker is easy to get at, as also are the carburettor and sparking plugs. The big-ends can be adjusted through the inspection door on top and the cylinders decarbonized without dismantling any part of the engine. Should it be desired to remove the cylinders at any time, it can be done in a few minutes from above. The reverse gear is of the self-adjusting type, running on ball bearings, and needs no attention. A feature of the Pup

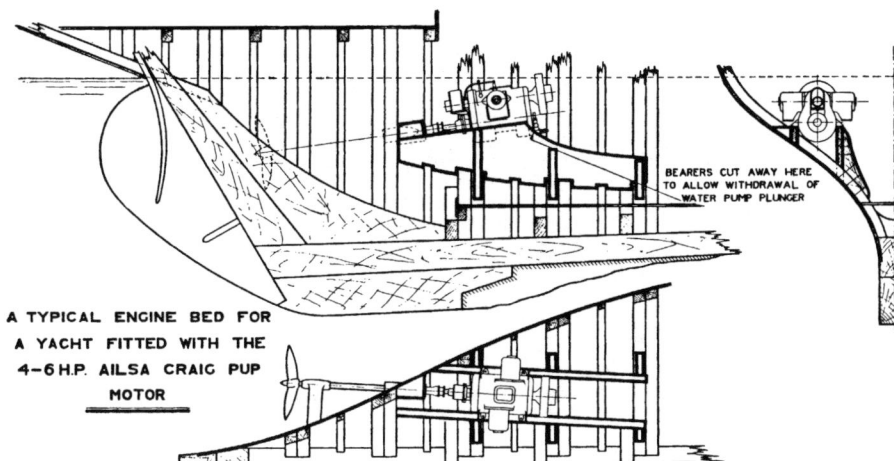

BEARERS CUT AWAY HERE
TO ALLOW WITHDRAWAL OF
WATER PUMP PLUNGER

A TYPICAL ENGINE BED FOR
A YACHT FITTED WITH THE
4—6 H.P. AILSA CRAIG PUP
MOTOR

Ailsa Craig "Pup" installation

engine is its smooth silent running, and owing to the perfect balance of the reciprocating parts it is claimed that it can be run even without bolting down to the bearers.

The reverse gear is operated by two self-adjusting metal-to-metal cone clutches, kept in engagement by an automatic device. When running all out, the engine can be thrown right over from ahead to astern and back again without fear of damage. When in the neutral position the propeller shaft is absolutely free to revolve on two ball bearings without friction or drag. The Pup is an economical engine to run, as it consumes less than half a gallon of petrol per hour, and is in every way a sound engineering job.

When installing an engine in a yacht, the following points should be kept in mind. It is not as a rule desirable to bore the stern-post for the propeller shaft, which should either be placed an inch or so to one side of the stern-post, or under the quarter of the vessel. The latter is probably the better plan, as it eliminates the necessity for cutting away the rudder, and a better flow of water to the propeller is obtained.

Then there is the question of propeller drag to be considered, particularly in the case of a yacht with fine lines. There are two ways of dealing with "drag": First, by permitting the propeller to revolve freely while sailing; and secondly, by the employment of a folding two-bladed propeller. Of these the former is usually the better method, as the power absorbed, being no more than is required to turn the propeller, is negligible. In the case of the Pup engine it is particularly small and a further advantage is that the reverse action can be retained. A folding propeller must of necessity be two-bladed, which renders a reverse impracticable, as the blades fold up immediately.

For yachts of from 8 to 10 tons, which require a rather larger engine, I would recommend the Ailsa Craig "Kid Junior." This is also a very compact motor and

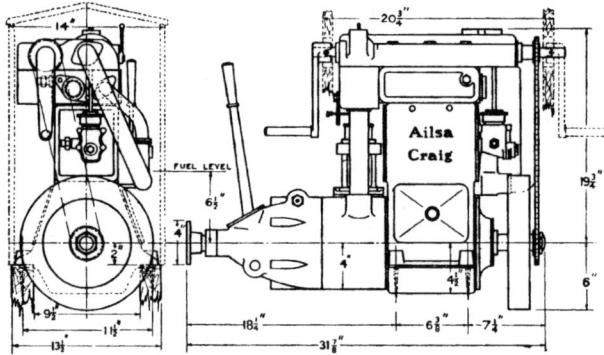

Ailsa Craig "Kid Junior"

will stow under a self-draining cockpit floor quite easily. In some yachts it would be possible to instal this engine below an ordinary cockpit floor if the latter were raised a few inches.

The Kid Junior is of a different type to the Pup, being a four-stroke twin-cylinder engine running on paraffin, its rating being 6-8 h.p. The engine has overhead valves and, as in the Pup, all the parts are easily accessible from above. The Kid Junior will drive an average 10-tonner at from five to six knots, it is easily started, and can be thoroughly relied upon to yield satisfactory service. The dimensions are indicated on the installation plan.

The Ailsa Craig Motor Co., have a fine range of engines suitable for auxiliary purposes, and those who require something more powerful than the Pup or the Kid Junior will probably find what they want in the "Kid", of 10-14 h.p. (Model de luxe 14-20 h.p.), or the "Z4" of 7-12 h.p. Both of these models are four-cylinder four-stroke engines and have a well-deserved reputation for reliability. I have not space to give particulars of them, but if you think of having an auxiliary motor installed in your yacht, I would advise you to write to the Ailsa Craig Motor Co., Ltd., Strand-on-the-Green, Chiswick, London, W., who will advise you as to the most suitable engine for your vessel and also as to the best way of installing it.

*   *   *

[1935] Whether you have a paraffin or petrol engine must be a matter of personal choice, for each has its good points. The paraffin engine is more economical but is apt to make the yacht stink. We had a paraffin motor in *Fancy* and periodically had to pour many buckets of water into the bilge and pump it out again to keep the bilge sweet. But paraffin is, I think, a safer fuel than petrol and personally I prefer it. As regards efficiency I don't think there is much to choose between them. Great progress has been made in the development of marine engines of late years and there are many reliable small auxiliary motors, both petrol and paraffin, now on the market. As it is quite impossible to give particulars of all, I shall confine my remarks to two well-known makes – one a paraffin engine and one a petrol – which I know to be extremely reliable and efficient. The make of which I have had personal experience is the Kelvin, manufactured by the Bergius Co., Ltd, of Glasgow. *Fancy*'s engine was a twin-cylinder of 7 horse-power and, although twelve or fifteen years old, it was quite reliable. As my interest is in sailing rather than motoring, the engine was only used when sail could not be carried with advantage; but on one occasion, being anxious to get to Pin Mill from Fambridge when there was a flat calm, we made the passage under power the whole way and the engine ran like a sewing machine.

The Kelvin engines are not only extremely popular with yachtsmen but extensively used in fishing smacks and other commercial craft all round the coast. More than twenty thousand of them have been produced by the Bergius Co., and they are noted for their reliability and long life. They are most substantially made of the best materials and, I should say, as nearly 'fool-proof' as any engine could be. Thousands of Kelvin engines are in constant use in fishing boats, working under conditions that afford the severest test. Exposed to salt water and dirt and maintained by unskilled labour, the engine of a smack is in use for many hours every week, running at full speed for long periods and slowly, on paraffin, for hours on end. That this make of engine is more commonly used in fishing smacks than any other is sufficient evidence of its remarkable reliability, for the fisherman must have a reliable engine, as his living depends upon it.

The engine we had in *Fancy* was of the four-cycle type, with poppet valves. It started on petrol but after running for about half a minute the fuel could be changed to paraffin. The lubrication was automatic, the oil being contained in the crankcase, supplemented by a small tank with a drip feed. The engine, which had a reverse, could be started and controlled from the cockpit, and the propel-

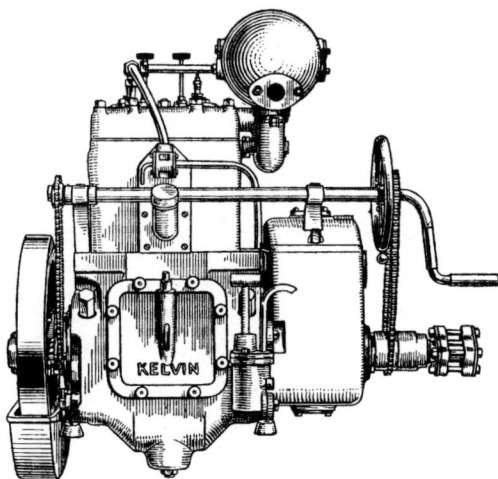

Kelvin-Ricardo 7½-hp engine

ler, which revolved freely when the yacht was sailing, was installed on the port side of the stern-post. In that connection it may be remarked that it is desirable to instal the propeller at the side rather than in an aperture, as the efficiency of a side propeller, owing to the free access of water to it, is much higher than that of one surrounded by heavy timber. A propeller installed in an aperture also causes noise and vibration, owing to the proximity of the blades to the woodwork. An aperture weakens the construction of the vessel and adds to the cost of building, and, if the engine is far aft, the withdrawal of the propeller-shaft involves removing the engine or the rudder.

Although the drag of a propeller revolving freely retards the progress of a yacht under sail to a certain extent, it is not serious. All the same, it would be advisable, when installing an engine, to have it fitted with a folding propeller. Tests made by the Bergius Co., with a 15-inch two-bladed folding propeller, fitted behind a stern-post 3 inches thick, at a speed of six knots, gave the following results: With blades folded, the drag was 3¼ lb.; with blades open and revolving, 9 lb.; with blades open and held vertically, 19 lb.; and with blades open and held horizontally, 21 lb.

If therefore you wish to obtain the best results when under sail, you should have either a folding or feathering propeller of some sort.

My engine was an old one of a type now obsolete, the Company having brought out a much improved model known as the Kelvin-Ricardo 7½-hp paraffin engine with poppet valves. The Bergius Co., make a wide range of auxiliary engines, both paraffin and petrol, which have a fine reputation, but I refer particularly to the Kelvin-Ricardo as it is installed in a number of yachts I know and the owners without exception speak very highly of it. Full particulars of the Kelvin-Ricardo engines can be obtained from the Bergius Co., Ltd, 254 Dobbie's Loan, Glasgow, C4.

The Watermota petrol engines, manufactured by Messrs. W. D. Fair & Co., range in size from 3 to 20 h.p. and are of the two-stroke type. Although I have had no personal experience of them, friends who have used them for years speak very highly of their performance and reliability. The 3 h.p., of course, would only be suitable for a very small cruiser, up to, say, 4 tons, and craft of from 4 to 7 tons would need the 6 h.p. engine. The 3 h.p. engine has a single cylinder and is supplied either with a clutch or reverse, and for a small extra charge a feathering propeller can be had. It is a very compact little engine and therefore specially suitable for auxiliary power for a small cruiser. It weighs but little more than 80 lb. complete and the price is extremely reasonable. The 6 h.p. engine has twin cylinders and is also very compact. It should be possible to instal this engine under the cockpit floor of most cruisers of 5 tons upwards. It is quiet and smooth running, cheap to buy and economical to maintain. It is claimed that it will run at full throttle for five hours on two gallons of petrol. Both of these engines are lubricated on the petroil system, half a pint of oil being mixed with each two gallons of petrol used. Full particulars of the Watermota engines can be obtained from Walter D. Fair & Co., Pembroke Engineering Works, Hampton Wick, Kingston-on-Thames.

Whatever kind of engine you select, it is of the first importance that it should be properly installed and the job should only be entrusted to a man who has had previous experience of such work. If the alignment is not perfectly correct, trouble is sure to ensue, and the bed must be firm and substantial. There should be a metal tray under the engine to catch oil, and if kept full of cotton waste, it will absorb any oil that drips or is thrown from the engine. By the way, the remark I made early in this chapter to the effect that an oil engine was apt to make the vessel smell was based upon my experience with an engine built as long ago as 1922 which had seen many years' service. I believe that the modern paraffin engine, if kept clean, is free from that offence. The fuel tank should be placed well above the level of the carburettor and as far away from the exhaust pipe and engine as practicable. I saw a yacht some time ago which had the petrol tank installed immediately above the exhaust pipe, which struck me as highly dangerous. I don't profess to know much about engines, but I do know that petrol tanks sometimes develop leaks.

If an auxiliary engine is kept in decent order, it should start readily. If it fails to do so, don't 'bust' yourself in trying to make it. It is obvious that there is something wrong and the sensible thing to do is to ascertain the cause of its failure. If the proper mixture of gas and air is reaching the cylinders, the compression is all right, and the plugs are sparking, the engine must start. Failure of the ignition is the most common cause of trouble in this respect and you should therefore test that first. Remove the plugs from the cylinders and lay them on top, with the cables attached. Then turn over the engine and see if the plugs spark. If not, they are probably dirty and require cleaning with a wire brush. If, after this treatment, they still refuse to spark, there may be a 'short' caused by damp inside the plug. The best way to dry a plug thoroughly, both inside and out, is to hold it in a clean flame for a minute or two. Your Primus stove will be very handy for this, as you can burn some methylated spirit in the cup, holding the plug in the flame with a pair of pliers. Should this fail to do the trick, it may be that the contact breaker of the magneto is not functioning properly and it should be examined and the points cleaned and adjusted, if necessary.

Should the 'mixture' not be reaching the cylinders, it is probably due either to water in the carburettor or a speck of dirt in the jet. In the former case the carburettor should be drained and wiped out, and in the latter, the jet should be cleared. Lack of compression may be due to a stuck-up valve or a broken or stuck-up piston ring – probably the former, as poppet valves occasionally get stuck-up with burnt oil.

When an engine fires only on one cylinder, the cause is almost invariably a dirty plug. The quickest way to find out which is the faulty cylinder, is by touch.

Place your finger on the insulated part of the plug you suspect, and if it is almost cold, you will know that it is not sparking. If you do not care to risk burning your finger you can obtain the desired information with the aid of a wooden-handled screw-driver. Hold the screwdriver so that it touches the cylinder-head and the plug. If it has no effect you will know that that is the faulty plug, whilst if the engine stops it will indicate that the plug you have 'shorted' is the active one.

I have referred only to the more common causes of engine failure but if you apply to the makers of your engine they will probably supply you with a booklet dealing with faults and their cure. The Bergius Co., issue such a booklet and I expect that other manufacturers do so also.

The small yacht owner must not think that because he has an engine, it will take him home under any conditions, because unless it is an exceptionally powerful one it will do nothing of the sort. He cannot, for instance, expect a small motor to drive his ship against half a gale of wind and a rough sea, for it is not intended to do that sort of thing. In my opinion the only excuse for using the engine is when the wind is so light that you cannot sail over the tide, in the case of accident, or if circumstances render it necessary for you to reach port quickly. If you get into the habit of using the engine whenever you have a foul wind, you will sacrifice one of the chief pleasures of yachting, namely, steering to windward, and also add very considerably to the expense of your pastime.

In every yacht that has an engine an efficient fire extinguisher should be carried in a place where it can easily be got at in case of need. Indeed, I think there should be two, as in the event of a fire you might not be able to reach the extinguisher if it were in the cabin and you were in the cockpit. By keeping one in the cabin and another in the cockpit, abaft the engine, you would be in a position to get an extinguisher in almost any circumstances. You should be careful, too, to see that they are fully charged, as the stuff evaporates to a certain extent. A fire extinguisher that has been hanging up in the cabin for years without attention, may be half empty.

CHAPTER 31: *Gear for the Single-hander*

Man, being a gregarious animal, loves to herd with his fellows, and it is therefore rather surprising that so many who cruise in small craft elect to sail alone. It might be thought that those who go in for single-handed cruising are of an unsociable disposition, preferring their own company to that of anyone else. But I do not think that that is the case, for whenever I meet them ashore I find them extremely sociable and chatty. The fact is that there is something very fascinating about handling a yacht alone, and when the habit has been acquired it is likely to persist. I think the chief charm is the feeling of complete independence.

Having no one but yourself to study, you can get under way or bring up when you like, go anywhere you fancy, and sail or remain at anchor as the spirit moves you. Anyhow, it is very desirable that you should be able to sail your boat without assistance should the occasion arise, for then, if the friend you have invited fails you at the last minute, your plans will not be entirely upset.

I have done a lot of single-handed cruising in my time and have always enjoyed it, although I must admit that there have been occasions when I would have given a lot to have had a companion. In moments of difficulty and danger it is a great comfort to have someone with you, but in ordinary circumstances I cannot say that I have ever been oppressed by feelings of loneliness. My cruising, however, has for the most part been confined to trips round the coast, and having friends at almost every place I put into, I have seldom been at a loss for company when the day's sailing is over and I am brought up in one of the delectable havens that I delight in visiting. But I cannot understand the mentality of such men as Slocom, Voss and Gerbault, who voyage alone round the world. Such cruising must entail great discomfort, and with nothing to look at day after day and week after week but the sea, I should think it must become extremely boring.

Personally when I go cruising, I like to keep the coast in sight so that I can enjoy the passing scenery and note my progress. There may not be anything heroic about such cruising, but I am sure that it is infinitely more pleasant. The jolliest form of cruising that I know is that in which a fleet of small craft, all sailed single-handed, go away together, bringing up in the same anchorage every evening. The owners then have the enjoyment of handling their craft alone during the day and can forgather and discuss the events of the trip in the evening. Incidentally there is an element of racing about it to add zest to the passage, for when several yachts are sailing in company they are almost sure to race each other. The man who is left astern may pretend that he was not racing, but, of course, the others will know that he had done his damnedest to get in front.

If you intend to make a practice of single-handed cruising, it is desirable that you should have a vessel suitable for the purpose. The question of size is, of course, an important one, and in that connection it may be remarked that it is not always the smallest boat that is the easiest to sail single-handed. What you want is a vessel in which it is easy to get about, and a boat with a heavily-cambered cabin-top and narrow side decks cannot be said to fulfil that desideratum. There seems to be a great divergence of opinion on the subject of the best size of yacht for single-handed work, for one sees big men with very small craft and little, spare men handling huge vessels. For instance, one friend of mine, a man of 6ft. 4in. in height, had a tiny canoe yawl with a lifting cabin-top, whilst the late Mr. Frank Cowper for many years sailed such craft as *Lady Harvey* and *Zayda* alone, vessels verging upon 40 tons T.M. In the former case the boat was, in my opinion, too small, whilst in the latter she was far too large.

As I have often pointed out, it is a physical impossibility for one man to sail a boat like *Lady Harvey* and at the same time keep her in decent order, and if one attempts to do so, one department or the other must suffer from neglect. Personally, I think that a single-hander should be of not less than 3 tons nor more than 10 tons T.M., and the ideal will be found somewhere between those limits. In considering this question of size, the weight of the ground tackle must not be overlooked, for if you have an anchor so heavy that a windlass must be used to weigh it, you may get into trouble. It is often necessary to sight the anchor quickly when getting under way from a congested anchorage and you cannot do that if you have to use a windlass with comparatively slow delivery. Then, the mainsail must be of a size that can be conveniently handled by one man. These are points that to a large extent must determine the size of the vessel you select for single-handed work.

Qualities that are desirable in craft carrying a full complement of hands may be just the reverse in a vessel that is to be sailed by one man. There is the question of handiness, for instance. We call a yacht handy when she is quick in stays, but to the single-hander a boat that spins round like a rater is a darned nuisance. With only one pair of hands with which to do everything, one wants more time in which to do it. The ideal single-hander, therefore, is one that comes round slowly but surely when in stays. With a vessel possessing this quality you can lash the tiller when you go about and, as she comes round, tend the sheets comfortably with both hands. If, on the other hand, she flies round the moment you put the helm over, you will probably have to keep one hand on the tiller and tend the sheets as best you can with the other. Another desirable feature in a single-hander is that of sailing herself for long periods with the tiller lashed. Years ago I owned a 7-ton cutter which would sail herself when close-hauled, or on a reach, until the cows came home, as the saying goes, and she was far easier to handle alone than many smaller craft I have had. She was a boat with a long, straight keel and plenty of forefoot, and although comparatively slow in stays, could always be relied upon to come round, even in a heavy sea, when I put the helm down. If you want a boat for single-handed sailing, I should advise you to look out for a craft of the old-fashioned type with a straight stem and considerable length of straight keel, as such vessels usually make far more comfortable single-handers than the modern type of yacht with overhangs and short keel.

Some men who go in for single-handed cruising devise all sorts of fancy gadgets which they think will render their work easier, but I am inclined to doubt whether such fitments are of much value. The late Marquess of Dufferin went to considerable lengths in that direction, with the result that his *Lady Hermione* was a veritable box of tricks; they are described in a later chapter.

To my mind, the gear of a single-hander cannot be too simple. The fewer ropes you have to handle the better, but it is essential that all the gear should run freely. With that end in view the blocks should be of a size larger than is really necessary for the ropes and fitted with patent sheaves. Every sail should come down with certainty the moment you let go the halyard, and if your blocks are large you will have no trouble from swollen ropes. Flexible wire running gear is extremely efficient and does not stretch, but it entails so many purchases that I do not think it desirable for single-handed work.

The only special equipment required for single-handed sailing is some means of securing the tiller when your work takes you away from the helm. For this purpose I use an ordinary jam cleat on the tiller in conjunction with the usual tiller lines. One turn of the line round the cleat will secure the tiller in any desired position and it can be released in a moment. If your yacht has an iron tiller – a beastly contraption – you may have some difficulty in attaching the cleat. In such circumstances you must either drill bolt holes through both cleat and tiller, or else seize the cleat to the tiller with marline. Personally, I hate an iron tiller, and when I buy a boat thus fitted, I immediately scrap it and fit an oak one. I dislike intensely the 'whip' of an iron tiller, and if the boat has a raked sternpost, the weight of an iron tiller will sometimes put her about when you let go of it.

The headsails of your single-handed boat should be fitted with the Wyke-ham-Martin gear of the latest pattern, which both reefs and furls. I have personally tried this out and can vouch for the effectiveness of the reefing device, if properly fitted. If your headsails are equipped with the Wykeham-Martin gear you will not have to shift them when you reef the mainsail, a great boon when one is alone.

I have often heard it suggested that single-handed cruising is a dangerous pursuit, and so it is if you do not take special precautions against falling over-board. If you should happen to fall overboard when the yacht is sailing with her helm lashed, your fate is sealed. You should therefore cultivate the habit of never letting go with one hand until you have grasped something with the other. If you have to work on the foredeck in heavy weather, tie a rope round your waist before doing so.

Some owners who make a practice of single-handed sailing think it desirable to modify the gear of their vessels with a view to easier handling, but I doubt very much whether they reap any material advantage from the alterations they make. A case in point is that of the lead of the halyard falls. In quite a number of small craft used for single-handed work that I have seen lately the halyards and topping-lift are led through blocks at the foot of the mast aft to the cockpit. The idea, of course, is that all the sails can be handled without leaving the tiller. In theory it is no doubt an ideal arrangement, but let us consider for a moment how it pans out in practice.

When getting under way you can either set your mainsail before weighing the anchor or you can't; it all depends upon the conditions of wind and tide obtaining at the time. Let us suppose, however, that your vessel is riding head to wind and tide and you are thus in a position to set your mainsail whilst at anchor.

In such circumstances it is quite immaterial where your halyards are belayed, as you can take as long as you like over the job and get everything coiled down before you even think about weighing the anchor. It is obvious, therefore, that no advantage is derived from having the halyards led aft under those conditions. Now let us consider what happens when you are riding to your anchor with the wind against the tide. When such conditions obtain, the anchor must be broken out before making sail. Will you reap any benefit if your halyard falls are belayed in the cockpit? I think not. It is obvious that you will have to go forward to get the anchor and it seems to me that it is far quicker and more convenient to set the mainsail and belay the halyards at the foot of the mast while you are on the foredeck. If the halyards are led aft you will have to make a journey to the cockpit before you can even commence to set the mainsail and that entails a loss of time that can ill be spared. Very often, when such conditions obtain, one gets under way with a headsail, the mainsail being set when clear of other vessels at anchor. If you know your job you will, in the absence of the Wykeham-Martin gear on your headsail, have sent up the sail in stops before getting the anchor, and it does not matter very much where the halyard is belayed. I think, however, you will find it more convenient if it is belayed forward, as you can then guide the sail clear of other gear as you hoist it. If, from laziness or lack of experience, you attempt to set a jib from the cockpit without first putting the sail in stops, you are pretty certain to have trouble. I saw an instance of it quite recently. It was a little yacht of about 3 tons which was riding to a mooring with the wind against the tide. The owner, having prepared the jib for setting, slipped his mooring, and then scrambled into the cockpit, where the halyards were belayed. As soon as he commenced to hoist it, the sail began to slat violently in the wind and got foul of the shrouds and crosstree, with the result that the boat drove on to the mud and stayed there for seven or eight hours. Now, if the halyard had been belayed forward he could have guided the sail clear of the crosstree as he hoisted it and all would have been well.

With regard to the actual setting of the sails I am sure you will get better results when they are belayed forward, for when they are led aft to the cockpit there is the additional friction of the extra blocks to contend with. Leading over the cabin-top, too, the falls are not well placed for the application of your weight and strength. No man can effectively apply his weight and strength to a rope that is breast high. You can put your foot against the bulkhead and pull until you are black in the face, but I am pretty sure that you will not set the sail so well as you would if the halyards were belayed to a fiferail at the foot of the mast and you 'swigged' on them in the usual manner.

So much for the setting of the sails, and now let us consider the question of lowering them. It would, no doubt, often be convenient when single-handed to be able to lower the mainsail from the cockpit, but in my experience it cannot be done. There is so much friction on the halyards that the sail will not come down unless assisted, and if you have got to pull the sail down, you can do it better when up forward than from the cockpit. As a matter of fact it is usually more convenient to lower the sail when you are up forward, for when bringing up, either to your anchor or a mooring, you have to do it from the fore-deck. A jib, of course, cannot be lowered from the cockpit, for it would be almost certain to go overboard, unless it were hanked to the stay. Even if it were, I doubt whether it would come down without assistance. Personally I am convinced that it is a mistake to lead the halyards aft, either in a single-hander or any other boat, and when I have bought yachts thus fitted I have invariably shortened the halyards and belayed them to a fiferail near the foot of the mast.

When rigging a small yacht for single-handed work, simplicity is much to be desired. Running gear should be reduced to a minimum, for the fewer 'strings' you have to handle the easier it is to sail the boat. When I come to build my 'dream ship,' if ever I do, she will be a sloop of about 4 tons, either with a gaff mainsail or Bermudian. At present I am somewhat undecided in my mind as to which rig would be the better. I am very fond of the gaff mainsail, but at the same time the extreme simplicity of the Bermudian appeals strongly to me. With such a mainsail, all the running gear necessary to set it consists of a halyard and a topping-lift. Those two ropes and a halyard for the foresail would constitute the whole of the yacht's running gear really essential, but I should always have a spare halyard for setting a spinnaker or balloon foresail. I have reached a time in life when I can no longer get aloft and that extra halyard would be my stand-by. If I carried away one of the other halyards, I could hoist the sail affected by means of the spinnaker halyard, and although it might not set very well, it would probably enable me to get into port.

The foresail of my ideal single-hander would, of course, be fitted with the Wykeham-Martin furling and reefing gear and thus equipped it would seldom be necessary to visit the foredeck, except when getting under way and bringing up. A small yacht rigged as I suggest would be extremely easy and comfortable to sail alone and could be got under way in five minutes if her sails were tanned and there was no mainsail cover to remove.

For ordinary week-end cruising and pottering around the coast I do not think one wants any special device for steering when single-handed, as one can lash the tiller when a job has to be done on deck, and as regards feeding, one usually makes shift with a snack at the helm. Should you want a square meal that necessitates cooking, you can always heave to, provided that you do not mind the loss of time. You need not even do that if your boat steers herself well. In my *Seabird* I often cooked a steak and potatoes, had my meal and washed up, whilst the boat sailed steadily on towards her destination; but she was exceptionally gifted in that way, and it is not every small craft that can be left to her own devices for so long, even with a beam wind. The time when the single-handed sailor most feels the need of some steering device is when picking up moorings, for when he

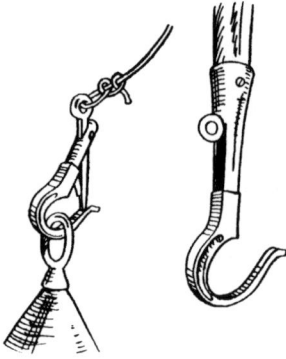

'Grab-it' boathook

leaves the tiller to run forward to get the buoy, he may find it a few feet out of his reach. I felt this particularly in *Seabird*, for she had a good deal of freeboard and I lost sight of the mooring buoy when I was some distance away. There was thus a certain amount of guess-work about it and occasionally, if unlucky, I found the buoy just out of reach. With the idea of eliminating this trouble, I rigged tiller lines leading through blocks on the quarters to the fore-deck, but it was not an unqualified success as the lines were apt to kink and foul in the blocks. I therefore resorted to an old dodge that I had employed in small craft many years before. I used a short warp, about 6 fathoms in length, with a spring hook on the end. When approaching the mooring, I made one end of the warp fast to the bitts and led it, clear of everything, into the well. By these means I was able to pick up the moorings from the cockpit, without leaving the tiller. I merely leant over the side and hooked the warp on to the buoy and let the boat ride to the warp until I had stowed the headsails. I thus had a clear fore-deck when getting the riding scope aboard and did not get my headsails wet. That plan worked admirably and I seldom experienced any trouble, but a certain amount of care and judgment was necessary to bring the boat within reach of the buoy.

Since those days there has been placed on the market a thing called the "Grab-it" boathook, which is obviously a refinement of my spring hook idea. It is a very ingenious device that I have personally tried and found most useful when picking up moorings. The head of this boathook has a hook with a spring tongue to prevent the buoy-rope coming out when secured, and on the other side a strong becket, to which is spliced a short warp. The head is loose on the shaft, being kept in place by a spring. When one has grabbed the buoy-rope, a pull releases the shaft of the boathook from the head and the yacht is left riding to the warp, which is, of course, securely fastened to the mooring buoy, or buoy-rope. When the boathook is used for other purposes, the head is kept on the shaft by means of a pin that passes through both.

CHAPTER 32: *Self-steering Downwind*

In an idle moment the other day I was turning over the pages of a back number of a yachting magazine and came across an article that interested me a good deal. It was an account of a single-handed voyage from Banagher, Ireland, to Las Palmas made by Captain Otway Waller in his 6-ton yawl *Imogen*, a smart little craft built about twenty years ago from the design of the late Mr. Albert

Strange. As I expect you know, Mr. Strange designed a number of small cruisers, characterized by particularly beautiful lines which rendered them easy and comfortable in a seaway. It was not, however, the boat or the nature of the cruise that interested me so much as an ingenious device adopted by Captain Waller, by which the vessel was made to steer herself when running before the wind. Given a fair length of keel, most yachts will steer themselves with the tiller lashed when on a wind, or reaching, but, with the single exception of Captain Slocum's famous *Spray*, in which he sailed round the world, I have never heard of one that would do so for any length of time when the wind was dead aft. My old *Seabird* would sail herself almost indefinitely with the wind on the beam or quarter, but if the breeze was right aft I could not leave the helm for more than a few minutes, and how Captain Slocum made his *Spray* do it I can't conceive.

Captain Waller started away from Ireland with the intention of sailing round the world, but was compelled by ill-health to abandon his project when he arrived at Las Palmas. During the passage of some 1,600 miles, however, he had ample opportunity for thoroughly trying out his steering device, which, he says, was an unqualified success. Briefly, it may be described as follows: When the wind was aft, the mainsail was stowed and in its place were set two small spinnakers, one on each side of the mast. Each of these sails contained 120 sq. ft. of canvas, the area of the two together equalling that of the mainsail. Each spinnaker boom measured 15ft. by 2¾in. and was furnished with guys fore and aft. The sails were fitted with the Wykeham-Martin furling gear. When furled they lay up and down the mast and when set the clews were sheeted to the ends of the booms. The after guys, or sheets, led through single blocks on the yacht's quarters and were secured to the tiller as illustrated. In operation the device works in the following manner:

When the wind is dead aft the booms are more or less squared and the pull on both being equal, the tiller remains amidships. Should the vessel sheer off her course, bringing the breeze on the quarter, one spinnaker feels the pressure more than the other and its boom runs forward a little, pulling over the tiller with it.

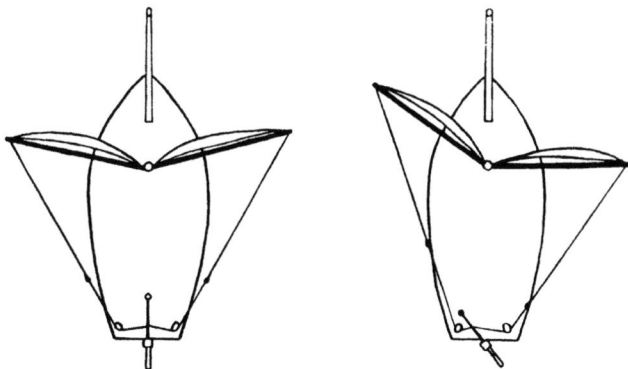

Capt. Waller's device for downwind self-steering

Answering the helm, the yacht comes back on to her course and the two booms resume their former position. It will be readily imagined a vessel steered by this device is inclined to yaw about a good deal, but as the steering arrangement always brings her back, she in effect steers an approximately straight course. I expect you noticed that I said that the booms were 'more or less' squared when the wind was right aft. It would, of course, be impossible to have them actually at right angles to the keel, for if they were so, the device could not function. As the two spinnaker booms are connected, both of the after guys being fastened to the tiller, it is obvious that as one boom goes forward the other must come aft. If both spars were squared the shrouds would prevent either from coming aft and the other could not therefore go forward. By guying them both forward a little, space is available for the necessary movement.

In *Imogen*, when the yacht was under her mainsail, the spinnaker booms were left in situ but topped up a little to keep them clear of the seas when the vessel rolled, and both spinnakers were furled. Captain Waller, it may be mentioned, carried the spinnaker booms in this manner all the way to Las Palmas. The only trouble he experienced was from chafe of the after sheets, or guys, where they led through the quarter blocks, and that he remedied by splicing in lengths of wire. In the course of his voyage Captain Waller covered 105, 107 and 106 miles respectively on three successive days without the helm being touched, with the wind right aft. The invention may be rather suggestive of the Round Pond in Kensington Gardens, but in view of the results obtained, I think it must be regarded as a thoroughly practical device which should be a boon to those adventurous spirits who delight in single-handed ocean cruising.

CHAPTER 33: *An Example of Ingenuity*

Those who make a practice of sailing alone seem to be somewhat divided in their opinions as to the best way in which to equip a small cruiser for the work. The majority, I should say, are in favour of simplicity in the matter of gear and endeavour to reduce the number of ropes to a minimum. There are those, however, who adopt every conceivable labour-saving appliance they can think of, but I am inclined to think that they usually find most of the gadgets employed more bother than they are worth.

I doubt whether anyone has gone to such lengths in that respect as did the late Lord Dufferin in his little cruiser *Lady Hermione*, which was a veritable box of tricks. Most of the fitments he adopted were extremely ingenious, whilst some were certainly useful. The handy little Dufferin winch, for instance, is still used in small yachts and something very like it is often found in large racing craft. As this famous little cruiser was in many respects an extremely interesting craft, I make no excuse for extracting from the Badminton Library book on Yachting the description of her written by Mr. James McFerran, or, at any rate, such portions of it as deal with the fittings.

The *Lady Hermione* is a yawl-rigged yacht built by Forrest and Son of Wivenhoe to the order of her owner. She is 22 feet 9 inches long between perpendiculars, 4 feet 2 inches in depth, has a beam of 7 feet 3 inches, and a registered tonnage of 4 tons. She is built with mild-steel frames, galvanised so as to resist the corrosive action of sea-water – a mode of construction which has recently been adopted for torpedo-boats – and is sheathed with East Indian teak and coppered. A novel feature in the hull of so small a boat is its division into water-tight compartments by transverse and longitudinal bulkheads, composed of galvanised steel plates riveted to the steel frames. These bulkheads form a large forward compartment, two compartments on each side of the cabin, and a compartment at the stern, thus rendering the vessel watertight as long as they remain intact.

On deck, forward and aft, are hatchways, which give entrance to the bow and stern compartments respectively. The hatches to these openings, which are kept constantly closed at sea, are fastened down with strong gun-metal screws fitted with butterfly nuts, the screws being fastened to the deck and made to fold down on it with a joint when not in use. The coamings to the hatchways, as well as the inner edges of the hatchways themselves, are lined with indiarubber, so as to render the covers perfectly water-tight. Access to the side compartments is obtained by means of manholes opening from the cabin, and covered with steel plates screwed into the bulkhead. In the event of the yacht shipping water, it is removed by a pump leading through the deck near to the cockpit and within easy reach of the steer-man's hand. The cover of the pump works on a hinge and lies flush with the deck when closed. The pump-handle is made to ship and unship at will and is in the form of a lever, which renders the operation of pumping more easy than in the ordinary form of pump usually employed in small boats.

Stepping on board the *Lady Hermione*, the visitor, however much he is accustomed to yachts, is struck by the number and apparent complication of the contrivances which meet his eye, the interior of the vessel looking, as a witty naval officer once observed on being shown over her, 'something like the inside of a clock'; but after a few explanations the usefulness and practical efficiency of the various devices become evident. The principle which has been adhered to throughout in the rigging and fittings is that all operations connected with the handling and management of the boat shall be performed by one person without the application of any considerable physical force. It has been laid down as a *sine qua non* that everything shall work perfectly in all weathers and under all conditions of wind and sea. The result of the owner's ingenuity is that the sails can be hoisted and lowered, the sheets attended to, the anchor let go and weighed, and the tiller fixed and kept fixed in any desired position without the necessity of the one person who composes the crew leaving the cockpit. The arrangements for carrying out these objects will now be described in detail.

The first contrivance that claims attention is that for keeping the rudder fixed at any desired angle. On the deck aft, about a couple of feet in advance of the rudderhead, are fitted two brass stanchions. These support a brass bar which on its lower side is indented with notches similar to the teeth of a saw and of a depth of about half an inch. On the tiller there is fitted a brass tube or cylinder made so as to slide backwards and forwards within a limit of some 8 or 10 inches and bearing on its upper surface a triangular fin of brass. When it is desired to fix the tiller in any particular position, the cylinder is instantaneously slipped back until the fin catches one of the notches of the bar, and the tiller is thus securely fixed. The tiller is unlocked by simply flicking forward the cylinder with the hand, the locking and unlocking being done in a second. The toothed brass bar, it may be mentioned, is curved so that the fin may fit into any desired notch, no matter at what an angle it may be desired to fix the rudder. The cockpit of the yacht being somewhat small, it was found that when there was a lady passenger on board the movement of the tiller interfered with her comfort, and in order to obviate this difficulty a steering wheel has recently been fixed on the top of the cabin immediately in front of where the helmsman stands.

When the wheel is used a short tiller is employed, with steel tackles leading from it through pulleys and fairleads to the wheel itself. The axis of the wheel carries a brass cap fitted with a screw, by half a turn of which the steering appartus can be locked or unlocked, and the helm fixed in any position. If it is desired at any time to substitute steering with the tiller for steering with the wheel the process is very simple. A brass handle of the requisite length and bearing a cylinder and fin as above described is screwed on to the short tiller, and the tiller ropes are cast off, the whole operation being performed in a few seconds. The wheel – the stand for which slides into brass grooves on the cabin-top – can also be unshipped and stowed out of the way in a very short time.

Many forms of tiller grip have been adopted by single-handed yachtsmen, but LordDufferin's method strikes me as by far the most simple and efficient of any I have seen or read of, although it could not be used conveniently in every boat. The indented brass bar must, of course, be curved in order that the brass fin on the tiller may engage at every angle of the tiller. A certain amount of deck-room between the rudderhead and after-coaming of the well is therefore necessary, and this would not be available in many transom-sterned yachts. But for a boat with sufficient deck-room aft the idea strikes me as altogether excellent.

Getting a yacht under way single-handed is often something of a problem on account of the physical impossibility of being at both ends of the vessel at once. In the absence of any special gear frequent journeys between tiller and anchor chain are sometimes necessary. When one is young and active this does not matter very much, but when one is no longer in the first flush of youth exercise of this nature is not viewed with favour. The late Lord Dufferin got over the difficulty in a very ingenious manner in *Lady Hermione*, the fitments he devised enabling him to let go or raise the Martin patent anchor without leaving the cockpit.

The fittings are described in the Badminton volume as follows:

The anchor when stowed rests upon two crescent-shaped supports, which project from the bulwarks just forward of the main rigging. These supports are fixed to a bar or tumbler lying close to the inside of the bulwark, and arranged so as to turn on its axis. Fixed to the tumbler inboard there is a small bar, which fits into a socket attached to the covering board. On the socket is a trigger from which a line leads along the inside of the bulwarks to within easy reach of the cockpit. By pulling this line the socket is made to revolve so as to release the arm; the weight of the anchor forces the tumbler to turn on its axis, bringing down with it the crescent-shaped supports, and the anchor falls into the sea. The chain cable runs out through the hawse-pipe in the bow, and across the hawse-hole a strong steel plate or compressor, with a notch cut in it to fit the links of the cable, runs in grooves. By pulling a line which leads to the cockpit this compressor is drawn over the hawse-hole, and the cable is thus effectually snubbed. When the anchor has to be got up or it is required to let out more chain, the compressor can be drawn back by another line, which also leads to the cockpit.

Equally as ingenious as the means of letting go the anchor is the machinery employed for weighing it. The windlass used is an ordinary yacht's windlass, except that on its outer end on its starboard side it carries a cogged wheel. Close alongside the windlass there rises from the deck a spindle cut with an endless screw, the threads of which take the teeth of the cogged wheel. This spindle runs through the deck and has at its lower extremity a cogged wheel fitting into another cogged wheel attached to a shaft, which runs aft on bearings in the ceiling of the cabin to the cockpit. At the cockpit end it is furnished with a large wheel, on turning which the motion is communicated through the shaft and a system of cog-wheels to the Archimedian screw rising up through the deck forward, and this screw in its turn revolves the windlass, and the anchor comes merrily home. The slack of the chain as it comes in drops perpendicularly through the hawse-pipe to the chain-locker below and requires no attention or handling. The machinery for getting the anchor possesses great power, and even when the anchor has a tight hold of the bottom, the wheel in the cockpit can be turned almost with one finger. The wheel is made to ship and unship, and when not in use is hung up to the side of the cabin.

It would appear to have been Lord Dufferin's desire to work *Lady Hermione* entirely from the well, and with that object in view practically all the gear was so arranged as to be within easy reach of the helmsman. The only operation that could not be performed from the well was fishing and catting the anchor, which entailed a journey forward to hook on the Spanish burton by which the anchor was raised. Every halyard and sheet in the yacht led to the well, the leads being very neatly arranged. At the foot of each mast was a brass fairlead containing a number of sheaves through which the halyards were led to belaying-pin racks in the well, the falls being stowed in boxes containing a number of compartments made to receive them. Each halyard was passed through a hole in the pin-rack before being belayed to keep it clear of its neighbour, and each belaying pin had the name of the rope for which it was intended engraved on a small brass plate to prevent confusion.

To reduce labour to a minimum Lord Dufferin devised a particularly handy little winch, of which a number was used in various parts of the vessel. These ratchet winches were made to ship into grooves on the deck so that they could be moved about from place to place as required. No fewer than ten were to be found in *Lady Hermione*. Two were placed on deck on each side of the cockpit for the headsail sheets, four on the cabin-top for the halyards, and two on the deck forward of the cabin-top for general purposes. The winches were worked with ratchet handles, to which were attached strong steel springs to ensure the ratchets biting in the cogs. They were remarkably powerful for their size and took up but little room.

In order to prevent the sheets fouling the deck fittings forward, brass guards were placed over every projection, and to reduce the risk of falling overboard a steel wire life-line was run round the vessel, above the rail, in stanchions. On the fore side of the mast of *Lady Hermione* was fitted a ladder made of steel wire with wooden treads. This extended from deck to cross-trees, being set up with rigging screws. To keep his lordship's feet warm in cold weather a charcoal stove was placed beneath the cockpit floor, whilst to keep off the sun on hot days a large umbrella was fitted over the cockpit in a socket. A spirit compass (and bin-nacle) was placed on the cabin-top, whilst a 10-foot Berthon dinghy was carried inside the cabin. Brass crutches on the rail were used for carrying spars when at sea and supporting the mainboom when at anchor. As a precaution against bad weather a hatch was provided to cover the cockpit. This hatch was in sections which were hinged together, its two halves being also hinged to the backs of the seats in the cockpit on either side. When in position the hatch covered the entire cockpit with the exception of a small circular opening left for the helmsman. This circular opening could also be closed if desired by means of a wooden hinged cover made for the purpose. As Lord Dufferin used the yacht for day sailing only, no berths or seats were fitted in the cabin, the only furniture being cupboards and racks for stowing a few necessary articles.

If I have devoted a good deal of space to a description of *Lady Hermione* it is because the fitments and arrangements of the vessel were so extraordinarily ingenious. It must not be assumed, however, that I think such a multitude of fittings necessary or even desirable for single-handed sailing, and I frankly admit that my interest in the yacht and her equipment is for the most part academic. If I found myself the owner of a craft like *Lady Hermione* I should be appalled at the complication of gear, and I feel pretty certain I should soon develop the trait possessed by Davies, the hero of Mr. Erskine Childers' fine novel, *The Riddle of the Sands*, namely, a fancy for dumping things over the side. Lord Dufferin fitted his craft with all the running gear found in a large yacht, and an idea of the quantity of gear can be gleaned from the fact that there were no fewer than ten fairlead sheaves placed at the foot of the mainmast for leading ropes aft to the helmsman. And, in addition, there was all the mizzen gear to be taken into account. It is not perhaps altogether surprising that his lordship should have found it necessary to label the various ropes to prevent confusion. The thing that tickles me most, however, is the umbrella. Surely Lord Dufferin was the only sailorman who ever put to sea with an umbrella, with the possible exception of Robinson Crusoe. Still, if a man has a fancy to go yachting with an umbrella, why shouldn't he?

Lord Dufferin was by no means singular in having his halyards led aft to the well, as it is quite a common practice in single-handers. Personal experience has, however, taught me that very little advantage is to be derived from it. In theory it is no doubt an excellent proposition to be able to set or lower the mainsail without leaving the well, but, unfortunately, theory and practice do not always walk hand in hand. When I bought the little canoe-yacht *Snipe* the main and peak halyards and topping-lift led aft through sheaves at the foot of the mast, but I soon came to the conclusion that the practice was a mistake and abandoned it for the following reasons: In the first place I found it next door to impossible to set the mainsail decently, as with the halyard falls leading over a breast-high cabin-top one could not get a fair pull on them. I have no doubt I could have set the luff sufficiently taut if I had put my foot against the bulkhead to secure additional leverage, but had I done so my foot would probably have gone through into the cabin. When it came to lowering the mainsail, the extra friction of the fairleads prevented the sail coming down with its own weight. This entailed climbing on to the cabin-top to assist it, thus nullifying the advantage that should have been derived from having the halyards belayed aft. In the case of the foresail the system is even more impracticable. If there be any weight in the wind when setting the sail it will take charge, and slatting with great violence may imperil the bowsprit and masthead. In such circumstances it will be impossible to set it properly, even if it does not get foul of something – say the bowsprit bitts or anchor stock – which would necessitate a journey along the deck to clear the sail. If one attempts to lower the sail from the well, it is almost certain to blow overboard. But even if the disadvantages I have pointed out could be eliminated, is there any real benefit to be derived from leading the halyards aft? I think not.

When getting under way it is necessary to go forward to break out the an- chor, and it seems to me that it is a positive disadvantage having to run aft to set the sails after the anchor has been sighted. Even Lord Dufferin, with all his complicated machinery, failed to devise any means of fishing and catting the anchor other than by hand, which entailed a journey forward. When bringing up, too, one must go forward to let go the anchor, and so here, again, it is more convenient to have the halyards belayed on or near the mast. When arguing this point with men who believe in leading the halyards aft for single-handed work, I have often been met with the remark that it is a great convenience to be able to lower the peak if caught in a bad squall when running before the wind without leaving the tiller.

So, no doubt, it is in theory; but in practice you can't do it. Every experienced yachtsman knows that the peak of the mainsail will hardly ever come down without assistance when the vessel is before the wind, and for that reason it is customary to fit a peak downhaul – a rope leading from the gaff-end to the boom. In most yachts you will find this downhaul secured to the boom within a few feet of the clew of the mainsail, and ere it can be reached the boom must be hauled in almost amidships, which is just what one would not wish to do in a bad squall. If the downhaul is attached to the boom near the gooseneck, as it should be, the single-handed yachtsman must leave the tiller to get at it. Finally, the main and headsail sheets are quite sufficient ropes to have lying about in the well of a small craft without the addition of the coils of three halyard falls and the topping-lift. It may also be remarked that leading the halyards aft means more rope, which makes for additional expense, whilst the constant chafing on the edge of the cabin-top does not add to the beauty of the latter.

Wherever the halyards are led it is essential that the ropes should be belayed in a very handy manner so that they may be cast off at a moment's notice. Cleats on the mast are, to my mind, an abomination, and pins in a spider-band are not much better. The best arrangement that I know is a fife-rail with good strong pins that are not placed unduly close together. The rail should be fitted just abaft the mast and bolted through a strong deck beam or otherwise the strain of the halyards may lift the deck. I think it better to place the fiferail abaft the mast rather than forward of it, as in the latter position it is apt to foul the headsail sheets. Failing a fiferail such as I suggest, two short pin-racks, one on each side of the mast, can be used, although they will be more likely to foul the headsail sheets than would a single pin-rack abaft the mast.

CHAPTER 34: *The Dinghy*

A dinghy of some sort is a necessity for even the smallest cruising yacht as it affords the only means of communication with the shore, but most owners will agree that it is an unmitigated nuisance. When under way it is often a source of anxiety, and when at anchor its unpleasant habit of bumping into the yacht causes loss of sleep and temper. Towing a dinghy, moreover, will reduce the speed of a small yacht by something like 25 per cent. But if you have an ordinary wooden dinghy you must tow it, as there is seldom room on deck of a little ship to carry it on board.

When I owned the 2½-ton *Snipe* many years ago, I solved the problem by using a 7-foot Berthon folding dinghy when I went cruising. At sea, I carried it in the cabin, stowed on one of the bunks, having first moved the cushion on to the other bunk. Lashed to the cot frame, it travelled well there and was not much in the way, as I could sit on the opposite bunk. It could be opened and launched in a minute and folded and stowed equally quickly. Berthon boats don't seem to be used much for yachting purposes nowadays, which seems strange as they provide the solution to a very difficult problem.

Of course, there are snags in connection with such dinghies. One is its unsuitability for kedge work and the other its liability to being punctured. The Berthon dinghy is a 'floaty' little boat, looking something like half a walnut shell, and a 7-foot one will carry two men in fairly smooth water – I once for experimental purposes crowded three into mine and she took us across Felixstowe Dock in safety, although if anyone had sneezed we should have been for it, as the saying goes. But for laying out or lifting a kedge, she is the wrong shape, being sharp at both ends. I used to manage it somehow in smooth water but it was a tricky business, and when it was rough I preferred to borrow an ordinary dinghy for the job. With reasonable treatment a Berthon dinghy should be immune from puncture, but unfortunately, the small boys who infest the hard at most yachting centres cannot resist the temptation of playing the fool with such a boat, and of course there is a risk of holing it on a pile when going alongside a hard, if you are not careful. As it has a double skin it is difficult to repair and it usually means sending the dinghy to the works, although I believe some bootmakers can do the job. If the outer skin is punctured, water gets between the skins and makes the boat heavy. Many different kinds of folding boat have been introduced for the benefit of small yacht owners, but the Berthon is still probably the best.

In the absence of a folding boat, you will in all probability have to use a wooden dinghy and tow it. As, when you go ashore, you will usually have to handle it yourself, it should be light. I once had a heavy elm dinghy and when hauling it up a hard it nearly broke my heart – to say nothing of my back. Weight does not necessarily mean strength and if well built a light dinghy will be strong enough to last for many years with decent treatment. The best material is spruce, but mahogany top-strake, transom and thwarts will enhance her appearance.

There is every temptation to have the smallest dinghy possible, particularly as she will cost less than a larger one. Seven feet should, however, be the minimum length and personally I do not care to use one of less than 8 feet. A 7-foot dinghy of good design will carry two people of average weight safely in smooth water, but she is rather too small in rough weather. If she is a foot longer she will tow nearly as easily and the extra foot will make a deal of difference to her seaworthiness. A safe load for an 8-foot dinghy is three people in smooth water and two in rough, although, of course, a good deal depends upon the boat's shape and freeboard.

A type of dinghy that has become popular of late years is the so-called pram. Beyond the fact that, instead of the usual sharp bow, she has a fore-transom, she is nothing like the Scandinavian pram; indeed, many of them are like nothing on earth. Still, if well-designed, she makes quite a useful tender for a small yacht. She is certainly a tricky little beast to get into, if you are not used to her antics, and a little carelessness may put you in the 'ditch.' A good pram dinghy, however, tows steadily, has fair carrying capacity and rows reasonably well; moreover, she costs rather less than one of normal type.

Another kind of dinghy that has made its appearance of late years is the flat-bottomed boat, something like the dory, of which you have no doubt read in Kipling's *Captains Courageous*. Some time ago I bought one of these dinghies to see how I liked it, and soon found that I did not like it at all. Its only merit was that it was very cheap, costing only about half the price of an ordinary dinghy. I found that this boat was hard to pull, would not steer as the wind caught her bow and drove her off her course, and towed very badly. She certainly slid over the mud easily but, owing to her flat bottom, pulling her down a hard was a labour that might have appealed to the late Mr. Hercules but not to me. Her worst feature, however, was her lack of grip on the water when streamed astern of the yacht. Quite a light breeze served to blow her over the tide into the yacht and the constant bumping was an intolerable nuisance.

Most owners of small yachts covet a dinghy that can be carried on deck, and many have boats specially built for the purpose. The only place in which a dinghy can be stowed on board of a little craft is on the cabin-top, and as the boom has to clear it, the boat must be a very shallow one. When laden, such a dinghy has so little freeboard that she is liable to be swamped in any but perfectly smooth water. But the average yachtsman regards a dinghy as merely a means of getting ashore and seems to think anything that will float will serve the purpose. I saw a rectangular contraption recently that looked more like a pig-trough than a boat, but as it could be stowed on his cabin-top the owner was quite happy. It should be remembered that the sea is not always smooth and at times you may have to land in rough water, or lay out a kedge in heavy weather; it is even within the bounds of possibility that the dinghy may some day have to be used as a life-boat. I have every sympathy for the owner of a miniature cruiser who desires to carry his dinghy on board, but the cabin-top is not a suitable place on which to stow it. The weight and windage of a dinghy in such a position affects both the stability and sailing performance of the yacht, to say nothing of the boat being horribly in the way. In small craft you go to and from the fore-deck by way of the cabin-top, as the side-decks, if any, are usually so cluttered up with spare spars, etc., as to render them unavailable for the purpose. If you want to carry a dinghy on board a little ship of that kind, I would recommend you to use a folding boat, like the Berthon.

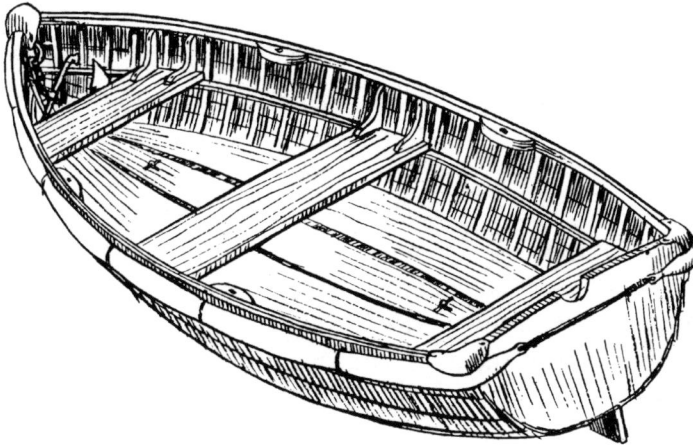

Dinghy with fender and rubber pads

Of course, carrying a dinghy of normal shape on deck is quite a practicable proposition in larger yachts of, say, 7 tons and upwards. To get the boat on board and turned over is rather difficult, but it can be done with the aid of the runner, or main halyard, or both. The rail of the yacht should be protected from damage by a shoe of hard wood, which can be slipped over the rail before commencing operations and subsequently removed.

I would recommend you to have fitted round the dinghy, just below the gunwale, a long fender of canvas, stuffed with kapok or some other suitable material, as it will save both the dinghy and yacht from being knocked about. The stemhead and corners of the transom should also be protected with rubber pads, which can be bought at almost any yacht chandler's shop. To avoid the risk of the rowlocks being lost, they should be fitted with lanyards. The lanyard should be

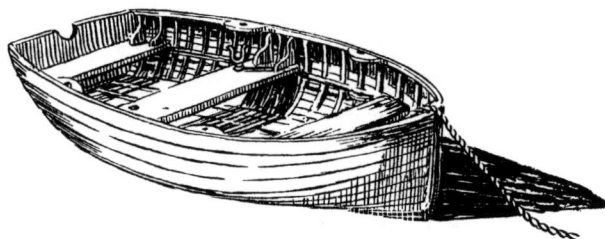

Holes in dinghy thwart for rowlocks

spliced round the neck of the rowlock and the other end made fast to the inwale of the boat. The rowlocks are apt to catch in the floorboards if left lying loose in the boat and it is a good plan to bore two holes in the rowing thwart, one at either end, large enough to take the rowlock. If the rowlocks are slipped into these holes, they will always be ready to hand and not get trapped in the floorboards.

The dinghy should have a score in the transom for sculling over the stern. Even if you seldom use it for that purpose, it will be invaluable for under-running the kedge warp.

The boat should be equipped with a small anchor with a folding stock and a good length of rope for anchoring it when you go ashore. Some hards are of inordinate length, that at Pin Mill, for instance, being 367 yards at low water spring tides. The longer the warp, the longer will you be able to get your dinghy when the tide is flooding. Keep a coil of small rope under the stern thwart. If you land on the flood tide, you will be able to make the rope fast to the crown of the dinghy anchor and secure it high up the hard. Your dinghy will thus be available for a longer period than if you merely anchored her in the usual way.

The towing painter should be of bass rope, as it has more spring than manila or hemp. Other useful items of equipment are a bailer and a sponge, although most owners seem to make shift with an old tin.

When pulling a dinghy down the mud at the side of the hard, the painter should first be passed under the fore-thwart, for if you tow from the stem it will

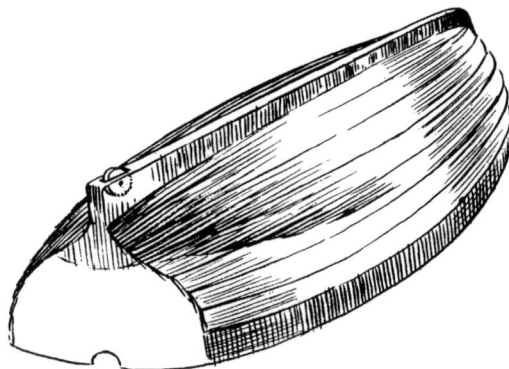

Roller in heel of dinghy

426

pull her into the hard and you will have to stop every yard or two to push her out again. "Elementary, my dear Watson," as Sherlock Holmes was wont to remark, but it is one of those obvious little things that the novice is apt to overlook. I think hauling a dinghy up and down the hard might be facilitated if a roller were fitted into the after end of the keel, as shown in the illustration. With such a roller, you could lift the bow and run the boat down the hard with one hand.

Here is another tip for the beginner – when going alongside the yacht with your bag and various parcels of food, etc., pass the painter round the yacht's rigging to hold her bow in while you get your luggage on board, otherwise, in your

Towing dinghy with a following sea

struggles to keep the dinghy's bow to the yacht, you may drop overboard some of your goods, and perhaps also yourself. If the boat's bow is not kept in to the yacht, the tide will sweep her away.

When at sea don't tow on too long a painter – about 5 fathoms should be sufficient. When close-hauled or reaching, the dinghy seldom gives any trouble, but when running before a following sea, it can be a perfect little devil and cause you much anxiety. The scend of the sea will bring it rushing down on to the yacht, threatening to damage the stern of the latter or stave-in her own bow. Or she may charge up alongside and then, when the painter tautens, her head will be pulled round with such a jerk that she will ship a lot of water. In course of time she may fill up altogether and break adrift. When dinghies are lost at sea it is nearly always while running in heavy weather.

Under such conditions a dinghy will tow best with two short painters led to the quarters of the yacht. A light warp should also be towed from the stern of

At anchor — bucket over stern of dinghy

the dinghy, as it will have a considerable restraining influence on her antics. As you may not need it all the time during your passage, the drag-warp should be made fast to the ringbolt in the stern of the dinghy and led to the yacht, where it can be coiled down on the after deck. Then, if you have occasion to use it, you merely have to drop it overboard. Failing this, you would have to haul the dinghy alongside to attach the drag-warp and that would entail heaving-to.

Some owners fit a canvas cover right over the dinghy when at sea, but that idea does not appeal to me very much. Not only would it be extremely trouble-some to fit or remove such a cover, but if the dinghy broke adrift it would render it very difficult to pick her up again, as there would be nothing to hang on to with the boathook. Moreover, one might want to use the dinghy in a hurry, as, for instance, if one got ashore and had to lay out the anchor.

But if the dinghy is sometimes a nuisance when under way, it is more often so at anchor. If the wind is against the tide, it has a nasty habit of driving up and bumping into the yacht to the detriment of her topside paint. That is annoying at any time and intolerable at night. You may be awakened by a vicious bump, which sounds worse than it really is as a boat is like a sounding-board. You prob-ably say to yourself, "Damn the dinghy" and turn over and try to go to sleep again; but you can't stand it for long and sooner or later you will get up and go out to do something about it. The usual method is to hang a bucket over the stern of the dinghy, but if the wind is fresh that is seldom entirely satisfactory, and when the tide begins to get slack it is next door to useless. A more effective expedient is to stream the boat on a long bass warp, which, floating on or near the surface, forms a big bight which has a far greater restraining influence than any bucket. Even that will be ineffective when the tide gets slack, but there is a chance that the dinghy may blow out right ahead and clear of the yacht. If you use a warp for this purpose, however, you have to dry it again before you can stow it away and that is irksome, although certainly better than being bumped all night. If you adopt this method you must be careful to see that you have plenty of room round you, or otherwise your dinghy may bump some other craft. That happened to me once and the crew of the bumped yacht, like Queen Victoria, were not amused and said so; although in words couched in rather stronger terms than those of our late august sovereign.

Another way of defeating the machinations of the little devil is to rig the spinnaker boom over the side and make her fast to the end. To do this, lower the spinnaker boom over the side, using the spinnaker halyard as a topping-lift, and lashing the spar to the rigging. In these days of short spinnaker booms, the spar is seldom long enough to keep a dinghy clear of the yacht if secured to the end, but she can be made fast by a short line to the middle thwart, the ordinary painter being belayed on the yacht's bow. In comparatively smooth water this is, perhaps, the most satisfactory expedient of all, but if it is really rough it cannot be recommended, for if sufficient slack be left in the line by which the dinghy is made fast to allow for the rolling of the yacht, it would probably not be possible to avoid occasional contact between the two. If insufficient slack were allowed, the thwart of the dinghy might be torn out when the yacht rolled away from her. I have tried all of these methods and taking them all round I think perhaps the warp idea is the most satisfactory.

Nowadays, my dinghy is protected by a fender all round and rubber pads on the stem and transom, and she cannot do much harm either to herself or the yacht. When she strikes the yacht it is only a soft blow that does not disturb me unduly; so I just let her bump and be damned. But then my craft has a transom

At anchor — streaming dinghy on long warp

At anchor — spinnaker boom rigged as a boat boom

stern. If the yacht had an overhanging stern, or a bumpkin, it would not be wise to let the dinghy come into contact with her, as she might come down with such a wallop as seriously to injure it.

In these days of crowded anchorages, you may have to bring up a long way from a landing hard and if your dinghy has a sail, much hard rowing will be saved. Of course, in the absence of a centreplate she will not sail to windward, and an ordinary iron centreplate would make her very heavy to tow and handle on the hard. A wooden dagger-plate, however, adds very little to the weight and does not take up much room. Even if your dinghy has no plate, I think it will pay you to carry a small sail in her for use with a fair wind. If the wind is foul when you go ashore it will probably be fair when you return to the yacht, so the sail would save rowing one way at least; and sometimes you would have a 'soldier's wind' and be able to sail both ways. But if you have a dagger-plate in the boat you will get a lot of fun sailing about the anchorage and exploring local creeks. The mast and spars should not be too long to stow in the boat and it is advisable to have the dinghy sail tanned, so that you can leave it in the boat when at sea and thus avoid cluttering up the decks. An outboard engine, no doubt, is very useful, but personally I will have nothing to do with them until some means of effectually silencing the exhaust has been discovered. Nothing tends to destroy the amenities of yachting so much as the horrible noise made by an outboard motor, which is calculated to rack the nerves of anyone within half a mile, and I would sooner row my dinghy than make myself an intolerable nuisance to other people.

CHAPTER 35: *Clothing*

My views on the subject of clothing are, I am afraid, rather unorthodox, but I cannot help wondering why so many men who go sailing should think it necessary to rig themselves out in fancy dress. This liking, however, seems to be inherent in our race, for there is nothing of which young children are so fond as 'dressing-up.' I refer, of course, to what is described by the tailor as 'regulation yachting dress,' and in my opinion nothing more unsuitable for the purpose could have been devised. Salt water always leaves a stain on blue serge, whilst a yachting cap is easier lost overboard than any other form of headgear I know.

Even if 'regulation yachting dress' were the most suitable for sailing, is there any reason why men should strut about ashore in it? In my experience the practical yachtsman who sails his vessel himself seldom wears yachting costume, and if he does he changes into something more suitable as soon as he gets on board. I can only think that in many cases it is mere swank, born of the desire to advertise the fact that the wearer owns a yacht. That, to my mind, is merely silly, for there is nothing heroic in owning a yacht, although it is a very delightful thing to have. Moreover, it does not always convey the impression intended, as nowadays something very similar to a yachting cap is worn by chauffeurs, railway porters, underground lavatory attendants, and others. I once saw a butcher in Southend standing outside his shop shouting 'Buy! Buy! Buy!' and he wore a smart yachting cap, complete with white cover and the flag of the Commodore of the Royal Yacht Squadron!

The most suitable costume for the practical yachtsman in summer is a grey flannel suit, or a sports coat and grey flannel trousers. Such a costume will not show salt stains, can be cleaned, and even when wet does not feel cold to wear. He should also wear a flannel shirt, and if necessary, a woollen sweater. For headgear, an ordinary golf cap takes a lot of beating, or, if the sun is very hot, a white cotton hat, such as is worn by paid hands in racing yachts. That is all one wants afloat, but a fairly respectable suit should be kept on board to wear ashore, should one put into a fashionable seaside resort. As a matter of fact any old clothes can be worn on board, as there is no one to see and criticize them, but to go ashore looking like a moth-eaten scarecrow, as some men do, is to bring discredit on the sport.

For youngsters I don't think there is anything to beat shorts. All a boy needs when sailing in summer are shorts, shirt and shoes, with a sweater to put on when the air becomes chilly. These are inexpensive garments which are easily washed, serviceable to wear and look nice. But shorts are only suitable for youngsters. The sight of an obese old man in shorts, to my mind, borders upon the obscene. Young girls, too, are best attired in shorts when afloat, as a skirt impedes their movements. For the same reason women, when sailing, should wear trousers, but they should be properly cut. I often see women dressed in men's flannel trousers and they look beastly. The anatomy of a woman differs considerably from that of a man. Where she has bumps he has hollows and vice versa, and it is obvious that trousers cut to fit a male figure will not fit a female properly.

Shoes are something of a problem. Rubber soles, particularly of the crepe-rubber variety, are suicidal on wet painted decks and might easily lead to your falling overboard. In the past I have had many a heavy fall when wearing crepe-rubber shoes and although they are extremely durable, I now think it folly to wear them afloat. Soles of ordinary rubber, too, afford anything but a secure foothold on wet decks. The most satisfactory shoes I have ever used had soles composed of a mixture of rubber and fabric, but the only really satisfactory solution to the problem is to paint the decks with non-slip paint, which, having silver sand mixed in it, gives one a sure foothold under any conditions.

Sea-boots should on no account be lined. Some brands are lined with a sort of felt stuff and, although they are warm and comfortable to wear, you will never be able to get them properly dry again should they once be 'drowned.' It is wise to have your sea-boots a very easy fit, so that if you fall overboard you can get them off. But if they are a sloppy fit they are apt to churn the heels and make holes in your socks. In some French ports special socks are sold for wearing inside sea-boots and sabots. They are made of chamois leather and just cover the foot and heel, saving one's ordinary socks from undue wear. Whether such things can be obtained in this country, I don't know, but they should not be difficult to make.

Nowadays in hot weather many yachtsmen wear next to nothing at all and I have even seen men prancing about on deck in their 'birthday suits.' This cult of the nude is being carried too far. Some time ago my wife and I were in a village shop and a man came in wearing nothing but shorts and canvas shoes. My wife was disgusted and remarked to me, "If that is how yachtsmen dress, I don't think much of them," and I was bound to agree. Later, we saw this man driving a car to the station to meet a train and he was still in the same state of semi-nudity.

People nowadays seem to think that getting the body scorched by the sun is beneficial to health, but personally I don't believe it and it may cause acute discomfort. I was reading in an old *Royal Cruising Club Journal* the other day, the late Mr. H. R. Wallace's account of his single-handed cruise from Brightlingsea to Ardglass in 1928 and came across the following:

> I'm old enough to know that one should get sunburned by degrees only. I had spent the greater part of Saturday clad in trousers only, and the result was the most painful sunburning that I've ever had. To this was added an attack of indigestion. Unable to lie down because of the tenderness of my

skin, I could not stand upright because of the searing pains in my inside. By rights I should have anchored when the tide began to run South, but for some five hours I was incapable of doing anything save sit doubled up on the cockpit floor, groaning idiotically. At 7 p.m. I think I must have become demented, for taking off my trousers (my topsides would not bear the touch of clothes at all), I took a header into the water. The shock of the cold water on blistered neck and shoulders nearly shook the wits out of me; however, I got on board again somehow.

Girls who go in for this sun-bathing usually do so because they think a brown-tinted skin attractive, but they guard against any ill effects by smearing their skin with oil. Men, however, seldom take such precautions and I think many must suffer acutely for their rashness.

The average oilskin strikes me as a very unsatisfactory garment, as the makers are usually too stingy with the material in the skirt. When you row a dinghy, your knees are exposed and get wet and when you climb on deck it is quite likely that you will rip most of the buttons off, probably taking a strip of the fabric out of the coat at the same time. A practical oilskin coat should be very full in the skirt and have no buttons below the waist. A friend of mine has had one of poncho type made from his own design which has proved a great success. The upper part of the coat is very like that of a fisherman's smock, but with an opening large enough for the head to go through comfortably. The slit extends for 8 or 10 inches down the chest and can be buttoned up to the neck like an ordinary oilskin coat. Below that there is no opening, the material being unbroken all round the skirt, which has a gusset at each side, to give ample play for the legs when moving about. When sitting down, the skirt falls over and between the knees and it is impossible for your legs to get wet.

This oilskin seems to me a vast improvement upon the ordinary kind, as it will keep you dry when working on deck or pulling the dinghy, while the absence of buttons on the lower part reduces the risk of damage. If you are likely to have much work to do on deck, a short coat and trousers would probably be more practical, but the trousers are a nuisance to get on and off and I have found that in the case of a shower one is tempted to chance getting wet rather than take the trouble to struggle into them. If these oilskin trousers were made very baggy they would be more useful. It must be remembered that they have to be worn outside one's sea-boots, which necessitates considerable width of leg.

The best oilskins I have had of late years are those known as the Fish brand, stocked by Gardiner & Co., 1 Commercial Road, London, E1. These, I find, will not begin to get sticky before they have had about three seasons' use. An oilskin coat, when not in use, should be hung up on a coat-hanger, so that the air can get to it. But that is not possible in a small boat, and if the coat is folded up and stowed away in a locker it is likely to get sticky pretty soon. I did not think there was any cure of a sticky oilskin until I read an article by Mr. Percy Woodcock, in which he recommended streaming the oilskin overboard for a day or two. I was rather sceptical about this, but at the end of the war I found my old oilskin in the store. It was a solid bundle of stickiness and seemed in a hopeless condition, after being stowed away rolled-up for six years. Even before the outbreak of war put a period to yachting, the oilskin had become so sticky that I had decided to scrap it and it was only by an oversight that it still existed. Well, here was an opportunity to try out Mr. Woodcock's tip. To straighten it out was a job that took both time and patience, but I managed it in the end with one small tear. Then I fastened a rope on to the oilskin and streamed it overboard for 36 hours. On hauling it on board again I found that every trace of stickiness had gone and that old condemned oilskin coat served me for another season. Whether such treatment will effect a permanent cure for stickiness I cannot say, as by the end of the season the fabric was so rotten that I finally discarded the coat. I noticed, however, before doing so that it had become slightly 'tacky' and it seems to me possible that in course of time the stickiness might return. But even so, if you can get another season's use out of an old oilskin, it is well worth doing.

If you sail in the winter you should study comfort rather than appearance and wear what will keep you warm. I know of nothing better for the purpose than trousers of heavy pilot cloth, thick woollen underclothing, flannel shirt, leather waistcoat lined with the stuff of which they make teddy bears and with sleeves, a tanned canvas smock as worn by fishermen, a Balaklava helmet, thick knitted socks, preferably over a thin silk pair, sea-boots and a muffler of some sort. This may seem a lot, but you will want every bit of it in a biting nor'easter if you are to keep reasonably warm.

Don't go about the boat with bare feet; it is a foolish practice in which many yachtsmen indulge. If you stub your toes against a cleat it will hurt like hell, and there are worse risks than that. In the days of my youth I was sailing an old converted ship's boat in the Thames Estuary and my companion, wanting something from the fo'c'sle, jumped down the forehatch on to a broken bottle that was lying on the floor. That bottle had been left there by the caretaker, probably to conceal the fact that he had drunk the whisky it had contained. Well, my friend gashed his foot right across the sole and, having severed an artery, bled like a stuck pig. It was during the winter, and as most of the gear had been taken ashore, I had nothing on board suitable for bandages. I did the best I could with the paper off the butter, a tea-cloth and a towel, but the boat soon resembled a shambles, for he must have lost pints of blood. I had to beat back to Hole Haven in a strong wind and rough sea ajid as the boat, like most conversions, was a perfect pig to windward, it was some hours before we arrived there. By that time my companion was about 'all in,' but fortunately I found some friends there in another boat. As we were unable to procure a trap, four of us carried the cripple all the way to Benfleet on a hurdle, and as he was a hefty lad, that three-mile journey was no picnic. After a doctor had sewn up and bandaged his foot we took him home and he was laid up for six weeks. Well, that is the sort of thing that may happen to you if you prance about on board with bare feet.

A Yarn

&

The Great Gale

When I had had *Wave* for about two years, I came in for a windfall in the form of a small legacy and decided to devote some of the money to altering her. I had had no end of fun in the little boat, sailing in the river, with an occasional trip to the Blackwater when the weather was fine, and thought she was worth spending a little money on. I hoped that the addition of waterways and coamings aft would enable me to cruise to Pin Mill again, or even farther, with some degree of confidence, while new and larger sails would make her faster. In the autumn, therefore, I sailed her round to Paglesham and left her at Shuttlewood's yard for the work to be carried out during the winter.

The proposed alterations comprised waterways and coamings, new and rather deeper keel, new mast and spars, cabin-top and decks strengthened and re-covered with canvas, new stemband, new standing rigging and running gear, removal of the thwarts and the addition of a proper pump. At the same time her ballast was to be removed and the bilge cleaned and black-varnished and the topsides burnt off and repainted. The new sails had a total area of 230 sq. ft., or about 90 sq. ft. more than the old ones. I also had one or two lockers put into the cabin and replaced the 'donkey's breakfasts' with air beds. She was to be ready early in February and on the tenth of that month I arranged to fetch and sail her back to Fambridge.

I was concluding a visit to my people in London when the appointed day arrived, and had a very bad cold and sore throat. When I mentioned that I was going sailing I was called a silly young fool and had to listen to the sort of rude remarks one usually hears from one's elder brothers. Their words of wisdom, however, fell upon deaf ears, for I had not been afloat for four months and felt that I could wait no longer; but before that trip was over I had quite come round to their way of thinking.

I was accompanied by a youngster named Louis, the young brother of an old school friend. At that time he knew nothing about boats but was frightfully keen on having a sail, even in the winter. He certainly had a bellyful of sailing on this occasion and long before we arrived at Fambridge wished that he had stayed at home.

Paglesham in those days was rather difficult of access, the nearest station being five miles distant at Rochford. It seemed to me, however, that the best way would be to go to Burnham, ferry over the Crouch and walk across Wallasea Island. But before we reached Paglesham we had come to the conclusion that we should have done far better to have gone to Rochford and walked the five miles. It was blowing fresh from the westward, mizzling with rain and altogether a most depressing sort of day. Laden with bags and various packages of gear, that trip across Wallasea fairly broke our hearts. The island was inter-sected with dykes and like a maze. Here and there were planks across the dykes, but they took a lot of finding and we wandered far and wide in our search for them. It took us longer to cross the island than it had to travel from London to Burnham, and it was nearly 2 p.m. before we ultimately arrived at our destination.

On going to the yard we found that *Wave* was not nearly ready. She had only just been launched and even her ballast had not been properly stowed. Her mast had not been stepped, rigging not made and there was no gear on board. Shuttlewood had not expected me, owing to the bad weather, and had deferred the completion of the job until the following week. It seemed impossible to get her ready by the following morning, but after two men and myself had worked hard until 8 p.m. things began to look more hopeful.

We slept at the Plough and Sail that night and turned out at six o'clock the following morning to find it blowing a heavy gale from west-south-west – the real thing, with a lot of weight in it and not a summer breeze that yachtsmen so often call a gale. It was too early to get breakfast at the inn, so we at once routed out Shuttlewood's foreman, who said it was madness to start in such weather. But as I was insistent, he came down to the waterside and set about completing the work we had left overnight. By 9.45 a.m. *Wave* was ready for sea and with her new paint and spars looked very smart. I had, of course, bent the old sails, reserving the new suit for the summer. We were anxious to get away without loss of time, but thought it wise to have something to eat first. Our breakfast consisted of some very stale sandwiches, which I had bought at Liverpool Street station the previous day, and almost neat whisky out of my flask. We soon decided that a litde of it went a long way and had finished our meal in ten minutes.

Having weighed the anchor, we set the small working jib, and while Louis steered I double-reefed the mainsail. By the time I had set it, we were in Key Reach, and with the wind off shore and smooth water *Wave* probably travelled faster than she had ever done before in her life, although the tide was against her. On hauling our wind round Branklet Spit, we met the full force of the gale and *Wave* lay in almost to her coamings. Here the tides meet and in heavy weather a succession of big seas are encountered. On this occasion the seas were not only the biggest I have ever seen in the Burnham river but extraordinarily short and steep. As we hauled in the sheets the little *Wave* leaped at the first like a chaser, flinging her bow high into the air, but before she could get into her stride the next was upon her and buried her to the mast. The water poured over her deck and cabin-top, quite a lot finding its way into the cockpit. For the next ten minutes or so she was like a half-tide rock, but gradually the seas became more regular and she rode them buoy-antly. But by that time we were both pretty well wet through.

Under the double-reefed mainsail *Wave* was buried to the coamings and required frequent luffing to keep the water out of the cockpit, but was making extraordinarily good weather of it for such a small craft. Then, as we approached the north shore of the Crouch a furious squall swept down the river and she was quite overpowered. Her jib was blown literally to ribbons and with no headsail the boat got out of hand and drove ashore. So there we were; stranded on a lee shore with the seas breaking over us and with no dinghy to lay out a kedge. It was a desperate situation that called for a desperate remedy, so I jumped overboard as I was and pushed her head round. The temperature of the water fairly made me gasp, but I got her off. Indeed, she sailed off so fast that I had difficulty in climbing on board again.

Back in the boat, I set the tiny spitfire jib and thinking that she would not balance with so little headsail, pulled down the third reef. It proved an error of judgment, for she would not handle under such reduced canvas, as the area of sail was insufficient to counteract the windage of the hull and spars. When I tried to put her about, she missed stays and we nearly got ashore again, but I had just enough room to wear her. Having thus got her on to the other tack, I left the jib aback and shook out the reef again. After that she went splendidly, but Lord! it was wet. Sailing hard with her lee deck awash, she smashed the crests of the seas into a continuous shower of spindrift and Louis was soon as wet as myself, although he was wearing his overcoat, having no oilskins. That was quite a smart coat when we started, but long before we arrived at our destination any self-respecting scarecrow would have rejected it with scorn. By the time we reached Burnham my companion was a picture of misery. Wet through to the skin, his teeth chattered with cold and the growing pallor of his face foretold the early loss of his breakfast, such as it had been.

The anchorage at Burnham presented a wild scene as we sailed through. Several yachts were dragging their ground tackle, while those which were holding on bravely to their moorings were pitching bows under. One large cutter had parted both her cable and kedge warp and was driving stern first through the fleet. Had she not drifted on to a mooring, which her crew were able to secure, she would surely have gone ashore and sustained serious damage. We passed close to *Rani*, a new yacht which my friend Pain Clark had had built. She had only been launched the previous day and my brother and several others, who had gone on board to a christening party in the evening, had had to spend the night on board. I have sailed the waters of the Crouch for forty-five years, but have never seen the river in such a state as it was on that wild February morning. I had hoped to leave *Wave* at Burnham, but as there was no chance of finding a safe berth or getting ashore we had no alternative but to plug on to Fambridge.

It was with feelings of relief that we came to Creeksea, for then we could reach through Cliff Reach in comparatively smooth water, as the wind was then off shore. Relinquishing the helm to Louis, I took the opportunity to bail out some of the water with the bucket. There was so much in her that I began to wonder how much had come over the top and how much through her bottom. With covering board awash, *Wave* fled up Cliff Reach like a scared cat and that part of the trip was all too short. We entered Easter Reach with the wind almost on end in a terrific squall. The boat lay over almost on her beam ends and the water poured into the cockpit over the lee coaming. For a moment it was a toss-up whether she turned turtle or not, but when I let go the mainsheet she righted. The water was now over the bunk in the cabin, and as she drove across the river with her jib aback we pumped and bailed for all we were worth. Easter Reach was a sight that morning. The short hollow seas curled over and broke, the tops being blown off in blinding spindrift. Wild horses chased each other, and down to leeward the seas broke on Bridgemarsh Island, sending clouds of spray high into the air..

Having bailed out as much of the water as we could, we let the jib draw and resumed our journey. Although the squall had blown over, there was still sufficient weight in the wind to lay the boat in to the coamings. Masses of icy-cold water flew aft from the weather bow and slapped us in the face until we fairly gasped, but the flood was now making up strongly, and gradually we won our way up to Fambridge, arriving just as the tide was on the turn. We picked up a vacant mooring, but as it failed to hold the boat we let go again and dropped our anchor. That also failed to hold *Wave* and it looked as if we should drive ashore. Fortunately we drifted close to the mooring of a 10-tonner and, grabbing the buoy with the boathook, I soon had the chain on board and made fast.

Having arrived safely at our destination, we thought that our troubles were over; but not a bit of it. *Wave* pitched like a mad thing, fairly standing on her head, and as I knelt on the foredeck stowing the jib, she pitched me overboard. Numbed with cold and weighed down by my sodden clothes, I had a rare struggle to get back again, even with my companion's help. Had I been alone it would have been impossible, as I seemed to have no strength left in my arms. This second ducking was about the last straw, and had anyone come along and offered me a 'fiver' for *Wave*, he would have had her, provided that he agreed to put me ashore. Louis was perhaps in a worse state than myself, for there was little to choose between us as regards wetness and he was horribly seasick, a malady to which I fortunately am not addicted.

Our main object in life was now to get ashore, but we had no dinghy and there was not a soul about. Nearly two hours elapsed, during which we shouted and tootled on the foghorn, before we attracted attention. That was not surprising as the land near the river was in flood, owing to a breach in the sea-wall, and the nearest houses were some three hundred yards distant. At last we saw someone climb on to the roof of a barn and wave his arm and we knew then that we had been seen.

We sat shivering in the cabin for another half-hour and then two sailing friends of mine appeared on the sea-wall, having made a perilous trip across the floods in a shooting-punt. They were in their shore clothes, but at once began to launch a boat to come to our assistance. No sooner was the dinghy afloat, however, than she was blown away down the river and they had to land on the mud far to leeward. In addition to the wind they had to contend with a strong ebb, but nothing daunted they launched another boat and tried again. But the result was just the same and they landed on the mud close to the first dinghy. Twice more they tried in other boats with no better luck and there was now quite a flotilla of dinghies anchored on the edge of the mud. There was then no other boat available but the ferry-boat, and this, with much labour, they hauled over the mud for about a hundred yards to windward before launching her. Needless to say we watched their operations with the keenest anxiety. Bows on to wind and tide, they rowed their hardest, gradually edging out into the tideway. At first they rather more than held their own, but when the boat began to feel the full strength of the tide they lost ground and our hearts sank into our boots.

Would they do it? No, they had just failed to reach *Wave* and we were plunged into the depths of despair. But our spirits rose again when we saw that they had managed to grab a 5-tonner moored some way below us. I unrove the mainsheet and halyards and these, attached to a warp, were just long enough. I tied the lifebuoy on to the end and floated it down to them and, by giving *Wave* a sheer, managed to bring it within their reach. We were then able to haul them up to us, and so, after waiting for rather more than three hours, we had at long last obtained the means of getting ashore.

We landed nearly a quarter of a mile below the hard and waded through the soft mud to the sea-wall. Louis was so done up that he did not even remove his shoes and socks or turn up his trousers. Our rescuers had used no fewer than five dinghies and incidentally quite spoilt their good clothes. They had certainly done their 'good deed' that day. On getting ashore, we all adjourned to the inn for a good stiff tot of hot rum, while a meal was being prepared for us, and later Louis departed for home rigged out entirely in my clothes, even down to shoes. Not the least extraordinary feature of this trip was the fact that my cold was completely cured.

When I look back to this adventure in *Wave*, I cannot help thinking that the trip from Paglesham to Fambridge on such a day was a rather remarkable feat for a 16-ft. boat to have successfully accomplished, for it was a severe winter gale in which many vessels were lost, including one on the Maplin Sands, from which the crew was taken off by the Southend lifeboat. But later, when

I came to try out *Wave* in normal weather, I was forced to admit that I had quite spoilt her by the alterations. She was little, if any faster, much wetter and leaked a good deal, particularly when sailed hard to windward. She had evidently derived a good deal of her strength from the thwarts and after their removal she could no longer withstand the heavy lateral stress involved in sailing to windward. She was rather tender, too, under the enlarged sail plan and inclined to gripe. I cured that to some extent by having a cloth taken out of the mainsail, but she was still hard-headed in a fresh breeze.

Far from being discouraged by this strenuous passage, Louis took very kindly to sailing and subsequently had many cruises with me. In later years he owned various craft ranging from 3 to 10 tons and became a very keen and able yachtsman ✺

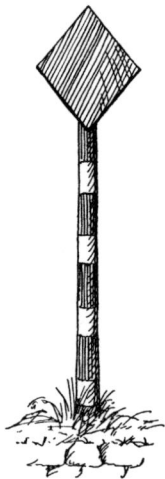

Hole Haven Beacon

Part V: DOMESTIC ECONOMY

CHAPTER 36: *The Cabin*

Some people might think the term domestic economy rather inappropriate when applied to yachting, but I don't think it really is, for by the exercise of a little ingenuity the cabin of a small yacht may be made a veritable 'home from home,' as the advertisements say. It is true that the space is limited, but if it is laid out to the best advantage the owner can have everything about him that he needs. After all, did not Diogenes live in a tub? Still, there are cabins and cabins, and while some convey the impression of comfort and homeliness, others that I have seen would be rejected by a pig with scorn.

There is a certain type of yachtsman, if you can call him such, who delights in posing as what our American friends term a 'tough guy,' and in some extreme cases he is so tough as to be hardly decent. His boat, usually a converted smack or ship's boat, is dirty and ill-kept, and he goes about unshaven and unwashed and wearing clothes at which a self-respecting scarecrow would look askance. Strangely enough, men who do that sort of thing are often quite smartly dressed and eminently respectable when at home.

Years ago I knew a baronet who owned a 'little old tore-out' and aped the 'tough guy.' One day he went into the public bar of a waterside inn for a bread-and-cheese lunch, and when he had finished his frugal meal, he asked for a cigar. The publican offered him a villainous-looking weed which even he was not tough enough to tackle. "Haven't you something better than that?" he asked. The land-lord, looking at him doubtfully, replied, "Well, yes I have, but they are twopence." The bold bad Bart. used to tell this tale against himself with much gusto, but it is difficult to understand the mentality of men who go out of their way to defy the common decencies of convention.

Some time ago I was invited on board a converted smack which was anchored close to my craft. I like to visit other men's boats, as one can often pick up useful tips and see interesting gadgets in that way. On this occasion, however, I was not interested but merely disgusted, for her cabin was in an appalling state. There were no cushions on the bunks, everything was grimed with filth and the boat fairly stank. The only thing in the way of fittings that I could see was a rusty tin lamp hanging on the mast with a smoked and cracked glass. There were no cots or any other form of beds, the crew evidently sleeping in their clothes on the bare locker lids. On the floor was an old Primus stove in a filthy state, some dirty enamelled plates and a rusty frying-pan coated with congealed fat. Articles of clothing, boots and shoes were heaped on the bunks, and among them I noticed a piece of bacon and a number of egg-shells. The crew had evidently been dining. It is not only among the small yacht-owners one finds people with piggish habits. A friend of mine once bought a yacht of nearly 40 tons from a certain well-known single-handed yachtsman, and on taking delivery of the vessel was troubled by a disgusting stench. On investigation it was found that a locker in the fo'c'sle was nearly full of bacon and cheese rind, potato peelings and grease, evidently the accumulation of months, and the whole mass was crawling with maggots. Cleaning out that locker was a job that might have defeated the efforts of Lewis Carroll's "seven maids with seven mops."

There is not the slightest reason why you should not be comfortable and live decently in the cabin of even a pocket cruiser of only 2½ tons, but as the space at your disposal is not very great it is essential that you should be methodical and tidy in your habits. Much, too, depends upon the arrangement of the cabin, and that offers considerable scope for ingenuity. As it is almost impossible to design a yacht successfully round a cabin plan, it would serve no useful purpose if I gave here specimen plans, and so I will confine my remarks to various items of equipment that make for comfort and convenience, with suggestions as to where they should be fitted if practicable. It cannot be stated too emphatically, however, that the cabin lay-out must be fitted into the yacht and not the boat built round a cabin plan.

First let us consider what particular items of furniture are necessary, or at any rate desirable, for our comfort and convenience. Of course, my ideas on the subject may differ from yours, but the things I consider most important are a comfortable bed at night and comfortable sitting accommodation by day; a cupboard in which I can hang my shore clothes, a pantry in which to stow the crockery, an adequate cooking outfit and a roomy locker in which to stow stores, etc. Whether all of these desiderata can be provided must depend upon the space you have at your disposal.

In most small yachts there is a bunk on each side of the cabin, which form seats by day and beds by night. By the way, these are sometimes termed sofas, settees or just seats, but I prefer to call them bunks. There are, however, objections to sleeping on the bunks. In the first place they are apt to be uncommonly hard, unless sprung (a rather rare refinement in small craft). After long use as seats the cushions get hard, and although they may be all right for sitting on, they are not sufficiently comfortable as beds. Then, it is difficult to keep the blankets in place during the night and if you are a restless sleeper you will probably awake in the small hours of the morning to find all your blankets on the cabin-floor. A final, and perhaps the most important objection, is the difficulty of disposing of the blankets during the daytime. If you stow them away in kit-bags they take up the deuce of a lot of room and will be horribly in your way all day; if you fold and stow them at the head of the bunks, they will not 'stay put' but probably fall off on to the cabin floor when the yacht is under way, and they may get wet. The

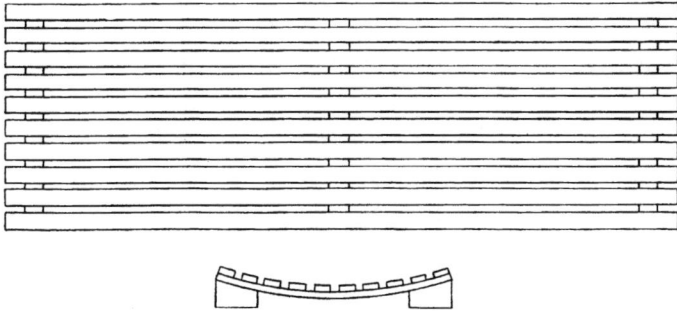

Concave slatted bunk

comfort of the bunks, however, will be enhanced if they are composed of battens and slightly concave.

In my opinion the best bed you can have afloat is a pipe-cot, in conjunction with a good horsehair mattress. I have used such a cot in my boats for many years and I sleep as comfortably afloat as in my bed, with its Vi-spring mattress, ashore. Most yachtsmen are familiar with the pipe-cot, or fo'c'sle-cot as it is sometimes termed, but for the benefit of the beginner, perhaps I should mention that it consists merely of a rectangular frame made of galvanized iron piping, to which a canvas bottom is tightly laced. One side is hinged to the side of the yacht, just above the bunk, and the other suspended by lanyards from the roof. By day, it is folded back to the side of the cabin, with all the bedding and blankets inside. At night you have only to lower it into position and there is your bed ready for you to get into. The lanyards keep the blankets in place at night, and when the cot is stowed it affords a comfortable back to rest against when sitting on the bunk. The accompanying illustration shows pipe-cots both ready for use and stowed. Now, here are a few hints about pipe-cots.

If you buy one at a yacht-chandler's it will cost you thirty shillings or more, but the materials are comparatively inexpensive and can easily be made up. The cot I have in my present boat *Iolanthe* was made for me by a friend, who had the

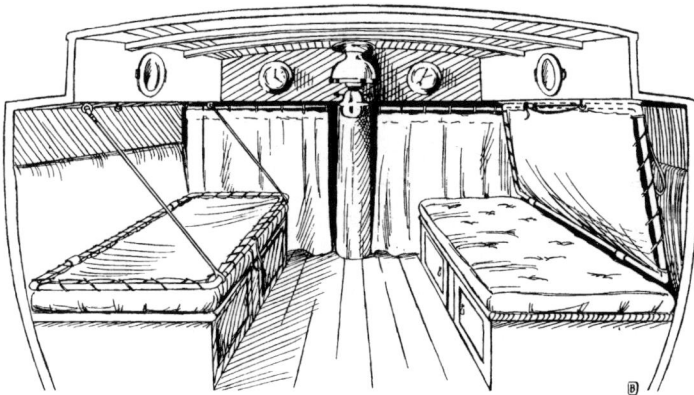

Pipe cots, lowered and stowed

necessary tools for threading the joints. It is 22 inches wide and 6 feet long. The galvanized piping – 16 feet of ½-inch – cost 4s. 6d., four elbows for the corners is. iod., and the canvas bottom, made by my sail-maker, 8s. 6d., making the total cost 14s. 9d. I use with it a good horsehair mattress, 3 inches thick, and it makes a most luxurious bed.

It is the usual practice to hinge the cot direct to the lining of the cabin, but that entails bending the side of the frame to fit the contour of the boat, not an easy matter if you make the cot yourself. Such a method of fitting moreover has other objections. It renders the stowage of the cot more difficult, as it has to be pushed back to the side of the boat by force and that is apt to squeeze the mattress out of shape. And if the stowed cot is to make a comfortable back to rest against when sitting on the bunk, it should be as nearly perpendicular as possible. In my boat I had the cot-hinges mounted on 4-inch chocks of wood and could thus use a rectangular frame. Fitted in that manner, there is more room to turn over when sleeping, and the cot, when stowed, is almost vertical and comfortable to lean against.

The cot lanyards should be of 1¼-inch rope, one end being spliced round the frame and the other fitted with a hook. A pair of sister-hooks will provide the hooks, if you force open the thimble with a cold chisel and separate them. A third lanyard is required to hold back the cot to the side of the boat when it is stowed and that is best fitted with a hook also. This lanyard should be attached to a screw-eye in the shelf just under the deck and in the centre of the cot.

To sum up, the folding pipe-cot is cheap, comfortable to sleep on and affords

Canvas cot

the only really satisfactory way of disposing of your bedding during the day. The last mentioned is a real problem in a small yacht, for the cabin cannot be kept tidy if blankets are left lying about. One man I know found a solution to the problem in a galvanized iron dustbin, which he lashed down to the fo'c'sle floor, but it took up a deal of valuable space and was something of an eyesore.

Another form of bed used in small yachts consists of a strip of stout canvas, one side being attached to the lining of the boat and the other mounted on a wooden batten, of which the ends engage in chocks. I don't think it very satisfac-

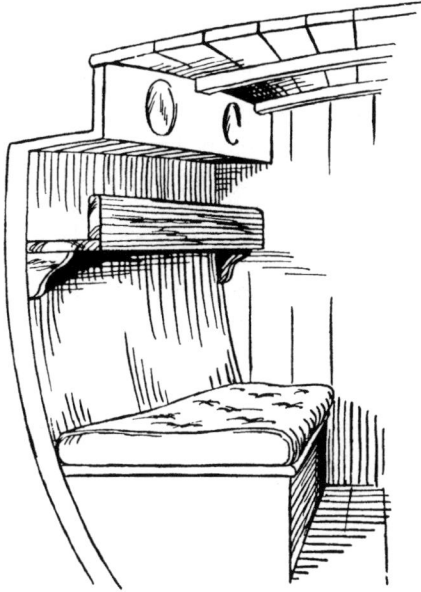

Shelf below side-deck

tory, however, as the batten is apt to whip and slack up the canvas, or may jump out of the chocks and deposit you on the floor.

However comfortable your bed may be, you are not likely to sleep soundly unless you have a soft pillow. You cannot expect Morpheus to do his stuff properly if you rest your head on a rolled-up coat, or a pair of sea-boots. I myself use two small pillows, stuffed with down. They are about the size of a baby's cot-pillow, and when not in use are stowed in the cot with the other bedding. In my *Iolanthe*, the bedding, when stowed, is covered by a sheet of Willesden canvas, which keeps everything perfectly dry. It has a few eyelets down one side, and as the cabin is not lined, I hitch the canvas to hooks in the shelf at night, to protect the blankets from moisture generated by condensation. The mattress and blankets are kept in position by a strap, when the cot is stowed.

Some owners object to pipe-cots in the cabin on the score that they are unsightly, but that objection can be overcome by covering them with art serge. In *Fancy* the cots were completely hidden during the daytime by upholstered cushions, similar to those on the bunks, which formed backs to the seats. By night the cushions formed mattresses for the cots. As the cots were slung at least a foot above the bunks, there was plenty of room below to dispose of one's clothes.

In an earlier chapter I drew attention to the great benefit derived from a raised deck, or over-all cabin-top, which not only enormously increases the size of the cabin but also enables you to sit back comfortably even in a little yacht of 2½ tons. Many small yachts, however, are still built with a cabin-top of the coach-roof type and few such craft of less than 5 or 6 tons afford sitting headroom under the side-decks. You consequently have to sit on the edge of the bunk, like a stage curate at a tea party, with the coaming cutting into the back of your neck. It is most damnably uncomfortable and after an hour or so becomes positive torture. Even pipe-cots will not give you the necessary back rest, if the side-decks are wide. I owned a 5-tonner years ago of that type and mitigated the discomfort by fitting shelves below the side-decks of the same width. These shelves had deep lee-boards, which provided the desired back rests. Although rather hard to lean against, they provided a solution to the problem, and probably would have been quite comfortable if they had been upholstered. The shelves were very useful for stowing long things like charts and burgees, which are often difficult to dispose of.

The clothes cupboard should be fitted with a shelf at the top for shaving gear and other toilet requisites, and there should be sufficient depth below to hang a suit. A brass rod can be fitted athwartship a few inches below the shelf for hanging trousers on, and the cupboard should have a sill, say, 4 inches deep, so that the door will clear the bunk cushion. There should be room at the bottom of the cupboard for shoes. In a little ship about the only place where sufficient height

Hanging clothes locker

can be found for such a cupboard is on the after bulkhead. If you sail single-handed, the cupboard need not be more than about 9 inches from back to front, but if it has to accommodate the clothes of two people, it must be about a foot. There should be hooks at the sides for coats.

In the absence of a proper cupboard, you will have to keep your shore clothes in a suitcase, where they will be badly creased. Suitcases too, are a beastly nuisance in a small yacht, as they always seem to be in the way. Apart from clothing one always has to take a certain amount of stuff, such as provisions, when going away, even for a week-end. I use a canvas bag for the purpose, which when emp-

Pantry for 2½-tonner

tied can be folded up and stowed away in a locker. The boat is thus kept free of suitcases.

A pantry is very desirable even in the smallest cruiser, for if the crockery is stowed loose in a locker, breakages can hardly be avoided. It is convenient, too, to have everything of that sort compactly stowed and ready to hand. My pantry is quite small and yet contains everything I need. There are compartments for dinner plates, small plates and saucers, while cups and mugs are hung on hooks at the sides and back. The teapot lives on top of the saucers and jugs hang on hooks. Across the back of the pantry is a compartment for pots of jam, marmalade, tea, etc. Small as the pantry is, it contains 8 plates of various sizes, 2 cups and saucers, 2 pint mugs, 2 jugs, teapot, pots for mustard, pepper and salt, 2 egg-cups, jars for butter, tea and coffee, a pot of marmalade, and a tin of household milk – sufficient for two people.

Well, that I think is a very suitable pantry for a little pocket cruiser of 2½ tons, like *Iolanthe*; but in larger craft you of course have space for something more elaborate. The one illustrated below would serve admirably for a yacht of 6 or 7 tons. The upper door lets down and is held in a horizontal position by chains at the sides, thus forming a useful table. In the upper part of the pantry are compartments for plates of different sizes, cups and saucers, and a bread locker. The lower portion is in the form of a cupboard, containing five tin drawers for tea, sugar, butter, etc., a wire egg tray (holding two dozen), meat tray, zinc drawer for knives and forks, and spaces for jars, condensed milk, etc. Altogether it is a compact, well-designed pantry, holding everything essential and in such a way as to reduce the risk of breakage to a minimum. These pantries are supplied by Messrs. Simpson, Lawrence & Co. of Glasgow, nicely made with teak-framed doors and Cyprus panels, the mountings being of brass. The overall measurements are as follows: breadth 22 inches, and height 32 inches, the depth being 21 inches at the top and 10½ inches at the bottom. The sides are

Pantry, standard pattern

Pantry for 7-tonner

left extending a couple of inches beyond the back so that they may be cut to fit almost any boat. When ordering, it would be as well to indicate the position in the yacht that the pantry is to occupy, as, if necessary, the depth can be decreased at one end to fit the contour of the yacht.

Messrs. Simpson, Lawrence & Co. also stock smaller pantries, and if you have not sufficient space for the one I have described, I would suggest that you procure their catalogue in which you will probably find one suitable for your requirements. A pantry as shown below would, I think, be very suitable for a yacht of about 5 tons.

The table question is one that often gives the small yacht owner pause to think. What one wants is a table that is firm and substantial and yet capable of being removed and stowed in a compact form. A small swing table is a devilish contrivance, for one barks one's shins on the weight and when the yacht is heeled in a breeze, the table is either on a level with one's chin or else in the neighbourhood of one's boots, according to the side at which one happens to be sitting. A table that is slung from the roof by lanyards is equally unsatisfactory, as it has a playful habit of discharging its contents on to one's lap.

Pantry for 5-tonner

450

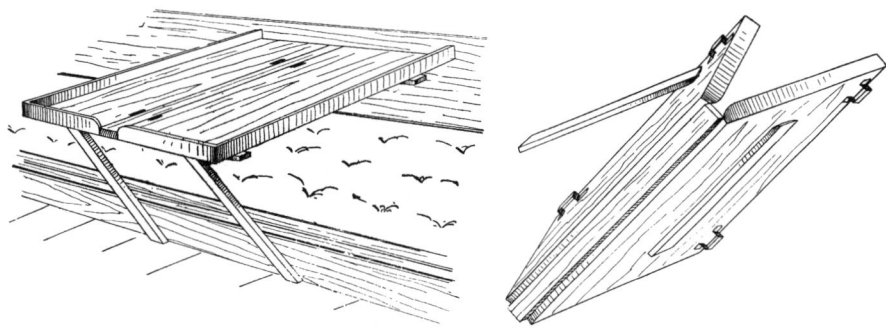

Side table, mounted and partly folded

I think the best form of table is one made to step into the keelson, for, if properly fitted, it is firm and occupies but little space, particularly if made with flaps to fold down when not in use. The legs should be hinged to the top so that it may be stowed compactly when unshipped. A form of table often used in small craft is as shown opposite. One side is hooked to the lining of the boat and the other supported by means of legs, which rest in the angle formed by the bunk-riser and the floor. The principal objection to this kind of table is that it will only seat three and those sitting at the sides are not very comfortably placed.

A very simple form of table that I used for many years with complete success is that shown below. The mast end of the table is supported on a batten of wood, hinged to the mast by a single screw. When the table is in use this batten is, of course, in a horizontal position with the end of the table resting on it; but when the table is taken down, the batten folds up and down the mast out of the way. The trestle legs are hinged so that they can be folded against the top and are kept from collapsing, when the table is in use, by a strut.

If a fixed table be adopted, it will be necessary to use fiddles when having a meal under way, should the weather be rough or the yacht heeling very much. These fiddles are merely racks made to fit the table and containing partitions for plates, glasses, etc. By the use of such fitments a meal can be comfortably enjoyed when the yacht is heeled to a considerable angle without risk of things being upset.

A tablecloth adds considerably to the homeliness of the cabin. It should be made of the same material as the curtains and if you can persuade one of your womenfolk to embroider the corners, so much the better. As a tablecloth

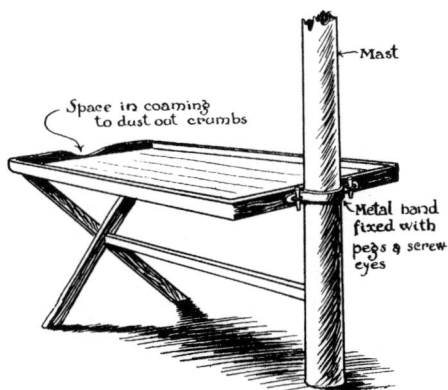

Table for small cruiser

is apt to slip off the table when the yacht is under way, it should be kept in place by means of clips, or by drawing-pins stuck in the edges of the table.

Most owners, I think, cover the cabin floor with linoleum, but I am sure that is a mistake, as it tends to harbour damp. It is much better to paint or varnish the floorboards and lay a rug, or strip of carpet on top, as it can be taken up when you leave the yacht. It is less trouble to shake a rug overboard than to sweep the floor, and the rug, or carpet, gives the cabin a comfortable homely appearance. A strip of Wilton stair carpet will serve the purpose in most boats and will last for years. It is economical in the long run to get good carpet or rugs. If you buy a cheap one, the colours will probably run and it will look like a dirty old rag in a few months. When I had the 2½-ton *Snipe*, nearly fifty years ago, I bought two little Turkey rugs for the cabin floor and those rugs, I believe, are still in use in *Shearwater*, a larger edition of *Snipe* which Mr. Munro had built some years ago as successor to the smaller craft. I am, of course, assuming that your yacht is reasonably tight; if she leaks badly it would be inadvisable to use rugs on the cabin floor. In my present boat I have a strip of Wilton carpet, cut to fit the floor and strongly bound at the edges.

I think the best material for cushion stuffing is either horsehair or kapok, but if they are to keep their shape they must be well made and plentifully buttoned. From the point of view of comfort I don't think there is much to choose between them, but kapok is rather cheaper and cushions stuffed with it will also serve as lifebuoys in case of need. Flock should be avoided for upholstering as it soon gets lumpy and hard. Of course, if you can afford them, Dunlopillo cushions, made of rubber of the Sorbo type, are the most comfortable of all, but they are rather expensive. Apart from being soft to sit, or sleep, on, they keep. their shape well and are impervious to damp.

The material with which the cushions are covered must be largely a matter of personal fancy. Rexine, or some other sort of leather cloth, is perhaps the most serviceable and being practically waterproof is less affected by damp than most other materials. Velvet cord is durable and looks nice but only suitable for a dry boat, as any drips from the decks would soak into the cushion. Velvet cord, too, collects dust and requires frequent brushing.

And now a word or two about the sanitary arrangements. Personally I dislike under-waterline wc's, as unless kept scrupulously clean they are offensive and they often give trouble. Of course, if you have ladies on board a w.c. is essential, but it should be enclosed if possible. A bucket, used in the cockpit, is

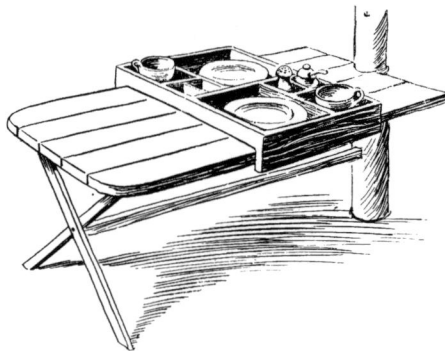

Table fiddles

452

Shelf for crockery

infinitely more sanitary and takes up but little room. If you are something of a sybarite, you can use a loose seat on the bucket. In little yachts of under 5 tons there really is not room for a w.c., although one is often installed in the fo'c'sle. In such a position it takes up a great deal of valuable space, is unhygienic and, owing to lack of headroom, extremely uncomfortable to use. I could say a lot more on this subject, but as it is a rather intimate one perhaps I had better not.

Not the least important item of cabin furniture is the lamp, which must be gimballed. Unfortunately most of the cabin lamps supplied for small yachts give a very poor light and are apt to cause eye-strain when one is reading. I have had a score or more gimballed lamps in my time but could count on the fingers of one hand those which gave sufficient light to read by without eye-strain. The light from a poor lamp can, however, be much enhanced by hanging a shaving mirror behind it. You can buy a suitable mirror at Woolworths, but see that it has a metal frame, for it is not desirable to place highly inflammable material like celluloid near a light.

It beats me why paraffin cabin lamps should be so unsatisfactory, for after all the space to be illuminated is only about 7 feet square. Yet, strangely enough, if you go to a lamp shop you can buy a wall lamp that will give a splendid light. I expect manufacturers would say that such a lamp would be top-heavy if gimballed; but, hang it all, what's the matter with a blob of lead on the bottom? The cabin lamp of *Fancy*, when my son and I bought her, gave a light of the dim religious order, so we bought an ordinary wall lamp, with a duplex burner, to supplement it. That illuminated the cabin brilliantly, but as it was not gimballed we could only use it when at anchor. We slung it on the bulkhead, with a smoke-catcher suspended from the roof above and it was altogether a success. In a little boat of 3 or 4 tons there is not sufficient headroom to use a wall lamp of that sort, as it has a tall glass and if fitted at a safe distance from the cabin-top it would be much too low down. Atmospheric gimballed lamps, with a mantle, are now procurable and give a fine light, but they are rather expensive and some of them make a humming noise when burning, which is irritating. Most of them seem to have rather tall chimneys, which render them difficult to fit in the cabin of a small boat. Fitting the lamp, indeed, often presents difficulties. If it is a stumpy one and the fore-coaming deep, it can be fitted there, but it must have a large smoke-catcher over it, or it might burn the cabin-top. In *Iolanthe* the lamp is fit-

Method of fitting cabin lamp

ted on the coaming and although it had a large smoke-catcher over it, I found that it was beginning to scorch the cabin-top. So I fitted an asbestos cooking-mat over the smoke-catcher and that did the trick.

If the fore-coaming is within an inch or two of the mast, the lamp can be fitted to the latter, but very often the mast is too far away. In such a case the difficulty can be overcome in the following manner. Screw a piece of hard wood, say 4 inches wide, to the fore-coaming and fit the lamp to that. To stiffen it up, another piece of wood of the same width can be screwed to the bottom and extended to the mast, thus forming a bracket. This extension can have holes in it for a couple of tumblers, thus providing a glass-rack that will not be in the way.

If room permits, there should be a sideboard at the end of each bunk with a cupboard beneath. There should be a deep ledge round the sideboard to keep things from rolling off when under way. The cupboards will be very useful for stowing stores, etc. and in one there might be a small cellarette to hold three or four bottles of wine and spirits, if you can afford such luxuries in these expensive days. An aneroid and clock can be mounted on the coaming of the cabin-top, or fore-bulkhead if the yacht has a flush deck. The clock should be an eight-day one, otherwise you may find that it has run down when you go on board. Some clocks will not start when wound up unless shaken and that entails unshipping the clock, which would be a nuisance if you often had to do it. But eight-day yacht clocks are expensive and you may jib at the cost. Well, here is a tip that will save you money. If you go to a large garage, or scrap merchant's yard, where they break up obsolete motor-cars, you will be able to buy an old car clock for a few shillings. I have one in my boat that cost five shillings; a friend bought one in excellent condition for only half a crown. They are eight-day clocks and mine keeps excellent time. As these clocks are sunk in the dashboard of the car, it is necessary to make a case if you want to fit one on the coaming, as it would be inadvisable to cut a hole in the coaming for the purpose. A case is easily made, as shown in the illustration.

If not essential, a bookshelf is certainly desirable in even the smallest cruising yacht. You may not be a great

Sideboard

reader, but you must at least carry a few volumes, such as pilotage books and a nautical almanac. If you sail much alone, the shelf should be large enough to accommodate say a dozen Penguin books, in addition to the works of reference to which I have referred. When you have read them, you will probably be able to exchange them with some other yachtsman for books of a similar type. The bookshelf should be fitted athwartship if possible, for otherwise the books might fall out when the yacht is heeled. If you are compelled by lack of space to fit it fore-and-aft, there should be a removable batten to keep the books in place when under way. In addition to the bookshelf, there should be a shelf, or shelves, for stowage of small items of everyday use, such as pipes, tobacco and one's loose change. There should be such a shelf for each person on board, so that each can keep his things separate. They need not be very large, but should have a deep ledge to keep things from falling off.

A few pictures will add a finishing touch to the furnishing of your cabin and I would suggest for the purpose the miniature reproductions in colour of the fine paintings of famous sailing ships by the late Mr. J. Spurling, issued by the Blue Peter Publishing Co. They should be framed and mounted on the coamings, between the scuttles. To preserve them from damp the backs should be covered with brown paper and varnished. Another indispensable item is an ashtray, and when I say ashtray I don't mean one of those footling little things of about 2 inches in diameter, but one of really serviceable size, in which you can de-

Case for car clock

posit odds and ends of rubbish, as well as tobacco ash. I use one of Woolworth's bulb-bowls and it answers admirably and is not easily upset. By the way, when speaking of clocks I omitted to say that you will need, in addition to the eight-day one, an alarm clock to wake you if you have to catch an early tide.

I think a fore-bulkhead a mistake in a small yacht. It is better for the boat to be open right through to the stem. The doors in a fore-bulkhead are usually very small and difficult to get through, particularly if you are what is often described as 'a fine figure of a man.' I admit that a fo'c'sle, and the gear that is usually stowed in it, is not particularly sightly, but it can be shut off with a curtain of art serge to match the tablecloth.

The owner of a little 'pocket' cruiser may wish to take, say, his daughter or sister away with him but is debarred from doing so by lack of cabin accommodation. This difficulty could be overcome by hanging a fore-and-aft curtain down the centre of the cabin, thus dividing it into two cubicles. In the morning he could dress in the cockpit, leaving the cabin to the lady. A cockpit tent would be desirable for use on wet days. If three or four cup-hooks were screwed into the cabin-top beams, the curtain could be put up or taken down in a moment. Although I am all for making the cabin as snug and homely as possible, I abhor ornate chromium-plated fittings, silk lampshades and arty cushions. The aim should be to make your home afloat comfortable, but not like Dicky Gloster's rooms at college – "more like a whore's than a man's," as Kipling said.

CHAPTER 37: *Planning the Cabin*

In the last chapter I wrote of various items of cabin furniture necessary, or at least desirable, for comfort and convenience, and we have now to consider where they should be installed. That, of course, will depend a good deal on the size and design of the vessel. If you are having a yacht built for you the accommodation plan will be prepared by the designer, who will do his best to follow your suggestions, but you should not tie him down too rigidly or the result may be disappointing. The inexperienced amateur is apt to attempt the impossible feat of putting a quart into a pint pot. He forgets that a yacht has not straight sides like a packing-case, and although the plan may look feasible enough on paper it may be quite impracticable.

Sketching the internal accommodation of a small yacht is a fascinating occupation, but you should not allow your ideas to run away with you. If you crowd into the plan everything you think you would like, the various items may be too small to be of practical use. Remember that the space at your disposal is strictly limited and you will be wise to eliminate from your scheme anything that is not really necessary for your comfort and convenience. If you study the accommodation plans of the yacht designs reproduced in this book you can hardly fail to glean hints that will be useful when planning your own cabin.

There is no more popular craft afloat than the little 'pocket' cruiser of from 2½ to 4 tons. Most of them are built from standard designs, although in some cases the cabin lay-out can be arranged to suit the purchaser's ideas. It may be of service to the potential owner of such a boat if I give particulars of the way in which I planned the cabin of my own 2½-ton *Iolanthe*. It has proved so satisfactory that I cannot think of a single thing that I would alter if I were building another similar craft.

Iolanthe is one of Dan Webb's well-known Blackwater sloops, but was built to my own specification, which included oak frame, pitch-pine planking, oak transom, and teak cockpit, coamings and bulkhead. Her approximate dimensions are: Length, 18 feet; beam, 6 feet 6 inches; draught, 3 feet, and headroom in cabin 4 feet 6 inches. As I sail alone, I had only my own comfort to consider when planning the cabin, although the arrangements have proved quite adequate for two people, when I have occasionally had a companion.

I decided that my chief requirements were a comfortable bed, a locker in which to hang my shore clothes, a pantry, a cupboard for stores and a bookshelf. Most of these were described in the last chapter and I will now tell you where and how they were fitted, so as not to encroach unduly on the cabin space.

I found that the only place in the boat where there was sufficient depth for a hanging clothes cupboard was on the after bulkhead, so I fitted it there on the starboard side. As it measures only 9 inches from back to front, it takes up little room and did not interfere with the installation of a pipe-cot on the same side.

The next thing to claim my attention was the pantry, which I designed to fit the crockery. It occurred to me that if I planned the pantry first I might not be able to get plates, etc., to fit in the compartments. I therefore bought the crockery first and having measured the various items, designed the pantry to accommodate them. As a result, everything of that sort that I need is compactly housed and there is no waste of space.

The pantry is fitted at the top of the bulkhead on the port side and below it is a large store cupboard. The illustration (overleaf) shows the after bulkhead, with the clothes locker, pantry and store cupboard fitted. At one side of the store cupboard are stretched expanding curtain wires, about 3 inches apart, between which are confined sundry spare tins of jam, marmalade, meat, etc. They are firmly held by the wires and are not dislodged in the roughest weather. These expanding curtain wires, by the way, are useful for a variety of purposes on board and can be bought at Woolworths and most ironmongery shops. They are easily cut to the required length and eyes are screwed into the ends, so that they can be attached to small cup-hooks.

The store cupboard was not carried right down to the bunk, as that would have made the latter too short for sleeping purposes, if I had a companion. There is a space of about 15 inches between the bottom of the cupboard and the bunk, to accommodate a sleeper's feet, and the bunk is a full 6 feet in length. When alone, as I usually am, this space is very useful for stowage, as there is room for the bread tin, my portable typewriter and writing case.

The space between the clothes locker and the side of the boat is filled by two shelves, one for books and the other for odds and ends. The bookshelf is certainly not very large, but it will hold a Lloyd's Register, one or two books of pilot directions and some half-dozen Penguin books.

Having provided a bed, clothes locker, pantry, store cupboard and bookshelf, all that remained was a cooking galley, and that presented something of a problem, as there was no suitable place left for an enclosed galley. If a galley is to be of any practical use it must be large enough to house a gimballed Primus and an oven stove, and such a galley is out of the question in a yacht as small as this. I therefore abandoned the idea and installed a gimballed Primus just forward of the port bunk. Fitted to the side of the boat, it does not take up much room and although just inside the fo'c'sle, is within easy reach from the cabin. For slow

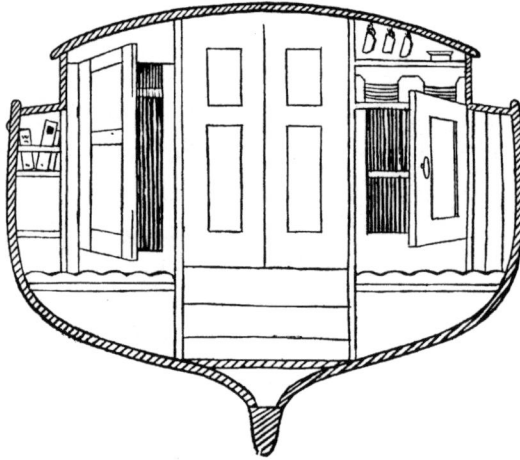

After bulkhead of *Iolanthe*

cooking I bought a Beatrice oil stove and a Staines Model Roaster, of which I will tell you more in the chapter on cooking. The oil stove I at first installed just in the fo'c'sle on the starboard side, but subsequently found it more convenient to cook on the step leading into the cabin from the cockpit. When not in use, the oil stove lives in the stern locker, being kept in position by expanding curtain wire.

The floor of the fo'c'sle in these boats is raised to the level of the bunks, thus forming a platform, beneath which are two large lockers. One of these contains the cable and the other houses all the cooking utensils. Right forward is a shelf, on which I keep spare sails.

The cabin table is of the type described in the last chapter, one end being supported by a batten on the mast and the other on folding trestle legs. It can be removed and folded in a moment, but is so little in the way that I seldom take it down except when cleaning the cabin. The gimballed lamp is fitted on the fore-coaming and there are ventilating scuttles in the coamings. The entrance to the cabin is closed by two sliding fashion-boards, with two small doors above.

The cockpit of *Iolanthe* is deep and comfortable. There are small lockers under the side-decks and large open ones beneath the seats. To keep things in

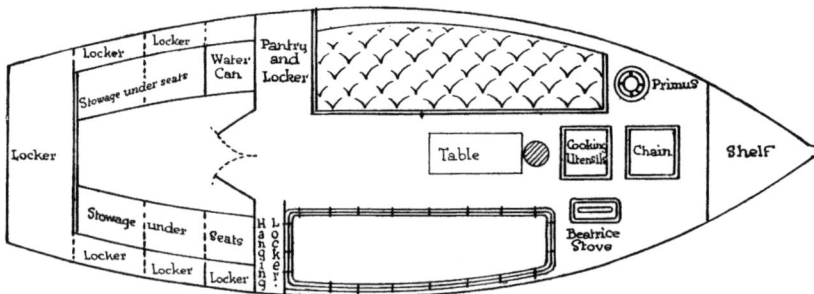

Iolanthe cabin layout

458

place in the open lockers, each is fitted with two teak battens, of which the upper fits in slots and is removable. These lockers hold a lot of stuff. On the port side I stow a 20-fathom warp, the riding light, my sea-boots and a 4-gallon water-can; and on the starboard side two buckets, a paraffin can, the washing-up bowl, a deck scrubber and the lead and line. There is also room in that locker for another water-can. In the small lockers under the side-decks I keep a small stock of bo-sun's stores, a box of tools, the rowlock for the sweep and various odds and ends, such as cleaning materials. In the large stern locker I fitted a shelf, with a deep leeboard, to form a larder, in which perishable goods keep very well. There is also room in the locker for the oil stove, a brush and pan, spare rope and a third water-can, should I be going away for some time.

Well, that is the lay-out of *Iolanthe* and after several seasons' cruising in her I cannot think of any improvement that I could make. There is a place for everything and everything is in its place and ready to hand. I can find anything on board in a moment, even in the dark, and nothing is displaced in rough weather.

Of course, in larger yachts you have more room to play with, and in a vessel of 6 or 7 tons there will be space for a proper galley, sideboards, a roomy pantry

Iolanthe cockpit

and a w.c. The best place for the galley, I think, is at the after-end of the cabin, and the pantry can be opposite to it. The engine can be housed under the cockpit floor and if possible it should be started and controlled from the cockpit. It is a nuisance having to remove the companion ladder to start the engine, as is the case in most small yachts.

In *Fancy*, a 7-ton Falmouth Quay Punt which I owned in partnership with my son, the engine was installed under the bridge deck and took up a great deal of space. One could get all round the engine and there were shelves at the sides for tools and spare cans of oil. A door in the after bulkhead gave access from the cabin to the engine room, which was also accessible from the cockpit by removing two or three of the floorboards. As she drew approximately 6 feet and had a transom stern, straight stem and straight keel, she was 'all boat,' as the saying goes. She had 6 feet headroom in the cabin and about 5 feet in the fo'c'sle, but owing to the large amount of space devoted to the engine, there was not so much room in the cabin as in many craft of her tonnage. Still, I think it was laid out to the best advantage and we certainly had everything we needed for comfort.

The bunks were about the same height from the floor as an ordinary chair, and just the right width. One could, of course, sit back under the deck with inches to spare and there were cushions to lean against. Behind these back cushions were folding pipe-cots, which let down over the bunks for sleeping purposes and were completely hidden when folded back during the daytime. Securely bolted to the floorboards was a large mahogany table, with flaps. When these were opened there was room for five people to dine in comfort-two on either side and one at the end. Below the table-top was a long locker for charts and burgees, mounted on canes.

At the fore-end of the starboard bunk was a sideboard, and opposite, on the port side, the pantry, with a large locker below for cooking utensils. The cooking galley, which was not enclosed, was in the fo'c'sle, on the port side; and opposite, on the starboard side was installed what the house agent terms 'usual offices' and the Americans a 'toilet.' Forward of that, on the starboard side was a pipe-cot. Next to the galley, on a small shelf, was a 3-gallon water-jar, which originally contained ginger-beer. These jars, having a tap, screw-stopper and handle, are very convenient for storing drinking water and can be bought for a few shillings.

As the cook had the pantry and cooking utensils on one side of the stoves and a supply of fresh water on the other, he could sit and ply his gentle art (as the Fleet Street reporter might say) with every comfort and convenience. The main supply of water was kept in 4-gallon cans under the cockpit floor. At night the fo'c'sle was lit by a gimballed lamp and by a deck-light in the daytime.

At the fore-end of the cabin was a bogey stove, which was a great comfort during the early and late months of the season, when it is often cold and damp. On the starboard side of the engine room was a place for hanging wet oilskins, so that they could drain into the bilge.

Although *Fancy* was comfortable enough for two, or even three people, so much space was sacrificed to the motor that there was not much scope for ingenuity in the way of cabin arrangement. In the absence of the engine there would have been room for a second cabin; but in a craft of that size and weight an auxiliary engine is almost essential. Such a vessel is too heavy to be propelled with a sweep and there are occasions when one must have the means of keeping steerage way-as, for instance, when drifting through a crowded anchorage like that at Burnham on a strong tide with no wind.

Although the after-end of the cabin is generally considered to be the best place for the galley, I am not at all sure about it. It seems to me that the fore-end is more convenient in some respects, for anyone cooking aft is in the way of others who wish to enter or leave the cabin. When cooking forward, too, the smell is carried off through the open fore-hatch But wherever you have your galley, the pantry should be close to it, as also should the cooking utensil locker.

If you have fixed water-tanks built into the boat, the best place for them will be under the cabin bunks, where the weight will not affect the trim of the yacht. Water could be drawn from them by a small semi-rotary pump in the fo'c'sle. The tanks should be connected by a pipe leading under the floor to ensure the same level being maintained in both. Personally, I prefer to carry water in the convenient galvanized cans supplied for the purpose. They hold a little less than 4 gallons and being furnished with a spout, screw stopper and handle, are very convenient. It is only at large ports that tanks can be filled by means of a hose-pipe and it is comparatively seldom that small yachts visit such places. More often their anchorages are in estuaries and creeks, and so cans must be carried in addition in order to fill the tanks. If you have to use cans for filling the tanks, why not keep the water in the cans and dispense with the tanks?

In many small yachts the locker accommodation is quite inadequate and in some cases almost non-existent. In one 5-tonner I bought there was not a single locker or cupboard in the cabin, other than the lockers under the bunks, which are practically useless for stowing anything but bottles and tinned stuff. There were lockers in the cockpit, under the side-decks, with access from the cabin by means of little doors about 6 inches square. To get anything out of these lockers, one had to put one's arm through the little door and grope for it; or else go out into the cockpit to get what one wanted-not very pleasant on a wet day. There was, however, a large door in the fore-bulkhead, meant for tending the stove that was installed in the fo'c'sle. I got over the locker difficulty by fitting a large cupboard in the fo'c'sle behind this door, shifting the stove farther forward. The upper part of the cupboard was fitted as a pantry and the lower half served as a store cupboard.

This question of lockers is a very important one, for unless you are able to stow things away properly you will have no real comfort.

The storage of perishable goods, such as meat, butter, etc., often presents difficulties in small craft. Perhaps the best thing is a meat-safe lashed down on the deck or cabin-top. It should be shaped like a miniature skylight, but of course with no glass in it. There should be a space of about half an inch between the sides and the deck, so that a free current of air can pass through it, and channels under the hinged lids to drain off any water that may get through.

It is the usual practice to hang cups on hooks in the pantry and although they travel safely enough they are apt to rattle and make an annoying noise when the yacht is brought up in rough water. A method adopted by Mr. Stanley Knowles in his yacht *Diana* strikes me as neat and efficient. Wooden bosses, made to fit the cups, are mounted on a shelf which slides into the pantry near the top. As the cups are thus securely held they do not rattle and as there is only a space of about 1 inch between the cups and the top of the pantry they cannot get adrift.

Stowage of cups

That this is a safe method of stowage will be gathered from the fact that he has been using the same half-dozen cups since 1921.

CHAPTER 38: *Heating*

If it is your intention to start your sailing season early and prolong it beyond September, a stove in the cabin will be essential to your comfort. Sleeping in the cabin of a small yacht without a stove on a frosty night is only to be endured by those of a spartan turn of mind, for when one's bed is on a level with, or even below, the waterline, the cold in its intensity approaches within measurable distance of that of the refrigerators in which so much of our Prime Southdown mutton comes from New Zealand.

Setting aside the question of personal comfort, a stove is necessary to the welfare of the yacht and her gear in winter. In the absence of a stove everything on board will soon be saturated with the moisture generated by condensation, a state of affairs that can only lead to mildew and general mouldiness. If a yacht is to be kept in commission during the winter without fear of deterioration, she must be kept dry inside, and that can only be done by means of a stove. This brings us to the question, what is the best form of stove for the purpose?

The only kinds of stove available to the small yacht owner are those which consume coal (or kindred fuels) and oil. Of these the coal stove wins every time. It gives far more heat than one burning oil and possesses much greater drying power, whilst it is certainly far more cheerful to live with. The worst that can be said against it is that the fuel is rather dirty to handle and bulky to stow, but those objections are readily overcome. Coal is best stored in ore bags, which are small sacks made of stout, closely woven canvas, through which the dust will not work its way. When a bag is empty it can be folded up and stowed away in a locker, and space is thus economized. As regards handling, it may be mentioned that a housemaid's glove is a very efficient substitute for tongs or shovel. The type of coal stove selected calls for serious consideration, and one should not be influenced too much by thoughts of economy. The ordinary 'bogey' stove, which one sees in the cabins of most small craft in the winter, is cheap to buy and burns well if generously stoked. It, however, soon gets red hot and renders the cabin insufferably warm, whilst if you do not keep it well filled the fire may go out.

Another objection to the 'bogey' type of stove is that it will not burn throughout the night without attention. You may stoke it up chock-full before turning in, but it is sure to go out if left to its own devices, and then you will wake up about 3 a.m. with that curious prickly feeling all over your body that is peculiar to sleeping in small yachts in the winter. But a 'bogey' dries up the cabin beautifully, and the cheerful glow of the fire imparts to the little saloon an appearance of homeliness that is very comforting on a cold winter night. Coalite, perhaps, makes a better fuel for these little 'bogey' stoves than coal, as it does not burn quite so fiercely; but it is not readily obtained at the little water-side villages that cruising yachtsmen delight to visit. By the way, the best method of lighting a coal fire is by means of a handful of cotton waste steeped in paraffin. This is far better than fooling about with damp wood and the Daily Mail.

The stove must be carefully installed to eliminate the risk of fire, all woodwork in its neighbourhood being protected with asbestos millboard and copper sheathing. If the stove is close to the mast, a piece of asbestos millboard should be tacked round the latter and the stove must be securely lashed down with wire to prevent its shifting when the yacht heels.

If the chimney is fitted with a fisherman type of cowl adjustable to the wind, do not leave the fire burning when you go ashore if the tide is likely to turn during your absence, for when the vessel swings the cowl will not be properly adjusted Some years ago a yacht was seriously damaged by a fire that occurred in that way. The draught down the chimney blew out flames which set fire to some woodwork and the outbreak was only discovered just in time to save her from total destruction.

If you lose the cowl, or the one you have is unsatisfactory, a piece of board lashed to the weather side of the chimney will prevent the fire smoking. I used a bit of board all one winter in *Fancy* and found it quite as efficient as the cowl.

The chimney will need sweeping occasionally and it is a filthy job if you do it in the ordinary way with a brush. The stove-pipe above deck can be removed and swept overboard, but to unship the portion between the stove and the deck is a bother and difficult to do without shaking a lot of soot into the cabin. The best way of cleaning the chimney is to burn the soot out. First lay the fire with dry sticks and a rag steeped in paraffin to ensure its burning. Then spread a piece of newspaper over the top and shut the door tightly. Sweep the chimney by pushing the brush down from above and then light the fire. The soot will soon be burnt away without making any mess in the cabin. It is not advisable to do this in a crowded anchorage as it will make a lot of smoke which might be the source of annoyance to others.

When the stove is not in use, the upper portion of the chimney should be removed and the hole in the deck filled with a wooden tampion. If you leave the pipe *in situ* when under way it may foul the foresheets.

The ideal stove for a yacht's cabin is one burning anthracite as, with a little attention night and morning, it can be kept alight indefinitely. For a yacht used

Fisherman's cowl

only at week-ends it is particularly suitable, as it can be kept burning during the week in the owner's absence. If the caretaker, when he goes on board night and morning to put up and take down the riding light, shakes out the ashes and stokes it up, the fire can be kept in throughout the winter. The cabin gear, bedding, etc., will then always be bone dry and the owner will not run the risk of contracting rheumatism through sleeping in a damp bed. The anthracite stove yields only a moderate heat, but it is quite sufficient for comfort and will keep at bay the mildew fiend. Being entirely enclosed, a stove of this nature can safely be left burning whilst the yacht is under way, as there is no fear of live coals falling out and setting the boat on fire. With a 'bogey' stove, on the other hand, one must draw the fire before getting under way, which entails the troublesome job of relighting it after bringing up.

An excellent little anthracite stove is the Bontesse, made by Messrs. Smith & Wellstood, and nowadays anthracite can be procured almost anywhere. The fuel may cost rather more than ordinary coal, but it goes much further, and so there is not a great difference in the ultimate cost.

Oil stoves are not altogether suitable for cabin purposes, as the heat generated has not the same drying power as that produced by a coal stove. Neither are they as wholesome, for in the absence of a chimney the atmosphere is to a certain extent vitiated. Moreover, unless kept scrupulously clean they smell. To keep the outside of the reservoir perfectly free from paraffin is not an easy matter afloat, as the motion of the boat causes the oil to splash about and ooze out through the burner. That, at least, is how I account for the fact that I have never yet been shipmates with an oil stove that did not stink – if I may be permitted to use an expressive word that is looked upon askance in polite society. The best form of oil stove for heating purposes is, I think, that known as the Valor Perfection, of which the smallest size is quite large enough for the cabin of a 5-tonner. This stove has a circular wick

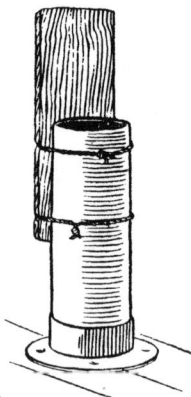

Makeshift cowl

464

which cannot be turned up too high, and burns with a blue flame that throws out considerable heat and smells less than most other oil stoves.

An atmospheric oil stove of the Primus type is not suitable for heating purposes, as it scoffs up most of the oxygen in the air when used in a small cabin. I remember many years ago passing the night with a friend in the 2½-ton *Snipe*, whose cabin measured 7 feet by 6 feet, by barely 4 feet headroom, and as we had no proper heating stove we tried the experiment of burning the Primus. After a time the cabin lamp began to burn dimly and threatened to go out altogether. As I could see that the lamp, which had a glass reservoir, was more than half full of oil I could not make this out. Then I had an idea. I pushed back the cabin slide and let in some fresh air. The lamp immediately began to perk up and burn brightly again. This rather intrigued me and I repeated the experiment several times, until at last my companion protested, saying that if he had to commit suicide he would sooner wait until he got home and could use the more fashionable gas oven. So we put out the Primus and sat shivering, wrapped up in blankets.

I think I have dealt with all the usual cabin fittings used in small craft with the exception of cooking stoves and ventilators, which are of sufficient importance to demand separate chapters.

CHAPTER 39: *Cooking Arrangements*

Those who go cruising nowadays in small yachts enjoy much more comfort than yachtsmen of the last generation, as their vessels are of better design and many labour-saving appliances have been devised for their benefit. In no respect is this more apparent than in their cooking arrangements. In the days when I first started cruising we had to depend upon sooty oil stoves, which took about half an hour to boil the kettle and required constant watching. Although apparently adjusted to a nicety at the outset, the flame had a disconcerting way of burning up and smoking, with the result that the cooking utensil was thickly coated with lamp-black and everything in the cabin covered with a deposit of smuts. Cooking under way was quite out of the question and even at anchor the result as often as not was of the order that has been described as 'a burnt offering or a bloody sacrifice.' Fortunately those days are no more, and with the aid of efficient stoves the owner of even the smallest cruiser is able to get a satisfactory meal without much trouble. If the yacht is of, say, 6 or 7 tons, there should be plenty of room for a properly equipped enclosed galley, containing two stoves – a Primus for boiling purposes and a wick-stove for slow cooking. Of these the Primus, at least, should be gimballed and, if there is sufficient room, the other as well.

Personally, I do not care for ovens in boats, as they are so difficult to clean. To get the grease out of the corners is not an easy job and unless the oven is kept scrupulously clean it will smell. If you want to cook a joint, or chicken, the oven must be a fairly large one – a good deal larger than the meat pan, as there are hot-air chambers all round it. Some of the oven stoves sold for yachts, however, are mere toys and of little practical use. When we bought *Fancy* we found on board a small oven stove fitted with two Primus stoves and affixed to the door was a brass plate inscribed, "This oven will not roast or bake." As it was also too small for warming plates, it did not seem to fulfil any particular use, so we scrapped it. You may ask, "How can you cook a joint if you have not an oven?" Well, there are other ways, of which I will tell you later.

I reproduce a drawing of a galley I designed for the fourth edition of *Cruising Hints* as I do not think that I can improve upon it so far as the general arrangement is concerned. In the illustration, however, Mr. Carr has made the door giving on to the well too small. It is not merely intended for starting the stove, as he supposed, but for inspection purposes and should be about a foot square. The galley is in the form of a cupboard, extending from the floor to the roof of the cabin. This should give a height of about 5 feet, and if built out flush with the cabin door, it should have a depth of about 2 feet 6 inches. The galley should be about 2 feet 9 inches wide, and divided by a shelf placed, say, 2 feet 3 inches from the floor. In the lower portion will be kept the cooking utensils and it should therefore have a separate door. The upper portion is the galley proper and should have a mushroom ventilator fitted in the roof, and there should be a second door in the bulkhead so that cooking can be carried on from the well in fine weather and when under way.

For the sake of cleanliness the upper compartment of the galley should be lined throughout with stove-enamelled iron plates, fitted over asbestos millboard, so that grease can be wiped off with a hot damp cloth. Suspended in gimbals between the bulkhead and the galley side should be a wooden tray, covered with an enamelled iron plate, to carry the stoves. If the tray be about 15 inches wide, there should be sufficient clearance either way when the yacht is heeled in a moderate breeze. As, however, it may occasionally be necessary to cook when the vessel is heavily listed in a hard wind, there should be extra bearings for the gimbals, say, 3 inches on either side of the central ones. If these extra bearings are used, it will, of course, be necessary to shift the gimballed tray every time the yacht goes about. It would only be on very rare occasions that the extra bearings would have to be used, as, in any ordinary weather, the central ones would give ample clearance for the tray. The dimensions I suggest must only be regarded as a rough guide, as they will depend upon the space available and the kind of stoves used. If space permit, a plate rack made of stout brass wire netting can be fitted 3 or 4 inches from the top of the galley.

In a small yacht a coal cooking stove is out of the question, as it would take up too much space, whilst the stowage of a sufficient quantity of coal would present difficulties. The choice of fuel is therefore reduced to paraffin and methylated

Galley

spirit. The latter is expensive, not always procurable in small water¬side villages, and, in my opinion, dangerous. I once had the unpleasant experience of finding myself penned up in the cabin of a yacht that had no fore-hatch, whilst a roaring fire blazed in the well. Fortunately it burnt itself out without doing much damage, but I registered a vow that I would never use spirit stoves in a yacht again.

An enclosed galley takes up an unconscionable amount of room in a small yacht and is really not necessary. Apart from cooking joints, etc., its main use is to prevent the spluttering of grease about the cabin and to retain the smell of cooking. But if you use in place of the oven a Staines Model Roaster, of which the lid is always kept on when cooking, there will be no spluttering and very little smell. Our cooking arrangements in *Fancy* were quite adequate, occupied little space and needed little attention. We used a Model Roaster, in conjunction with an ordinary Beatrice oil stove, and a gimballed Primus. The cook could sit comfortably on a seat opposite the stoves, which were situated in the fo'c'sle, and the pantry was next to the stoves. Any smell of cooking was carried off through the fore-hatch just above.

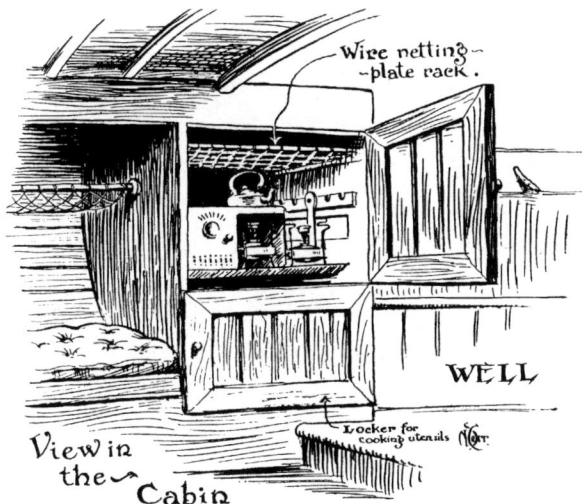

Before describing the Model Roaster, I must say a few words about the Primus stove, which has long been regarded as an essential item of equipment in any yacht. I think I must have been one of the first yachtsmen to use Primus

Cooking arrangements on *Fancy*

stoves afloat, as a friend brought me one from Sweden in the early 'nineties. Since then I have always had at least one of them in every yacht I have owned, and nowadays it would be difficult to find a yacht without such a stove. The Primus is extremely efficient, gives great heat and requires no cleaning other than an occasional wipe over and pricking out the burner. When I went on board my boat after she had been laid up for more than five years during the war the Primus started just as easily as if I had been using it every day.

Most sailing men have an intimate knowledge of the Primus stove, but for the benefit of recruits to yachting I will give a brief description of it and a few hints as to its use.

The stove is very easily manipulated and if treated with reasonable care seldom gets out of order. It consists of a brass oil reservoir, from which a tube projects, surrounded by a small metal cup. At the top of the tube is the burner, and in the reservoir a little pump and a valve. When the stove is used the *modus operandi* is as follows: The reservoir having been three-quarters filled with paraffin, the filler cap is tightly screwed down, and the cup round the burner filled with methylated spirit, which is ignited. The burning spirit heats the tube and the burner above and when it has nearly burnt away the valve is closed and a few strokes on the pump are given. This has the effect of forcing the paraffin up the tube, which is sufficiently hot to vaporize it so that it issues from the burner in the form of gas under high pressure. The more the stove is pumped the greater the heat, and it is possible to boil a quart of water in rather less than four minutes. The valve in the pump can be opened or closed by turning a small thumb-screw. Should a smaller flame be desired for frying purposes, the valve is opened to reduce the pressure, and when the flame is of the required size it is closed again. To put out the stove, the valve is left open until the air is exhausted and the flame extinguished.

Having described the stove, a few words as to its treatment may not be out of place. To work efficiently it is essential that the nozzle of the burner shall be quite clear and free from grit and special prickers are provided for clearing it. If one exercises a little care the stove will only need the use of a pricker every few weeks. When the nozzle gets stopped up it is usually due to a bit of grit being forced into it from inside the reservoir and the more one pumps the firmer is the obstructive particle jammed in the burner. The only way in which it can be dislodged is by means of a pricker, and even then there is always a chance of its being forced back again when the stove is subsequently pumped up. The remedy is always to use a funnel with a gauze filter when filling the reservoir. Another point to be noted is that when lighting the stove the burning methylated spirit must not be in a draught, for if the flame be blown aside it will not heat the burner sufficiently to vaporize the paraffin. Then, when you start to pump, the unvaporized oil catches alight and flares up. This looks rather alarming but is not really of much consequence, for if the valve be opened the flame will soon die down and go out. The makers supply a shield which clips round the burner to exclude draught, and if there is any suspicion of a draught you should use it. If you have not one of these special draught-excluders, a very good substitute can be made out of a coffee tin with the bottom removed. A couple of notches should be cut in one end and when used the tin should be dropped over the burner with the notched end downwards; and when you remove the tin be careful to take hold of it at the bottom, or you may burn your fingers.

Primus, showing home-made draught shield

If you take reasonable care of it, a Primus stove will last for many years, although it will occasionally require a new nipple, and at long intervals a new burner. To fit a new nipple a special spanner is required and I should advise you to get from Messrs. Condrup Ltd., a box of accessories, which costs but a trifle and contains, in addition to the spanner, a supply of nipples, washers, prickers, etc. They also supply a brass methylated spirit can with a long curved spout and an aluminium funnel with a gauze filter for filling the stove. Filling the methylated spirit cup from a bottle is rather awkward, and by using the brass can much waste will be saved. There are two kinds of Primus stove; a noisy one and a silent one, and of these the former is the more efficient for yachting purposes, although I have no doubt the silent one is quite satisfactory in a house. As one often has to boil a kettle when under way, I consider it essential that the Primus stove should be gimballed and I know of no better gimbals than the 'Mol-Con,' supplied by Messrs. Condrup Ltd. They can either be screwed down to the floor, or bench, or fitted to a bulkhead or side of the boat, as indicated by the dotted lines of the illustration. I always keep my kettle on the gimballed stove and have never known it to fall off in any weather.

Messrs. Condrup Ltd., stock a large range of oven stoves of various types and sizes and a special toaster, by means of which you can make four slices of capital toast and boil eggs on the top at the same time. I should advise you to get their catalogue, in which you will find many ingenious and interesting gadgets calculated to enhance your convenience and comfort.

In a very small yacht you may have to cook in the cockpit with a Primus stove and frying-pan. In such circumstances it is difficult to avoid fat being spluttered, but the evil can be mitigated by spreading under the stove a newspaper. If you do that, however, you should put weights on the paper to hold it down, otherwise it might get blown up and set alight. Don't cook chops in a frying-pan in the cabin if you can possibly avoid it, as the smell of stale mutton fat clings like the proverbial ivy and will be offensive for days. And the smell of herrings can hardly be described as a delicate perfume.

About ten years ago I discovered a cooking appliance that has completely revolutionized my culinary operations afloat and which I think will satisfactorily solve the problems of every small yacht owner. It is known as the Staines Model Roaster and Cooker, and supplied by the Staines Kitchen Equipment Co. Ltd., 94 Victoria Street, Westminster, SW1. With this cooker you can cook almost any

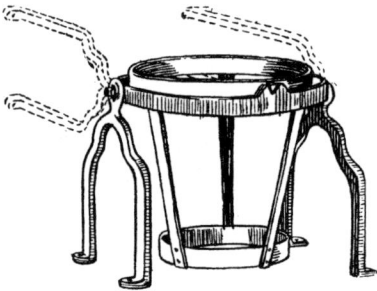

Primus gimbals

darned thing you please, as it roasts, boils, stews, steams and fries equally well and with the minimum of trouble and attention. It is best used over an ordinary Beatrice oil stove (single wick) such as can be bought at almost any ironmonger's shop.

The Staines Roaster looks something like a big pie-dish with a lid but the sides are double, thus forming a hot-air pocket. It is made of steel coated with a very hard glass enamel, which does not crack or chip. I have had one in use in my yacht for the past ten years and it is still in quite good condition. As it is seamless and has no corners, it can be very easily cleaned after use with a little hot water and a dish mop. The lid being a good fit, there is never any spattering of grease and you can therefore cook in the fo'c'sle or cabin without offence. For steaming, a wire grid, made of some rustless metal, is supplied and altogether I regard this roaster as one of the most valuable contributions that has been made towards the equipment of small yachts for many years.

The Junior model, before the war, cost 10s. 6d., carriage paid, and is quite large enough for a small yacht, as it will cook a joint of 4 or 5 lb. in weight, or a chicken of 6 lb. Its dimensions are as follows: Length (including the handles) 15 inches; width, 9 inches; and height (including handle), 6 inches. In addition to roasting joints and poultry, it will steam or fry fish, cook stews or hash, eggs and bacon, steam puddings (in basins placed inside the roaster) and kippers, etc. In fact, it will cook almost anything to perfection and requires little or no attention. The printed instructions supplied with the cooker tell you to allow twenty minutes per pound weight when roasting a joint or chicken, but I think that is perhaps rather an underestimate, and I usually allow twenty-five minutes per pound. A stew takes about two hours or rather less. When buying a Staines Roaster you should ask for the leaflet of instructions, which tells you how to cook all sorts of things, and with a little experience you will find that you can add considerably to the list.

Since I bought my Staines Roaster I have scrapped most of my other cooking utensils, merely retaining a kettle and a spare saucepan. I use it in conjunction with a single-wick Beatrice oil stove and having also a Primus for boiling the kettle, I reckon I have as efficient a cooking outfit as one could wish in a small yacht. In the absence of gimbals, I anchor the Beatrice stove to the bench with two short lengths of expanding curtain wire, stretched tightly over the oil reservoir and secured to cup-hooks. Steps must also be taken to eliminate the risk of the roaster falling off the stove. This can be done with similar wires from the handles to hooks on the bench, or better still by a very neat fitting designed and made by my old friend, the late Mr. L. R. Huggins, as shown in the illustration overleaf. Mr. Huggins gave me the following instructions for making the gadget:

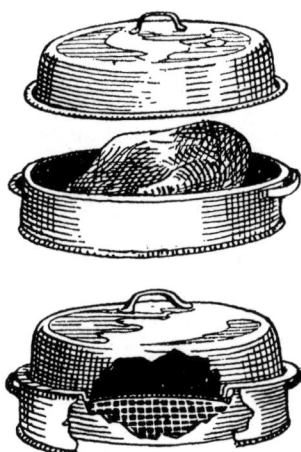

Staines Model Roaster, showing air pocket

"Material: ½-inch × ⅛ inch strip iron. Drill ⅛-inch holes and use copper rivets, countersinking for heads. AB and CD should rest just inside the outer studs at the end of top of stove; JK and LM should clamp outside the top. The bends at the ends of AB, CD, JK and LM should be cut diagonally across strip to fit round the cooker and top of stove respectively; the strip can be bent cold in a vice or with two screw hammers. The best way to get everything to fit is to place the cooker on a piece of cardboard, draw round it with a pencil and cut out a template. Place template on top of the Beatrice stove in correct position and tap on studs lightly with a hammer. This will leave small dents in the template. Mark where A and B and C and D should come and bend strip so that it fits fairly close to template. EF and GH can then be laid on template and marked to fit in correct position. It is a good plan to lay the template on a book, so that the hooks of AB and CD point downwards, otherwise it would be quite easy to make a mistake. Finally, rivet on JK and LM."

The cooking galley is often lined with zinc, but that seems to me an unsuitable material for the purpose. Not only is zinc subject to corrosion but it also has a rather rough surface, to which grease will cling and be difficult to dislodge. I think a galley should be lined throughout with stove-enamelled steel plate. Such plates, enamelled white, are used for putting round gas stoves and can be bought at most ironmongers. A wipe over with a hot damp cloth after cooking will keep the galley clean and takes very little time.

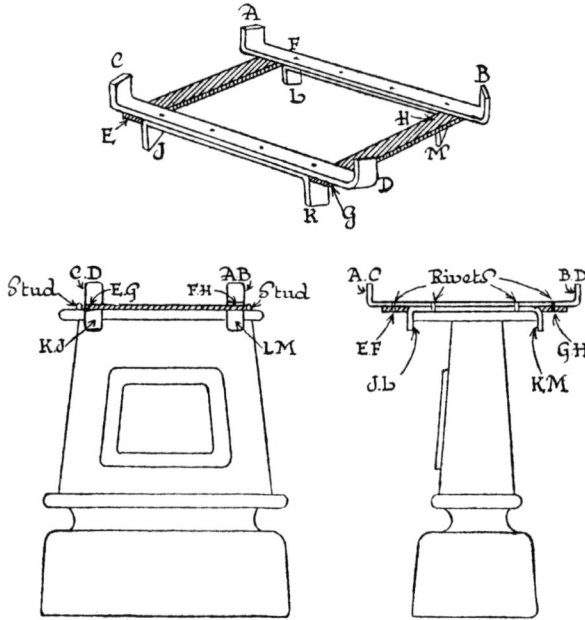

Gadget for holding roaster on stove

In one yacht I know, Mr. T. M. Felgate's *Majority*, the galley is lined with white tiles, which look very neat and hygienic, but I am inclined to doubt whether the tiles will remain in place for very long. Most yachts work a little when sailing to windward and I cannot help thinking that some of the tiles will come unstuck sooner or later. It would of course depend a good deal on the construction of the vessel. In most cruising craft the working is so slight as to be unnoticeable but some lightly built racing yachts wring so much that cupboard doors cannot be opened or shut when the boat is under way. But whatever material is used, the lining should be backed by asbestos millboard to eliminate the risk of fire. A mushroom ventilator should be fitted in the roof of an enclosed galley to carry off the fumes of cooking.

It is, of course, desirable that both stoves should be gimballed but in many small craft there is not room to gimbal the slow-cooking stove as well as the Primus. Even if you don't cook under way, it is important that the stove should be quite level, otherwise the fat will run to one end of the pan and your joint, or whatever you are cooking, may be burnt in one place. If you use a Beatrice stove, anchored to the cooking bench with spring wires, it can easily be levelled up by forcing wedges under the stove where necessary. Little wooden wedges, such as those used for windows to prevent their rattling, serve admirably for the purpose.

A very useful cooking utensil is the Welbanke Boilerette, as it requires no attention. If you have a gimballed stove, a stew can be put on before getting under way and when you bring up some hours later a good hot dinner will be awaiting you. This boilerette cooks by steam under pressure and all of the goodness is retained in the meat. An old boiling fowl cooked in a Welbanke will be as tender as a spring chicken, and all you have to do is to see that the water in the jacket does not boil away. I had several of these boilers before I discovered the Staines Model Roaster and found them very satisfactory, although, of course, they are only suitable for such things as stews.

Another ingenious cooking utensil, of somewhat similar type to the Welbanke Boilerette, is the Pentacon, which cooks by steam under high pressure. It is said to roast a chicken in six minutes and a joint in from twelve to fifteen minutes. No attention is required, a valve being set for the required time, which whistles when the time has elapsed. It is claimed that an entire meal can be cooked together without the flavour of the various items being affected. This all seems very wonderful, but as I have never used a Pentacon, or know anyone who has, I cannot say whether it really does all that is claimed for it.

Most small yacht owners cook with paraffin, which perhaps is the most suitable fuel for such craft, which for the most part seek anchorages in out-of-the way creeks. Paraffin can be bought in almost any village and it is not therefore necessary to carry a large supply, and it can also be used for lighting. In larger vessels, however, bottled gas is very convenient, as the stove can be lit by just putting a match to it. The containers take up more room than can be spared in a miniature cruiser, but in a yacht of 7 or 8 tons bottled gas is undoubtedly a boon.

I was recently on board Dr. Ives's *Tartar*, 7 tons, and was much impressed by his Botto-gas plant. He is a handy man and had fitted it up very cleverly. The gas cylinder was installed in one of the lockers under the bunks and the gas led through tubes to the cooking stoves and neat little lamps in various parts of the ship. To light the stoves or lamps you merely turn a tap and apply a match, just as if you were lighting the gas in a house. The cylinder is a fairly large one, but as it is housed in a locker that is of very little use except for storing such things as bottles and tins, it is not at all in the way.

One of the main objections to the use of bottled gas is the difficulty of replenishing the supply, should a cylinder be exhausted while one is away cruising, as replacements can only be obtained at the more important ports. Dr. Ives, however, tells me that this objection is more imaginary than real. When installing the plant, he bought two gas cylinders, one being retained by the suppliers. When the cylinder in the yacht is nearly empty, he sends a card to the suppliers instructing them to forward the other cylinder to some place he proposes to visit in the near future. He is thus able to substitute the new cylinder for the empty one, returning the latter to be refilled. There are several different brands of bottled gas now on the market, but the Botto-gas is in long cylinders, which are more easily stowed than some of the others. The lamps Dr. Ives uses are quite small, but, fitted with mantles, give a brilliant light.

CHAPTER 40: *Catering and Cooking*

If you cruise round the coast, as most small yacht owners do, there is no necessity to carry a large supply of provisions on board, as you will have frequent opportunities for replenishing the larder. At most places you visit there will be a shop, or shops, available and fresh food is infinitely preferable to anything out of a tin. Still, it is prudent to carry a small supply of tinned stuff to fall back on in case of need. Sometimes you may not reach your anchorage until after the shops have shut, or possibly you may find that it is early closing day. It is only fair that shop employees should have a half-holiday once a week, but it is a pity that the early closing days are not uniform. Many times when cruising have I been compelled to go short of food owing to early closing, and it is for that reason that I have, in the section on Headquarters, given the early closing day at every port.

There is seldom any difficulty in obtaining supplies of such things as eggs, butter and vegetables, for if there is no shop available they can usually be procured from a farm, and if you happen to run short of bread the landlord of the local inn will usually oblige you with a loaf. It is not so easy, however, to get fresh meat, as at many waterside villages the butcher only comes from some neighbouring town on two or three days a week. It is therefore advisable to have something on board as a stand-by. In that respect it may be remarked that a dish of eggs and bacon makes a more satisfying meal than something out of a tin with a fancy name. In the past most tinned food seemed to taste the same, the only difference being in the labels. But we have learnt a lot from the Americans about canned food during the war and some of the products now available, such as Spam and Cook's brand of sheep tongues are excellent; as also are sardines and tinned fruit. By the way, if you have to fall back on a tin of bully beef, you will find it more palatable if you make a stew of it, with onions and carrots.

When starting on a cruise it is my practice to take with me a cold joint and a piece of boiled bacon, which I have cooked at home. If you do that you will not have to bother much about catering for some days. A leg of lamb will provide two people with dinner for three days; it can be eaten cold, with potatoes and salad, for two days and on the third day it can be hashed. The bacon is particularly useful as it will serve both for breakfast and lunch. When your initial supply of food is exhausted you will have to scheme meals from day to day, and no doubt will come to the conclusion that catering is the devil of a business. But the experience will make you think more sympathetically of the housewife ashore, who, poor woman, has to plan meals day after day for a family all her life.

Breakfast and lunch are comparatively easy, as for the former eggs and bacon are more or less standard, while for lunch you can always fall back on sardines, or bread and cheese, if you have nothing in the way of cold meat on cut. It is dinner that is the main trouble, but the problem is much simplified if you have a Staines Model Roaster. Here are a few suggestions: Leg or shoulder of lamb; ribs of beef, rolled; rabbit, if in season; two or three pounds of neck of lamb (best end) boned and rolled; chops; cutlets; stewed ox-tail; boiled beef; and liver and bacon. Any of those can be cooked without much trouble and the list will give you a good variety on which to ring the changes. Occasionally, too, you might have a chicken or duck. I should not advise you to go in for rump steak unless you can get it at some large town, for in my experience the rump steak usually sold by the village butcher is as tough as old boots. For a change you can have fish, steamed or boiled, such as hake, cod, halibut, turbot, haddock or salmon; Canadian salmon, by the way, is cheap and quite good. Fish, however, is not easily procured, even at fishing ports, as most of it is sent to the London market, but you can sometimes buy it cheaply from a smack. If I seem to harp unduly on eating, it is not because I am by way of being a gastronomist, but because the morale of the crew depends so much on their being adequately fed. If you are caught out in heavy weather things look much worse when you are hungry. Some men seem content to exist on 'thumb-pieces' and snacks when cruising, but such Spartan conditions are calculated to mar the pleasure of the holiday.

Now for a few general hints on catering.

Bread: Best kept in a square biscuit tin, such as you can buy for a shilling from your grocer. Half a loaf a head per day is an adequate allowance, but if you have youngsters with you, you will need more. Growing boys eat a devil of a lot and want it, and in their case the ration should be increased to three-quarters of a loaf, or even a whole one. If you buy long loaves and cut them in halves, you can stow three in the tin and they will be quite eatable when four or five days old. If you have an oven stove, stale bread can be reconditioned by damping it and putting it in the oven for a little while.

Butter: (or Margarine) Best kept in a 2-lb. jam-jar, but in very hot weather a butter-cooler should be used. You can get one (or at any rate could before the war) for sixpence at Woolworth's, made of terra-cotta with a glass dish. It should be soaked in cold water for a few minutes before the glass dish is put in, and kept in the larder rather than in the cabin.

Eggs: A great stand-by and a good supply should be kept on board. They should be stowed in proper egg boxes, with a separate compartment for each egg. These boxes, made of stout cardboard, can be bought for a few pence.

Salt: The only salt I know that will keep in decent condition in a yacht is Cerebos, which is put up in a tin with a patent pourer. A sixpenny tin will last for months.

Mustard: This can now be obtained in collapsible tubes already mixed, which saves trouble. The only brand I know, however, is mixed with tarragon vinegar, like French mustard, and personally I do not care for the flavour.

Cheese: If bought in the piece it is apt to get hard and I think it better to buy it in boxes. It is put up in segments, wrapped in tin-foil, and will keep in good condition for some weeks. Blue Cap is a good brand.

Vegetables: Such vegetables as potatoes, carrots and onions, are best stored in a canvas bag, or large fish mat, which can be hung up in the fo'c'sle out of the way. Tomatoes, however, might be squashed if stowed in a bag with the other vegetables and should be kept in the larder, in a tin, or basin. New potatoes can be easily scraped with a knife, but old ones must be peeled. A stainless steel peeler is the best implement for the purpose, and will also serve for peeling apples. The average cruising man dispenses with green vegetables as they are too much trouble to cook. As a rule he has only two stoves and if meat is being cooked on one and potatoes on the other, a second vegetable is impracticable. To compensate for this lack of green stuff, it is desirable to have lettuce as often as possible. Good lettuces are usually procurable from cottages at most waterside villages.

Potted Meat and Fish: Many brands of potted meat and fish, put up in small jars, are obtainable and a few should be kept on board. The best brands I know are Shippam's, Brand's and St. Ivel, and they give a relish to one's tea or lunch.

Fruit: A plentiful supply of fruit, such as apples, prunes, plums and bananas, should be carried. Stewed plums, damsons and apricots make a very good substitute for a sweet at dinner and are very little trouble to stew. If you use prunes or apricots of the dried variety, they should be well soaked before stewing.

Cakes: Cakes of all kinds, made by Lyons, can now be obtained at almost any village shop and are very good when fresh, particularly the Swiss rolls. They should be kept in a tin, like the bread. Lyons also make small fruit tarts which are acceptable.

Milk: Everyone became familiar with milk powder, known as Household Milk, during the war and personally I much prefer it to the condensed variety, as I think the latter spoils one's tea or coffee. To those who do not take sugar in tea, the sweetened condensed milk is positively nauseating. For a good many years before the war I used on board a brand of milk powder known as Milkreem, supplied by the Wilts. United Dairies Ltd., and found it excellent. The Household brand of war days is skimmed milk and seems quite as satisfactory, although a good deal more of it is required to make the same quantity as Milkreem. About two heaped teaspoonfuls for each person should be allowed. The powder can be easily mixed in about three minutes, preferably with a fork. Care should be taken to put the powder into the water and not the water on to the powder. If you use condensed milk, two holes should be punched in the tin, one to pour from and the other as an air vent.

An opened tin of condensed milk can make a horrid mess if capsized in a locker, and you should take steps to prevent such a mishap. One way is to stick pieces of adhesive tape over the holes, but that is rather a nuisance. When I used condensed milk, I used to put the open tin in a can with a handle and sling it from a cup-hook in the cabin-top. It travelled well like that and even if any was spilled it only went into the can and made no mess. Perhaps the simplest method, however, is to put the tin of milk in the teapot before getting under way.

Drinks: What you drink when cruising must be largely a matter of personal taste. Beer is perhaps the best for meals and it is satisfactory to note that several brewers are now putting it up in cans, which can be dumped overboard when empty. You thus avoid the necessity for leaving a deposit of twopence on each bottle, with the subsequent accumulation of a large number of empty bottles. The deposit can only be recovered by returning the bottles where they were bought, and as more often than not you do not revisit the place, the money is lost. When I bought a boat some years ago I found that the lockers under the bunks and fo'c'sle seats were crammed chock-a-block with empty stout bottles. There were dozens and dozens of them, and as each represented twopence I dumped a small fortune overboard, but as I didn't know where they were bought, I had no alternative. The beer in tins, or at any rate that which I have tried, is in excellent condition and the innovation should be a boon to yachtsmen.

Methylated Spirit: As methylated spirit is not easily procurable in country villages, it is advisable to carry a good supply. As it is only used for starting the Primus stove, a pint should suffice for a cruise of three or four weeks. A drop of methylated spirit on a rag will clean the glass of a ventilating scuttle better than anything.

Glass Jars: The glass jars in which Canadian and Australian honey is put up make splendid containers for tea, coffee, sugar, rice, etc., as they have screw-on metal lids and are of a size convenient for stowing in the pantry or store cupboard.

Cleaning Lamp Glasses: There is nothing so efficient as newspaper for cleaning lamp glasses.

Fresh Water: The strictest economy should be practised in the use of fresh water, for it is often difficult to replenish the supply. At many places which the owner of a small yacht loves to visit, the only source of supply is the local inn, or a cottage, and it is often necessary to take the cans ashore in the dinghy and perhaps carry them for some distance. As a 4-gallon can, when full, weighs more than 40 lb., it is an irksome job and the less frequently you have to do it the better. Fresh water should only be used for drinking, cooking and shaving and an allowance of three-quarters of a gallon a day for each person should be ample. Plates and dishes can be washed-up quite well with hot sea water.

Marine Soap: Ordinary soap is practically useless in sea water, as it will not lather. There are various brands of sea-water soap on the market, but I have never yet struck one that was really satisfactory. Some years ago I discovered by chance that the Trusoap, produced by Truslove & Co., of Colchester, which is intended for house-cleaning, was equally efficacious in salt water and have used it for washing purposes afloat ever since. I find it far better for the purpose than any marine soap I have tried.

Paraffin Cans: I have a fine paraffin can which I bought some years ago from an itinerant oilman. It has a curved spout and handles, both at the top and side, and one can fill lamps without the aid of a funnel. As there is a screw stopper on the spout, paraffin cannot leak out when the yacht is under way. By the way, it is inadvisable to store water in petrol cans if you have an auxiliary engine, as some owners do, as it may lead to a serious accident. Some years ago, at Maylandsea, one of the crew of a yacht by mistake filled the kettle with petrol instead of water and put it on a Primus stove to boil. The result was an explosion, which caused the death of one of the party.

Towels, Teacloths, etc.: These should be hung up to dry immediately after use. Little spring clothes pegs, which you can get at Woolworths for a few pence a dozen, are very useful for this purpose, as they can be clipped on to any rope and will hold the cloth securely even in a fresh breeze. If, after the kettle has been boiled, you wrap the teacloth round it, the cloth will be quite dry by the time you have finished your breakfast or tea.

Blankets: These should be hung over the boom to air at suitable opportunities. The best time to do this is when you get up in the morning, but if there is a heavy dew or damp mist you may have to wait until later in the day. The edges of the blankets should be clipped together with clothes pegs to prevent their being blown overboard. If by ill chance a blanket does go over the side, the only thing to do is to take it ashore at the first opportunity and soak it in fresh water before drying it, otherwise it will always be damp when there is moisture in the air.

Not being Mrs. Beeton, I don't propose to write a treatise on the art of cookery, but will try and give you a few general hints that may be of use. I shall assume that you have a Staines Model Roaster and a Primus stove for boiling.

Joints: The most suitable joints for cooking in the roaster are a leg of lamb; best end of neck of mutton, boned and rolled; ribs of beef, boned and rolled; and loin of lamb. The instructions supplied with the roaster tell you to allow twenty minutes per pound weight, but if you like your meat well cooked, you should allow rather more, say twenty-five minutes per pound.

First rub some salt on the joint and then put in the roaster a lump of dripping, about the size of a golf-ball, or rather larger. While the fat is getting hot, smear the joint all over liberally with dripping. When blue smoke begins to rise from the fat in the roaster, put in the joint and cover it. At first the stove should be fairly high, but far short of smoking point; and after the joint has been in a few minutes, the wick should be turned down quite low. Experience alone will teach you the right amount of flame, but roughly speaking it should not be more than about ½ inch high. The joint will need no basting, but should be turned every half-hour. Cut potatoes into slices and at half-time put them in the fat round the joint and they will then be nicely done at the same time as the joint.

About twenty minutes or so before the joint is due to be dished up, put on a saucepan of water to boil, placing the dish and plates on top to get warm. If you change them about occasionally you will be able to get them all nicely hot. Having dished up the joint, pour off some of the fat into a basin for future use and empty the remainder overboard. Put some of the boiling water from the saucepan into the roaster and clean it with a dish mop and, of course, the lid also. This should be done at once, while the roaster is hot, for if you wait until it is cold it will be much more trouble. Fill up the saucepan again and leave it on the Primus to boil for washing-up purposes while you have your dinner.

Chicken or Rabbit: A chicken or rabbit can be cooked in the same way, but personally I think a rabbit is better stewed. If you want a cabbage or other green vegetable as well as potatoes, it can be cooked in the saucepan. The plates can be warmed over it and the water used for cleaning the roaster. For washing up, boiling sea water does very well and in that connection it may be remarked that drinking-water should be used sparingly, as one cannot stow a large quantity in a small craft and it is a nuisance having frequently to replenish your stock when away cruising.

Fruit: To stew plums or other fruit, place the fruit in the cooker with sugar and water and stew slowly until the fruit is quite soft.

Fish: Fish is best steamed and for this purpose the grid should be used. Water should be put into the cooker up to the base of the grid and when boiling, put in the fish, either whole or in cutlets or fillets. Cook for about ten or fifteen minutes, according to the size of the fish or thickness of the cutlets, with the lid on. Fresh herrings, kippers and dried haddock can be cooked in the same way, but haddock or kippers should be smeared with butter when dished up. Fish, such as soles, plaice, hake, cod, etc., can be fried if you have sufficient fat. Put the fat in the cooker and when it boils (i.e. when blue smoke begins to rise) put in the fish and cook for from ten to fifteen minutes, according to thickness, turning the fish at half-time. Kippers only take about five minutes to cook, and should be turned once. Keep the lid on the roaster when frying fish, or anything else.

Eggs and Bacon: Put a little lard in the roaster and when it has melted add the rashers. When the bacon is done to your liking, push the rashers to one end and break the eggs into the centre. These will take about three minutes to cook and should be removed carefully with a fish slice. Slices of bread can be fried in the fat until a golden brown and the eggs and bacon served on them.

Tomatoes and Kidneys: Tomatoes, or kidneys, and bacon make a pleasant change for breakfast and are easily cooked. They should be cut in halves and fried in the fat. As they take rather longer to cook than bacon, they should be put in five minutes earlier. The kidneys should be skinned and the stringy bit of fat removed before cooking. If the tomatoes are large, they should be cut in slices.

Boiling: The cooker can be used for boiling such things as fish, a piece of bacon or pickled pork, beef or mutton. When the water boils, turn the stove down low enough to keep the water simmering. When fish is done the flesh will begin to come away from the bones. Eggs can also be boiled in the cooker.

Stews: A tasty stew can be made of neck of lamb, steak, or the remains of a joint, chicken or rabbit. Slice up potatoes, onions and carrots and cut up the meat. Put a layer of the vegetables at the bottom of the cooker, then put in the meat and finally another layer of potatoes. Place the lid on the cooker and shake it to mix the contents. Then add water and place on the stove, having first sprinkled the contents with salt and pepper to taste. Cook slowly for an hour and three-quarters. A rabbit, when stewed, should be cut up first – you can have this done when you buy it – and pickled pork, or streaky bacon, cut into cubes, should be cooked with it. Finally, add about half a teaspoonful of browning to the gravy before serving. A dash of Worcester sauce will enhance the flavour.

Hash: Another way of using up the remains of a joint is to hash it. First fry the vegetables, such as onions and carrots, in a little fat for a few minutes. Then put them in the cooker with the cut-up meat and a couple of rashers of bacon, cut up small, adding salt and pepper and a dash of Worcester sauce. Simmer gently for three-quarters of an hour and add a dash of browning before serving.

Curry: This can be cooked in the same way as hash, omitting the vegetables and Worcester sauce. Stir in some curry powder and serve with boiled rice and chutney, if you have any.

Rice: To boil rice, place a teacupful of rice in a quart of boiling water and boil furiously until the rice is quite soft. This will take about twenty minutes.

Sausages: First place in the cooker a bit of lard about the size of a walnut and when it has melted put in the sausages and cook slowly until they are browned all over. Some people prick them first to prevent bursting, but I don't think that makes much difference. The bursting proclivities of a sausage depend upon the amount of bread in it.

Rump Steak: This is best cooked in a frying-pan over a Primus stove. Most yachtsmen when frying a steak commence operations by placing a large piece of fat in the pan, and the result is a flabby tasteless slab of meat that may satisfy hunger but certainly will not charm the palate. Now, in my arrogance, I will tell you how a steak should be cooked. First take a clean frying-pan, and when I say clean I mean what a good housewife would consider clean and not what many yachtsmen would pass as such. A chap once remarked to me, "We never clean our frying-pan because the grease keeps it from rusting" – personally, I would prefer the rust. The pan should be of the ordinary tinned iron variety and not one of those enamelled things, which are apt to chip. Place the pan on a Primus stove that has been well pumped up, and when the pan is hot, put in your steak, without grease of any sort. Push the steak about in the pan to prevent its sticking until the outside is slightly charred. Then turn it over and do the same to the other side. Then turn down the stove and cook slowly until done. By this method all the gravy and goodness will be retained in the steak, which will taste like one that has been grilled. It will take from ten to fifteen minutes to cook, according to the thickness.

Eggs: There are many ways of cooking eggs, the most common, of course, being boiling. Now, if you are going to have boiled eggs for breakfast or tea, the quickest way of cooking them is to put them in the kettle. When the kettle boils the eggs will be done. I have heard it said that tea made from water in which eggs have been boiled gives one warts in the stomach, but that is all bunk. I have cooked eggs in that way for more than half a century and so far as I know I have no warts in my stomach. If you boil the eggs separately they will take from four to four and a half minutes if really new laid. If of the shop variety they should be boiled for from three and a half to four minutes.

To scramble eggs, melt a piece of butter about the size of a golf ball in the roaster, or frying-pan, and having beaten up the eggs in a basin, add two table-spoonfuls of milk and a pinch of salt. Pour the mixture into the pan and keep stirring until the eggs are set. Serve on buttered toast.

Eggs can be poached without any special implement. Boil some water in a saucepan and then stir it vigorously. Break the egg into a cup and drop it in the vortex of the stirred water. It will be poached in about two minutes and can be removed unbroken with a fish-slice and served on a piece of buttered toast, or with bacon.

To make a savoury omelet, break two eggs into a basin; add salt, pepper, minced onion or finely chopped parsley, and whip briskly with a fork. Melt an ounce of butter in a clean pan and pour in the ingredients which must be fried quickly until just set. When done, double over and remove with a fish-slice to a hot plate.

Braising: If you have neither a model roaster nor an oven, a small joint, such as a leg of lamb, can be cooked quite well by braising in a saucepan. Melt about half a pound of dripping in the saucepan until blue smoke begins to rise. Then put in the joint and cook slowly, allowing about twenty minutes per pound weight. The joint should be turned over at half-time and the lid kept on the saucepan while cooking. You should get the butcher to cut off the bone at the knuckle end, as otherwise you may not be able to get it into the saucepan. A chicken can be cooked in the same way.

Of course, there are many other dishes that can be cooked quite easily afloat, but those I have mentioned will give you a varied diet while away on a cruise of three or four weeks' duration. Before leaving this subject I would urge you to make a practice of always cleaning your cooking utensils immediately after use.

If done while they are hot, it takes but a minute or two, but if left until cold, it is likely to be a darned unpleasant job. To get under way with a lot of dirty cooking utensils and crockery lying about is a filthy habit that should not be tolerated by anyone in charge of a yacht.

Before sitting down to a meal you should put a kettle of sea water on to boil and wash up as soon as you have finished. Spoons and plates with egg on them, however, should be soaked in cold water. If you do this you will find that the egg comes off quite easily, while with hot water it is extremely tenacious.

All cutlery used afloat should be of stainless steel of good quality. As such knives are not cleaned on a board, they are apt to get rather blunt after a time, and should be sharpened occasionally on an oil stone. But if the knives are really good ones, this should only be necessary at the beginning of the season. I would advise you to buy a proper bread-knife with a saw edge, as attempting to cut a crusty new loaf with an ordinary knife is a most unsatisfactory business. A bread-knife with a saw edge will cut any sort of loaf cleanly and efficiently and will never get blunt. I have had one in use in my house for nearly twenty years and it still cuts as well as ever.

CHAPTER 41: *Ventilation*

There are few things in connection with a yacht of greater importance than ventilation, yet there are few things to which the average owner of a small cruiser devotes so little attention. Adequate ventilation is necessary for the well-being of both vessel and crew, for in its absence the hull may be attacked by that deadly enemy dry rot, while lack of fresh air is certainly not conducive to good health. A small cabin, measuring perhaps 7 feet square, with from 4 to 5 feet headroom, may be the temporary abode of two or more persons, and in that confined space they must live, cook and sleep. Under such conditions the air soon becomes vitiated unless steps are taken to provide proper ventilation.

It is, of course, better for the boat if the interior is unlined, but as the naked ribs of the vessel are not particularly ornamental and moisture is apt to be generated by condensation and trickle down the sides, wetting the cushions and blankets, it is customary to line the cabin portion of the yacht at least. The lining should not extend below the bunks and a gap of about two inches should be left between the top of the lining and the shelf. It is desirable, too, that a few holes should be bored in the lining itself, and others, of about 1 inch in diameter, in the bunk risers. If the bunks are to be used for sleeping purposes they will be more comfortable if slightly concave, and if made of slats instead of boards they will allow air to get to the underside of the cushions. A group of ventilation holes should also be bored in every cupboard door.

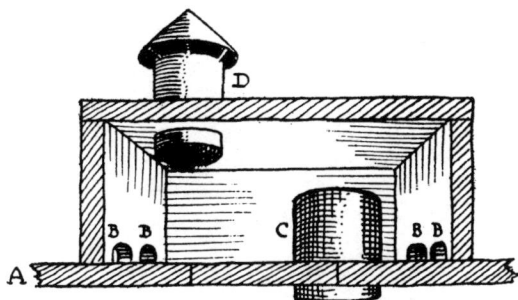

A. Deck.   B. Scuppers.
C. Pipe through deck
D. Ventilator pipe with cowl

Dorade ventilator

The effective ventilation of a small cabin presents something of a problem, as means must be devised of letting in air and at the same time keeping out rain and spray. The method usually employed is either a skylight or scuttles in the coamings and of these I think the latter preferable. Small skylights almost invariably leak – at least I have never been shipmates with one that didn't – and must be closed when it rains. Even if open but an inch or two, rain will find its way into the cabin on a wet day and make things unpleasantly damp. If the yacht has a flush deck and access to the cabin is by way of a companion, the difficulty is enhanced, as both skylight and companion hatch must be closed. In such circumstances the atmosphere in the cabin after a few hours is likely to rival that of the black hole of Calcutta, of which we read in our school days.

In such a vessel a ventilator of some sort is essential, and it must be of a type that can be left open on the wettest day without risk of rain entering through it. Probably the best for the purpose is that known as the Dorade, named after the famous ocean racer in which it was first used. This is an ordinary cowl ventilator, but instead of being fitted direct to the deck, it is mounted on a rectangular box, installed over the pipe that leads through the deck. Any rain or spray driving through the cowl is trapped in the box and runs away through scuppers. The pipe into the cabin extends a few inches above the deck, and it is impossible for any water to get below unless the ventilator is entirely submerged. The Dorade ventilator is extremely efficient, but rather bulky for a small yacht.

A hood over the companion hatch, as used in the ocean racers *Dorade* and *Stormy Weather*, would be an aid to ventilation in a flush-decked yacht, as the hatch could be left open in wet weather. But the hood shown in the illustration would only protect the companion hatch when the yacht was riding head to wind. If it were fitted to slides at the sides of the hatchway, the hood could be run forward and turned over so that it would shelter the open hatchway when the wind was blowing from astern. With scuttles in the coamings, the problem of ventilation is not so difficult of solution, particularly when access to the cabin is

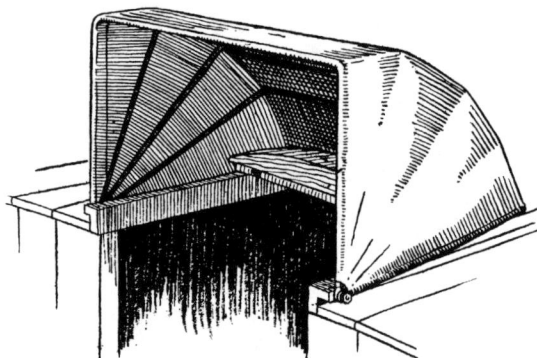

Hood over companionway hatch

by way of a door from the cockpit, as it usually is in craft of less than 5 tons. It is often possible on a wet day to open some of the scuttles or the door. If the wind is on the beam, the lee scuttles can be opened, and should the yacht be lying head to wind, the cabin door can be left open. If she is riding stern on to the wind, the fore scuttles are available and, of course in fine weather any, or all, of the scuttles can be open and the door also. Another advantage of scuttles is that one has a view on either side and ahead, while with a skylight one can see nothing unless one goes outside.

Water is apt to accumulate through condensation on the inside of scuttles in the coamings and drip on to the cushions. This can be prevented by the adoption of an idea of Mr. Percy Woodcock's. He fits below each scuttle a brass drawer-pull, such as used on the drawers of a kitchen table. The drawer-pull is inverted, thus forming a cup which will effectually catch the drips. When the receptacle is full, Mr. Woodcock says it can be mopped out with a cloth, or bit of cotton waste, but I think it would be a better plan to drill holes through the coaming through which water would drain away.

But whether your ship has scuttles or skylight, all must be closed when she is left, as it is impossible to foretell from what direction the wind may blow dur-

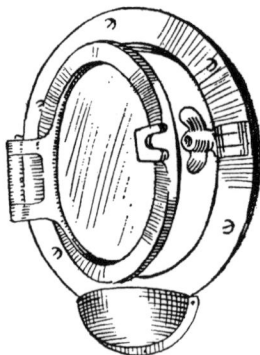

Scuttle drain

ing your absence. In such circumstances when you re-join the vessel after an absence of some days you will be assailed by that unpleasant odour, a combination of paraffin, stale cooking and bilge water, peculiar to small craft that have lacked ventilation. It is desirable, therefore, that every cruising yacht should have some form of ventilator that can be left open without fear of rain driving into the cabin. When my little ship *Iolanthe* was built, I had fitted in the cabin door what I call a 'shop-blind' ventilator, because it looks like a miniature edition of the sun-blind used by the shopkeeper to protect his window. It is extremely effective, and costs next to nothing to make. A rectangular piece is cut out of the door and hinged at the top, water-proof canvas being fitted at the sides. It opens to an angle of about 45 degrees and is kept open by a hinged strut engaging on the door. It is always left open when I am not on board and it has never let in a drop of rain in any weather. This simple ventilator not only keeps the cabin aired in my absence, but is useful when I am on board, as when there is a fresh breeze aft, I can shut the cabin door and open the ventilator, thus getting all the air I need without a draught.

'Shop-blind' ventilator

A sliding hatch on the cabin-top can also be used to ventilate the cabin when untenanted if so fitted that it can be drawn aft for about 3 inches beyond the door, as the gap thus left will let in air without risk of rain getting through. When the hatch is level with the door the aperture is, of course, closed.

It is seldom that any provision is made in small yachts for ventilation of the sail locker, although there is no part of the boat that needs it more. Not only are spare sails that are seldom used kept there, but it also houses the rudder-trunk, perhaps the most vulnerable part of the vessel. Access to the locker is usually by means of a door and there is no ventilation of any kind. It is not surprising in such circumstances that sails are attacked by mildew and rudder-trunks rot. Occasionally a mushroom ventilator is installed on deck over the locker, but such ventilators are not infallible, and in heavy rain let in a certain amount of water. Fitted in that position, too, such an excrescence is apt to foul the mainsheet when gybing.

I think a small 'shop-blind' ventilator, about 6 inches square, would meet the case, if fitted in the door, particularly if it were augmented by a few holes bored through the locker bulkhead. If the holes, about 1 inch in diameter, were just below the cockpit seats they would be protected from rain and spray and would ensure a steady flow of air through the locker.

Ventilation by sliding hatch

A fore-hatch is a great aid to ventilation. If hinged at the fore end it can usually be propped up a few inches on a wet day. Even if a little rain drives in it will only fall in the fo'c'sle where it will not do any harm. But unless carefully constructed, a fore-hatch will leak when the yacht is sailing to windward in rough weather. It should fit over a deep coaming, and the sides come right down to the deck. A deck-light fitted in it will serve to brighten a part of the ship which is usually rather gloomy.

The fore-hatch of the average small cruiser strikes me as a very indifferent contrivance. It is usually merely a lid, fitting loosely over coamings about 2 inches high, and it is surprising what a lot of water can get through when punching to windward against a short head sea. But to design a fore-hatch that will be absolutely tight when the deck is streaming with water is not by any means an easy matter, for if it fits too tightly it will be difficult to open and close. The first Marquess of Dufferin, in his remarkable single-hander *Lady Hermione*, accomplished it by screwing the hatch down with gun-metal screws, fitted with butterfly nuts, on to a bed of rubber; but rubber, when frequently in contact with sea water, soon perishes. I am inclined to think, however, that a fore-hatch could be made reasonably tight if the coamings were, say, 6 inches high, and the sides of the hatch came right down to the deck, fitting over the coamings like the lid of one of those cardboard boxes in which note-paper and envelopes were packed before the war. That might involve difficulties in hinging it to the deck but it should not be beyond the wit of a designer to evolve a satisfactory way of doing it.

I think it important that the hatch should be permanently hinged to the deck, for otherwise it might be lost overboard. Of course, a loose fore-hatch is usually provided with bolts by which to secure it when at sea, but you may forget to fasten them. That happened to me some years ago when I was beating through the Wallet in dirty weather in a 7-ton Falmouth Quay Punt I then owned. The hatch was washed off and although it was kept from going overboard by a lanyard, many gallons of water poured into the fo'c'sle before I could get it properly secured. If you lost your fore-hatch in heavy weather, you would be in a pretty fix.

Many of the little 'pocket' cruisers which have become so popular of late years are not supplied with a fore-hatch, and apart from the question of ventilation, it is very useful. For instance, one can stand in the hatchway when changing a headsail, and it also affords a second exit from the cabin. The latter may not seem of much importance, but it might become a matter of urgent necessity, as the following incident will show.

Some forty years ago I was lying in Mersea Quarters in a small yawl that had no fore-hatch and was boiling a kettle on a spirit stove on the cockpit floor. The kettle seemed to take an unconscionable time to boil, so I removed it to investigate the cause. The flame of methylated spirit is practically invisible in strong sunlight and I thought the stove had gone out. Concluding that the spirit had all been consumed, I proceeded to pour some more into the stove. The immediate result was a mild explosion, which startled me so much that I dropped the bottle of methylated. In a moment the whole cockpit was a sheet of flame. I hastily backed into the cabin and shut the door. Then I was appalled by the thought that I was imprisoned in the cabin, with a roaring fire without and no means of escape. It was a horrible situation which I have never forgotten, but fortunately with methylated spirit it is only the vapour that burns and provided that there is nothing above little harm is done. When the fire had burnt itself out, I was glad to find that the damage was negligible, consisting merely of a slightly scorched mainsail cover and blistering of the varnish on the cockpit seats and cabin door. That incident was due solely to my own carelessness, but in these days of auxiliary motors the risk of a fire in the after part of the ship cannot altogether be ignored and it is well to have a second exit from the cabin.

A fore bulkhead is neither necessary nor desirable in a small yacht. Not only does it render access to the fo'c'sle difficult but is apt to rob that part of the vessel of adequate ventilation. In the absence of a bulkhead, the fo'c'sle is to all intents and purposes part of the cabin and air can circulate freely throughout the vessel. As the fo'c'sle of a little cruiser is used mainly for stowage purposes, it is apt to be rather unsightly, but can be hidden from view by a curtain, which can be drawn back when the yacht is left. As I remarked in a previous chapter, it is better to paint or varnish the cabin floorboards than cover them with linoleum, as the latter is apt to harbour damp.

These little things may not amount to much in themselves, but if neglected will in the aggregate lead to a general mustiness, unpleasant to smell and inimicable to the welfare of the ship. If the interior of a little yacht is to be kept sweet and dry she must be adequately ventilated, and it is worth while taking a little trouble to attain such conditions.

A Yarn

ə◌

About Snipe

The first time I ever saw *Snipe* was on a depressing Sunday afternoon in the year of Queen Victoria's Diamond Jubilee. It was raining and blowing hard from the westward, and I had not long picked up my mooring after a particularly juicy trip up the river in *Wave*. Then, as I was stowing the mainsail, I saw a little canoe-sterned cruiser beating through the anchorage and paused to watch her. With her lee decks just awash, she was going grandly, sailing fast and staying with the precision of clockwork. Her fore-deck, it is true, was running with water, as she cut through the tops of the short seas, but I noticed that it ran harmlessly away down the side-decks and nothing but spray entered the cockpit. I fell in love with her at sight and registered a silent vow that one day I would own her.

As she sailed by, I recognized her owner as a man I knew slightly, so, after he had brought up and stowed away, I rowed off and asked if I might look at her. He invited me on board and I learnt that her name was *Snipe* and she had just made a passage round the Whitaker from Queenborough. If I had been impressed by her sailing qualities, I was perhaps even more so by her cabin, which, after *Wave*'s, seemed quite palatial, as there was about a foot more beam and eight or nine inches more headroom. It looked extraordinarily snug and cosy, and although *Snipe* must have had a bit of a 'dusting' coming round the Whitaker on such a day, everything seemed dry. And so, in the American jargon that passes for English to-day, I fell for her and made up my mind that if she ever came into the market I would buy her, if by hook or by crook I could raise the necessary funds.

It has been said that if a man desires a thing earnestly and constantly, that which he desires will sooner or later be granted to him, and God knows I coveted *Snipe* from the moment that I saw her. I had a presentiment that she would one day be mine, and so it came about, although I had to wait for two years before I was able to gratify my desire. She came into the market soon after I had first seen her, when her owner acquired a much larger vessel, but at the time I was 'broke to the wide' and she passed into the hands of a stranger, who took her round to the Orwell.

Later, my circumstances improved and, being then in a position to buy a better boat than *Wave*, I scanned the advertisements in the yachting papers every week to see if *Snipe* was offered for sale. Week after week and month after month went by without mention of her, although I heard from time to time that she was still at Pin Mill. After waiting for nearly two years I had almost given up hope of ever getting the boat, when one Friday afternoon I saw in a yachting paper a note to the effect that *Snipe*'s owner had bought a 20-ton yawl. I thought it possible that he might feel disposed to sell *Snipe* now that he had another craft and decided to go and see him. Arranging to be away from my office, I journeyed down to Pin Mill the following morning, with my cheque-book in my pocket.

I was the only passenger to land from the steamer at Pin Mill, and when I asked the ferryman if he could tell me where I could find Mr. C, he replied, 'That's him on board that yawl,' and pointed to a yacht of about 20 tons lying near by. 'He's only just bought her,' he added. I asked him to take me alongside.

"'Ere's a gentleman wants to see you, Mr. C."

I thought he looked a trifle surprised at seeing a stranger, so I hastened to explain that I had heard he had bought a new boat and had come from Fambridge to see if he was open to consider an offer for *Snipe*. He invited me on board, which I thought promising, but my hopes were dashed when he remarked, "I am afraid you have had your journey for nothing as I have no intention of selling *Snipe*. I mean to keep her for sailing about in the evenings."

"Surely," I said, "a dinghy or half-decked boat would be more suitable for that."

"Possibly," he replied, "but I have *Snipe* and she will serve the purpose quite well. She's a very nice little boat and I really don't want to sell her."

There seemed nothing more to be said and I was about to leave him, when he suggested that I should stay and have lunch with him. As I had breakfasted very early, I gladly accepted his invitation and climbed on board. While the paid hand was getting the meal ready, Mr. C showed me all over the yacht and told me of various alterations he proposed to make in her accommodation.

As we sat down to lunch he remarked, "I'm awfully sorry that you have had such a long journey for nothing. What a pity you did not write to me first." I explained that I had been waiting for two years in the hope of buying *Snipe*, and when I saw that he had bought another craft I did not like to waste any time lest someone should buy her over my head. With which, we left the subject and talked of other things.

Mr. C told me that later in the summer he proposed to cruise to the Baltic in his new ship and hoped to get the alterations finished before he went. "I want to do the job myself," he remarked. "I'm rather keen on carpentering, but shall only be able to work in the evenings as I am otherwise engaged during the day."

"Well," I said, "if that's the case, you are not likely to do much evening sailing in *Snipe*. Don't you think you had better sell her to me?"

He was silent for a few moments and then replied: "What will you give for her?"

I could not really afford to pay more than £50, although I fully expected that if she were for sale the figure would be at least £70. But, as a basis for bargaining, I replied £35.

After a long pause, he said, "All right, you can have her. I don't suppose I should use her much if I kept her."

You could have knocked me down with a feather, as the saying goes.

Then he continued, "She is in perfect condition but I am afraid rather short of equipment, as I have taken off the stoves and a few other things which I can use in this boat. But you had better come and see her."

So we got into the dinghy and rowed off to *Snipe*. I saw that she had bunk cushions, cots and mattresses, and a riding-light, and other things that were wanting I could supply from *Wave*. As we sat in the cabin, Mr. C remarked, "I have a new 7-ft. Berthon dinghy you can have for £4 if you like. It has only been in the water once, but it won't be of any use to me now."

So, for £39 I bought *Snipe*, then only four years old, and a brand-new Berthon dinghy. We went back to the yawl and I wrote out a cheque, receiving a formal receipt in exchange and thus returned home the owner of *Snipe*. I seem to have been in luck just then, for within the following week I sold *Wave*.

As I had bought the boat at such a low price I felt justified in spending some money on fitting her up to my liking. Her topsides were white, which I thought made her look rather tubby, so I had them burnt off and repainted black, with a gold line, which much improved her appearance. Her sails, too, although in quite good condition, did not set sufficiently well to satisfy me, so I ordered a new suit from Cranfield, which set to perfection. Then I turned my attention to the cabin.

The cushions were re-covered with red Pegamoid and the folding cots with dark blue serge. As there was no fore-bulkhead, I divided off the fo'c'sle from the cabin with a dark blue serge curtain, and a cloth of similar material covered the table. For the floor I bought two little Turkey rugs, which, incidentally, are still in use in another boat after forty years' service, which goes to show that it is economical in the long run to pay a good price for a really good article. At the after end of the port berth I fitted a store-cupboard, with a pantry above, and on the starboard side a hanging clothes locker. Between the mast and the port side of the boat were two shelves, which carried books, the compass, when not in use, and various other things, and just abaft the mast I fitted a small cellar-ette to hold three or four bottles. An aneroid and eight-day clock to match were mounted on the fore coaming and in the roof I fitted a brass mushroom ventilator. The folding pipe-cots were supplied with horsehair mattresses, covered with Willesden canvas, and made extremely comfortable beds, although not very wide.

The cockpit was deep and comfortable, with lockers under the side-decks and room beneath the seats for the stowage of a water can, buckets, etc. There

Snipe

was a big locker under the stern seat in which warps were stowed and abaft that another for spare sails. When I bought her, she carried a roller jib, but I scrapped that at once, as I thought and still think a roller jib an abominable contrivance in a cruising boat, particularly when she has a fairly long bowsprit. The new jib was fitted with the Wykeham-Martin furling gear which had just made its appearance. I think *Snipe* was one of the first craft to carry it, as Mr. Wykeham-Martin sent me one of the earliest sets made to try out. I soon came to the conclusion that it was one of the most valuable fittings ever devised for small yachts and have used it ever since in all of my boats. I have written so much about this furling gear in my books and elsewhere that it is not necessary to say more now, but that its merits are appreciated by yachtsmen generally will be gathered from the fact that it is now extensively used in small craft all over the world. The mainsail was fitted with Turner's roller reefing gear, which has been retained until this day, although I myself now prefer to reef with a tackle and pendant in the old-fashioned way.

When the alterations had been completed, *Snipe* was as jolly a pocket cruiser as one could imagine. With her shining black topsides, set off by a gilt line, her new canvas, narrow plank decks with teak covering board, varnished teak hatch, coamings and cockpit fittings, she looked a smart little yacht and I was very proud of her.

I cruised in *Snipe* for three delightful years and then two friends offered me practically double what she had cost me. I had no idea of selling, but they were persistent and I came to the conclusion that I should be a fool if I rejected such an offer. So I yielded to temptation and *Snipe* passed out of my ownership. Before the week was out I was sorry and have continued to regret parting with her ever since. In selling this little ship that I loved so much, I felt, and still feel, that I was no better than the man in Hardy's novel who sold his wife at a fair.

Although now forty-three years old, *Snipe* is still bravely sailing the seas and in good condition. But she has always had owners who loved her and kept her up. Whenever anything has needed renewal, it has received attention, and she has thus had new garboards, stem and sternpost and, I think, one or two new planks. She must, however, have been uncommonly well built in the first place to have lasted so long. Of the two dozen small craft I have owned in my time *Snipe* was the favourite, for I have never had another that gave me so much pleasure to sail or inspired such confidence. Apart from that, she was very comfortable to live in, and the only thing she lacked that I should have liked was a cooking galley. But I managed very well without it, cooking on two Primus stoves in the cockpit and using a well-tent on wet days. By dispensing with the store-cupboard and pantry, I could have found room for a small galley, but an enclosed galley of inadequate size is a mistake, and in a little ship one is perhaps better without it 🙢

Part VI: MAINTENANCE

CHAPTER 42: *Fitting Out*

The life of a yacht depends very largely upon the manner in which she is kept up, and an owner who neglects his ship is, to put it bluntly, a fool. If properly looked after there is no reason why she should not last a lifetime, provided of course that she was built of sound materials in the first place; but if neglected she may go to wrack and ruin in a comparatively short time. Even a small cruiser is property of some value, which it is surely worth while to take care of; but apart from that the owner's personal safety may rest on the soundness of the craft and her gear.

To ensure that everything alow and aloft is sound and in good order, the yacht should receive a thorough overhaul every year before she goes afloat and I would strongly advise the owner to do at least some of the work himself. By fitting out the vessel himself he will not only save money but get an intimate knowledge of the craft and her gear that he could not obtain in any other way. If you fit out the boat yourself, every item of her gear will pass through your hands and you will be able to put to sea confident that everything is all right. I once had a small craft fitted out for me by a waterman, as I wanted to compete in a race and there was not time to do the work myself. The result was disastrous, as I had barely crossed the starting line when the mast went over the side. As there was not any great weight in the wind at the time, I was more than a little surprised at the accident, but when I came to investigate the matter the cause was at once apparent. The shrouds were in pairs, each pair being seized at the hounds, or rather they should have been; but the waterman had omitted to do it. It appeared that he had temporarily tied each pair with a piece of marline, meaning to put on proper seizings later, but, being called away from the job, had forgotten about it. I learnt from that experience that when employing others it is prudent thoroughly to inspect their work before putting to sea.

STANDING AND RUNNING RIGGING

Fitting out a small yacht takes a good deal of time, but it is an interesting job and helps to pass the winter months when your yacht is out of commission, and incidentally enables you to acquire a working knowledge of what is known as marlinspike seamanship. I propose to deal with such matters as knotting and splicing in a later chapter.

If you live at a distance from your boat, you will probably only be able to work on her at week-ends and even then the extent of your operations will be dependent upon the weather. It is advisable therefore to begin work as soon as you lay up in the autumn. I should recommend you, when you lay up, to take all the running gear home with you, and you will then be able to work on it in comfort during the long winter evenings. By the way, when you remove the gear from the yacht, do not unreeve the halyards but merely unshackle the blocks, and if you have any doubts about being able to identify the various halyards, tie a label to each.

When you have got the gear home, examine all the rope carefully to see if any of it requires renewing. Twist the rope against the lay so as to expose the inner side of the strands. If they look dry and frayed and the rope seems to have no elasticity, it should be condemned and new rope purchased. It is possible, however, that the rope may seem quite sound although one end of it is thinner than the other. Should that be the case the halyard should be 'end-for-ended,' or in other words, turned round so that what was the standing part becomes the fall, and vice versa. When a halyard is in use, a considerable portion of it is coiled down on deck and consequently gets but little wear, while the part that is aloft and under strain is stretched thinner. By 'end-for-ending' you are able to get another season's wear out of the rope before it is finally discarded. It has always been my practice to end-for-end my running gear at the conclusion of its first season and scrap it after the second season. This may seem rather extravagant, but I don't believe in using running gear to the point of destruction, as it may carry away when you are at sea in heavy weather. Many small yacht owners do not think of replacing rope until it breaks, but they are the men who are always in trouble.

Having looked over your gear and decided what must be renewed, measure up the quantity of new rope you will require. Running gear, when of rope, should be of yacht manila or lightly tarred Italian hemp. It is customary to use four-strand rope for this purpose, as, being laid up round a heart, it is said to keep its shape better than three-strand; but, personally, I don't think there is anything in that theory. Of late years I have used three-strand, which seems to serve the purpose equally well. It is wise, however, to use blocks that are at least one size larger than absolutely necessary, for if the halyard be too tight a fit in the block it may not render freely in wet weather. My old friend the late Mr. G. U. Laws, once met with serious trouble in that respect when taking a 6-tonner from the Crouch to Northumberland. He got caught out in very heavy weather and the halyards had swollen to such an extent that the mainsail could not be lowered until he went aloft with a knife and cut the halyards adrift. When purchasing the new rope, remember it is measured by circumference and sold by weight.

Having settled these preliminaries, you will be ready to start operations. It is best, I think, to begin with the blocks, which will have to be scraped and varnished. To do this, it will be necessary to remove them from all the gear, and as you may subsequently have difficulty in identifying the different halyards, each should have a label tied on to it when you remove the blocks.

Before beginning to scrape a block, you should knock out the pin and remove the sheave, placing both in a tin of oil after you have thoroughly cleaned them. Now you can turn your attention to scraping the shell of the block. Some people use a knife, or pieces of glass for scraping, but I don't think there is anything to beat an ordinary three-cornered scraper. To get good results, however, you must keep it sharp. It is best sharpened with a file, subsequently running a knife along the edge to remove any burr. The old varnish will scrape off quite easily, but if the weather has got into the block, you will have to remove a certain amount of wood to get it clean; but don't scrape off more than absolutely necessary. Always scrape with the grain, and when the block is quite clean, rub it down thoroughly with glass-paper until the surface is perfectly smooth.

When all the blocks have been scraped and rubbed down, they can receive the first coat of varnish. This should be the best yacht varnish, for it is false economy to buy cheap paint and varnish. If good results are to be obtained the varnish must be applied thinly and each coat allowed thoroughly to dry before the next is applied. Varnishing is best done in warm weather, but during winter such conditions are seldom obtainable and on a cold day the varnish will be too thick for good work. You can, however, overcome this difficulty by standing the tin in a saucepan of hot water.

The blocks should receive three coats, or even four, if you contemplate keeping the yacht in commission well into the autumn. When varnished the blocks should be threaded on to a string and hung up to dry. When the final coat is thoroughly dry, the sheaves can be re-fitted. The pins are square at one end and round at the other, and when you removed the sheaves you tapped the round end. When re-fitting you must tap the square end, taking great care not to damage the new varnish. When the pin is nearly home, put something over it, say a piece of canvas, or a thin piece of wood, to protect the varnish. If a pin is a rather sloppy fit in the block and might work out, it is advisable to fit a disc of brass or copper over it. The disc should be about the size of a farthing and have three small holes drilled in it near the edge, so that it can be attached to the block with little brass screws, as shown above.

Having finished the blocks you can turn your attention to the rope. If you are renewing the halyards, it is merely a question of carefully measuring off the new rope, splicing one end into the block and whipping the other end. If you have decided to use the halyards for another season, you can now proceed to turn them end-for-end. If the halyard is already rather short, you had better draw the splice, but otherwise you can cut it, as you will then be able to make a neater end to the fall. Having thus detached the rope from the block, take the end that was the fall and splice it on to the block. You should turn in your splice as neatly as possible. Dip each strand thrice, then halve the strands and dip again. Finally, halve the remaining strands and dip once more. That should give you a nice tapered splice.

The splice may be served or not, as you please. Personally, I have given up serving splices, as I do not think anything is gained by doing so, and in my view a well turned-in splice is more pleasing to the eye than any service. If you decide to serve the splice, the serving should be put on tightly with the aid of a serving board.

A particularly neat and effective service board was devised some years ago by Mr. Thornley King, of Messrs. William King & Sons, the well-known yacht-builders of Burnham-on-Crouch. I have tried this serving-board and found it a most fascinating implement with which to work. Fitted on the back is a reel, on which the marline is wound, and this reel is furnished with a spring and wing-nut, by means of which the tension can be adjusted to a nicety. The marline leads from the reel through a fairlead to the work, and all one has to do is to pass the implement round and round the rope one is serving. The drawing shows the serving board in operation. A feature of the device is that one can stop in the middle of the service if one wishes, for the board can be left on the work without loss of tension.

Blocks nowadays are usually fitted with internal metal strops, but if you have any with grommet strops, the strops should be scrutinized. As they will probably be covered with canvas or leather, you may be tempted to omit this examination, but it is prudent to do so, as, although the covering may appear to be in good order, the hidden strop may be unsound, if you have any doubt about the condition of a strop, scrap it and make a new one. I shall deal with such matters as splicing and grommets in a chapter on knotting and splicing in the Seamanship section. If you make a grommet strop it should be just large enough to take the block and thimble when they are seized in. Should the strop be the slightest bit

King's serving-board

too large in the first place, the block would probably come out after the strop had stretched. As each halyard is completed, coil it down neatly and label it, to avoid confusion when you come to rig the yacht again.

Having finished the overhaul of your running gear there is not much more that you can do at home, unless you wish to make some new cabin fittings, such as a bookshelf or cupboard. You can pass the winter evenings very pleasantly in your workshop occupied on such jobs, provided of course that you have a workshop. Even if you have not, you should be able to do a certain amount of fitting out at home. One owner I knew, who lived in a flat, used to spread a dust-sheet over the hearth-rug and scrape his blocks in the drawing-room; but then his wife was as keen on sailing as he was himself.

If you have a yacht of 6 or 7 tons, with a coal stove in the cabin, there is no reason why you should not do your fitting out on board. There are worse places than the cabin of a yacht on a winter night, when the fire burns brightly in the 'bogey,' and if the vessel is well covered up in your absence during the week, your cabin gear will take no harm. Things may seem a trifle damp when you go on board the following week-end, but after the stove has been lit for half an hour everything will be as dry as a bone.

MAST AND SPARS

The next job to tackle will be the mast and spars. If the yacht is laid up at a yard, there will probably be a long shed in which you can work; otherwise you will have to do the job in the open air, selecting fine days for the purpose. I take it that the mast will have been lifted before the yacht was covered up, and if it has been well protected with varnish during the season, it should not need scraping. The less spars are scraped the better, as it tends to reduce their strength. Grown spars are difficult to obtain in these times, and masts and spars for small yachts are usually cut from balks of timber. As the main strength of a spar is in the outer skin, the latter are not nearly so strong as grown spars, which have little more than the bark removed. If you are fortunate enough to possess grown spars, you should take care of them and scrape them as little as possible.

Before beginning cleaning operations, examine the spars for cracks. Longitudinal cracks are not of much consequence unless very wide and deep, but they should be filled to keep out the wet. The best kind of filling, I think, is Jeffrey's 'Seamflex' plastic marine glue. This never sets hard and for that reason is better than putty or white lead for this job. It is easily applied with a putty knife and in cold weather can be softened by warming, or rubbing between the hands. If the crack extends diagonally almost from one side to the other, the spar is probably sprung, and should be replaced.

If the spar is in good condition, a good rub down with glass-paper will suffice to remove the old varnish, but if the weather has got into it, making black marks, the spar will have to be scraped. For rubbing down purposes, I can recommend the wet glass-paper which, I believe, is used by manufacturers of motor-car bodies. It may cost you sixpence or sevenpence a sheet, but one sheet will suffice for the mast of a 5-tonner. It is used with water and does the job much quicker than the ordinary dry variety.

When scraping a spar you should scrape with the grain of the wood and away from knots, removing no more wood than you can help. The aim should be to remove the dirt and perished varnish, but if the weather has got into the spar you can't help cutting away a certain amount of wood. Man being by nature a somewhat impatient animal, you may be tempted to take a plane to a spar that is in very bad condition, but if you do that sort of thing you will soon spoil the spars. When you have scraped them clean, you must rub down the spars with glass-paper of medium coarseness to begin with, but finish with a finer one. When perfectly smooth, the spars can be varnished and if possible fine weather should be selected for the purpose. If you have to work in the open air, you must have a fine day, and remember what I told you about standing the varnish can in hot water, if the weather is cold. At least three coats, preferably four, should be applied thinly, each coat being allowed thoroughly to dry before the next is applied. Use the best spar varnish, such as that supplied by Noble & Hoare, or John Mathews & Co.

If the mast has been left in the yacht during the winter, it will certainly have to be scraped, and you will have to go aloft in a bosun's chair to do it – a chilly occupation, if the weather happens to be of the 'brass monkey' order. The mast of a small yacht should always be lifted out of her when she is laid up, for it not only saves a deal of scraping, but much work aloft when re-fitting, as all of the rigging and running gear can be placed on the mast before it is stepped. If there is no crane available, the mast can be lifted with a tackle and sheer-legs. Don't forget to put the hoops on the mast before stepping it. You may think that remark rather superfluous, but professional riggers often omit to do so and sometimes fail to notice the absence of the hoops until the yacht has been completely rigged and they come to bend the mainsail.

THE ANCHOR CABLE

When fitting out the anchor cable should be unshipped so that any turns may be taken out. These turns are caused by the vessel swinging to the tide and at the end of a season the inboard end for a few fathoms may be wound up almost solid. When you put the chain back on board, don't forget to weather-bitt it, or you may subsequently lose your anchor and cable. In many yachts there is an eye-bolt in the keelson to which the chain can be shackled, but it is better to secure the chain to the bitts, or foot of the mast. After a round turn has been taken round the mast, or bitts, the end of the chain can be secured with a couple of half-hitches, the end link being tied with a bit of cord. If the cable is shackled to an eye-bolt the pin of the shackle may get rusted up solid, owing to the presence of bilge water, and if it became necessary to slip the cable, you would not be able to do so. That such a contingency is not altogether beyond the bounds of possibility will be gathered from the following incident:

The owner of a certain 4-tonner went out fishing on the West Coast of Scotland one evening, accompanied by a young lad. Having reached their fishing ground, they anchored in 7 fathoms, riding to their full scope of chain. They enjoyed good sport for an hour or so, and then as a choppy sea had got up, they decided to return home. Suddenly there was what the owner describes as "a rasping thudding that shivered the yacht from stem to stern, as if she were on the rocks." The chain was straight up and down and as rigid as a bar of iron. It was evident that it had fouled a rock and the tide was making fast. Already the yacht was pinned down by the bow, and the situation began to look very ugly.

Obviously, the only thing to do was to slip the cable, but on going below to cast it off, the owner discovered that it was secured to the keelson with a heavy rusty shackle. When he tried to unscrew the pin his spike broke, and then they were in a nasty fix. The flooding tide was rapidly reducing the free-board of the yacht forward and elevating her stern, the wind was freshening and darkness coming on. So they decided to try and sail out the anchor.

Having set the mainsail and jib, the sheet of the latter was hauled a-weather. As the mainsail filled, the yacht lay over until the water lapped into the cockpit. Then the chain, bursting the fairlead on the stemhead, sprang round to the starboard rigging and the bows were then flush with the water. Again they hauled the jib a-weather and the yacht lay over until several planks were under. Then, with a crash, the hawse-pipe in the deck burst and the chain ripped the deck across to the rail, a few feet from the now submerged bow. The chain was sawing through the rail and the yacht heeled to an alarming angle. In desperation they filled on her once more and, a squall striking the boat, she at last broke her chain and was free.

Well, that strikes me as a pretty close call and should be a warning to owners not to weather-bitt the cable with a shackle. In such a predicament the only way in which the yacht could be released would be by severing the chain, but the necessary implements are not likely to be included in a small yacht's equipment. A chain can be cut with a cold chisel or a hack-saw, or, in the absence of such tools by breaking a link. To do this, hold a link endwise on a hard surface and give it a few hefty welts with a heavy hammer – but then I don't suppose you would have a heavy hammer on board.

CHAPTER 43: *Painting and Varnishing*

Painters can be divided into two classes – those who paint properly and those who merely slap on paint, and I fear that many yachtsmen who fit out their own craft belong to the latter category. If good results are to be achieved you must use the best materials and carefully prepare the surface before you start. A rough surface makes for a rough and unsatisfactory finish and if the surface is not quite dry the new paint may blister, as it probably will if the paint is applied too thickly. But first let me say a few words about brushes. Some yachtsmen are inclined to be casual about the care of paint and varnish brushes and often, when the job is done, put them away in a locker without thoroughly cleaning them. Then, when they have more painting to do, they find the bristles of the old brushes all stuck together, and as likely as not throw them away and buy new ones. Such a practice is not only extravagant but foolish, for better work can be done with an old brush that has been well cared for than with a new one.

When buying brushes get the best, preferably of the 'rubber-set' variety. It is false economy to buy cheap brushes, as the bristles are apt to come out and spoil the work. A new brush should be rubbed on coarse glass-paper to remove any stray bristles, and as it will probably be too soft, a piece of string tied tightly round the bristles about a third of the way down. When the brush has worn a little, the string can be removed.

After use the brush should be placed in a jar containing a half-and-half mixture of linseed oil and turpentine. The bristles should not touch the bottom of the jar; the best way of preventing this is to drill a hole through the handle and pass a bit of wire through it, so that the wire rests on the mouth of the jar. Before using the brush again, it should be thoroughly cleaned in turpentine, or paraffin if you have no turps.

In the early spring the weather is seldom suitable for outside painting, as you want a dry sunny day for the job and at that time of year such days are rare indeed, but there is no reason why you should not paint the cabin and fo'c'sle, if they need it. Inside painting, however, should not be necessary every year. Very often all that is needed is a good scrub down with hot fresh water and Trusoap, or Vim. Still, it has to be done every two or three years.

If the old paint is in good condition but merely dirty, you can paint over it, after it has been well rubbed down with a damp cloth and powdered pumice, but you must be sure that the surface is quite dry before the fresh paint is applied. If there are any blisters, cut them out and apply paint to the bare spot until the level is brought up to that of the surrounding surface and rub down until quite smooth.

Storing a paint-brush

When painting, work first with the grain, then across and finally with the grain again. You should apply the paint thinly, taking care that no 'tears' are formed. When the paint is quite dry, rub it down and having dusted it, put on a second coat. After each dip, draw the brush across the edge of the tin to remove surplus paint. Rub down the second coat lightly and then put on the final coat of enamel. Applying enamel is rather tiring, as the brush clings more than with ordinary paint, but there must be no break in the work. For instance, if you are enamelling a bulkhead, do not stop until you have finished it, otherwise joins will be visible and spoil the appearance. The enamel should not be applied too thickly but well worked in, first with the grain of the wood, then across, and finally with the grain again. The interior of the cabin is usually painted white for the sake of the light, but make sure that the paint is zinc white, as lead white turns yellow after it has been exposed to the light for some time. If the coamings are bright varnished, care must be taken to keep the paint clear of the varnish. This can be done by using a strip of tin, or cardboard; hold it in your left hand and move it along to protect the varnish as you paint.

If the cabin paint is in a bad state, it should be burnt off with a blow-lamp down to the bare wood. After all of the old paint has been removed with the lamp and scraper, the surface must be thoroughly rubbed down and dusted before beginning to repaint. You should first apply a coat of priming, then two coats of undercoating and a final coat of enamel. Each must be quite dry and rubbed down before the next coat is applied.

If, at any time, you wish to change the colour from a light to a dark shade, or vice versa, the old paint should be burnt off. It is never satisfactory to put a light colour over a dark, or a dark over a light shade, as sooner or later the original colour will begin to show through. This remark applies particularly to the top-sides of a yacht, as the dinghy scraping against them will at once bring the old colour to light.

When you have got your cabin painted and fitted up, the days will be drawing out and it will be time to think about outside work. If the yacht has been properly covered up during the winter, it is not likely that the bright parts, such as coamings hatches and lockers, will need scraping, but if she has been left uncovered in a mud berth, they certainly will. If the bright-work is in good condition, all that will be required is a good rub down and a couple of coats of varnish. When rubbing down, use medium glass-paper stretched over a flat piece of cork, measuring about 6 inches by 4 and 2 inches thick. By this means you will be able to rub a much larger surface and it will be less tiring to the hand. When the bright parts have been thoroughly rubbed down, they should be dusted before applying the varnish.

If possible, select a bright sunny day for varnishing and commence operations as early as you can after the woodwork has dried. If you put on varnish on a surface that is not perfectly dry, the varnish will subsequently 'bloom,' a fault that may also arise from putting on the varnish too thickly, or applying it on a cold moist day. If the varnish is too thick in the tin for a thin application, stand the tin in hot water, or wait for a day when the conditions are more favourable; never attempt to thin varnish by adding linseed oil. Blooming can sometimes be got rid of by sponging down with a mixture of vinegar, methylated spirit and linseed oil in equal parts, but if it is really bad, there is no alternative but to scrape off the varnish and do it again.

After prolonged storage varnish may be rather thick, in which case it is better to apply to the makers for something with which to thin it, rather than try and do it yourself with linseed oil or turpentine. Linseed oil will affect its drying qualities, while turps, will deprive it of much of its gloss, and both are detrimental to the lasting properties of the varnish.

If the brightwork is in a bad state, it will have to be scraped, and, with a considerable area to deal with, a Skarsten scraper will be found more effective than an ordinary three-cornered one. This scraper is fitted with a renewable blade, made of the best quality steel and curled over. The blade is bent while the steel is soft and then hardened and tempered, being finally ground like a razor blade. It can be sharpened with a file in the usual way, and when finally worn out, renewed for a few pence. As there is a large range of these scrapers, varying in width of blade and shape of handle, you can get one suitable for almost any job.

A Skarsten scraper must be used with care otherwise you will take off too much wood. It should be held in the hand in one of three positions, according to the nature of the work. If the weather has got into the wood and a heavy cut is necessary, the tool must be held at an angle of about 80 degrees, while for smooth finishing work it should be used nearly flat. For a medium cut the position will be midway between the two.

When you have finished scraping, you must rub down the surface thoroughly with glass-paper and dust the work before applying the first coat of varnish. Four coats in all will be desirable and each should be rubbed down lightly with fine glass-paper before the next is applied; and, of course, each coat must be quite dry before the next is put on. The varnish should be applied freely, but well crossed and worked in with the brush, finishing with the grain of the wood. Care should be taken to prevent the varnish running or 'tears' being formed.

If you want your boat to retain her smart appearance throughout the summer, the brightwork on deck and in the cockpit should receive a fresh coat of varnish in the middle of the season. Before applying this coat, the surface should be rubbed down very lightly-just enough to remove the gloss and give the new varnish something on which to bite.

I would not recommend you to paint the topsides or deck yourself, as painting so early in the year is at the best a chancy business. If you attempt to do the job yourself it is quite likely that a shower of rain may ruin your work before it is finished. It is much better to have this outside painting done for you, as the man, being always on the spot, is in a better position to select a suitable day. The decks should not be painted until the very last, when the mast will have been stepped and the vessel rigged. It is essential that painted decks should be bone dry before they are walked on, otherwise the paint will be damaged and the job will have to be done again.

Now a word or two about the colour of the topsides. I expect you have wondered why so many yachts are painted white. Well, there is a very good reason for it. White repels the rays of the sun, while black and other dark colours attract them. It is quite a common thing for the topside planking of yachts painted a dark shade to open under the heat of a hot sun, particularly if the vessel is rather lightly built. I have known several cases of boats painted black, or some dark shade, suffering in that way and when subsequently painted white they remained perfectly tight. Of course, white topsides are apt to get dirty unless they receive a great deal of attention. Streaks of dirt appear below the scuppers and brown rust-stains beneath the chainplates, and a white yacht usually needs a coat of paint on her topsides in the course of the season. I think perhaps a cream, or oyster shade, is preferable to white, as it will repel the sun and not show dirt quite so much as dead white. The dinghy should be painted to match the yacht, but should be bright varnished inside. If she has a mahogany top-strake, that may be left bright and will enhance her appearance.

There is nothing that mars a yacht's sailing so much as a foul bottom, for if covered with weed or nuns it seriously reduces her speed and makes her sluggish in stays. Unless coated with some efficient anti-fouling composition a boat will foul very rapidly during the summer months, and if that trouble is to be avoided a really good anti-fouler must be used and properly applied. I have used all sorts of compositions in my time, ranging from the cheapest to the most expensive, but it is only of late years that I have discovered one that approaches within measurable distance of perfection. This is Kobe Green, manufactured by the International Paint and Compositions Co. Ltd. It is, I believe, about the most expensive on the market, but in the long run it is probably the most economical.

Before I discovered Kobe Green I almost invariably had to have my boat scrubbed and recoated three times every season, and in some years four times, but now I go through the season with only one scrub and one coat of the antifouler; and Fambridge, where I keep my craft, is a bad place for fouling.

The cost of having the anti-fouler put on will be the same even if you use the cheapest brand, and if you have to have your yacht scrubbed and recoated three or four times in the course of the season, your cheap composition may in the end be more expensive than the best. Surely it is a sounder proposition to use the best quality and thus save all the bother of putting your craft ashore for scrubbing purposes at frequent intervals.

The suppliers of Kobe Green claim that if a yacht is coated with it when she is commissioned in the spring, she will remain quite clean until she is laid up at the end of the season, and I think she would in ordinary circumstances. But my season is a rather long one, as I usually go afloat just before Easter and do not lay up until the end of October, and, as I say, Fambridge is a bad place for fouling. Still, I manage to make one coat a year suffice, by adopting the following method.

Vessels do not foul very much while the water is cold and so when I go afloat towards the end of March, I put nothing on her in the way of anti-fouling composition and find that she will keep clean until May, when the temperature of the water begins to rise. Then she is scrubbed and coated with Kobe Green and requires no further attention throughout the season. When laid up at the end of October there may be a few stray roses, or hairy teats as they are sometimes called, on her bottom, but those drop off while she is in her mud berth during the winter.

The efficiency of an anti-fouling composition depends a good deal upon how the stuff is stored and applied, and if the man who puts it on is a casual sort of chap, it may not be given a fair chance.

In most anti-fouling compositions powerful poisons are employed and these being comparatively heavy, sink to the bottom of the drum or tin. When the yacht-chandler or waterman lays in his stock he places it in store and I suspect that in most cases it is not touched until wanted for use. Drums and cans containing anti-fouler should be turned end-for-end periodically, say, once a week, in order to keep the contents adequately mixed and if this is neglected the principal ingredients will sink to the bottom of the container. This perhaps would not matter very much if the anti-fouler were thoroughly stirred before use and while in use. I am inclined to think, however, that the average waterman often fails to do this, with the result that what our American friends call 'the doings' are left in the tin and subsequently thrown away. When this happens, the owner probably says that the stuff is no damn use and tries another brand. That is the only way in which I can account for the variable results so often obtained from the same brand. One tin may keep a yacht's bottom clean for months, while another of the same brand may prove so ineffectual that the boat will require scrubbing again in a few weeks. To get the best results, the anti-fouler must be stirred all the time it is being applied, but that means the employment of two men to put it on-one to stir and one to apply it, but you seldom see more than one man engaged on the job.

In Kobe Green, however, the ingredients are so finely ground that they remain in suspension, and although it is advisable to stir the stuff occasionally when applying it, there is very little risk of the poisons being unevenly distributed over the yacht, or left behind in the tin. I know several owners who have attempted to reduce the cost of Kobe Green by omitting the special undercoating with the result that their boats soon fouled. Such a policy is penny wise and pound foolish, for it is imperative that the undercoating be used, as it is an important part of the anti-fouling process. To omit it is to court failure and it is not fair to the manufacturers. All that is necessary to obtain consistently satisfactory results is to use the correct undercoating and rigidly to adhere to the recommended covering capacities, i.e. not more than 550 square feet to the gallon for the undercoating and 350 square feet to the gallon for the anti-fouling composition.

The cabin-top, which is usually covered with canvas and painted, should be white, to repel the heat; and the decks, if painted, should also be a light tint. The actual colour must be a matter of personal taste, but primrose, or a light shade of buff, looks well. If the decks are painted, but not covered with canvas, they will probably need re-painting in the middle of the season to keep them tight, as in hot weather the planks are liable to shrink a little and the film of paint over the seams may crack. I am of the opinion that the only way to keep the decks of a small yacht perfectly tight is to cover them, either with painted canvas or brown linoleum, cemented down to the deck with a mixture of varnish and white lead.

Coamings, cockpit lockers and cabin doors of teak or mahogany should be varnished, but if made of pitch-pine or any other comparatively cheap wood they will look better painted. There is a varnish paint sold that so closely resembles teak that at a few yards distance it can hardly be distinguished from the real thing.

CHAPTER 44: *Laying Up*

The care of a yacht when laid up during the winter months is of as much, possibly greater, importance than when she is in commission. If not properly looked after she will deteriorate more during this period of inactivity than in the course of several seasons' sailing, and it will therefore pay you to give some attention to the manner in which she is berthed and her gear stored.

Your first consideration, no doubt, will be that of locality. If there are reasonable facilities for laying up a craft at your sailing headquarters, it will, of course, be most convenient for her to winter there; failing that, you will have to seek a berth for her elsewhere. If you contemplate having some structural repairs or alterations carried out during the winter, it will probably be best to lay her up at the yard where the work is to be done.

The best way of laying up a yacht is to haul her out and berth her ashore under cover, but that is not always practicable and the average owner, particularly if he has to study expense, must rest content with a mud berth on the saltings. Most small yachts, indeed, pass the winter in mud berths, and, provided that they are covered up and well cared for, take no harm. Some owners leave their craft afloat at moorings during the winter, but I don't think that altogether wise, for the nights are long and there is a risk of their being run down in the dark by some passing vessel. There is also a risk of damage from ice during a severe winter. Ice floes will saw right through the planking of a vessel at the waterline and I have known several yachts sunk in that manner. Moreover, it is desirable that a yacht should be out of the water for a few months during the year to allow her to dry.

When a yacht is laid up in a mud berth, or anywhere in the open, it is essential to her welfare that she be covered up, for if left uncovered all the brightwork on deck and in the cockpit would have to be scraped before being varnished in the spring, and that would involve a deal of work and considerable expense, unless you did it yourself. But if properly covered, a rub down and a couple of coats of varnish would probably suffice. A cover, too, will keep the interior of the yacht dry, and as the cabin doors and hatches can be left open, the vessel will be well ventilated throughout.

The cover should be of waterproof canvas and made to fit the boat. It should extend from end to end of the vessel and cover the topsides down to the waterline. The cover should be laid over a ridge-pole, say 2 feet 6 inches above the deck, and laced down to a rope passed right round the yacht below the waterline. The ridge-pole can be supported by a crutch stepped through the mast-hole and another crutch aft. The ends of the cover should be left open, as also should all doors, hatches and lockers, for the sake of ventilation. Before the cover is put

Yacht laid-up in a mud berth

on the mast should be lifted and stored in the spar shed, if there is no crane available, the mast can be lifted out of the vessel with the aid of sheer-legs and a tackle. With those preliminary remarks, I will now describe the whole process of laying up a small yacht.

The first thing to do is to unbend the mainsail, which, of course, should only be done on a fine day. Then take it ashore, together with the other sails, and put them into the store. You should make sure that both canvas and bolt ropes are bone dry before putting them away, for otherwise they might be attacked by mildew. It is a common practice when storing sails for the winter to put some newspapers with them to prevent damage by rats and mice. Such vermin prefer paper to anything else for nest-making, and if adequately supplied are more likely to let your sails and cushions alone.

The next job, I think, should be to lift the mast, and the yacht must be berthed under the crane for the purpose. First remove the gaff and boom and disconnect the shroud and stay lanyards. Then stop all the running gear and standing rigging to the mast and knock out the mast-wedges at the deck. The mast will then be free for lifting by the crane. When out of the boat, it should be stripped of gear, each halyard being neatly coiled and a label attached indicating exactly what it is and the name of the yacht, if the gear is to go into a common store with that of other vessels. This will eliminate the risk of confusion when you come to re-rig the boat in the spring. The bowsprit, if any, should then be taken out and its gear treated in the same way.

The yacht can now be installed in her mud berth. She must be securely moored 'all-fours,' or in other words, with warps from her bows and quarters. Take care that the posts to which the warps are belayed are firm in the ground. You will probably need a good spring tide to get her in her berth, and if the berth is a good one she will only float at high water spring tides.

It is the usual practice, when laying up a yacht for the winter, to remove everything on board and store it ashore, but unless you are going to re-paint the cabin in the spring, that is hardly necessary. If the vessel is properly covered up such things as crockery, cooking stoves and utensils, buckets, lamps, etc., will winter just as well on board as in a store, and if you take them ashore you will only have to bring them back in the spring. I assume, of course, that the local people are honest; in some districts you could not leave anything on board without risk of their being stolen. Such items as bedding, blankets, cushions, books, the clock and aneroid and navigating instruments should however be stored ashore. We will assume, however, that you are going to paint the interior of the yacht in the spring and therefore decide to strip her of everything. Unless you have a private lock-up store, I would advise you to buy one or two cube sugar boxes from the local grocer, in which to pack the various items. They can be purchased at tri-fling cost and by keeping all your things together in that way, there will be less risk of items being mislaid or lost. The spars, too, should be lashed together and labelled with the name of the yacht before being put in the spar shed, otherwise they may be mixed up with those of other craft and be difficult to identify.

As there are several jobs to be done to the hull before the cover can be put on, the mast-hole should be covered with an enamelled plate, or something of that sort, to keep out the rain. The most important of these jobs is to clean out the bilge and give the bottom inside a coat of black varnish. Before this can be done the inside ballast must be removed. The bilge should then be thoroughly scrubbed out, care being taken that the limber-holes are quite clear – a pointed stick will be found a useful implement for clearing them. Then two coats of black varnish should be applied.

If the inside ballast is of lead, all that will be needed is to scrub it with water and a hard brush, but if of iron, the pigs should be black-varnished. If the yacht is hauled out, or legged on a hard, for the winter the ballast should not be re-stowed until she is fitted out in the spring. If left on board when the vessel is not either water-borne or resting in a mud berth, its weight might tend to distort her lines. When re-stowing the ballast the greatest care must be taken to put it back in its old position, for otherwise the trim of the yacht will be affected, so it is advisable to mark the pigs in some way when removing them. When the bilge has been cleaned and black-varnished and the ballast re-stowed, the cover can be put on.

Should the yacht have an auxiliary motor, the engine must also receive atten-tion. The fuel tank must be emptied, the carburetter drained and the engine well greased. The magneto should be removed and stored in a dry warm place, such as the kitchen at home. Remove the sparking plugs and pour a little oil into each cylinder; then turn over the engine a few times by hand. Don't put back your good plugs, as they will winter better at home, but substitute old ones that you have discarded, as they are only needed to keep out the damp air.

It is customary to leave the engine *in situ* during the winter unless it is sent to a motor works for a thorough overhaul. Should you do that, you should advise your underwriters and arrange to be held covered, as a motor works is not a store within the meaning of the policy, but what is known as a 'hazardous risk,' for which a higher premium is charged. Some years ago there was a disastrous fire at Burnham and a number of yacht engines were destroyed. The question arose as to whether they were covered by the yacht policies and the matter went to arbitration. The arbitrators held that it was not, as it is not common practice to remove a yacht's engine and send it to a motor works. As the extra premium to cover the risk is trifling, it is better to be safe than sorry.

And now let us return to the storing of the yacht's rigging and running gear. Before the shrouds and stays are stored away, they should be coated with a mixture of boiled linseed oil and petrol, put on with a soft brush. This mixture will penetrate right into the heart of the wire rope, and, the petrol evaporating, a skim of linseed oil will be left on every tiny wire of which it is composed. It may take two or three days to dry but will preserve the wire from rust. Having been treated in this way, each shroud should be coiled in large coils, labelled, and hung up in the store. Flexible wire halyards can be treated in a similar manner but the mixture should be petrol and vaseline.

Bunk cushions, when stored, should be stood on edge. If they are stowed flat, with other things on top, it will tend to make them hard. The same remark, of course, also applies to mattresses. If you do not take the running gear home to overhaul during the winter, the coils should be hung up in the store. By the way, before the yacht is covered up all metal work should be well greased.

During the winter, if there is a coal stove on board, a fire should be lit in the cabin from time to time, the cover being partially folded back to permit of the chimney being shipped. If there is no stove, the cover should be turned back for a few hours on fine dry days occasionally.

CHAPTER 45: *Preventive Maintenance*

Provided that she be strongly and faithfully built of well-seasoned wood, the life of a yacht depends almost entirely upon the manner in which she is kept up. If the owner has her periodically examined, and such repairs and renovations executed as are necessary, the vessel will last almost for a lifetime; but, if neglected, she will only be fit for the scrap-heap in a matter of fifteen years or so. The Marquis of Ailsa's famous old 40-tonner, *Bloodhound*, is staunch and seaworthy after nearly forty years' sailing, and still a prolific prize-winner, but the majority of her contemporaries met their fate at the hands of the shopbreaker many years ago.

The prudent owner does not grudge his craft an occasional coat of paint, for he knows that if her hull be not well covered with paint and her spars and blocks with varnish, they will soon deteriorate under the ravages of the weather. To paint the yacht once a year when fitting out is not sufficient to keep her in good condition, and another coat in the middle of the summer is usually necessary. The spars, if they receive three coats of good varnish in the spring, will not require any further attention until the end of the season; but all large cracks should bo stopped with white-lead to keep out the weather. Longitudinal cracks, unless very large and deep, are of no consequence, but if transverse they are serious, and the spar should be condemned.

Every other season the outside paint on the topsides should be burnt off, and the boat well rubbed down and a coat of priming applied before she is repainted. Whenever the bottom is scrubbed, a fresh coat, or even two coats, of anti-fouling composition should be applied. The services of a competent shipwright should be enlisted every three or four years to thoroughly examine the vessel's fabric and replace anything that should show signs of decay. A yacht's planking and timbers should be beyond suspicion, and if any soft spots be found, the plank or timber affected should be taken out and renewed.

All iron-work must be closely scrutinized from time to time, particularly the keel bolts. Iron bolts should never on any account be used to fasten a lead keel, for the two metals when in contact set up galvanic action, and under such circumstances keel bolts will be corroded right through in a few years. Lead keels have been known to drop off through this cause, and the owner should therefore make it his business to ascertain the nature of his keel bolts. If of iron, they should be replaced by others of yellow metal at once. Even when the lead keel is secured with yellow metal bolts, the owner must exercise a certain amount of vigilance if the floors are of steel, as the latter will set up corrosion when in contact with yellow metal. I think this difficulty might be overcome by the use of vulcanized insulating washers between the floors and the bolt nuts, although I have never heard of the experiment being tried. Shroud-plates should be securely bolted right through the planking and timbers of the vessel, and not merely screwed on, as is sometimes the case in small yachts. These plates, by the way, are better made of hard brass or phosphor bronze, for if of iron they rust and sully the topside paint. Nothing detracts so much from the appearance of a white yacht than streaks of brown rust below the chain-plates.

There is nothing so conducive to the generation of dry rot in the fabric of a yacht as lack of ventilation, and every means should therefore be taken to ensure a free current of air to the planking and timbers of the craft. For this reason a yacht's cabin is, I think, better left unlined; but should the owner, for the sake of appearance, prefer to have the boat's side ceiled, holes should be drilled in the lining at frequent intervals and a narrow space left between the ceiling and shelf. The chief objection to an unlined boat is the moisture which on cold nights accumulates on the planking from condensation. It is easy, however, to prevent one's blankets, etc., from getting damp by fitting battens to the timbers a few inches apart. If the skin of the yacht be of hard wood and kept nicely varnished, it looks very smart, and varnished battens of a different kind of wood will enhance, rather than detract from, the general appearance.

When the weather is fine and dry, not only the cabin, but the lockers should be periodically opened, in order that they may be well aired. Wet warps should not on any account be stowed away in lockers, for such a practice will not only rot the warps themselves, but, by keeping the locker in a constant state of dampness, foster the generation of mildew and rot.

There is nothing, perhaps, which causes the owner of a small yacht so much discomfort as a leaky deck or cabin-top, and yet, unless one resorts to the somewhat drastic remedy of covering them, it is almost impossible to keep them tight. The reason of this is that, being comparatively thin, the decks work as one walks on them, and will not retain the caulking for any length of time. Another place which is very liable to leak is along the sides of the cabin-top. On a small craft one is obliged to walk on the cabin-top a good deal, and this causes the coamings to work, thereby forcing the caulking out of the seams all round. This leakage can be prevented by fixing a narrow strip of oiled silk right round the cabin-top so that it overlaps both deck and coaming. This strip must be well stuck down to both deck and coaming with varnish, and if covered with a beading of wood, will not be seen. In order to keep the cabin-top itself tight, it should be covered with thin sheeting tightly stretched and painted until it is quite smooth. White will be the best colour, as it will keep the cabin cool in summer. Brown linoleum is far and away the best material with which to cover the decks of a small boat, for if well laid it looks neat, is quite impervious to wet, and easily kept clean. It has a far smarter appearance than painted canvas, and I think wears very much better. It is not a difficult matter to cover a yacht's decks with linoleum, and I have known several amateurs tackle the job with unqualified success. The following is the method recommended to me by a firm of yacht builders who make a speciality of this work:

Ordinary brown linoleum of good quality is the material usually employed for the purpose, and it is stuck to the deck with a cement composed of white-lead and varnish. Before laying the linoleum, the edges of the deck planks must be planed down until a perfectly smooth surface is obtained. The rail and all deck fittings should be removed, and the linoleum put on in as few pieces as possible. Wherever there is a join, the edges must be closely tacked down and covered with a thin fillet of wood, the edges of which should be well rounded off in order to reduce the liability of one's tripping over the obstruction. The white-lead and varnish should be generously applied, for if the linoleum be not firmly cemented down the wet may get beneath and rot the decks. After the linoleum has been laid, the rail and deck fittings can be put back, and the job is then completed. Should there be any cleats on deck, the linoleum in the immediate vicinity should be protected by means of brass plates or thin pieces of wood. It is better to leave the linoleum unvarnished, for it will be less slippery when wet, and will, I understand, wear better in its natural state.

CHAPTER 46: *Leaks and their Cure*

There is probably nothing more depressing to an owner than a leaky yacht. Apart from the annoyance of having to pump her out frequently in order to keep the cabin dry, it is apt to prey upon his mind. He wonders all the time whether the trouble is developing and constantly pulls up the floorboards to see how much water she has made since she was last pumped out. That sort of thing completely spoils one's pleasure, and if your boat is leaking you will be wise to put her on the hard and try to trace the leak. Locating a leak is often more difficult than stopping it, but where water goes into the boat it will come out again, and if you put her on the hard and examine her bottom carefully at low tide you will probably be able to trace the source of the trouble. If it is a bad leak, the water will spurt out in a continuous jet that is easily seen, but a small leak will only 'weep' and is not so readily located. Leaks in a carvel-built boat seldom present much difficulty as, more often than not, they are caused by defective caulking in one of the seams. The remedy in such a case, of course, is re-caulking, and if you have had no experience of such work, you will be well advised to get a shipwright to do the job, as an inexpert amateur can do a lot of harm with a caulking-iron.

The leak may be due, however, to a crack in a plank or a nail hole, and in such circumstances it can be cured by means of a tingle. It is quite a simple matter to put on a tingle, and if it is done properly a permanent cure is effected. In the days of my youth I owned many leaky boats and cured innumerable leaks with the aid of tingles. The materials I used ranged from the biscuit tins of Huntley & Palmer to sheet copper – it all depended upon what I had available and the state of my pocket, which in those days was usually pretty empty. The best material, however, is thin sheet lead, as it can be hammered with a mallet to a close fit over the leak.

Having located the leak, mark the spot and then cut a piece of sheet lead of suitable size. If it is merely a nail hole that has to be covered a patch about 3 inches square will suffice, but if it is a crack the patch should be oblong in shape and extend for about 2 inches beyond each end of the crack and be about 3 or 4 inches wide. The lead patch must be backed with brown paper and bedded down with either tar, Farotex or Ryto. Farotex and Ryto are very much the same sort of thing and I don't think there is anything to choose between them. The stuff is really intended for repairing leaky roofs, but is also excellent for boat work. It is sticky, messy stuff to handle but is very effective and can be applied to wet wood. Having placed the lead tingle over the hole or crack, so that the leak comes approximately in the middle of the patch, hammer the lead gently with a mallet until it is a close fit. Then apply a generous coat of the Ryto, or tar, over the leak to form a seating for the tingle and stick a piece of brown paper on to it. Now smear the tingle with Ryto and press it into place. Having tapped the tingle gently with the mallet, drive in copper tacks all round the edges, spaced about ½ inch apart. The copper tacks, if sharp, will easily go through the lead, but if you use sheet copper for your tingle, you will have to drill holes round the edges for the tacks. All that you now have to do is to run a sharp knife round the edges of the tingle to remove surplus brown paper, and if you have done the job properly the leak will be permanently cured.

Leaks in clinker-built boats are not so readily stopped, as they usually occur under the lands, where they are not so easily located. If the leak is under a land, the usual method is to fit a land-tingle. That is a strip of wood placed beneath the affected land, but to be effective it must be very well fitted. I have, however, often cured leaks of that sort with a lead patch, hammered to fit over the land. Of course, if the leak is caused by a split or a nail hole in the middle of the plank a lead tingle can be applied as easily as on a carvel-built boat.

Leaks in the deck or cabin-top may not be dangerous, but they are darned annoying all the same. It is not pleasant, when lying in your bunk at night, to have rain persistently dripping on your face, or wetting your blankets, but, as I pointed out in a previous chapter, the only way in which you can ensure tight decks in a small yacht is by covering them with painted canvas or linoleum. Even if you do that there is a possibility of a tiny leak developing in the cabin-top, but if you can locate the leak it is easily stopped.

Tracing a leak in the deck or cabin-top is not so easy as it sounds, as the water may drip quite a long way from the point of ingress. It will trickle along the underside of the plank until it meets some obstruction, say a beam, and will then drop. But if you dry the plank with a sponge and watch carefully, you will probably be able to locate the leak. You can then stop it at once by pressing into it a bit of Jeffrey's 'Seamflex.' This is a plastic marine glue, which never sets hard. If you rub it between your hands it will become as soft and pliable as putty. It is excellent stuff and I would advise you to keep a small tin of it on board for emergencies; it is supplied in white, yellow, black and mahogany colours. An alternative to Seamflex for stopping small leaks in the deck is plasticine, a sort of wax beloved by children for modelling purposes, which can be obtained at Woolworths.

A place where leaks commonly occur is where the coamings join the deck. If, when seated in the cabin, you look at the cabin-top while someone is walking on it, you may notice that the beams appear to give under his weight. It is really the coamings that are working, and this in course of time forces out the caulking. The trouble is easily cured. Run a strip of oiled calico, or wide tape, right round the coaming, so that it overlaps both deck and coaming. The strip must be well stuck down with varnish and then covered by a quadrant beading of hard wood.

The beading can be fixed either with copper nails or brass screws. Use plenty of varnish and the thicker it is the better. I adopted this method in several boats and in every case it completely cured the leak.

If you cannot cure the leaking propensities of an old boat by the application of tingles, the position is by no means hopeless as you can fall back on Portland cement. That however should be regarded as the last resort, for although you may by such means make her reasonably tight, she will be damned for selling purposes. None but the veriest 'mug' would buy an old boat that had been cemented, for any yachtsman of experience knows that such drastic treatment would not be adopted unless the vessel was in a pretty bad way. Many old smacks, however, are kept in work by such means and some literally sail on their concrete. In one old smack I once examined on the hard, the cement was plainly visible through holes in the planking. Mind you, a certain amount of cement is by no means a bad thing in a yacht, as it tends to keep her bilge clean and sweet. It was the practice of the late Mr. Claud Worth to have the bilge of a new yacht cemented when she was built for that reason, but I should advise any owner who does so to obtain from the builders a certificate to the effect that the cement was put in at the time of her construction, otherwise it may have a detrimental effect if the yacht is offered for sale.

Many people hold the view that when cementing a yacht it is important that the planking should be quite dry before the cement is put in. They say that if the planking is wet the cement will not adhere to the wood, which will rot. Some years ago, however, I consulted the Cement Marketing Co., on the subject and they told me that it was of no importance provided that there was no oil on the damp planks. They further informed me that to obtain the best results the cement should be mixed with three times the bulk of clean sharp sand. I followed these instructions, using their Ferrocrete, and the result was quite satisfactory, although the interior of the boat was anything but dry when I did the job.

The yacht I operated upon on that occasion was a lightly built centreplate craft of 5 tons, which worked and leaked badly when sailed hard to windward. I could no doubt have cured her of that defect by having some additional floors put in, but as she was an old boat I did not care to go to the expense. I therefore cemented her bottom up to the bunks with concrete about 2 inches thick, and her bottom, thus reinforced, worked no more.

A Yarn

Snipe's Trial Trip

Having bought *Snipe* I had to get her round to the Crouch and, as the weather seemed to be set fair, I thought I might as well take a holiday and have a short cruise before bringing her home. I invited Louis, who had often sailed with me in *Wave*, to accompany me, and he was fortunately able to get away from the City for a week. The alterations which I described in the last chapter had not then been carried out and so we had to take a good deal of luggage with us. When we arrived at Ipswich and had collected all our gear into a pile on the platform, we looked at it with dismay. It included two suit-cases, two large kit-bags full of blankets, a compass in a box, a lead and line, a 2-gall. stone jar for water, a case of charts, two Primus stoves, a kettle, frying-pan and saucepan, and various other packages. I still had to collect a kedge and warp that I had ordered by post. How to convey all these impedimenta to Pin Mill was something of a problem. To take it by water seemed outside the sphere of practical politics, for it was a considerable distance from the station to the steamer, and as the latter merely slowed down to drop passengers into a ferry boat at Pin Mill, I thought we should not be very popular if we caused delay by the transhipment of so many packages. So we ruled out the steamer and decided to go by road.

There were, of course, no motor buses in those days and we had some difficulty in procuring a conveyance, but eventually managed to hire a rather decrepit old four-wheeled cab, in which we set out for Pin Mill with our luggage piled high on top. The poor old horse seemed to find the load rather more than he liked and our journey was a slow one. When we came to a hill we had to get out and walk, and more than an hour was occupied in covering 6 miles.

When we arrived, we found that *Snipe* was lying at moorings on the outskirts of the anchorage, near the Cat House, so leaving our luggage at the hard, we put off in the little Berthon dinghy, with the idea of bringing the yacht down to a berth nearer the causeway. The little collapsible boat, both from its shape and colour, looked rather like half a walnut shell, but it carried us bravely. It had no thwarts, the man rowing sitting on a small cork cushion, and with the weight thus carried low, it proved a buoyant little craft. When we reached *Snipe* and climbed on board, Louis at once went into the cabin and exclaimed:

"Golly, what a ship! Why! look, Skipper, I can sit up with my hat on."

The accommodation certainly did seem palatial after the close quarters to which we had been accustomed in *Wave*. We wasted no time in getting her under way. Slipping the mooring and unrolling the jib, we dropped down nearly to the hard, but not knowing the river, I stood in too close and *Snipe* took the ground. The tide was ebbing fast and our efforts to push her off proving unsuccessful, it was obvious that we should not be able to get away that afternoon. Still, it did not matter much as we had a deal to do in the way of getting things stowed and buying food.

Having laid out the anchor, we proceeded to get our gear on board. This took a good many journeys in the little dinghy and by the time it was all on board, *Snipe* had taken a pronounced list. Seeing that there would be no comfort until she floated, we decided to go ashore and do our shopping and then have tea at the Alma Inn. So we walked up to Chelmondiston and bought bread, meat, butter and various other perishable stores. On returning we found that *Snipe* had dried out and it would be some hours before we could get on board. So we had tea at the inn and afterwards played billiards on an old half-size table. It was the most curious table on which I ever played, as the balls had a natural bias towards the pockets, and we made some prodigious breaks. One might have thought that it had been specially designed for use in a pub. to encourage rapid scoring, but as a matter of fact no charge was made here for playing on it.

Snipe was not afloat until after eight o'clock, and we then went on board and ran down to a berth below the hard, among the barges, bringing up by a charming wood, in which the nightingales were singing fit to bust their little hearts. Then we had to stow away our gear and cook steak and potatoes. It was consequently nearly 10 p.m. before we had our dinner. After we had finished our meal and washed up, we sat in the cockpit and smoked. It was a clear moonlit night and under such conditions Pin Mill presented a scene of enchanting loveliness which we were loath to leave, and it was not until the clock at Orwell Park chimed the hour of midnight that we turned in.

We found the canvas cots most comfortable; so much so, indeed, that we did not wake the next morning until after nine o'clock, but as there was no wind and the tide flooding, it did not matter much. After a swim we dallied with our breakfast and watched the vessels passing up the river to the docks at Ipswich, for even in those days Ipswich was quite an important grain port.

Presently a light breeze sprang up and at high water we got under way. At first our progress down the river was slow, as the wind off the shore was impeded by the trees, and we came to the conclusion that the Orwell, despite its beauty, provided very poor sailing in its upper reaches. We did little more than drift through Butterman's Bay, where a large four-masted barque lay at the buoys discharging cargo into barges. On rounding Collimer Point, we found a fine true breeze in Sea Reach and had a slashing sail nearly out to the Cork Lightship. Then we turned back, having decided to find a berth for the night in Felixstowe Dock. I was delighted with *Snipe*'s sailing qualities as she seemed to have a good turn of speed and was as handy as a top. I had never been in Felixstowe Dock before, and when we sailed in I did not know where to berth, but a man on board a rather disreputable-looking yawl of about 35 tons, which was lying next the quay, invited us to moor alongside of her. Luffing head to wind, *Snipe* just carried her way into the appointed berth, coming alongside so gently that, as Louis said, she would not have crushed an egg. Having moored fore and aft, we put out fenders and congratulated ourselves on having secured such a comfortable berth.

Our neighbour proved to be the late Mr. Frank Cowper and the yacht was named *Zayda*. She was an old-fashioned vessel with straight stem and flat counter, fitted with a fidded topmast and long bowsprit. Mr. Cowper was, as usual, alone, which accounted for the rather neglected appearance of his yacht, for it is a physical impossibility for one man to sail and keep a vessel of such size in smart condition. It was sufficiently marvellous that he was able to sail a heavily sparred 35-tonner single-handed and, as he told me, he did not care a hang about 'spit and polish.'

After dinner Mr. Cowper invited us on board, and as we sat smoking in the saloon of *Zayda* he told us of some of his adventures in *Lady Hervey*, an even larger yacht, in which he had cruised all round the British Isles, entering almost every river and creek en route, to obtain data for his well-known series of Sailing Tours. When we mentioned that we were going to try and find our way into Walton Creek, at the back of the Naze, the next day, he said that he was going there himself and would pilot us. We were jolly glad of this, for in those days there was nothing to guide one through the intricate channel but the 'look of the land,' as they say, and if you don't know what the land looks like – well, where are you?

This channel, at the back of the Pye Sand, is very narrow in parts and extremely tricky, but nowadays it has been rendered quite simple by the series of small buoys which the Walton and Frinton Yacht Club instituted some years ago. In the 'nineties the only landmarks we had to guide us were a dairy house and a clump of bushes, which were difficult to locate even if you knew where to look for them, and so one had to trust mainly to the lead to keep one off the sands.

The next morning, when we left the dock, *Zayda*, with her big spread of canvas, soon took the lead and we followed in her wake, gradually being left farther astern. With a leading wind we soon crossed Dovercourt Bay and then we saw *Zayda* run ashore just outside the entrance to the creek, and as the tide had started to ebb, she stayed there. As we approached, Mr. Cowper rowed to meet us in his dinghy to warn us. It was quite unnecessary, with *Zayda* making such a fine mark, but very sporting of him all the same. We got into the creek without any difficulty, and as there are no obstructions to pick one up when once inside, were soon anchored just by the Twizzle, another creek running at a right angle to Walton Creek. *Zayda* dried out and did not get in until late at night.

It would be difficult to imagine a snugger berth than this at the back of the Naze, for you can bring up under a weather shore under almost any conditions, as if the wind is blowing straight up or down Walton Creek you can lie in the Twizzle. There is a hard close by, on which you can land and walk along the promenade into Walton, about a mile distant, where there are plenty of good shops, if you want to replenish the larder. Nowadays, there is another hard a little way above the old one at the Foundry and also one at the club in the town, which can be reached in the dinghy at about two hours flood.

After lunch, we went ashore to spend the afternoon and do some shopping. As the water jar was nearly empty, we took it with us, and on landing I asked a boy where we could obtain water. He said that he could get some for us, so I gave him sixpence and told him to put the jar in the dinghy when he had filled it. The following morning at breakfast, we discovered that the little devil had filled the jar from the creek and so we had to go without tea and later go ashore for fresh water.

Walton, of course, is a popular seaside resort and vast crowds of people throng there during the season, but this backwater behind the Naze is deserted by all but yachtsmen, and of them one sees but few during the week. The anchorage is consequently extraordinarily quiet and you can go ashore and leave your yacht, feeling confident that neither she nor the dinghy will be interfered with during your absence. The town itself is neither beautiful nor interesting, and we decided, after spending a night in the creek, to go to Aldeburgh.

As we first had to go ashore for water, it was nearly ten o'clock before we were ready to get under way. The flood-tide had then about an hour and a half to run, but we had a fair wind. We rather welcomed the foul tide as we thought that if we had the bad luck to get aground outside the creek it would enable us to refloat the boat more easily, and in view of our very limited knowledge of the channel such a contingency was more than likely. For the first time we carried the dinghy on board, I found that I could pull her out quite easily with one hand, as she was so light. Laying her across the cockpit coamings, we folded her in a few seconds and then passed her down into the cabin. Having transferred one of the bunk cushions to the other bunk, we placed the dinghy on that side, lashing her to the cot-frame to keep her steady. The absence of the dinghy astern made a noticeable difference in the speed of the yacht and in future I always carried the Berthon on board when making a passage.

With a nice breeze aft, we were soon outside the creek and, as it was getting on for high water and we took frequent soundings, we managed to reach the Pye End buoy without misadventure. We then had nothing to worry us, as at that state of tide there was plenty of water for *Snipe* over everything. The tide turned when we were near the Beach End bell buoy and as the ebb gathered strength our speed materially increased. Soon we were passing Bawdsey Haven, which is the mouth of the River Deben, and noticed a big house standing out prominently on the point, making a fine seamark. This mansion, which I subsequently learnt was the residence of Sir Cuthbert Quilter, seemed to stand upon a rocky cliff, which surprised us as rocks are seldom seen on this part of the coast. Some years later, when I came to visit Felixstowe Ferry, the village on the other side of the Haven, I was told that this rocky cliff was artificial, the stones having all been transported there. Nevertheless, the effect was very imposing and the rock garden one of the most beautiful I have ever seen.

It was a glorious May morning, and as we sailed over the sparkling sunlit sea we felt that it was good to be alive. The breeze held steady and true and with the spinnaker set we travelled fast. There was just enough sea to make sailing exhilarating and *Snipe*, rolling slightly, ran before the wind as steadily as a train. Soon we were passing the Bawdsey seamark, a tall tower which can be seen for many miles, and then had but 6 or 7 miles to go before we came to Orford Haven, or, as it is more commonly called, Shingle Street.

We arrived off the Haven in the early afternoon and hove-to to await the pilot, as these are treacherous waters. We had no pilot jack, so lowered our burgee half-mast, a signal recognized by the pilots as indicating that their services are needed. We waited for more than an hour but nothing happened, and I was beginning to think of trying to get in without a pilot when we saw a white boat coming out of the Haven under a lug sail.

As we waited, I studied the entrance through my glasses and it certainly seemed a weird place. Great piles of shingle were the prominent feature, and everywhere, as far as I could see, was broken water, which perhaps is not surprising as the ebb at spring tides runs out of the river at 7 knots and meets the coastal ebb.

In a few minutes the pilot came alongside and making his boat fast astern jumped on board. He told us that he had seen our signal, but the ebb was then running too hard for us to get in. Even now, he said, he could not take us right in, but would put us in a berth where we could lie safely until the tide had slackened sufficiently for us to proceed up the river.

As we crept along the edge of the steep-to bank, the motion of the boat caused the shingle to fall in. Even on a fine day like this there was a good deal of broken water, and in heavy weather it must be a hell of a place. The pilot told us that in bad weather they could not go out and had to direct vessels from the shore with flags. Keeping within a few feet of the shingle bank, where the tide was comparatively slack, we managed to get just inside the entrance, but when we met the full force of the tide we began to go stern first and had no alternative but to anchor. We gave her a big scope of chain and the anchor held, but *Snipe* rode uneasily in the strong tide, sheering about wildly. Pocketing his fee of five bob and an extra bob as a tip, the pilot left us, having given us directions how to proceed when the tide turned.

We then got the dinghy out of the cabin and launched it. As she lay astern, she cocked her nose out of water just as if she were being towed by a fast motor-launch, so strong was the tide. As the wind had fallen rather light, it seemed likely that we should have to wait some time before we could proceed, so we had tea and then decided to go ashore. We had but a few yards to row, but even so were swept down some distance before we reached the beach. When the dinghy grated on the shingle, I jumped out with the painter on to the steep-to bank. To my dismay the shingle slid from under my feet and I sprawled full length. I could feel myself sliding back into the water and it was only by a great effort with hands and feet that I managed to save myself. Crawling cautiously for a few yards over the treacherous shingle, I found firmer ground and was able to stand up and hold the painter taut for Louis to cling to as he landed.

As we looked back we thought that Shingle Street was a very good name for the place as there was shingle everywhere – shingle on the shore and great mounds of it rising out of the seething water. The River Ore, of which this was the mouth, is also very strange as for some 9 miles it runs parallel with the coast, being separated from the sea by a bank of shingle, so narrow in places that one could throw a stone over it. At Aldeburgh the river turns at a right angle and runs inland, being navigable on the tide as far as Iken. Curiously enough, it is at Slaughdon Quay, just by Aldeburgh, that the shingle bank is at its narrowest, and it seems extraordinary that the river has never broken through there.

We walked towards a row of cottages and there met the Coastguard officer, with whom we stopped to chat. He seemed pleased at finding someone to talk to and invited us into his cottage, where he entertained us hospitably with bottled beer. He told us many strange things about the Haven, which he said was a desolate spot in the winter, as we could well believe. Every change of wind, he said, affected the entrance, and the channel frequently altered. It had not changed materially for some months, he remarked, but there were indications that it would soon shift farther north. His forecast proved correct, for when I sailed past a few weeks later, I saw that the entrance was fully half a mile farther north, and where we had entered on this occasion was a great mound of shingle, perhaps 30ft. high. On leaving him, our friend half-filled the dinghy with vegetables from his garden, which kept us supplied for the remainder of our cruise.

When we returned on board the tide had turned, so we got under way and proceeded up the river. The Ore, or Alde, is a good sailing river as the

Orford Ness lighthouse

tide only runs fiercely near the mouth and there are no mud-flats of any consequence to trap the unwary. About 3 miles from the mouth, the channel is
split into two by Havergate Island. There is plenty of water in both channels,
but we took the southern one as being the more direct route, and so came to
the pretty village of Orford, with its fine old castle, where we brought up for
the night.

Some time before, a friend had remarked to me, "If you ever go to Orford
make a point of dining at the Crown and Castle, as George Hunt always does
you well," and remembering this I decided to have dinner ashore for a change.
So after we had stowed away and put up the riding-light, we landed and made
our way to the Crown and Castle Hotel. Apparently George Hunt "did us
well" on this occasion, for it is recorded in the log: "Dined at the Crown and
Castle, where they gave us a dinner fit for the gods: soup, boiled salmon, loin
of lamb, asparagus, sweets and cheese, for half a crown a head."

After dinner we sat and 'talked boats' with Mr. Hunt, who was himself a
yachtsman, until nearly closing time, and then returned on board and turned
in.

We got up at about eight the next morning and after a swim and breakfast
went ashore again to see the sights, as we thought it would be a pity to leave
Orford without inspecting the Castle. Only the keep remains, but that is in a
good state of preservation. It is very old, but how old I cannot say, as we were
told that no reliable record of its origin can be traced. One enters by a door on
the first floor of the great round tower, of which the walls are said to be 20ft.

thick, approached by a flight of external steps. There are four storeys and on the third is a furnished room, fitted up by the Marquess of Hertford when he owned the property. At the time of which I write the Hunt dinner was held in this room, which is also a favourite resort of picnic parties. This Marquess of Hertford, by the way, is said to have been the original of Thackeray's Marquess of Steyne in Vanity Fair.

Climbing to the top of the tower, we had a wonderful view of the North Sea and surrounding country. Across the bank of shingle that separates the river from the sea, which is here about a mile wide, Ordfordness Lighthouse stood out prominently, and inland was the Manor of Sudbourne, where the Marquess of Hertford formerly resided and George IV received news of the death of Princess Charlotte. On our way back to the Quay, we looked at the picturesque old church, which dates from the eighth century. The chancel is separated from the nave and lies in ruins, while a portion of the tower has fallen.

Returning on board, we got under way, bound for Aldeburgh. It was a hot day with but the lightest of airs from south-east, but we had no great distance to go. We had not proceeded very far when we ran aground on a mud-flat. Attempts to push her off with a sweep proving unavailing, I laid out the kedge with the dinghy. I found it rather a tricky job in the little sharp-sterned Berthon, but by slinging the anchor over the stern, secured by a line, managed to drop it safely. With the aid of the kedge, we soon hauled *Snipe* off and resumed our journey, but the wind had by then completely died away and there was a flat calm. By taking it in turns to row with the sweep, we managed to save our tide up to Aldeburgh, where we brought up off Slaughdon Quay, close to a cluster of fishermen's cottages. This proved a nice snug berth, with a landing hard near by and only a short walk from the town of Aldeburgh.

Nowadays, Aldeburgh is a pleasant seaside resort, of which the principal attraction is a fine golf course, but in the Middle Ages it was an important town. The chief object of interest is the old Moot Hall, dating from the fifteenth century. It formerly stood in the centre of the town, but is now on the beach, a fact that brings home to one the serious nature of the coast erosion in East Anglia.

Aldeburgh seemed a very pleasant little place and we should have liked to stay there for a few days, but time was slipping away and our holiday drawing to a close. We decided therefore to make a start for home the next morning and with that end in view laid in a fresh stock of provisions and filled up with water.

After breakfast the next morning, we beat down the river almost to the mouth, where we brought up just by the bathing-place of the Colonial Agricultural College. We had a good berth there, although the tide ran rather hard on the ebb. After a late lunch, I set up the rigging and did various odd jobs about the boat, which kept me engaged until tea-time. In the evening we went ashore and arranged with the pilot to take us out the next morning and also visited our friend the Coastguard officer.

We got under way the next morning at 10 a.m. and shortly afterwards, having picked up the pilot, left the Haven. The fine weather still continued, although the wind was foul for Felixstowe Dock, whither we were bound. It was, however, a nice sailing breeze and as the tide had not yet turned we should have the whole of the flood to help us on our way. Moreover, as we had hitherto been favoured with fair winds, I rather welcomed the prospect of a good beat to windward, so that I could thoroughly try out the boat on that point of sailing.

Having dropped the pilot, we hauled in the sheets and brought *Snipe* on to the wind. As the ebb had only about half an hour to run, I decided to make a long board off the land in order to get the full benefit of the flood when it started to make. There was plenty of water for *Snipe* over the Cutler Sands even at low tide, so we sailed on the starboard tack until close to the South Cutler buoy, some 4 or 5 miles from the land. When we started the sea was comparatively smooth, but the breeze freshened on the young flood and knocked up a considerable sea for a little ship. Heeled nearly to the covering board, *Snipe* sailed splendidly, although the showers of spray that came aft from her weather bow compelled us to put on our oilskins. The way in which she sailed over the seas imparted much of that sense of power that one gets from larger vessels, and I began to feel a confidence in the little ship that I never after lost.

When near the South Cutler, we put her about on to the port tack, which was the more favourable, and were pleased to find that Bawdsey Haven now lay well under our lee bow. As we drew in to the land we smoothened our water, so, while I steered, Louis opened a tin of sardines, and we had lunch. When we went about again, we were half a mile to windward of Bawdsey Haven and with our next board out to sea, weathered the Cork Lightship.

Our next board towards the land took us over the Platters, where we found a hollow confused sea. As it was now about half flood there was water everywhere for a little craft like *Snipe*, but it was a wet trip. She sloshed through the tops of the steep seas in great style, her foredeck running with water, but nothing green came on board. We had to make one more longish board out to sea and then could lay Landguard Point. An hour later, we entered Felixstowe Dock, where we made fast to a buoy at the top of the dock, taking a stern line ashore. Despite our oilskins, we had got pretty wet while crossing the Platters shoal, but our clothing soon dried in the hot sun, and after tea we went ashore and played billiards at the Pier Hotel.

When we turned out the following morning we found a cold grey day with a northerly wind, which I welcomed, although regretting the absence of the sun. I had a healthy respect for the Wallet, as the experience I had there in *Wave* was still fresh in my memory. A northerly breeze would enable us to reach through, and with the wind off shore we could expect to find smooth water. We were both due back at our work on the following Monday morning and, as it was now Saturday, we only had two days' holiday left. We therefore planned to go to West Mersea this day and make the passage home to Fambridge on Sunday.

It was a cheerless morning and we both shirked bathing. For one thing the temperature of the air was not exactly alluring, and then there was a filthy scum on the surface of the water. We agreed that it was not sufficiently tempting and contented ourselves with what Louis called a 'wash and brush up' with the aid of a bucket. I was anxious to get away as soon as possible, as there was a destroyer alongside the quay taking in coal and *Snipe* was receiving a liberal coat of dust. I wanted to get out into the harbour and give the decks a good wash-down with clean seawater to remove the harbour stains.

But we had not got up very early, and by the time we had had breakfast and stowed the dinghy in the cabin it was just on ten o'clock. The ebb, however, would run for about two hours yet, longer than we should need it, so as soon as we got outside the dock we hove-to and gave the boat a good scrub-down. When we had made *Snipe* respectably clean, we let the jib draw and laid our course for the Naze. As is often the case with a northerly wind, visibility was extraordinarily good and the Naze and its tower stood out so sharply that they looked quite close, although really about 7 miles away. There was a nice little breeze and with the spinnaker set *Snipe* made capital progress, sailing in company with quite a fleet of barges, with which we managed to keep up. We reached the Naze soon after eleven and there parted company from the barges, which headed towards the Wallet Spitway, evidently being bound for the Thames.

After rounding the Naze we had to shift the spinnaker on to the bowsprit-end, but it continued to pull the boat along grandly and, with the flood tide now making, we began to travel fast. We covered the 6 miles between Walton and Clacton piers in just an hour, and as the conditions were so perfect, we decided to cut out West Mersea and carry on to the Crouch. We therefore began to leave the shore and make for the Knoll buoy. As we lost the protection of the land the water got rougher, and when we opened out the estuaries of the Blackwater and Colne we found quite a big sea.

We passed the Knoll buoy at half-past one and entered the Crouch at about 3 p.m. Then the breeze freshened, causing us to hand the bowsprit spinnaker and set the working jib. This change, however, did not seem to make much difference to the speed of the boat and we reached up the river at a rare bat. It was just after four o'clock when we brought up in Cliff Reach for the night. We had sailed 35 miles and thought it enough for one day.

A Yarn

Having put the dinghy overboard, we boiled some eggs and had a good tea, for which we were more than ready, having had only a hunk of bread and cheese since breakfast. Later, we landed on the sea-wall and went for a walk to get an appetite for dinner. We did not stay ashore very long, however, as it was miserably cold and began to rain. The weather was obviously breaking up at last and we felt jolly glad that we had come straight back to the Crouch and not put into Mersea. The wind was backing and piping up and when, on returning on board, I tapped the glass, I found that it had fallen three-tenths of an inch since the morning. But we were back in our home waters now and did not care a hoot if it snowed, as they say. That evening, as we sat playing cribbage in *Snipe*'s cosy cabin and heard the wind moaning in the rigging, we were even more thankful to be so near home.

When I looked out the next morning at about 8 a.m. I found that it was blowing the best part of a gale from the westward and the glass had fallen a further half-inch during the night. In such circumstances bed seemed the best place, so I turned in again and slept until nearly eleven. We came to the conclusion that it was then about time that we got up and had breakfast, but on investigation found that the larder was nearly as bare as Mother Hubbard's. That was a curious meal – a sort of combination of breakfast and lunch. By abstaining from shaving we had just enough water to make tea, and the rest of the menu comprised one egg, which we scrambled and divided between us, the scrapings of the jam and marmalade pots and the last remnant of the cheese. The only bread we had was the top of a loaf that had been left at the bottom of the tin and was probably five days old; it was still sweet, but died hard.

Having staved off the pangs of hunger, we rolled down a big reef in the mainsail and set the small jib. As we were on a lee shore, we sailed out the anchor and then started to beat up to Fambridge. We only had about 5 miles to go but it was a thrilling sail. In the harder squalls *Snipe* was laid in to the coamings, but she travelled fast and handled to perfection. Before we reached the anchorage we were both wet through, but that did not matter as the cruise was over and we had our dry shore clothes to change into.

And so we brought *Snipe* home, after one of the jolliest little cruises I can remember. She had more than fulfilled my anticipations as she had proved a fine sea boat, with a good turn of speed and a most comfortable little cabin.

As my summer holiday was due in little more than a month, I at once started on the improvements referred to in the last chapter. The new sails were ordered and so promptly delivered that I was able to get the mainsail nicely stretched, and when the eagerly awaited date arrived everything was ready for the cruise ❧

Part VII: SEAMANSHIP

CHAPTER 47: *Learning Seamanship*

Can seamanship be learnt from books? That is a question often asked and I think most yachtsmen would answer it in the negative, for it is very certain that you can't handle a yacht efficiently unless you have had practical experience. All the same, a lot of the theory of sailing can be acquired from books and also the names and use of the various ropes that form the running gear. In seamanship theory and practice must walk hand in hand, for the one is complement to the other. If it is true that you can't learn to sail a yacht without practice, it is equally true that in the absence of theory you have nothing to practise.

I would advise the beginner therefore to get a good book by a reliable author and study it closely. Read it as you did, or were supposed to do, your text-books at school, making notes of things that strike you as of outstanding importance. But if your study is to prove of value the book must be a really practical one. Ask some experienced yachting friend to advise you in its choice, or if you don't know one, write to one of the yachting journals for advice on the subject. The editors of all our yachting journals are practical yachtsmen of wide experience and will be pleased to help you.

As you read, you will probably say to yourself, "What is all the song and dance about? It all seems quite easy and simple." So it may on paper, but things are not always what they seem. The tides, for instance, are important factors, as also is the behaviour of the vessel under varying conditions of wind and water. Such matters can only be learnt from practical experience. The same applies to navigation. On looking at a chart, the beginner may think it all delightfully simple-just going from one buoy to the next and as easy as walking down Regent Street. But a chart gives a bird's-eye view of a wide tract of sea and all of the buoys and marks are plainly visible to the eye. In practice, however, it is very different. More often than not when you come to a buoy the next is not visible and you have to steer a compass course, making due allowance for the set of the tide and leeway; or you may have to beat to windward. You will see, therefore, that there are many things that can only be learnt afloat, and the question arises, how can you obtain the necessary practical experience?

Well, I can suggest three ways: (1) By employing a professional to teach you; (2) by sailing for a time with friends; (3) by buying a boat straight away and working out your own salvation. Let us consider these different ways.

As I discussed the employment of a paid hand in Part 1, I need say no more, except that even at the best your progress would not be very rapid. You see, it would be against the man's own interests to teach you much, for he would know that as soon as you had learnt sufficient to do without him, he would lose his job. Moreover, it would be a very expensive way in which to learn.

Sailing as a guest with friends would be better, if you have any willing to take you, but you would probably only be invited from time to time, unless you could fix up a working partnership, of which I have something to say in Part I. Even then I doubt if you would learn very much, as the owner, being skipper, would be responsible for the handling of the yacht and you would never be called upon to act on your own initiative. I don't suppose you would learn much more than steering and tending the headsail sheets, although you would no doubt become an expert in washing-up after meals and kindred domestic chores.

If I favour the third method, it is not merely because that was the way in which I learnt myself, but because many of our most prominent yachtsmen acquired their knowledge in a similar manner. It is a hard school but an extremely efficient one, for lessons learnt from practical experience are not readily forgotten. An outstanding example was that great amateur seaman R. T. McMullen, the pioneer of single-handed cruising. In recording his early experiences in the little 3-ton *Leo*, he wrote:

> I could not get under way, or go in among the ships to bring up, without having a taste of brimstone in the mouth from excessive anxiety. I envied the bargemen their coolness and evident self-possession, and looked forward to the time when I should feel the same confidence. My plan was to persevere in sailing by day or night in all weathers, and never let want of confidence stand in the way. In this manner, getting into scrapes and getting out of them, I learnt more of practical sailing in a few months than I should have learnt in several years if I had hired a man to take the lead in everything.

Like most beginners, McMullen got into every conceivable kind of scrape, such as running aground and getting athwart the bows of another vessel. One mishap almost cost him his sight. Having neglected to mouse the sister-hooks of the mainsheet of the lugsail, one came adrift and caught him in the eye as the boat was in stays. He was so badly injured that he had to seek the aid of watermen to sail the yacht home, and his eye was out of service for nearly a month.

That his progress in seamanship was rapid will be gathered from the fact that a few years later he sailed that same *Leo* from the Thames to Penzance and back. Under date of August 10, 1855, the following entry is recorded in the harbour books at Penzance: "The Leo, 3 tons, McMullen master and owner, 6d.," the sum being paid by the Harbour Master and entered as a curiosity. It is interesting to recall that it was for that trip McMullen invented the sail now known as a spinnaker. Well, that was how McMullen learnt, and now let us see how that other famous yachtsman, Claud Worth, acquired the rudiments of seamanship. As his father looked askance at his sailing ambitions and would not buy him a boat, Worth, at the age of twelve, decided to build one himself. He tells us in his book *Yacht Cruising,*

> She was an eight-foot canvas boat. The keel, stem and sternpost were made from pieces of deal fencing rail, and were halved together and screwed. The ribs were of green ash, because it was found that these would bend better than the dry wood. A large dipping lug was made from an old bed sheet, and she was launched on the Great South Holland 'drain.' With a younger brother and sister as ballast, she sailed quite well with the wind abeam.

A few years later he converted a 22-foot ship's boat, in which he and two friends cruised from the Wash to the Solent. "As a youngster," he wrote, "I ran appalling risks from crazy boats and inadequate gear, because no one could understand that one must sail in anything rather than not at all."

If a youngster approaches sailing in that spirit, nothing will stop him. He will get a boat of some sort by hook or crook and either become a fine sailor or a corpse – as the fates decree.

Given a suitable boat – I discuss that question in Part I – I am sure that the best and quickest way of learning seamanship is to teach yourself. As McMullen very truly said, it is by getting into scrapes and getting out of them that one learns, for one has to use one's brains and act on one's own initiative.

Should you run your ship aground you will have to devise means of re-floating her. If you succeed you will have definitely learnt something, and even if you fail your endeavour has not been altogether wasted, for you will know that the plan you tried was futile, knowledge that will prove invaluable on future occasions. Indeed, I am not sure that the novice does not learn more from his failures than from his successes.

But you must not leave it there if you would profit by such incidents. You should try and find out just what you did wrong. If you can't, explain the circumstances to some experienced yachtsman and ask him how you were at fault. He will not mind discussing it with you in the least, for the average yachtsman thinks that the next best thing to sailing yachts is to talk about them. But be sure that the man you select as your mentor is really experienced and not just a 'windbag.'

If you elect to teach yourself, be content with a comparatively small craft, for if you allow your ambition to run away with you and buy a yacht of some size, the lees of your courage may run out when it comes to getting her under way. That happened to a man I knew years ago who bought a 14-ton yawl. When at home he had visions of cruising round the coast in her, but when on board he had not the pluck even to try to get her under way. After some months he and a friend, who knew no more about it than himself, did get her under way, but piled her up before they had gone a quarter of a mile. Having spent a miserable night in the heavily listing yacht, they were ignominiously rescued by a local waterman and taken back to their mooring. That was the end of his sailing activities, for he sold her at a considerable loss.

The yacht in which you first adventure should not be more than 4 tons and rigged as simply as possible. Such a craft will provide reasonably comfortable accommodation and you will not be afraid to get her under way. If you aspire to something larger, it will be time enough to gratify your desire when you have learnt to sail the smaller boat with some degree of confidence.

If you confine your activities to the sheltered waters of a tidal river and give other craft a wide berth, you will not come to any harm. The worst that is likely to befall you is to run aground occasionally. Should that happen you will be in no danger, although you will probably have an extremely uncomfortable time, for a yacht ashore is not the sort of place that one would select for a rest cure. But there is one thing I must impress upon you. You should have your mooring laid on the outskirt of the anchorage and well clear of other craft. Not only is this wise from your own point of view, as you will then have plenty of room when getting under way and bringing up, but it is a positive duty you owe to other users of the anchorage. If you had your mooring in the thick of the vessels, you would be a menace to the safety of those in your immediate neighbourhood, to say nothing of your own ship. It is true that by having a berth on the fringe of the anchorage you will probably be a long way from the landing hard, but that can't be helped and the rowing exercise will do you a power of good, as they say.

CHAPTER 48: *Preparation*

More than a little of the success or otherwise of a cruise depends upon preliminary preparation and you will be well advised thoroughly to overhaul your little ship before starting your holiday. First make sure that her bottom is perfectly clean, for the presence of weed or nuns, or even slime, will seriously mar her sailing qualities. If you examine her in still water you will be able to see the bottom for a foot or two below the surface and if she is quite clean as far as you can see, you can safely assume that she is also clean where you cannot see, at any rate so far as weed is concerned. Seaweed can only flourish where there is a certain amount of light and consequently first makes its appearance on a boat near the waterline. It is true that nuns have an affection for the keel and garboards, but in my experience anti-fouling composition repels their attentions longer than it does weed and, if the bottom near the waterline is free from weed, it is not likely that there will be nuns on the lower part of the hull to any appreciable extent. If you notice that the bottom is a little slimy, you may be tempted to say to yourself, "Oh, it's only a little slime and not worth bothering about." But believe me it is, for it is a sign that the anti-fouling composition is beginning to lose its effect and in a short time the yacht may be filthy. To start on a holiday cruise in a dirty boat is foolish, for the presence of foreign matter on her bottom will make her sluggish and unhandy. And it will get worse from day to day, probably causing you so much annoyance that you will put her ashore for a scrub. That will entail the sacrifice of a whole day out of your all-too-short holiday. If, therefore, you are not quite confident that she is perfectly clean, have her scrubbed and a fresh coat of anti-fouling composition applied before you start.

The rigging and gear should also be submitted to a close scrutiny. If the shrouds are unduly slack, set them up, but not as taut as fiddle-strings, for it is better to allow the mast to take the initial strain. All halyards, sheets and purchase falls should be examined and replaced if of doubtful soundness. Make sure that strop seizings are sound, and re-whip any rope-ends that need it. If you notice a loose whipping, remove it and put on a fresh one, and if any of the sails requires repairing, have it attended to. Possibly the head of the mainsail has stretched a little, and if that be the case, take up the slack and re-lace it. See that the sheaves of the blocks are thoroughly lubricated, and if you carry a gaff mainsail, grease the leather on the jaws with tallow. Lubricate all moving metal parts, not forgetting the cable roller on the stemhead. Attentions of this sort, although individually trivial, make for general efficiency and will enhance the success and pleasure of your cruise.

If you have an auxiliary engine, make sure that it is in thorough working order, for a motor you cannot start is mere junk, occupying valuable space. An hour devoted to overhauling the engine will repay you later. Clean it up and renew the oil in the crank-case. Thoroughly clean the points of the plugs and make sure that the gaps are correct for efficient sparking. See that the petrol and oil tanks are full and that you have an ample spare supply of fuel and also a couple of new plugs.

Make sure that there are no small leaks in your decks or cabin-top, for there is nothing more irritating than a steady drip of water on your face on a wet night. If it does not drip on your face it will wet your blankets. A small leak can be temporarily stopped by pressing plasticine in it – if you can find the leak, which is not always easy. I always carry a lump of plasticine for that purpose, although I have not had to use it for some years. If the hot sun has cracked the paint film over the seams of the decks, apply a fresh coat of paint, and make sure that it is thoroughly dry and set hard before you walk on it.

Then turn your attention to the stowage question. First sort out the contents of the lockers and dump overboard that accumulation of useless junk that you are sure to have collected, such as shackles without pins, broken sister-hooks, bits of rotten rope, rusty nails and small pieces of soap. Few of us are like Davies, in *The Riddle of the Sands*, who had a mania for throwing things overboard. Generally, when we replace a broken fitting, we keep the old one with the idea that it may come in useful some day; but it seldom does and there is not room in a little ship for old junk.

Having done this, re-stow the lockers, putting the things that are most frequently used in the most accessible places. If you stow the lockers methodically, you will be surprised at the amount of space you have available for the extra stores you will need during your cruise. And in that connection I would remark that most yachtsmen take far more stuff away with them than they ever use. Particularly does this apply to clothing. Some men who have sailed with me have brought away an equipment more suitable for a honeymoon than a short cruise in a small yacht and their superfluous luggage has been an infernal nuisance. You should take, not what you think you might want, but as little as you can possibly do with.

Carry as much drinking water as you can conveniently stow and use it with the greatest economy, as getting a fresh supply is often very troublesome. If you intend to cruise round the coast you will need very little in the way of tinned provisions as you will be able to replenish the larder at frequent intervals. Carry just one or two tins of meat and if circumstances compel you to use one, replace it the next time you go ashore. You should, however, keep a good supply of eggs and bacon on board. A dish of eggs and bacon makes a darned sight more satisfying meal than anything out of a tin, and bacon will keep for quite a long time even in hot weather.

It is my practice when starting on a cruise to take with me a leg of lamb and a piece of boiled streaky bacon, which I have cooked at home, and thus I do not have to do much in the way of cooking for some days. The joint can be eaten cold for a couple of days and subsequently hashed, whilst the bacon is useful both for breakfast and lunch. See that you have a good supply of methylated spirit for starting the Primus stove and a few spare prickers. Bread, if stored in a biscuit tin, is quite eatable when a week old.

The secret of successful cruising is working the tides. If there is sufficient wind to drive your boat through the water at a speed of 5 knots and you have a 3-knot tide in your favour, your speed over the bottom will be 8 knots; but if the tide is against you, it will be reduced to 2 knots. I am assuming, of course, that the wind is fair; if it were foul and you had to beat to windward, your progress, if any, in the latter case would be negligible. You will see how extremely important it is that you should work the tides. Indeed, your life afloat must be governed by the tide table rather than the clock. You must get under way when the tide serves, no matter at what ungodly hour that may be, have your meals when you feel hungry and go to bed when you feel tired, but such departures from the conventional are not the least fascinating features of cruising in little ships.

When cruising alone, a certain amount of preparation is desirable before starting on a passage. You should study your journey overnight, making notes of the buoys and landmarks you will pass, the courses you may have to steer, the set of the tide at different points and hours and of any other information you may happen to require. The notes are best made on a slate, or in a small notebook which you can keep in your pocket. In the event of encountering bad weather you might not be able to leave the helm, in which case you would find your notes of great value. Even if the weather remains fine, they will save you a lot of trouble.

When making a passage you can't afford to waste a minute of a fair tide, so be sure that you are under way when the tide serves, no matter how early that may be. You should turn out of bed at least half an hour before tide-time as you will have certain preparations to make. It is desirable, for instance, to have something to eat before you start if it is an early hour of the morning, as at that time of day vitality is at its lowest ebb and you need something to buck you up. I do not suggest that you should cook a meal at, say, 3 a.m., but you should certainly have a snack of some sort, such as a hunk of cake and a cup of coffee. Then, if you are wise, you will prepare food to consume en route, for should you encounter bad weather you might not be able to leave the helm for many hours. If you are adequately fed you will be able to view bad weather with equanimity, but if hungry and cold you are likely to wish that you had taken up fretwork, instead of sailing, as a hobby. It is my practice to make some sandwiches before starting on a single-handed passage and wrap them in greaseproof paper to keep them fresh. These I stow in one of the cockpit lockers together with something to drink and am thus able to get a meal when hungry without leaving the helm. What to drink is a matter of personal taste, but there is not much the matter with a bottle of beer, or coffee in a thermos flask, which will keep hot all day.

You should also see that you have everything you are likely to want ready to hand. The compass should be shipped in its place on the bulkhead, lead and line in the cockpit, your notes and chart in a handy place and also tobacco, pipe, cigarettes and matches. Place just inside the cabin your oilskin coat and sou'-wester, so that you can get them in a moment in case of need, and see that you have at least one earing rove and the reef-tackle in position on the boom. Make sure that you have handy short lengths of suitable rope for preventer lashings in case you have to reef, and spare sails, such as the small jib and balloon foresail, just inside the cabin. Thus prepared you won't care if it snows, as the saying goes.

But the great thing is to work your tides to best advantage. It may be that you will want the ebb to take you to a certain point, say 5 miles distant, where you should pick up the flood. Don't think that you will only require about an hour of the ebb, for you will probably need a good deal more. In the early hours of the morning in fine summer weather there is often very little wind or none at all, so you should allow two, or even three, hours. If there is no wind you can shave and attend to other domestic matters as you drift and if you reach the position you want before the flood has begun to make, and there is not enough wind to enable you to stem the tide, you can drop your anchor and have a proper breakfast. Always, if anything, be ahead of your tide rather than late if you want your cruising to be a success. "We must take the current when it serves, or lose our ventures," said Shakespeare, a remark peculiarly applicable to yachtsmen.

CHAPTER 49: *Trim and Ballasting*

I doubt very much whether the average small yacht owner gives much thought to his vessel's trim. When buying the boat he probably assumes that she is in her proper trim and if her weather helm is excessive he regards it as a trait peculiar to her which cannot be remedied. It has often struck me, when sailing another man's yacht, that she might be considerably improved by a little readjustment of her ballast, but the idea of experimenting in that way does not seem to occur to many owners. It stands to reason that if the helm has to be kept nearly hard up in a strong breeze on the quarter, the speed of the craft must be seriously affected. Besides, it is extremely tiring to the helmsman.

It is quite possible that when a second-hand boat is bought she may not be in her designed trim. In all probability she has frequently had her inside ballast removed for the purpose of cleaning the bilge and it may have been re-stowed incorrectly. It is very easy to make a mistake of that sort and I am afraid that some yacht caretakers are not as careful as they might be when re-stowing ballast. If he can get it all stowed away under the floorboards the man is apt to rest content and does not worry about the subsequent performance of the yacht. Every yacht, I think, should carry a little weather helm, but if she is decently balanced she should not increase it unduly when heeled in a fresh breeze. If she does, she is either badly designed or badly trimmed. The balance of a yacht depends mainly upon her extremities. If she has a fine bow she should have a fine stern to match, but sometimes a designer, with a view to increased accommodation, is tempted to give her too heavy quarters, and as a result she is 'hard-headed' when well heeled. The old-fashioned type of craft, with straight stem, deep forefoot and full quarters, often gripes abominably with a strong quartering breeze, but much has been learnt about designing of late years and the modern vessel is seldom gravely at fault in that respect.

Theoretically, a yacht designed under Admiral Turner's metacentric shelf system seems ideal, for she carries no helm at all and will, or at any rate should, sail herself for long periods with the helm free and does not develop weather helm when heeled. But in practice I don't think such perfect balance desirable, for I am pretty sure that unless a helmsman can 'feel' the boat he cannot get the best out of her. Moreover, steering a craft that carries no weather helm at all is as uninteresting as steering a motor-boat, which bores me excessively. In my view a yacht should always carry slight weather helm but, if properly balanced, should not materially increase it when heeled in a fresh breeze. But that is only my personal opinion, with which many experienced yachtsmen will not agree.

If excessive weather helm is objectionable, lee helm is far more so. I know of nothing more damnable than steering a vessel in heavy weather when she carries lee helm. It is not only a most unpleasant feeling but positively dangerous. Fortunately the yacht that naturally carries lee helm is comparatively rare, but it is not uncommon for a Bermudian-rigged boat to do so when her mainsail is close-reefed. The effect of reefing a sail of that type is to throw the centre of effort farther forward, and it is possible that a Bermudian yacht that carries slight weather helm under full sail may develop lee helm when the sail is reefed. When converting a yacht from gaff rig to Bermudian it is important that the new sail plan should be designed by an expert, for the correct relative positions of the centres of effort and resistance cannot be ignored.

Now let us see what can be done to cure a yacht which is badly trimmed. We will take first the case of a vessel that has too much weather helm. Most small yachts have a certain amount of inside ballast, and it will be as well first to see what we can do by a redistribution of the weight. If the vessel has a tendency to gripe, the weight should be moved farther aft, with a view to trimming her more by the stern. In many cases this in itself will not be sufficient but it will certainly improve matters The next step, I think, should be to try the effect of pulling the masthead farther forward by setting up the masthead stay as taut as possible. This may not make much difference, but 'every little helps,' as the old lady said in the story you probably heard when you were a schoolboy. If, after these alterations, the boat still carries too much weather helm, we shall have to see what can be done by modifications to the sail plan. We can either increase the area of the head-sails, reduce the size of the mainsail, or both. The best thing to do will depend a good deal on the sail plan. If your mainsail is a large one and the boom extends several feet over the stern, I think it would be preferable to reduce its size by having a cloth taken out of it and shortening the boom and gaff to fit. Another way would be to scrap the gaff mainsail altogether and substitute a Bermudian, which in most cases tends to throw the centre of effort farther forward. But that is an expensive expedient, as it will probably entail a new and longer mast in addition to a new sail. You could, of course, also reduce the area of the after canvas by cutting down the hoist of the mainsail a foot or two, but if the reduction is too drastic the boat will be under-canvassed and slow in light weather. On the whole, I think I should prefer to increase the area of the headsail by lengthening the bowsprit and using a larger jib. If that proves insufficient you might in addition slightly reduce the size of the mainsail as well. Should all of these expedients fail, nothing remains but to have the mast shifted farther forward. That, of course, is likely to prove a rather expensive matter, as it will entail a new mast-step, a fresh hole cut in the deck, and an alteration in the position of the chainplates. But it is certainly the most effective cure, and when the other methods I have indicated fail, there is no alternative, although possibly cutting away some of the forefoot might tend to improve matters.

Now let us consider the boat that carries lee helm. The procedure should be the same as when dealing with weather helm but, of course, reversed. The effect should be first tried of shifting the ballast farther forward, as this will tend to trim her by the head and give her a better grip of the water forward. If that is insufficient, the forestay and masthead stay should be slackened and the runners set up taut with a view to bringing the masthead farther aft. This alteration in trim should make an appreciable difference, and as lee helm is usually easier to rectify than weather helm, it may suffice. But if the yacht still shows a tendency to fall off from the wind, some modification in the sail plan should be tried. The simplest plan is to reduce the area of the headsail, and the effect should be tried of sailing her with the whole mainsail and a small jib. If that proves satisfactory, you can have the bowsprit shortened and use the second jib as your working sail. You will, however, require a smaller sail to set when the mainsail is reefed. Of course, the same result could be obtained by enlarging the mainsail, but that would be far more expensive, as it would probably entail the provision of new and longer spars.

If the methods I have suggested fail to cure the lee helm, there are still two remedies left open to you. You can either have the mast shifted farther aft or else have a piece of deadwood affixed to the forefoot. I think I should prefer the latter, as it would not be very expensive, and if the excrescence failed to achieve the desired end, it could easily be removed.

A slight readjustment of the ballast often makes a tremendous difference in the speed and handiness of a yacht, and if you are not perfectly satisfied with the sailing of your boat I should advise you to experiment a little in this way. A peculiarity of some craft, notably those with a fin keel, or no forefoot, is to fall off after staying. I had a yacht once that did that to such an extent that the wind was almost on her beam before she gathered way on her new tack. That is a serious fault, for when beating over a foul tide it may cause her to lose nearly all the distance she had gained to windward on the previous tack. I found the only way to counteract this trait was to wait until she gathered way before getting in the headsail sheets. By such means I checked her paying off unduly, but as I had to sheet the sails when they were full of wind it made for hard work. If I had kept the boat I should have had the space between the fore-end of the fin and the stem filled in with deadwood, which I think would have cured her.

Apart from the question of griping, many small yachts would be better sea boats if their ballast were spread out more fore-and-aft. If the weight is concentrated too much in the centre of the vessel, although it may make her lively and dry in a seaway, it is apt to detract from her speed and comfort. The motion of a yacht with all her ballast stowed amidships is very violent in a rough sea and she seems to plunge twice into the same hole, so to speak. The ballast should be so stowed that she lifts and falls to the rhythm of the seas. If she does that, her motion will be more sedate and she will keep travelling. It would be a mistake, however, to stow the ballast too near her extremities, for that would make her too sluggish and, failing to lift quickly enough, she might ship green water. Any vessel that habitually ships heavy water in a rough sea is undesirable, if not actually unsafe, so the aim should be to strike the happy medium. Here again, experimenting is called for, as it is only by trial and error that the best results are likely to be achieved. One of the chief advantages of having all the ballast outside in the form of a keel is that it is always in the right place provided, of course that the designer has made no error in his calculations.

Another thing I would advise owners to do is to check the leads of the headsail sheets. I often see small yachts with the leaches of their foresail and jib flapping when on a wind and believe that in most cases it is due to the fairleads being incorrectly placed. When ordering new headsails the owner probably only supplied the maker with the luff and foot measurements of the old sails. But the new sails may be of slightly different shape, in which case the lead of the sheets will not be fair. If possible the sailmaker should be asked to come on board and take the measurements himself. He will then be able to note the positions of the fairleads and cut the sails accordingly. This, I think, is far the best plan, for if the lead is not right, you can throw the blame on him and get him to rectify matters.

According to the well-known aerodynamic expert, Manfred Curry, the correct position for the fairlead should be determined by prolonging a line drawn through the clew of the sail at a right angle to the luff. If you have not read Curry's book *Yacht Racing*, you should certainly do so at the first opportunity, as it is extraordinarily interesting and instructive.

I am inclined to think that many small craft have their headsail sheet leads too far inboard. I suppose the idea is to sheet the sails closer with a view to making the vessel point higher when close-hauled; but it is quite wrong. If the sails be sheeted too harshly, although the yacht may appear to point high, her speed will be checked, for she will make more leeway and will not, in fact, go where she looks, as we say. The backdraught from the headsails, too, will impinge on the lee side of the mainsail and tend to reduce its efficiency. Manfred Curry in his book makes the following remark:

The jib increases the effectiveness of the mainsail when it directs a strong current of air along and parallel to it, thus catching up and carrying off the unfavourable return current or back flow of the eddies; but it decreases the effectiveness of the mainsail when it merely spills air on to it, which flows into the region of the partial vacuum in the lee of the mainsail and thus weakens its suction pull.

In most cruising yachts I think it will be found that the head-sail sheet fair-leads are best placed as close to the rail as possible. Curry has, indeed, patented a form of outrigger by means of which the lead of the jib-sheet can be placed outside the boat, and he maintains that by its use the efficiency of the jib is great-ly increased. I believe that outriggers for headsail sheets are prohibited by our racing rules, but I see no reason why they should not be employed in a cruising craft. Curry's outriggers are designed to slope upwards so that the sheet is never in the water, however much the boat may heel. Many yachtsmen, I think, are apt to sheet their jib too harshly when going to windward, and this tendency would be checked by the use of outriggers.

The modern overlapping headsail must also, I think, be attributed to Man-fred Curry, and although at present mainly used in racing yachts it will, I have no doubt, soon come into favour in cruising craft, for it is undoubtedly very ef-ficient. It is essential, however, that it should be correctly sheeted, for other-wise the overlap will do more harm than good. Years ago it was considered bad practice to carry anything in the nature of a balloon sail if the wind was much forward of the beam and it was even considered a doubtful policy to carry a jib-topsail to windward. Such ideas, however, have now been exploded and racing craft carry Genoa jibs to windward with great effect. Such sails, I think, are now cut to set flatter than was formerly the case and stand well on a wind.

CHAPTER 50: *Bending and Setting Sails*

THE MAINSAIL

To bend a gaff mainsail, start with the head of the sail. First seize the throat-cringle to the eye-bolt on the underside of the gaff and then haul out the peak to the other end of the spar with the peak-outhaul. This can be of hambro-line, spliced into the peak-cringle, and must be passed a number of times through the hole in the gaff and the cringle and finally several times round the end of the spar and the cringle before making it fast. As I have explained previously, it is better to attach the head of the sail to the gaff with a separate stop of marline at each eyelet, but if you use a long lacing it can be of hambro-line. There is only one cor-rect way to lace a sail, so that the lacing will lie snugly against the bolt-rope, and that is as illustrated. Having bent on the head of the sail, the luff can be seized to the mast-hoops with marline. If the sail has a laced foot, it is laced to the boom in a similar manner to the head. The clew-outhaul should be of manila rope and belayed to a cleat under the boom. It is unnecessary to fit a purchase to the out-haul of a small yacht's mainsail, as, if it cannot be hauled out sufficiently by hand, the reef-tackle can be used. Should your sail have a loose foot, the outhaul should

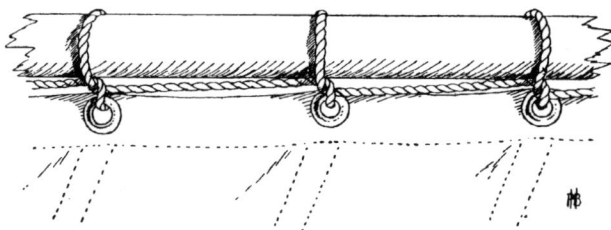

Mainsail head lacing to gaff

be of rather stouter rope, since the strain is not distributed over the whole length of the boom, as it is when the sail is laced.

When setting, the first thing to do is to remove the sail cover, and if the lacing is in one long length you will find it a rather finicking job. It is far more convenient to have the lacing in several short lengths, as that will save time both when removing and replacing the cover. It is surprising that some better way of securing a sail coat has not been devised. Why not press studs, for instance? The married man who is not unfamiliar with such requests from his wife as 'Do me up behind,' will know what I mean, but for the benefit of the bachelor perhaps I should explain that press studs are little fastenings used on ladies' dresses. They are as elusive to male fingers as the 'Scarlet Pimpernel' and love to hide behind folds of chiffon, or whatever the stuff is called. But when found, they close with a satisfying click. Well, that is the sort of thing I have in mind but, of course, much stronger and on a larger scale, the cover would have to be a little wider than usual to enable the edges to meet comfortably below the boom, but I feel sure that thus fitted it could be removed or put on in half the time. Or, how about zip fasteners? A foot or so of the cover would have to be sewn up at the end to form a bag to slip over the boom and that would entail removing the topping-lift first; but it would take less time to unshackle the latter than one usually wastes messing about with a lacing. As zip fasteners seem to be used for almost anything nowadays, even clothing, it seems to me a practicable proposition. After that digression, let us get on.

When you remove a sail cover, start at the outboard end and roll it inside out, so that it will be ready to put on again when you bring up. Never fold a sail cover, for if you do it will get worn in the creases and let the wet through. A sail coat that leaks is worse than no cover at all, as it will foster the generation of mildew. Some people, when taking off the cover, wrap it round a mopstick and it is not a bad plan.

To set a gaff mainsail, first hook on the main and peak halyards and overhaul the mainsheet, that is to say, pull the rope through the blocks so that the boom has a few feet of play, and then top up the boom a few feet with the topping-lift. Keep an eye on the boom crutch, if of the scissors type, to see that it does not go overboard. Now haul on the main and peak halyards together, so that the gaff rises more or less horizontally. When the throat is nearly in position, belay the peak halyard temporarily, while you 'swig' on the main until the luff of the sail is as taut as you can get it. Having belayed the main halyard, turn your attention to the peak once more. Peak up the sail until pronounced wrinkles appear in the throat, then belay and coil down the halyards neatly, taking care to coil them clockwise. All hawser-laid ropes, by the way, must be coiled clockwise, or with the sun, otherwise they will kink. The only ropes coiled anti-clockwise are cable-laid, such as hemp warps and lead-lines.

When setting a gaff sail, don't be afraid of hoisting the peak well up; you can't expect a boat to sail decently to windward with her mainsail setting like a pair of pants on a clothes-line. If you set it properly most of the wrinkles in the throat will be taken out when the topping-lift is slackened and the sail feels the weight of the boom, and the remainder will disappear when the halyards have stretched a little, as they soon will, if of manila.

If your gaff-jaws are of the old-fashioned wooden crutch type, the gaff should be well above the horizontal when you swig up the throat. With such a gaff, the main halyard is shackled to an eye-bolt on the spar several inches from the jaws, instead of being attached to the jaw fitting itself, as is the case with saddle gaff-jaws. If the gaff were horizontal when you set up the throat, subsequent peaking of the sail would cause the jaws to drop a little and slack up the luff. When the sail has been set, either hitch the halyard coils on their belaying pins or tuck them under the falls, to eliminate the risk of their being washed overboard when under way. Finally, slack up the topping-lift sufficiently to prevent the sail being girt on it when full of wind.

Now, here is a warning. It is customary, when going aloft in a gaff-rigged vessel, to use the mast-hoops as steps, but if the hoops are rather large it is possible for your foot to slip through the hoop. That happened to a friend of mine some years ago. He was single-handed in his 7-ton cutter and lying in Bradwell Creek. It was early morning and there was nobody about. Having set his mainsail, he found it necessary to go aloft, and as usual, swarmed up by the mast-hoops. His foot slipped through one of the upper hoops and he could not get it out. He managed to get his shoe off but his foot was firmly imprisoned, and as there was no help available, he was in a difficult, even dangerous, position. Eventually, with a violent wrench, he contrived to extricate his foot, but his ankle muscles were badly strained in the process and he was lame for some weeks. So if you go aloft in that way, be very careful and remember that the mast tapers and the hoops will fit more loosely near the hounds.

Setting a Bermudian sail calls for little comment, as, after topping the boom, all you have to do is to haul on the halyard until the luff is as taut as you can get it. Should the wind be aft and you have to set the sail after the anchor has been weighed, the best plan is to hoist the head of the sail a little and then luff head to wind before setting it. If you try and set the whole sail with the wind abaft the beam, it is sure to foul the rigging. A gunter mainsail is set differently to a gaff sail as the yard is first hoisted until it is up and down the mast. The sail is then set with the main halyard. As the peak halyard is shackled to a long wire span, it adjusts itself as the sail is hoisted, although it may need a little trimming subsequently with the peak halyard.

THE TOPSAIL

Topsails are not much used in small yachts nowadays as most owners prefer to have a rather larger mainsail and dispense with the extra gear. Still, the topsail is by no means obsolete and the recruit should learn how to set and hand one. But first a word or two about the gear. The topsail halyard is led over a sheave in the masthead and when not in use is made fast to the rigging, one part on each side. The sheet is led through a sheave on the end of the gaff and secured to the boom when not in use. The tack-purchase is usually left on the sail. The head of the sail is laced to a yard and the halyard attached to the yard at a position determined by trial and error. When the correct spot has been ascertained the spar can be marked for guidance on future occasions. The sheet is secured to the cringle in the clew. Sometimes a topsail has a jack-yard on the clew to increase the area, in which case the sheet is attached to the jackyard instead of to the clew cringle. Now to set the sail.

A topsail should be set, or handed, on the weather side of the mainsail, so that you can see what you are doing, and also to prevent its getting foul of the rigging as it is hoisted, as it probably would, if set to leeward. Now, here is a useful tip. Seize a thimble to the foot of the yard and before sending the sail aloft, pass the end of the halyard through the thimble. That will keep the yard straight up-and-down the mast as it is hoisted and reduce the risk of its fouling the rigging and other obstructions. Having bent the halyard to the yard and the sheet to the clew, hoist away until the yard is at the masthead, hauling on the sheet as you do so. If the topping-lift happens to be on that side, you must be careful that both the halyard and sheet are inside it when you bend them on to the sail. Having belayed the halyard, haul out the clew with the sheet and bowse down the tack with the purchase; it is better to get the tack down before hauling the sheet right out.

A jackyard topsail is not by any means an easy sail to set well, and unless it sets almost as flat as a card it will not stand on a wind. Some times a guy from the end of the jackyard to the boom is used to prevent the former sagging to leeward, and the set of the sail may be improved if the mainsail be peaked up a few inches above normal before the topsail is set and subsequently dropped into its proper position.

Many small yacht owners, I think, refrain from using a topsail because, apart from the trouble of setting it, the long yard is a cumbersome thing to stow when not in use. Quite a serviceable topsail, however, can be set fisherman fashion on a comparatively short yard in the following manner. A bull's-eye is fitted to the upper side of the gaff close to the jaws and through it is rove an endless rope, long enough to pass loosely below the boom. To this, when setting the sail, the foot of the yard is made fast, the rope taking the place of the usual tack tackle. After the topsail has been hoisted, the yard is brought into place up-and-down the mast by means of the endless rope, which is then belayed and the clew hauled out as usual. A small topsail can be set in this manner with very little trouble and it will set quite well enough for cruising purposes.

If the yacht has a reasonably long masthead, a jib-headed topsail can be set without a yard and will help the vessel along considerably. In the absence of a yard, the halyard is, of course, made fast to the head of the sail.

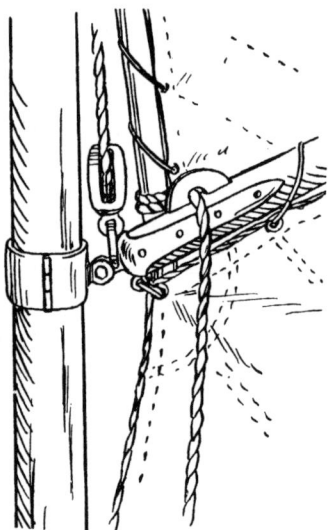

Topsail set fisherman's fashion

THE JIB

Most small craft now have a standing bobstay which needs no attention, but if it is fitted with a tackle, you must make sure that it is set up before you start to set the jib, otherwise you might pull the bowsprit out, or at least steeve it up excessively. You should also see that the runners are set up, otherwise you will pull the mast forward when purchasing the jib.

The jib halyard of even the smallest yacht should be of flexible wire rope, for if of manila it will stretch and allow the luff of the sail to sag to leeward. No vessel will sail decently to windward unless the luff of her jib is bar taut. As much of the virtue of the wire halyard would be lost if the manila rope of which the purchase is composed were to stretch, there should be no more of it than absolutely essential. When the sail is set there should not be a drift between the purchase blocks of more than a few inches, so that the stretching of what little manila rope is used will be negligible. If the purchase on the end of the halyard be fitted so that the fall leads from the lower blocks, instead of from the upper, as is usual, much more power can be used and the sail well set.

The halyard is just a length of flexible wire rope with an eye spliced in each end. To one end the head of the jib is shackled and to the other the purchase. When you bend on the sail, the other end of the halyard will be aloft and some means of pulling it down must be provided. Of course, the purchase could be permanently shackled to it, but that would involve a great waste of manila, to say nothing of a considerable coil of rope cluttering up the foot of the mast when the sail was set. All that is needed is a line attached to the halyard by which to haul it down; then the purchase can be hooked on and the line removed. In my own boat I keep a line specially for the purpose and as it has a spring hook on the end, it can be snatched on to the halyard in a moment. By the adoption of this method, only a few feet of manila are needed and when the sail is set the two blocks of the purchase are only 3 or 4 inches apart and there is nothing to stretch. Of course, before the sail is lowered the down-haul must be hooked on again. With those preliminary remarks, we can proceed to set the jib.

First hook the tack of the sail to the traveller on the bowsprit and then bend on the halyard. Having hauled the tack out to the end of the bowsprit, belay the outhaul and then bend on the sheets to the clew, leaving them quite slack. Now hoist the sail by pulling on the halyard down-haul; hook on the purchase and after you have got the luff of the sail bar-taut, belay the fall of the purchase to one of the pins on the mast-band. The sail is then set and you can remove and stow away the down-haul.

If your jib is not fitted with the Wykeham-Martin furling gear – it will be if you are wise – you should cultivate the habit of setting the sail in stops. This is done as follows: Spread out the sail and fold it so that the clew cringle just over-laps the luff rope, then roll up the sail neatly to the luff rope and secure it with rope yarns or seaming twine at intervals of about 18 inches. The sail then looks something like an elongated sausage. The tack is hauled out to the bowsprit-end on the traveller, the head hoisted with the halyard, and the sheets shackled to the clew cringle. Care must be taken when setting a sail in stops that the sheets are quite slack, otherwise the stops may be prematurely broken. A sail set in this manner is ready for immediate use and yet is not in one's way when working on the fore-deck. When the services of the sail are needed, all one has to do is to haul on the sheet and the rope yarns break away.

The foresail is set in much the same way as the jib, but the luff hanked to the forestay and the tack secured to the stemhead. Some-times the foot is laced to a boom, with the sheet travelling on a fore-horse, and the sail looks after itself when tacking. That, of course, is an advantage when the yacht is sailed single-

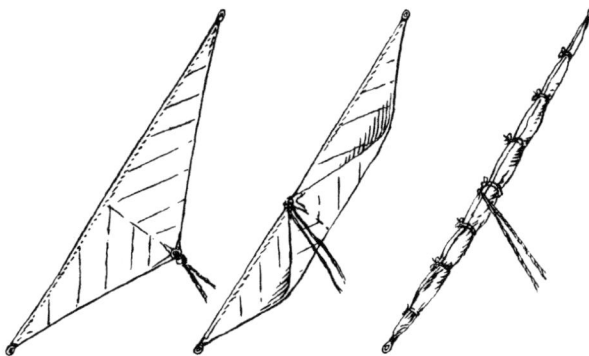

Setting jib in stops

handed, but it entails a reduction of area as the boom has to clear the mast when the vessel is in stays. For its area the foresail is the most powerful sail in the ship and it is open to doubt whether the enhanced handiness is sufficient compensation for the sacrifice in area. And that is not the only point for consideration. Aerodynamic experts stress the importance of the foresail overlapping the luff of the mainsail, maintaining that such overlap increases the effectiveness of the mainsail. Whether there is anything in that theory I am not prepared to say, as I am not a scientific cove myself; but I do know that a foresail with a boom is much more trouble both to set and stow than one without, and I should not adopt it myself unless I wanted to sail a craft of say 8 or 10 tons single-handed. The operation of Wykeham-Martin gear for jib or foresail is described in the earlier chapter on Roller Headsails.

THE BALLOON FORESAIL, OR GENOA

The balloon foresail is a most valuable sail, as with the wind on or abaft the beam, it will pull a boat along grandly. If well cut it can also be used with effect with the wind about two points forward of the beam; and when running it can be set across the vessel, fisherman fashion, in place of a spinnaker. Of course, as its area is less than that of a spinnaker, it is not so effective but very useful if you have not got a spinnaker, or are single-handed. When employed in this manner, the tack is secured to a shroud plate on one side of the boat and the sheet led outside the rigging on the other. As it needs no attention when the mainsail is gybed, it is, in my opinion, a better proposition for single-handed work than a spinnaker. A balloon foresail, which nowadays is often called a 'Genoa,' should not be cut too low on the foot and should be sheeted as far aft as possible if the wind is anywhere forward of the beam. If sheeted too far forward the back-draught from it is apt to impinge on the lee side of the mainsail and rob the latter of a good deal of its driving power. The clew of the sail can with advantage reach as far aft as the runner, but the foot should not be so low as to shut out the helmsman's view to leeward, as it often is in racing craft. It must be remembered that it is the racing owner's aim to use as much untaxed sail area as the rules permit, and the foot of the Genoa is consequently almost on the deck. As a balloon foresail is not intended for windward work, it is fitted with a single sheet, which must be passed round to the other side when going about.

THE SPINNAKER

The spinnaker is a very useful sail when running before the wind as it enables one to set a very large area of canvas, but it is not an easy sail to set or hand, and for that reason not suitable for single-handed sailing. As the luff extends from the masthead to the end of the spinnaker boom and the foot to the other side of the mast, its area is almost as great as that of the mainsail. Indeed, in racing yachts, which use the modern parachute spinnaker, it is very much larger, but I

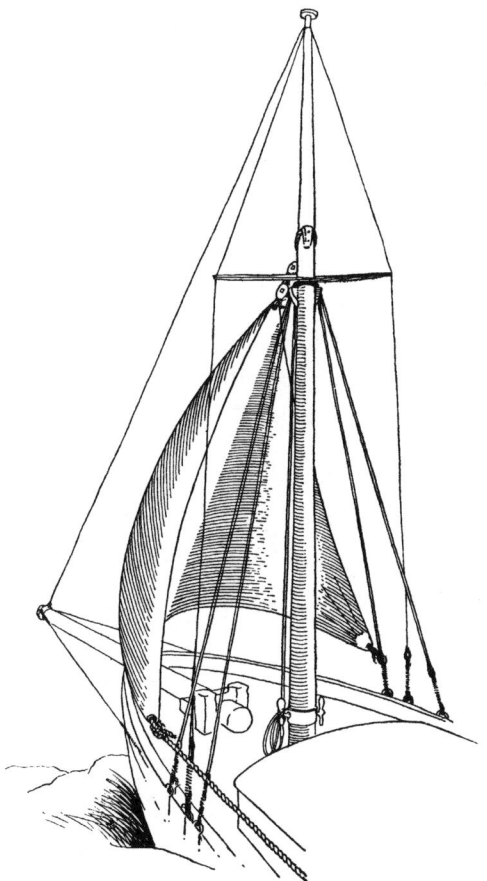

Balloon foresail set for running

am referring to the ordinary spinnaker of the cruising yacht. Although the origin of the spinnaker is usually attributed to the racing yacht Sphinx, which used the sail in 1866, it was really invented by McMullen in 1855, who wrote of it in *Down Channel* as follows:

> In 1852, contemplating longer passages, I gave Leo a topmast; and in 1855, wanting more sail for running before a light wind, I invented a sail which for want of a better name I called a studding sail, but which was known about twelve years later as a spinnaker, when it came into use amongst larger yachts for match-sailing. It is made of very light material in the form of a jib, and sets from the topmast head to the deck where it is boomed out like a squaresail. As it is a sail that endangers the topmast, except in the lightest winds, I discarded it in 1865.

But the rather curious name was undoubtedly derived from the yacht Sphinx, which was called 'Spinks' by the crew and longshoremen. So the sail came to be known as a 'spinker,' and later 'spinnaker.'

In larger vessels the spinnaker boom is fitted to the fore side of the mast with a gooseneck and when not in use is topped up along the mast, but in small cruising yachts it is better to have wooden jaws on the spar to engage on the mast. As the sail is apt to lift, it was a common practice for one of the crew to sit on the boom to prevent its skying. But this skying can be eliminated if the inboard end of the boom be engaged on the mast higher than the outboard end, particularly if a fore-guy is also used. If the two guys are set up taut, one against the other, it is impossible for the boom to lift. When the mainsail is gybed, the spinnaker has to be shifted over to the other side, a rather troublesome job in a short-handed vessel.

THE JIB TOPSAIL

In these days when topmasts are obsolete the jib topsail is seldom seen in small craft, although a small one can be used effectively on the tall mast of a Bermudi-

Lead of spinnaker guy

an-rigged yacht. It is hanked to the masthead stay and fills up the gap above the jib, but seldom sets well enough to be of much use when close-hauled.

THE SQUARESAIL

For ocean cruising the squaresail is very useful, as a vessel will run much more steadily under it before a heavy following sea than under her mainsail, and the risk of an accidental gybe will be eliminated. For coastwise cruising, however, it is less efficient than a spinnaker, as when used in conjunction with the mainsail a portion of the squaresail is blanketed, although the effective area can be increased by pushing the weather clew out with a long pole. Of course when the squaresail is set in heavy weather the mainsail is stowed. As the coastwise cruising yacht seldom experiences conditions when a squaresail can be used with advantage, it is hardly worth carrying in such vessels.

The squaresail yard should not be longer than four-fifths of the hoist of the mainsail, and the sail should have a row of reef-points by which its area can be reduced by about one-third. The sail should be set upon a jackstay of wire, leading from the hounds and set up to a strong eye-bolt in the deck a foot or two forward of the mast. The halyard should be made fast to a wire sling on the yard.

The squaresail is a beast of a sail to handle in a strong wind, unless it can be brailed up first, and for that reason I think it should be attached to the yard with wooden hoops, in much the same way that the luff of the mainsail is attached to the mast. The sail could then be set by means of outhauls led through blocks at the yard-arms. Inhauls, led through blocks at the centre of the yard, would also be necessary for stowing it. To stow the sail, one would haul on the inhauls until it was bunched in the middle of the yard and then pass one of the falls round the sail a few times and make it fast. I think that a squaresail rigged in this manner would be quite tractable in a strong wind. But, as I say, it is a sail that is quite unsuitable and unnecessary for ordinary coastwise cruising.

Running under squaresail

THE TRYSAIL

A trysail is a very useful sail to keep on board, particularly when you have a new mainsail that you wish to avoid reefing. Being intended for use in heavy weather, it is made of stout canvas and has a loose foot. There are two kinds of trysail used in yachts, one having a short gaff and the other being of the thimble-headed variety. Of these the former is much the better. In my experience a thimble-headed trysail is something of a snare in a little craft, as if the vessel should be hove down in a heavy squall she will probably not handle under it.

When a yacht has been designed to carry a gaff mainsail, the substitution of a trysail has the effect of throwing the centre of effort farther forward, which will make her less handy than under normal conditions. Moreover, there is not sufficient driving power in a small jib-headed sail to counteract the windage of the hull when the vessel is heeling to a considerable angle. I once saw a smart little 3-tonner of the bulb-fin type get into a horrid mess under such conditions, and since then I have lost all faith in the efficiency of a thimble-headed trysail in heavy weather.

The gaff of a gaff trysail should not be longer than half the length of her usual gaff. It is fitted with jaws and parrel, the luff being laced to the mast. Neither form of trysail has a boom, the sheets leading through blocks on the vessel's quarters. Should you set the trysail merely to move from one berth to another in the anchorage, or for a short trip down the river, it will be more convenient to secure the clew of the sail to the made-up mainsail and boom, using the ordinary mainsheet, but in heavy weather the mainsail should be lashed down to the rail and the proper trysail sheets used.

CHAPTER 51: *Getting Under Way*

Before getting your ship under way you must make up your mind as to what canvas you will set, and owing to your lack of experience you may be in doubt whether to reef or not. In such circumstances the best thing to do is to play for safety and reef. Remember that it is less trouble and more comfortable to reef the mainsail while the vessel is riding to her moorings, or anchor, than when under way, and if you find that the reef is unnecessary it is an easy matter to shake it out again.

If, on the other hand, you discover that the reef was wanted; well, you can pat yourself on the back for having done the right thing and think what a clever chap you are. It is not of much use asking the opinion of someone else who, not knowing your boat, will probably consider the matter from the point of view of the capabilities of his own craft. It is far better to rely on your own judgment in such matters; but if you err, let it be in the direction of safety.

Should you make an error of judgment and set too much canvas, do not hesitate to rectify your mistake as soon as possible. Don't run away with the idea that others will think you timid if you reef, for if they know anything about the game they will not. Even if they do, what does it matter? It is better to be a coward than a corpse anyway, so use your own judgment and be hanged to the critics. Never carry on out of mere bravado, for by so doing you will only expose your inexperience. The seasoned yachtsman does not 'carry on' unless he has some definite object for doing so and, knowing the risk he runs, you may be sure that he is competent to cope with any situation that may arise. To make your poor little ship wallow under a press of sail is not heroic; it is merely silly. If it be your object to get the greatest speed out of her, you will not attain it by burying her lee decks. Most yachts reach their maximum speed before their decks are awash and their progress is retarded when they have to drag the lee rail and rigging through the water. Moreover, a little ship that is unduly pressed is apt to rebel and become unmanageable.

Some time ago I saw a little yacht, which had been bought by a novice, get under way at Fambridge in a strong wind under whole mainsail and working jib, when she should have had a pair of reefs and small jib. Her owner could do nothing with her and in a few minutes she had charged on to the seawall, where she remained for many hours. Yet that boat was a handy little craft, designed by Harrison Butler, which would have revelled in such weather had she been properly canvassed.

The most comfortable conditions for reefing are when the yacht is lying head to wind and tide at her moorings, or anchor. First hoist the sail about half-way up so that you can get a good view of your work; then secure the reef cringle on the luff to the boom with a short length of rope. In my own boat I have sister-hooks stropped to the gooseneck for the tack and when I reef it is merely a matter of shifting the sister-hooks from the tack to the appropriate reef cringle. Now bend the reef tackle on to the earing (also called a pendant) of the particular reef you propose to take down. Then haul on the fall of the tackle until the reef cringle of the sail is boused down to the bee-blocks on the boom. Then make the earing fast to the cleat on the boom, if there is one, or with a hitch round the boom. For additional security, take a short length of rope and lash the cringle to the boom. Now you can tie up the points with reef-knots, and see that they are reef-knots and not grannies.

If the sail has a loose foot you have merely to roll up the foot of the sail to the points and tie them; but if it has a laced foot, you will have to haul the sail down to the boom before you can tie the points, and if there is any wind in the sail that is not so easy. Some people will tell you, indeed I think I have read it in text-books, that the points of a laced sail must be passed between the foot-rope and the boom before they are tied, otherwise the sail may be torn. You can take it from me that that is all bunk; it has been my practice for half a century and more to tie the reef-points of a laced sail under the boom and I have never yet torn a sail. Just think for a moment. When one has to reef it is usually in bad weather, and the lacing, wet with rain or spray, will have shrunk tightly on to the boom. To pass the points under the sail one would first have to prise up the foot-rope with a spike and it would take the deuce of a long time to get the reef down. Having taken down the reef, the mainsail can be set in the usual manner. I shall have something to say about reefing under way in the chapter on Heavy Weather.

The manner in which you must get your craft under way will depend upon the conditions obtaining, and no hard-and-fast rules can be laid down. Not only must you study the wind and tide but also obstructions to sea room, such as other vessels brought up in your immediate neighbourhood and shoal water under your lee. So far as the wind and tide are concerned, however, I can give you a rule from which you should never depart unless compelled to do so by exceptional circumstances. Well then, here it is:

If the wind is before the beam you can set your sails before getting the anchor, or slipping the mooring, as the case may be; but should it be on or abaft the beam, you must not set any sail until the anchor has been weighed or the mooring slipped.

The reason why you must not make sail before getting the anchor when the wind is on or abaft the beam is that the sails would cause the vessel to drive past her anchor, which could not then be broken out, as the yacht would be sailing it farther into the ground. If you attempted to weigh the anchor under such conditions you would be pitting your strength against the weight of the vessel, plus the pressure of the wind on her sails, and you will be a strong man indeed if you can do that.

The reader may ask, if the wind is on the beam, could not the boom be run off so that the sail held no wind? The answer to that question is in the negative, as they say in the House of Commons, because the boom can't be squared right off, as the after shroud is set up a little way abaft the mast; so, no matter how much you slackened the mainsheet, the sail would still hold some wind. In a light air, however, you might set the mainsail 'scandalized,' that is to say, with the boom topped up and the peak lowered, so that it held insufficient wind to force the yacht over the tide.

Another question that might be asked is, if riding to a mooring, why should not sail be made before getting under way? – there is no question of weighing the anchor as you have merely to slip the mooring chain. Well, of course you could, but as soon as you began to hoist your sails the yacht would charge about all over the place and the mooring chain would scrape her topside paint; and if the moorings were laid unduly close to one another you might even foul some other craft.

And now we will consider the best means of getting our ship under way under various conditions. I shall assume that your jib is fitted with the Wykeham-Martin furling gear, as most small craft are nowadays, but if not you should set the sail in stops, in the manner I explained in the last chapter.

TO GET UNDER WAY FROM A MOORING
RIDING HEAD TO WIND AND TIDE

First take a good look round to see if there are any obstructions to be avoided. Having satisfied yourself that there is nothing of that sort to worry about, you proceed to get under way. Following the rule given above, you have set the mainsail and jib (the latter furled) and the foresail is hanked to the forestay and ready to set. Then, pass the mooring buoy under the bowsprit shroud (if any) and stream it. That is to say, let it drift astern as you pay out the buoy-rope. You must be careful to see that the buoy goes clear and does not get hitched up on anything, such as the dinghy painter, or the propeller if the yacht has an auxiliary engine. I myself always pull up my dinghy to the transom of the yacht and temporarily make her fast there until I am under way. To be hung up by your dinghy after you have slipped the mooring is an ignominious situation from which it is not always easy to get clear.

Although on this occasion there are no obstructions near you, you have decided to fill on the starboard tack or, in other words, to cast the yacht's head to port. By the way, a vessel is said to be on the starboard tack when the wind comes over the starboard side and on the port tack when it blows on the port side. As you have decided to fill on the starboard tack you have streamed the mooring buoy on that side. Had it been your intention to fill on the port tack, you would have streamed it to port, passing the buoy beneath the bobstay if necessary. You see, if the buoy is to windward there is less chance of its getting foul of anything. Now, I am afraid I must make another digression. By the new international helm orders, which came into force some years ago, the wheel, rudder and vessel's head all turn in the same direction. But a small yacht is still steered with a tiller and in order to avoid any misunderstanding, when I refer to the helm in this book I mean the tiller. For instance, when I say starboard the helm, I mean put the tiller to starboard; the boat's head of course would turn to port.

To resume our discussion on getting under way, we have decided to fill on the starboard tack, so the helm is put over to starboard and the yacht's head at once begins to sheer to port. Then the mooring is slipped and the jib unrolled and sheeted to starboard for a moment to assist her head to pay off still more. Then let go the jib sheet and belay it on the other side, when the yacht will begin to forge ahead. If your course is to windward, you have merely to trim the sheets and proceed, but if you wish to travel down wind, the helm should be kept up and the mainsheet paid out handsomely until the vessel is before the wind. If your boat has runners, the lee one must be let go to allow the boom to go forward. Then the foresail can be set and sheeted home. For the benefit of the beginner perhaps I should explain that to put up the helm is to push the tiller towards the windward side of the boat; when pushed to leeward, the helm is said to be put down.

In the example I have quoted, I assumed that you had a crew and could send a hand forward to slip the mooring. If you had been alone, you would have lashed the helm to starboard to sheer her head to port and then gone forward to slip the mooring when her head had paid off sufficiently, and then returned to the helm. In such circumstances it would perhaps be advisable to unroll the jib first, so that you could hold it over to starboard to help her head round, if necessary. As you had plenty of room all round you, the operation was a simple one, but suppose the mud was close at hand to starboard, while to port there were other vessels brought up so near to you that you could not get under way in the manner indicated without grave risk of fouling one or other of them. Then, what are you to do? Well, the safest way would be to swing the yacht on her mooring. Have the sails ready for setting, but not set. As the mud is so close to starboard, you have no alternative but to swing the boat to port. Having led the buoy-rope under the bowsprit shroud and outside the rigging, make it fast near the vessel's stern. Then put the helm over to starboard and as her head sheers to port, slip the mooring chain and let her swing on the buoy-rope. When she has swung nearly round, slip the buoy-rope and unroll the jib. Sail under it until clear of the obstructing craft and then set the mainsail. As you will have to luff up into the wind to set the mainsail properly, you must wait until you have ample room before you set it.

As the reader will no doubt have gathered, the operation of getting under way is much simplified when the yacht is riding to a mooring. Starting from an anchor makes a much bigger call on the yachtsman's seamanship and in the early stages of his sailing career the novice is likely to find himself up against many a pretty problem. A little thought, however, will usually enable him to extricate his ship from a tight place and he will soon learn to handle her with some degree of confidence.

TO GET UNDER WAY FROM AN ANCHOR
RIDING HEAD TO WIND AND TIDE

The first thing to do is to 'heave short,' or, in other words, get in some of the cable, as it is easier to haul a vessel against the wind when she has no sail set. Having hove short, set the mainsail and see that the jib halyard is properly set-up and the furled sail ready for immediate use. We will suppose that you have decided to fill on the port tack, so as soon as the anchor has been broken out of the ground, you must port the helm. When a vessel is riding to the tide, and for a few moments after the anchor has left the ground, she can be sheered either way at will. By putting your helm to port, therefore, the yacht's bow will be cast to starboard, and to assist her to pay off on the desired tack, you should unroll the jib and sheet it to port, so that it is aback. As she will then be hove-to, she can be left to her own devices, if there are no other craft in the immediate vicinity, while you haul up the anchor and stow it. When that has been done, you can let draw the jib and proceed on your course, setting the foresail at your leisure. The method I have described is comparatively simple, but the near presence of other vessels may render it impracticable.

Suppose, for instance, that you had been hemmed in on all sides by other craft at anchor. The more you consider the situation the less you like it. If you got under way in the usual manner you would risk fouling one or other of the near by vessels, whichever way you cast your yacht's head. You are, in fact, in what might reasonably be described as a 'tight place' and you wonder how you can extricate your boat from her hampered berth. Well, one way would be by what is known as dredging. The operation is carried out as follows: The cable is hove short until the vessel begins to drag her anchor, which is kept just trailing over the ground by paying out or shortening in cable as required. By these means the boat is made to drift slower than the tide, and so long as such conditions are maintained she can be steered and kept under control. This is a method often practised by barges when passing under a bridge with all their gear down on deck. It is a pretty manoeuvre, but all the same I should not recommend you to try it unless you are quite sure that the bottom is clear of moorings and other obstructions, for if you got your anchor hitched up on a heavy mooring chain, you might have a lot of trouble in clearing it.

If the wind were blowing from dead ahead you might set the mainsail before commencing to dredge, but otherwise no sail should be set until you are clear of the obstructing vessels.

If it were merely a case of having a vessel at anchor on either side of you, the position would not present any great difficulty, as you would only have to drop astern until you were clear of them. Still, it would call for a certain amount of care. The following would be the best method: Weigh the anchor and let her drop astern until clear of the other craft. Then to make her pay off on the desired tack, back the jib and reverse your helm for sternway. For instance, if you wish her to pay off to starboard, unroll the jib and sheet it to port, at the same time putting the helm to starboard.

TO GET UNDER WAY FROM A HAMPERED BERTH

That is simple enough, but the situation I want you to consider is one in which you are lying in a crowded anchorage, with vessels brought up quite close on each side and others just astern. You are riding head on to wind and tide and hemmed in on all sides. As there are moorings laid all over the river, you dare not dredge. What, then, are you to do? Well, I can suggest several methods. If you have a reasonable amount of room, you might be able to get clear by the use of a headsail and sternway. Suppose that you have decided to cast your boat's head to port. Set no sail, but have the jib ready for setting. Break out the anchor and then unroll the jib, sheeting it to starboard. As she gathers sternway, put your helm to port and the yacht will practically turn on her heel. Keep the jib aback and the helm to port until she is nearly before the wind, then let the jib draw and right the helm as she begins to forge ahead.

When clear of the obstructing vessels you can set the mainsail and foresail and proceed on your way.

Another, and perhaps safer way for a novice, would be the following: Heave short on the cable and bend a warp to it with a rolling hitch. Lead the warp clear of the bowsprit shroud and rigging to the stern, where it should be securely belayed. Then slack out cable handsomely, thus allowing the yacht to swing round until she is riding to the warp stern first. Haul in on the warp until the chain is reached and then break out the anchor and get it up on to the counter. As soon as the anchor is up, unroll the jib and run before the wind until you have sufficient room to set the mainsail. The only objection to this method is the trouble involved in having to take the anchor and chain forward again.

Still another way of getting clear would be to run off a warp to one of the vessels abeam and swing your own craft on it, but you would probably need a very long warp for, after you had made it fast to one of the neighbouring craft, you would have to slack it out as you hauled in your cable. Still, by joining two warps you could no doubt get the necessary length.

Let us assume that you have hove short on your cable and run off a warp to a neighbouring yacht on your starboard side. First weigh your anchor, paying out warp to enable you to do so. Then, as soon as the anchor has been broken out, start to haul the yacht stern first on the warp. As you do so, put the helm over to port, for sternway, to assist her to swing. By the time you approach the vessel to which you have made fast, your own ship will have swung almost round, and then, if there is someone on board the former to cast off your warp, you will be able to set the jib and run under it until you have room to set the mainsail. If there is no one on the other craft to release your warp, you would have to pass it round her rigging, bringing the end back to your own vessel and making both ends fast to her stern. You would then be in a position to recover your warp by slipping one end.

TO GET UNDER WAY WITH WIND AGAINST TIDE

The easiest conditions for getting under way are with wind against tide. Have the sails ready for setting, but set no sail at all until after you have got the anchor. Then, if your course is to leeward, set the jib and, when you have ample room, the mainsail and foresail. If your course is to windward, begin to set the mainsail as soon as the anchor has left the ground. If the crew are smart, the sail should be set by the time the yacht has come on to the wind, or pretty nearly so, and no distance will be lost, as would be the case if the yacht were run to leeward under a headsail, while the mainsail was set.

TO GET UNDER WAY FROM A LEE SHORE

A particularly awkward situation in which one may sometimes be placed is that of being anchored on a lee shore, when the yacht is wind-rode and has a mud flat close under her stern. As she is riding to the wind and not to the tide, she will not take a sheer, whilst the mud flat behind her is so close that sternway is out of the question. In the absence of sheer or a sternboard, you could not rely upon her filling on the desired tack if you got under way in the usual manner. Indeed, you would almost certainly be blown ashore before you could get the yacht under control. You will admit, I am sure, that this is a devilish awkward situation, calculated to give any novice a headache. But it is not really so bad as it sounds, for, if you 'know your stuff,' you can make the boat do most of the work herself. The only satisfactory manner of getting under way in such circumstances is by sailing out the anchor, for while you are doing so, you leave the shore farther and farther behind you.

To carry out the operation you must proceed as follows: Set the mainsail and jib and then work up to the anchor in short boards, hauling in cable as it slackens and going about when the strain comes on the chain again. After two or three little boards, which of course will be but a few yards in length, the yacht will sail right over her anchor. As she does so, snatch a turn of the chain round the bitts and she will sail the anchor clean out of the ground. Then, as she sails on towards open water the anchor can be got on board and the foresail set. This is a most interesting operation which even a novice can attempt with confidence, as he can't very well go wrong. The vessel being under control before the anchor leaves the ground, it does not matter which tack she is on when it is broken out. You either succeed in getting your anchor or you don't. If successful all is well; but should you fail to break out the anchor, you can slack out the cable and let her drop back into her old berth and try again.

I have frequently used this method of getting under way when single-handed, with complete success. As one cannot be at both ends of a boat at the same time, it is necessary to handle the craft without the aid of her rudder. To the beginner this may seem a difficult proposition, but in reality it is quite simple. Having set the mainsail and jib, haul the jib sheet aweather and belay it aback; the mainsheet being trimmed as for sailing to windward. With the sails thus sheeted, the yacht will forge ahead until the anchor is broad off on the bow. The strain on the cable will then pull her head round until her sails fill on the other tack and she begins to sail towards her anchor.

As soon as she is about, haul in the cable, which, as she gathers speed, will come in so easily that you can hardly get it in fast enough. When she is over the anchor, snatch a turn of the chain round the bitts and let her sail the anchor out of the ground. To carry out this manoeuvre successfully single-handed an intimate knowledge of one's boat is necessary, as much depends upon the correct adjustment of the main and jib sheets; but with a little practice you will find it quite easy and, as I have remarked, there is no risk of a novice getting into trouble while attempting it.

Before closing this chapter on getting under way, a few words must be said on anchor stowage. Many small yacht owners just haul the anchor up to the stemhead and then lift the crown and lash it to the rail. That, I think, is bad practice, as the weight of an anchor right on her nose does a small craft no good in a seaway. In such a position, too, the jib sheets are liable to foul it when the yacht is in stays. A far better plan is to stow the anchor on deck, in the neighbourhood of the mast, by one of the methods described in the chapter on Ground Tackle.

If, when lifting the anchor on board, it is passed outside the bowsprit shroud, all you will have to do when you bring up is to drop it overboard and it will run clear of everything.

If the anchor is a C.Q.R. the position in which it is carried is not of so much importance as it is so light. I carry mine on the fore deck, resting in chocks, and that seems as good a place as any.

CHAPTER 52: *Under Way*

Now for a few hints on handling your boat when under way. If you take a pride in your vessel and wish to get the best out of her, you will always set just the amount of sail that she can carry to best advantage according to the weather obtaining at the time. And in that connection it may be remarked that every yacht has her limitations in the way of speed. If you pile on canvas after she has reached her utmost speed, she will not go faster but probably slower. Most yachts attain their greatest speed when the deck is about level with the water, and if a vessel be pressed beyond that point she will commence wave-making that will have a considerable retarding effect upon her progress.

A yacht with several planks of her lee deck awash, moreover, is further hampered by having to drag her rail and lee rigging through the water. It is quite a common experience in one-design racing for a boat with a reef in her mainsail to sail right away from rivals carrying whole sail in a strong breeze. Should you have any doubt whether your craft will carry her whole mainsail, you will be well advised to start with a reef, for it is far less trouble to shake out a reef under way than it is to put one in.

HELMSMANSHIP

For sheer enjoyment I doubt if you will find anything in the world of sport to equal that of steering a yacht to windward in a fresh breeze. It is not only extremely exhilarating but also calls for considerable skill on the part of the helmsman. Take the case of two yachts of similar size and design; the one sailed by an expert and the other by a novice. Running and reaching, the performance of the two would not differ to any marked extent, but when sheets were gathered in for a beat to windward the expert would come into his own and soon leave his opponent far astern. The skill of a helmsman is therefore judged by his ability to sail a boat to windward. Some men are born helmsmen and will get far more out of a yacht after a few months' practice than others who have had years of experience.

The chief fault of the novice when steering to windward, is that of 'pinching' the boat. Instead of minding his own business, he watches other craft near by and thinks they are pointing higher than his own vessel. And so he keeps hauling on his sheets until he has them pinned in as taut as it is possible to get them. As the result of this treatment the yacht may point higher but her sails constantly lift, she travels much slower through the water and she sags away to leeward. It is true that the modern racing yacht will stand a good deal of harsh sheeting, but the average cruising vessel will do nothing of the sort. To sail efficiently she must have a foot or two of slack in her mainsheet when going to windward, or she will not go where she points. The amount of slack that should be allowed cannot be arbitrarily fixed, as no two boats are alike, and it can only be learnt by experiment and experience what suits her.

It is unwise to allow yourself to be influenced by what another craft is doing, for she may not have the same wind as you. There is nothing more unstable than the breezes that blow over these islands, and you cannot rely upon another yacht a hundred yards away holding the same wind as your own vessel. I remember once, when running down the Crouch with the wind right aft, meeting another boat which was running up the river and we were both carrying spinnakers. We sailed on thus until there was only a gap of about fifty yards between us, when we were both becalmed. That will give you an idea of how fickle the wind can be, and although the instance I have quoted was quite exceptional, you will readily understand that it is not by any means unusual for there to be a variation of a point or so in the direction of the wind a short distance away.

Although you should not allow the sailing of another boat to influence you unduly in the handling of your own, it will pay you to observe the performance of others in your immediate neighbourhood, as thereby you may often have a useful object lesson. You may see, for instance, a barge coming along with her foresail bellying out like a bag, and presently she will pass you, although your boat is lying points nearer to the wind. This will probably strike you as amazing and you will wonder how she does it. The explanation is that the barge is sailing while you are doing little more than drift to leeward. By pinning in your sheets you may succeed in pointing within, say, four points of the wind, but the boat is not going where she looks, as we say. She simply sags away to leeward and at the same time all the speed is knocked out of her.

The novice when sailing to windward is apt to rely too much upon his burgee, which is often a very unreliable guide. The little flag at the masthead may appear to be blowing out almost in a line with the keel of the yacht, giving the impression that you are sailing very close to the wind, when, as a matter of fact, your vessel is too full. The best guides are your sails and the feel of the wind on your face. And here a word must be said regarding sail trim.

It is only by experiment that you will find the best position for the boom when beating to windward, as no two boats are alike in that respect. Even with cruisers of the old straight-stemmed type some will stand harsher sheeting than others, but, in my experience, practically every cruising yacht is at her best when a foot or two of slack is given to the mainsheet. As regards the headsails, it is best to sail with the sheets a trifle slack. The best method for the novice is, perhaps, to ease out the jib sheet until the sail begins to lift and then haul it in a few inches until the jib is drawing nicely. The foresail must be sheeted a little flatter, or otherwise the back-draught from the jib may cause it to shake. Take the mainsail as the standard, and trim the jib so that it will lift just before the mainsail; then trim the foresail from the jib.

If you trim your sails as I suggest, you will be able to steer by the luff of the jib. As soon as you see a slight shiver of the luff you will know that you are sailing rather too near the wind and must bear away a trifle to send the sail to sleep again. Your burgee will warn you if you get too far off the wind. After a time you will find that you need no other guide but the feel of the tiller and the wind on your face.

There are few things less stable than the wind, at any rate in our part of the world. What we call a steady breeze is seldom anything of the kind, as it varies slightly in strength and direction. But the little puffs or squalls that come along are the helmsman's opportunities, for they allow him to sail his craft a little closer to the wind. As the breeze freshens, the helmsman should slightly ease the strain on the tiller and allow her to eat into the wind, keeping an eye on the luff of the jib to see that she does not come up too close. As the puff dies away, it will probably be necessary to bear away again to keep the sails asleep, but in the meantime several yards will have been snatched to windward without in any way impeding the speed of the vessel.

To get the best out of a yacht when beating to windward the helmsman must exercise constant vigilance and make the most of every little squall that comes along. In course of time and after much practice, he will luff into squalls in the manner I have indicated almost by intuition, and his sense of touch will become so highly developed that the sails will never lift at all, although the yacht is being sailed as close to the wind as she can be with advantage. I have often noticed novices sawing the tiller about from side to side, evidently under the impression that they help the boat thereby; but far from assisting they are actually impeding her. If there were anything in it, you may be sure that our crack helmsmen who steer big racing yachts would do it, but they don't. The less the rudder is used the better for the ship.

Most yachts carry a certain amount of weather-helm; that is to say, they have a natural tendency to come up into the wind. To counteract this the helmsman must keep the tiller slightly to windward. Although this weatherhelm makes for safety, it has a certain retarding influence. In a well-balanced boat the weather-helm will be very slight on the wind in a light breeze but increase a little as the yacht heels. Racing yachts are often designed to carry no weather-helm at all in light weather, and some I have sailed have even carried lee-helm. A boat possessing that trait is unsatisfactory to steer, as you can't "feel" her, while in heavy weather it is positively dangerous. A boat carrying lee-helm usually completely baffles a novice, who will be apt to get her right off the wind.

A lot has been said and written of late years about Admiral Turner's metacentric shelf system of designing, which, it is claimed, ensures such perfect balance that the vessel will sail herself for long periods with the helm free. That seems ideal in theory but, to my mind, is undesirable in practice. I am sufficiently old-fashioned to believe that every yacht should carry slight weatherhelm, not only for safety but because it enhances the pleasure of steering. I am sure that no helmsman can get the best out of a boat to windward unless he can feel her, and personally I find steering a metacentroid as uninteresting as steering a motor-boat. The weatherhelm, however, should not be excessive, for a yacht that "gripes" badly when reaching with the wind on the quarter is very tiring, while the position of the rudder must reduce her speed. And now, after that digression, let us get back to steering.

In a strong wind and rough sea a yacht should be sailed with slacker sheets and rather fuller than usual. The great thing is to keep her moving, for in a rough sea she will not handle reliably unless a good head of speed is maintained. You will no doubt get plenty of spray over you, but never mind that; salt water hurts no one and is invigorating rather than otherwise. Above all, don't be alarmed if water invades the lee decks, for that is what they are there for. But if the vessel be hove down until the water threatens to invade the cockpit, she must be eased by luffing. Don't, however, luff so much as to lose way. The pressure can be relieved by luffing just enough to spill some of the wind out of the mainsail; that is to say, until the luff of the sail is lifting whilst the after part is still drawing. By careful handling it should be possible to nurse her through an ordinary squall in that way; but if it is one of long duration it will be wise to reef.

Steering when the vessel is reaching presents no difficulties, as it is merely a question of laying a course. Having put your boat on her course, slack out the sheets until the sails begin to lift and then haul them in a trifle until they are drawing nicely. Then all you have to do is to keep the yacht steadily on her course. It is the easiest form of sailing there is, and that is probably why a breeze that enables the boat to reach either way is called a 'soldier's wind.'

Steering when running is equally simple, provided that you do not get by the lee. A vessel is said to be by the lee when the wind blows on the same side as that on which she is carrying her boom. The novice must be careful not to let his boat get much by the lee, as it might result in an unpremeditated gybe. Should the wind be strong, an accidental gybe might result in serious damage, as the boom would fly over with tremendous force.

STAYING

The modern yacht, with her deadwoods cut away, is extremely quick in stays and will often put herself about if you merely let go the tiller. The old-fashioned type of cruiser, however, often requires careful handling when in stays, particularly if the water be rough. As your first boat will probably be of the latter type, a few hints on staying her in rough water may not be out of place. It should be your aim to sail her round and you should not therefore stop her way by putting the helm hard over. Before attempting to stay her, ramp the boat along and get a good head of speed and then look out for a 'smooth.' If you watch the seas you will notice that every now and then there will be several waves larger than the general run and these are usually followed by one or two little ones, which the sailorman calls 'smooths.' Push over the tiller slowly and not too far at first, or you will knock the way off the boat. Let fly the jib sheet as she comes head to wind, but don't release it as long as the sail is drawing, for it is helping her through the water. Your aim should be to sail the yacht round, for if she loses her way she is pretty certain to miss stays. When the head-sails begin to lift let go the jib sheet and then give her a little more helm.

There is a moment when a vessel is in stays when the jib sheet can be hauled in and belayed with one hand, and that is when the clew has just blown clear of the forestay. Should you miss this opportunity, you would have to get the sheet in when the sail was full of wind, which would be uncommonly hard work if the sail were a large one. As the clew of the jib blows across the forestay, haul it in the other side and belay it and then do the same to the foresail sheet. Keep your helm over until she is nicely full on the new tack and then right the tiller. If your boat is very unhandy, it may be advisable to leave the foresail aback until she is safely on the new tack.

If you are beating to windward in an unhandy vessel in rough water it is possible that she may miss stays when going about and get 'in irons.' A vessel is said to be in irons when she lies head to wind and will not fill on either tack, having lost all way. Should this happen when you have plenty of sea room under your lee, haul the headsails aback, ease the mainsheet a little and reverse the helm for sternway. By such means you will soon get her going again. Then ramp her along for a bit and try again to stay her.

Should, however, she miss stays when beating up a river and there is shoal water close under her lee, it would be folly to make a second attempt to wend her. If she failed to go about when she had a full head of speed, she would be much more likely to do so when she had but a few yards in which to gather way.

If she failed a second time, as she would be almost certain to do, you would have no room to retrieve the situation and would probably find yourself hard and fast ashore before you could do anything.

If your vessel misses stays in the circumstances I have mentioned, there is only one thing to do and that is to 'wear' her, and waste no time about it. To perform this manoeuvre, the helm must be put up and the mainsheet paid out freely, the lee runner being let go to allow the boom to run off. When the yacht is right before the wind, haul in the mainsheet as quickly as you can in readiness for the coming gybe (described below), whilst a hand stands by to tend the runners. As the boom comes over, as it will do with considerable force, the runner which was previously slackened must be set up whilst the other is released. After the mainsail has gybed, ease over the headsails and trim the mainsheet as she comes on the wind again. Of course, by wearing you will sacrifice a good deal of distance to windward, but that is better than getting ashore.

RUNNING

When running before the wind in a yacht with a gaff mainsail the boom should be off as far as it will go, short of touching the shroud. The lee runner, of course, must be slackened right away to allow the boom to be squared off, but the weather runner should be set up taut. The headsail sheets should be quite slack, although when the wind is right aft those sails are blanketed by the mainsail and of no service. Indeed, if they are fitted with the Wykeham-Martin furling gear, they may as well be rolled up, as they can be set again in a moment should they be needed. So long as the wind is dead aft, or coming over the weather quarter, steering will present no difficulties, as all you have to do is to keep the yacht steadily on her course. Should the wind draw round on to the lee quarter, however, you must be very careful, as an unpremeditated gybe might spell disaster.

If the best is to be got out of your craft when running, the position of the crew is important. The old-fashioned type of vessel with a straight stem was apt to bury her head when running under a press of canvas, and it was the custom to bring all of the crew aft on to the counter to correct as far as possible this tendency to bore. I have seen the same practice followed in modern craft with overhanging pram bows; but that is quite wrong, as such vessels are apt rather to cock their noses out when running than bury them. To put the weight aft in such circumstances shortens the waterline and causes her quarters to drag, conditions not conducive to speed.

If your yacht has a flaring overhanging bow, therefore, place your crew amidships, or thereabouts, and thus get the full benefit of her sailing length. I remember it was found that the disposition of the crew in this manner made a considerable difference to the speed down wind of the America's Cup challenger, *Shamrock III*. When handling the spinnaker of a small yacht, care must be taken to keep the end of the boom out of the water, for should it be allowed to dip into the sea by mishandling, the spar will be broken off short against the rigging like a carrot.

GYBING

Gybing a yacht is the reverse of staying her. In tacking, the vessel is luffed until the wind is brought on to the opposite bow, but when gybing she turns stern on to the wind which is brought on to the opposite quarter. In the latter operation the mainsail swings across the deck, covering in its journey almost half a circle. If there is a strong wind, the boom, unless checked, will come over with terrific force, which may lead to serious trouble for the boom itself might be broken or the yacht even dismasted. You will see therefore that the operation of gybing is extremely dangerous unless carried out with the greatest care.

As soon as the yacht begins to get by the lee, or in other words, when the wind begins to blow on the same side as that on which she is carrying her mainsail, you should gybe her. It is foolish to run by the lee for any but the shortest distance, as, apart from the risk of an accidental gybe, it reduces the yacht's speed considerably.

First haul in the mainsheet until the boom is nearly inboard, at the same time luffing sufficiently to prevent a premature gybe. When the boom has been hauled in, the runner which has hitherto been the lee one must be set up and the other slackened off so as not to impede the travel of the boom when it comes over. Don't forget to do that, for if the boom struck the taut runner, one or the other might be carried away. Now you are ready for the gybe. Put up the helm gently and as the boom begins to come over, snatch a turn of the mainsheet round a cleat or bollard, or otherwise you may not be able to hold it. As the boom flies over, the yacht will show a tendency to broach-to – in other words, to turn strongly to windward such that she lies broadside to weather and may dip her lee rail under and risk swamping – so you must antipate this with the helm. As soon as the mainsail has gybed, ease out the mainsheet and pass the headsails over. Take care that no one's head is in the way when the boom gybes, as a blow from the spar might cause serious injury. And don't forget what I have just told you about taking a turn of the mainsheet round a cleat. To emphasize the importance of this I will tell you a little story.

Many years ago a friend of mine was sailing single-handed a 7-ton cutter down Channel. She was of the old plank-on-edge type, heavily sparred and carrying a large mainsail. Having to gybe in a squall, he omitted to take a turn with the mainsheet, which ran through his hands so fast that they were badly skinned. Being unable to touch a rope with his raw palms, he had no alternative but to seek the assistance of a smack, which towed him into Dover and subsequently 'mulcted' him for £50 salvage. Moreover, he was unable to use his hands for many weeks after the accident. Just one more warning. Keep clear of the coils of the main-sheet as the boom comes over. A story is told of a hand of a first-class racing yacht being cut in halves by getting entangled in the mainsheet during a gybe. That is probably an exaggeration, but all the same the mainsheet of even a small cruising craft could give you a pretty nasty nip. Do you remember what R. L. Stevenson has to say on the subject in *The Ebb Tide*? Captain Davis, when addressing the unspeakable Huish, remarks:

> "Where would you have been if the boom had swung out and you bundled in the slack? No, sir, we'll have no more of you at the mainsheet. Seaport towns are full of mainsheetmen; they hop upon one leg, my son, what's left of them, and the rest are dead."

Although I have laid some stress on the dangers of gybing, I don't want to make you nervous about it. Provided that reasonable care be exercised, there is no undue risk, and after you have carried out the operation a few times you will think nothing of it. The thing to avoid is the possibility of an unpremeditated gybe all-standing, and fortunately one usually has a certain amount of warning. There is a moment just before a yacht gybes when all the strain goes off the tiller, which lies lifeless in your grasp. If the helm be then put down quickly the impending gybe can sometimes be averted. But you should never let your ship get so much by the lee as to make an accidental gybe possible. As soon as you feel the wind drawing round on to the same side as that on which she is carrying her boom, gybe at once. You will not only be taking a seamanlike precaution but doing the best for the boat, as there is a definite loss of speed when sailing by the lee. How are you to know when the boat is getting by the lee? Well, the burgee will tell you; and so will the feel of the wind. When the wind is right aft you will feel it on the back of your neck, but when you are by the lee you will feel it on your cheek.

The casual helmsman is apt to say to himself, when the wind begins to draw round to the lee quarter, "I need not bother about gybing yet as she can't gybe herself until the wind is nearly on the beam." There he is quite wrong. In the first place the boom is never at right angles to the keel, as the after-shroud prevents its being run off so far. Then there is the possibility of the boom being swung aft a little by the motion of the yacht if the sea is at all rough. The motion of a lively little yacht in a heavy sea is quite sufficient to swing the boom several feet aft; so you will see that it is quite possible for her to gybe herself long before the wind is on the beam. This fact is so well known and appreciated that it is customary in small vessels when making an ocean passage, to guy the boom forward with a line when running, in order to check this tendency of the spar to swing aft.

Gybing in really heavy weather, of course, calls for extra care, as the slightest mistake might bring disaster in its train. For this reason it is sometimes more prudent to bring the yacht on the wind and stay her, bearing away again when she is on the other tack. Of course, there are times when one has no choice in the matter. For instance, there may not be room to stay, in which case one has no alternative but to gybe and chance it. Even so, it is possible to minimize the risk by reducing sail before gybing.

In the old days it was a common practice to trice up the tack to the throat, by means of the tack tricing line which led through a small block on the gaff just below the jaws; but now tricing gear is seldom seen except occasionally in smacks. It can only be fitted to a sail with a loose foot and probably the introduction of the laced-foot sail was the cause of its disappearance. As an alternative to tricing up the tack the peak can be lowered, but that is not desirable unless the yacht is carrying such a press of canvas that a reduction of sail is absolutely necessary.

When the peak is lowered the gybe becomes a double one. First the boom comes over and then the gaff, and as the latter is more or less free, it flies farther forward than it would in a normal gybe. There is thus a risk of damage either to the gaff itself or the crosstree. If a gybe has to be negotiated with the peak of the sail lowered, the mainsheet should be pinned in amidships as the boom comes over and not released until the gaff has gybed.

Then the sail can be eased out gradually as it is peaked up again. Rather than gybe with the peak lowered, some yachtsmen prefer to lower the throat, but if you do that you will have difficulty in re-setting the mainsail, as the peak will have to be lowered before you can hoist the throat back into its proper position. The peak, on the other hand, can usually be set again without trouble.

When discussing spinnakers in the chapter on setting sails, I referred to the tendency of the spinnaker boom to sky, and pointed out that if it were fitted with both fore and aft guys, which were set up taut, and the inboard end was higher than the outboard, it could not sky. But the spinnaker of a small yacht is usually set on a comparatively short boom which has an after guy only. If this guy be led through a fairlead near the runner, the comparatively sharp angle seems to minimize this skying trait.

The spinnaker boom of the small cruising yacht of to-day has no topping-lift and usually jaws instead of a gooseneck: it is consequently comparatively easy to handle. When the sail has to be shifted over to the other side after a gybe, the boom is allowed to go forward and is then unshipped from the mast. It is then run aft along the deck, until it can be pushed out the other side of the forestay. While this is being done, the head of the sail is lowered and secured to the other part of the halyard. With a smart crew the job can be done in a few seconds. Even in the big racing cutters the operation does not take so long as one would think. I once timed the crew of the famous *White Heather II* as they shifted the spinnaker in the course of a race on the lower Thames and they took just under forty seconds.

HEAVING-TO

Heaving-to is the sailor's equivalent to the soldier's marking time, for the vessel remains practically stationary. When hove-to she can be left to look after herself while the crew reef the mainsail or do anything else that may be required. A vessel is hove-to by first having the wind forward of the beam, and then one of the headsails sheeted to windward, which will prevent her travelling through the water. This can be effected by simply hauling it there if conditions permit or, more likely, by putting the vessel about without touching the headsail sheets. The mainsail attempts to drive her up into the wind, but the headsail, being aback, checks her progress. The two forces acting against each other keep the vessel almost stationary and nearly head to wind; many vessels will nonetheless continue to move through the water. If the yacht is a cutter it is better to back the foresail when heaving-to. As a rule the helm may be left free, but some yachts will not lie-to quietly unless the tiller is lashed a little to leeward.

When heaving-to for reefing purposes the mainsheet should be pinned in to keep the boom steady and enable you to reach the reef-points comfortably, and she will probably forge slowly ahead. Should you have to heave-to owing to bad weather, the boom should be well over the quarter.

REEFING

Shorten sail on the first indication of the approach of bad weather. Do not hang on to your whole mainsail until the yacht is overpowered, for under such conditions reefing will be infinitely more difficult. Moreover, the vessel will sail faster and make better weather of it when her decks are clear of water than she would with her lee rail and several planks awash. Having hove-to, the topping-lift should be set up and the boom sheeted hard in to prevent it kicking. Then the main and peak halyards should be slackened up sufficiently for the required reef to be taken in. Secure the luff-cringle to the boom, haul down the reef pendant with the tackle, which, by the way, should always be kept in readiness on the boom, and secure the pendant. For additional security a lashing should be passed through the reef-cringle and round the boom. If the sail has a loose foot, all that remains to be done is to roll up the foot neatly and tie the points with reef-knots. If the sail is laced to the boom, the tack must be secured before the clew is hauled down and you must be very careful that the cringles are well boused down to the boom. Should there be a few inches of slack the sail might be torn by the points, if the latter are tied under the boom, as they usually are. Some men make a practice of tucking the points between the sail and the boom before tying them, which certainly makes a very neat reef, but it takes too long and is really not necessary. I would refer the reader to what I have written on the subject of reefing gear in the section on equipment.

On single-handers and other craft that are sailed short-handed, at least one reef ear-ring should be kept always rove and the reef tackle in its place under the boom. When the first reef has been pulled down, the second reef pendant should be at once rove in case of need. If the pendant and reef tackle are stowed away in a locker, as is often the case in small yachts, they may not be forthcoming when wanted in a hurry.

Should you have to reef when beating up a river you may not have time to tie the points before reaching shoal water, but if you have got the tack and reef pendant secured, you can hoist the peak of the sail and put the vessel about and then tie down the points at your leisure whilst she heads away from the shore.

When shaking out a reef the process of reefing must be reversed. That is to say the points must be untied before the reef pendants are slackened, or otherwise the points may tear the sail. The topping-lift must be set up before letting go the pendant, to take the weight of the boom, and must not be eased up until the sail has been set.

After taking a reef in the mainsail it may be necessary to shift jibs in order to restore the balance. In the case of an old-fashioned type of yacht with a straight keel, it is seldom that one has to shift jibs until the second reef is taken in the mainsail, as such craft usually develop more weather helm when pressed. Experience alone can teach you what sail trim your boat likes, but as a rough guide I would suggest trying the No. 1 jib and whole foresail when you have one reef in the mainsail; reefed foresail and No. 2 jib when the mainsail is double-reefed; reefed foresail and No. 3 jib when the mainsail is close-reefed. Some yachts, however, do better with a No. 3 jib when the mainsail is double-reefed.

When setting a No. 3, or storm, jib there should be a wire span between the halyard and the head of the sail. If the halyard be shackled direct to the sail, there will be a long drift of manila rope which will stretch considerably and allow the luff of the sail to sag away to leeward. No yacht can be expected to sail decently to windward unless the luff of her jib is bar-taut, and that can only be achieved by a wire halyard, with a purchase, of which the blocks are no more than a foot or so apart when the sail is set. The span can be spliced permanently into the head cringle of the sail as shown earlier, and the length of the luff cum span should be the same as that of the working jib.

For a passing squall the yacht may be eased by lowering the foresail, which is an extremely powerful sail. Indeed, stowing the foresail is nearly as effective as taking a reef in the mainsail, but it is bad practice to sail a cutter without her foresail for long distances, as the vessel would probably sail far better with a reefed mainsail, foresail and small jib. I sometimes see a yacht in heavy weather sailing under a double-reefed mainsail and large working jib, with no foresail. It is, of course, less trouble to tend one pair of headsail sheets than two, but a vessel cannot be expected to perform respectably under such canvas. Under such conditions she should have a double-reefed mainsail, foresail (possibly reefed) and storm-jib, set half-way along the bowsprit. Under such canvas she will point higher, travel faster, be more handy and dryer. In bad weather the aim should be to concentrate the sail area, so far as possible, inboard. In a hard wind and rough sea, a big jib slatting violently is quite enough to make a vessel miss stays.

CHAPTER 53: *Heavy Weather*

"If you can't get into port before the seas get dangerous," said McMullen, "get as far from the land as you can and see it out at sea." The wisdom of that advice has been proved over and over again, and although it needs some pluck to turn your back on the land when the weather looks ominous, I am sure it is the right thing to do. I will try and tell you why.

In the open sea, waves do not break unless there is some special cause to make them, such as a tidal current or sudden change in the depth. The tops of the seas may break and invade the decks, but they are merely surface water and not likely to do serious damage. In shoal water, however, the seas assume a much more dangerous character, as they change from undulations to moving masses of water which, as they approach the shore, turn over and break with terrific force. Many fishing smacks and other small craft have been lost in trying to make port under such conditions and there can be no doubt that the majority would have come through in safety had they remained at sea.

When far from the land, where the waves are long and the water deep, a small vessel will be safe so long as she offers little or no resistance to the seas, but if you try and force her against them, they may break and overwhelm her. Curiously enough, it is when running before a heavy sea that the little ship is most likely to come to grief. One might think that the faster she ran away from the overtaking sea the less resistance she would offer to the waves and the safer she would be. Indeed, many old seamen formerly held the theory that sail should be crowded on in such circumstances to keep ahead of the seas. That idea, however, is nonsense, as in a gale of wind the seas travel at something like 30 miles an hour, far faster than any vessel can sail. It is obvious therefore that no craft under sail could keep ahead of the seas.

But let us consider why it is dangerous to run at high speed before a following sea. Every vessel has a maximum speed according to her length and displacement and if it be attempted to drive her beyond that speed, she starts wave-making on her own account and those artificial waves upset the rhythm of the true seas, causing them to break. In such circumstances a little ship may be pooped with disastrous results. When the yacht begins to steer hard and show a tendency to broach-to, sail should be reduced. Under short canvas she will need less steering and the seas will pass harmlessly beneath her.

Another factor, I think, that contributes to the breaking of a following sea is the action of the rudder. If the yacht is run too hard she needs a lot of helm to keep her straight and that tends to affect the true seas. I think this theory is confirmed by the fact that towing warps astern, or carrying a spinnaker to balance the mainsail, enables a small yacht to run with safety at a comparatively high speed as it tends to reduce to some extent the artificial wave-making to which I have referred. In the course of a Fastnet Cup race some years ago the cutter *Maitenes*, overtaken by a gale, ran for a long distance, with warps towed astern, at a speed of 10 knots. Ahto Walter, too, during one of his long voyages in the little *Ahto*, ran for many hours at high speed with a small spinnaker set. In the first of these instances I have quoted I think the restraining influence of the warps kept the yacht from yawing about, whilst in the other, the spinnaker balanced the mainsail and kept *Ahto* steadily on her course. The friction of warps towed at speed is very great, as will be gathered from the fact that in *Maitenes* it was found impossible to get the warps on board when they were no longer needed and they had to be cut adrift. They could no doubt have been hauled on board by bringing the vessel to the wind, but as she was competing in an important race, that was not to be thought of. Notwithstanding these instances I have quoted of yachts running at high speed before a heavy following sea, it is a risk not warranted when cruising, and I think most experienced yachtsmen will agree that in the absence of special circumstances it is wiser to shorten sail, or even heave-to or get the sea-anchor overboard. Well, so much for theory and now let us turn to practice.

First, let me say a few words about the canvas that should be carried when sailing in a strong wind and heavy sea. I frequently see small yachts in such weather staggering along under a double-reefed mainsail and large working jib, with no foresail set, which is definitely bad. No vessel can be expected to sail decently to windward under such a combination of sails, particularly if the luff of the jib is quite slack and sagging to leeward, as it often is. Not only will the yacht hold a very poor wind, but she will labour heavily in the rough sea, make a lot of leeway and be very wet and unhandy, even to the extent of missing stays, as the slatting of the big jib will prevent her coming about. The adoption of such a sail plan must be attributed either to ignorance or laziness, it being less trouble to handle one pair of sheets than two.

If the weather conditions demand a double-reefed mainsail, appropriate headsails must be carried if the vessel is to sail satisfactorily, and they should comprise the foresail (possibly reefed) and a small storm jib, set half-way along the bowsprit. I, of course, refer to craft with two headsails, but if your boat is a sloop, you will merely have to set your small jib instead of the usual working sail. Canvassed in the manner I have indicated, your little ship will be lively and dry, point higher, travel faster and be infinitely more handy when going about.

It is of the greatest importance that the luff of the jib should be bar-taut when sailing to windward, and that desideratum can only be achieved by the use of a wire halyard. A small jib set on a manila or hemp halyard is a hopeless proposition, as the rope will constantly stretch, owing to the long drift between the head of the sail and the block on the mast. Even with a wire halyard there should be as little manila in use on the purchase as possible, and there should be a wire span between the head of the sail and the halyard block, as explained in another chapter.

When close-hauled in a rough sea the yacht should be sailed a little fuller than in smooth water and with rather slacker main and fore sheets. The jib, however, should be sheeted rather more harshly, for should it be necessary to luff for a dangerous sea, it will help her to pay off again. Before going about, the yacht should be ramped along for a minute or two to ensure a full head of speed, and you should wait for a 'smooth' before putting down the helm. Every now and then, usually following one or two extra big seas, there is a patch of comparatively smooth water, and it is then that the boat should be stayed. Don't put the helm down too far at first, as it is desirable to gain as much distance to windward as possible as she comes round. When she is nearly head to wind, you can give her a little more helm. As soon as the clew of the jib clears the forestay, haul in the headsail sheets and you will then be able to get them belayed before there is any weight of wind in the sails.

If, when sailing to windward, you encounter a dangerous-looking sea, you should luff so as to meet it not quite end-on, bearing up again as soon as it is well under the yacht. When reaching in a heavy sea, you should carry rather less sail than you would in smooth water and be on the alert for threatening seas on your beam. These can be dealt with by luffing or bearing away, so that they are taken either on the bow or quarter. It does not matter which, but it is as well to vary your tactics, for if you always luffed or bore up you would be taken far out of your course.

Most yachts' mainsails have three rows of reef points and some four, but few little yachts will sail satisfactorily with more than two reefs down in heavy weather, owing to the windage of the top-hamper and the sail being partially becalmed in the trough of the sea. Under such conditions a trysail is more effective as it has greater hoist than a close-reefed mainsail and the absence of a boom makes for enhanced stability. Some yachtsmen, however, sacrifice much of the benefit derived from the trysail, by lashing the clew to the made-up mainsail, but that is bad practice. When the trysail is set, the main boom should be lashed down to the rail and double sheets, led through blocks on the quarters, used for the trysail.

A trysail may not be used very often, but is a useful sail nevertheless. It will come in handy, for instance, while you are stretching a new mainsail. To reef the new sail before it was thoroughly stretched would probably ruin it, but if you were caught out in a strong wind you might have to do so to get home. But if you had a trysail on board you could set that instead and eliminate the risk of spoiling the new mainsail. The knowledge that you were thus prepared for such a contingency would encourage you to sail on days when otherwise you would not care to venture and the stretching process would thus be accelerated.

There are two forms of trysail in use in yachts and it is a matter of opinion which is the better. One has a short gaff and the other is a thimble-headed sail. Personally, I prefer the former as I think it more effective although, perhaps, rather more trouble to set. The absence of peak seems to rob the thimble-headed sail of the driving power necessary to counteract the windage of the hull and top-hamper, and I have known more than one little yacht, handy enough under normal conditions, get quite out of hand in heavy weather under such a trysail. With a sail of that kind, too, the centre of effort is shifted farther forward and may even make the vessel carry lee-helm, a feature objectionable at any time and positively dangerous in heavy weather. When setting a trysail the usual halyards are employed and the luff attached to the mast either by a lacing or toggles.

Possibly the reason why the gaff trysail is not so popular with small yacht owners as the thimble-headed sail, is that it is rather more trouble to set, but if kept ready for use it really does not take very long. The gaff need not be longer than, say, half the length of the ordinary gaff and the sail should be kept already bent to it. As the spar will probably be too long to stow in the sail locker, it should be slung in the fo'c'sle, with the sail made up on it and the sheets bent on in readiness for setting. The jaws must be fitted with a parrel line and wooden balls. The hoist should be about the same as that of the mainsail, but as the sail is much shorter on both head and foot than the mainsail, its area is only about half that of the latter. As it will not often be used, it would be advisable to have it tanned to preserve it from mildew. It should be made of stout flax canvas and the luff rope of hemp, in preference to wire, to facilitate stowage. Some owners, with a view to economy, sometimes have a trysail made out of an old mainsail, but that is unwise, as it is obvious that canvas already condemned is not likely to last very long when exposed to heavy weather.

When the conditions become so bad that the yacht can no longer be sailed with safety, she must be hove-to, with the foresail a-weather and the main boom over the quarter. She will also probably require the helm lashed a little to lee-ward, but the amount of helm and mainsheet allowed her must depend on the type of yacht and can only be determined by experiment and experience. A yacht of the old-fashioned type with a straight keel and ample forefoot will usually lie-to quietly, making little or no headway, but many modern craft are perfect pigs to heave-to. Unless there is a man at the helm to restrain her antics, such a boat will at one moment fall broad off the wind and sea and then come to again with a rush. When heaving-to the aim should be to keep her from sailing ahead, for should she meet a wave with any force she might ship it green. When well hove-to, the vessel should make no appreciable headway but simply soak to leeward, leaving a wake on the weather side which will have the effect of smoothing the water a little.

It is doubtful if any vessel of less than 20 tons can be hove-to safely in a really heavy gale, as a smaller craft would be becalmed in the trough of the sea and probably overpowered on the crest. The alternative in such circumstances is to ride to a sea-anchor.

The sea-anchor, or drogue as it is sometimes called, has been the salvation of many small craft caught out in heavy weather far from the land, and, in my opinion, no little ship should set out on a deep-water cruise without one. The kind most commonly used is in the form of a conical canvas bag, sewn to an iron ring at the mouth and having a small hole at the apex. There is a rope bridle at

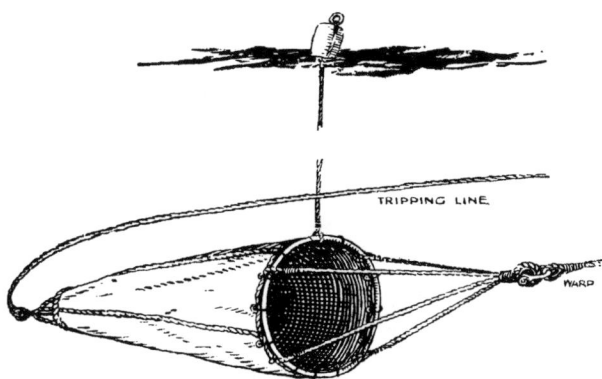

Sea-anchor — ordinary type

the mouth to which the riding warp is attached and the sea-anchor is kept from sinking too deeply by a small buoy secured to the ring by a few fathoms of line. A sea-anchor has a tremendous grip on the water and should keep the vessel riding about four points off wind and sea.

The Voss pattern, which I personally prefer as it is more convenient to stow away in a small yacht, is a canvas bag of pyramidal shape, the mouth being extended by crossbars of hard wood, bolted together in the form of a St. Andrew's cross. This type also has a small hole at the apex but does not need a buoy. A small lead weight is sewn in a pocket in one side of the mouth to sink it below the surface. When not in use, the Voss sea-anchor can be stowed in a comparatively small space. The crossbars are folded and the bag wrapped round them. It can, if preferred, be made with iron crossbars, but in that case a buoy would be needed.

Captain Voss also introduced a sea-anchor with a flat ring of hard wood at the mouth, which he recommended for use in craft of less than 30 feet in length. The ring is weighted to sink it.

Whatever type of sea-anchor you use, it must be immensely strong as it has to withstand enormous strain. It should be made of the stoutest canvas and every seam heavily roped, the ropes being extended to form the bridle to which the riding warp is attached. As most of the sea-anchors stocked by yacht-chandlers are

Sea-anchor — Voss type, shown head-to-wind and running

mere toys, it is, perhaps, better to have one specially made by a sailmaker. There seems to be a considerable divergence of opinion as to the correct proportions, and I think it depends a good deal on the type of yacht in which it is to be used. If the vessel has a fair amount of forefoot and her mast stepped well in her – not less than two-fifths of the waterline measurement from the bow – the diameter at the mouth should be, I think, about one-eighth of the waterline measurement. If she is of modern type, with but little forefoot, it would probably have to be a good deal larger to be really effective. The position of the mast, too, is extremely important, for if the centre of effort of the top-hamper is much forward of the centre of lateral resistance, the yacht will take a lot of holding to the wind and sea. Indeed, I am inclined to think that the majority of modern yachts will not ride by the bow at all and would do much better riding by the stern.

The late Mr. Claud Worth recommended a sea-anchor with a diameter at the mouth of one-tenth the waterline length, but I think his estimate was based mainly on his own experience of riding to a sea-anchor which was gained in his early days in small craft of the old-fashioned type with ample forefoot. The sizes advocated by Voss were as follows: For a vessel of 20-foot water-line, diameter 20 inches; length of bag, 30 inches with a 2-inch hole at the apex. To these figures 1 inch should be added to the diameter and 1½ inches to the length of bag for each extra foot of waterline length, increasing the size of the hole in the apex proportionately. It will be seen that the length of bag should be approximately one-and-a-half times the diameter at the mouth. A tripping line should be attached to the apex with any form of sea-anchor to facilitate getting it on board again, and it is important that it should be kept clear of the riding-warp. The tripping line is best made of bass rope, which is light and floats on or near the surface. Worth recommended stringing a few corks on it, which seems a good idea. The riding warp should be of stout manila of about 30 fathoms in length. For a yacht of about 20-foot waterline measurement the circumference of the warp should be 2½ inches, and for a craft of 30-foot waterline, 3 inches.

Steps must be taken to protect the riding warp from chafe. A parcelling of canvas would not be much good for that purpose as it would soon chafe through and it would be better to use a length of chain on the inboard end. A common practice is to unshackle the bower anchor and use the end of the cable for the purpose, but it is more prudent to keep a short length of chain specially for the job. Some time ago a yacht riding to a sea-anchor and using the end of her cable was drifting down on to a lightship and it became necessary to get way on her. When the crew attempted to get the sea-anchor on board they were unable to do so – I take it that they had omitted to attach a tripping line to it. They consequently had to slip the cable, thereby losing some 40 fathoms of chain in addition to the sea-anchor and warp.

In most cases some sort of riding sail aft is desirable. If the yacht is a yawl or ketch, a small mizzen might be used, but in a cutter or sloop the matter presents some difficulty. A storm jib could, however, be set up to the main horse and sheeted forward, or in a Bermudian boat a few feet of the head of the sail might be hoisted, the remainder of the sail being stowed and secured with tyers. The merest rag of sail will serve to hold the vessel to the wind provided that it can

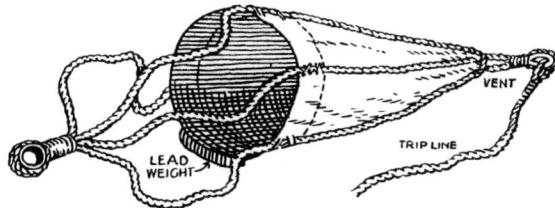

Sea-anchor — Voss round type

be kept full, but if it slats violently it will probably be blown to shreds in a very short time.

A sea-anchor of the Voss type can be effectively used when running before a heavy following sea. When employed in that way, it is towed astern of the vessel by its tripping line, apex first, so that it offers but little resistance. On the approach of a dangerous sea, the tripping line is slackened, allowing the sea-anchor to turn over and come into action. This holds the yacht's stern steady and prevents her broaching-to. When the sea has passed safely beneath her, the sea-anchor is tripped again. In this way Captain Voss took an open boat repeatedly across the dreaded Sumner Bar in heavy weather without shipping a drop of water.

Many yachtsmen are sceptical as to the utility of a sea-anchor, but I think it will be found that when it fails to 'do its stuff' efficiently it is because it has been attempted to ride by the bow in a craft of unsuitable type, as, for instance, one of light displacement with practically no forefoot and her mast stepped far forward. Experience has proved that such yachts will only ride satisfactorily by the stern. Given the right sort of craft and a sea-anchor of suitable dimensions, the efficiency of the sea-anchor is beyond dispute. Let us consider for a moment the evidence of yachtsmen of wide experience who have ridden out heavy gales in small craft to a sea-anchor. Claud Worth, when making a single-handed passage in *Tern*, 6½ tons, got caught out in the Channel in the great gale of September 1896 and rode it out in safety to a sea-anchor. Describing the experience, he said:

> After she was fairly astream of her drogue she shipped no more heavy water. She stood first on one end, then on the other, but climbed each sea safely. The wind tore off the tops of the seas, and the spray came in sheets, everything white as far as one could see. Daylight; no land visible. At about 11 a.m. wind suddenly veered to W. and blew – I don't want to pile on superlatives, but I have been in a pampero off the Plate, and a heavy gale of wind in the South Pacific, and I have never known the wind so strong or the seas so steep and so near breaking. A large barque, the *Rose Ellen* of Wilmington, passed quite close, running up Channel under bare poles, with rags of the lower main topsail streaming from the yard. Managed to change my clothes and to feed.

The strength of the wind on that occasion was force 9 by the Beaufort scale and the sea-anchor used 38 inches in diameter, or one-ninth of the waterline length of the yacht.

The fact that the windage of *Tern's* mast and boom, [Mr. Worth added] was little, if at all, forward of her centre of lateral resistance, undoubtedly had much to do with her riding so well to the drogue. Her drift was about a mile an hour. A vessel with cut-away forefoot and mast far forward would require a very large drogue and some sort of riding sail aft to keep her head to the sea.

Then we have the testimony of Mr. W. E. Sinclair, who frequently rode to a sea-anchor in heavy weather in the little 4-ton *Joan*, in which he made a number of ocean cruises. During a homeward journey from Funchal, when 18 days out, he tried the sea-anchor for the first time and says he was delighted with the result.

It answered admirably. Practically no water came aboard. We had no need to pump out and for a good deal of the time the sliding hatch was open just as we were accustomed to have it in calm weather. We were able to get a good long sleep.

After that Mr. Sinclair frequently used the sea-anchor, which always worked well, and when clear of the land he felt quite safe. It was his practice to set a small jib-headed mizzen as riding sail and he says that she kept steadily 4 points off the wind and it never shook. "She rode," he declares, "like the much quoted duck is supposed to ride," and her drift seems to have varied from half a mile to a mile an hour, according to the conditions obtaining.

In the absence of a sea-anchor, a little ship may be left to her own devices under bare poles, provided that she has any amount of sea-room under her lee. As she drifts she will usually take up a berth with the wind on her beam, or a point or two abaft the beam. Mr. Sinclair more than once allowed *Joan* to drift in that manner, notably on an occasion when the sea-anchor had been lost, and she came to no harm. Let me quote once more from his delightful book *Cruises of the Joan*:

When the wind and waves grow too strong for a little boat to sail she must stop. In general, if a small boat is left with no sail up she will ride up and down the waves in safety. The wind blows violently and she goes before it. The waves help her in the same direction and she offers no resistance. Because she does not resist these forces she is safe. Spray and wave-tops will be swept over her and she will be very wet outside, but with the cabin door shut she can be a dry home below. The Joan had often ridden out bad weather in this way without giving us cause to be alarmed, and with a sea-anchor out and a small sail hoisted astern she had ridden out several gales in what we called comfort.

A small yacht, however, can only be allowed to drift in that manner if she has almost unlimited sea-room to leeward. In a heavy gale her drift might amount to as much as 3 miles an hour, or, say, 70 miles in a day, and the gale might last for 4 or 5 days. Ahto Walter in one of his cruises let his little ship drift after he had lost his sea-anchor and she was driven about 150 miles off her course before the gale had moderated sufficiently to allow her to proceed under sail.

Oil can be used with great effect to smoothen the surface waves in heavy weather; indeed, pouring oil on troubled waters is proverbial. Captain Voss recommended for this purpose a good-sized canvas bag about three-quarters filled with cotton waste steeped in fish oil. A few holes are bored in the bag, which should be suspended over the bow if the yacht is riding bow-on to a sea-anchor, or over the stern if riding by the stern. When hove-to, the bag should be hung over the weather bow, or preferably there should be two bags. One could be suspended from the weather bow and the other from the weather quarter.

I remarked earlier in this chapter that seas do not break in open water unless special circumstances cause them to do so, but in heavy weather crests form on top of the waves. These crests, blown by the wind, may break on board but seldom do any serious damage as there is not much weight in them. Sometimes, too, the wind may change during a hard blow and waves from the direction of the new wind will then develop on top of the swell of the old sea. This imparts a peculiar corkscrew motion to the vessel, extremely uncomfortable to the crew and trying to all but the strongest stomachs. The influence of the old sea will be felt for a considerable time before it finally dies away.

No one should venture on deck in bad weather without first taking the precaution of tying a life-line round his waist. I have no doubt that the younger generation will regard this advice as grandmotherly, but neglect of such a precaution might easily lead to loss of life. Mr. Uffa Fox and another member of the crew of *Typhoon* were washed overboard during a voyage across the Atlantic, and one of the hands of *Ahto* was washed out of the cockpit near Ushant, through disobeying their captain's orders to put on life-lines, and narrowly escaped drowning. Apart from the risk of being washed overboard there is that of falling overboard, for in rough weather the deck of a small yacht offers but precarious foothold, owing to the violent motion.

Too little attention is paid to this matter in small craft. Every little ship that cruises far from the land should have permanent life-lines rigged above the rail from stem to stern. They may be unsightly, but they make for safety, and that should be the first consideration.

CHAPTER 54: *Anchoring and Stowing Away*

There seems to be an idea current among yachtsmen that, legally speaking, a vessel riding to a single anchor is not properly brought up, but that is not quite the case. The Board of Trade have made no regulation, nor are there any general statutory requirements under which a ship must be moored with two anchors, such matters being fixed by the 'custom of seamen,' although, of course, in restricted areas regulations may be made by the local harbour authority. But every ship is entitled to a clear berth, that is to say, room to swing to the tide or wind. If she is riding to a single anchor that involves a clear space with a radius of her own length plus scope of cable, with a bit to spare to allow for the fall of the tide. If she is moored with her kedge out astern, so that she rides first to one anchor and then to the other, as the tide changes, her clear berth

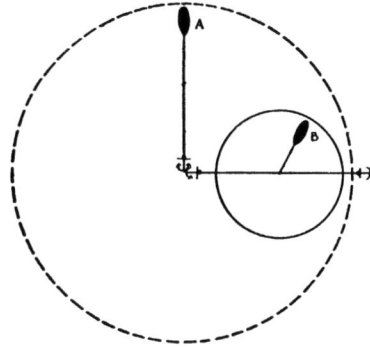

Clear berth of vessel anchored (A)
and moored (B)

will consist only of her length and cable radius, with a bit to spare, as she will remain in practically the same spot when the tide turns. In the illustration the large circle shows the clear berth of a yacht riding to a single anchor, and the small circle inset, the clear berth of one moored.

When a vessel has taken up a clear berth, any other anchoring after her must not encroach upon that berth, taking into consideration her own radius of swing. If she does so she gives the first-comer a foul berth and would be held responsible for any damage that might ensue through the two craft colliding. It will be seen therefore that the berth belongs to the first-comer and any vessel that brings up too close to her must either shift or take the consequences.

Provided that there is plenty of room to swing clear under all conditions of wind and tide, there is nothing to prevent a vessel riding to a single anchor, but in a congested anchorage – and there are few recognized anchorages that are not crowded nowadays – there is not sufficient room for her to do so and she should lay out a kedge. Apart from the legal aspect, it is selfish and unsportsmanlike to ride to a single anchor in a crowded yacht anchorage, thus causing inconvenience and danger to the property of others, and an owner who does so will very soon get himself disliked.

When mooring, the kedge should be laid out astern on the quarter on the opposite side to the anchor hawse; the yacht will then ride alternately first to the anchor and then to the kedge as she swings each tide. If the two anchors were laid out ahead from the bows, the yacht would take up nearly as much room as if riding to a single anchor.

It is customary to moor up and down stream. But sometimes, when wind-rode in an exposed anchorage, the kedge is laid out to relieve the bower anchor. A yacht thus situated should be moored with open hawse to windward – that is to say, with an anchor put from each bow and some distance apart. The simplest way to do this is to pay out a big scope of cable on the bower, and then set a headsail with the sheet belayed a-weather. This will cause the craft to forge away from the anchor, when the kedge can be dropped. Then, when the sail has been stowed, cable should be paid out on the kedge whilst it is hove in on the bower until there is nearly the same scope to each. It is advisable, however, to have a few fathoms more on one than the other, for should the anchors drag together, one will then back the other without fouling.

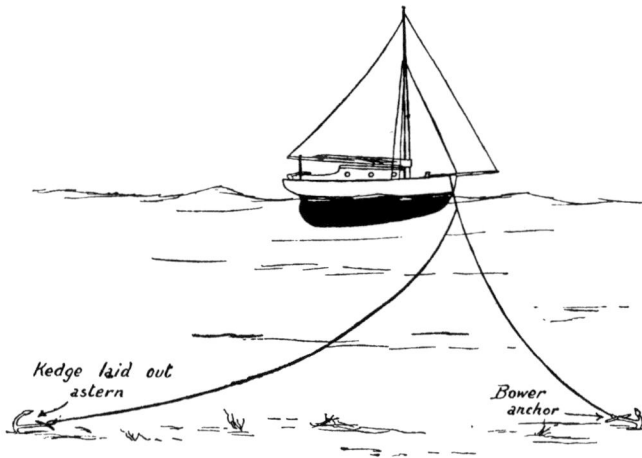

Mooring with kedge

Many yachtsmen appear to be obsessed by the herding instinct and whenever possible bring up close to other craft. I have frequently anchored when there has not been another yacht within sight and before nightfall have been surrounded by a fleet, although there were plenty of equally good berths available anywhere within a mile or more, and sometimes the late arrivals have even given me a foul berth. You may ask, what does it matter so long as they keep clear of you? Well, I will tell you, and if in doing so I have to refer to matters of a rather intimate nature, you must forgive me.

Nowadays, many yachts have women on board and their presence may be the source of much inconvenience and discomfort to others at close quarters. Few small craft of 5 tons or less are fitted with a lavatory, and in its absence one has to make shift with a sanitary bucket in the cockpit. In ordinary circumstances that is quite a satisfactory arrangement, but when you are surrounded by other yachts, with girls sitting about on deck, it becomes impossible and you may be subjected to dire discomfort. Even if it is merely a matter of bathing, you have to retire to the cabin to dress, and removing a wet bathing-costume will make things unpleasantly damp.

Registered vessels over a certain tonnage have to use anchors of specified weight adequate for the size of the ship, as found efficient by experience and duly certified by a competent authority, but the small yacht owner is not subject to such restrictions. It is up to him, however, to see that his ground tackle is sufficient to hold his yacht in any weather likely to be experienced in the course of the season. Should his vessel drag and damage some other craft, the inference is that his ground tackle was either inadequate or improperly used, which in either case would constitute negligence. It is a common practice in such circumstances to plead 'Act of God,' or in other words that the accident was inevitable and beyond human control, but in my opinion such a plea could only be successfully maintained in a gale of abnormal severity, such as that experienced in September 1935, when literally hundreds of yachts were lost or damaged all along the south coast.

The wind on that occasion attained a velocity of about 100 miles an hour and accidents were so numerous that the leading yacht underwriters came to an agreement that each would bear his own loss. But storms of such severity are very rare during the yachting season and a yacht's anchor should be adequate to hold her in any ordinary summer gale. If it fails to do so, surely the owner should be held responsible, particularly when other vessels in the neighbourhood are securely held by their ground tackle and do not drag.

The inexperienced yachtsman is apt to make a frightful hash of bringing up. He either gives some other craft a foul berth, or, after he has anchored and stowed his sails, finds that there will be insufficient water to lie afloat at low tide. He consequently has to move and that often entails setting his sails again. More often than not, I think it is due to lack of preparation. For instance, the conditions of wind and tide may necessitate the mainsail being lowered before the anchor is dropped, and having nothing ready it may not be possible to get the sail down in time. The yacht consequently travels beyond the selected berth before the anchor is down and holding.

When approaching the anchorage, the topping-lift should be set up, the halyard coils removed from the belaying pins and capsized ready for running, and the anchor got over the bow and clear of the bobstay. Thus prepared, there will be no delay in getting the mainsail down. It is also wiser to take a sounding with the lead before anchoring, rather than after. Now I will try and give you a few hints on the best method of anchoring under various conditions.

First of all let me impress upon you that the anchor should not be dropped while the yacht is stationary, for if you dump several fathoms of chain on top of it, it is almost certain to be fouled. Even a C.Q.R., which cannot be fouled when in the ground, might be if you dropped a lot of chain onto it before it had had a chance of cutting into the bottom. It is immaterial whether the vessel is forging ahead or dropping astern, provided that she has some way on.

Then there is another point. You must know what depth of water you will need for your ship to lie afloat at low water and as you approach the anchorage should make a rough calculation. You will probably know what the range of tide is for your district and can calculate how much the tide has to rise or fall at any hour by what is known as the 1, 2, 3, 3, 2, 1 rule. If the range be divided into twelve parts, the tide will rise or fall approximately 1 part in each of the first and last hours, 2 parts in each of the second and fourth hours and 3 parts in each of the third and fourth hours. Suppose that the range is 12 feet and you bring up at two hours ebb. By the rule the tide will fall another 9 feet, which must be added to the draught of your boat. Thus, if she draws 3 feet, you will need at least 12 feet, or 2 fathoms, of water when you anchor, if she is to lie afloat at low tide. But it is not wise to anchor in such shoal water; you must leave a margin in case the wind changes during the night, converting your berth from one under a weather shore to one on a lee shore. Should that happen, as it often does, your boat might be blown nearer the shore and take the ground.

Well, with those preliminary remarks, we can get on a bit. Let us suppose that you are beating into the anchorage with a fair tide. Having selected a good clear berth, sail a little way beyond it and lower the mainsail. Then run to the berth under a headsail, sounding as you go. Having reached it and ascertained that the depth of water is right, stow the headsail and wait until the boat begins to drop astern on the tide before letting go the anchor. Check the chain as the anchor touches the bottom and pay it out gradually until she has a full scope. In ordinary circumstances the scope should be three times the depth at high water, or rather more if your anchor is a C.Q.R..

Had you been beating over a foul tide, you would merely have had to luff into the berth and wait for sternway before dropping the anchor. As the yacht would be lying head to wind and tide after she had brought up, the sails could be stowed at your leisure.

If running with fair wind and tide, haul your wind as you near the chosen berth and luff into it, letting go the anchor just before she is head to wind. She will then run out most of her scope before she loses way and the friction of the chain over the stem roller will drive the fluke of the anchor well home. If running with a fair wind over a foul tide, lower the mainsail before you reach the berth and sail to it under a headsail. The headsail should be stowed before dropping the anchor, which you must not let go until she has sternway.

If you are reaching with the wind on the beam, you can lower the mainsail before reaching the berth and sail into it under a headsail, which should be lowered and the anchor dropped after the yacht has gathered sternway. An alternative method is to stow the headsails just before reaching the berth and luff into it. Then let go the anchor, at the same time lowering the mainsail, which must be got down before the yacht has swung to the tide, or she will charge about all over the place and possibly break the buoy-rope.

The most trying conditions that one can have for picking up a mooring are when the yacht is driven up with a strong tide and no wind. I think the best method to employ in such circumstances is to send the dinghy out ahead with a warp to tow the yacht. Steerage way will thus be secured, and when the mooring is reached the man in the dinghy can make fast the towing-line to the buoy rope; then those on board the yacht, by hauling vigorously, will be able to sight the chain and secure the yacht before any great strain is thrown upon the mooring.

With wind against tide, unless the yacht be wind-rode, it is advisable to give a sheer to prevent her fouling the anchor, in other words, to lash the tiller a little to one side or the other. In such circumstances the boat should be sheered to windward if the breeze is not dead aft. Should the wind, however, come right over the transom, she may be sheered either way. If, however, you bring up in a crowded anchorage, you should sheer the same way as the other craft; there is usually a local rule about this.

Having brought up, the sails and gear must be stowed and everything made shipshape for the night. Start with the mainsail, which we will suppose is a gaff sail with a loose foot. First ship the boom in the crutch and set up the mainsheet and then, if you are not going to put on the sail cover, ease up the outhaul a bit to allow for shrinkage by rain or dew. You will be wise, however, to put on the cover to keep the sail clean. Belay the peak halyard so that the end of the gaff is just clear of the boom and then haul the foot of the sail over the boom. Haul the leach forward and lay it on the foot, having got all of the sail on one side of the boom. Now stand on the opposite side and leaning over, get a grip on the sail with your hands spread apart and shake vigorously. Repeat this, getting a grip lower down each time, until the whole sail is neatly rolled up. You should press your knees against the boom as you shake to keep the foot and leach from falling off. When the sail has been stowed, secure it with the tyers, which should be passed round the sail and gaff only, except that at the gaff-end which goes round both gaff and boom. Three tyers should be sufficient, although a fourth may be desirable near the boom-end. If the sail has a laced foot, you have merely to haul the leach forward and roll up.

I think the best way to stow a Bermudian sail is to flake it. The sail should be folded backwards and forwards across the boom, gradually reducing the size of the 'flakes' until the whole sail is on the boom. Then pull up the lowest flake on either side to form a skin and pass the tyers round sail and boom. When stowed the sail is of course a good deal higher near the mast, but the cover is made to accommodate that.

Having stowed the mainsail, unshackle the halyards and put on the cover. With a gaff sail it is the usual practice to remove both halyards from the gaff, but I don't think it really necessary to take off the main halyard. I merely slack it up a little and tie it in the collar of the cover. Any water that gets in just trickles down the mast and does not touch the sail, which is several inches away, owing to the presence of the mast-hoops. With a Bermudian sail the halyard should always be removed before putting on the cover.

Now stow away the headsails. If the jib is fitted with the Wykeham-Martin furling gear, it can be left up, but a tyer should be put round it near the clew, in case the rolling line should get adrift from its cleat and allow the sail to unroll, and the halyard should be slackened a few inches. It is not wise, however, to leave the sail up throughout the summer, as some owners do, as the leach cloth will get dirty and be stretched out of shape. The fore-staysail of a cutter is best stowed away in the sail locker, with its sheets attached. If left bent for the night, it should be neatly rolled up and raised from the deck by a lanyard made fast to the rigging.

After the sails have been stowed, the halyards and other gear on the mast should be frapped, to keep them from tapping against the mast, which makes an irritating noise and causes unnecessary chafe to the ropes. You can either frap them by winding one of the halyards round and round the mast and other gear, before belaying it; or you can use lanyards attached to the rigging, the latter method for preference. In my own boat I have lanyards of hambro-line permanently seized to the shrouds on either side and secure the halyards and other ropes with them so that they do not touch either the mast or rigging. The halyards and topping-lift should be belayed quite slack, otherwise a shower of rain might shrink and take all the life out of the rope. Finally, coil the mainsheet and hang it up to the boom crutch. Having stowed away, you can go below and cook that juicy steak, for which I have no doubt you have a hearty appetite after your day's sailing.

A FOULED ANCHOR

There are few more annoying mishaps than that of getting your anchor foul of a heavy mooring and such an incident is by no means uncommon in these days of crowded anchorages. If, before letting go your anchor, you look round and note the position of craft at moorings and vacant mooring buoys, you should not often be trapped in that manner, but at some places the moorings are laid athwart the tide and constitute a snare for visiting yachtsmen, who naturally conclude they are laid up and down stream in the usual way. Then again, moorings are sometimes lost and lie on the bed of the sea, a veritable trap for the unwary. Walton Creek, at the back of the Naze, for instance, is a graveyard of lost anchors and chains and on many occasions I have got my anchor foul of some obstruction there.

At low water, when you are foul of a mooring, it is usually possible to heave up the obstructing chain on your anchor until you can sight it. If you are able to do that the remedy is simple. You have merely to pass a stout rope round it – the end of a warp will do very well – and make fast to the bitts. Then by lowering the anchor a foot or so, it can be pulled clear of the mooring chain. Hang on to the mooring until you are ready to get under way and then slip it. That is all very simple, although it will probably make you sweat a bit heaving up the obstruction.

It is possible, however, that it may be high water when you discover that your anchor has fouled a mooring. It is very certain that you will not be able to lift the obstructing chain high enough to sight it under such conditions. Then what are you to do? Must you wait until low water and waste the whole of a favourable tide? Well, I will tell you how I coped with such a situation once with complete success. I had brought up overnight in Walton Creek in my 7-ton cutter *Seabird* and the next morning when I tried to get the anchor I found it foul of some heavy obstruction. It was high water and being bound north I wanted all of the ebb tide. To have waited until low tide would have meant wasting the whole of the ebb and deferring my start until the next day. That was unthinkable, so I and my companion started to heave in cable with the windlass. There was little chance of being able to sight the obstruction, but we went on heaving in chain until we could get no more. The yacht was then pinned down by the head and the cable straight up and down and as taut as a bar of iron. Feeling down the cable with the boathook, I found that it was a mooring chain we had fouled and it was hanging on our anchor about 5 feet below the surface. Then I got out the lead and line and dropped the lead ahead of the obstructing chain. Hooking the line below the mooring chain with the boathook, I hauled it on board and thus had a line round the obstruction. The rest was easy. Bending a warp to the lead line, I hauled it round the mooring chain and made it fast round the bitts. Then I slackened the cable a foot or two and my companion, taking it out along the bowsprit, hauled the anchor clear. Finally, we got the anchor on board and having made sail, slipped the mooring chain and were away with little loss of time.

Even if we had not been able to reach the obstruction with the boathook, I don't think the position would have been hopeless. I should have fastened a tripping line to the crown of the kedge and lowered the latter until I could hook the mooring chain with it and then made the warp fast. I should thus have had two anchors foul of the mooring, but the kedge would have had a rope on its crown by which it could be tripped. By slackening the cable and taking it out ahead in the dinghy the anchor could have been hauled clear. Then the mooring chain could have been dropped to the bottom and the kedge recovered with the tripping line. That necessity is the mother of invention is a true saying and by a little thought one can often find a way out of a difficult position.

CHAPTER 55: *Moorings*

That it is a great convenience to have a permanent mooring at one's headquarters no yachtsman would deny, and it is the right of every British subject to lay down moorings in navigable waters. That fact was established by a famous test case in 1897. The action was brought by the Essex Yacht Club against the sublessee of the foreshore, to restrain him from interfering with members' yachts and their moorings. Claiming that the laying of the moorings was a trespass which he had a right to abate, he had not only cast the yachts adrift but also pulled up the moorings themselves. The verdict was in the yacht club's favour and the defendant appealed.

When the appeal was heard, the judgment of the lower court was confirmed, the Master of the Rolls, in the course of his judgment, saying:

> That mode of anchoring (fixed moorings) is within the ordinary course of navigation and the right of anchoring granted to an individual – it is not a right to be granted by the Sovereign, it is a right belonging to the country as part of it, a right that everybody (unless an enemy) should use those navigable waters in any ordinary navigable way, and amongst these ordinary and navigable ways is from time to time to anchor a ship, and to anchor it by either of the two ways which are perfectly well known, namely, by an anchor they can take up at any moment, or by an anchor they may leave at the bottom of the sea, with a buoy and a chain left there as a mooring in order that they may go away for a time and come back. This is a public right of everybody navigating navigable waters.

The other Lords Justices concurred, their ruling being on much the same lines as that of the Master of the Rolls, and the appeal was dismissed.

It would appear from the judgment in this test case that the owners or lessees of fisheries have no legal right to prohibit anchoring or mooring on their fisheries, yet some time ago a certain oyster company publicly announced their intention of prosecuting anyone who anchored or moored within the limits of their fishery.

On receipt of this notice the local yacht clubs took legal advice and a letter was sent to the company asking on what particular case or statute they relied for their claim to prohibit mooring. In reply they stated that their claim was based upon the Sea Fishery Act of 1867. The clubs' solicitors pointed out that there was no such Act and the company's representatives then said that they had made a mistake and the act to which they referred was that of 1888. On reference to this Act it was found that although various penalties were mentioned for damaging or interfering with oyster layings, there was a clause in the same Act to the effect that nothing in the Act should vary or alter the rights of ships or vessels to anchor or moor on any oyster beds, as permitted in common law. This was pointed out to the company and so far as I know nothing further on the subject was heard by the clubs.

Now, if a yacht owner is legally entitled to lay down moorings in navigable waters, why should he have to pay the oyster companies a yearly fee for the privilege of doing so? It seems to me a gross imposition, but for the sake of peace yachtsmen in many districts have for a good many years past allowed themselves to be mulcted in that manner. Individual yacht owners cannot be expected to shoulder the burden of fighting the oyster companies over this matter, but the local yacht clubs might very well combine and take action. I believe that if the clubs said to the oyster companies, "we intend to lay moorings without payment and if any of the yachts or their ground tackle are interfered with we shall take immediate action," nothing further would be heard about payment.

I have dwelt on this matter at some length because it is one that affects many hundreds of yacht owners. No one, I am sure, would wish to inconvenience the oyster companies more than necessary, but yachtsmen are jealous of their rights and the companies would be well advised to adopt a more conciliatory attitude.

Although one has the right to moor in navigable waters, it must be clearly understood that the mere fact of laying down a mooring does not give one a right to the berth. The actual anchors and chains of which the mooring is composed are the property of the man who lays them down and no one else has any right to touch them without his permission, but he has no claim on the water or ground surrounding them. His rights in fact are precisely the same as if he brought up to his anchor, and if on returning to the anchorage he finds that another vessel has anchored so close to his mooring that he cannot use it without giving the other vessel a foul berth, he must refrain from picking it up. But if, in such circumstances, he has no legal right to use his mooring, I think most yachtsmen would recognize that he had a moral one, as he had gone to considerable expense in laying down the mooring. If he politely asked the first-comer to move so that he could pick up his mooring, it is probable that his request would be granted; but he must remember that he is asking a favour and not demanding a right.

To pick up another man's mooring without permission is not only unsportsmanlike but definitely illegal. That was laid down by the Master of the Rolls in the case to which I have referred above. I will quote his actual words:

"You will say that nobody has a right to injure my chain or cut away my buoy, and you will say, and in my opinion rightly say, *no person has a right to use my buoy and my anchor in order to fix his own ship to it, and thereby anchor his own ship.*" (The italics are mine.)

There is nothing in yachting so disturbing to the amenities as this use of other people's moorings without permission. There are unscrupulous yachtsmen, and unfortunately their number seems to be growing, who make a practice of grabbing any mooring they happen to see vacant, regardless of whether the owner may return and want it, or whether it is of sufficient weight and strength to hold the vessel; and what is more they frequently go ashore, leaving the yacht unattended. In such circumstances the owner of the mooring, if he returns during their absence, must either anchor or jill about for perhaps an hour or two until it pleases the 'mooring-snatchers' to return and get their vessel under way. Recently a friend of mine at Fambridge went for a short sail, leaving his dinghy on the mooring. When he returned he found a strange yacht on his mooring and her crew had gone ashore in his dinghy. As an example of consummate impudence, that, I think, would take a deal of beating; but those who do such things are not sportsmen – they are not even gentlemen.

Then again, big yachts often pick up the moorings of small craft with the result that the anchors are drawn together and have to be relaid at the owner's expense. I recently saw a yacht of over 70 tons pick up the mooring of a 3-tonner and drag it half-way across the river.

Mind you, no yachtsman would be so churlish as to grudge the use of his mooring to a visiting yacht, provided that it was of sufficient weight and strength to hold the vessel and he did not want to use it himself. Indeed, most owners when away cruising like their moorings to be used during their absence, as it keeps the buoy rope free from weed. But if you value your reputation as a good sportsman you should, before picking up a mooring, ascertain whether the owner is likely to return and whether it is of sufficient weight to hold your craft. There is usually a waterman, or some local yachtsman, about from whom you can get this information.

Having satisfied yourself on these points, get the chain on board. This last may seem rather superfluous advice, but I have known many instances of buoy ropes being stranded through yachts riding to them. Unless you know definitely that the owner of the mooring will not return, do not go ashore leaving no one on board. If you remain on board and he happens to return, you will be able to slip the mooring without causing him inconvenience.

It must be understood that my remarks on the subject of anchoring and mooring rights do not apply to waters governed by a competent authority. In such ports the mooring and anchoring of vessels are controlled by the Harbour Master, and you have no alternative but to berth where and as instructed by him.

PICKING UP A MOORING

There are few things in connection with seamanship which the novice approaches with such apprehension as picking up a mooring, yet it is not really very difficult. It is true that under certain conditions of wind and tide it calls for a certain

Tide   Wind

A. Lower mainsail.

B. Bear up under headsails.

C. Run to mooring under
     headsails.

Mooring
Buoy

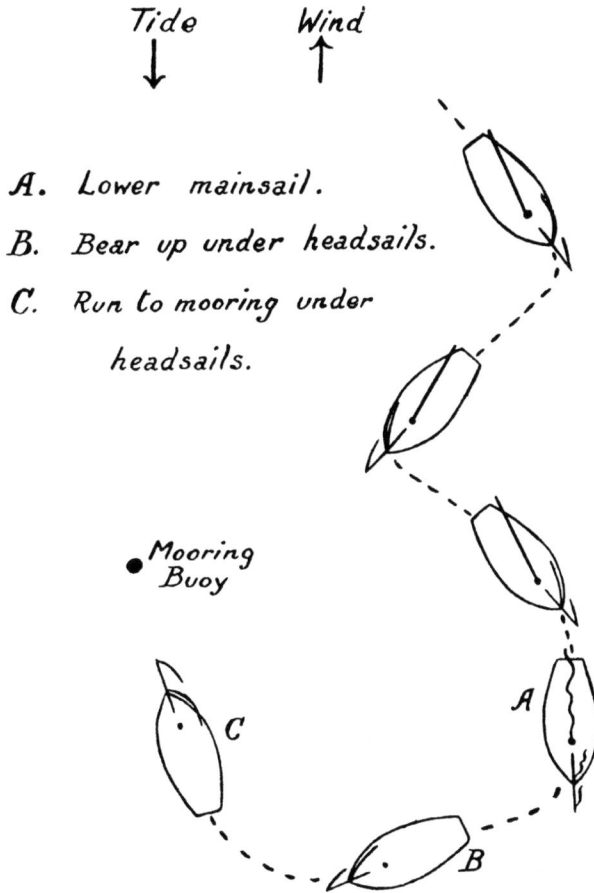

Picking up a mooring — beating with a fair tide

amount of judgment, but more often than not it is as easy as shelling peas, as they say. The trouble of most beginners is that they do not use their brains. They seem to think they have only to sail up to the mooring and pick up the buoy. The result is sometimes disastrous and sometimes amusing-at any rate for onlookers.

The error most commonly made by the novice is to attempt to pick up a mooring while sailing with wind and tide, but that is all wrong. It cannot be too strongly stressed that a mooring must be picked up against the tide. Even if you succeed in getting hold of the buoy while sailing with wind and tide, it is extremely unlikely that you will be able to hold it, as no man is strong enough to hold a heavy yacht when her sails are full of wind and she has the tide under her. I can understand a novice making that mistake once, but how he can go on doing the same thing week after week right through the season, beats me. Yet some of them do. Many years ago at Fambridge, the owner of a certain 5-tonner provided us with entertainment almost every Sunday evening. He was obsessed by the idea that moorings should be picked up with the wind and tide, and often spent

Wind   Tide

A. Begin to haul wind.

B. Luff head to wind and

shoot up to mooring.

Mooring
Buoy

B

A

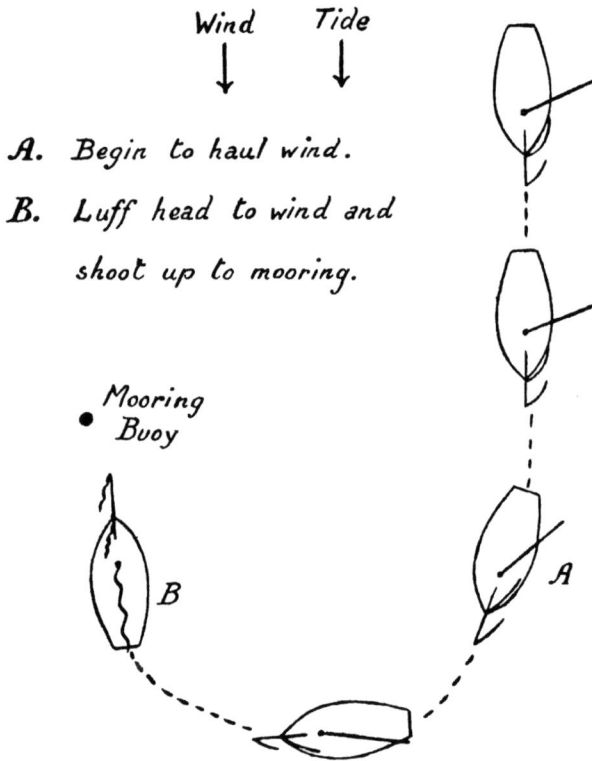

Picking up a mooring — fair wind and tide

an hour or more in fruitless efforts to moor his ship. His crowning performance occurred one Sunday afternoon, when he had with him a guest who evidently had had no previous experience of sailing. Having lost his boathook, the owner had instructed his visitor to hang over the bow and pick up the buoy by hand.

In accordance with his usual practice, he came sailing down to the mooring under whole sail, with a fresh breeze aft and a snoring ebb tide beneath him. Being an ex-2½-rater she was a fast boat and must have been travelling at something like seven or eight knots. Well, she came flying down to her mooring at top speed with the hapless visitor hanging over the bow. He grabbed thebuoy with praiseworthy accuracy, and we heard the owner shout "Don't let go." His guest had evidently been trained to obey orders and hung on nobly. A moment later he was in the 'ditch' cuddling the buoy, whilst the yacht continued her mad career down the river. When we picked up that lad, he was saying a good deal more than his prayers.

Well, having told you how not to do it, I will try and tell you how it should be done under various conditions of wind and tide. The easiest conditions are when beating up to the mooring with a fair tide, so we will start with that. Beat some little way past the mooring, then lower the mainsail and run back to it under a headsail. When the buoy is but a few yards distant, stow the headsail, and if

Tide

A. Haul wind.

B. Luff head to wind and lower mainsail.

C. Bear up under headsails.

D. Reach up to mooring under

headsails.

Wind

B

Mooring
Buoy

C

D

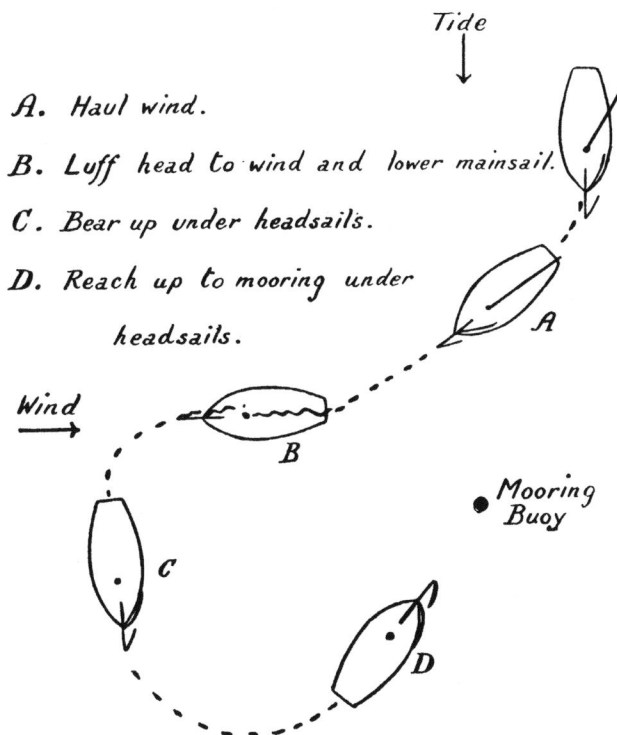

Picking up a mooring — wind on beam, method 1

you have judged it correctly, the yacht should lose her way just as she reaches the mooring. Then all you have to do is to pick up the buoy with the boathook and haul the chain on board. If the wind is light and you find, after lowering the mainsail, that the boat cannot stem the tide under a headsail alone, hoist the peak a few feet. In a dead light air, it may be necessary to run back to the mooring under the mainsail, and in such circumstances the peak must be lowered just before you reach the mooring.

If you are coming up to the mooring with a foul tide, all you have to do is luff on to the buoy and pick it up. As she will then be riding head to wind and tide, you can stow the sails at your leisure.

Now we come to what are perhaps the most difficult conditions for a novice, namely, with a fair wind and tide. As the buoy must be picked up when the yacht is head to wind and tide, you must allow sufficient room for rounding her up into the wind. You should therefore direct your course a little to leeward of the buoy and begin to haul your wind when the buoy is approximately on your beam. To bring the yacht head to wind and tide, and lose way just as she reaches the buoy, calls for nice judgment and a knowledge of your vessel, but with a little practice you will soon become expert. It is not really so difficult as it sounds, for, as you round her up, you can regulate the speed with the mainsheet.

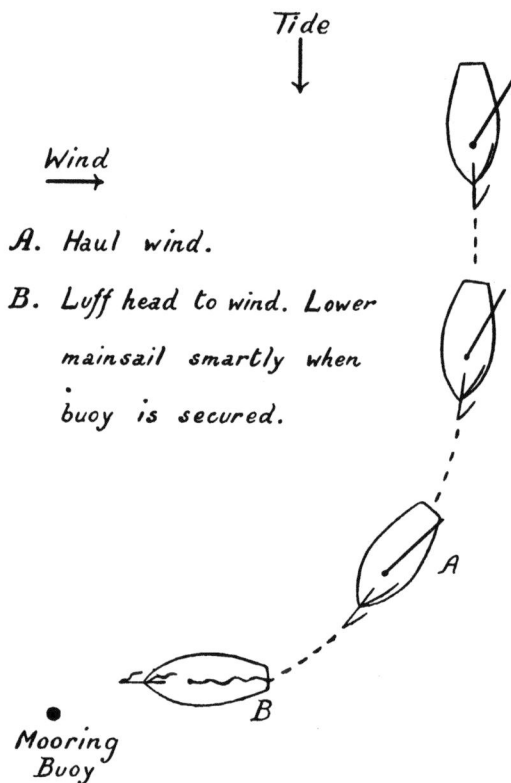

Picking up a mooring — wind on beam, method 2

Although I have only referred to picking up moorings when running and beating, the method when reaching is much the same. If the wind is abaft the beam, you should act as if you were running with the wind aft, and if it is before the beam, proceed as if you were beating. If the wind is actually on the beam, you have the choice of two methods. You can either luff to windward of the buoy, lower the mainsail and pick up the mooring under a headsail against the tide; or you can shoot up to the buoy from leeward under the mainsail, lowering the sail smartly as soon as the buoy is on board. The former is the safer method for a novice, as it is essential in the latter case to get the mainsail down before the yacht has swung to the tide.

CHAPTER 56: *Running Aground*

The yachtsman who has never run his craft ashore is a *rara avis* indeed, for even the most experienced do it sometimes, while to the novice it is an incident of frequent occurrence. It may arise through ignorance of the locality, mishandling the yacht, or from sheer carelessness. I think, however, the most common cause of such a mishap is holding on too long on a board towards the shore, particularly when beating over a foul tide. As you approach the shore you find rather slacker water and are tempted to make the most of it. Very often you are actually in the act of going about when the vessel strikes the ground, which seems very bad luck. But it is no good getting cross about it, for after all it was your own fault. You should either have gone about sooner, when you had ample water, or else have sounded with the lead as you approached shoal water.

The recognized method of taking soundings is with the hand-lead and line. The lead commonly used in small yachts weighs 5 or 6 lb. and the line is marked at intervals by different kinds of material, so that you can see at a glance the depth of water. A proper hand-lead, as used in bigger vessels, weighs 14 lb. and the line is 25 fathoms in length, but a lead of such hefty proportions would be out of place in a small craft. All that the yachtsman, who confines his cruising to coast-wise passages, needs is a lead of about the weight I have indicated, on a line of some 10 fathoms in length. It should be marked at every fathom with a different sort of material, so that the depth of water can be ascertained at a glance. To avoid kinking, the line should be cable-laid and, incidentally, should always be coiled anti-clockwise.

To heave the lead when the yacht is under way, you must cast it well ahead of the vessel, so that it is on the bottom and the line taut to your hand and straight up and down when you are immediately over it. The coils of the line should be held in your left hand so that it will run freely and when you feel the lead strike the bottom, as you will, you must gather in the slack of the line. If you heave the lead to leeward you are less likely to get wet.

A quicker way of taking soundings when in shallow water is by means of a pole, or boathook, and if much of your sailing is done in rivers and estuaries, it is worth while carrying on board a light bamboo rod of, say, 8 or 10 feet in length. Rings should be painted round it in different colours to indicate the depth, an exceptionally conspicuous one, such as a black band, two inches wide, at a depth of one foot greater than the yacht's draught. You will then know, when sounding, that so long as that band is submerged, you have nothing to worry about.

The method you employ to refloat the yacht must depend upon the conditions under which she took the ground and as they are infinitely variable, no hard-and-fast rules can be laid down and any hints I give must be regarded merely as suggestions. You must not think, if she has taken the mud when beating on a flood tide, that you have only to sit and smoke your pipe until the rising tide floats her off, because it won't. Most yachts draw more water aft than forward, and if you do nothing to help her, her head will blow round and she will drive farther on.

If your boat took the ground when in the act of going about and is sufficiently far round to enable you to back the headsails, she will come off in a few minutes if the tide is flooding. Failing that, if the bottom is fairly hard, you may be able to push her head round with a sweep. If the ground is soft mud, however, it is doubtful if you will be able to do much good in that way, for the mere act of extricating the sweep will pull her back again. In such circumstances the only thing to do is to take the anchor out in the dinghy, with a good scope of chain, and drop it in deep water. Then, as the tide makes, you will be able to haul her off. The mainsail can be left up, with the boom run off so that the sail holds no wind, but the headsails should be furled.

If the tide is ebbing and your boat draws no more than about 3 feet 6 inches the best thing to do is to jump overboard and push her off. The headsails should be furled, or the sheets let go, so that the sails hold no wind, and don't wait to take off your clothes, for every minute is of importance. Go in as you are and get under the bowsprit. Heave up with your shoulder, at the same time pushing the bow round until the sails can be sheeted home on the new tack. The yacht will then sail off and if you are not 'nippy' in getting back on board, you may be left behind. It is a drastic method but extremely effective, and getting wet will serve to remind you not to stand in so close another time.

An alternative method is to take out the anchor in the dinghy and try and haul her off, but as that will take time, there will be an element of doubt about the issue.

Now let us consider the case of the yacht going ashore when running before the wind. In such circumstances she will go on pretty hard and her keel cut deeply into the mud. The only way is to haul her off stern first. Lower all sail and then take the kedge out in the dinghy and drop it astern of the yacht. Then rock the vessel from side to side to loosen her keel in the mud, and if she draws more water aft than forward, it will tend to reduce her draught if one or two of the crew go out on the bowsprit. Then, if the tide is flooding you will soon be able to haul her off with the kedge. Should it be ebbing, however, you will not have much chance of refloating her and will have to wait until the next flood.

If you are running when you get ashore and can gybe over the mainsail, the yacht will probably sail off at once, but unless you were running by the lee, it is doubtful whether you will be able to force the sail over against the wind far enough to gybe. In such circumstances, you might lower the sail and reset it on the desired side, but you would have to be quick about it if the tide were ebbing.

If you get ashore at, or near, high water, and fail to refloat the yacht, you can take it from me that you are in for a darned uncomfortable time, unless of course she is a vessel of barge type, which will sit almost upright on the mud. You will have to wait for something like twelve hours before the succeeding flood has risen sufficiently to refloat the boat, and I can tell you that there are few less comfortable places than a heavily listed vessel ashore. You can't sit on the bunks or cook a meal and all you can do to mitigate the discomfort is to put one of the bunk cushions on the cabin floor and wedge yourself against the bunk-riser. But before thinking of your own comfort, you must look to the welfare of your ship.

The most important thing is to make sure that she lists inwards, particularly if she draws a good deal of water. If such a yacht lists outwards on a shelving bank, she will lie over to such an extent that the water may invade her cockpit before she can lift to the next flood tide. That must be avoided at all costs, so you must take steps to make her list the right way while she is still water-borne. If you have run aground on the foreshore, you will of course list her towards the shore, but if she is on a horse, or flat, at a distance from the shore you may be in doubt. You should therefore sound all round her with the boathook and then make her list towards the shallowest water. To ensure her settling down in the desired position, lash the boom and made-up mainsail to the rigging. Then, if you have not already done so, lay out the anchor, while there is still water for the dinghy. The direction in which you lay it out will depend upon the way she went ashore. If there is any water in the bilge – there is sure to be a little – pump or bail out as much of it as you can, for when the yacht is resting on her bilge any water in her will rise over the bunk and wet the cushion, if you have not taken the precaution of removing it. It is also advisable to prop up the water- and oil-cans, so that the contents cannot leak out. You don't want to lose your supply of drinking water and if the contents of the paraffin-can are drained into the bilge the boat will stink to high heaven for weeks. Then if the boat will be aground during the night, you must think about illumination, for it is probable that you will not be able to light the cabin lamp, as the gimbals will not operate sufficiently. In such circumstances a candle is indicated.

If you got ashore at high water, you will be wise to study the tide tables in your nautical almanack, for it is possible that the tides may be taking off and there will be less water at the next high tide than when you went ashore. Should that be the case there will be a grave risk of the yacht being neaped and not float again until there is another big tide. If the tables show that the tides are taking off, you must take steps to reduce her draught by lightening her. You can do this by removing some of the inside ballast and putting it into the dinghy. It is a tiring, dirty job, but if you fail to get her off on the next tide, you may have to wait for days or even weeks.

I once had the bad luck to get a boat neaped for rather more than four months, and although it happened some twenty years ago the episode still lingers in my memory. In those days I owned an old converted ship's boat of about 6 tons T.M. which drew barely 3 feet of water. Having at that time only recently taken up my quarters at Burnham I did not know the river very well. One day in the early winter I was beating up the river on the top of the tide, and at the upper end of Cliff Reach, seeing a wide expanse of water before me, sailed gaily on towards Bridgemarsh Island. So far as I knew there was deep water right up to the sea-wall, and so I held on until the wall was but a few yards distant before putting the helm down to go about. To my astonishment the boat suddenly stopped and I realised that I was hard and fast ashore. The ebb was running fast, and before

I could do anything the vessel began to list and I knew that there was no hope of refloating her that tide.

When the water had run off I found that I was 40 or 50 yards from the edge of a big salting projecting from the eastern end of the island. A glance at the tide tables revealed the fact that the tides were taking off, and when, on returning to Burnham, I heard that it was the biggest tide that had been experienced for eighteen years, I realised that my boat was likely to stay where she was for some time. Although it was a forlorn hope, I went on board at the next high water to attempt to get her off, but the tide only just lapped round her keel. Day after day as I passed the spot in the train on my way up to town I could see my unfortunate craft perched amidst her rural surroundings and had to put up with much chaff from my travelling companions. Occasionally we could see a cow standing on the seawall gazing pensively at the derelict, an incident that never failed to amuse my friends.

It was not until the spring came round that I saw a prospect of refloating the boat. Late in March the tables showed a tide that should be the biggest of the year, and I determined to make strenuous efforts to get her off that night. And it was high time. The owner of the land threatened to seize the boat as flotsam. Whether he could legally have done so I cannot say, but the threat was quite sufficient to spur me on. For some days before the attempt I visited the spot and made the most careful preparations. I dug a trench for the vessel's keel right down to the edge of the saltings and marked out the passage with withies. I removed all the ballast, which was of scrap iron of the most varied description, and placed it in a heap at the edge of the saltings, and finally I chartered a big sailing tripper irom Burnham to lend me assistance. When the eventful night arrived I was rejoiced to find the wind blowing fresh from the north-west, a quarter that favours big tides in that district. The tide came up bravely, but even so it was evident that it would be a near thing, and so I set every stitch of sail I could with the idea of reducing her draft by listing. We waited until we dare wait no longer before making the attempt. Then, when we considered the moment had arrived, I began to heave on the windlass whilst the tripper endeavoured to tow her off. For a minute or two there was 'nothing doing,' as the saying goes; then she began to move very slowly. Yard by yard we hauled her over the saltings until with a rush she leapt into deep water. With no ballast on board she was naturally very crank, but I contrived to cast off the tow rope and luff her up just in time to save her from turning turtle. Then I grabbed the sails down and let her swing to her anchor. With the assistance of the watermen I got the ballast on board and stowed away and the boat was on her moorings at Burnham long before breakfast-time. But Lord, how she leaked! The dry easterly winds had opened her topsides and she was not fit to sail for days; but she 'took up' again in time, and was little the worse for her long sojourn amongst the buttercups and daisies. I have never got a yacht neaped since, and sincerely hope I never shall.

Of course, if all of the ballast is outside in the form of a keel, you cannot lighten the yacht very much, but you can remove all portable heavy things and further reduce her draught by listing her. The best way to do that would be to run out the boom, topped up a little, and lash it to the rigging. Then, when making your attempt to refloat her, the weight of one or two men out on the boom would list her considerably, reducing her draught by several inches. The anchor should have been carried out to the full extent of the cable at low water and buried in the mud to ensure a good grip. Then, at the top of the tide, by heaving on the windlass, you may be able to refloat her, if you have dug a trench for her keel. But, when all is said and done, getting a yacht ashore on the top of the tide is the devil of a business and you should be extra careful when approaching shoal water round about high tide and allow a good margin for safety.

Earlier I pointed out the danger of allowing a yacht of deep draught to list outwards. That happened to me with my first yacht, a narrow-gutted 4-tonner, drawing 6 feet of water. I and another boy had sailed her from Gravesend down to Hole Haven and having brought up in the narrow creek, we went ashore to spend the evening. On our return we found that the yacht had blown out of the channel and taken the ground. She had almost dried out and was listing outwards at a most alarming angle. As it was obvious that she would not lift on the flood without assistance, we took up a couple of floorboards from the cabin and nailed them over the lower side of the cockpit, backed by an old sail. When the tide came up this temporary hatch leaked more than a little but saved the situation, for by vigorous bailing, we managed to keep the water under until she lifted to the tide. I have told that yarn at length elsewhere and only refer to the incident now to show the novice that it is possible to cope with most difficult situations by the exercise of a little thought and ingenuity.

Well, there are a few hints which may be useful if you are so unlucky as to get your ship ashore; but they are only suggestions and you must think things out for yourself and devise the best scheme you can for refloating her, according to the conditions under which she stranded.

CHAPTER 57: *Safety Precautions*

If you happen to fall overboard when sailing with a full crew, you probably escape with nothing worse than a wetting, for if your companions know their job they should be able to rescue you within a few minutes. But when alone such a mishap might very easily prove fatal, as there is no one to pick you up. More often than not when the single-handed yachtsman falls overboard the vessel is sailing herself with the helm lashed while he is doing a job on deck, and unless he is lucky enough to grab the dinghy as it passes, the yacht will sail on and leave him to his fate. When you are alone, therefore, you cannot be too careful and precautions must be taken which in other circumstances might be regarded as superfluous. One hand for yourself and the other for the ship should be your motto, and you must cultivate the habit of never letting go with one hand until you have grasped something with the other.

Let us consider for a moment how it is that one comes to fall overboard. Such accidents, I think, can usually be attributed to one or other of the following incidents :

(1) Slipping on a wet deck.
(2) Being thrown off one's balance by a sudden lurch of the boat.
(3) Tripping over something.
(4) Being knocked over by the boom.
(5) Struggling with a headsail in a strong wind.
(6) Being washed overboard.
(7) Stepping on a rope.
(8) The breaking of a rope on which one is hauling.

I will take these various contingencies in order and suggest means by which the risk may at least be reduced, if not entirely eliminated.

(1) The decks of most small yachts are painted, and paint when wet is extremely treacherous to walk on. Crepe rubber shoes in particular border upon the suicidal on wet painted decks and ordinary rubber soles are not much better. I have tried many kinds of shoes but have yet to discover any that can be regarded as perfectly safe under all conditions. It is better, therefore, to approach the problem from a different angle. The solution will be found in the use of non-slip paint on the decks and cabin-top. Such paint is made by the International Paint Co., and having some gritty substance, such as silver sand or pumice powder, incorporated in it, gives a firm stance under any conditions of weather. If you prefer it, you can make any paint non-slip by sprinkling it with silver sand when it is in a tacky state. When applying non-slip paint it is essential to keep stirring it, as otherwise the sand will sink to the bottom of the tin and the non-slipping qualities be lost.

Decks covered with non-slip paint should not be washed with a mop, as the fluff comes off and adheres to the deck. And, as I know from experience, it is the devil to get off again. It is better to wash down with a scrubber, which, however, should not be used too vigorously as deck paint is apt to wash off a little if brushed too hard.

Wet varnish is as treacherous as wet paint and as the cockpit seats are usually varnished you may come an awful cropper if you jump down on them on a wet day. The remedy will be found in the Solent non-slip varnish made by John Mathews & Co. This, like non-slip paint, has some gritty substance in it and must be well stirred when applied. Until you get the knack, it is a little difficult to put on evenly, and Messrs. Mathews tell me that the best way is first to distribute the varnish as evenly as possible with heavy strokes of the brush and then finish off with very quick light strokes.

(2) Being thrown off your balance by a sudden lurch of the vessel is a contingency that cannot be foreseen, but if you cultivate the habit of expecting something of that sort to happen, you will not be altogether taken by surprise should it occur. The wise car driver gets into the habit of always expecting to meet something on a blind corner, and I see no reason why a yachtsman should not be equally alert with regard to the antics of his craft.

It is when climbing on deck from the cockpit that you run the greatest risk of falling overboard, as, until you can reach the runner, or rigging if the yacht has no runners, there is nothing to which you can cling. I will tell you later in this chapter how to guard against that risk.

Another occasion on which you might easily be thrown overboard by the motion of the boat is when pumping. Most small yachts are fitted with an ordinary deck pump situated at the side of the cockpit and to operate it you must stand either on deck or on the cockpit seat. You consequently have nothing to cling to but the plunger, and a sudden lurch of the ship might cause you to fall overboard, taking the plunger with you. Such pumps, although cheap, are not to be recommended as, apart from the risk to which I have referred, they throw little water and have to be primed. It is far better to have a semi-rotary or diaphragm pump mounted on the bulkhead and discharging through the topside. Neither of these pumps requires priming and you can sit in the cockpit and pump with one hand with comparative ease and safety. In my own little ship I have one of Simpson, Lawrence & Co.'s diaphragm pumps which discharges 10 gallons a minute, and I find it excellent.

(3) Tripping over something on deck is usually the result of carelessness. You cannot very well avoid having a few obstructions on deck, but you soon get used to their presence and elude them by intuition. But there is one trap against which I would warn you and that is having turn-up ends to your trousers. They are apt to catch on cleats and trip you up and may be responsible for even worse dangers. Some years ago a single-handed yachtsman, when bringing up at West Mersea, got his anchor caught in the turn-up of his trousers as he dropped it and it pulled him overboard. He managed to catch the rail as he fell and hung there with the anchor suspended from his trousers. Owing to its weight, he was unable to pull himself up, nor could he shake the anchor free. It was a very nasty predicament, but fortunately another yachtsman anchored near by saw that he was in trouble and managed to rescue him when he was nearly exhausted. The moral of that little story is, don't wear trousers with turn-ups when sailing boats.

(4) If you would avoid being knocked overboard by the boom, keep your mainsheet belayed and watch the antics of that spar. Quite recently I saw a man

set his mainsail before getting under way and as he neglected to belay the main-sheet the boom was unrestrained. As he walked aft, the spar caught him a wal-lop on the backside and knocked him overboard. Such incidents may add to the gaiety of the nation, but they are rather disconcerting to the person principally concerned, and are best avoided.

(5) The risk of falling, or being washed, overboard when shifting jibs in heavy weather cannot be ignored and calls for special caution. It is prudent when thus occupied to tie a lifeline round your waist, for at the best your stance on the heav-ing fore-deck is likely to be somewhat precarious.

(6) The risk of being washed overboard can be averted by the use of lifelines, to which I will refer later. Such accidents usually occur when working on the fore-deck, but there have been cases of men being washed out of shallow self-draining cockpits. That, of course, could only happen in very bad weather, but if you were caught at sea under such conditions it would be prudent to have a lifeline round your waist when at the helm.

(7) Should you inadvertently step upon a rope it will be like a roller under your foot and may cause you to lose your balance. It is when walking along a narrow side deck that it is most likely to occur, as there is so little room available for your feet and you may step on one of the headsail sheets. It is better therefore to go forward by way of the cabin-top as you have more room and it is, or should be, clear of loose ropes.

(8) If a rope on which you are hauling should break, you may turn a back-somersault into the 'ditch,' but if your yacht is properly maintained such an ac-cident should not occur. Gear in sound condition does not carry away in that manner; it is only rotten rope that does so. It is false economy, particularly when single-handed, to use gear that is not perfectly sound.

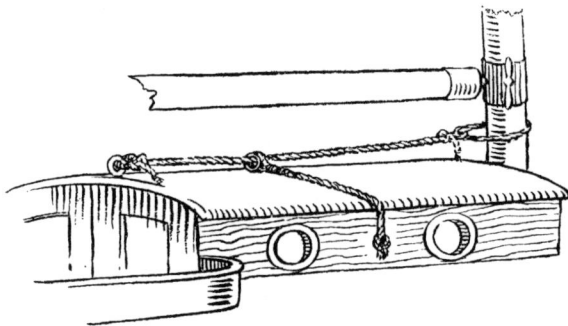

Lifeline on cabin top

In my own boat *Iolanthe* I guard against the risk of falling overboard by the use of a lifeline rigged in the following way. A rope extends from the mast aft along the centre of the cabin-top, and on it is threaded a short man-rope free to travel fore-and-aft. The man-rope has a double-wall-and-crown knot in the end to ensure a good grip and can be used on either side of the vessel. When going forward, I grasp the man-rope and do not let go until I have hold of the rigging, and when returning, I cling to it until I am safely back in the cockpit. Many small yachts have wooden handrails on the cabin-top, but as you cannot reach them

Temporary lifelines

when walking on the cabin-top, they are not of much use, except to keep things from rolling overboard. Now with my lifeline arrangement you can walk forward freely on the weather side of the cabin-top, where you are not impeded by the boom, and clinging to the man-rope gives you a sense of security. It is a very simple precaution, but you should make a practice of always using it, in fine weather as well as foul, for it is when least expected that accidents occur.

If the yacht is to be used for ocean cruising, lifelines should be permanently rigged all round the boat, say at about 2 feet 6 inches above the deck. It would perhaps be advisable to have them double, as one might fall under a lifeline rigged as high as that. In the absence of permanent lifelines, temporary ones of rope can easily be rigged by attaching them to the forestay and shrouds and leading them aft to the ends of the main horse. Permanent lifelines should of course be of wire and if threaded through white rubber hose-pipe they will enhance the appearance of the yacht and the rubber will help to preserve the wire from rust.

If the single-handed yachtsman adopts the precautionary measures I have indicated, he need have little fear of falling overboard. My younger readers may think I am over-cautious, but a long experience has taught me that one cannot be too careful when sailing alone, even in the finest weather.

A fruitful source of accidents is carelessness in laying out and weighing a kedge with the dinghy, and such mishaps are not by any means confined to beginners. Many yachtsmen who should know better habitually stand up in the boat to drop the kedge and thereby ask for trouble. At the best a small dinghy affords a precarious stance and to stand up in one while holding a heavy anchor is dangerous, particularly in rough water. Yet it seems to be a common practice to row away from the yacht with the kedge and coiled warp in the dinghy and when all of the warp has run out to stand up with the kedge and throw it overboard. Such proceedings have led to many yachtsmen getting a well-deserved ducking and more than one have lost their lives.

As the dinghy of a little cruiser has to be towed, it must of necessity be very small, as otherwise it would retard the yacht's progress inordinately, and when using it for anchor work the greatest care must be exercised. When laying out a kedge using the dinghy, you should sling it over the stern, secured to the ring-bolt with a piece of rope. Coil down the warp and capsize the coil so that it is ready to run freely, and then row away from the yacht in the desired direction. Keep your foot on the warp, if you are alone in the dinghy, so that you can regulate the speed at which it is paid out, and when you get to the end of the scope, drop the kedge by slipping it.

The methods employed by many yachtsmen when weighing a kedge also call for criticism. They kneel, or even stand up, in the stern of the dinghy to break out the anchor, thereby running a considerable risk of either falling overboard or swamping the dinghy. The weight of a man in the stern of a little dinghy is sufficient to depress it until the freeboard is reduced to but a few inches, and when he hauls on the warp he may pull her stern right under. The best and safest way in which to break out the kedge is to haul the warp taut and then, having taken a turn with it round the rowing thwart, crawl up forward. This will have the effect of depressing the bow and the leverage of the boat will be sufficient to break out the anchor. If there is not enough slack in the warp to take a turn round the thwart, it can be lashed to the ring-bolt in the transom of the dinghy.

In concluding this chapter I would urge the single-hander to keep on board a small first-aid outfit. You may never meet with a serious accident, but when handling gear you can't help chipping bits out of your hands at times, and a bandage, or a piece of sticking plaster, will save your white sails from being sullied with bloodstains. It is also wise to keep a flask of brandy on board, but it should be regarded strictly as a 'medical comfort' and not used except in case of need. By the way, in the absence of iodine, a cut finger should be held over the side, as seawater is an excellent disinfectant.

Safe way to lay out a kedge

CHAPTER 58: *Man Overboard*

When one comes to think about it, it is astonishing how few fatal accidents occur in yachting. Every season scores of inexperienced youngsters tempt Providence in small craft, of which some are of doubtful seaworthiness, and come to no harm. They get into horrid scrapes, but somehow or other contrive to get out of them, and it is thus that they learn seamanship. We have all had to go through the mill, but there is this to be said about it: One learns far more from one's mistakes than from one's successful achievements. And one's seafaring education is never completed, for the moods of the sea are infinitely variable, and there is something to be learnt almost every time one gets under way. It is this, I think, that makes sailing so extraordinarily interesting and fascinating.

Although fatal accidents are comparatively rare, it would be folly to suggest that sailing is devoid of risk. If it were, we probably should not think nearly so much of it, for a slight element of risk undoubtedly adds zest to a sport. Still, there are quite sufficient risks in the game that cannot be foreseen and guarded against, and it is folly to add to them by neglecting reasonable precautions against accident. But custom is apt to make us callous and we do not think of the possibility of an accident arising until it has occurred. The greatest risk we run, I think, is that of falling overboard, and for that reason it is the custom to carry a lifebuoy. Many owners, however, seem to think that the chief use of a lifebuoy is to display the yacht's name and club initials. It is certainly very convenient for that purpose, but is not of much use as a means of saving life if securely lashed to the rigging, as it so often is. A lifebuoy, if it is to be of any practical use, must be of efficient size and readily accessible in case of need. It should be kept within easy reach of the helmsman and not secured by any sort of lashing. If the vessel is travelling fast when a man falls overboard, the lifebuoy must be thrown within a few seconds if it is to be of any use, and that cannot be done if you first have to get out your knife and cut away sundry lashings. In my own boat I carry my lifebuoy under one of the cockpit seats and in case of need the helmsman would merely have to stoop and pick it up, but my cockpit is an exceptionally roomy one and the seats are wide. An excellent place in which to carry the lifebuoy is on the sliding hatch of the cabin-top. A friend of mine carries his lifebuoy in this manner, it being kept in its place by means of three teak pegs in the hatch, over which it fits loosely. Three small brass angle-irons would serve very well for the purpose and would be easier to fit than wooden pegs.

It is usually in heavy weather that men fall overboard, for wet decks afford but a precarious foothold when one is wearing rubber-soled shoes, particularly of the crepe rubber variety. When a man has to go forward in a heavy sea to hand the jib or any other job of that sort, he should take the precaution of tying a rope round his waist. This may sound rather suggestive of a baby in a perambulator, but it is much easier to haul a man on board with a rope than to pick him up after he has gone adrift. Particularly should one take this precaution when sailing single-handed. If you fall overboard when sailing alone and the tiller is lashed, as it usually is when you leave the helm to do a job on deck, you have not an earthly chance as the yacht will sail right away from you. Even in fine weather the single-handed sailor should cultivate the habit of never letting go with one hand until he has grasped something with the other.

If, in spite of these precautions, one of your crew falls overboard, keep cool (if you can) and act promptly. The first thing to do is to throw him the lifebuoy, pitching it as close to him as you can without hitting him on the head. Then put your helm hard up and gybe. No matter what point of sailing you are on, always gybe, for by so doing you will get the vessel into the right position for picking him up quicker than by any other method. If you don't believe me, just work it out for yourself, either by drawing diagrams or with matches on the table.

You must remember that you have to bring the yacht head to wind and close alongside of the man in the water, for you cannot pick him up when ramping along at top speed. I know that it requires a certain amount of nerve to gybe a vessel quickly in heavy weather, but when it is a question of saving life it has got to be done. All the same there is no reason why you should not exercise some degree of care in carrying out the operation. To gybe 'all standing' under such conditions would be courting disaster, and you certainly won't be of much help to the man struggling in the water if you carry away your boom or lose your mast.

Therefore, see that the runner is set up before you let the boom come over, and for goodness' sake take a turn of the mainsheet round a cleat or bollard as you gybe, or otherwise you may flay your hands and be helpless. As soon as you have gybed, haul your wind and bring the yacht round in a circle. If the manoeuvre has been carried out smartly the boat should come head to wind close alongside the man in the water. If you gybe promptly and handle the vessel efficiently there is no reason why he should not be back on board in five minutes, but if you stay her and mess about generally, you may be the best part of half an hour over the job.

Should you fail to pick up your man at the first attempt and you have someone else with you, send him away in the dinghy. By the time the dinghy reaches the unfortunate individual in the water he will probably be getting a trifle exhausted and not able to help himself very much. To haul an exhausted man, whose clothes are sodden with water, into a small dinghy is a ticklish business and in such circumstances I think it would be better to secure him to the boat by means of a rope – the painter passed through the stern ringbolt would serve the purpose – and then tow him to the yacht. If any trouble is experienced in getting him on board, hike him out with one of the halyards.

I hope you will never have to pick up a man overboard, for in any circumstances the operation can hardly fail to cause you a good deal of anxiety, but you cannot afford to ignore the fact that such a contingency may arise at any time. Every owner should therefore practise the manoeuvre occasionally. When you are out for a sail with no particular object in view, you should throw the lifebuoy overboard and see how long it takes you to recover it. This should be practised when close-hauled, reaching and running and you will learn far more in this way than from anything that I can tell you. Even if you never have to pick up a man, the time devoted to practice will not be wasted, for you will learn how far your vessel will carry her way under various conditions and the knowledge thus gained will be very useful when picking up moorings or berthing alongside a quay.

More often than not, when a man falls overboard he is able to catch hold of the dinghy, if the yacht is towing one, and he is then easily recovered. But, even so, he cannot be considered safe until on board the vessel again. If she is travelling fast, he may not be able to retain his hold for very long and he certainly cannot climb into the dinghy whilst it is in motion. As soon as it is seen that the man has grasped the dinghy, the yacht should be brought to the wind and hove to. The dinghy can then be hauled alongside and the man pulled on board the yacht. In concluding these remarks I would offer a word of advice to the hapless man who falls overboard. If a lifebuoy is thrown, swim to it and hang on; but if not, don't lose your head and swim after the yacht, for you can't catch her and will only exhaust your strength. Just turn on your back and float or paddle about gently until you are picked up.

CHAPTER 59: *Damage to the Rig*

In the old days of long bowsprits and fidded topmasts accidents were not uncommon, for such spars were often carried away, but in modern craft mishaps should be of rare occurrence if the gear is sound and maintained in decent order. When they do happen they are usually of a comparatively trivial nature and temporary repairs can be effected with such materials as you have on board unless, of course, you are so unfortunate as to lose your mast.

Your supply of bosun's stores should include a length of new rope long enough to replace any halyard or sheet in the yacht, an assortment of spare shackles and thimbles, one or two blocks, marline, whipping twine, a hank of hambro-line and some copper wire. With these, you should be able temporarily to repair almost anything in the way of gear likely to carry away. If you break a halyard, the obvious thing to do is to reeve a new one, but if you have not the necessary rope, the broken halyard can be repaired with a long splice, which will render through the blocks. The same remark applies to a broken sheet. If, like me, you are too old to go aloft, you could at a pinch use the spinnaker halyard in place of any other that had carried away. By clapping a 'handy-billy' purchase on the fall you could set the sail well enough to get you home.

Now let us consider a few other likely mishaps and see what could be done in the way of temporary repairs. Should a shroud break, the yacht must be thrown round on to the other tack immediately, if the mast is to be saved. Having done that, heave her to with the foresail aback while you consider what you can do to remedy the damage. More often than not when a yacht is dismasted it is due to a flaw in a rigging screw, or the stripping of the thread; or possibly to a shroud having got adrift from the cross-trees. If the shroud itself breaks it will probably be at one of the splices, where water has settled and rusted the wire.

Should the accident be due to a faulty rigging screw, substitute a rope lanyard; or if it is a lanyard that has broken, reeve a new one. But supposing that it is the wire itself that has broken? Well, if it has carried away at the lower end, I think the best thing to do would be to bend back the broken end and put on several seizings, thus making an eye. Into this your handy-billy could be hooked and the shroud set up to the chainplate with it. If the shroud has gone at the hounds, it will be more difficult to effect a repair. You might, however, make a loop in the broken end by seizing it and then lash it to the mast, above the hounds with a stout rope. That, of course, would make the shroud too short to be set up either with a rigging screw or lanyard, so you would have to do it with the handy-billy. You should then sail her gently to the nearest port to have a new shroud fitted. A handy-billy, by the way, is a spare purchase consisting of a double block and a single, with hooks on the blocks, or at any rate on one; the other may have a tail-rope for attaching it. A handy-billy should be carried in every cruising yacht, as it can be used for a variety of purposes when a little extra power is needed.

A broken runner could be temporarily repaired in the same manner, but if it has gone at the lower end, the block should be seized into the loop. Should it be the purchase that has given out, it would merely entail reeving new rope through the blocks.

Should the forestay carry away – an unlikely accident – the yacht should at once be put before the wind. If she is a cutter, the chain cable should be unshackled from the anchor and the end secured to the mast above the hounds. The chain could then be set up to the bowsprit. Of course, when you arrived in port you would have to bring up to your kedge and warp, while you got the chain down and shackled to the bower anchor again.

If the forestay of a sloop is carried away it will probably be due to the loss of the bowsprit, for if the bowsprit goes it takes the forestay with it. In such circumstances I think the best procedure would be to pass the forestay through the gammon-iron and set it up to the mast with a tackle. You could probably set a small foresail, tacked to the gammon-iron, to get you home.

The most serious accident, of course, is the loss of the mast. I have only been dismasted twice in the course of my sailing career, and on both occasions I was in port. Once, I had my mast knocked out by a barge when at anchor at Queenborough, and the other time was when I was starting in a race and had not crossed the line. If the mast were lost at sea in rough weather, I think the first job should be to clear away the wreckage, as the broken spar banging into the vessel might imperil her safety. First cut away the shroud lanyards, or unshackle the rigging screws, as the case may be, and unreeve the runner falls. Then cut the lanyard holding the masthead stay to the bowsprit-end and cast off the tacks of the jib and foresail. The wreckage will then be held only by the forestay and the yacht can ride to it for the time being. If it is not too rough for dinghy work, man the boat and commence salvage operations. The sails should first claim your attention. Cut away the lacings and outhauls of the mainsail and get it into the dinghy and then unbend the headsails. It will probably be a long and difficult job and if the sea is very rough you may have to wait until the weather moderates. Having salved the sails, unreeve the running gear and remove the gaff and boom from the mast. Having got these on board, you should attempt to save the broken mast, as the fittings can be used on the new mast when it is made. To get it on board will entail heavy work, but it can be done by parbuckling. Two or three short lengths of rope should be made fast on the deck of the yacht and passed under the mast, as it lies alongside. Then by hauling on these ropes simultaneously the spar can be rolled up on to the deck and secured.

Having salved all of the gear, the next consideration will be how to make a port. If you have an auxiliary motor, you will of course proceed under power, but if not you will probably have to wait for some passing vessel to take you in tow, and if that happens to be a smack or trading vessel it is likely to cost your underwriters a pretty penny in the way of salvage. If it is another yacht that picks you up, she will probably render you assistance without thought of payment, for dog does not eat dog. It is a regrettable fact, however, that there are a few yacht owners of an avaricious turn of mind who in such cases demand their pound of flesh and one leading insurance company has thought it necessary to warn owners, before accepting help from another yacht, to ascertain whether any claim for salvage, or towage, will be made, and if so to make a bargain before accepting such service. I would remind owners, too, that the crew of a life-boat are entitled to claim salvage for services rendered to a vessel, although not for saving life.

CHAPTER 60: *Tides*

"We must take the current when it serves or lose our ventures," wrote Shakespeare, a remark peculiarly appropriate to cruising in small yachts, for unless you work your tides you cannot make successful passages.

If your ship is a miniature cruiser of, say, 3 tons, her maximum speed through the water will not be much in excess of 5 knots and if you have a 3-knot tide against you, you won't get very far, even with a fair wind; and if both wind and tide are foul, you may make no appreciable progress at all. If, on the other hand, the tide is with you, you will be able to get quite a long way, even in a little boat. You will readily appreciate therefore that the tide may be your greatest friend or your deadliest enemy.

When cruising in small craft you must order your life afloat by the tide tables rather than the clock. It will sometimes entail turning out of bed at some ungodly hour to catch the tide, but that is really no hardship, for those early hours are often the cream of the day. But you should make a practice of having something to eat before a daybreak start, for vitality is then at its lowest and you need something to buck you up. If the tide serves at 4 a.m. set your alarm clock to wake you at 3 o'clock, or a little later. You will then have time to have a snack and a hot drink and get everything ready, and will not waste a moment of the favourable tide.

Should you only need the ebb to carry you, say, four miles out of a river in order to pick up the flood on the coast, don't think that an hour's ebb will be sufficient, for it probably won't. During the early hours of the morning in fine weather there is seldom much wind and often none at all, so if you are wise you will allow three hours. If you get out of the river before the flood has begun to make and there is not sufficient wind to stem the last of the ebb, you can bring up and have a proper breakfast while you are waiting. Always be a bit ahead of your tide rather than late if you want your cruising to be a success.

In your nautical almanack you will find tables showing the time of high water and rise of tide at the principal ports for every day of the year, and also a comprehensive list of tidal constants, which will enable you to find the time of high water at most places round the coast. You have merely to add, or subtract, as the case may be, the tidal constant from the time of high water at some standard port, such as Dover or London Bridge. But you will often want to know the depth at times other than high water. If you know the range of the tide, you can calculate the depth at any hour by that 1, 2, 3, 3, 2, 1 rule I told you about in the chapter on anchoring. It will only be approximate but near enough for practical purposes if you allow a small margin for safety.

The rise of tide, both at springs and neaps, for the district is given in the chart, but not the range. That, however, is easily calculated. But perhaps I had better first explain the difference between the rise and the range. The rise is that from low water at ordinary spring tides to high water and the range the rise of the tide from its low to high water level. The range of a spring tide is therefore the same as the rise, but at neaps it is not, for neaps do not rise so high nor fall so low as springs. You see, the rise of a neap tide is calculated from low water spring tides, which is called the chart datum, and as it does not fall so low as at springs, the range is a good deal less than the rise, although at half-tide the depth is the same with both.

Now, as I say, the range of a spring tide is the same as its rise, as shown on the chart, and the range of a neap, or one smaller than a spring tide, can be calculated in the following manner. Deduct from the neap rise half the spring rise and multiply the result by 2. For example, suppose the spring and neap rises shown in the chart are 16 feet and 12 feet respectively:

Neap rise	12ft.	
Subtract half the spring rise	8ft.	
	4ft.	× 2 = 8ft. (neap range).

Having found the neap range, the depth at low water neaps can be ascertained by deducting it from the spring rise and dividing the result by 2 – thus:

Spring rise	16ft.	
Subtract neap range	8ft.	
	8ft.	÷ 2 = 8ft. (depth at LW neaps).

This, of course, must be added to the sounding shown in the chart, which is the depth at low water spring tides.

Now, suppose you are in a district where the spring rise is 16 feet and the rise of tide for the day, according to the tide tables, is 12 feet. It is 2 hours flood and you want to know how much water there is. By the rules I have given you find that the range is 8 feet and the depth of water at low tide is 4 feet. To this you must add the rise for the two hours that have elapsed since low water. By the 1, 2, 3, 3, 2, 1 rule this would amount to $^3/_{12}$ or ¼ of the range, namely 2 feet, which must also be added to the sounding shown in the chart.

Although quite simple, this may seem rather complicated to the novice, so I will set out the various stages of the calculation in detail:

Rise according to the tide table	12ft.	
Subract half the spring rise	– 8ft.	
	4ft.	× 2 = 8ft. (range).

Spring rise (as shown in chart)	16ft.	
Subract range	– 8ft.	
	8ft.	÷ 2 = 4ft. (depth from chart datum).

Depth from chart datum	4ft.
Rise during 2 hours of flood	
(by 1, 2, 3, 3, 2, 1 rule,	
namely ¼ of the range)	+ 2ft.
Sounding in chart, say	+ 3ft.
	9ft.

If the sounding given in the chart is 3 feet, as suggested, the actual depth of water at the moment will therefore be 9 feet. The diagram shows the rise and range of both spring and neap tides.

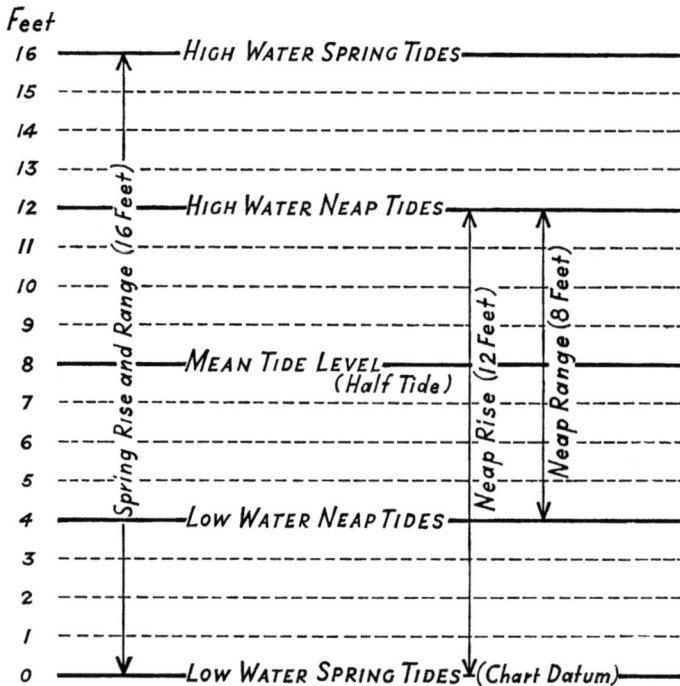

Tidal rise and range

It must be clearly understood that the results obtained by the use of the rules I have given must only be regarded as approximate, as it is a very rough and ready way of calculating. It is assumed, for instance, that the duration of a tide is 6 hours, but it is really rather more than that. The round figure of 6 hours is taken so that it can be divided into twelve equal parts for ready reckoning. In some districts the duration of the flood and ebb differs, the tide flooding for 7 hours and ebbing for 5 hours. In such circumstances, instead of taking hourly periods, you must allow 70 minutes on the flood and 50 minutes on the ebb.

Then again, the level of the tide may be affected by strong winds from certain quarters, or by barometric pressure. If the normal height of the barometer be taken at 30 inches, a fall of an inch may increase the height of the tide by a foot in the open sea, or perhaps twice as much in an estuary, while the rise of an inch may reduce the height of the tide to a similar extent. In the Thames Estuary a heavy gale from NW may cause the tide to rise 3 feet or more above the normal, while a strong SW gale will cause a corresponding fall below the usual low water level.

CHAPTER 61: *Strange Harbours*

To the inexperienced yachtsman, entering a strange harbour is apt to be a rather hair-raising business, for he has not the slightest idea as to what he will find after passing through the entrance. He knows neither where he must berth nor how, or what room he will have for manoeuvring. Of course, if his vessel has an auxiliary engine the matter is much simplified, as he can go in under power; but we will assume that he has not and must handle the yacht under sail alone.

The great thing is to be adequately prepared to meet any contingency that may arise, for if you have everything ready that you can possibly want, you will be able to cope with almost any emergency and enter with some degree of confidence. You should make your preparations before reaching the harbour and not attempt to enter until they are complete.

Should you be carrying your dinghy on deck, launch it and see that the sculls and rowlocks are on board, as you are almost sure to want the boat for carrying out warps. Get out a couple of warps and having coiled them carefully, make one fast to the bitts forward and the other aft. Then remove the coils of the halyards from the belaying pins and capsize them on deck so that they will be ready to run if you have to get the mainsail down in a hurry, and take up the slack of the topping-lift. See that your sweep is ready for immediate use and the rowlock shipped in the rail; also clear the anchor for letting go. Have fenders handy in case you have to go alongside a quay, or some other, vessel. If the harbour is one where there is not much water, look out for the tide signal. At most tidal harbours

signals are hoisted to indicate the depth of
water and you must make sure that there is
sufficient for your craft. At the larger ports,
too, a signal is often hoisted when vessels
are leaving the harbour and you should
watch for that, as you don't want to get
mixed up with several large smacks coming out, as may be the case at such places as
Lowestoft. Having ascertained that there
is sufficient water and no vessels coming
out, you can enter. But before doing so you
must make up your mind what sail to carry
and that will depend upon the conditions
of wind and tide obtaining. At many artificial harbours the tide sets strongly across
the mouth and allowance must be made
for this cross-current. At Lowestoft, for in-

Quay berth — method 1

stance, the ebb sets strongly across the entrance from south to north and the
flood from north to south. If entering on the ebb you must therefore hug the
south pier, and if on the flood, the north pier.

If there is a fresh breeze blowing straight into the entrance, you might stow
the mainsail and go in under headsails, but if the wind is blowing across the
entrance, or straight out of the harbour, you will have to keep your mainsail set
until well inside, otherwise you might be swept on to one of the piers, but you
must be ready to get it down quickly. Unless the wind is blowing straight down
the harbour, you are pretty sure to be blanketed by the piers, in which case it will
be prudent to send a man out ahead in the dinghy with a warp and tow in, or you
might propel the yacht with the sweep. If your progress is slow, all the better, for
it will give you time to look round and find out where yachts have to berth and
how; but you must of course keep steerage way.

Arrangements differ at various ports. At some, yachts ride to a buoy, or dol-
phin, by the bow with warps out astern to the shore; at others they have to anchor
and carry out warps to the quay, while at Lowestoft, where they lie in two tiers,
those in the outside tier moor to dolphins ahead and to a stout warp, stretched
across the basin, astern. In the back tier, they moor ahead to the warp and astern
to the pier. At some places one has to berth alongside the quay and at others
against piles. So you see you must be prepared for all sorts of contingencies.

If you enter a harbour where yachts lie alongside the quay, it will save you a
lot of trouble if you can tie up to some craft already berthed, for then you will
not have to tend your warps. It would be as well to ascertain, however, that she
will not be leaving before you, for if she wanted to go out first, you would have to
shift to allow her to do so.

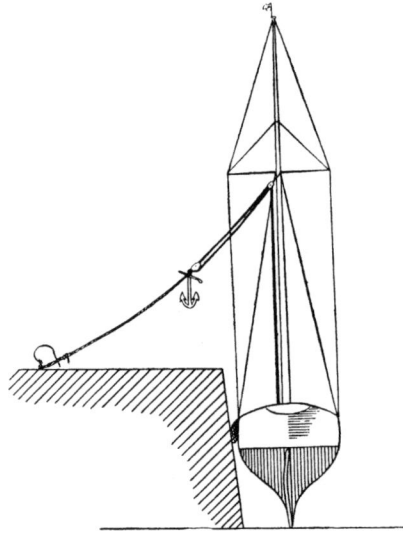

The most unsatisfactory berth of all is against the quay in a tidal harbour that dries out at low water, as, when the yacht takes the ground you have to ensure her listing in towards the quay. It may not be convenient for you to remain on board until she has settled down, or she may take the ground in the middle of the night. I can suggest two ways of making her list in towards the quay automatically and they are both comparatively simple.

One method is to take the main halyard ashore and belay it to a bollard. Then sling a weight – say the kedge – on the halyard, as shown in the illustration. The weight will be quite sufficient to make the vessel list inwards when she takes the ground.

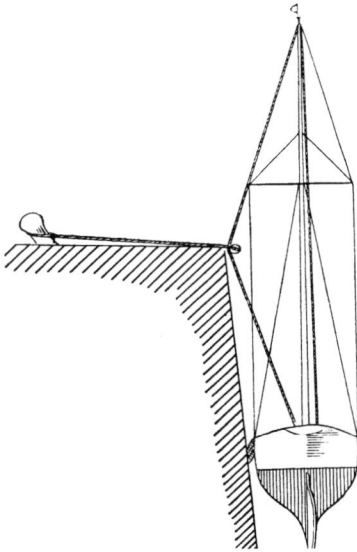

Quay berth — method 2

The other method is to make fast ashore a rope with a block on the end in such a manner that the block comes just over the edge of the quay or pier. The spinnaker, or topsail, halyard should be rove through the block and set up taut to one of the chainplates. As the yacht drops with the tide, an increasing strain will be put on the halyard, causing her to list towards the quay.

When lying alongside a quay or pier, or even another vessel, you must use fenders to prevent your topsides being rubbed. Should you be lying against a piled pier, it would be very difficult to arrange the fenders in such a way that they would remain against the piles. The best plan is to hang a spar over the side, outside the fenders, as shown in the drawing. But if there is any sea running in the harbour, it will be prudent to use a breast warp. By laying out the kedge abeam, you will be able to haul off the yacht sufficiently to prevent her bumping into the pier.

The small yacht owner will be well advised to keep out of artificial harbours as much as he can, as most of them are extremely unsatisfactory. You have to pay harbour dues, your boat gets filthy and you are at the mercy of the weather. Should it blow hard, you may be penned in for days, and I can tell you that many harbours in heavy weather are anything but the havens of rest they are supposed to be. A swell will come in through the entrance, making your little ship roll about intolerably, and you may have an anxious time in keeping clear of other vessels.

And in some harbours you will suffer from a disconcerting lack of privacy, as there will be a small crowd of girls watching you at your necessary domestic duties – amusing to them, no doubt, but darned annoying all the same. And then there is the difficulty of disposing of your garbage. You can't dump it overboard into the basin, for if you do it will stay there, so at intervals you have to put the pail in the dinghy and row outside the harbour to get rid of your rubbish.

Finally, there is the bother of getting out, if you are moored in a tier. If there is anyone on board the yachts next to you, you can ask them to slack up their warps to let you out, but out of pure cussedness they are usually untenanted. So you have to shove each warp in turn under your keel with a sweep and run a very good chance of getting hung up in the process. Once, at Lowestoft, I got a warp firmly jammed between my rudder and stern-post and had the deuce of a job to clear it.

I should advise you therefore to seek an anchorage in some river or creek wherever possible. You will then enjoy decent privacy and should the weather be too bad to permit of your putting to sea, you will at least be able to get a sail in the sheltered waters of the river. Of course, if you are bound from, say, the Thames Estuary to the Solent, you must either put into harbours or keep the sea, as there is no river or inland water in which you can find a berth until you come to Chichester Harbour. McMullen objected so strongly to being cooped up in a harbour that on more than one occasion, in *Procyon*, he deliberately left Dover in bad weather and saw it out at anchor in the Roads, considering the violent motion of the yacht infinitely preferable to the dirt and inconvenience of the harbour.

Fenders used with spar, against piles

CHAPTER 62: *Watermanship*

In the course of my cruising last summer I noticed a good many exhibitions of indifferent watermanship, which at the time I thought rather deplorable. On further reflection, however, I have come to the conclusion that this inexpert handling of dinghies must be regarded as an indication that there are a good many recruits coming into the sport just now, for in no way does a novice display his lack of experience so much as in the control of a boat under oars. An expert waterman when boarding a yacht acts almost by intuition. He gauges the strength of the tide to a nicety, and rounding up the dinghy at the right moment, comes gently alongside the vessel, with the dinghy head-on to the tide. The novice, on the other hand, often makes an awful hash of it. He either bashes into the yacht, to the detriment of her topside paint, or else rounds up the dinghy too soon and cannot reach her. Should he make the latter mistake it is probable that he will give a furious dig with one scull and charge the yacht end-on. Failing that, he will let the dinghy drop astern and have to start his manoeuvring all over again. To bring a dinghy alongside a yacht decently is, like everything else, a matter of practice, and I think, therefore, that when you see anyone make a mess of it, you can safely assume that he is a novice.

Everyone, of course, has to learn by experience, but all the same it is astonishing what a lot of work the novice often gives himself by his lack of forethought. I witnessed a case in point in the Blackwater last summer. A small cutter brought up near the east end of Osea Island, right in the middle of the river, and a man and a girl put off in the dinghy to land on the Island. There was a fresh easterly wind and a strong flood tide, and after an easy trip to the shore, they landed on the beach, near the little pier and went shopping. About an hour later they started away to return on board. As I say, there was a fresh easterly breeze, which was now against them, and they also had to contend with a strong spring flood, running about 3 knots. The yacht was anchored the best part of a mile away and, to my amazement the man, who was rowing, pulled out into the full strength of the tide. He seemed to make little or no progress and I did not think it possible that he could reach the vessel. But he was a strong man with plenty of perseverance and after rowing for nearly an hour he managed to get alongside his craft. Watching through my glasses I saw him climb on board and then collapse from sheer exhaustion.

Now, that yacht could have brought up within fifty yards of the shore in slack water, and even if the owner was a stranger to the district, as probably he was, he should have known it, for my craft and several others were lying there. It should have been obvious to him that if there was water there for us, there was for him.

Having made the initial mistake of anchoring so far from the shore, he made a second and worse one in rowing out into the tide when he returned to her. He should, of course, have rowed up close in-shore, where he would have found comparatively slack water, until well above his yacht, before edging out into the tide. That is the sort of thing that the novice does, but he soon learns about tides from such experiences.

Another thing the novice has to learn is that when coming alongside a yacht, it is the man in the bow of the dinghy that must hold on to her. He must unship his scull as he comes alongside and grasp the vessel's rail, whilst his passenger gets on board and takes the painter. Yet how often one sees the passenger hang on whilst the man who has been pulling fiddles about with his sculls! The result is that the dinghy's head, caught by the tide, swings away from the yacht and the man in her stern has to let go. These are the first principles of watermanship, which all who go sailing in tidal waters must learn as soon as possible. Another thing that the beginner should note is that when alone in a dinghy he should row from the centre thwart and not from the bow. A dinghy that is trimmed by the head is not only hard to row but extremely difficult to steer. Moreover, in rough water, a dinghy thus trimmed is unsafe. If you have a heavy passenger in the sternsheets, it is usually better to row from the bow thwart rather than from the centre one, for, if the boat is trimmed too much by the stern, she will cock her nose out of water and the wind will tend to blow her head round. Another thing a novice has to learn is how to pull a dinghy. He has probably been accustomed to sculling up-river skiffs, which are long and narrow, but a dinghy is a short tubby little boat which calls for a different method of propulsion. When pulling a skiff, one takes long strokes and feathers close to the water. But that style of rowing is not suitable for sea work in a dinghy. In such boats one should pull with comparatively short strokes and feather high. Short quick strokes will take a dinghy along much faster than long slow ones, whilst if you feather too low your sculls will catch the tops of the waves. These hints, no doubt, are very elementary, but may be of use to novices who have not yet got the hang of handling boats in tidal waters.

It is not, however, only the novice that comes to grief in a dinghy, for I can recall quite a number of accidents in which experienced yachtsmen have lost their lives. These casualties have usually resulted from one or other of the following causes: Overloading, changing seats, and carelessness in laying out a kedge in heavy weather. Now, with regard to the question of overloading. The owner of a small cruising yacht, having to tow his dinghy, naturally selects the smallest one that will serve his purpose. Any dinghy, when towed, seriously retards the progress of a little cruiser, and for that reason the tender of a craft of 4 or 5 tons seldom exceeds 9 feet in length. Such a dinghy will carry two people comfortably, and three if the water is smooth. In rough water, however, three people in a 9-ft. boat borders upon the dangerous, whilst to carry four or five is positively suicidal. Yet one often sees it done and, if the boat happens to be wet and the journey but a short one, some of them may even stand up. In my opinion anyone who stands up in a dinghy in any circumstances is a damned fool, and he who makes a practice of it is pretty certain to get a ducking sooner or later. Mind you, there is often a great temptation to overcrowd a dinghy. The yacht may be lying a long way from the hard, with wind and tide against you, and your party may number, say, four. You know that your dinghy will carry three all right, but you feel a bit doubtful whether she will take four. To make two trips means a lot of hard rowing and sacrifice of time, and so you decide to chance it. Well, you may do that sort of thing time after time with impunity, but it is not safe and one of these days you may have an accident.

A time when accidents due to overcrowding often occur is when returning on board after a festive evening at the club. You may be asked by two or three men, who have no dinghy of their own, to put them on board their vessel, and do not like to refuse. These self-invited passengers may not be 'tight' in a police-court sense, but they have probably had enough to induce that 'don't care a damn for anyone or anything' sort of feeling, and as the thwarts are wet with dew they insist upon standing up. I can recall several fatal accidents that occurred in such circumstances, and it is a wonder that there have not been more. Years ago an accident of that nature occurred on a dark night in winter at a well-known East Coast yachting resort. The dinghy capsized within a yard or two of the yacht, but all of the party managed to get on board with the exception of one man, who apparently sank like a stone. When his body was subsequently recovered, it was found that he had in the 'poacher's' pockets of his overcoat, a joint of beef, a bottle of whisky, two syphons of soda water, a pound of sausages, and various other items.

To change seats in a small dinghy is a very risky proceeding and should never be attempted unless absolutely unavoidable. If you have to do it, don't on any account stand up, but crawl past each other, keeping your weight as low down as possible. If you have a very long row to the yacht, or hard, it is probable that for a considerable part of the journey the shore will not be very far distant. Should that be the case, the best plan is to run the dinghy on the mud whilst you change seats.

Many accidents, some of them fatal, have occurred to yachtsmen when laying out a kedge and they have almost invariably been the result of sheer carelessness. This is the sort of thing that happens. The yachtsman takes into the dinghy the kedge and warp, one end of the latter being made fast to the yacht. Then he rows off, paying out the warp as he goes. When all of the warp has run out, he hastily ships his sculls, seizes the kedge and, standing up, throws it overboard. As likely as not the water is rough and the little dinghy dancing about with considerable liveliness. To stand up at all under such conditions would be foolish, but to do so when holding a heavy anchor is sheer madness. Several yachtsmen of the widest experience have lost their lives in that manner and yet hundreds continue to lay out kedges in that haphazard way. The only safe method of laying out and weighing a kedge with a small dinghy is described in the chapter on Safety Precautions.

CHAPTER 63: *The Rule of the Road*

No one should go afloat in charge of even a small yacht until he has acquired a working knowledge of the Regulations for Preventing Collisions at Sea, commonly termed the 'Rule of the Road.' It is a duty he owes both to himself and other users of the sea and a plea of ignorance would not absolve him from the consequences of any neglect in that respect. I do not mean to suggest that he must learn by heart the whole code, for it covers a good many pages and as it is mainly intended for big ships, much of it would be superfluous to the yachtsman. But it is essential to know those portions of the code which deal with the prevention of collision. They are quite short and easily learnt, but before quoting them a few preliminary explanations will be advisable.

A vessel is said to be under way within the meaning of the rules when she is not at anchor, made fast to the shore, or aground. The term 'steam vessel' includes any vessel that is mechanically propelled and an auxiliary vessel when under both sail and power ranks as a steamer. A vessel is close-hauled when she is sailing as close to the wind as she can and when she is not close-hauled she is said to be 'running free.' She is on the port tack, or gybe, when carrying her boom to starboard, and on the starboard tack, or gybe, when carrying her boom to port. The steering rules are as follows:

ART. 17. When two sailing vessels are approaching one another, so as to involve risk of collision, one of them shall keep out of the way of the other as follows, viz:

(A) A vessel which is running free shall keep out of the way of a vessel which is close-hauled.

(B) A vessel which is close-hauled on the port tack shall keep out of the way of a vessel that is close-hauled on the starboard tack.

(C) When both are running free, with the wind on different sides, the vessel which has the wind on the port side shall keep out of the way of the other.

(D) When both are running free, with the wind on the same side, thevesselwhichistowindwardshallkeepoutofthewayofthevesselwhich is to leeward.

(E) A vessel which has the wind aft shall keep out of the way of the other vessel.

ART. 20. When a steam vessel and a sailing vessel are proceeding in such directions as to involve risk of collision, the steam vessel shall keep out of the way of the sailing vessel.

ART. 21. Where by any of these rules one of two vessels is to keep out of the way, the other shall keep her course and speed.

Note: When, in consequence of thick weather or other causes, such vessel finds herself so close that collision cannot be avoided by the action of the giving-way vessel alone, she also shall take such action as will best aid to avert collision.

ART. 22. Every vessel which is directed by these rules to keep out of the way of another vessel, shall, if the circumstances of the case admit, avoid crossing ahead of the other.

ART. 24. Notwithstanding anything contained in these rules, every vessel overtaking any other shall keep out of the way of the overtaken vessel.

Those are the rules which mainly concern sailing yachts and if you adhere to them strictly you are not likely to collide with any other vessel.

In studying these rules you will notice that the term 'reaching' so often used by yachtsmen, is not mentioned; a vessel is either close-hauled or running free. Bearing that in mind, the rules are quite clear and call for little explanation. If you are not sailing as close to the wind as you can with advantage, you must remember that you are running free within the meaning of the rules and act accordingly. If you are reaching and meet another vessel also reaching from the opposite direction, you must not say to yourself, "She has the wind more free than I have and she has to give way," for that has nothing to do with it. If you are not close-hauled and have the wind on your port side, it is your duty to give way. If the approaching vessel has the wind on her port side, she will have to give way to you.

There is only one situation that I can think of that does not seem to be covered by the rules; that is when two vessels are close-hauled on the same tack and risk of collision is involved through the leeward vessel sailing closer to the wind.

It is a situation often met with in racing and sometimes when cruising when yachts are beating to windward in a river. It is provided for in the YRA racing rules, but there is no mention of converging in the Board of Trade regulations. Should you find yourself in such a position, I think, if you are the windward vessel, you should give way, as you would under clause D when both vessels were running free.

If, when beating to windward, you are on the port tack and are meeting another vessel which is on the starboard tack, watch her closely and if possible observe her position in relation to some fixed object ashore. If she materially changes that position, you will probably go clear, but if you have any doubt about it, you should go about in good time. Should you make an error of judgment and find at the last minute that you cannot clear the approaching vessel, put your helm down. Even if you are unable to keep clear by such means, you will only strike her a sidelong blow, which is not likely to do much damage, and don't forget to apologize, for you were at fault.

Bearing Article 22 in mind, you might bear away with the idea of passing under her stern, but this is one of those cases where the circumstances do not admit of your complying with that rule. If you attempt by bearing away to go under her stern and have not room, you will strike her end-on with devastating force and the consequences may be very serious.

If you are overhauling another vessel and you are more than 2 points abaft her beam, you are an overtaking vessel within the meaning of the rules and must keep out of her way. At night, you can determine whether you are an overtaking vessel by her lights. If her sidelights and masthead light (if she is a steamer) are screened and you can only see her stern light, you are overtaking.

Remember that if you have your engine running, you are a steamer within the meaning of the rules, even if you are sailing as well, and if at night must carry the regulation lights. I referred to these in the chapter on navigation lights, so need not do so again; but it is necessary for you to know the regulations regarding steam vessels. The only rules you need trouble about are the following:

When two steam vessels are meeting end-on, or nearly end-on, so as to involve risk of collision, each shall alter her course to starboard so that each may pass on the port side of the other.

When two steam vessels are crossing so as to involve risk of collision, the vessel which has the other on her own starboard side shall keep out of the way of the other.

In narrow channels every steam vessel shall, when it is safe and practicable, keep to that side of the fairway or mid channel which lies on the starboard side of such vessel.

As it is sometimes not easy to determine whether a vessel under sail has her engine running also, a new regulation was adopted some years before the war, whereby it was ordained that a vessel under both sail and power should display in a prominent position aloft a shape in the form of an inverted cone. As I had noticed that yachts were not complying with this new regulation, I interviewed the Board of Trade on the subject. They told me that they were still awaiting the agreement of one or two other countries (the rules are international) and the rule would not come into force until an order in council had been made.

So far as I know the order has not yet been made and I have never seen a vessel carrying the prescribed cone. It is, however, extremely important that a helmsman should know definitely whether a vessel under sail he is approaching has her engine running or not. If she has, then it is her duty to give way; if she has not, then it may be your obligation to keep clear. Should you have any doubt whether she has her engine running, it will be safer to assume that she has not.

Although by the rules a steamer must always give way to a vessel under sail alone (unless of course the latter is overtaking, which very seldom happens) prudence will tell you not to shove your little ship under the bows of, say, the *Queen Mary*, as it is sometimes impossible for a big ship to give way. What seems to you a wide stretch of water, may be an extremely narrow channel for a ship drawing perhaps 30 feet or more, and even if she were able to give way, you cannot expect her to run the risk of getting ashore in doing so. It is wise therefore to give big vessels a wide berth.

I think, too, it is only sporting to give way to barges in narrow waters, for they are on business while the yacht is on pleasure. If a barge has frequently to give way to yachts in a crowded river, such as the Crouch, she may fail to reach her destination on the tide and incur a serious loss of time.

I will conclude this chapter by quoting Article 27 of the BOT regulations:

"In obeying and construing these rules, due regard shall be had to all dangers of navigation and collision, and to any special circumstances which may render a departure from the above rules necessary in order to avoid immediate danger."

You must not think that holding the right of way relieves you of all responsibility, for it does not. I know it is extremely annoying when a vessel that should give way to you fails to do so, but if you 'ram the blighter,' as you may be sorely tempted to do, you will place yourself in the wrong. You would be acting against the spirit of Article 27 and probably be held guilty of contributory negligence.

CHAPTER 64: *Marlinspike Seamanship*

Every small yacht owner should make it his business to acquire sufficient knowledge of knotting and splicing to enable him to keep his vessel's gear in order and effect repairs should anything carry away while at sea. The more intricate work of this description is best learnt by ocular demonstration, but as I propose only to deal with such comparatively simple splices and knots as are really necessary, I hope the reader will be able to follow how they are made from the diagrams. But ropework is a rather fascinating pursuit and you will probably desire to attain a more extensive knowledge of the art. Should that be the case, I would advise you to get some expert to show you, as the more elaborate knots are difficult to explain on paper and still more difficult to illustrate.

SPLICING AND WHIPPING

The best implement for splicing rope is a fid of hard wood, such as lignum vitae, as it is less likely to damage the strands than a metal spike; but for small stuff like hambro-line, the spike on your knife will serve. For splicing wire, however, you must use a metal marlinspike. For laying on a service you will need a serving board, or serving mallet. When splicing rope you must splice against the lay, but wire rope is spliced with the lay. With those preliminary remarks, I will pass on to a description of how the splices are made.

Short splice: This is used to join two ropes permanently together. Unlay the strands of both ropes for 3 or 4 inches and 'marry' them, so that the strands interlock (left figure). Now take a strand, pass it over the one opposite to it and under the next (right figure). Do the same with all of the strands of both ropes until each has been dipped twice. Then cut away half the yarns of each strand and dip again. Halve and dip what is left and cut off the surplus close to the rope. Singe off any loose fibres with a lighted match and finally roll the splice under your foot to smooth down the work. If properly made the splice will look neat and be nearly as strong as the rope itself.

Short splice

Eye splice: Unlay the strands for about six inches and lay back on to the rope so as to form an eye of the required size. Now take the middle strand you have unlaid and dip it under one of the laid-up strands. Working from right to left, do the same with the next strand. Then turn the rope over and pass the third strand under the remaining laid-up strand. If you are splicing a thimble in the eye, the

Eye splice

splice must be pulled up very taut round the thimble otherwise the latter may come out when the splice has stretched a bit after use. You will be able to get it tighter if you use the spike as a lever. The novice, when splicing, will find it helpful if he first ties up the end of each strand with whipping twine.

Long splice: This is used for repairing a broken rope that is required to reeve through a block, as it does not materially increase the size of the rope. Unlay the strands about three times as far as you would for a short splice and marry the strands. Now unlay one of the strands still farther, taking care not to disturb the

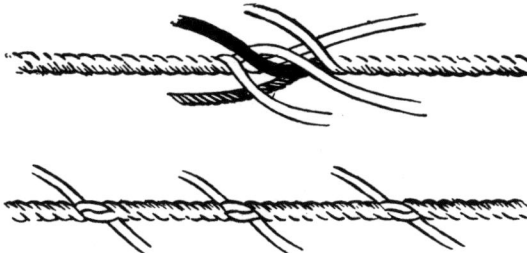

Long splice

lay more than you can help, and lay up in its place the opposite strand. Halve the two and tie with an overhand knot. Do the same with all the strands (top) then halve and dip before cutting off the surplus (bottom).

Whipping a rope's end: Take a length of whipping twine about 18 inches long

Whipping

and lay the end along the rope. Hold it in position with your thumb while you lay on the first few turns. When you have put on about two-thirds of the whipping, working towards the end of the rope, lay back the other end of the twine on the rope and whip over it, passing the bight over the rope's end each turn. When you have laid on sufficient turns, say four or five, haul the end of the twine taut. The rope will then be neatly whipped with both ends of the twine tucked under the whipping. It is the usual practice to cut off the ends of the twine close up to the whipping, but I prefer to tie them together before cutting, as I think it adds to the security of the whipping.

The ends of sail-cover lacings are best whipped with a needle, sail-maker fashion, as otherwise they are apt to come adrift. They have to be very close to the end of the cord, which would otherwise fray out and make it difficult to pass the cord through the eyelets of the cover. If not sewn on they soon get loose and come off.

Serving: A service is put on over a splice in much the same way as whipping a rope, but must be laid on very tightly with a serving board. You should work up towards the eye and take the last few turns by hand. It is not really necessary to serve a splice, but it is usually done for the sake of appearance.

Wire splicing: Wire rope can be spliced either with a short or long splice but seldom is, as it makes the rope too short and the splice is of rather doubtful strength. For wire splicing you need a metal spike, pliers, a hammer and vice, and as wire rope has six strands and a core, it is more complicated to splice than manila or hemp rope. There are many ways of splicing wire but it must always be done with the lay to avoid undue bending of the strands. A common method of splicing an eye in wire is to lay back three of the strands on each side of the rope, tucking in the third strand from the right, then the third from the left and so on, the last strand being tucked under two strands. Then proceed as usual until each strand has been tucked at least five times. Then beat the splice with a hammer to make the strands fit tightly. When completed, the splice should be parcelled, by wrapping insulating tape round it, and then served. The service should finally be varnished to keep out wet.

Before beginning a wire splice, each strand should be tied up, otherwise they will unravel, and a lashing put round the rope to limit the unlaying of the strands. Wire splicing is a difficult, and often rather painful, job for the inexpert, and most yachtsmen prefer to have it done for them by a professional rigger.

SEIZINGS AND STROPS

Seizing: This is used to secure a block in a strop, or a thimble in an eye, and a length of stout marline should be used for the purpose. Having made a small eye in the end of the marline, take a number of turns round both parts of the rope below the block or thimble. The turns should be put on neatly and each hauled as tightly as possible, using your spike as a lever. When the seizing is sufficiently wide, put on another layer of turns, working back over the others. These are called 'riders' and lie in the interstices of the first layer. Then take a couple of

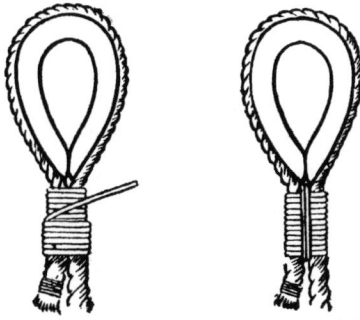

Seizing

turns round the seizing between the two parts of the rope and finish off with a clove hitch.

Grommet strop: To make a grommet for stropping a block, unlay a strand

Grommet strop

from a rope, being careful not to disturb the lay of the extracted strand. Then lay up this strand again and you will have a ring of rope like a deck quoit. To finish it off, tie an overhand knot, thin down the strands and tuck them into the strop. The length of strand required should be rather more than three times that of the finished strop.

Selvagee strop: A very neat and strong strop can be made of marline in the following way. Drive two nails into a stout plank at a distance apart determined by the size of the strop required. Then take a ball of stout marline and having secured the end to one of the nails, wind it tightly round and round the two nails until the strop is of suitable thickness. The strop should then be tied up with seaming twine in six or eight places to preserve the shape before it is removed from the nails. A selvagee strop of this kind can be covered either with can-

Selvagee strop

vas and painted, or with leather. If covered with leather, soak the latter first, as leather stretches when wet and shrinks as it dries.

KNOTS, BENDS AND HITCHES

Now we will pass on to knots and hitches. These are not easy to illustrate, but I think the plain outlines used will be clearer to follow than any fancy drawings or photographs. To enable the reader to differentiate between the end of the rope and the standing part, the former is in all cases shown whipped.

Overhand knot: This requires no description other than the diagram. It is of

Overhand knot and reef knot

little use by itself but forms the basis of the reef knot and is also employed when making a long splice or a grommet.

Reef knot: As its name implies, it is used for tying the points of a sail when reefing. It should be noted that the standing part and end both pass through the bight the same way, otherwise it would be what is commonly termed a 'granny.' A reef knot should not be used for joining two ropes of different sizes, as it is unreliable for that purpose.

Clove hitch: This is one of the most useful hitches in existence as it can be

Clove hitch and half hitch

used for a variety of purposes. It consists merely of two half-hitches and the diagram shows clearly how it is made. You will note when making it that the end travels in the same direction throughout.

Half-hitch: This is not of much use by itself, although sometimes employed for making a temporary loop in a rope, the end then being seized to the standing

Two half hitches

part. To make it you merely pass the end round the standing part and through the bight.

Two half-hitches: Practically the same as a clove hitch, being merely a half-hitch repeated. It is most useful for securing a dinghy painter, making fast a rope to a ring and many other purposes.

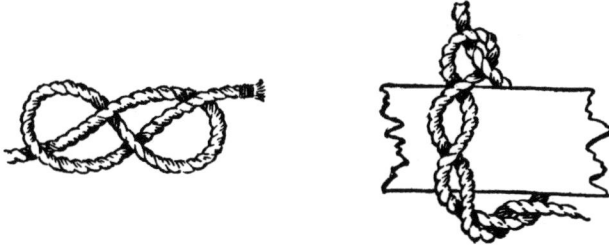

Figure-of-eight knot and timber hitch

Figure-of-eight, or Flemish knot: This is made at the end of a rope to prevent its being pulled through a fairlead or block. Pass the end of the rope over and under the standing part and tuck it through the bight from above.

Timber hitch: Used for attaching a rope to a spar, or the topsail halyard to the yard. Pass the end round the spar and under and over the standing part. Then take several turns round its own part.

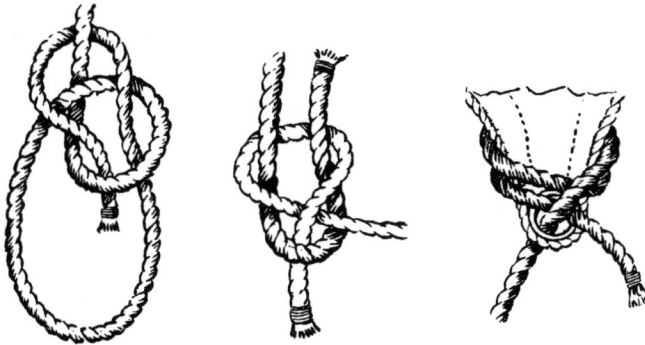

Bowline, common bend and sheet bend

Bowline: This is one of the most useful hitches extant as it never slips and can always be undone easily. It is used for securing a warp to a buoy and many other purposes. Make a small bight and pass the end of the rope through it, then round the standing part above and back through the bight from below.

Common bend: This is often used for joining two ropes together. Double back the end of one rope and then pass the end of the other through the bight thus formed, round both parts and tuck it under its own part.

Sheet bend: This is very much like the common bend, but the cringle of the sail is substituted for the bight.

Rolling hitch and fisherman's bend

Rolling hitch: This is an exceedingly useful hitch as it will not slip on a spar or rope. It is used for attaching a tail block to a rope, making fast the signal halyards to the shrouds and many other purposes. Take a turn round the spar or rope to which you wish to make fast, bringing the end below the standing part. Then take another turn above the first, jamming it between the first turn and the standing part. Finish off with a half-hitch over all for the sake of security.

Fisherman's bend: Used for securing a warp to a kedge. Pass the warp twice through the ring of the anchor, then over the standing part and finally through both of the turns on the anchor. To make all secure, finish off with a half-hitch round the standing part, or tie the end to the standing part with a bit of marline.

Topsail halyard bend

Topsail halyard bend: As its name indicates, this is used for attaching the halyard to the topsail yard. Pass the end three times round the spar, then over the standing part, down through all three turns, then over the last two turns and under the third.

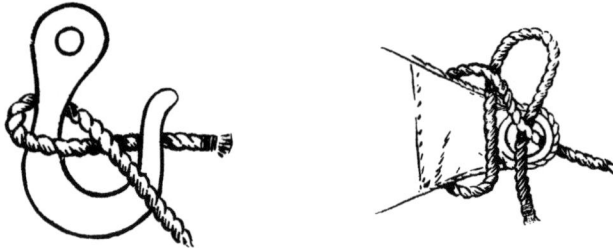

Blackwall hitch and slippery bend

Blackwall hitch: Used for securing a rope to a hook. Pass the rope round the back of the hook and tuck the end under the standing part in the hook, so that it is jammed by the standing part. This is a quick method of attachment but is not recommended if the rope is wet as in such circumstances it is liable to slip.

Slippery bend: This is similar to the common bend but the end is doubled before being tucked under the standing part. By pulling on the end it is immediately released.

Sheepshank

Sheepshank: Useful for shortening, or taking the strain off a stranded rope. The rope is doubled and brought down again so that you have three parts. A half-hitch is then taken at each end.

Wall-knot, shroud knot, crowning a wall-knot

Wall knot: This forms the basis of the double-wall-and-crown and shroud knots. The strands of the end of a rope having been unlaid for a few inches, the second strand is laid over the first and the third over the second. The third strand is then tucked through the bight of the first from below and all three strands are then pulled tight.

Shroud knot: This was extensively used in olden times for repairing a broken hemp shroud. It can be employed for joining two ropes together, or repairing a broken lanyard. Unlay the strands of each rope for 5 or 6 inches and marry them. Then make a wall knot with each set of strands. As one knot will pull against the other, the result is a strong and neat union.

To crown a wall knot: Lay one strand over the top of the knot, then lay the second strand over the first and the third over the second and through the bight of the first. You now have a single-wall-and-crown and by following the lead round will get a double-wall-and-crown, a very handsome knot for the end of a manrope.

Back splice: Unlay the strands for a few inches, make a wall knot and then splice the ends into the rope, dipping each three times. This makes a good permanent fixing for the end of a rope instead of whipping.

Grocer's hitch: This is a very useful but little-known knot which until quite recently I was under the impression that I had invented when a small boy at my prep. school. Having enjoyed what I thought was its exclusive use for more than sixty years, I was more than a little surprised to receive a parcel secured with the hitch. After some little research, I have discovered that it is known as the grocer's hitch, or slide knot, although I have yet to come across a grocer who makes use of it. The hitch is merely a figure-of-eight knot made round the standing part and pulled tight. It can be used for lashing two spars together, tying up parcels, securing the parchment top of a partly-used pot of jam and many other purposes. In my motor-cycling days I found that it was the only hitch that would hold a package securely on the carrier. It can be hauled very taught without slipping and yet, curiously enough, a pull on the loose end will free it at once. A half-hitch should be made round the standing part with the loose end for additional security.

Grocer's hitch

To renew a reef point: Having removed the broken point from the sail, take a piece of hambro line of suitable length and whip the ends. Then, holding the line in the middle with both hands, separated by about an inch, give a sharp twist

Renewing a reef point

against the lay. This will cause the strands to separate and form little rings, looking rather like the leaves of a shamrock. Now pass the line through the vacant eyelet in the sail until the rings lie close up to the canvas and then sew them to the sail. Of course, if you use four-stranded hambro line there will be four rings.

BOSUN'S CHAIR

The usual bosun's chair consists of a bit of board slung on rope bridles, but it is neither comfortable to sit on nor easily stowed away. I recently saw in one of Uffa Fox's books an illustration of one made of canvas, which seems a much better proposition. When not in use it can be folded up and stowed away in a locker, and there is a pocket in the side to hold tools. The canvas is 3 feet 6 inches long

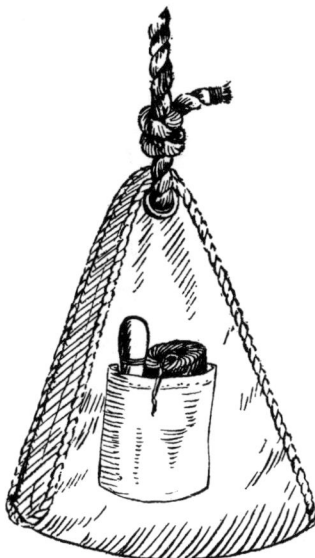

by 12 inches wide, tapering to the ends, where there are eyes for the bridle of 1¾-inches rope. Apart from the question of comfort, there are no corners to foul the rigging as it is hoisted.

MOUNTING A BURGEE

To mount a burgee on a cane, so that it will swing clear of the truck, first remove the cord which, for some reason or other best known to themselves, the manufacturers always put in the flag, and substitute a length of stiff wire, about four inches longer than the hoist of the burgee. Sew the wire tightly to the flag and bend over the ends of the former at right-angles. Now bend the ends into loops, a small one at the top and a larger one at the bottom. The upper loop will revolve on a screw driven into the head of the cane, and the lower one round the cane itself. The top of the cane should be rubbed down smooth with glass paper and the edge slightly bevelled, to insure the flag revolving freely. If you use a brass screw-eye, instead of an ordinary screw for the top fitting, you will be able to employ the same cane for other burgees if you belong to several clubs.

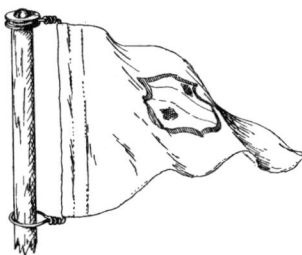

A Yarn

❧

Cruising in Company

In our youth we are apt to regard the summer holiday as the crown of the year and await its advent with ever growing eagerness. In that summer of 1899 I looked forward to my holiday cruise with exceptional impatience, for *Snipe* was still something of a new toy and I had arranged to sail in company with several other craft. We contemplated a cruise to Lowestoft and as none of us had been so far north before, the passage promised to be a bit of an adventure. In addition to *Snipe*, the fleet was to include *Viper*, *Walrus* and *Rani*.

Walrus had been recently bought by my brother, O. V. Cooke, to replace *Norah Creina*, which he had sold. She was a cutter of 3 tons, built by Burgoine in 1885 from a design by Clayton, and the amount of gear and sails she had was appalling. Her mast was supported on each side by three shrouds, a runner and a preventer backstay, and her equipment of sails included, in addition to the mainsail, two jackyard topsails, two thimble-headed topsails, two jib topsails, working and balloon foresails, five jibs and a spinnaker. Notwithstanding her spread of canvas she was not very fast, and *Snipe* could always beat her, except in dead light airs, when her large sail area gave her an advantage.

Rani had been built the previous year from the design of her owner, J. Pain Clark, the creator of many desirable small yachts. She was a speedy little sloop of 3 tons, so our boats were all of much the same size, with the exception of *Viper*, a converted ship's lifeboat of 7 tons, owned by the brothers Viner.

I was accompanied on this trip by one whom I will call the Passenger, as that seems to me the most appropriate designation for him. He was an amusing companion but knew little of sailing, and was one of those people who only enjoy work when someone else does it. He left me to do the cooking as a matter of course, and after every meal settled himself comfortably with pipe and book while I washed up. He had never sailed with me before and never did again, as before the cruise was over I was heartily sick of him.

In accordance with my usual practice, I kept a log of the cruise in diary form, which I now reproduce with a little amplification.

July 8th. – Arrived on board at 10.30 a.m. after a perilous passage in the Berthon dinghy, which was heavily laden with a large case of stores and various other packages. Having unpacked the case and stowed everything away, I cleaned the brasswork (I wonder how long I shall keep up this spit and polish business!) At 11.30 I got under way and with a light W.N.W. breeze ran down to Burnham over the tide, bringing up shortly after one o'clock.

Rowing over to *Rani*, I learnt from Clark that the rest of the crowd would not be down until late in the afternoon, so I returned to *Snipe* and had lunch.

Having washed up, I went ashore and on going to the club was seized by the press-gang, or, in other words, Bertie Robinson, who insisted upon my crewing for him in *My Lady Dainty*. We got a good start but had not gone far when Bertie rammed a smack at anchor – and did it properly, too. There was a rending crash and in a moment we were enveloped in sails. *Dainty's* mast was over the side, the spinnaker boom broken, the foredeck torn up, the mast-step carried away and the foresail torn. After we had cleared away the wreckage, we got a boat to tow us back to the mooring and I then went ashore to meet the Passenger. I found that he had just arrived, complete with a damn great portmanteau, at which I looked askance. I suggested that he should take out what he wanted and leave the bag at the club, but he would not hear of it, saying there was nothing in it that he would not want.

We had tea at the club and shortly afterwards my brother and his crew arrived from Town. As *Viper* had come down from Fambridge during the afternoon, we were all there, ready to start, but as it was getting on towards low water, we decided to wait until the night tide. So the Passenger and I went off to *Snipe* for dinner. With much difficulty I managed to stow his portmanteau – one of those old-fashioned things that opened in the middle – up forward and then got dinner ready. The menu consisted of cold lamb, peas and new potatoes, apricots and cream, and cheese and biscuits, washed down with Burgundy and soda and followed by coffee and sloe gin. After dinner, the Passenger read the evening paper while I washed up and then we, in company with the other crews, adjourned to the club and spent a very convivial evening. As we were going to get under way at about 1 a.m. it did not seem worth while going to bed, so we spent the intervening time in visiting the other boats.

July 9th. – We all got under way by arrangement at 1.30 a.m. There was not a breath of wind but a strong ebb carried us down the river. At Shore Ends we got a light S.W. breeze, which took us nearly to Clacton, but the ebb had then finished and we had to bring up. There we lolloped about for nearly three hours, during which we cleaned up the boat – or rather, I did – and had breakfast. To while away the time, I discoursed more or less sweet music on a flageolet (rather less than more, was the Passenger's verdict) that attracted a thrush which settled on the foresail stowed on deck. The bird stayed for quite a long time and 'left his card' before leaving.

At last a nice little breeze filled in from the eastward and took us past Clacton Pier. *Snipe* and *Walrus* just managed to fetch along the coast, but *Viper* had to make several boards. The speedy little *Rani* had by this time left us far astern. We carried the breeze until we had just passed the Naze and then it died away and I had to row with the sweep nearly all the way to

Felixstowe Dock, where we found *Rani. Walrus* and *Viper*, arriving some time later, brought up outside the dock. After dinner we went ashore for a stroll but did not stay long as we began to feel tired, having been up all the previous night, and turned in at ten o'clock. Very hot day and tedious passage.

July 10th. – We did not turn out until 10 a.m. and discovered that *Rani* and *Viper* had departed for Lowestoft – What energy ! Got under way at half-past eleven and found *Walrus* waiting for us outside the Dock, so we ran up to Pin Mill with a nice southerly breeze. We cursed ourselves for our laziness as the conditions were ideal for the passage to Lowestoft. As long as we had the breeze right aft, we ran side by side with *Walrus*, but when we hauled our wind round Collimer Point, we at once began to leave our consort and arrived at Pin Mill leading by about 300 yds. We both brought up and went ashore to buy meat and bread and then returned on board for lunch. At 4 p.m. we got under way and had a slashing sail down to Felixstowe Dock, incidentally giving *Walrus* a good trouncing. On entering the dock I missed the buoy and just touched another craft. We did no damage to her but broke off one of the bowsprit shroud beckets of our cranse iron. After we had moored, I temporarily re-paired the damage with a strop. We then walked over to Felixstowe and it was so late when we got back that we did not have our dinner until after nine. As we intended to start for Lowestoft in the early hours of the following day, we did not turn in properly, but lay in our cots reading.

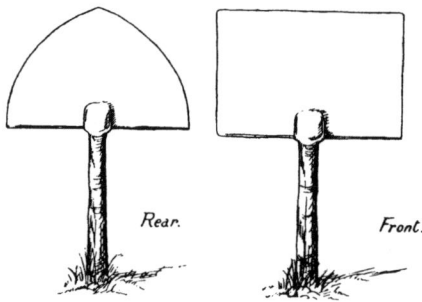

Rear.   Front.

Woodbridge Haven leading marks

July 11th. – At 3 a.m. we rowed out of the Dock and found *Walrus*, which had brought up outside, just getting under way. There was a light S.S.E. breeze which carried us to Bawdsey Haven and then it died away leaving us becalmed.

This was particularly annoying as it seemed likely that we should fail to save our tide round Orfordness, which is the crux of the passage to Lowes-toft. The flood runs very hard round the Ness, and unless you have a smart fair wind you cannot get round. To make matters more difficult, the farther north you go, the less ebb you carry. The ebb, however, was running strongly when the wind petered out, and with the aid of occasional puffs we managed to get as far as the Orfordness Lighthouse before the tide turned. We had only about half a mile to go to get round the Ness, and having come so far it would have been heartbreaking if we had had to go all the way back. *Walrus*, with her larger spread of sail, had got some way ahead of us and was nearly round and I was determined not to give up without a struggle. It is bold water round Orfordness, the shingle beach being as steep as the side of a house. A little yacht can stand in within a yard or two of the shore and I could see my brother actually poling *Walrus* along the beach with a sweep. With topsail and spinnaker set *Snipe* wooed the gentle zephyr and at the same time I pulled like blazes with the sweeps. Lord! how I sweated under the scorching sun. Yard by yard we won our way and ultimately squirmed round the point.

Having got round Orfordness we found much less tide, and presently, as if in reward for my labour at the oar, we got a grand southerly breeze which sent us along at a fine gait. We began to overhaul *Walrus* and passed her just before we came to Dunwich. The Passenger was asleep in the cabin, and as we passed Dunwich I meditated upon the devastating effect of coast erosion in this district. According to Stow, Dunwich was once the capital city of East Anglia, but it now lies buried deep beneath the waters of the North Sea. In mediaeval times it could boast of fifty-two churches, a king's court, a bishop's palace and a large harbour full of shipping. All that now remains to remind one of its past glory are a few cottages and a solitary church. Even this church is threatened with extinction as it stands on the very edge of the cliff and may at any moment topple over into the sea. Already most of the churchyard has fallen and the bones of deceased Dunwichites lie bleaching on the strand beneath. (Note. – This last remaining church of the fifty-two mentioned by Stow was blown down in a gale during the Great War.)

The erosion has not by any means been confined to Dunwich, for the avaricious sea has taken toll both to the north and to the south. The West Rocks, off Harwich, for instance, mark the site of the ancient town of Walton and that barn-like church St. Peter's-on-the-Wall, at the mouth of the Blackwater, is all that remains of the Roman city Othona. Farther north, at Pakefield, the coast is also crumbling away despite valiant efforts to save it, and there can be no doubt that in the fight between man and nature man has come off second best.

But these rather melancholy thoughts were soon dispersed by the joy of sailing, for *Snipe* was putting her best foot foremost and steadily dropping *Walrus*. Southwold, with its tall lighthouse, was already in sight and but 5 miles distant and we covered those 5 miles in quick time, as the tide was comparatively slack in Dunwich Bay. As we approached Southwold we stood in closer to the shore to have a look at Walberswick, a favourite haunt of artists. It is an extremely picturesque little village, but here again we noted evidence of the destructive action of the sea, for the piers seemed to be dilapidated and the harbour derelict. Like Bawdsey and Orford Havens, it has a bar that silts up and shifts, for the River Blyth has not sufficient scour to keep the entrance clear.

We had now reached the last stage of the journey, being but 11 miles from Lowestoft, and the Passenger, having slept peacefully for some hours, woke up and announced that he was hungry. "Shall I take the helm while you get some grub out?" he suggested, adding, "I could do with a bottle of beer." I thought he might very well have got lunch ready himself, seeing that he had done nothing in the way of work since we started, but as I was hungry also, I fell in with his proposal, and bringing the necessary things out into the well, we had lunch *al fresco*, so to speak. By the time we had finished we were close to Covehithe Ness and began to look for the South Barnard buoy, which marks the end of the Barnard and Newcome Sands. We soon located it and leaving the buoy to starboard, entered the Covehithe Channel, which lies between the sands and the shore.

I suggested to the Passenger that he should wash up, to which he replied, "Oh, I will just put the things in the bucket; we can easily wash them up when we get in." That 'we' rather amused me, as I knew very well that the job would eventually fall to me. As I hate having dirty things lying about when under way, I gave the helm to my companion and washed up there and then.

And so we sailed on, close to the shore, past pretty little Kessingland and Pakefield, and Lowestoft at last hove in sight. As I had never been there before and had not the slightest idea what the harbour was like inside, I hove-to off the entrance and launched the dinghy. Then, determined to have everything that we could possibly want ready to hand, I got the topsail down and the anchor over the bow, coiled down a couple of warps, cleared the halyards, put a fender ready in the cockpit and cleared the sweeps. Then, letting the foresail draw, sailed boldly in. I need not have troubled, for as we approached the yacht basin a couple of watermen in a boat came to meet us and taking a line towed us into a berth in the tier and moored us 'all fours,' while I lowered the sails. As I felt pretty tired after being up all night and the long sail, I thought the two bob I gave them money well spent. We berthed next to *Viper*, which had arrived the day before, and *Rani* was on the other side of her. *Walrus*, which we had beaten by fully a mile and a half, berthed next to us when she came in, so we were all together.

There is something extraordinarily satisfying about a successful passage in a small yacht, particularly when one is a comparative novice, and as I stowed away the gear and put on the mainsail cover, I felt very much like Columbus must have done when he discovered America. That night we all dined together at the Suffolk Hotel and exchanged experiences. *Viper*, we learnt, had created something of a diversion when entering the harbour the previous afternoon. She sailed in with her topsail and every other stitch of sail set, and her crew, to their horror, found they were sailing into a sort of *cul-de-sac*. Right ahead was the quay on which stands the Royal Norfolk and Suffolk Yacht Club; to starboard was another quay and to port the tier of yachts in the basin. They could not get the topsail down as it was laced to the topmast and were altogether in the devil of a tight place. In a vain hope of bringing her round, they put the helm hard down, but there was not room and she charged into the tier, catching a white steam yacht a sidelong blow. The only damage that resulted, however, was a long streak of black paint on the steam yacht's topside and the loss of one of *Viper's* bowsprit shrouds. The relations between *Viper's* crew and the skipper of the steam yacht after the collision were not exactly cordial, but they subsequently made peace over a pot of beer and by the time we arrived all was well.

We spent the evening on the pier, listening to the band, and turned in early.

July 12th. – It was certainly very jolly lying in the basin, with a good band discoursing cheerful music on the pier just by, but it had its inconveniences. Lying just below the pier as we were, our domestic activities seemed to be a source of considerable public interest, which was rather embarrassing. Then, too, there was the difficulty of getting rid of our rubbish. We could not with any decency dump it overboard in the basin and so periodically I had to row outside the harbour to empty the bucket. We could wash at the club, where we had been made honorary members, but could not have a swim unless we went to the beach and hired a machine. We therefore decided to seek a more private berth on Oulton Broad.

At eleven o'clock we took in our warps and rowed *Snipe* round to the swing bridge. We had to wait there for nearly half an hour before the bridge was opened, but having got through, we made sail and ran up Lake Lothing to the lock at Oulton Broad. The Berthon dinghy had a narrow escape from being crushed in the lock, but fortunately I noticed its precarious position in time to rescue it. Having got on to the Broad, we all brought up together and after lunch went ashore on a shopping expedition. Had tea on board and then rowed down to the Commodore Inn to get some bottled beer for dinner.

When it was time to prepare dinner the Passenger got into the dinghy and went off to pay a round of visits to the other boats, leaving me to get it ready as usual, and did not return until I shouted to say that it was ready. He was, however, good enough to express approval of the menu, which was as follows: Hors d'oeuvres (sardines), mock turtle soup, curried chicken (Halford's), new potatoes, peaches and cream, cheese and biscuits, followed by coffee and sloe gin. When we had finished, he sprawled on the cabin-top smoking a cigar and reading a detective story, while I washed up. Later, the whole crowd assembled on board *Viper* and had a convivial evening. We did not return to our respective ships until 12.45 a.m. Shocking hours!

July 13th. – We had arranged overnight that we would all sail to Beccles to-day, and so after breakfast we got under way with a very light breeze. We had a foul wind through the Dyke and found that there was not room enough for *Snipe* to beat to windward. She is as handy as a top but, as the main horse prevents the tiller from going over very far, she needs a fair amount of room in which to come round. We consequently kept getting on to the bank, and when pushing off for about the sixth time I shouted to my brother, "I'm sick of this damn ditch." "So am I," he replied; so we tied up at the Waveney Inn and went ashore for a morning beer and to discuss the situation. We came to the conclusion that sailing on the Broads was a footling business unless you had the right kind of boat for it, and decided to return to Oulton. *Viper* had already given it up but *Rani* went on and we saw her no more. Spent the afternoon in cleaning the boat thoroughly and in the evening we all went to Lowestoft to dine at the Suffolk Hotel, returning by the last train.

July 14th. – Spent the day at Lowestoft with *Viper's* crew, returning to dine on *Snipe*. Foregathered on *Walrus* in the evening.

July 15th. – Turned out at 8.30 a.m. and had a swim and then breakfast. We were returning to Lowestoft to-day with a view to starting our homeward journey to-morrow. Got under way and sailed about the Broad, while Ernest Viner took photos of *Snipe*. Later, in company with *Viper* and *Walrus*, we sailed for Lowestoft. We made a good job of negotiating the lock and bridges and, sailing right into the yacht basin, berthed in the tier without a scratch. Spent rest of the day ashore.

July 16th. – Turned out at 6.30 a.m. and after breakfast stowed the dinghy in the cabin and got our warps on board. Cleared the harbour at 7.45 a.m. bound for Felixstowe. It was a flat calm and I rowed *Snipe* with the sweeps nearly all the way to Southwold – who says one gets no exercise when sailing? – then a nice little breeze filled in from about E.S.E. and with the aid of the tide *Snipe* began to make good progress. Going this way, the duration of the flood tide is much extended, for the farther south one travels, so does the time of high water advance. A 10-tonner I know once sailed from Lowestoft to Burnham on one tide, but she was a very fast yacht and had a strong fair wind. Off Southwold we passed close to a lot of cormorants and several porpoises. I tried to take a photo of one of the latter, but fell into the cockpit and only took the sky.

Walrus, with the aid of a big jackyard topsail and her spinnaker set on the bowsprit-end, overhauled us off Aldeburgh and when we passed Orfordness had established a lead of about a mile. At Orford Haven we lost the flood-tide, having carried it for nearly eight hours, so we stood closer in to get slacker water.

We caught *Walrus* at Bawdsey Haven and again took the lead, but had a rather tedious sail from Felixstowe to Landguard Point as the tide was now running hard against us. *Walrus* came up to us again as we entered Harwich Harbour and we sailed into Felixstowe Dock side by side. We found a nasty confused popple on the pitching ground outside Harwich, but with that exception the sea was quite smooth all the way. Visited *Walrus* after dinner and had a great argument with O. V. as to the relative speed of *Snipe* and *Walrus*. Turned in at midnight after as glorious a day as one could wish for.

July 17th. – Turned out at half-past nine to find another grand day. After breakfast had a good clean up and then got under way in company with *Walrus* and sailed up the Stour as far as Parkeston Quay. There, we came about and reached out again over the flood, just fetching the Shotley Spit buoy, although *Walrus* had to make several boards. We then ran up to Pin Mill and brought up at 2.15 p.m. Whilst I got lunch ready, the Passenger went ashore to get some beer. Later, we all went ashore shopping and did not return on board until dinner-time. Spent the evening on *Walrus*.

July 18th. – The glorious weather continues and we have not had a drop of rain since we started our holiday. Long may it last! We did not turn out until half-past nine, and after a leisurely breakfast got under way with *Walrus* with a nice southerly breeze. Beat down the Orwell to Shotley Spit, where we met *Isobel*, one of the Fambridge boats, which had come round from Woodbridge. We reached up the Stour in company with her until some way past Parkeston Quay, where we parted, *Isobel* going on to Wrabness, while we returned to Pin Mill. It was another perfect sailing day with a nice balmy breeze. Went ashore shopping and then had a big dinner on board. In the evening *Rani* arrived from Lowestoft after a good passage, and Clark and my brother came on board *Snipe*, remaining until nearly midnight. As we had only a few days of our holiday left, we thought we had better be getting nearer home and so decided to sail for Brightlingsea on the morrow.

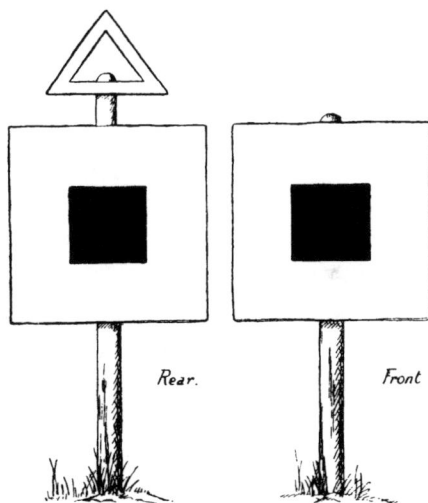

Orford Haven leading marks

July 19th. – Turned out at 6.30 a.m. and had breakfast. Then, having washed up and stowed the dinghy in the cabin, we made sail and got under way at 8.45 a.m. There was a light breeze from south when we started but as the day wore on it backed to S.E. and freshened. It was just high water when we got our anchor, and with the ebb running hard soon beat down to Harwich. Outside the harbour we found a nasty confused sea and one wave came on board and breaking on the cabin-top fairly soused us. We could just carry whole sail and *Snipe* went grandly on the beat out to the Naze. We then had the wind more free and could fetch through the Wallet. With her covering board just awash *Snipe* attained her maximum speed and I cannot remember ever having a better sail. On rounding the Bar, we had a fast run up Colne to Brightlingsea, bringing up in the creek after a splendid passage. *Snipe* fairly 'put it across' *Walrus*, beating her in by at least a mile and

635

a half, although we had left Pin Mill together. *Rani*, of course, beat us both, but she is such a fast little craft that we expect that as a matter of course. We all went ashore catering and then dined together at the Ship Hotel. We returned on board at half-past nine and put up the riding-light. Just as we were about to turn in a smack that had brought up uncommonly close to us, came foul of *Snipe*. I gave *Snipe* a starboard sheer, which took her clear, but felt a little doubtful whether we should lie afloat at low water. These smacks are an infernal nuisance, as they don't seem to care a damn where they bring up.

July 20th. – It is a curious fact that when sleeping in a yacht one usually wakes up when anything is wrong, and that happened to me at about 5.30 this morning. I had the feeling that we were moving, but for a time lay in my cot in that delightful state when one is neither quite awake nor yet quite asleep. I heard voices but in my semi-conscious condition took no notice for a time. At last I was fully awake and crawling from my cot went out into the well to see what was happening. To my astonishment I found that we were out in the Colne, apparently in tow of a smack.

"What the hell do you think you are doing?" I shouted. A man on the foredeck of the smack looked first at *Snipe* and then over the bows. Then he exclaimed:

"Lord lummy, Bill, we've got the little bo't's anchor." They had evidently hauled our anchor up with theirs and put to sea quite unconscious of the fact that they were towing *Snipe* after them. Leaning over the bow, he cleared our anchor and dropped it, and there were we, brought up in the Colne about half a mile from the creek. It would not have mattered much in ordinary circumstances, but we happened to have no bread on board and a visit to the baker's was imperative if we were to have any breakfast. It meant a hell of a long row in the dinghy against the ebb tide.

"What's up?" inquired the Passenger, who had been awakened by the sound of voices.

"Why, a bally smack has towed us right out into the Colne and we've got no bread."

"Oh well," he calmly replied, "it won't take you long to row ashore and get some."

"That be damned for a tale," I said. "We'll toss up for it."

For once in a way fortune smiled on me and the disgruntled Passenger had to get up and go in quest of bread, whilst I turned in again and had another hour's sleep.

More than two hours elapsed ere the Passenger returned and in anything but a sweet temper, as he had had to wait for a long time for the shop to open; but, personally, I rejoiced at having at last made him do a job of work.

We got under way after breakfast with a nice S.E. breeze and fetched down to the Bench Head buoy, washing down the decks and cleaning the brass ventilator as we went. Then we bore up and with spinnaker set had a fine run into the Blackwater. Off Bradwell we hove-to for lunch, but it was not a comfortable meal as the wind against the tide had knocked up a bit of a sea. One extra large wave upset the table, resulting in the loss of our beer and a broken glass. By the time we had cleared up the mess, the tide had turned and we went into Bradwell Creek on the young flood, followed by *Walrus* and *Rani*, which had come up while we were hove-to. We got in without trouble and brought up close to the quay, but *Walrus* ran hard on to the mud and did not float again for more than half an hour.

We landed in the afternoon and walked over to the village to replenish the larder, but as it was not the day that the butcher came over from Tillingham we could not get any meat and had to dine that night off a Halford's curry. These curries are very good, if you don't have them too often; but one gets tired of them after a time and of late we had eaten a good many. Visited *Walrus* after dinner for a short time and turned in at the respectable hour of 10 p.m.

July 21st. – Was awakened at 6 a.m. by a heavy shower of rain, the first we had had since we started from Fambridge, but it did not last long. Got up two hours later and after a swim scrubbed down the decks and then had breakfast. While thus engaged, *Nydia*, one of the Fambridge Y.C. boats, came in from Brightlingsea. There was a flat calm when we got under way and so I had to row *Snipe* out of the creek. We drifted up the river for about 3 miles and then brought up. It was a sweltering hot day, so we had another swim and basked in the sunshine until lunch-time. After lunch a little northerly breeze got up, so we weighed anchor and sailed up to Stansgate, where we brought up close to the Coastguard vessel. After tea we landed and walked to Steeple, a little village about 2 miles away, in quest of food, but did not meet with much success and again had to dine out of a tin. After dinner, while I was washing up, the Passenger sat in the well, with the binoculars glued to his face. He said he was studying the surrounding country, but I knew jolly well he was really looking at some girls bathing on the beach at Osea Island across the river. Found that there was a very strong tide on the flood, so gave *Snipe* the whole scope of 20 fathoms. The *Record Reign*, a fine new boomsail barge, passed us, going at a rare bat on the first of the ebb.

July 22nd. – As this was the penultimate day of our holiday, I thought we had better get back to the Crouch. So I turned out at 5.30 a.m. and got under way, leaving the Passenger asleep in his cot. There was a very light S.E. breeze and after beating down the river for some miles I let go the anchor and we had breakfast. When we resumed our journey the wind had freshened a little and we got some distance below Bradwell before the tide turned.

Beating over the flood was rather slow work, but after about two hours we felt our way on to the flats with the lead and managed to fetch across into the

Crouch. We brought up in the Roach, and *Walrus*, which had started with us, came in just an hour later. After tea, landed and walked across Foulness Island to the pub to get some beer for dinner. Dined this evening off a tin of Irish stew, which was very greasy. A little of it went a long way and most of the contents of the tin was consigned to the fishes. During the evening, *Rani, Norah Creina, Viper, Sunbeam* and *Dimsie III* came in and we visited *Sunbeam*. Later, Hugh Viner, who had recently bought *Norah Creina* from my brother, came on board. We turned in at about 11 p.m. and soon afterwards a violent thunderstorm came on and it poured with rain all night.

July 23rd. – This was the last day of our holiday and we turned out to find it still raining hard. The Passenger expressed a desire to return to Town from Burnham with my brother, so as soon as he had dressed, I dumped him and his bag on board *Walrus*; without much regret, I am afraid, as I had come to regard him as a lazy blighter. I registered a silent vow that I would never again take away with me anyone whom I did not know very well for a holiday cruise. Fearful that he might change his mind, I got under way at once and beat up to Fambridge in the rain, picking up my moorings at half-past twelve. Then I proceeded to have breakfast, and being uncommonly hungry ate up everything in the food line that remained on board.

During the cruise we sailed approximately 300 miles, not a great distance it is true, but I believe in taking things easily when away for a holiday. The weather was wonderfully fine until the last day and altogether we had a most enjoyable trip. Although my companion was inordinately lazy, he was a cheery cove and quite good company on the whole, but on subsequent cruises I preferred to sail alone, unless I could get some old shipmate to come with me ❧

APPENDICES

APPENDIX 1: *Desirable East Coast Anchorages*

It is essential to yachtsmen who reside in London to keep their boats at some place within comparatively easy access of Town, for otherwise travelling would take a considerable slice out of their short week-end holiday. It is no doubt probably mainly due to their accessibility that the waters of the Thames Estuary and rivers of Essex and Suffolk have become so popular. Quite a number of yachting stations have been established in those districts of late years and the majority can be reached in an hour and a half or less. At Burnham-on-Crouch, which has not inaptly been termed the Cowes of the East Coast, there are about a thousand yachts and many more higher up the river at Creeksea and Fambridge, while large fleets are also stationed at such places as West Mersea, Brightlingsea and Pin Mill.

It is not, however, my purpose to write of the advantages or otherwise of these places as headquarters, but rather to indicate spots where one may obtain a snug berth at night when cruising.

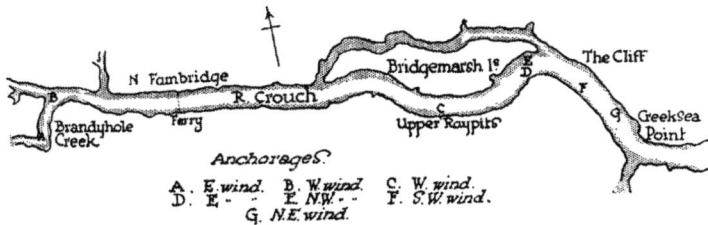

The Upper Crouch

The Crouch, although it has no great attractions to offer in the way of scenery, is a fine sailing river, for there are no trees near the banks to impede the wind, which comes true off the marshes. The whole river from Shore-ends to Brandy Hole, a distance of about 14 miles, is a safe anchorage, but as it for the most part runs east and west, the prevailing winds blow straight up or down and a strong wind meeting the tide knocks up a short hollow sea, which makes matters very uncomfortable. Before now, I have rolled my decks in at Fambridge in a 7-tonner while lying on my moorings. But these unpleasant conditions are easily avoided. Let us take the upper part of the river first. Fambridge Reach is long and straight with a drift of about 3 miles and lying almost due east and west. If a little yacht is lying at Fambridge, with a strong wind against the tide, she will usually take up a berth athwart stream and roll her heart out. In such circumstances if you remain there you will probably not be able to cook or stay in your bunk at night.

If you are wise you will clear out and seek a more comfortable berth elsewhere. Should the wind be easterly, you can run up to the top of the reach and then slip round the corner into Brandy Hole, where a yacht of 5ft. draught can lie afloat at any state of tide. There you will have the wind off shore and find smooth water and can lie as snug as a bug in a rug, as they say. The best water is just off the point on the west side. Another berth in a strong easterly breeze is at the top of Fambridge Reach, just off the spit that lies between Clement's Green Creek and Brandy Hole Reach. It will not be so smooth there as in Brandy Hole, but there is far less sea than lower down the river. That may seem strange in view of the long drift of 3 miles, but I think it can be accounted for by the fact the tide between the two channels is comparatively slack and it is the wind meeting a strong tide that knocks up a sea. This is also, of course, a good berth in strong westerly winds.

If the wind is westerly, as it more often is, you have the choice of several quiet berths. Either of the two I have mentioned above are available, but of course you will either have to beat to windward to get there, or run up under power. It is more convenient therefore to go down the river. In Short Poles Reach, which is the next below Fambridge Reach, you will get good protection off Raypits Farm, on the south side of the river. This reach is so short that there is never much sea there.

A quiet berth can usually be obtained in Cliff Reach in any wind except north-west and south-east, and it is the pleasantest reach in the river in which to anchor, as the north side is quite pretty, with its little brown cliff, studded with bushes and small trees. If there is any north in the wind, lie off the north shore, and if south, off the south shore. With a southeasterly breeze, the best berth is just round the corner in Easter Reach, close in under the point, where the shore is steep-to. Should there be a fresh north-west wind, lie at the top of Cliff Reach, just under the Bridgemarsh Island shore. Should you seek a berth on the north side of Cliff Reach you should anchor fairly low down, as at the upper part of the reach on that side of the river there is a patch of hard clay in which an anchor does not always bite. It is not an uncommon occurrence for the owner of a yacht that has anchored there over night to find himself on the south side when he turns out in the morning. I usually bring up a little above Tideways, the house with a private hard, and as the shore is fairly steep-to just there, one can anchor close in.

Burnham yachtsmen, when it blows fresh from east or west, have the alternatives of going up the river to one of the berths I have indicated, or down to the Roach, where a quiet berth can always be found in any wind. The bottom reach of this river, which lies at a right angle to the Crouch, affords splendid shelter from either east or west winds. If you want to land and walk across Foulness Island to the village, you should bring up just off the stone point, on which there are landing-steps. These steps are available for landing at any state of tide except for about an hour on either side of low water. You can bring up either below or above the landing, but as there is rather a lot of water above, it is perhaps better for a small yacht to anchor below. On the west side of the reach, you will find a good berth just inside Branklet Spit, where the shore is fairly steep-to. But there is good anchorage anywhere on that side. A favourite anchorage of mine is in Yokefleet, the first creek you come to on the port hand when sailing up the Roach. This is an extraordinarily snug berth in any wind and a haunt of wild-fowl. If you are keen on studying the habits of birds, you will find plenty to inter-est you here. The best place to anchor is just off the stone point, some little way up on the east side. You can lie afloat there in any craft drawing not more than 5ft. of water and can land on the sea-wall at most states of tide. The entrance to

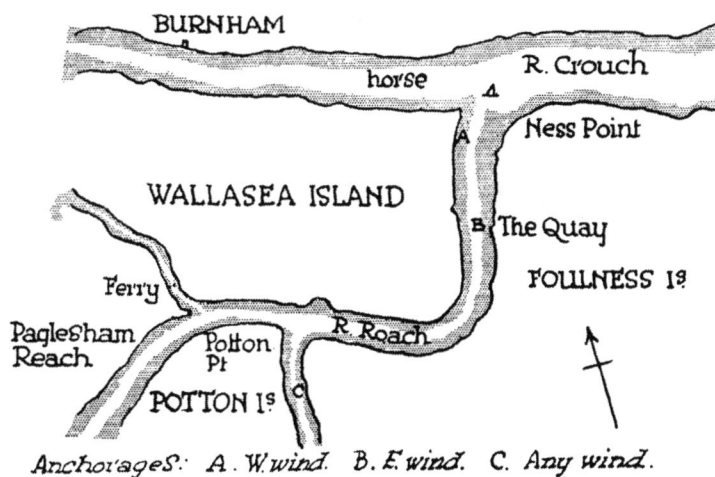

Anchorages: A. W. wind. B. E. wind. C. Any wind.

The Lower Crouch and Roach

this creek is narrow, there being a long spit running out from the point on Potton Island and a large mud flat extending from Foulness Island opposite. The chan-nel lies between the two and as soon as you are clear of the spit, you will find the best water on the Potton Island side. A yacht drawing 4 ft. or more cannot enter much before two hours' flood at spring tides.

Paglesham, situated on the north-west bank of the Roach, a little above Yoke-fleet, has but two objects of interest for yachtsmen – Shuttlewood's building yard and the Plough and Sail. The latter is an ancient pub that has long been a favour-ite haunt of Burnham yachtsmen, particularly day-boat owners, who sail round on Sunday morning and lunch at the inn before returning to their moorings. If you bring up at Paglesham, you should anchor off Shuttlewood's shed, as that is the best holding ground. Above and below that spot the mud is soft and there are beds of flag-weed.

Going north from the Thames, the next river is the Blackwater, of which the lower portion is a glorious expanse of sailing water, nearly 2 miles wide. The water is deep and clear as crystal and until you get above Tollesbury Pier there are no traps for the unwary. Unfortunately snug anchorages are not very numerous and what there are are for the most part unduly crowded.

Near the mouth of the river, the yachtsman has the choice of West Mersea on the north and Bradwell Creek on the south. West Mersea is nowadays an important yachting station, a great many craft being stationed there. The only really snug anchorages, the Thornfleet and Mersea Fleet, are consequently full up with the moorings of local yachts and it is as a rule impossible for a visiting vessel to

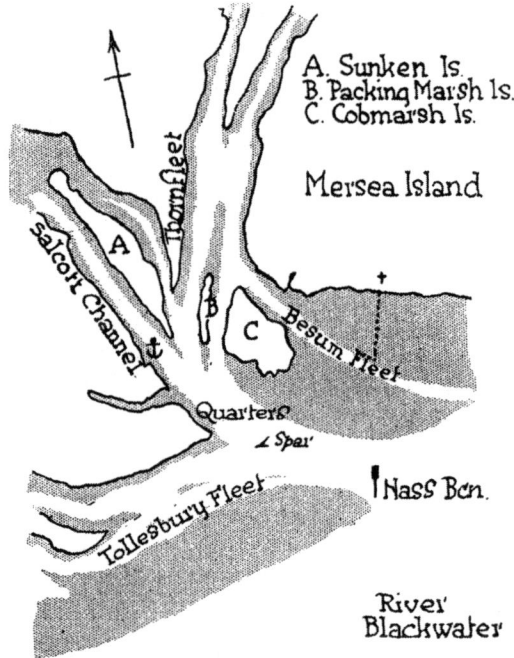

West Mersea

find a clear berth in either. The only alternative is to lie out in the Quarters, or Deeps, as they say locally. This is a pleasant enough berth in fine weather, but with strong easterly winds it is too exposed for small craft. Moreover, if you are anchored in the Quarters you have a deuced long row to get ashore, as the hard is at the old village, which curiously enough is known as Mersea City. From the Quarters to the hard is about three-quarters of a mile, roughly speaking, and if you have a foul tide both ways you are likely to come to the conclusion that rowing is an over-rated amusement. The best berth for a small yacht in the Quarters, is just in the entrance to Salcott Channel, but if you go too far up you are likely to have words with the oyster people.

On the other side of the river, Bradwell Creek is available for small yachts, but there is not room for many and as there are a dozen or more craft now permanently stationed there, a visiting yacht may not be able to find a berth where she can lie afloat at low tide. There are one or two holes where craft up to about 4ft. 6in. draught can lie afloat at all states of tide, but they are not easy for a stranger to find. Bradwell Creek is a very snug berth in all but strong north-easterly winds at high water, but the entrance is extremely intricate unless you know the leading marks, the trend of the channel being in the form of the letter 'S.' The last time I was in there I noticed that the channel had been roughly marked with posts, probably put in by men from the numerous large steamers that were then laid up in the Blackwater. At that time there were no fewer than 41 large steamers lying in the river, but they have now all gone, thanks to the improvement in

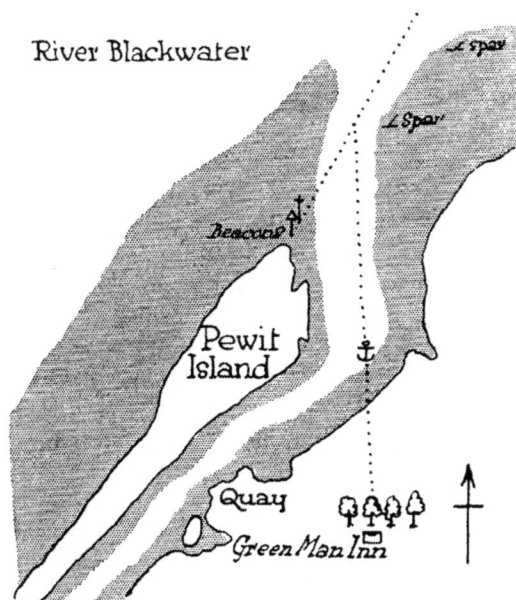

Bradwell Creek

the shipping trade. It is likely, therefore, that in the course of time these stakes will disappear and so it will be as well to indicate the leading marks.

When about to enter the creek, first make for the bathing huts on the shore, which are about a quarter of a mile to the east of the entrance. When about a cable and a half from the shore, look out for two small beacons that are stuck in the mud off the end of Pewit Island and get them in line. On your port hand there are, or should be, two small buoys or floating logs and when you reach the second one, look up the creek and locate the Green Man inn – a largish white house, with a diamond shaped sign-board on the front. In front of the inn is a row of small trees and you must get the second tree from the right in line with the signboard. That line will lead you into the creek and you follow it until you see on the mainland saltings two white stakes (formerly these were merely branches cut from a tree and splashed with whitewash, but have now, I believe, been replaced with proper stakes painted white.) As soon as you get the stakes in one, follow that line for a short distance until the quay is open and then let go your anchor. You should then be in one of the holes in which you will be able to lie afloat at low tide. As I have used Bradwell Creek on and off for the past forty years, the entrance does not present much difficulty to me, but a stranger should not attempt it on the ebb, but at about two hours' flood, when most of the banks are uncovered and the trend of the channel can be seen. But even then it is advisable to adhere to the leading marks I have mentioned as there is a treacherous horse a little way inside the entrance. The country at Bradwell is beautiful, being suggestive of Worcestershire rather than Essex, and there is a capital little grocer's shop in the village, which is about a mile from the Quay.

Higher up the Blackwater there is a delightful anchorage off Osea Island where the shore is sandy and steep-to. The best berth is a little below the small

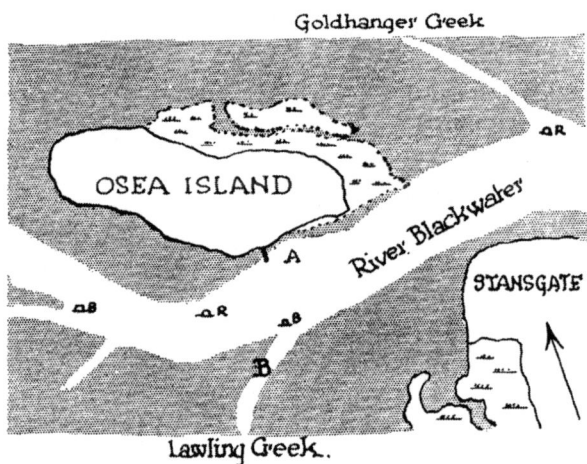

Goldhanger Creek

OSEA ISLAND

River Blackwater

STANSGATE

Lawling Creek.

Anchorages. A. N and W. wind. B. E and S. wind.

Osea Island

pier, close to a big black post in the foreshore, known as the Barnacle. This post was, I have been told, originally put in for the famous *Jullanar* to rest against, when berthed ashore for scrubbing purposes. You should bring up a little way below this post and about 50 yards outside it. You will then have a good berth, out of the worst of the tide and can land on the sandy shore of the island.

Osea Island is well wooded and coming into the Blackwater from the sea it reminds one of an atoll in the Pacific, as the trees appear to grow out of the water. The island is quite small and one can walk round it on the sea-wall in about an hour. With a strong north-easterly wind meeting an ebb tide, the river off Osea Island is apt to be rather too rough for comfort, but one can always slip into the mouth of Lawling Creek, on the opposite side of the river, if the berth off the island becomes untenable.

The next river, going north, is the Colne, of which the entrance is on the other side of Mersea Island. As the Colne runs nearly north and south it affords good protection from our prevailing westerly winds. Brightlingsea, being nowadays a very popular yachting centre, is unduly crowded, and in my opinion it is better to seek a berth in the Colne, under the Mersea Island shore. The best place to bring up is just above the police boat moorings, opposite to a sign on the shore bearing the words 'GOLF LINKS.' It will be prudent, however, to take a sounding before letting go your anchor, as there is a flat just there with a steep-to edge. There is very little water on this flat, but a few yards from its edge you will find several fathoms. You can land on the island here, but the hard is definitely of the sea-boots order. Should it come on to blow hard from the south or south-east, it

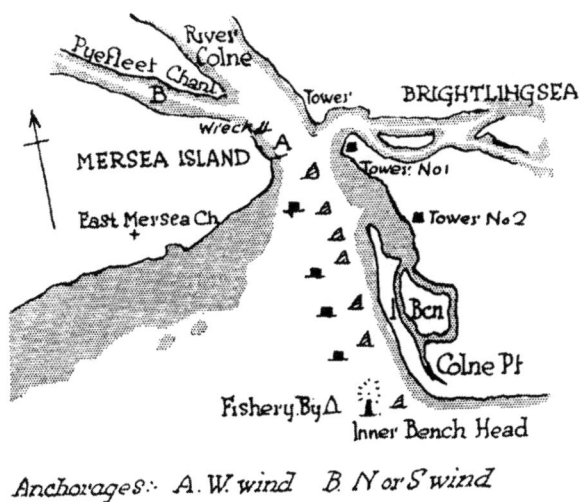

River Colne
Pyefleet Chanl
B
MERSEA ISLAND
Wreck
Tower
BRIGHTLINGSEA
A
East Mersea Ch
Tower No 1
Tower No 2
Ben
Colne Pt
Fishery.By
Inner Bench Head

Anchorages:- A. W. wind   B. N or S wind

River Colne

is an easy matter to get your anchor and slip round into the Pyefleet, a creek just above, where you will find a snug berth under almost any conditions.

A favourite anchorage of mine is in Walton Creek, at the back of the Naze, as one can always get a snug berth there, no matter from what quarter the wind may blow. In the 'nineties, when I first began to visit this creek, the entrance was exceedingly difficult to negotiate, as there was practically nothing to guide one but the 'look of the land,' as the fishermen say. Thanks to the enterprise of the Walton and Frinton Yacht Club, the approaches have been admirably buoyed and it is now comparatively easy for a stranger to find his way in.

The attractive feature of this anchorage is that you can always have the wind off shore, as you can either lie in Walton Creek, near the Foundry hard, or in the Twizzle, another creek that branches off at a right angle. You can either land at the Foundry hard or the lower club hard, a little way above it. At about two hours' flood, you can also row right up to the clubhouse in the town of Walton-on-Naze, which is convenient for shopping and filling your water-cans. There is a standpipe outside the club and you have merely to carry the cans across the path to your dinghy after filling. The bottom of Walton Creek, however, seems to be strewn with old anchors and chains, which are rare traps for your anchor. You should therefore take the precaution of bending a tripping line to the crown of your anchor before letting it go.

A few miles farther north we come to Harwich Harbour, a grand sailing ground for small craft. Here the rivers Stour and Orwell meet, forming a natural harbour large enough to accommodate hundreds of vessels of all sizes. There

Harwich Harbour

are not, however, many suitable berths for small yachts, but one can usually find one more or less protected from the wind. In fine weather small craft can lie fairly comfortably to the south and south-west of the Guard buoy, but I do not recommend it. Another berth is in the Stour off Shotley Pier, but that also is rather an exposed position for little ships in fresh southerly and westerly breezes. Another berth I have used from time to time is in the Upper Pound, between the north-west arm of the East Pier and the Railway Pier, but the mud there is filthy and your chain comes up in the most appalling state. In easterly winds, a comfortable berth can be obtained between the entrance to Felixstowe Dock and the Walton buoy, although you are likely to be disturbed by the wash from the L.N.E.R. steamers when they go out. When I want to lie in the neighbourhood of Harwich, I usually bring up just above Shotley Spit, in the Orwell. It is steep-to there and one can consequently lie pretty close in to the shore. The best berth is off, or just above, the hard, or, perhaps I should say, apology for a hard, as it is one that requires the use of sea-boots. In one spot below the hard there is a curious eddy for an hour or so on the ebb, which will cause a small yacht to travel round her anchor and pick it up. That happened to me during the night some years ago and the next morning I turned out just in time to find my boat drifting rapidly past the Shotley Spit buoy. Before we could bring her up again we were off Felixstowe Dock. That incident was not without its amusing side. Two friends of mine had arrived the previous evening from West Mersea in a half-decked boat, in which they proposed to sleep under a tent. As they had no food on board or any means of cooking, I invited them to breakfast the next morning. When they turned out to keep the appointment, they found that my boat, and incidentally their breakfast, had disappeared. I could not get back to them as there was a sluicing ebb and no wind and I had no engine. After a lot of mud-larking they managed to get ashore and buy some food, but to this day they believe that I pushed off and left them in the lurch on purpose.

But those who visit this district would do well to turn their backs on Harwich Harbour and sail some 5 miles up the Orwell to Pin Mill, the beauty spot of the East Coast. There, one might be in Devon or Cornwall, for both banks of the river are densely wooded to the water's edge. The anchorage is in a little bay out of the traffic, and during the summer months crowded to congestion. It is therefore best to seek a berth on the outskirts, either below the fleet or above, near the Cat House. My favourite berth is some little way below the hard, where the barges used to lie, and where the nightingales sing fit to burst their little hearts. It is rather a long way from the hard, but at or near high water one can land on the shore, which is fringed with sand, or you can row to the hard on the last of the flood and return on the first of the ebb, thus having a fair tide both ways.

It must be admitted that the landing facilities at Pin Mill leave a good deal to be desired, as the hard is of inordinate length – 367 yards at low water – traversing a mud flat that is extraordinarily flat. The hard itself is a good one, being constructed partly of concrete and partly gravel, and it is the flatness that causes the inconvenience. If you land at high water and remain ashore for some hours, you will find your dinghy perhaps a couple of hundred yards from the water and that is the deuce of a long way to shove a dinghy; whilst if you land near low water, you may find her anchored far from the shore when you want to return to your yacht.

With the exception of the upper reaches of the Orwell and the River Deben, our East Coast scenery cannot compare with that of, say, Devon and Cornwall, but mud has its advantages. If you get ashore on a mud bottom you are not likely to suffer anything worse than loss of time and inconvenience, but if you strike the inhospitable rocks of Cornwall you will probably lose your ship and perhaps your life also.

APPENDIX 2: *Tidal Constants*

I give below the tidal constants for a number of places round the coast, which may be useful if you have not a nautical almanac on board. To find the approximate time of high water, add to or subtract from the time of high water at Dover as follows:

Place	h	m	Place	h	m	Place	h	m
Aldeburgh	−0	40	Greenwich	+2	25	Naze, The	+0	26
Beachy Head	−0	7	Grimsby	−5	36	Needles, The	−1	48
Beaulieu River	−0	43	Hamble River	−0	10		+1	40
	+1	0		+1	51	Newhaven	−0	5
Benfleet	+1	41	Harty Ferry	+0	46	Pin Mill	+0	37
Berry Head	−4	57	Harwich	+0	35	Plymouth	−5	36
Boston	−4	47	Havengore	+1	1	Poole Harbour	−2	21
Bournemouth	−2	16	Heybridge	+0	58		+1	14
	+0	49	Hurst Point	−0	54	Portland Bill	−4	34
Bradwell Quay	+0	40		+1	17	Queenborough	+1	18
Brightlingsea	+0	32	Hythe	−0	17	Ramsgate	+0	13
Brixham	−4	57	Itchenor	+0	11	Rochester	+1	24
Burnham-on-	+0	46	Keyhaven	−0	40	Rothesay	+0	58
Crouch				+1	31	Salcombe	−5	23
Dartmouth	−0	49	Kingstown	+0	17	Selsea Bill	+0	8
Dungeness	−0	5	Largs	+0	50	Southend-on-Sea	+1	7
Emsworth	+0	27	Littlehampton	+0	19	Southwold	−1	6
Erith	+1	53	London Bridge	+2	39	Start Point	−5	23
Exmouth	−4	38	Looe	−5	35	Teignmouth	−5	5
Falmouth	+5	58	Lowestoft	−1	47	Walton-on-Naze	+0	28
Fambridge	+0	56	Lulworth Cove	−4	8	Weymouth	−4	8
Faversham	+1	7	Lymington	−0	51	Wivenhoe	+1	7
Felixstowe	+0	41		+1	0	Woodbridge	+1	11
Folkestone	−0	3	Margate	+0	55	Yarmouth (IoW)	−0	52
Fowey	−5	46	Mersea, West	+0	37		+1	9
Gravesend	+1	35	Mevagissey	−5	55	Yarmouth (Gt)	−2	10
Greenhithe	+1	43						

Where two constants are given they indicate the double tides peculiar to the Solent and adjacent waters.

APPENDIX 3: *Cruising Clubs*

Having his own cabin, which should supply all the comfort he wants, the owner of a cruising yacht has not the same need for a club as the racing man, who has to sleep and have his meals ashore. Nevertheless, most cruising yacht owners belong to a club of some sort in order that they may fly a recognized burgee. But, apart from that privilege, I do not think that the cruising man derives much advantage from membership in a club, unless its activities are mainly devoted to cruising interests.

Most clubs seem to concentrate upon racing nowadays and usually maintain one or more racing classes. Little or nothing is done for the cruising members beyond putting on a few handicap races in the course of the season, which seldom attract many entries, as the average cruising man does not care a hoot for racing. The cruising member, of course, has the right to use the clubhouse, but seldom does, as he likes to get away from his moorings as soon as possible. The clubs that really cater for the needs of the cruising man could almost be counted on the fingers of one hand, and perhaps a few brief particulars of some of them may be of interest.

THE ROYAL CRUISING CLUB

The premier club in the United Kingdom devoted solely to the interests of cruising is the Royal Cruising Club, founded in 1880 by the late Sir Arthur Underhill. At the outset Mr. Underhill, as he then was, filled the office of Vice-Commodore but was elected Commodore in 1886. He served in that capacity with great distinction until 1936 and was subsequently Honorary Commodore until his death in 1939. Such long service as senior flag officer of a yacht club must, I think, constitute a record. Under his guidance the club prospered exceedingly and membership in the Royal Cruising Club is regarded as a distinction much coveted by yachtsmen who follow the cruising side of the sport.

The work of this old-established club strikes me as altogether admirable, for the annual competitions for various challenge cups, awarded for the most meritorious cruises of the year, have undoubtedly done a great deal to foster and encourage cruising. Since the club's establishment, the members have cruised farther and farther afield and the burgee has been carried all over the world in vessels ranging from the late Lord Brassey's famous *Sunbeam* down to the late Mr. A. G. H. Macpherson's equally famous 8-tonner *Driac II*. Every year the club publishes, for circulation among the members, a journal containing accounts of the competition and other cruises made by members during the preceding twelve months, from which others who contemplate cruising in the same waters are able to glean much valuable data as regards pilotage. The trophies offered annually for competition are the Royal Cruising Club Challenge Cup, the Romola Cup, the Claymore Cup and the Founder's Cup, and none but a cruise of exceptional merit has much chance of winning any one of them. In the course of the summer one or two meetings of the club yachts are organized at some delectable anchorage on the South Coast such as Beaulieu, for the sake of social intercourse, and during the winter a dinner is held in London. The club has a fine library of nautical works at its London clubroom and also issues charts specially prepared for the use of its members.

THE LITTLE SHIP CLUB

Some years ago the idea occurred to one or two yachtsmen that it would be nice to have some place in London where sailing men could meet during the winter to 'talk boats,' and with that end in view they secured the use of a room at the Ship tavern near Charing Cross. The idea caught on and in 1926 the Little Ship Club was founded. From that modest beginning the club has in a few years developed into one of the most popular yachting institutions in the kingdom and now numbers upwards of a thousand members.

The club premises are now at Beaver Hall, Garlick Hill, Canon Street, EC, where, throughout the winter months, classes are held in navigation, seamanship, knotting and splicing and other subjects of practical use to yachtsmen. Frequent lectures are given on various nautical subjects and during the season cruises in company are arranged and a race organized for cruising craft from Brightlingsea to Ostend. The club also issues an exceedingly interesting and entertaining journal.

That the Little Ship Club has filled a long-felt want there can be no question and I think every young yachtsman should join it, as it will enable him to obtain practical instruction of a kind that will be invaluable to him. And as the club keeps registers of owners wanting crews and crews seeking berths, membership affords an opportunity for getting afloat for those who are not fortunate enough to own yachts of their own.

THE NARROW SEAS CLUB

This club was established in 1932 by a few yachtsmen who had seceded from the Little Ship Club. It has a clubroom in the City of London and its activities are similar to those of the Little Ship Club. Cruises are arranged during the season to Continental ports and I believe the club has now several hundred members.

THE CRUISING ASSOCIATION

Sooner or later the average small yacht owner gets tired of sailing about in his home waters and wishes to wander farther afield. His annual holiday cruise of two or three weeks' duration merely serves to whet his appetite and increase his longing for change of scene. When he reaches this stage in his yachting career, he will probably begin to cultivate the habit of sailing round to some port, perhaps fifty or sixty miles from his headquarters, where he will leave his craft until the following week-end. He may then return to his home waters or extend his travels a farther stage, as his fancy may dictate.

For anyone with a fair amount of leisure that is a delightful way of spending the summer, as one gets that constant change of scene which is the salt of life and fresh problems of navigation to titillate the interest. It, moreover, enables the week-end yachtsman to make the most of his all-too-short holiday cruise. Suppose, for instance, that he has planned a trip to the Scilly Isles. If he starts from his headquarters, the early and closing stages of the cruise must be passed in familiar waters that have lost a good deal of their interest for him, and lack of time may cause him to hurry when he would prefer to loiter. If, on the other hand, he began to work round the coast at week-ends, say a month before his holiday was due, he would be well on his way and have much more time available for exploring the waters he desires to visit.

Years ago I used to cruise in that way from port to port on the East Coast, being away from my headquarters for, perhaps, a month at a time. The railway company allowed the holder of a week-end ticket to use the return half from almost any port on their system on payment of the difference in the fare. It was a valuable concession as it enabled one to leave one's yacht at some distant port and return to town without undue expense. Visiting strange places in that way was delightful, but leaving one's boat in the care of strange watermen was sometimes the reverse. More than once I rejoined my ship, after a week's absence, to find that she had suffered damage through the negligence of the man in whose charge I had left her and on one occasion I had a new spinnaker ruined owing to the man failing to carry out my instructions to dry it. Anxiety as to the welfare of my craft during my absence in town rather took the gilt off the gingerbread, as the saying goes, and ultimately put a period to my wandering propensities.

Nowadays there would be no occasion to worry at all, as any yachtsman who desires to cruise from port to port can ensure that his vessel will be properly looked after by joining the Cruising Association. This extremely useful institution has an official boatman at practically every port frequented by yachts, and as the men are carefully selected and supervised by Honorary Local Representatives, they are thoroughly reliable. The regulations relating to registered boatmen are as follows:

(a) Registered boatmen shall be recommended by the sub-committee appointed for the purpose.

(b) The duties of the boatman, for which he shall make the charges agreed upon for his district, shall include drying canvas, if necessary, tidying decks, pumping out, lighting and hoisting riding lights, filling fresh-water tanks and breakers, stowing dinghy, taking due precaution as to putting out extra ground tackle (if on board) when necessary, and exercising general supervision over any yacht or boat belonging to any member of the Association during the time the yacht or boat is in the boatman's charge.

(c) In cases where the safety of a yacht or boat is imperilled the registered boatman shall, at the expense of the owner of such yacht or boat, take such steps as are necessary to protect her from damage, and advise the hon. local representative immediately, and telegraph to the owner of same. Any dispute arising over any extra charge for such services (which shall not in any case be considered as salvage), which the hon. local representative may be unable to adjust, shall be referred to the council, and the boatman shall accept the decision of the council as binding upon him.

(d) A registered boatman, on his services being requisitioned, shall request to see the member's card, and shall not be bound to perform the service required of him by any member of the Association until the production thereof or until such member shall have satisfied the hon. local representative for the district that he is a member of the Association.

(e) In the event of a registered boatman having grounds for believing that a member's card is being used by an unauthorized person, he shall immediately report the matter to the hon. local representative.

(f) Every registered boatman shall be supplied by the hon. local representative with an official badge and flag, which shall remain the property of the Association. In each succeeding year he shall be furnished with a new badge, but shall return the old badge to the hon. local representative to be forwarded to the central office before being supplied with that for the ensuing year.

(g) Any registered boatman who transfers his official badge or flag shall be struck off the list of registered boatmen.

(h) The dinghy shall be taken care of, as part of the vessel to which it belongs, and shall not be subject to any extra charge.

(i) Registered boatmen shall fly over their station at the waterside the boatman's flag of the Association, to indicate their position on shore.

(j) Registered boatmen shall immediately go off to any vessel on which they see the red rectangular flag with white diamond hoisted.

(k) Members shall be entitled to pay at the weekly rate for any period, and in this event a fraction of a week shall be reckoned as a week.

(l) The day and week shall commence at midnight.

Any member having a complaint to make against a registered boatman, shall make it in writing to the hon. local representative and to the hon. secretary.

The tariff of charges is printed in the Year Book and a member thus knows exactly what he will have to pay and the service he will get for his money. The charges vary according to district but are very reasonable. Should the visitor need information or assistance outside the sphere of the boatman he can apply to the hon. local representative. This is really wonderful service, but it by no means exhausts the activities of the Cruising Association. There is a clubhouse in London where members can obtain the fullest information about cruising grounds in and around the British Isles and adjacent waters and where there is housed an extremely comprehensive library of nautical works. The library contains many very rare and valuable books, as, for instance, a first edition of Hakluyt's *Voyages* with the rare account of 'The Voyages of Sir Francis Drake into the South Seas,' which was suppressed by Queen Elizabeth and is only to be found in a few copies. Such works as that are, of course, far too valuable to be taken from the library, but most of the books can be borrowed by the members.

The Handbook, of nearly five hundred pages, is a most useful compilation, comprising sailing directions, passage notes and much other information of value to the cruising yachtsman. Clear and concise directions are given for entering nearly every port round the coast, charts showing the approaches to harbours and illustrations of leading marks being furnished for the benefit of strangers. The Year Book, in addition to the tariff of charges for registered boatmen, contains tide tables for the year, lists of members, hon. local representatives, and registered boatmen, of which there are upwards of 170, besides corrections and addenda to the Handbook and other useful matter.

Another admirable feature is a register of members who are willing to take amateur crews and of amateurs who are desirous of berths in members' yachts. This strikes me as a capital scheme, particularly as the Association enlists Cadet Members, between the ages of fifteen and twenty-two, at an annual subscription of half a guinea. A lad joining the Association as a cadet can enter his name in this register and thus obtain cruising facilities that he could get in no other way. It seems a most practical way of securing recruits to the sport and should be brought to the notice of every public school in the kingdom.

The Cruising Association is not an exclusive social club but exists to encourage yachting in every way. The social side, however, is not altogether neglected, as the members dine together every year, and a journal, known as the Cruising Association Bulletin, is published for circulation among the members. This excellent journal contains accounts of the cruising activities of the members and much other matter of interest to yachtsmen who follow the cruising side of the sport. Three valuable trophies are offered for competition every year. These are the Love Challenge Cup, which is awarded for the best log of a yacht cruise under sail, with or without auxiliary power; the Dugon Cup for the best log of a cruise under mechanical power, with or without auxiliary sails; and the Knight Cup for the best log of a yacht cruise made single-handed.

I have dwelt at some length on this Association because I consider it to be of real use to those who sail round the coast. Indeed, what the Automobile Association is to the motorist, the Cruising Association is to the cruising yachtsman and every owner who wanders from his home waters should make a point of joining it. It is of far more practical use than any ordinary yacht club and the Handbook alone is worth the annual subscription of two guineas.

APPENDIX 4: *Flag Etiquette*

The owner of a small yacht who cruises round the coast need not include in his equipment many flags. Indeed, he can get on very well with nothing but a burgee, but should he occasionally 'go foreign' it would be advisable also to have an ensign to indicate his nationality. He might, too, include a pilot jack, although that is not really essential, as dipping the burgee half-mast will usually bring off a pilot. Many owners, however, seem to have a mania for displaying bunting and carry on board, in addition to an ensign and burgees, a complete outfit of signal flags and fly them on every possible occasion. I recently passed a small schooner which was flying a burgee on each mast, an ensign at the peak of her mainsail and two rectangular flags at the ends of the fore-cross-trees – one I took to be the owner's private flag, but what the other was goodness only knows. This flag-flying craze is a harmless amusement that hurts no one, although, if you indulge in it, there are certain rules that should be followed and I will give a few hints on flag etiquette for the guidance of the novice.

The Burgee: The burgee is flown from the mainmast head, both when under way and at anchor. It is hoisted at 8 a.m. from March 21 to September 20 and at 9 a.m. from September 21 to March 20 inclusive. It is always lowered at sunset when at anchor, but when the yacht is under way the burgee is usually flown as long as there is sufficient light to see it. The flag is only flown when the owner is on board, or ashore in the immediate neighbourhood, and it must not be flown when the vessel is lent or under charter, unless the borrower or charterer is a member of the club. If the yacht is sold, the burgee should be removed before she is handed over to the buyer. If you belong to several clubs you should have a burgee for each and fly that of the club in whose waters you happen to be. The burgee is never used for saluting purposes, but is half-masted in the case of general mourning. The flag should be attached to a cane, so that it will fly clear of the truck.

The Red Ensign: The red ensign may be flown by any British vessel, either under way or at anchor. When at anchor it should be flown from a staff at the stern and when under way from the peak of the mainsail. As a Bermudian sail has no peak, the ensign is flown under way from the leach of the sail about two-thirds of the way up. On yawls and ketches the flag is usually displayed at the head of the mizzen mast, although some purists maintain that it should be flown from the peak of the mizzen. Formerly, a red ensign flown at the mainmast head was recognized as the signal to intimate that the vessel had come from abroad, and was kept flying until she had been cleared by the Customs. Since January 1, 1934, the proper signal has been flag Q of the International Signal Code by day, and a red light over a white light not more than 6 feet apart, by night. I have no doubt that the red ensign at the masthead would still serve to bring off the Customs officer at most ports, but it is better to comply with the regulations and make the proper signals.

The White Ensign: Yachts belonging to the Royal Yacht Squadron alone are permitted to fly the white ensign of the Royal Navy.

The Blue Ensign, and Red Ensign Defaced: Certain yacht clubs hold Admiralty warrants entitling them to fly the blue ensign, either plain or defaced, and the red ensign defaced, but the fact of being a member of such a club does not in itself entitle an owner to do so. He must first obtain, through the secretary of the club, from the Admiralty a warrant for his own yacht. The laws relating to the use of Admiralty warrants are strictly enforced and are printed on the back of the warrant, as follows:

This Warrant shall be carried on board the said Yacht, and shall at all times be revocable at their discretion.

This Warrant shall have no force or effect when

(a) the said Yacht ceases to be duly registered as a British Ship in accordance with the Merchant Shipping Acts, 1894 to 1925, and any Acts replacing or amending the said Acts; or

(b) the said Yacht is being sailed otherwise than by the Owner mentioned herein in person; or

(c) the said Yacht is used for any Commercial Purpose; or

(d) the Owner of the said Yacht ceases to be a member of the Yacht Club.

An Admiralty Warrant can in no circumstances be issued for a vessel which has not been registered as a British Ship in accordance with Part I of the Merchant Shipping Act, 1894, or to anyone who is not a British subject.

If a Yacht is owned conjointly, all the joint Owners must belong to the Club to be eligible for a Warrant.

When the Yacht is sold or the Owner ceases to be a member of the Club, the Warrant must at once be sent to the Secretary of the Club, who is responsible for its immediate return to the Admiralty.

The Special Ensign may not be flown unless the Owner is on board, or in effective control of her when she is in harbour or at anchor near the shore. It may be flown only while the Warrant is carried on board the Yacht.

The Special Ensign may be flown by any boat which belongs to the Yacht and can conveniently be hoisted on board her.

If the owner belongs to more than one Club to which Warrants to use a Special Ensign are granted, he must apply for a separate Warrant from each Club.

A Yacht which is ever used for any Commercial Purpose is ineligible for a Warrant.

A Yacht which is never used for cruising (houseboat, etc.) is ineligible for a Warrant.

The penalty for flying the white, blue (plain or defaced), or red ensign defaced without warrant is a fine not exceeding £500 for each offence, and any commissioned officer on full pay in His Majesty's naval or military service, or Customs officer, may board the vessel and confiscate the flag.

Private Flags: Some yachts carry the owner's private flag, which is flown from the foremast head of a schooner, with the burgee at the main. In yachts of other rig it is usually flown from the cross-tree. The Board of Trade have drawn attention to the fact that the private flags used by several yacht owners are either identical with the alphabetical flags of the Code or are so similar that they may be mistaken for such flags. It will be appreciated that, if a private flag is read as a signal, confusion and possibly serious inconvenience may be caused. It is accordingly suggested that yacht owners who have adopted private flags either identical with or similar to the Code flags should consider the desirability of adopting new flags which cannot be mistaken for Code flags under any circumstances.

Racing Flags: The distinguishing flag flown from the mainmast head when racing is rectangular in shape and of fancy design. It is carried as long as the yacht is engaged in a race and hauled down if she retires from the contest. In the past many yachtsmen adopted flags from the International Code as racing or private flags, but since the new code came into force in 1934 the practice is undesirable, as will be gathered from the following notice issued by the Board of Trade:

The Pilot Jack: This is a Union Jack with a white border. When used as a signal for a pilot, it should be hoisted at the mainmast head.

The Blue Peter: (Code letter P) This is a blue rectangular flag with a white centre, flown when a vessel is about to sail.

The International Code: Small cruising yachts seldom make use of these code flags for any but decorative purposes on festive occasions. The ship is usually dressed 'rainbow' fashion at anchor, with the pilot jack as the lowest flag at the bow. Burgees, strictly speaking, should not be used, although they often are when the supply of flags is somewhat short. The ensign of a foreign country is never used when dressing ship unless she is dressed in honour of that country, when it is flown at the mainmast head.

The Union Jack: The Union Jack is reserved for the Royal Navy and must not in any circumstances be flown on a yacht.

APPENDIX 5: *Morse Signal Code*

A working knowledge of the Morse code is extemely useful and should be acquired by every yachtsman. Signals can be transmitted, or read, by day with a flag, by night with a flash lamp, and in thick weather by a fog horn:

Letters

A	• —	H	• • • •	O	— — —	U	• • —
B	— • • •	I	• •	P	• — — •	V	• • • —
C	— • — •	J	• — — —	Q	— — • —	W	• — —
D	— • •	K	— • —	R	• — •	X	— • • —
E	•	L	• — • •	S	• • •	Y	— • — —
F	• • — •	M	— —	T	—	Z	— — • •
G	— — •	N	— •				

Numerals

1	• — — — —	6	— • • • •
2	• • — — —	7	— — • • •
3	• • • — —	8	— — — • •
4	• • • • —	9	— — — — •
5	• • • • •	0	— — — — —

—   indicates a long of about 3 seconds' duration

•   indicates a short of about 1 second duration

Preparatory signal to attract attention:	— — — — — — — — etc
Answering signal, or 'I understand':	— • — • — • — • etc
Interval between each flash or sound:	1 second
" " " letter	3 "
" " " word	6 "

APPENDIX 6: *Weather Portents*

My knowledge of the science of weather forecasting might be described, without putting any great strain upon the truth, as 'superficial.' Even that, perhaps, would be a complimentary estimate, as more often than not when I have expected fair weather, it has turned out particularly foul. If I had a comprehensive equipment of instruments and knew how to use them, it is possible that I might be more successful, but I only carry an aneroid on board and that by itself can, I think, merely serve as a rough guide. If, on turning out in the morning, I find that the glass has fallen half an inch or so – well, I stay put, or at least do not venture far from sheltered waters. By adopting this policy I have, no doubt, occasionally missed a passage that I might very well have made, but, on the other hand, it has saved me from many a 'dusting.'

Unless one has made a study of weather forecasting and has all the necessary instruments, better results are likely to be obtained by observation of natural phenomena. There is undoubtedly more than a modicum of truth in some of the old saws about the weather that have come down to us through the ages. Here are a few of the better-known weather portents:

A red sunset presages fine weather, while a red sunrise may be taken as an indication of coming bad weather. The sun rising or setting behind a bank of clouds is said to foretell rough weather.

A bright yellow sky at sunset is a sign of wind and a pale yellow of rain.

The presence of heavy dew at night is usually followed by fine weather.

A halo round the moon suggests wind and probably rain also. 'Wind dogs,' seen to windward in the morning are an indication of a coming gale.

Distant objects seen very clearly with a hard edge suggest northerly winds, and the ragged streaks of cloud known as 'mares' tails' foretell strong winds or a gale from the direction from which they radiate.

In fine summer weather the wind follows the sun, being from the north-west in the morning and south-east in the evening. If the wind comes from the west in the morning and backs against the sun, bad weather usually ensues.

A dark blue sky is a sign of wind and a light blue of fine weather. The presence of porpoises up a river is supposed to indicate coming bad weather, but, personally, I am inclined to think that it merely indicates that there are fish in the river.

Streamers of cobwebs in the rigging are a sure indication of a coming south-east breeze – at any rate that is so on the East Coast – with fine weather.

A phosphorescent sea is also a sign of fine weather.

Such portents, particularly if confirmed by the barometer, may afford some guide to the weather that is likely to be experienced.

GLOSSARY

£. s. d.	British currency up to March 1971 was 'pounds, shillings and pence'; the stylised L represents the Latin 'libra' (pound weight, hence lb), and the abbreviation d for pence represents denarius, plural denarii, a small Roman silver coin. There were 20 shillings to the pound, twelve pence to the shilling, and coins of these values existed: ¼d (farthing), ½d (halfpenny, pronounced hayp'nny, often spelt ha'penny), 3d (threepenny piece or bit), 6d (sixpence), 1s (a shilling), 2s (two shillings, or a florin), 2s 6d (a half-crown). 2d was pronounced 'tuppence', 3d 'thruppence' or by some 'threppence'. In slang, a 6d piece was a 'tanner', a shilling was a 'bob' (plural the same), a pound was a 'quid' (plural the same). So 'five bob' was five shillings, 'ten quid' was ten pounds. The sum of £5 3s 6d would be spoken "five pounds, three-and-six". 7s 4¾d would be "seven and fourpence three-farthings". The guinea was a quaint unofficial unit of retail pricing equal to one pound plus one shilling; it conferred a spurious respectability on products so priced, and diverted attention from the higher price in pounds: 20gns = £21.
apron	Centreline component linking inside of the stem to the keel, and in some craft accepting fastenings of the plank ends
athwart	Across
backstay	Standing rigging component supporting mast from astern
ballast	Internal or external weight, normally iron or lead, imparting righting moment to the hull when heeled
balloon foresail	Downwind sail, smaller precursor to the spinnaker
bass warp	Heavy-duty general-purpose rope which floats
battens	Strips of timber in pockets on the leach of a sail with roach, to prevent it flapping
beacon	Static post embedded in the seabed in coastal waters to form a navigation mark
beam	Maximum breadth of a vessel; transverse structural component at deck level
beam-ends	A yacht is on her beam ends when heeled to almost 90 degrees
bear away	Steer away from the wind
bear up	Raise the tiller, ie to bear away, not to head up
beat	Make progress against the wind by tacking to and fro
becket	On a block, a metal eye at one or both ends enabling it to be shackled or lashed to something
bee-block	Fixed block where a spar forms one side of the shell, resembles a letter b or B
belay	Of a rope or cable, to secure to a cleat or other fixed point

belaying pin	Hardwood or metal peg inserted in fife-rail or spider-band, to which a line is belayed using a figure-of-eight arrangement; pulling out the pin is intended to free the line instantly
bend (-on)	Attach a sail to a spar by means of a light line
Bermudian rig	Rig in which the mainsail comes to a point at the head, adjacent to the mast, and having no gaff or other form of yard aloft
Berthon dinghy	Proprietary folding wood-and-canvas boat
bight	Large loop in a rope
bilge	The part of a boat's sectional shape where the topsides merge into the bottom planking; the cavity beneath the cabin sole
bilge stringer	Longitudinal structural timber inside the frames at bilge level imparting stiffness to the hull
binnacle	Generally brass illuminated enclosure for the steering compass
bitts	Pair of stout timber posts on the foredeck for belaying the anchor cable
blind block	Block with no rotating component, the rope rubs against the solid core it as it is pulled through
block	Wooden shell incorporating one or more rotating wheels, or sheaves, forming part of a boat's rigging
board	Each leg of a sequence of tacks
bobstay	Fixed wire or sometimes rod from bowsprit end to stem near the waterline, to take upward stresses on the bowsprit
bollard	Pillar on deck or quayside for securing mooring line
boom	Horizontal spar holding the clew of the sail out from the mast, and so maintaining its shape
boom foresail	Foresail sheeted to a short boom pivoted at the fore end, so self-tacking
bosun's chair	Device for sitting in to be hauled up the mast to perform maintenance or repairs
bower anchor	The boat's principal anchor
bowse	To haul down and fasten a line under load using some form of mechanical advantage such as one or more blocks or simply a doubling of the line around part of the item being secured
bowsprit	Spar projecting from the bow, enabling a jib to be set from it
breaker	Small wooden barrel normally containing water
bridge-deck	Structural feature strengthening vessel at the cabin entrance, and which must be stepped over to gain entry
bright-work	Varnished woodwork

broach-to	When running, to bury the bow and slew round putting wind on the beam, rolling and possibly capsizing the boat
built-down	Of a hull, having a keel integral to the hull form, not a fin or bulb-fin arrangement
bulkhead	Transverse structural 'wall' within the hull
bull's eye fairlead	Annular hardwood shape, normally lignum vitae, mounted in metal or on a strop, and through which a line such as a foresail sheet passes
bulwarks	Low continuous barrier around the perimeter of the deck, normally of planking attached to vertical projections of the boats major frames
bumkin, bumpkin	Spar or structure projecting from the stern, normally of a yawl, to provide an outboard sheeting point for the mizzen
burgee	Small, often triangular, club flag flown at the masthead
by the lee	To sail 'by the lee' is to have the wind abaft the beam and on the same side as the mainsail, ie the sail is to windward, presenting the danger of an unintended gybe
cable	Anchor chain; unit of distance (220 yards)
cable-laid	Of a rope, made from three strands laid together left-handed, each being itself three-strand, hawser-laid; used for towing and other heavy applications
canoe stern	Stern coming to a point; strictly, with a stern-hung rudder – an inboard rudder makes it a canoe counter
canoe-yawl	A canoe-sterned vessel of yawl rig
capstan	Type of windlass with vertical shaft for retrieving anchor or other heavy duty applications
carlines	Longitudinal timber components forming foundation for the sides of a coachroof
carvel planking	Planking where each plank lies adjacent to, but not overlapping, the one above or below it, the seams being caulked for watertightness
caulking	To caulk is to seal the gaps between the planks of a carvel-built vessel using certain traditional materials; the resulting filling is called the caulking
causeway	Raised path enabling dry progress across a tidal area at most or all states of the tide
ceiling	Non-structural planking on the inside of a yacht concealing the hull internals; should not be complete from top to bottom, so that air may circulate freely

centre of effort	The theoretical point on the sail plan at which the wind force on all the sails may be regarded as occurring; its relationship to the centre of lateral resistance determines the helm balance of the vessel; the issue is by no means as straightforward as this description suggests
centre of lateral resistance	The theoretical point on the hull's longitudinal section at which its lateral resistance to motion may be said to operate; generally and simplistically, the geometrical centre of the immersed section, however it moves according to the yacht's motion at sea
centreplate, centreboard	Steel or timber component which may be lowered or raised to alter a boat's lateral resistance and so optimise performance on or off the wind
chafe	Wear due to friction, commonly of sails and rigging, especially from repeated rolling on a long run
chainplates	Metal plates attaching the shrouds to the hull
chine	Some hulls are planked with distinct areas of simple curvature and twist; each cross-section of the hull shape is a polygon, and the chines are the longitudinal junctions between these areas of planking (or sheet material such as plywood)
chord, anchor	The mearurement across the fluke tips of an anchor of Admiralty or Fisherman's pattern
claw-ring	On a yacht with roller-reefing and a boom extending well aft of the stern, the claw-ring grips the boom and rolled sail and provides anchorage for the mainsheet
cleat	Fixed device to which a line such as a jib-sheet or mooring rope may be secured
clench	Of a planking nail used without a roove, to bend over and bury the sharp end to make it secure - this is clench-building. Cooke uses the word to mean to rivet the end over the roove.
clew	The trailing corner of a sail, be it foresail, main, mizzen or topsail
clinker planking	Planking where each plank overlaps the one beneath it and is fastened to it as well as the frames; generally a lighter form of construction than carvel, the resulting stressed skin requires less heavy internal framing; watertightness is imparted by the fit of the planks, not by caulking
close-hauled	Sailing close to the wind, with the sails hauled well in towards the boat's centreline
club-headed	*See* jackyard topsail
coaming	Vertical planking forming the lip of the cockpit and the sides of the coachroof
companion (-way)	Entrance into the accommodation

counter	Type of stern which projects above the waterline and aft of the sternpost
covering boards	The planks forming the periphery of the deck
cringle	A brass-lined hole at the edge of a sail to take a line such as a reef pendant or outhaul
cross cut sail	Sail with the seams at right-angles to the leach, thought to give the best airflow
cross-trees	Spars projecting out from the mast at some height, forming part of the standing rigging, and enabling the shrouds to form an effective angle with the mast
cutch	Red dye with preservative properties extracted from a tree grown in India; used for tanning sails
cutter	Rig with two or more foresails
cwt	Hundredweight, 112 lbs, 1/20 of an imperial ton
dagger-board, -plate	Board or plate which can be adjusted straight up and down through the keel, and can be completely removed; not being hinged it is liable to damage from collision with rocks etc., so a spare may be carried
dead-eyes & lanyards	Archaic means of securing the shrouds to the hull
deadwood	Timber filling the acute triangle between the ballast keel and the timber keel, towards the stern
deep-heeled	Of a boat, having much greater depth at the stern than the bow, i.e., with considerable drag to the keel
deviation, compass	Correction to be applied to the compass reading to allow for magnetic disturbance of, typically, the yacht's engine; this varies with the boat's heading, and a deviation card is carried, bearing the information determined when the compass is 'swung' when on a mooring
diagonally cut headsail	Or 'mitre cut'; with the cloths running at right angles to the foot and leach, meeting on a seam running perpendicularly from clew to luff
dipping lug	Lugsail where the yard projects well forward of the mast, and must be lowered and shifted to the other side when going about
displacement	The actual weight of the vessel, crewed and supplied. Equals the weight of water the hull displaces, or the weight of the volume of water equal to the immersed volume of the hull
dog-house	Small shelter at the fore-end of the cockpit / aft end of the coachroof
donkey's breakfast	Straw bedding

downhaul	Line for securing down, or getting down, part of the rig, for example the tack of the mainsail, or the gaff
drag	The downward slope of the keel from bow to stern
draught	The depth of the vessel at its lowest point
dredging	Controlled progress in reverse, downwind or downtide in confined quarters, by hauling in the anchor until it intentionally drags
dress	To treat sails with a preservative such as cutch
drift	In one sense, the distance between the fixed and moving ends of a purchase; the shorter this can be, the better, especially to minimise the effect of stretch in a halyard arrangement; a metal rod driven through a tight hole drilled through two timbers, to fasten them together permanently
earing	*See* pendant, reefing
early closing day	In England, shops used to close at lunchtime, for the rest of the day, on one day per week, varying with the locality; this was to enable staff to do their own shopping (presumably elsewhere) and/or to compensate them for working on Saturday
ensign	Type of flag flown to indicate a yacht's nationality and certain other status
ere	Prounced 'air'; archaic, 'before' or 'by the time that'
explosive hulk	*See* powder hulk
eyes of the boat	The extreme forward end of the fo'c'sle or forepeak
fair tide	A tide which serves our progress in the desired direction
fairlead	Static fitting guiding the run of a line such as a jibsheet or mooring rope
fall	Of a rope such as a halyard, the part hanging down which needs securing
fastenings	Screws, nails, rooves etc used to hold the boat together
fidded topmast	Topmast removable by lifting slightly then lowering past the fitting, or fid, where its bottom end, or heel, sits
fiddle	Raised, generally folding, lip to a table preventing things sliding off
fife-rail	Wooden rail fixed to deck or bulwark, with holes to hold belaying pins
fishing & catting, anchor	Getting hold of the anchor when weighed, and tying it back against the bow of the vessel
fit out	Ready a vessel for the coming sailing season

flake	To fold a sail in zig-zag fashion; to lay out on deck, zig-zag fashion, the calculated length of chain for an imminent anchoring operation
flare	Of the hull, the extent to which it is wider at the gunwale than at the waterline
flax	Fibre made from a plant grown generally in India, and used to make rope or canvas
floor	Transverse structural component linking the keel to the lower planking
fluke, anchor	The blade-like end to the arms of an anchor of Admiralty or Fisherman's pattern
flush deck	Deck having no raised coachroof, hatches for entry below, and possibly a skylight
fo'c'sle	Originally 'forecastle' from medieval fighting ships; the interior portion nearest the bow
forefoot	The forward end of the keel profile
foul tide	Tide which impedes our progress in the desired direction
frame	Of the hull, a transverse component around the inside of the planking; sawn or grown frames are few in number and form a permanent part of the building jig and final structure; steamed frames are inserted, typically every 6 to 12 inches along the hull, after the planking is installed
freeboard	The height of the gunwale above the waterline at any point
fretwork	Possibly therapeutic handicraft involving sawing decorative shapes from thin sheet timber
gaff	The wooden yard supporting the head of a gaff sail
garboard	The plank on either side immediately next to the keel; the hardest to fit, due to their twist, and generally the likeliest to leak
gas buoy	A buoy illuminated using bottled acetylene gas
genoa	Large headsail overlapping the main
gimbals	Swivel mounting for a lamp or cooker enabling it to remain level in one or both planes as the boat moves
gimlet	Small hand-tool for making holes in material such as leather or wood
girt	Girdled about
go about	*See* tack
gooseneck	Metal attachment between boom and mast such that the boom can swing laterally and vertically
goose-winged	With main and foresail on either side of the boat when running, generally with foresail 'poled out'

gridiron	Metal structure on which a barge is settled for work on its flat bottom at low water
gripe	To have a tendency to turn upwind, i.e., to exhibit strong weather helm
grommet	Continuous loop of rope employed to link things flexibly together
ground tackle	Anchors and their chains
gudgeon	Hollow inverted cup-shaped metal fitting which sits on a pintle (q.v.) forming, for example, the 'hinge' attaching the rudder to a dinghy
gunter	Spar on the upper luff of a triangular main or mizzen sail enabling it to be set on a shorter-than-otherwise mast, and the entire rig when removed to perhaps be stowed within the boat's length
guys, spinnaker boom	Lines preventing the fore-and-aft movement of a spinnaker pole when deployed
gybe	With the wind aft of the beam, to steer such that it passes from one side of the boat to the other, necessitating careful control of the boom as this happens; an uncontrolled gybe can be dangerous to vessel and crew
halyard	Rope used to hold up a sail; derivation 'haul-yard'
hambro line	Three-strand hemp or flax light cord
handy	Manoeuvrable; particularly, quick in stays (i.e., to go about)
handy-billy	Portable rope purchase
hank	Usually metal fitting like a dog lead clip or of piston form, securing a foresail to its stay
hard	Area of tidal ground hard enough to dry out a vessel to work on it
hard-headed	Having strong weather-helm
haul one's wind	To steer closer to the wind, hauling in the filled sail as one does so
hawse	Anchor cable (ie chain)
hawse-pipe	Metal fitting in the bow through which the anchor hawse passes
hawser-laid	Rope in which three strands are laid up against the twist
headboard	Of a bermudian sail, the stiff area at the head of the sail, to which the halyard is attached
headsail	Triangular sail set before the mast

heave-to	To stop the boat by putting her about without touching the jib sheets, such that the wind impinges on the backed headsail(s), the main is blanketed, and the boat moves forward little if at all, enabling operations such as reefing the main to be performed safely; the longer the keel, the better a boat will heave-to
heel	The foot of, for example, a mast, rudder, topmast; of the boat itself, to lean with the wind
heel-rope	Line attached to the heel of a topmast, to initiate and control its lowering
hemp	Natural fibre used in rope-making
hitch	Any method of attaching a line to a rigid object such as a spar, using just the line itself
hoist	To raise; also the distance through which a sail is raised
horn timber	Timber attached to the sternpost and supporting a projecting stern
horse	Generally metal or wire guide along which a mainsheet or foresail sheet block can move; a shoal in a tidal river which may dry out
hounds	The point on the mast at which the shrouds attach, normally to a metal band with eyes attached
hove	Part tense of heave
hull speed	maximum speed of a hull through the water, determined by its waterline length and found emprically to be, in knots, around $1.41 \times \sqrt{WL}$ (in feet)
in irons	A yacht is 'in irons' if it fails to go about, and will not fall away onto the orignal tack, so is stuck in a kind of limbo
inboard rudder	One whose post is inside the hull, the rudder generally not being visible from the outside when the boat is afloat
jackstay	A strong line along which another line is able to slide, retaining a sail, or a crew member, in position
jackyard topsail	Topsail employing one or two wooden yards to maintain its shape and allow a larger shape than the mast and gaff alone might facilitate
jib	The foremost (or only) foresail
jib-headed	Of a sail, pointed at the top, and having no yard
kapok	Tropical plant fibre, very light and trapping of air; retains warmth and was used to fill lifejackets
kedge	Secondary anchor generally used for hauling off a grounded vessel, or forming a mooring in conjunction with the main, or bower, anchor

keel	The structural 'spine' of the boat, to which the floors and frames attach; informally, the shaped piece of iron or lead ballast suspended from it by bolts.
keelson	Internal 'false keel' above and parallel to the keel, and above the frames and floors, and helping to stiffen and hold it all together
ketch	Vessel of ketch rig, ie two masts, the hindmost, the mizzen, being proportionately larger, and further forward, than in a yawl; for a given sail area, possibly more easily handled sails than in a sloop
knee	Grown or perhaps laminated wooden reinforcement for any angle in the boat's structure, oriented downwards (hanging) or sideways (lodging)
lands	The lower edges of clinker planks
lanyard	Small line used to make one thing, such as an oar crutch, captive to another, such as a boat; line used to link wire shroud to the chainplate
lay up	To put the boat 'to bed' for the winter, either ashore or in a mud berth
leach	Trailing edge of a sail
lead-line	Weighted line with marks along its length, for measuring depth of water
leading marks	Two static features ashore which, when aligned as seen from the vessel, ensure a safe route through hazards such as rocks or shoals
lee helm	Tendency for the boat to turn away from the wind; very undesirable
lee shore	A shore to leeward of the boat, and so a potential danger
lee-board	A board either side of a (normally flat-bottomed) vessel, lowered to restrict leeway – the tendency to lose ground downwind
lee-cloth	A cloth supported by a wooden rod or just a line, raised at sea to hold a sleeper in his or her bunk
leeward	The downwind direction
leeway	distance lost to leeward by a sailing vessel
lie-to	*See* heave-to
life-line	Line attaching a crew member to the vessel; deck perimeter line strung between posts called stanchions
light dues	A former tax on registered yachts above a certain tonnage, to support the maintenance of buoyage and lighthouses
limber-holes	Holes fore-and-aft through a boat's timbers permitting water to flow rather than accumulating in one place

linoleum	Abbrev: Lino. Durable and flexible flooring material made from solidified linseed oil mixed with various fillers, on a canvas or hessian backing
linseed oil	Oil derived from flax seeds, with a multiplicity of uses, including preserving timber, and as a component of paints and varnishes
list	Of a boat, to take on a sideways lean due to poor weight distribution
loose-footed sail	A main or mizzen sail attached to its boom at the ends only, allowing the sail to take a natural shape when filled
luff	The fore-edge of a sail; to steer into the wind
lug	Type of sail with a yard at the head which projects before the mast instead of being pivoted to the mast at one end like a gaff
manila	Tropical plant fibre used to make rope; durable and resistant to salt water damage; liable to shrink when wet, causing problems with any knots made when dry
marline	A light cord made from two loosely-twisted strands; used for whippings and seizings
masonite	Type of hardboard made from compressed fine wood fibres
mast hoops	Wooden hoops able to slide up and down the mast, and to which the luff of the mainsail is attached
mast-step	The solid wooden base where the heel of the mast fits
match-boarding	Tongue-and-groove boarding
metacentric theory	Admiral Turner's method for the analysis of yacht hull characteristics based on simple geometry; whilst it can yield impressive results, it is not infallible; some apparently ideal designs prove not to be so, and vice-versa; it takes no account of the dynamics of yacht motion and wave forms at sea; T. Harrison Butler was an adherent, and describes the theory in his book Cruising Yachts: Design and Performance
miss stays	To fail to make it through the wind when going about, resulting in the boat 'falling away' again or just getting 'stuck in irons'
mizzen	Hindmost of two or more masts; the sail attached to it
moulded	Of a frame or curved timber, the dimension measured radially through it it, e.g., 1" moulded
mouse	Light lashing across the opening of a hook to prevent the hooked item coming off
neap tides	In the cycle of the tides, those of smallest range and force of current
neaped	To be neaped is to run aground at the top of a spring tide, and be stuck there until at least the next one, or even longer, sometimes many weeks

nun	A conical unlighted buoy; a marine organism attaching itself to a boat's bottom
on / off the wind	Having the wind before or abaft the beam
one-design class	Racing class with a strict design rule, intended to eliminate boat differences as a source of competitive advantage
outhaul	Line locating an item of rig horizontally, e.g., the clew of the mainsail towards the boom end, or the traveller on the bowsprit
over-blocked	Having too many blocks; more blocks mean more mechanical advantage, but this is rapidly frustrated by the increased friction, which can make it difficult or impossible to lower a sail
overhaul	To manually feed line through a block in anticipation of it being taken up
painter	The line attached to the bow of a dinghy
worming, parcelling & serving	Protection of the lower ends of shrouds (typically) from the elements, and from causing chafe to running rigging, by means of three sequential processes: 'Worming' is to 'fill in' the channels between the strands of a rope by winding light line along them, 'parcelling' is to wrap the wormed rope with tarred canvas or similar, and 'serving' is to wrap tarred line or similar around the whole assembly.
parrel beads	Hardwood beads threaded onto a loop of line locating a sail's yard against the mast, and facilitating raising and lowering with minimal friction
pay off	Of a boat, to turn away from a headwind, typically when leaving a mooring
peak	Of a gaff sail, the highest point, at the aft end of the gaff
pendant, reefing	Short line holding a mainsail's leach cringle down to the boom when reefing
perpendiculars	Length between perpendiclars is that from the waterline at the bow to the waterline at the sternpost
pigs	Moveable ingots of internal ballast, generally iron or lead
pintle	Partner of the gudgeon (q.v.) - the PIN-like fitting on a dinghy stern forming part of the rudder's 'hinge'
pipe-cot	Sleeping berth made from a trapezoidal shape of metal piping with fabric stretched across, generally hinged up out of the way, with bedding contained, when not in use
pitch	To rock in a fore-and-aft direction
plank-on-edge	Term describing outmoded slim, deep hull form of late Victorian yachts
plough steel	Grade of steel originally made for a plough manufacturer in Leeds, England, and suitable for wire rigging on yachts

plumb	Vertically in alignment
point, of compass	The compass rose is divided into 32 points, each equating to 11.25 degrees; if dealing in points rather than degrees, it is not generally necessary to specify a course to steer with greater accuracy than the nearest point
pointing higher / lower	A yacht able to be steered closer to the wind than another is said to point higher
powder hulk	Decommissioned vessel, often dating from the age of sail, used to store explosives afloat
pram	Type of dinghy with a transom at each end; capacious for its length
preventer	Line rigged from somewhere near the bow to the end of the main boom when running, preventing an uncontrolled gybe
preventer lashing	Lashing around the bunched-up after end of the reefed mainsail, preventing the reef undoing should the pendant fail
purchase	An arrangement of one or more blocks giving mechanical advantage to a rope being hauled on
raised deck	A deck allowing useful headroom across the full width of the boat, resulting in higher topsides and more windage, but requiring no coachroof; popularised by many Maurice Griffiths designs
reach	Point of sailing with the wind on or near the beam; the fastest point is a beam reach, since this imparts the maximum forward thrust; the apparent wind force does not change with speed, and the yacht will accelerate to be limited only by her 'hull speed', not by an falling off in apparent wind as will occur with the wind aft of the beam
red ochre	Pigment made from haematite (an iron oxide)
reef	To reduce sail in anticipation of stronger wind
reefing bowsprit	One which retracts inboard to facilitate reduction of jib sail area
reeve	To thread a line, generally running rigging, through the sheaves etc along its course; past tense rove
reverse curve	An s-shaped curve somewhere in a boat's section; generally improves water flow at the expense of difficulty in planking
riding light	Light hoisted in the rigging to make the boat visible at anchor by night
riding sail	Sail hoisted to make a boat lie comfortably at anchor or on a mooring, in a wind
rigging screw	Device for tensioning the foot of a shroud
roach	Convex curvature to the leach of a sail; maximises its area and performance, but requires battens for stiffening

roll	to rock from side to side; an affliction to be endured when running for any length of time
roove	The flattened conical ring of copper over which the inboard, pointed end of a planking nail is rivetted
rudder trunk	The strong wooden housing for the rudder shaft
run	To sail downwind
runners	Running backstays, only the windward one is necessary and set up; the mainsail needs to sweep where the other would be
running rigging	Ropework involved in hoisting and controlling the sails
samson post	Stout post near bow or stern to which mooring lines or the anchor cable can be secured
save one's tide	To succeed in utilising the tide in gaining one's objective; failure to do so may necessitate anchoring to wait out the tide
scandalize	To depower the mainsail by raising the boom and/or dropping the peak, keeping it ready for deployment
scantlings	Specification for the dimensions and materials of a vessel's structural parts
schooner	Rig having at least two masts, of equal height or with the after one(s) taller
scope	Of anchor cable: The ratio of cable let out to depth of water; light anchors relying on burying themselves require a more horzontal pull, and so a larger scope to achieve this, than heavier anchors
scuttle	A sealable opening in a boat's topsides or cabin side
sea-anchor	A device to stabilise a vessel and minimise its downwind drift when the conditions are too heavy to sail in; needs plenty of sea-room
sea-room	Leeward distance to the nearest danger, generally shoals, rocks or land
seaway	'In a seaway' means in the rough conditions likely to be met at sea
seize, seizing	A seizing is a light lashing attaching a line to another line or some rigid item such as a spar
self-draining cockpit	Cockpit whose floor is sufficiently far above the waterline for drains to be able to empty it; this is not achievable in smaller yachts, and it is arguable that the shelter of a deep cockpit is a more useful safety feature
shackle	Small loop of metal closed by means of a threaded rod, employed in rigging; fastened and unfastened using a shackle key; to connect using a shackle

shake	Longitudinal split in a spar, not generally harmful to its functioning
shank	Of an anchor, its shaft
sharpie	Generally flat-bottomed shoal-draught hull form of single-chine construction
sheave	The rotating portion of a block; 'patent' sheaves employ bearings to reduce friction (but give themselves away with noise)
sheer	The profile of a yacht's gunwale, and a key aesthetic element of its design
sheerpole forestay	Forestay attached at the bow to the apex of a pair of poles hinged to the gunwales further back, allowing a mast in a tabernacle to be lowered and raised using a type of sheerlegs
sheet	Line used to control the clew of a sail
shelf	The beam shelf is the longitudinal member onto which the boat's beams are fitted
ship / unship	To mount or unmount some part of the boat or its gear
shoal-draught	Of small draught, suitable for shallow waters
shrouds	Wires (generally) holding up the masts, or providing lateral support to the bowsprit or bumkin
sided	Of a frame or curved timber, the dimension measured across it, e.g., 3" sided
single-part, two-part etc	Number of strands making up a rope purchase
sister-hooks	A pair of hooks pivoted together or capable of being locked together, such that each forms the mousing for the other; they both hook through the same cringle or other fitting
sloop	A single-masted, fore-and-aft-rigged sailing boat with a short standing bowsprit or none at all and a single headsail set from the forestay
slow in stays	Taking her time to come about; not necessarily a bad thing, especially when single-handing
smack	Traditional and powerful fishing craft employed in England and the eastern United States until well into the 20th century; many survive today to be cruised and raced by enthusiasts
soldier's wind	A fair wind both going out and returning home
sound	To measure depth of water using a lead-line or pole
Spanish burton	A purchase comprising one double and two single blocks giving a 5-1 reduction ratio but presenting a technical challenge to the user; may form the origin of the services expression 'gone for a burton', meaning, of a person or object, to have suffered a misfortune

spar	Generic term for mast, boom, yard, gaff, bowsprit, bumkin etc
spider-band	Metal fitting around the mast near its base, holding belaying pins (fixed or removable) to which halyards etc are secured
spinnaker	Large headsail used downwind
splice	To join one rope to itself or another by unravelling and re-laying
spline	Thin strip of wood used to fill an open seam between planks, or modify a boom used in roller reefing
spoon bow	Bow whose profile is strongly convex above the waterline
spring tides	In the cycle of the tides, those of greatest range and force of current
springs & lines	When tying up alongside a dock or other vessel, spring lines prevent fore-and-aft motion of the boat; the bow spring links the bow to a point on the dock well aft, stern spring does the opposite; bow and stern lines hold the boat near the dock, and run more or less perpendicular to the dockside
sprung	Of a spar, strained and split by bending so as to make it seriously weakened or useless; of a plank, angled away from the hull due to failed fastenings at the end
stanchion	Post typically supporting lifelines around the deck perimeter
standing rigging	Rigging which supports the masts, and provides lateral support to bowsprit & bumkin
stateroom	Enclosed sleeping cabin
stay	Standing wire rope supporting mast or bowsprit etc; to go about
staysail	On a cutter, the foresail between jib and mast; a mizzen staysail sets before the mizzen mast on a ketch, yawl or schooner, and generally has its tack secured to the windward rail, forming a funnel with the mainsail; it has to be lowered and relocated when going about
stem	The vertical timber at the bow of a yacht
stem the tide	To make headway, or at least hold one's ground, against the tide
stemhead	The top of the yacht's stem
step / unstep	To erect or take down a mast
stern-hung rudder	A rudder whose mountings are at the extreme aft end of the boat
stern-post	The part of the vessel on which the rudder pivots, whether an inboard or stern-hung rudder

stock, anchor	The stock of an anchor so-equipped is a metal rod fitted transversely through the shank at the opposite end from the flukes and right-angles to them, designed to make the anchor topple on the seabed so the flukes dig in; it is generally slid through and pivoted to lie along the shank when stowing the anchor
strop	A rope or metal loop or link around, for example, a block enabling it to be attached to something
swatchway	A channel of deeper water across a shoal, often unmarked but known to locals, and perhaps having leading marks on shore associated with it
sweep	A type of large oar used singly with both hands, as in a whaler, or when propelling a becalmed yacht (only one need be used)
t and g	Tongued and grooved (boards)
tabernacle	Hinge arrangement at the base of a mast enabling it to be lowered to negotiate bridges
tack	The foreward lower corner of a sail; to go about
tackle	Pronounced *tay*ckle; a small rope purchase
taffrail	Functional and often decorative stern rail on a vessel
take the ground	To settle more-or-less upright without damage on drying ground
take up	Of planking, to absorb water when immersed, so as to expand and become watertight
tallow	A solid lubricant made from beef or mutton fat
Thames Measurement	Expressed as a tonnage, this is a volumetric measure of boat size, based on the number of 'tuns' or barrels which might be stowed aboard. The tonnage is arrived at using the formula $((\text{length - beam}) \times \text{beam}^2)/188$ (dimensions in feet) and it gives a useful measure of the usable room in a boat; it does not indicate the boat's weight or displacement
thimble	Metal lining which fits inside a loop in the end of a rope or wire
throat	Of a gaff sail, the point at the root of the gaff
thwart	Seat mounted across a boat
tide-rode	At anchor, being orientated principally by tide rather than wind; this is a function of prevailing conditions, underwater shape, and the windage of the above-water parts of the boat
tie-bolts	Threaded metal rods with nuts employed to secure carlines to the half-beams between which they sit
tiller lines	Lines from the tiller around the deck so the boat can be steered by the singlehander when attending to something forward; sometimes attached to the sails so as to effect a form of self-steering

timbers	Structural wooden parts of the boat
tingle	A crude wooden or metal patch fixed to the outside of a hull to block a leak
toggle	Something like a duffel-coat fastener, through a loop in the end of a line
tonnage	*See* Thames Measurement
top up	To raise the boom using the topping lift
tophamper	Gear aloft imparting unwanted weight and windage
topping lift	Line(s) enabling the boom to be raised
topsail	On a gaff-rigged boat, a triangular sail 'filling in' the space between gaff and mast, or the projection upwards of it.
topsides	The outside of the planking above the waterline
transom	Flat or curved panel forming the stern of the boat
trap	Two-wheeled horse-drawn passenger vehicle
traveller	Rig attachment point able to be drawn up or along a spar
trice up	Of a boomless or sprit sail, to furl it up theatre-curtain fashion leaving the gaff or sprit in place; done with Thames barges, where the permanently rigged sprit may weight 3 tons or so, and bawleys, which are gaff rigged with no boom
trim	The balance of the boat, in the sense of weight distribution, or of sail forces
tripping line	A line attached to the head of an anchor by which it might be freed from the seabed if fouled; line attached to the apex of a sea anchor by which it may be hauled back in
truck	The top of the mast
trysail	Small heavy-weather sail to replace the main
tumblehome	Hulls with tumblehome at some point have their widest point below the gunwale
tumbler fid	A self-actuating base fitting for the topmast
turn over the tide	Make progress against the tide
una	Rig with one mast in the eyes of the boat, and one sail
vang	Line from deck level or a mizzen mast to the aft end of a mainsail gaff to limit its falling to leeward and improve the sail's performance
vertical cut sail	Sail where the cloths run parallel to the leach or trailing edge
Vi-spring	Proprietary interior springing for a mattress or cushion
w.c.	Water Closet, ie toilet

warp	Strong rope used for towing, mooring, manouevring in congested harbours
waterman	Skilled small-boat handler employed to provide ferrying and general services to larger vessels
weather helm	Tendency to turn into the wind
weather shore	Shore to windward of the boat, posing no immediate danger and a possible source of shelter
weather-bitt	To secure the inboard end of the anchor cable
weatherly	Having good windward ability
whip purchase	Purchase where one end is fixed and the other is pulled in a different direction, serving to constrain, for example, the end of a foresail boom
whip, whipping	Binding around the end inch or so of a cut rope to prevent it fraying
whole sail breeze	Exhilarating breeze not requiring reefing
Willesden canvas	Proprietary treated canvas from the Willesden Paper and Canvas Works, Willesden, north London
winch	Rotary mechanical device to apply useful gearing or friction to a line such as a sheet being hauled on
windage	Unwanted tendency to be affected by the wind
windlass	Mechanical device with transverse axis by which the anchor may be hauled up
wind-rode	When anchored or moored, being orientated principally by wind rather than tide; this is a function of prevailing conditions, underwater shape, and the windage of the above-water parts of the boat
windward	Direction from which the wind is blowing
yard	Spar raised aloft to hold up a square or lug sail
yaw	To swing in the lateral plane
yawl	Two-masted vessel where, technically, the mizzen is mounted aft of the sternpost; in practice, it's more a question of sail distribution and proportion than where the sternpost is, many yawls have a stern-hung rudder

INDEX

INDEX

The THAMES ESTUARY

circa 1900

LOWESTOFT

SOUTHWOLD

SUFFOLK

ALDEBURGH

R. Alde

Orford Ness

Butley Creek

R. Ore

Shingle Street

Woodbridge Haven

WOODBRIDGE

R. Deben

Felixstowe Ferry

FELIXSTOWE

Pye Sand

WALTON on the NAZE

IPSWICH

R. Orwell

Pin Mill

R. Stour

HARWICH

Walton Backwaters

MISTLEY

WIVENHOE

COLCHESTER

ROWHEDGE

R. Colne

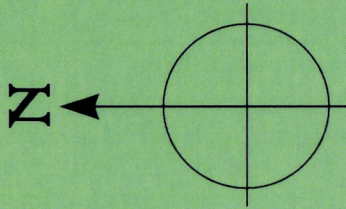

ESSEX

N